To Richard and Frank

Contents

Acknowledgments

The work of formulating and honing our arguments for this book entailed many informal get-togethers at our respective homes over a period of several years with the inevitable result that a considerable amount of excellent food was consumed in order that our brains might be nourished. This stimulus for thought would not have been so efficacious, however, without ongoing discussion and exchange of ideas with colleagues and friends on both sides of Mount Royal as well as further afield in just about every corner of the world. Special thanks go to Thomas Schlich, Abraham Fuks, Laurence Monnais, Nancy Hunt, Kenneth Weiss, and Ann Buchanan for reading drafts of one or more chapters. We are also indebted to the anonymous reviewers of the manuscript for their extremely helpful insights and encouragement. Special thanks go to Gillian Chilibeck, Megha Sedhev, Julie Désalliers, and Wilson Will for managing the immense bibliography and the inevitable challenges it at times posed. Our senior editor at Wiley-Blackwell, Rosalie Robertson, has been marvelously supportive throughout, as have Julie Kirk and Annie Jackson. We have drawn at length on the publications of numerous anthropologists, sociologists, historians, epidemiologists, philosophers, biologists, and others to ground our arguments and furnish the bedrock of this book, but the overarching orientation and the narratives that we have developed based on these incredibly rich sources are our own.

Introduction

It is commonly assumed that biomedical technologies, if equitably distributed, will dramatically improve the health and wellbeing of people everywhere. In principle we agree that this is indeed the case with respect to the majority of such technologies, but two major provisos need serious consideration. The first is that human bodies are not everywhere the same; they are the products of evolutionary, historical, and contemporary social change resulting from ceaseless interactions among human beings, their environments, and the social and political milieux in which they live. The second is that biomedical technologies are not autonomous entities: their development and implementation are enmeshed with medical, social, and political interests that have practical and moral consequences.

Three interwoven themes form the fabric of this book and illustrate throughout the significance of the provisos noted above. The first theme elaborates critically on a dominant orientation in biomedicine consolidated over the past three centuries that considers the human body, despite its outward differences, as everywhere essentially the same for the purposes of diagnosing and managing disease.[1] This assumption that the human body can everywhere be normalized began to take form when biomedical technologies were used, often on an experimental basis, by the colonial empires of the 19th century on colonized peoples. Today, the global reach of biomedical technologies is undeniable and, together with public health, is the prime means by which governments and developmental agencies aspire to ameliorate disease and disability everywhere. An unexamined assumption about the uniformity of human bodies continues to inform most biomedical practice.[2]

Second, we elaborate at length on the way in which culture, history, politics, and biology (environmental and individual), are inextricably entangled and subject to never-ending transformations – phenomena that we call "biosocial differentiation." Our position is that biological and social life is mutually constitutive, a position that is supported by evidence of the extent and significance of human biological diversity that we describe as local biologies. Research in epidemiology, population genetics, biological anthropology, and a small amount of work in cultural anthropology, together with remarkable new findings being produced at an exorbitant rate in molecular biology, have shown convincingly how evolutionary, historical, political, and social variables as well as individual behaviors can bring about changes in human biology, some transient and others long lasting. For example, the misuse of antibiotics has actually produced new pathogens and transformed others, bringing about so-called "emerging epidemics" resulting in new forms of biosocial differentiation.

Until recently, the majority of social scientists paid little attention to the material body in their ethnographic accounts, in effect placing its interior in a black box, off limits to investigation. Their assumption has been that the body "proper" – the standardized body subject to the laws of biology – falls outside their domain. Particularly since World War II, with its legacy of scientific racism and industrialized genocides, the issue of biological difference among human kind has become a potently charged one. As a result many social scientists are reluctant to address the issue of biological difference given how easily this may be framed in racial and racist terms, with negative social repercussions.

While we share this concern, we argue that empirically it is impossible to maintain a marked division between the biological body and its social context. The influence of social and political variables on human health is well recognized by the majority of epidemiologists and certain health economists, and highlights the socioeconomic and political ramifications of human wellbeing. We go further, however, and draw on the concept of biosocial differentiation to illustrate the dynamic process of embodiment – the lived entanglement – of local biologies, social relations, politics, and culture. In doing so we signal the limits of the approach commonly upheld in biomedicine that the human body is, for all intents and purposes, universal and amenable to intervention through standardized approaches to medical management and care.

To continue to ignore the possibility that human bodies may differ in biologically significant ways among groups will not, however, make the issue of racism go away. Such variations are not the result of a mistaken belief in essentialized difference among human kind (often glossed as "race"), but rather result from interactions among physical environments, social engagements, and individual bodies. Moreover, ignoring biological variation blinds us to the more insidious, perverse, and alarming consequences of political and economic processes that over time have resulted in intertwined social and biological vulnerabilities and forms of health inequalities not always captured in statistical surveys. Poverty, exposure to environmental toxins, and poor nutrition etch themselves over a lifetime into physical bodies and (as we shall see in chapter 13), the bodies of future generations.

The third theme is our resolute belief in the importance of ethnography for assessing the impact of biomedical technologies. Over the past 40 years medical anthropologists and other social scientists have written extensively about the introduction of biomedical technologies all over the world, documenting how such technologies are perceived at local sites and put to work in practice, and with what effects. Some of this research makes abundantly clear the positive effects of biomedical technologies, but a great deal more leads to startling cautionary tales about the limits of a standardized, largely unreflective approach to the delivery of health care, especially when local knowledge and aspirations are not taken into account. Clearly, it is essential to develop and sustain an approach to global health in which priority is given to a reduction in poverty and inequities, especially gender inequities. Health must be a basic human right, and its promotion and preservation demand that these inequalities be addressed. However, our argument is that such an approach should be complemented by the following: first, a clear-sighted recognition of unexamined assumptions embedded in the normative technological practices of biomedicine; second, an understanding of local aspirations and perceived priorities about individual and community wellbeing; and third, an acknowledgment of significant global biological diversity including close attention to how this is produced over evolutionary and historical time and, further, as a result of contemporary human activities both local and global. In what follows in this Introduction, we first situate our specific arguments in the context of a widely perceived need for global improvement in human health and wellbeing. We then address the concept of culture as it is used in this book, followed by some reflections on ethnography and its value as a research tool. In closing we set out the contents of each chapter.

Improving Global Health: The Challenge

It is abundantly clear that many biomedical technologies bring about globally significant changes for the better with respect to health outcomes. However, effective though a large number of biomedical technologies may be, a simple technofix leaves unchallenged the common-sense assumptions set out above. The ethnographic findings adduced in the following chapters suggest that these assumptions must be challenged if the world is to be made more equitable in terms of health and wellbeing.

The constitution of the World Health Organization (WHO) states that "the enjoyment of the highest attainable standard of health is one of the fundamental rights of every human being."[3] And yet newspaper reports daily make it patently obvious that large segments of the world's population do not enjoy these rights.[4] Clearly the inequitable distribution of global economic resources is in large part responsible for this situation, exacerbated by structural adjustment loans and conditions imposed on countries slated for development by the World Bank, the International Monetary Fund, and other powerful institutions.[5] The effect of these inequities and conditions, despite numerous pledges to reduce disparities, has been that the number of people living in absolute poverty over the past decade, the majority without access to health care, has burgeoned by over 100 million at a time when the total world income increased by 2.5 percent annually.[6] Furthermore, this has happened at a time when biomedical technologies have become increasingly dispersed and are made use of worldwide.

In light of the dramatic and growing divergences in wellbeing between the increasingly wealthy and the desperately poor, wherever they live, efforts to improve global health have taken on a new urgency – in fact, the health of the world's poor has become something of a *cause célèbre*, as captains of industry, academics, retired politicians, and rock stars seek to marshal resources for the needy, making the most of media exposure to assist them. Yet the quest for global health continues to be compromised locally by poverty and the spread of conditions that foster ill health. Access to basic nutrition is increasingly conditioned by global economic forces that affect the availability of food. The price of food, for instance, depends on multiple factors, among them economic policies, agribusiness, and changing patterns of land use, over which individuals and even local governments have little or no control. Privatization of access to clean water in very many places has added to the travails experienced by people with few or no resources, enormously compromising their health. Increasing global warming adds to this burden.[7] It is against this backdrop that efforts to improve the health and wellbeing of people are taking place.

In addition to attempting to provide basic food supplies, water, and sanitation, governments are expected to ensure that biomedical technologies are readily available, including immunization and indispensable medication including antibiotics and pain-killers. Increasingly, however, as the media reminds us every day, money is spent on weapons as a result of local conflicts, leaving ever fewer resources for medical care. Furthermore, regulations implemented in the name of security as a response to threats of terrorism, real and imagined, have brought about restrictions by local governments on the movement of peoples as they attempt to flee from violence and abject poverty, resulting in a phenomenal rise in refugee and squatter populations.[8] Epidemics of infectious disease thrive in conditions of poverty and instability, and today have the potential to wreak widespread havoc in a matter of hours, striking even the world's wealthiest – as demonstrated by the case of Atlanta lawyer Andrew Speaker in 2007, who was infected with a lethal strain of extremely drug-resistant tuberculosis (XDR-TB), leading to a frantic search for other exposed passengers on transatlantic flights.[9]

In summary, the health of people everywhere is inextricably entangled with global politics, social issues, and economics.[10] Moreover, poverty, malnourishment, and poor sanitation are associated with high infant and maternal mortality, a greater exposure to pathogens and toxins, a larger number of illness episodes, and shorter life expectancies.[11] These outcomes have been documented repeatedly over the past decades, and have become a major focus for governments, non-governmental organizations (NGOs), and interest groups that seek to improve health today.

Biomedicine as Technology

This book does not deal with inequities in health provision per se, but focuses instead on biomedical technologies and the way in which their application brings about radical changes, not merely with respect to individual bodies but in society at large. Unlike basic requirements such as clean water, biomedical technologies are not fundamentally essential for life. It is not necessary to have an extended discussion about the possible unintended consequences of providing clean water equitably to people. In contrast, numerous biomedical technologies, whether they concern the recruitment of subjects into randomized controlled trials in developing countries to test medications that will be marketed in the West, testing a fetus with the intention of practicing sex selection if it is of the "wrong" kind, or "pulling the plug" of a respirator sustaining the life of a patient in persistent vegetative state, raise profound moral questions, very often with legal and political consequences. Even something as apparently simple as taking a pill to treat an infection may have major repercussions on communities as a whole. A nationwide survey in Canada recently showed that it is not uncommon for people to self-medicate with leftover antibiotics present in their households, thus encouraging the spread of drug-resistant super-bugs. Furthermore, one in three Canadians wrongly believes that antibiotics are effective against viruses, and yet two-thirds of Canadians report that they have a clear understanding of when and how antibiotics should be taken.[12] Furthermore, in hospital settings where, one would assume, antibiotics are correctly administered, epidemics of antibiotic resistant bugs have repeatedly emerged and spread into communities – the result, it appears, of a lack of hygiene among health care professionals.[13]

Our position is that biomedical technologies are not autonomous entities, the effects of which are essentially uniform whenever they are put into operation. Professional choices about the use of specific technologies – when exactly to put them into practice, and how to interpret the results and effects that they bring about – are combined with broader societal variables including culturally informed values and constraints, specific local and global objectives, economic disparities, and inconsistent or non-existent regulations. These variables ensure that the far-reaching effects of biomedical practices of all kinds are understandable only in context, notably at sites of implementation. Drawing largely on ethnographic research, our objective is to illustrate the impact and repercussions associated with the application of several biomedical technologies in many locations, north and south, east and west, including some that are well established and widely used, and others more recently developed. Discussion will highlight professional and popular discourse about these technologies and the effects of their implementation on individuals, families, communities, and nations. Local and global policy-making in connection with their use will also be examined. Such discussion cannot be separated from a reciprocal consideration of the broader global interests and objectives of organizations such as the WHO and UNESCO, governments of both wealthy and poor countries, special interest groups, multinational business and industry, medical communities, and NGOs, all of which at times facilitate or else impede the distribution of technologies. Throughout this book our attention will be directed toward the vibrant entanglements of human activity in connection with biomedical technologies. However, we give relatively little attention to the minutiae of activities in laboratories – gene splicing, micromanipulation of human gametes, drug preparation, and so on; nor do we examine the marketing of biotechnological products. Our focus is on taken-for-granted objects of knowledge in the worlds of medicine, public health, and health policy, and their usage in practice. We also discuss the ways in which various practices and technologies are legitimated, and in particular the value judgments (often unrecognized) embedded in this type of discourse. In creating our arguments, we draw extensively on historical and ethnographic research, because the impact made by biomedical technologies of all kinds cannot be understood without an appreciation of how they are incorporated into the historical trajectory and everyday social life of the locales in which they arrive. We will show that it is impossible to assess the effects of technologies without obtaining extensive first-hand accounts from affected populations about their experiences in adopting (or being forbidden to adopt) specific biomedical technologies.

While quantitative survey research can result in findings that assist in the implementation of innovative changes in health policy-making, our position is that evidence in the form of accounts given by local peoples should also be drawn on in creating policies because the promise of and the actual effects of biomedical technologies embedded in the social relations and moral landscapes in which they are applied. Ethnography and other forms of knowledge that explicitly engage the views of local actors provide insights into the ways in which the global dissemination of biomedicine and its specific local forms transform not only human bodies, but also people's hopes and aspirations in ways that may well have broader repercussions for society at large, a point that will be developed in several of the following chapters.

Does Culture Exist?

Throughout this book the concept of culture will be drawn on, at times explicitly, at other times implicitly, as an analytic tool in the discussions that follow. The idea of "culture" has a tortuous genealogy, in part as a result of its separate origins in several European languages from approximately the 14th century and its continued use since then in several different ways. From the time that anthropologists first took up this concept in the mid–19th century they have created hundreds of definitions of culture, and continue to debate and discuss its worth.[14] For this reason, a brief discussion follows about this slippery concept and how we make use of it in this book.

The anthropologist Clifford Geertz, writing about the concept of culture in the 1990s, stated that the task of "other-knowing," that is, the work of many anthropologists, "is a delicate business."[15] As part of the escalating process of globalization, borders dissolve and boundaries that are drawn to demarcate self from other – whether justified in terms of politics, economics, or the idea of culture – tend to become less meaningful and, in many instances, actively open to dispute. The assumption, held formerly by the majority of anthropologists and others, that in a named culture everyone participates equally in local socioeconomic arrangements, exhibits similar behavioral patterns, and adheres to shared values is no longer tenable. The majority of anthropologists now agree that assigning individuals to named essentialized cultures is not a valid exercise and, although many medical anthropologists have in the past given priority to "culture" as an explanatory concept in connection with matters relating to health, it has now become obvious to most that this concept has serious limitations. For one thing, in privileging culture, anthropologists have often set to one side a consideration of political and economic contributions to health and illness, notably the impact of inequities and discrimination on wellbeing and longevity.[16] But beyond this fundamental difficulty is another, bearing on the culture concept itself, involving a vexing debate about what exactly is being conveyed by using culture as an analytic tool.

More than any other eminent anthropologist Clifford Geertz has wholeheartedly supported the concept of culture. Over a decade ago, clearly feeling defensive, he set out to defend his continued support for its utility:

> Everyone, everywhere and at all times, seems to live in a sense-suffused world, to be the product of what the Indonesian scholar Taufik Abdullah has nicely called a history of notion-formation ... one can ignore such facts, obscure them, or pronounce them forceless. But they do not thereby go away. Whatever the infirmities of the concept of "culture" ("cultures," "cultural forms" ...) there is nothing for it but to persist in spite of them.[17]

The anthropologist Marilyn Strathern, writing for a largely medical audience, also defends the use of culture, and argues that the concept "draws attention to the way things are formulated and conceptualized as a matter of practice or technique. People's values are based in their ideas about the world; conversely ideas shape how people think and react." She goes on: "ideas always work in the context of other ideas, and contexts form semantic (cultural) domains that separate ideas as much as they connect them."[18] In common with many other anthropologists, including ourselves, Strathern is adamant that if this slippery concept is to be made use of, then it must be applied ubiquitously, to all societies and to all aspects of knowledge, including scientific knowledge.

Other writers stress that culture should be understood as neither static nor totalizing; culturally informed values are subject to dispute, are never distributed equally across named groups of people, and are inevitably made use of in relationships of power, moral order, and the maintenance of inequalities.[19] However, borders and boundaries can no longer easily be demarcated and, given the global economy, are best interpreted as a "complex, overlapping, disjunctive order."[20] Arjun Appadurai argues that a major problem today is "the tension between cultural homogenization and cultural heterogenization."[21] He points out that by homogenization is usually meant "Americanization" and/or "commoditization"; however, he argues there is a second process that often goes unnoticed, one of "indigenization," a process that occurs when newly diffused ideas, knowledge, behaviors, technologies, and material goods are appropriated and actively transformed in order to "fit" with the cultural horizons of their new localities. Significantly, it has been shown repeatedly that artifacts, including biomedical technologies, can be introduced successfully to different locations without the simultaneous adoption of the logical use originally associated with them.[22] New meanings and social relations coalesce around transported artifacts, whatever the direction of their travel.[23] This is not an argument for the autonomy of artifacts (or for that matter for the autonomy of culture), but rather for their inherent heterogeneity as social objects, a point to which we will return in the following chapters.

Today, nation-states often draw self-consciously on the idea of a unique shared history and culture that holds their peoples to a common set of so-called "traditional" values that serve as a moral code for conduct. This idea of a unique shared history has been described by the anthropologist Daniel Valentine as "mythohistory"[24] and, when invoked, can have profound affects on the application of technology.[25] Nationalistic sentiments such as these serve to re-essentialize the culture concept at a time when anthropologists are voicing marked concern about its misapplication. Furthermore, it is noticeable that many people who formerly assisted in anthropological research as local "informants" react strongly today to being "treated as specimens of cultural difference and otherness."[26] Equally evident, the self-conscious fostering of the idea of a shared culture is, in most parts of the world, subject to interrogation or rejection by segments of the populations in question. In other words, the very idea of culture is being politicized and has become a touchstone for mobilizing dissent often in opposition to "outsiders."

In contrast, in health care settings in the West, in an effort to promote what is sometimes termed "ethnically sensitive health care," or "cultural competence,"[27] health care professionals in the U.S., Great Britain, Canada, and elsewhere are frequently encouraged to pay attention to the impact of culture and ethnicity on the knowledge and behavior of their patients. This practice can perhaps be characterized as the "medicalization of culture." Such an approach makes few allowances for the following: highly divergent countries of origin of immigrants who speak the same language; generational, educational, and value differences among immigrants; and embedded gender inequalities that can be profoundly damaging to the health of women and children. No standardized approach to acquiring "cultural competence" is adequate; the challenge demands a great deal of careful, context-sensitive reflection, rather than simply adding on clichéd notions of ethnicity as another variable in the patient history.[28]

Despite the promotion of so-called cultural competence, a widespread tendency persists among certain health care professionals and indeed many members of the public, evident at times in the media, of ethnically stereotyping "others."[29] Part of the reason for this in the world of medicine is the common assumption that "culture" is largely composed of non-rational and superstitious beliefs that inhibit the acceptance of scientifically grounded knowledge and practices, and that such beliefs must be circumvented in order to bring about patient compliance. In a recent essay Didier Fassin notes that health care authorities, including those employed by the WHO, frequently cite cultural beliefs as the reason why women choose not to cooperate with the modernization of maternity practices: "In incriminating culture, as certain health authorities willingly do, sometimes supported by anthropological data, they are in fact blaming victims while masking their own responsibility in the matter."[30] Using a case study from Ecuador, Fassin stresses that poverty and an inability to travel to biomedical facilities on the part of many indigenous peoples have much greater explanatory power in accounting for apparent non-compliance than does the idea of embedded cultural resistance. Fassin, himself a physician/anthropologist, noted that this situation was exacerbated by a lack of understanding and sympathy among local health care professionals. He argues that "culturalism," by which he means the assumption that culture is a unified entity and may be used to fully account for people's behavior, is made use of by powerful individuals and in institutions to divert attention from the social, economic, and political origins of ill health.[31]

Culturalism often ensures that "target populations" themselves are assumed to be the cause of difficulties encountered in trying to implement changes in health care; furthermore, Fassin argues, such an attitude denies people a right to be different in how they understand their bodies in health and illness. He decries the violence implicitly associated with culturalism, but concedes that it is possible to retain the idea of culture as a useful concept (in the form of widely shared values within a group of people), provided that it is used as an explanation of last resort and then only as a politicized concept – a study of culture must move out of the realm of moral assumptions, he argues, and into the domain of politics. It is then possible to better comprehend the dangers associated with adopting an attitude in which it is assumed that culture determines behavior. Furthermore, by politicizing culture, it is made evident how the concept, often linked with religion, is subject to being mobilized for nationalistic purposes by powerful groups, usually in opposition to perceived threats to society as a result of the "Westernizing" influences of modernity.

We agree wholeheartedly that the effects of inequities, discrimination, and injustice on health and on life itself must be exposed; these variables account, more than do any others, for the unequal distribution of disease, disability, and early death.[32] But recognition of the way in which culturalism contributes to the perpetuation of inequities and injustice within and among societies is crucial, especially when it is recognized that the majority of individuals today are no longer immersed in a situation where a dominant cultural ideology exerts a hegemonic hold over them. Increasingly, as a result of exposure to other ways of being, people in most parts of the world are able to reflect on their lives and exert agency in the hope of bringing about change. Although living under an oppressive political regime places major limitations on such activities, it is nevertheless clear that global communication technologies such as the Internet and the cultural ideas of many kinds that they disseminate have the power to influence how people virtually everywhere are able to imagine a better life for themselves.[33]

In his recent comprehensive genealogy of the anthropological uses of culture, Michael Fischer comes out in support of the concept. He argues that culture is, in effect, "an experimental tool" for anthropologists – one that assists in making "visible the differences of interest, access, power, needs, desires, and philosophical perspective[s]." Fischer goes on to note the importance of the concept of culture for understanding new developments in the life sciences: "in particular, as we begin to face new kinds of ethical dilemmas stemming from developments in biotechnologies, expansive information and image databases, and ecological interactions, we are challenged to develop differential cultural analyses that can help articulate new social institutions for an evolving civil society."[34] Many of these emerging institutions are assemblages whose networks straddle the globe and are by no means confined within one or more society. Increasingly facets of biomedical research are deeply embedded in such networks with repercussions for clinical care and the promotion of public health everywhere. Further discussion of such networks appears in Part III of this book.

A Word about Ethnography

Historically the practice of ethnography was devoted to providing detailed descriptions of the "exotic other" in order to "make the strange familiar." During the latter part of the 20th century, a second objective was made explicit, namely to use such descriptions to reflect on how "our own common sense is structured."[35] The anthropologist George Marcus, in writing about the techniques and uses of ethnography for a globalized world at the end of the 20th century, called for a significant shift in the orientation of ethnographers away from an emphasis on localized, discrete societies. He argued that if the findings of ethnographic projects are to have significance beyond anthropological circles then they should be multi-sited.[36] Marcus insists that no one site can any longer be regarded as insular; documenting the worldwide networks in which linked sites are embedded, and giving voice to all involved actors, powerful and otherwise, wherever they reside, is crucial. This does not necessarily mean literally visiting a string of field sites but rather documenting how larger forces past and present impinge on local sites. Giving voice to peoples without power whose opinions and experiences are rarely heard or known has been common anthropological practice. Such research continues to be important, but by taking a multi-sited approach, the many factors relating to an object or phenomena selected for investigation can be described, including the perspectives of experts, policy-makers and practitioners.

Marcus cautions that, particularly when portraying the positions of those in power, it is all too easy to fail to interrogate key categories that appear commonsensical and are used unreflectively by researchers. A multi-sited ethnographic approach readily opens up for questioning ontological assumptions about what is assumed to be "real" and fundamental, as well as epistemological assumptions about how we know what we know. One effect of this approach is to highlight the way in which scientists, health policy-makers, and publics are all caught up in culturally informed realities that are sometimes mutually reinforcing, and at other times divisive. Disputes among scientists and clinicians, as well as competing positions taken up by government factions, advocacy groups, and affected families and individuals, are made visible through ethnography and by means of archival research. For example, ethnographic research on HIV should engage experts and policy-makers who seek to change sexual behavior through HIV prevention programs, and not only the individuals who are targeted by these programs. Current debates about the role of male circumcision, abstinence, or condoms in HIV prevention require that the cultural beliefs and practices of NGOs, development agencies, and international organizations be examined in light of the expertise and critical perspectives (rather than the "culture") of their intended "beneficiaries".

A good number of medical anthropologists have made use of ethnography over the past 30 years to examine certain of the unexamined assumptions embedded in biomedicine, including the creation of biomedical categories of disease, the way in which populations are delineated, and other fundamental assumptions about what will count as natural facts. The idea of the gene, for example, is presently undergoing a transformation for many scientists, so that it is no longer recognized literally as a material entity, but rather as a working concept, with enormous social repercussions for predictions of and testing for genetic risk.[37] A "physical snippet of DNA" is the material entity that takes priority in the minds of many scientists today; this epistemological shift will be taken up more fully in chapter 13.[38] Similarly, until relatively recently it was believed that nerve tissue could not regenerate. That belief is now thoroughly overturned and brain "plasticity" is recognized among neuroscientists, also with significant social repercussions.[39]

This book is not itself an ethnography, but in creating our arguments we have drawn extensively on ethnographic research that we find particularly helpful in revealing entanglements among history, politics, and cultural values in connection with the global circulation of biomedical technologies. As noted above, it is abundantly clear that wherever they live, the vast majority of people are by no means passive recipients of new technologies, and inevitably a variety of disputes and responses are evident in any given setting. A considerable amount of our attention will focus in the following pages on these responses in order to highlight the severe limitations of a top-down approach to the implementation of biomedical technologies.

Throughout the discussion in the following chapters we pay considerable attention to the way in which culturally infused assumptions are embedded in scientific knowledge, health policy-making, and clinical care, with significant consequences for local populations. It is the cultures of organizations, of biomedicine,[40] and of other powerful actors that are often more pertinent factors in shaping the outcomes of public health initiatives than are the values embedded in targeted populations; yet such cultures of power and intervention are studied only rarely.[41] We highlight the several bodies of knowledge, unexamined assumptions, and expectations evidenced among the many actors involved in medically related projects, including politicians, NGOs, basic scientists, clinicians, patients, families, and communities.

We also consider the actual implementation of biotechnologies at local sites, wherever their origin – global, regional, or local – giving recognition to the ever-present possibilities for fluidity, transformation, and surprise. It is clear that culturally infused values have relevance both to the reception of biomedical technologies and the uses to which they are put, or alternatively to their rejection, as was the case while the Bush administration was in power in the United States for stem cell technology making use of discarded human embryos.

Outline of Chapters

The book is divided into four parts. In the first part, comprising four chapters, the relationship among technologies, the production of knowledge about the material body, and actual medical practice are considered with emphasis on historical, social, cultural, and political variables. The first chapter sets out different ways of characterizing technologies and in so doing highlights our position that biomedical technologies are neither morally nor socially neutral; rather, unexamined assumptions are embedded in the development of technologies and their implementation in practice that reflect prevailing social and political interests and cultural values. Furthermore, biomedical technologies encompass a broad range of practices and procedures that are made use of not only in clinical care, but also in both the production of scientific knowledge and standardized practices. Technologies are not, therefore, the straightforward application of scientific knowledge; furthermore, we argue that biomedicine itself is a technology.

In the second chapter we discuss the way in which, beginning in the 17th century, a systematic and ultimately scientific approach to knowledge about the body and its management began to emerge, resulting in what has come to be known today as biomedicine. This approach was grounded by knowledge produced by decontextualizing the body and subjecting it to an anatomical gaze resulting in the objectification of bodies. Furthermore, by the 19th century, the condition of individual bodies began to be judged in relation to so-called "norms" derived from statistical data based on the biological characterization of groups of bodies – or populations – with the result that disease came to be conceptualized as essentially everywhere the same. Thus, the science of biology became the standard, a set of agreed-upon rules, for intervening in the body.

In chapter 3 we outline several research themes prominent in the social sciences over the past half century that demonstrate, in stark contrast to a common assumption about the scientific neutrality of biomedicine, that medicine is a deeply social and political enterprise. Medical anthropology and medical sociology have made use of diverse theoretical orientations and methodologies over the years to produce a rich body of data; we elaborate on two themes: the phenomenon of medical pluralism abundantly evident everywhere in the world and the so-called medicalization of life, including the social construction of disease taxonomies and the significance of illness narratives; and the pursuit of health. These social science findings alert readers to the limitations of an approach to the body which assumes objective and standardized measures that do not unfailingly achieve desired results, and they also make clear what sets biomedicine apart from other medical systems.

Using ethnographic and scientific findings, we argue in chapter 4 for the recognition of local biologies. Evidence is presented that bodies are not everywhere the same because humans are inextricably entangled with historical, environmental, social, cultural, and political contexts, thus dislodging an assumption that bodies are readily "standardizable." We challenge the notion of biological universals using examples about the end of menstruation, the neurodegenerative condition known as *kuru*, the relationship between the experience of racism and low birth weights, and the reciprocal association of microbes and humans. These examples make clear that nature and culture are inseparably entangled and, further, that evolutionary, environmental, and social forces, including the application of biomedical technologies, transform the material body.

Part II of the book, comprising chapters 5 through 7, shows how biology has become as a standard for technological intervention on human bodies and populations. The impact of these technologies at local sites is documented with reference to historical and ethnographic materials. Central to our argument is a consideration of how the technological production of biomedical knowledge and its practices are entangled with practices by means of which power, wealth, health, and longevity are acquired both globally and locally. These chapters also make clear how the deliberate or inadvertent erasure of local biologies has serious implications for the management of ill health. Chapter 5 opens with a discussion of the history of the concept of "population" commencing with Thomas Malthus. The now defunct science of eugenics associated with the social engineering of populations is then considered and its transition in the mid–20th century to the "family planning" movement and thence to contemporary "population control." In recent years, numerous governments, in order to "acquire" modernization and economic development, have made systematic use of technologies designed to reduce excess population. The case studies of China, India, and Palestine are used as illustrative examples of the varied politics of population management, global and local. The dramatic impact of these technologies on everyday life is stressed and, on the basis of social science research, it is shown how the demand from above to dramatically reduce family size has exacerbated gender discrimination. Illegal use of fetal imaging technology to select against female births has resulted in a significant imbalance in the sex ratio at birth in several parts of the world. This situation raises the question of the global governance of biomedical technologies.

Chapter 6 discusses some aspects of the medical management of "critical events" including epidemics, famines, and fertility and birth, from the early 19th century with an emphasis on the European colonies of Africa. This chapter also reveals the way in which campaigns for infectious disease control and improved maternal and child health and nutrition paved the way for biomedicine to become the dominant medical system, even in places far from where it first arose. The public health measures that were put into practice in the colonies, once found to be successful, in turn influenced the introduction of similar practices in many of the major European cities. Chapter 7 describes the way in which the assumption of human biological equivalence worldwide provides the grounds for counting and comparing humans, in effect making human populations worldwide available as "laboratories" for generating biomedical knowledge. The assumption of a standardizable body permits specific material, political, and economic conditions at local sites, and the local biologies that result, to be effectively circumvented, with enormous moral and practical consequences. The knowledge acquired from these experimental sites, in particular those that conduct randomized controlled trials, is put to work in producing medications, the bulk of which may be consumed far from these experimental sites.

The third part of the book, comprising chapters 8 through 10, deals with techno/ biologicals, entities created out of living cells, tissues, and organs that facilitate research, or else substitute or replace faulty, inadequate, or failed body parts and mechanisms. The production and application of techno/biologicals challenge several fundamental assumptions about the natural and moral order, including that of the body as a clearly bounded entity; a well-demarcated distinction between self and other; and what constitutes biological parenthood. What was formerly assumed to be an unassailable distinction between the social and natural order can no longer be thought of in this way. Chapter 8 examines the types of "acquisitions" essential to the implementation of vital technologies, namely the global commodification of human bodies and body parts for use as experimental and therapeutic tools. The bio-economy associated with this form of commodification is considered and the question of who "owns" the body is discussed. The commodification of eggs and sperm is considered by two illustrative case studies, one about the "immortalization" of cell lines and a second about DNA data banking. Chapter 9 examines one specific form of bodily acquisition – the procurement of human organs and tissues for transplantation. The "bioavailability" of organ donors is discussed, as well as the complex global repercussions of both the sale and donation of organs for involved individuals, families, communities, and nations. Until recently, most organs for transplant have been obtained from human bodies diagnosed as brain dead. The creation of this concept and its application results in entities that are hybrids of life and death, entirely dependent for existence on technological intervention designed to ensure that biological life continues in a body where it is assumed the person is no longer present. Chapter 10 focuses on the beginning of life, and takes up the politically charged topic of reproductive health. Emphasis given by governments and international agencies to fertility control is in strong contrast to the paucity of research on infertility in most parts of the developing world, notably sub-Saharan Africa. The consequences for everyday life of ignoring infertility are discussed. Also examined is the global implementation of assisted reproductive technologies, with emphasis on the gendered, social, and political ramifications of these practices. Ethnographic findings from the United States, Egypt, Israel, and elsewhere are made use of to illustrate the significant challenges posed by these technologies to normative reproduction and who counts as kin.

The fourth and final part of the book examines how attempts to locate invisible and elusive agents of illness within the body – in the form of the unconscious or the gene – may falter, generate radical uncertainty, and have other unexpected consequences. We focus on how biological selfhood is resocialized in unexpected ways, and how these agents introduce new forms of personal responsibility for some while absolving others. These uses of biomedical technologies in fact challenge common distinctions made between body and self and self and other, and ethnographic examples show clearly how people's sense of "self" results both from embodied, biological phenomena and patterns of social relations.

Chapter 11 examines how the "self" is mobilized to therapeutic ends, and how biomedical technologies act as "technologies of the self" when used by individuals to heal themselves and others, and to achieve a better life for oneself and one's off-spring. Technologies that are used to uncover "pathogenic secrets," fashion biomedical practitioners' expertise, and foster social "empowerment" are examined to challenge common assumptions about a universal, inward self and the "objectivity" of biomedicine, including the idea that biomedicine's therapeutic power stems from biological efficacy alone.

In chapter 12 we consider the new genetics and the concept of "embodied risk." Technologies of genetic testing and screening make the genetic body knowable and, once again drawing on ethnographic findings, we examine the impact of learning about one's genetic heritage for sense of self and kin, political activism, and new forms of sociability. Preimplantation genetic diagnosis – the selection of fetuses following genetic screening for implantation and gestation – is also discussed in light of concerns about an emerging neo-eugenics.

In chapter 13, the significance of recent findings in molecular biology for challenging genetic determinism is outlined, as well as a discussion of directions taken by emerging epigenetic knowledge. The difficulties of calculating estimations of risk for future disease based on knowledge about susceptibility genes associated with complex common disease are discussed and illustrated with reference to ethnographic data about late-onset Alzheimer's disease.

The final chapter takes up the topic of biological difference, and the way in which findings in molecular genetics and genomics have resulted in a new round of politically charged disputes about race and ethnicity. We argue that because biological difference is real, as we have shown throughout the book using the concept of local biologies, to deny this reality is inappropriate and leads at times to poor medical care. Nevertheless to use essentialized categories of race to gloss biological difference is entirely inappropriate.

In conclusion we return to the argument we make for the entanglement of material bodies with history, environment, culture, and politics. We reiterate what has been stated in different ways throughout the book – that the human body in health and illness is not an ontological given but a moveable, malleable entity – the elusive product of nature and culture that refuses to be pinned down.[42] Without attention to this malleability and to the social and political contexts in which people live out their lives, technological interventions will often result in unintended consequences, and will exacerbate rather than heal global inequities and health disparities.

Part I
Technologies and Bodies in Context

1
Biomedical Technologies in Practice

In this chapter, we set out our argument that biomedical technologies are not merely devices or machines such as blood tests and X-ray machines that permit the routinized application of scientific knowledge; neither are they ethically and morally neutral. Biomedical technologies have histories that inevitably start with an idea or a random or unexpected observation that then initiates a series of experimental procedures. Many technologies never progress beyond this initial phase, but others are put into production and are then applied in medical care. However, the application of a biomedical technology does not simply depend on its medical use alone, but is deeply influenced by prevailing medical and political interests and cultural norms, as well as by overarching ideas about the most promising directions for progress and mastery of the natural world.

At the experimental stage, biomedical technologies enable manipulations that intervene in animal and human bodies to make previously unknown or inaccessible "objects" factually real. Very often extensive tinkering is necessary to produce these material entities or "techno-phenomena." The improbable chain of events in 1928 that led the Scottish researcher Alexander Fleming to observe the antibiotic properties of the rare mold, *Penicillium notatum*, is a well-known example of the humble origins of many biomedical technologies. Fleming rather carelessly left an open Petri dish smeared with *Staphylococcus* bacteria on his laboratory bench by an open window while he went away on a two-week holiday. When he returned a clear halo surrounded the yellow-green growth of the bacteria produced by a mold that had accidentally drifted into Fleming's London lab from a mycology unit one floor below. Various unconfirmed reports about the effectiveness of the mold had already been reported prior to Fleming's "discovery," but he was the first to grow a pure culture of *Penicillium* resulting in a new techno-phenomenon that he named penicillin. However, it was not until 1942 that sufficient observations and experiments had been carried out and sufficient quantities of penicillin produced for it to be put formally into production in the United States, and then initially only on a small scale. It took even longer for ordinary doctors to appreciate its value and learn that the drug should be administered intravenously to be effective.

Ludwig Fleck argued in the first half of the 20th century that phenomena that scientists work with are the products of technologies, practices, and preconditioned ways of seeing and understanding. Fleck's argument is that every scientific phenomenon exists only as a result of a technical intervention on the part of scientists,[1] and that creating a firm separation between the worlds of research and of application (such as is commonly done between the laboratory and the clinic) is entirely inappropriate. In other words, biomedical technologies are anchored as part of one or more "sociotechnical systems" that straddle institutions including hospitals, laboratories, biotech companies, and the state.[2] The phenomena that result from their application coalesce as accepted biological, clinical, and epidemiological facts associated with biomedical practice. Such routinized practices are transportable across vast distances, and are capable of marshalling yet more phenomena as a result of systematic interventions into patient bodies or populations of people, thus producing yet more facts. In other words, biomedical technologies bring about transformations, resulting in newly discovered knowledge about the material world that, in turn, influences subsequent interventions into it. This insight informs our position that the science of biomedicine is actively constructed by technology – biomedical technology. By extension this means that health-related matters are routinely "objectified" as technical problems, to be solved through the application of technology and the conduct of science and are, by definition, therefore, decontextualized in practice. Objectification tends to make opaque moral assumptions embedded in the uses to which any given technology is put and its actual effects on individuals and social groups, as the following chapters will show.

This approach builds on and extends the work in the 1960s and 1970s of the French philosopher Michel Foucault. As is well known, Foucault argued that, commencing in the 17th century, the management of individuals by the state began to be accomplished through the expansion of practices of regulation, discipline, and surveillance directed at individuals. At the same time, government of "populations" – of what Foucault termed *le vivant* ("the living") – was brought about making use of technologies of the census. Foucault coined the term "biopower,"[3] to describe the means by which government is exercised in the form of technologies that, while not "machine-like," are nonetheless systematic and codified, generating objects for management as well as new knowledge. Foucault's formulation encourages an examination of a broad range of practices that can be usefully understood as biomedical technologies. Shortly before his death Foucault introduced a distinction between, on the one hand, technologies of bodily governance that he termed "objectifying practices" and, on the other hand, technologies of the self used to transform one's own body and mind through, for instance, spiritual exercises, public acts of contrition, and confession.[4] Together, these technologies have resulted in forms of embodiment and experience that people today take to be "natural," resulting in the "making up" of kinds of people that did not previously exist.[5]

We argue that two significant developments make a straightforward application of Foucault's categories to contemporary biomedical technologies problematic. The first is the advent of what we call "techno/biologicals," technologies that are in part constituted from human biological material, thus troubling "natural" categories about self and other, and producing new forms of life. The second is the deployment of biomedical technologies outside the parameters of the state, whether in the developing world or in industrialized economies, by NGOs and private actors who seek to achieve specific health goals independently of a systematic government-monitored approach to public health. In light of these developments, understanding emerging forms of biopower requires careful scrutiny of biomedical technologies in practice.

Technological Mastery of the Natural World and Human Development

A belief that mastery of the natural world could be achieved through scientific investigation and the application of "machine power" was central to Enlightenment thinking.[6] By the 19th century, writers as different as Herbert Spencer and Auguste Comte explicitly associated developments in science and technology with progress and the advancement of human kind. Spencer argued that the degree to which people are able to control the natural world is an indication of the degree of their civilized status,[7] and the anthropologist Edward Tylor, in his book *Primitive Culture*, sought to rank cultures according to their ability in "adapting nature to man's ends," with savages at the lowest end of the spectrum and educated peoples of Western Europe at the highest end.[8] Of course there were a good number of well-known dissenters to a position that valorized the progress brought about by science and technology, but these people were, without doubt, in the minority.[9]

Signs of this "honorable" and "audacious" struggle against "brute matter"[10] were evident in Europe from the 15th century; the work of Leonardo da Vinci, Nicolaus Copernicus, Andreas Vesalius, followed later by Francis Bacon, Galileo Galilei, Isaac Newton, and many others, provides evidence of an epistemological upheaval characterized today as the "scientific revolution," one in which the world is made known through systematic investigation and transformed for the better by means of the application of technologies. In the 18th and 19th centuries this approach was indispensable to the industrial revolution in northern Europe, one of the principal intentions of which was to improve the wellbeing of the masses, if only so that they might be better able to endure excessively hard work.[11] It also brought about world-wide exploration and colonization, including the systematic extraction of wealth in the form of natural materials of all kinds, both for building and engineering feats and for scientific investigation in laboratories and medical schools.[12]

One strand of early scientific thought that became extremely influential in both British and Continental thinking of the 18th century, and is particularly relevant for the argument that we make in this book, culminated in Isaac Newton's experiments on optics, mathematics, and mechanics. Newton postulated a "world machine" created by God, a machine that set the whole universe in motion, one governed by immutable laws subject to human investigation. This mechanistic view of nature is both causal and deterministic and enabled Newton to argue provocatively that the force holding the planets in their orbits that can be expressed in a single mathematical equation is the same force governing matter on earth.[13] Newton has been described by many as a "disembodied scholar," one who lived an otherworldly life of detachment, although this characterization is currently being questioned; nevertheless he was most certainly a man "possessed by a love of truth,"[14] one who exemplified a rational approach to understanding the world about us as a unified whole.

A good number of truth-claims put forward during the Enlightenment, including those of Newton, are still with us today, and have a profound effect on the way in which science is conducted and biomedical technologies of all kinds are put into practice. Among them are the following: First, many people involved in the enterprise of "development" argue with little reflection that further technological mastery of nature is essential to continued progress and improving the state of the world economically and in terms of health and wellbeing. Second, many researchers in the biological sciences continue to assume that biology is subject to universal laws similar to those established for physics based on the insights of Newton. Third, it is commonly assumed in the medical sciences that the human body is readily standardizable by means of systematic assessments, bringing about a further assumption that the material make-up of the body is, for all intents and purposes, universal. Fourth, the global dissemination of knowledge, biomedical technologies, and ways of life and moral underpinnings associated with modern Western civilization are an essential part of an enlightened humanistic endeavor. Although people increasingly question these axioms, the dominant ideology holds firm.

Technology and Boundary Crossings

In common with technologies of all kinds, biomedical technologies have the prime function of enabling humans to act on the world and its people. However, simply observing this situation and leaving things at that immediately suggests that technologies are mere objects – in effect, autonomous entities. Marx noted the key corollary long ago: that by changing the shape of material things we inevitably change ourselves, and much of what we discuss in this book will make that evident. Biomedical technologies are, of course, designed expressly to facilitate human intervention into the workings of the body in health and illness; in implementation they change us, and even as they themselves are constantly modified, they change the world in which we live.

The use of complex, sophisticated technology is integral to biomedicine today – increasingly so as molecular biological knowledge and its associated computer technologies become ever more routinized.[15] Once technological interventions become the keys to diagnosis (very often of more importance today than the clinical examination per se) and to care, then inevitable changes result as to what counts as valid knowledge about the body, the doctor–patient relationship, and, indeed, the relationship among the body, culture, and society.

As mentioned above, the history of technological innovation, at least from the time of the Enlightenment, is usually portrayed in Europe and North America as a narrative of progress and of the betterment of individual and social life. The anthropologist Brian Pfaffenberger[16] has characterized this history as the "Standard View" of technology: tools, devices, and artifacts permit us to lead an increasingly rational, autonomous, and prosperous existence, liberated from constraints imposed by individual biology, oppressive human enemies, and the environment. Embedded in this Standard View are two sets of tacit meanings that at first sight are contradictory. The first assumes that the relationship of humans to technology is too obvious to need examination. Organizations, industries, technicians, craftspeople, and others simply make things that are in themselves neither good nor bad. This is what Langdon Winner[17] has described as "technological somnambulism" – an unreflective acceptance of technological innovation. The second approach, one of technological determinism, conceives of technology as a powerful and autonomous agent, inherent to progress, and therefore by definition an unquestionable good, but one that inevitably dictates the forms that human social life will take.[18] The very idea of an autonomous technology raises an "unsettling irony."[19] We humans have apparently lost out to the monster, but nevertheless rush eagerly ahead creating new devices in the belief that we will achieve yet more control and autonomy in our lives.

Of course utopian visions about the freedom that technologies will bring have not been entirely hegemonic, and all along they have been opposed by a counter-discourse depicting dystopias, replete with warnings about the consequences for society of technology gone wild. From the Frankenstein story of Mary Wollstonecraft Shelley, to Charles Dickens' *Hard Times*, H. G. Wells' *The Island of Dr Moreau*, Aldous Huxley's *Brave New World*, George Orwell's *Nineteen Eighty Four*, and Margaret Atwood's *The Handmaiden's Tale* and more recently *Oryx and Crake*, among many others, we read in novels and science fiction and see at the movies and on television the havoc and misery that technologies can potentially create. Inevitably it is at technologically manipulated margins between what is assumed to be the unassailable natural world and the encroaching boundaries of culture where concern and moral outrage is most evident in these dystopian accounts. Well over a decade ago, Pfaffenberger concluded that, as seen through a Modernist lens, technology is depicted as both creator and destroyer; an agent of future promise and at the same time of culture's destruction,[20] a position that has been reiterated repeatedly over the intervening years. Emerging technologies that enable us to "see into" the living body and to manipulate bodily boundaries and molecular formations formerly assumed to be absolutely inviolable exacerbate this tension.

Among those who in the early part of the 20th century perceived the effects of technological innovation principally as a form of dystopia was Lewis Mumford. In his extensive writings he was one of the first to sow the seeds of a more complex approach to our understanding of the relationship among technology, society, and culture and, with fascism very much in mind, he wrote critically about technology. Mumford referred to "our over-mechanized culture," a condition that he feared would lead to a "final totalitarian structure." He believed that the new international competitiveness associated with globalization would eventually produce a "dominant minority" who would manipulate the majority through the creation of depersonalized organizations constituting a "megamachine," something visualized by Mumford as an inclusive but "invisible" entity, embracing not only technical and scientific expertise and artifacts, but also the bureaucratic structures designed to organize and control the whole enterprise.[21] In an era of technologized and globalized neo-liberalism, and now with the collapse of the global economy, Mumford's writing reads as prophetic.

A tacit assumption embedded in both the somnambulist and autonomous visions of technology is that material artifacts are things-in-themselves, and therefore ethically and morally neutral – a position that Mumford so ably exposed, and one that today a good number of philosophers, sociologists, and anthropologists of science, ourselves included, argue against.[22] Biomedical technologies, ranging from embryos created by means of IVF (*in vitro* fertilization), tissue cultures, and genetic engineering, permit us to radically reconstruct what are assumed to be "natural" boundaries between culture and nature, often creating new entities – hybrids of what was formerly thought of as belonging distinctly in the domain of either nature or culture. A body diagnosed as brain dead continues to breathe with the assistance of a mechanical ventilator; it is warm, urinates, and defecates – such a "dead" body must be alive if organs for transplant are to be procured from it. The technological ability to determine the sex of a fetus prior to birth has brought about a significant demographic imbalance in some locations. The implementation of biomedical technologies also challenges what has generally been regarded in any one location as "normal" and morally "right": resort to sperm donors to accomplish pregnancy for example is often forbidden; buying organs for transplant is illegal in most parts of the world; and making use of psychopharmacological agents such as Prozac to "enhance" personality may be frowned upon.

Furthermore, what counts as normal and abnormal is open to interpretation on the basis of statistically calculated estimations of risk that can be subject to periodic recalculation as a result of new research findings. An example of this is the use of blood cholesterol levels to assess the risk of heart attack based on epidemiological studies of large populations that have demonstrated the association between cholesterol and heart disease. Recent research, much of it funded by drug companies that make cholesterol-lowering drugs, suggests that even lowering a "normal" cholesterol level can decrease the risk, a finding contested by some physicians.[23] At these nodes of uncertainty it becomes most apparent that moral and scientific judgments are intertwined.[24] We will return to this point repeatedly throughout the following chapters.

Biomedicine as Technology: Some Implications

By focusing on biomedical technologies, our purpose is to draw empirical and analytic scrutiny to the practical and everyday implications of biomedicine and the biosciences in the lives of people around the world. In so doing, we are in agreement with anthropologists and practitioners who view biomedicine neither as a monolithic, universal, static enterprise, nor simply as a particularistic and personalized practice. Wherever it is made use of, biomedicine, although standardized for universal application, must be individualized for use in actual clinical practice. It is this two-fold dimension we wish to capture from the outset, by drawing attention to the enterprise of biomedicine as itself a technology in the application of which judgments are constantly made.

No doubt what springs most readily to mind when thinking about biomedical technologies are machines such as mechanical ventilators, imaging technologies including X-ray machines and CT scans, as well as devices such as prosthetic limbs, cardiac pacemakers, tooth implants, and so on. However, our lives are filled with far more mundane biomedical devices and technologies including the basic physical examination, patient history-taking (including self-examination and self-history-taking), administration of injections, and the prescription of medications. These technologies are ubiquitous and affect everyone including many of the millions of people today designated as the "super poor." In practice such "simple" technologies have a number of features in common. Most importantly, they are highly portable and can easily be applied anywhere and used with little or no training, and often at relatively little cost. Furthermore, the undoubted efficacy of many pharmaceuticals, when appropriately prescribed and applied, makes them powerful tools, sometimes invested with magical qualities. Not surprisingly, then, the lives and hopes of people in virtually all parts of the world are touched to some extent by the promise of bio-medicine, even when the majority of its medications and more expensive technologies remain largely beyond the reach of most.

As noted above, biomedical technologies can be viewed as the products of ration-ally ordered sociotechnical complexes in which they must be embedded in order to function. Nikolas Rose refers to "hybrid assemblages of knowledges, instruments, persons, systems of judgment, buildings and spaces, underpinned at the program-matic level by certain presuppositions and assumptions about human beings."[25] Applying the genealogical method of Michel Foucault, Rose is explicit that technolo-gies have histories, and this simple recognition makes it evident that their application changes what it is to be human. In her study of the development of tissue culture, Hannah Landecker shows how biomedical technologies, particularly those that have emerged over the past century as a result of advances in molecular biology, transform, first of all, "what it is to be biological" and thence what it is to be human.[26] These formulations are very helpful, and we draw on them to argue that technologies should be understood as both produced through culture and as productive of culture.[27] This approach highlights the way in which meanings and moral imperatives are differen-tially attributed to the production of technologies over time and to the interventions on human life made possible by them. In other words, unexamined ideologies are often associated with the implementation of technologies. It also makes clear that we do not subscribe to a technological determinism although, quite often, new scientific insights and new technologies facilitate change and innovation in ways never before possible.

Legitimation of biomedical technologies involves the dissemination of rhetoric about their value; at the most fundamental level, it is assumed that they contribute to scientific progress and, further, that they fulfill human "needs." However, as Marilyn Strathern[28] has noted, the flurry of voiced opposition that surrounds the introduction of so many of the new biomedical technologies makes it clear that these hybrid entities are frequently assumed to be a threat to moral order. Hence, to justify such practices and damp down vented anxiety, legal constraints or, at a minimum, professional guidelines are produced to govern conduct in research laboratories, the clinic, and consulting rooms. Examples include rules about who is "eligible" for assisted reproduction or for organ transplants, or for medications that can be used not only to treat "deficiencies," but to enhance performance.

While, on one hand, citizens of democratic societies often assume that they have a "right" to have access to the full range of biomedical technologies in the name of health, on the other hand some individuals, apparently concerned more about personal enhancement than civic virtue, lobby government for unhampered access to technologies such as genetic testing, genetic engineering, reproductive technolo-gies, organ transplants, and even cosmetic surgery. Contradictions between what are thought of by some as individual rights and what might be understood by the authorities as in the best interest for society are not easily resolved. For example, couples who are apparently unable to conceive may wish to resort to the use of donor sperm, a practice that is not acceptable in many countries. Certain individuals who are on a list to receive an organ transplant may decide that they cannot wait any longer and decide to go abroad to buy an organ. The sale of organs is illegal in virtually every country in the world, and a further problem arises because such individuals must receive treatment when they return to their home country if the transplant is to function adequately, challenging the authority of physicians and governments. Furthermore, because technologies are themselves modified rather frequently, the practices they make possible inevitably change and hence the social and ethical aspects of the situation also change. For example, until recently it was not possible to freeze and store human eggs. Now that this can be done questions arise about under what circumstances should eggs be retrieved from women for storage, and for what purposes. Furthermore, as increasing moves are made worldwide toward the privatization of medical services, the question of national and international control over the implementation of technologies, and their growing economic cost, has become exceedingly acute.

Technologies of Bodily Governance

Biomedical technologies are not only found in clinics and hospitals. Indeed, it is the articulation of clinical practice with what we term, following Michel Foucault, "technologies of bodily governance" that makes the dissemination of biomedicine particularly effective. Such technologies deploy representative sampling, statistical assessment, and the application of probability to target entire social bodies – communities, nations, and, at times, the whole world. Foucault, writing about "techniques of power," charted the gradual emergence and regularization from the 18th and 19th centuries onward of state-controlled, systematically organized institutions – schools, the army, prisons, the family, hospitals, clinics, and other units for the administration of collective bodies. He described these changes in social organization as the formation of "biopower," central both to the emergence of capitalism and to the "controlled insertion of bodies into the machinery of production." For Foucault, biopower literally means having power over other bodies: "an explosion of numerous and diverse techniques for achieving the subjugation of bodies and the control of populations."[29] Foucault envisioned biopower as having two "poles," one of which he labeled "anatomopolitics" to express the increasing objectification and manipulation of the human body by means of medical examinations and drills, exercises, and techniques used in education, the workplace, and policing. The focus of attention of the second pole is the "biopolitics of population," in which groups constituted as named populations and sub-populations come to be defined as entities for management by the state. Foucault coined the term "governmentality" to refer to the way in which the exercise of power by the modern state came increasingly to include the active management of the population to stimulate its vitality, and the adoption of codes and techniques by individuals to govern their own lives, for instance, by adopting a "healthy" lifestyle.[30]

Although Foucault argued for two distinct poles of power, in practice they are inseparable: statistical compilations used in conjunction with the concept of risk are the tools made most use of in the fields of epidemiology and public health, and these compilations in turn profoundly influence clinical practice. Reciprocally, the creation of such compilations relies heavily on clinical data.[31] Emphasis is often given in epidemiology to what is known as the "social determinants" of health and illness, that is, to measures of poverty, inequality, discrimination, and stressors of various kinds, in order to explain why some people are more liable to become sick and die early deaths than others.[32] The proliferation of estimations of "risk" derived largely from epidemiological data means that we all are subject to warnings, primarily in the media and secondarily from our physicians, about any number of conditions to which we may be vulnerable, ranging from sexual dysfunction to obesity.

In his book *The Taming of Chance*, Ian Hacking argues that with the founding of the biometrical school of statistical research by Francis Galton in 1889 (who was also the founder of the "science" of eugenics) "the stage was set for ultimate indeterminism."[33] Hacking insists that the "imperialism of probabilities" with which we live today could only have come about in conjunction with a massive expansion of literacy, computation, book-keeping, the invention of the census, and the idea that people can be divided into different groups of populations. At first these populations consisted of deviant groups who did not "fit" with society, but they were later expanded to include citizens as a whole, for whose governance the state was responsible. Together, these activities constitute "technologies of data collection" that are intimately associated with the growth of a "research mentality" evident in Europe and North America of the late 19th and early 20th centuries, and that gradually fused with the political technologies of rule deployed in the European colonies.[34] Law-like regularities that can be observed statistically among groups of people provide a means of setting off "normal" from that which is considered deviant or "abnormal." Madness, disease, vagrancy, births, and deaths, must all be counted and categorized, in order that they may be – as it were – managed. Furthermore, individuals exhibit governmentality when they change their activities, consciously or otherwise, to those thought to be best suited to continued health and wellbeing.[35] It goes without saying, of course, that many people do not respond in a way that either the government or the medical professional might wish.

We will have more to say below and in the following chapters about Hacking's idea of "making up people,"[36] that is, the way in which people are classified into groups by authorities of one kind and another and how these classifications in turn affect the subjectivity and lives of the people so classified. And further, we will examine how these individual effects may at times in turn bring about changes in the original classifications (notably through the interventions of involved advocacy groups). Hacking argues that people subject to classification (and in contemporary society this includes us all in one way or another) are moving targets because, by being assigned to a class – abused as a child, a single mother, a refugee, a senior citizen – individuals are changed, and do not experience themselves as the same kind of person as they were prior to classification. Hacking calls this the "looping effect" – the manner in which science and bureaucracies "create kinds of people that in a certain sense did not exist before."[37]

One result of this looping effect is the proliferation of disease taxonomies. This phenomenon, together with the so-called "population problem" that preoccupies many governments today, contributes to the creation of batteries of statistics central to global health planning. Statistical modeling of troubling and threatening events, including maternal death during labor, projected HIV infections, estimations of future disease based on genetic testing, and so on, informs policies, and in so doing contributes to the looping effect and hence fashions identities; individuals are made into "at-risk mothers," "vulnerable to HIV," "at risk for prostate cancer," and so on.

Statistical methods made use of in epidemiology are sophisticated technologies designed to calculate individual risk for illness based on standardized estimates derived from population studies. Such estimates are made possible with the emergence of a state apparatus for enumerating populations through the census and making them available for study. Such an approach differs from classical divinatory technologies (consulting oracles or soothsayers and reading omens) in which accounts provided by experts about unfortunate events in the past and predictions of future danger are contextualized in the client's own life circumstances, resulting in highly individualized predictions. In contrast, population-derived epidemiological forecasts produce decontextualized probabilities about whether or not a breast cancer gene might cause breast cancer in the future, for example, or an elevated cholesterol level a heart attack. Such probabilities are of great value to insurance companies and health planners whose work depends upon reliable knowledge about populations. For example, actuarial and epidemiological data can predict with considerable certainty how many individuals in any given population will die in a year; however, these estimates cannot say who will die. Thus, risk estimates actually produce uncertainty when given to individuals, who are often baffled by or disbelieving of probabilistic calculations. The "tyranny of numbers" has often been criticized because their use is designed to create an objectivity and produce truth claims that must inevitably decontextualize and efface the reality of everyday life and experience; calculations of future risk for disease are a ubiquitous example of this kind of governance technology.

In an article published in 1985, entitled "The Median Isn't the Message,"[38] the renowned biologist Stephen J. Gould recounted how he had dealt with the acute anxiety he experienced on being diagnosed with abdominal mesothelioma, a deadly cancer. His first response was to go to a library and read up on the available literature that, once he had absorbed the information, "stunned him" for about 15 minutes. But Gould's rational brain soon took over, producing knowledge which, when combined with what he describes as his naturally optimistic outlook, permitted him to emerge from the library feeling reasonably encouraged.

In Gould's words, the literature could not have been more "brutally clear," in that the disease is incurable, and has a median mortality of about eight months after diagnosis. However, he set about questioning what a median mortality of eight months actually signified in his case. He suggests that to most people it would mean, "I will probably be dead in eight months," but insists that this is exactly the conclusion that should be avoided. We tend to view medians and means as hard "realities," Gould points out, and forget the most important thing, the variation that permits their calculation. Thus, if the median is the reality and variation around the median just a device for its calculation, then "I will probably be dead in eight months" may pass as a reasonable interpretation. But, Gould goes on, it is the medians and means that are the abstractions, and the variation that is the reality. He then figured out where in all probability he should be located amidst the variation, on the basis of his age (relatively young), his diagnosis at an early stage in the disease process, his access to the best possible medical treatment, and his strong desire to keep living. Gould then found himself in the "right skewed tail" around the median, indicating that he was among that group of diagnosed individuals who remain alive, often many years after diagnosis. In fact, Gould's calculations proved to be correct and he continued to live for a good number of years after his diagnosis.

Gould's case makes it very clear that the concept of risk is not at all self-evident because all such predictions have to be translated from statistical probabilities to "fit" the circumstances of individual lives. Moreover, health care professionals, patients, and involved families, may weigh contextual variables quite differently, added to which media reporting of risk estimates is often inaccurate.[39]

In geographical locations where material and financial resources to set up and sustain the massive apparatus needed to document, classify, and store population-based data are sparse, probabilistic technologies of governance raise yet other very serious difficulties. This is because in such locations the collection of statistics is patchy and often skewed by being disproportionately culled from certain "kinds" of people (pregnant women and urban dwellers, for example) who are the most readily available as sources for data collection – leading to enormous bias. Moreover, creating population-based data in resource-poor countries has special importance because such numbers, however they are obtained, are crucial in mobilizing financial and technical resources. Significantly, in contrast to wealthy countries, choices are rarely made locally today about the way in which the numbers will be mobilized with the objective of improving health, but are the result of technocratic decision-making at a distance, carried out largely by donor organizations and other international agencies. A similar situation applies very often to poor and isolated parts of well-off countries, including the rural United States and the Canadian Arctic where life expectancy rates are up to seven years lower than in these countries as a whole.

Technologies of the Self

Michel Foucault introduced the notion of technologies of the self when writing about Greek and Roman philosophy. He pointed out how, in classical times, philosophy extended beyond a system of thought to comprise a series of practices, including spiritual exercises, dietetics, and forms of self-control. Foucault defined these "technologies of the self" as practices that "permit individuals to effect by their own means or with the help of others a certain number of operations on their own bodies and souls, thoughts, conduct, and way of being," with the purpose of transforming the self in order to attain "happiness, purity, wisdom, perfection, or immortality."[40] Foucault's point is not simply that individuals have long sought out ways to thrive and better themselves, but that the situation changed dramatically with modernity, when state bureaucracies, supported strongly by professional disciplines (notably medical specialties), began to be systematically involved in projects to govern life, no longer leaving matters up to individual whim. Some scholars argue that these disciplinary practices are indispensable to the success of modern governance and "the production of a biopolitical body is the originary activity of sovereign power."[41] The promotion of the idea that individuals themselves should manage health gained prominence with the support of governments and members of the medical profession, including some deeply religious practitioners. In the 19th century organizations such as the "crusaders for fitness" associated personal salvation and health with correct living, diet, and exercise.[42] The doctrine of these "hygienic religions" was that, rather than simply praying for health, one should work for it. In North America, physician activists such as John Henry Kellogg and Horace Fletcher were explicit that changes in lifestyle would reinvigorate both body and spirit and promote a healthy nation.[43] The sociologist Peter Conrad argues that today "wellness" – the avoidance of disease and illness – has become a "virtue," for some, a secular path to salvation.[44] Obviously many people choose not to participate in activities purported to sustain health and enhance their body image for a variety of reasons, but equally it cannot be denied that media and television reporting, self-help groups, exercise facilities, and government and corporate initiatives of many kinds relentlessly target individuals about the importance of "working" at one's health. The promotion of biomedical concepts of health can be tentatively explored, following Foucault, as a technology of self.

A very different picture emerges when efforts to encourage individual responsibility for health are examined in a global context where the apparatus of the state is often weak, dependent on outside aid, or essentially non-existent. Today, private capital and foundations, NGOs, churches, and other religious bodies, and a host of other non-governmental actors increasingly promote technologies of the self globally. In the contemporary climate of neo-liberalism, these self-help practices are designed expressly to incite individuals to take responsibility for their own health and illness, even in situations where people are assaulted repeatedly by infectious and parasitic diseases and where chronic disease is on the increase. In response to neo-liberal initiatives, there is diminishing access to state-sponsored health care, and, where the economic means are lacking, access to the private clinics that have opened up to replace clinics formerly run by the state. Quite simply, as WHO figures show all too clearly,[45] the bodies of the poor are increasingly under threat and their health is inevitably fragile. In the absence of a well-functioning medical system, self-help groups are often the most readily accessible – at times the only – means to conjure up a potential for wellbeing in situations where people have little opportunity to change the demeaning and often violent circumstances in which they live. Chapter 11 will explore how, in such settings, where outside interventions are designed to assist primarily with economic development and secondarily with humanitarian assistance, self-help groups sponsored by NGOs and religious organizations have become vehicles for injecting ideas about personal responsibility for individual health in contexts where the notion that individuals can exercise control over their health is glaringly inappropriate.

Repeatedly in the chapters that follow we will see that people everywhere resist, circumvent, reinvent, and pragmatically adapt and adjust to the various biomedical technologies that appear in their communities. Theoretical arguments about biopower, including the assumed role of the state in the management of individual bodies and populations and the idea of technologies of the self, are inspired almost exclusively by the experience of modernization in Europe, in particular France. Their mechanical application to settings where state power takes very different forms – or where "government" is exercised to some degree by NGOs and humanitarian interventions – may conceal more than it reveals. As we will show, theories of "biopower" must be rethought if they are to be of global relevance.

We turn now to another set of practices that has been made possible only recently as a result of technological developments that came about from the latter part of the 20th century.

The Power of Biological Reductionism

The foundations of what would become scientific medicine were gradually set in place commencing in the 15th century in Europe, when the practice of anatomical dissection, much of it carried out as public spectacle, became customary practice. Early European anatomists were "consumed with disease and death"[46] because they were certain that knowledge obtained from the dissection of corpses (and on occasion from vivisection), would enable them to determine the causes of pathology lurking in the body. The organization of clinical medical training and practice continues to take place today largely on the basis of anatomical divisions of the body.

Commencing in the 18th century a major conceptual shift gradually took place in medicine bringing about a "vitalist" approach to the body focused on "life itself."[47] This approach was consolidated by a style of reasoning that drew on the emerging basic sciences of biology, notably physiology, and the gradual acceptance of the theory of evolution.[48] Emphasis began to be given to the body as an organically unified whole – a vital, integrated system that could be examined in the clinic by means of standardization of techniques and procedures. By extension, the notion of a social body was recognized: "made up of extracorporeal systems – of environment, of culture – ... conceptualized in terms of large scale flows – of air, water, sewage, germs, contagion, familial influences, moral climates, and the like."[49]

Toward the middle of the 20th century, under the influence of the "father of quantum mechanics" physicist/philosopher Erwin Schrödinger, another major conceptual move took place. This brought about a molecularized approach to medicine that overshadowed, but by no means entirely displaced, the vitalist approach. It also opened the door to an era of genetic determinism that remained dominant until the beginning of the 21st century. Schrödinger, following in Newton's footsteps, was convinced that the laws of physics, notably the second law of thermodynamics, must apply to the natural world, and he came to the conclusion that chromosomes could best be conceptualized as "some kind of code-script."[50] But Schrödinger went on to argue with himself, commenting that the term code-script is too narrow because it does not account for continuity between generations. In contrast to the inert matter of the physical world one must account for how the living world is able to resist decay and "keep going."

Schrödinger's answer to the problem was to endow chromosomes not only with a "law-code" but also with "executive power"; a second metaphor he used was to describe chromosomes as being both "architect's plan and builder's craft – in one."[51] Evelyn Fox Keller characterizes Schrödinger's effort as a "two-sided image of the gene, part physicist's atom and part Plato's soul," an image that was "immensely productive for geneticists, both technically and politically"[52] and one that has had enormous social repercussions. Although subjected to criticism by influential scientists for several decades, this reductionistic, determinist approach is only now undergoing some major rethinking, in large part due to surprising findings in the world of molecular biology that are bringing back, in some respects, an appreciation of vitalism in medicine.[53]

Techno/Biologicals

Over the past four decades it has become increasingly possible to manipulate the boundaries and demarcations of biological entities. Emerging technologies that we term "techno/biologicals" have the potential to challenge boundaries assumed to be unassailable – to perform "border crossings"[54] – between what is normatively accepted as nature or as culture, self or other, life or death. The application of such technologies inevitably results in hybrid entities, and questions are brought to the fore about what is normal or abnormal; what is moral and just, and what should be the limits, if any, of human intervention into the "natural world." In other words, techno/biologicals intervene powerfully on life itself. Donna Haraway, focusing specifically on the biotechnology industry, has argued: "bodies as objects of knowledge are material-semiotic-generative nodes"; their boundaries materialize in social interaction, and through this interaction bodies and body parts are constituted as objects; as sites for manipulation.[55] In the genetic laboratory such manipulation often results in "rigorous couplings across taxonomic kingdoms (not to mention nations and companies)."[56]

Among their many key applications, techno/biologicals enable the transformation of living cells, tissues, and organs into agents that facilitate research, or else substitute or replace faulty, inadequate, or failed body parts and mechanisms. Among such technologies are "immortalized cell lines" kept "alive" in nutritive media; the creation of transgenic and synthetic organisms; organ transplants; and extraction and preparation of stem cells for research purposes from embryonic tissue. There are similarities in the effects brought about by techno/biologicals with medical traditions where substances are trafficked between humans in order to enhance wellbeing and provide protection from danger. Practices of witchcraft, spirit possession, shamanism, and initiation rites, to name a few, often involve grafting, or the hybridization of humans, with entities taken from the material and spiritual worlds with preventive or therapeutic intent. And while many researchers argue that the effects of these practices are symbolic, evidence suggests that in many cases "real" bodily transformations take place (usually interpreted by outside observers as the placebo effect).[57] Such activities thereby transform body and society, and effectively challenge locally understood boundaries between self and other, and nature and culture. However, such indigenous practices cannot have the same portability as do techno/biologicals because the efficacy of healing ceremonies, witchcraft practices, and so on, is not detachable from the specific contexts where they are applied.[58]

Techno/biologicals of all kinds are quite different from earlier, ubiquitous forms of hybridization because they rely on procedures of standardization and normalization that facilitate the treatment or transformation of bodies deliberately decontextualized from history, society, and social relationships. It is this ability to treat bodies-out-of-context – on the twin assumptions that all bodies are essentially the same and that taxonomies of diseases and conditions are applicable anywhere – that gives these technologies great portability and translocal effectiveness in connection with many medical conditions. For example, in discussing the procurement and preparation of organs for transplant, Linda Hogle describes what she terms "donor enhancement."[59] Pharmaceutical agents are injected into brain dead donors in order to preserve cell integrity and inhibit certain functions while enhancing others. Hogle notes that due to these interventions, organs and tissues lose any particular or unusual features they may have had while functioning in a now deceased body, and are transformed into the equivalent of " 'off-the-shelf' reagents" – they become, in Hogle's words, donor-cyborgs.[60] Once removed from the donor body, the surgeon takes the organ to one side in the operating room and quietly works on it further, striving for easy insertion into another body.

Techno/biologicals clearly have the potential to intervene worldwide and refigure life everywhere. Eugene Thacker, a specialist in communication and culture who has written extensively about the biotech industry and genomics, asks in what way Foucaultian biopolitics might be relevant with respect to this particular industry. He notes – as have we done above in connection with the management of populations and individuals deemed at risk – that Foucault never made an explicit link between the poles of biopower (the pole of anatomopolitics and the population pole). Foucault made only the "general inference that both the science of statistics and the science of life (bio-logy) constitute a biopolitics, that is, a bioscience of the state."[61] Thacker argues that this nascent relationship noted by Foucault is magnified and developed in the biotech industry with the "integration and management of the relationships between biology and computers," that is, between genetics and informatics."[62] He writes that information generated from this relationship "is the point of mediation through which biopolitics regulates genetics and informatics into a sophisticated mode of governmentality or control."[63] Thacker points out that "Genome databases, biological 'libraries' of cell lines, patient databases, online medical services, and a host of other innovations are transforming the understanding of 'life itself' into an understanding of informatics." In this sense "life itself" is now "both material and informatic."[64] It is clear that this "upgrading," as Thacker puts it, of Foucault's argument for biopower is on a vastly different scale from what took place in the 19th and 20th centuries. And it must also be kept in mind how fragmentary at present is the penetration of such informatic-based medical care into many parts of the world. Most of the pills, therapies, diagnostic measures, and insurance practices noted by Thacker as the material output of this new informatic approach simply do not exist for the world's poor, although no doubt this will change to some extent in the future.

The relationship among governments, medical establishments, emerging biomedical technologies, biotech industries, and cultural values – often deeply associated with religious precepts – and the everyday lives of people living in most parts of the world today does not resemble that of 20th-century Europe. Furthermore, this is now a world where the accumulation of wealth by some is on the increase, while inequality and poverty are strikingly worse than in the 20th century, and where social security is largely non-existent. It is against this new reality that emerging forms of biopower demand attention and many of the contributions made by social scientists to this task are presented in some detail in the chapters that follow.

2

The Normal Body

The subject of this chapter is the emergence and transformation of medical practice over the past three centuries into the systematized body of knowledge commonly known today as biomedicine. The approach to human disease that characterizes biomedicine was neither an inevitable development nor the result of an orderly uncovering of the "true" causes of illness. Biomedicine is the product of particular historical circumstances in which systematic efforts began to be made to understand nature, making use of techniques designed to produce an objective description of the material world. Knowledge produced about the body and its management in health and illness was firmly situated in this domain of "objectified" nature. The whole process, part of more encompassing changes that took place with modernization in Europe, was described by Max Weber as "the disenchantment of the world."[1] A further crucial development came about when bodily variation began to be defined in terms of deviation from a statistical norm or average. Norm and normal, the statistical and the moral, came to be conflated in this understanding of variation as deviation. Individual bodies were "normalized" both biologically and statistically. Once the material characteristics of individual bodies were described and quantified, they were then assessed against "normal" values established by statistical surveys of "healthy" populations. The most obvious example of this process is the routine blood test, the results of which are interpreted according to "normal values" that distinguish "healthy bodies" from the pathological. If the standard reference for "normal" hemoglobin is between 120 and 160 g/L, individuals whose values fall below this range are likely to be diagnosed with anemia. What counts as "normal" in actuality is a statistical "average."

Equally, the idea of normal is understood as normative (what it takes to be healthy), and is also very often equated with what is morally right (the range where individuals "ought" to be). The fundamental tension between the normal and the moral remains largely unexamined to this day. Biology alone has come to furnish the standard by which difference is managed, using statistical techniques that distinguish between the "normal" and the "pathological." The work of human standardization by means of biology, discussed further in Part II, is an essential step that enables the global circulation of biomedical technologies including techno/biologicals, body parts, and "normalized" forms of personhood, all of which will be explored in later chapters. Before turning to an account of how the body came to be normalized, we begin with a striking example of how a medical mystery was solved long before the "normal" body was in place.

Cholera in the 19th Century

Before objects and events can be made phenomenologically real their very existence has to be recognized by a process of naming, ordering, and classification. Such recognition, including the diagnosis and management of episodes of illness, is the product of culture and does not emerge spontaneously from nature.[2] In other words, what will count as disease and illness comes about as the result of particular practices embedded in specific historical, political, social, and technical relationships.[3] In this chapter we will examine some of the evidence amassed, mostly by historians, that documents the gradual emergence of scientific medicine and especially its anchoring practice of standardization.

Steven Johnson in his book *The Ghost Map*[4] illustrates how it was extraordinarily difficult for both the medical authorities and policy-makers of the mid–19th century to recognize the water supply as the source of the disease that we know today as cholera. This was the case even when Dr. John Snow presented them with what can justly be called sound scientific evidence according to current-day standards. Prior to the mid–19th century it was believed that this deadly condition was caused by "miasma" – noxious emanations that resulted from the foul conditions and putrid stench perpetually present in incredibly densely populated cities such as London before sanitary facilities had been installed.

While an apprentice doctor in a mining area in northeast England, Snow was confronted with the cholera epidemic of 1832 that killed 32,000 people across the country before suddenly, inexplicably, petering out. It seems that Snow never forgot this experience[5] and, after he had set up practice in London, when cholera returned in 1848 he immersed himself once again in caring for patients struck down by the epidemic, all the while paying careful attention to who exactly contracted the disease and who was spared. He noted that it was not only the poor living in fetid and crowded surroundings who died, but also at times the middle classes. Snow began to be skeptical of miasma theory, and insisted that the disease so rapidly killing hundreds of people in central London must be caused by water, because only as a result of imbibing tainted water could so many people die who were often not directly in contact with one another.

Gradually a handful of doctors began to accept Snow's theories, but for the most part, despite publications, he was ignored. When the next epidemic struck in 1854, Snow decided to systematically compare the experiences of people who drank water from two different water sources, one polluted by London sewage and the other, further upstream, unpolluted. He was about to publish his findings that clearly demonstrated a stark difference in incidence of cholera cases depending upon a given water source, when the most swift and deadly attack of cholera ever recorded in London broke out in Soho, very close to where Snow himself was living.

Snow used a new tool of his day, that of "disease-mapping," in which he reproduced a street plan and marked the deaths from cholera house by house on the map, from which a clear pattern of infection started to emerge. Snow then interviewed selected people, both on the streets and in their homes, asking them, above all else, about the sources of their water. By supplementing the findings obtained by disease-mapping with this ethnographic approach, slowly, and with great persistence, Snow was able to establish that every one of the dead and dying in the area he had surveyed had imbibed water drawn from the same public source – the Broad Street pump. It also became clear that in this limited geographical area, several small, discrete pockets were left unaffected by the epidemic, one of which was the Lion Brewery, where no workers were struck down at all. It soon became evident that they drank only beer. With great reluctance, officials agreed to take the handle off the pump at Snow's insistence, although this did not bring about an abrupt end to cholera because the disease had already moved on[6] and most officials remained wedded to a miasmic theory of causation.

A local curate, the Reverend Henry Whitehead, began to support Snow's position after carrying out his own investigations in his impoverished parish and its environs. It was he who inadvertently detected the "index case," when he talked to a mother who had disposed of her infant's cholera-infected diapers, while the child was still alive, into a cesspool encased by rotten bricks that leaked fecal matter into the well that supplied the Broad Street pump. Even so, the powerful physicians who sat on the Board of Health continued to dismiss John Snow's findings as unsound, as did the prestigious journal *The Lancet*, largely because his findings went against the dominant medical theories of the day that attributed epidemics to "miasmas," or foul air. It was not until after Snow's death, when the next scourge of cholera hit the city causing over 4,000 deaths, that members of the Board of Health, "blinded" until that time by their belief in miasma, grudgingly acknowledged that the disease was indeed water-borne, and that the poor did not succumb most readily to the disease because of the "filth" they themselves created, as the Board had earlier declared. Eventually Snow was given due credit for his research that could not longer be disregarded once the *Vibrio cholerae* (the bacteria that causes cholera) was recognized.[7]

An Italian scientist Filippo Pacini isolated the *Vibrio cholerae* in 1854 when bacteriological techniques were first being developed. His finding went unnoticed by the establishment for several years, and Robert Koch, the German scientist who had earlier isolated the tuberculosis bacillus, was given credit for the discovery. After the existence of bacilli had been incontrovertibly demonstrated, strong claims began to be made about necessary causal factors contributing to specific disease states. This new approach to disease etiology opened the door to the idea of universal causation, and fostered a reductionist approach to the understanding of disease etiology. Louis Pasteur's contribution, also very important in this transformation, will be considered in later chapters.

It is clear that evidence for the germ theory of disease causation contributed greatly to the recognition of European medicine of the day as a science, leading people to assume that what were thought of as the superstitions and beliefs of previous generations of medical professionals would soon be a thing of the past. The increasingly rational, systematic approach to the accumulation of medical knowledge and its application that ensued from the latter part of the 19th century, in which knowledge about infectious disease had a singularly important role, has granted biomedicine therapeutic efficacy over a broad range of conditions relative to other medical systems. As this account shows, however, Snow was able to control a major epidemic before the discovery of *Vibrio cholerae*, and then this discovery helped pave the way for germ theories to gain widespread acceptance. Moreover it makes clear how unquestioned assumptions and truth-claims embedded in medical knowledge and practice of all kinds can be put into historical perspective – something to which we now turn.

Representing the Natural Order

In common with all other forms of medical knowledge, the orientation and practices of biomedicine as we know it today are a product of a particular historical, political, and social context that informed the way in which the natural order, including the human body, should be represented and worked upon. The historians Lorraine Daston and Katherine Park argue that for a period of about two centuries immediately prior to the Enlightenment it was assumed that wonder and passion assisted best in bringing about an understanding of nature. The time was marked by stories circulating about "wondrous therapeutics" and an explosion of professional medical services in the market-places of recently urbanized areas. The uniqueness of these therapies was what made them particularly attractive. Books documenting notable wonders continued to be widely distributed until well into the 17th century, and the collection and display of *materia medica* of all kinds were enormously popular, designed above all to demonstrate the particularity and individuality of objects. What was being invoked at that time, Daston and Park argue, was "an order of nature's customs rather than natural laws, defined by marvels as well as by miracles."[8]

Several fundamental changes gathered momentum toward the end of the 17th century in Europe, resulting eventually in a radically different approach to the natural order, one dependent for the first time upon the positing of uniform and inviolable laws. Wonders continued to happen occasionally, but they could no longer lay claim to any special ontological status outside "the strictly natural."[9] They became marginalized, lying at the boundaries of established scientific knowledge, either to be dismissed as nonsense, or else examined by the scientific method to establish their possible worth. Numerous techniques and therapies that come under the umbrella of what is today called complementary medicine nowadays fall into a similar marginal position.

Truth to Nature

This historical approach calls for recognition of scientific knowledge and practices that could only arise in what Lorraine Daston has called a "specific moral economy" that she argues is inevitably associated with the production of scientific knowledge.[10] Daston notes that this moral economy embodies an ideal of scientific objectivity that insists on "the existence and impenetrability" of boundaries between facts and values, between emotions and rationality; however Daston argues that this ideal is based on an illusion.[11] By moral economy Daston does not mean that ideologies and political self-interest inevitably penetrate the scientific endeavor (although frequently they clearly do). Nor is she suggesting that scientific knowledge is socially constructed, and can, therefore, simply be equated with other kinds of knowledge as a belief system. In using the concept of moral economy Daston implies "a web of affect-saturated values that stand and function in a well-defined relationship to one another."[12] She points out that even though moral economies of science "draw routinely and liberally upon the values and affects of ambient culture, the rewording that results usually becomes the peculiar property of scientists."[13] Daston is writing about "truth" claims made in connection with objectivity, measurement, replication, and so on, and also about the sciences of probability and the "making up" of populations designated at risk.[14] Theodore Porter notes that the ability to attain consensus allows a specialist disciplinary community to reach tacit agreement that its work is objective.[15] He adds: "its acceptability to those outside a discipline depends on certain presumptions, that are rarely articulated except under severe challenge." Specialists must appear, therefore, to be disinterested in what they do, that is, in contrast to medieval times, as being without passion.[16] In a related vein, when discussing "modernist sensibilities," Lawrence and Shapin argue that, after Descartes, knowledge was, in theory, disassociated from value; "knowledge itself" came to inhabit a "transcendental and disembodied domain."[17]

Recently Lorraine Daston and Peter Galison have published a co-authored book titled, simply, *Objectivity*. Their position is that the history of the idea of scientific objectivity when examined in fine detail is surprisingly short, commencing only in the mid–19th century. They set out to write this history with emphasis on "epistemic virtue," that is, the choices that are made and techniques that are used in order to comprehend nature and divide it into what are assumed to be fundamental, standardized, working objects. Epistemic virtue, designed to know the world and not the self, not only subsumes what is thought to be truthful and objective but also embodies certainty, precision, and replicability. Daston explains the difference intended between reference to "moral economy" and "epistemic virtue" as follows. She writes, "I see epistemic virtues as parts of (not substitutes for) moral economies." An epistemic virtue of objectivity, then, is just one part of a larger moral economy of science that also favors other practices including standardization and rule-bound procedures that are clearly defined and firmly enforced. What specific epistemic virtues and broader moral economies have in common is a fusion of ethical and epistemological elements.[18]

To develop their argument Daston and Galison refer to atlases made use of across a range of scientific disciplines from astronomy to medicine. They find that the struggle to represent nature takes three distinct turns from the mid–18th century on – three forms of epistemic virtue that they call "truth-to-nature," "mechanical objectivity," and "trained judgment." But no simple progression from one form of representation to another takes place; as the repertoire of epistemic virtues expands, each redefines and informs the others, rather than transcending them. The authors claim, "Epistemic virtues earn their right to be called virtues by moulding the self, and the ways they do so parallel and overlap with the ways epistemology is translated into science."[19] Carl Linnaeus is an early example of someone who used the truth-to-nature orientation – his method of classifying plants was "openly and aggressively selective."[20] His was an era of obsessive collecting of natural objects, closely associated with the early days of exploration and the founding of colonies, but the objective was to identify and depict only ideal types and to cast out everything thought to exhibit an anomaly. Scientists in Linnaeus' time attempted to control the activity of illustrators who depicted objects found in nature in order that only truthful representations be created.

Truth-to-nature continues to be valued in medicine and becomes entrenched when medical practice begins to be systematized in hospitals and clinics, and diseases come to be viewed as natural objects to be classified and described in the same manner as other natural objects. A move toward mechanical objectivity took place in the late 19th and early 20th centuries. This shift in orientation is characterized by a drive to repress any wilful intervention on the part of the observer in the process of representation. The focus narrowed to individual items and away from ideal types; and in order to accomplish objectivity, enormous diligence, control, and persistence were required on the part of the scientist – a morality of self-restraint. Of course it was evident to many that subjectivity could never be entirely eliminated, that the goal of objectivity was always unstable; nevertheless, with use of increasingly sophisticated technologies, an ideal of mechanical objectivity was seductive.

Throughout the 20th century this orientation has been supplemented by a specific epistemic virtue of trained judgment in which experience, and hence the subjectivity of the scientist accrued over time, are valued. Representation of nature to this day draws variously on the approaches of truth-to-nature designed to uncover universals; mechanical objectivity that seeks to represent particulars; and trained judgment associated with families or groupings of entities. Daston and Galison conclude: "fidelity to nature [in whatever way it is performed] is always a triple obligation: visual, epistemological, ethical."[21]

In summary, before the Enlightenment, nature was a "wonder" to be contemplated, riddled with symptoms of divine intervention.[22] Illness and disease that afflicted humans were not "natural" events (as we usually understand them today); although regularities were noted and some events were in effect mundane, many were intelligible within a framework of wonder and passion. With the Enlightenment, the idea took hold that nature and "man," while considered by most to be divine in origin, nonetheless obeyed natural laws. Nature became knowable and the description of its laws offered to many a greater understanding of divine perfection. The relationship of humans to nature shifted, and "wonder" gave way to "truth." With close observation, contemplation became "objectification" and the "truth" of nature was laid bare through systematic description. Vast taxonomies for classifying nature were constructed, and, as a result, at the same time an ethic emerged that valued objectivity above all else and, conversely, distrusted subjectivity.

The Natural Body

Historians are not unanimous about the moment that European medicine can first be described as scientific. As the example of cholera in the 19th century shows, Galenic humoral medicine, one belief of which was miasma, continued to be very powerful until the mid–19th century and even later. Nevertheless, from the 18th century on, a good number of medical thinkers abandoned humoralism and sought to ground medicine in a systematic approach to the natural sciences as set out by

Bacon, Descartes, and others. Furthermore, it was argued for the first time that "the improvement of health [was] essential to human emancipation – from fear, want, and suffering.[23] Eighteenth-century medical thinkers who sought to be scientific placed observation and experimentation at the center of their work, but the earlier approach of individuals such as J. O. de La Mettrie, who promoted the idea that the human body could best be understood as a machine, was dismissed by these new physicians as overly simplistic. Like de La Mettrie, these "vitalists" had abandoned the idea of divine intervention, and focused instead on the internal workings of the body to explain the origin of all types of conditions, including "irrational behaviour," but they postulated a "vital force" or a "structured nervous system" as the organizing principle of the body, and not a machine-like entity.[24]

Foucault argues that, from the 18th century, these early vitalists transformed the configuration of disease by firmly situating it inside the body. The human body was objectified, no doubt assisted by the work of anatomists over the previous several hundred years. Foucault suggests that in this "homogenous space" inside the body, time is abolished. He cites the famous English physician, Thomas Sydenham, who wrote: "he who writes the history of diseases ... must imitate the painters who when they paint a portrait are careful to mark the smallest signs and natural things that are to be found on the face of the person they are painting."[25] This is a space in which "analogies define essences" and "the distance that separates one disease from another can be measured only by the degree of their resemblance."[26] Similarity, it was argued, uncovers the rational order of disease so that doctors are dealing at the same time with what is natural and ideal.

Foucault describes this approach as "classificatory thought," solidified in hospitals and clinics that were built in part to advance this new understanding of the body.[27] It is an approach that circumvents the living patient and in which knowledge is amassed by opening up corpses and, we must add, by extensive vivisection of animals, especially in the 19th century. According to the historian Roy Porter, such taxonomies – classificatory thought – reinforced a growing conviction that diseases were "truly distinct entities, possibly localizable, possessing an ontological status perhaps analogous to chemical elements,"[28] and this in turn profoundly influenced the teaching of medicine. Classificatory thought, like the taxonomies of Linnaeus, grouped phenomena according to external similarities and sought to achieve "truth" through objective description of what was visible, but nonetheless enabled an approach that increasingly located the "truth" in relation to abstract understandings of disease and its causation. Symptoms would no longer be classified on the basis of similarity alone, but grouped into taxonomies according to the "pure" underlying disease that was thought to cause them. The "standard" disease was born.

A Numerical Approach

Along other lines, the beginnings of what would become systematic research into disease causation and the eventual formation of the disciplines of epidemiology and public health were evident as early as the 17th century. It was suggested that it might be possible to control human vulnerability to disease by mapping frequencies of disease according to location and climate, much as John Snow did a century later when he plotted the cartography of cholera deaths in search of clues as to how they might be associated with one another. Initially it was epidemic outbreaks that spurred this numerical approach to the body. This "medical geography" reflected the miasmatic ideas of the day as it sought to describe the associations between climate, geography, and disease. An important legacy of this approach is its methods; namely, the standardization of the statistical method. Porter emphasizes the disagreements and divisions that pervaded medical thinking of the time, but he nevertheless shows convincingly that by the closing years of the 18th century in England the systematic collection and storage or "banking" of medical facts at a national level had been proposed. The experimental method using patients as subjects was well established as the appropriate path to truth, and laboratory inquiry and findings were explicitly linked with clinical work. Porter concludes that these developments "encouraged medicine to move away from individual cases in search of the laws of health and sickness in wider contexts, examining climate, environment, and the rhythms of epidemics over the longue durée."[29]

Thus the interplay of medicine, sickness, and society gained importance, and questions began to be asked about why disease prevalence and incidence vary among groups of peoples and in different environments. Such an approach was not new. Hippocrates, after all, had asked similar questions, but a more sophisticated, systematic approach to these provocative problems was called for, including the possibility that individuals could be held responsible for their bodily condition resulting from inappropriate lifestyles or "pathological habits."[30] Porter argues that many medical experts of the day "were not merely proposing that disease had its cultural history, but were suggesting, in turn, that physiology and pathology were, in a sense, sedimented social history, and hence essential for a wider grasp of the dynamics of culture."[31] In practice, not all countries gave equal weight to the social factors contributing to disease; in France access to good food was stressed whereas in Great Britain greater emphasis was given to sanitation. The idea of a "natural history of disease" proposed at this time is inseparable from human behavior and, in stark contrast to the timeless, uniform disease entities slowly being isolated in the clinic, represents a division in theorization that continues to be evident today.

Historians will continue to debate the timing of the consolidation of medicine as science, and its relationship to natural philosophy and to what are now known as the social sciences and social epidemiology. But all historians of European medical history make it abundantly clear that practices of systematization of one kind and another – collection, classification, objectification, quantification, standardization, dissection, and experimentation – became increasingly routinized after the Enlightenment, contributing to an emerging body of medical evidence assumed to be grounded in universal laws and glossed under the rubric of science. Furthermore, medical practice was beginning to be relatively tightly regulated, often by secular rather than by religious authority, thus bringing about a degree of standardization.

Other Natures

This was in contrast to other parts of the world.[32] Certain of these practices, notably the collection and classification of therapeutic herbals, are evident to a greater or lesser extent in other literate medical traditions including Chinese, Ayurvedic, Islamic, and Galenic medicine. One of the most notable differences of long standing between European and other medical traditions is in connection with anatomical dissection. Although surgery was not uncommon in Ayurveda and, for a while, in very early Chinese medicine, religious and legal constraints against vivisection and dissection of the human body have been in place for well over a thousand years everywhere except in Europe. Anatomical practice, including the vivisection of animals and humans, was carried out in the ancient world in Alexandria, and then fell into decline for several centuries until the 13th century when it began to be practiced in medieval European universities. From the 16th century on, in an effort to create a "truthful" depiction of the interior of the human body, public dissection of corpses in the major medical centers of Europe and parts of the Ottoman Empire became routine. Dissection was confined to the relative privacy of medical classes only in the early 19th century.[33]

This practice has no counterpart elsewhere in the world, and no doubt accounts in large part for why the body came to be conceptualized apparently so readily at the time of the Enlightenment, as a bounded, decontextualized unit, the interior of which holds the secrets to an understanding of both health and disease. The comparative research of Shigehisa Kuriyama into Chinese and Greek medicine makes it abundantly clear how differently bodies were approached and represented in various medical traditions.[34] Although it was not always so, Kuriyama notes that after the second century CE significant and enduring differences became apparent between Greek and Chinese medicine. Kuriyama's position is that conceptions of the body are products not simply of different styles of thinking and reasoning, but equally of particular uses of the senses. Chinese medicine exhibited, Kuriyama notes, a "blind indifference to the claims of anatomy" as it unfolded in the West. He illustrates the way in which Chinese doctors, in contrast to Greek doctors, scrutinized living rather than dead bodies, making use not merely of their eyes, but of other senses, in particular that of touch.[35] Even though in both Greek and Chinese medicine it was thought that blood and breath gave vitality to the body, the medical gaze of Chinese doctors was confined to the surface of the body where "the skin shone as the site of privileged revelations."[36] Understanding of both the structure and function of the body in Chinese medicine was, and to a large extent continues to be to the present day, remarkably dissimilar from biomedicine – not only do the meanings ascribed to bodily signs differ profoundly but, more fundamentally, features recognized as signs of significance do not correspond.[37] Above all, the approach in Chinese medicine was one of introspection in which the doctor seeks to understand individual bodies in context.[38]

Kuriyama has also examined the effects of the translation and introduction into Japan in the 18th century of a well-known European anatomical text.[39] This translation opened the door in Japan for the first time to the idea that visual inspection on the basis of dissection could provide insight for understanding the human body. Kuriyama notes that skepticism in connection with the abstract, philosophical thinking about the body common in Chinese and Japanese medicine was already present in the minds of some influential thinkers of the day, and he cites the factional battles that erupted over the introduction of an anatomical approach. Similar to medieval Europe prior to the time of Vesalius, dissection of the human body could not legally be carried out by doctors in Japan. Such an act was regarded as highly polluting, with the result that the bodies of criminals had to be dissected by members of an outcast group whose usual work was as butchers and tanners. The account of the first dissection he ever attended given by a famous Japanese doctor of the time named Genpaku is highly instructive:

> In dissecting the human body, the custom till then was to leave everything up to … outcast people. They would cut open the body and point out such organs as the lungs, the liver, and the kidneys, and the observing doctors simply watched them and came away. All they could say then was: "we actually viewed the inside of a human body." With no signs attached to each organ, all they could do was listen to the dissector's words and nod.
>
> On this occasion too, the old man went on explaining the various organs such as the heart, the liver, the gallbladder and the stomach. Further, he pointed to some other things and said: "I don't know what they are, but they have always been there in all the bodies which I have so far dissected." Checking them with the Dutch charts, we were able to identify them to be the main arteries and veins and suprarenal glands.[40]

As Kuriyama notes, it is easy to understand how dissections of this kind contributed little to medical insight or innovation. Physicians merely confirmed what was already common knowledge to them (even where dissection is strictly forbidden it does not mean that no knowledge at all is circulating about body interiors). The anatomical text, in the form of an atlas, and not the dissection per se, provided instruction for the Japanese doctors – it was only on the basis of the represented images that they began to "see" the body in an entirely new way. Genpaku could not understand the written text, for he had no knowledge of European languages, but he could "read" the illustrations, and this experience transformed his entire outlook. He discovered for the first time a visual style of representation that attempted to emulate "reality," one that, to his mind, could have immediate utility for a new medical approach to the human body.[41] Kuriyama argues that no amount of exposure to an accumulation of empirical data in written form would have brought about such a profound transformation in understanding, as did this anatomical atlas with its densely depicted images. Ethnographic studies of biomedicine have made it clear that the ability to "see" and "feel" what is represented in biomedical texts – what medical students learn in the dissecting theater, or radiologists in the reading room – is a powerful dimension to the acquisition of biomedical competence.[42]

This example makes it very clear that an intimate relationship exists between medical knowledge and insight, technological manipulation, bodily representation, and the subjectivity of scientist/physicians, in turn informed by culturally shared values. "Epistemic virtues" are not limited to objectivity, and other forms of knowing nature may be regarded as superior, a position by no means exclusive to "exotic" medical systems. Throughout the 20th century there has been a persistence of non-standardized forms of medical knowing within mainstream biomedicine, in which reductionism and standardization are overtly resisted. Examples include psychoanalysis, psychosomatic medicine, Catholic humanism, social medicine, and neo-humoralism,[43] as well as the deliberate incorporation of alternative medical practice such as shamanism, acupuncture, and homeopathy into some hospitals and clinics. Such approaches conflict with the objective universalistic ideology of biomedicine, and provoke unease even as clinicians recognize the limitations of an approach derived strictly from scientific "evidence."

Interpreting the Body

The medical gaze cannot be thoroughly standardized; bodies and their ailments are not exactly the same, but the goal of clinical biomedicine is nevertheless one of pinpointing internal bodily truths. Arguments about how best to interpret bodily findings are a routine part of medical practice. For instance, clinicians customarily disregard abnormal results on routine blood tests if they do not "fit" the clinical condition of the patient or if they know from experience that these "abnormal" results do not usually signify pathology. And the physician anthropologist Barry Saunders has shown how interpretation in the practice of radiology is not a process of discovery so much as of debating the significance of images by confronting clinical and anatomic evidence.[44] The media makes it clear to the public at times that internal arguments in connection with epistemic virtue take place, although not in so many words, of course. In addition, there is dispute in connection with moral economies, sometimes in situations when there is little or no argument about objective evidence.

At stake is often what can be inferred from the documented objective findings for taking the next step, namely the care of the patient. For example, Japanese, American, and Canadian neurologists undertake essentially the same tests and measurements, use the same logical arguments, and draw the same inferences to make an "objective" diagnosis of irreversible loss of consciousness (known familiarly as brain death).[45] The validity and replicability of these diagnostic techniques are challenged by only a tiny minority of neurologists around the world, and only very rarely does the diagnosis have to be actively justified in medical circles. However, values of another kind, about what exactly counts as life and death, come to the fore as soon as the diagnosis is made. Bodies of brain-dead patients are often extremely valuable as potential organ donors but, in order that their organs are kept "alive," patients must stay tethered to ventilators, even after a diagnosis of brain death. Ventilator technology creates a hybrid entity that is both dead and alive. When Lock talked with Japanese physicians a few years ago, many concurred with the results of surveys of the Japanese public that a brain-dead body cannot be considered as no longer alive. Until 1997, brain death was not recognized legally as death in Japan, and brain-dead patients who are not organ donors are often kept on ventilators for several days or longer until such time as families agree that death has taken place.

On the other hand, American and Canadian critical care physicians, with some exceptions, conceptualize brain-dead patients as "good as dead," even though the body lying in front of them in the Intensive Care Unit continues to breathe, is warm, metabolizes nutrients, excretes, and exhibits other signs of "life" with the aid of the ventilator.[46] For these physicians, once a patient is diagnosed as brain dead and has entered a condition of irreversible loss of consciousness, then the "person" is no longer alive, no matter the condition of their body and, with prior permission, organs can be legally procured. Not all involved families are willing to cooperate, and one or two physicians demur, but the weight of public opinion strongly supports organ donation. In contrast, in Japan much more ambivalence about what brain death actually represents with respect to the condition of the person, and about organ donation from brain-dead bodies, is evident in all segments of society. It is, of course possible that this situation will change, but given the persistent very low rate of organ donation from brain-dead bodies in Japan this does not as yet appear to be the case.

Recognition of the epistemic virtue incorporated into the production of scientific knowledge, as well as broader cultural and on occasion religious values that pervade medical practice forces us to pose radical questions about the global application of biomedical technologies. Furthermore, ethnography makes it possible to examine the way in which scientific knowledge is selectively deployed in different contexts by drawing, either explicitly or implicitly, on historically, politically, and culturally informed moral economies in local settings. We moderns have never been modern, argues Bruno Latour, because values and judgments are embedded in the scientific endeavor,[47] and yet people everywhere are increasingly alert to the fruits of a sound scientific approach to the body in health and illness and many yearn for access to vital basic care and are all too impatient to accept whatever biomedicine can offer them.

How Normal Became Possible

Discussion thus far has focused largely on several significant developments that have taken place in European medicine since the Enlightenment, culminating in "the standardized body" so evident today, one that each of us is fitted into every time we seek out biomedical assistance. We now turn to one more important 19th-century development that has contributed enormously to the emergence of the standard body: the standardization of diseases. A tension has been present from classical times in European medicine between, on the one hand, an "internalizing" discourse that gives weight to recognition of bodily distress and its medical management and in which disease is decontextualized; and, on the other hand, an "externalizing" discourse that emphasizes familial, social, political, and environmental contributions to ill health.[48] Clinical and experimental medicine as we know it today adopts, almost exclusively, the former approach. During the 18th and 19th centuries the externalizing discourse, formerly grounded in Galenic medicine, was gradually transformed by the introduction of mathematical methods for estimating statistical probabilities, culminating in the formation of the specialties of epidemiology and public health in which the concept of risk is central for discerning variables exterior to the body that contribute to disease occurrence.

Another important development, explored further in chapter 6, is the rise of germ theory that, gradually starting in the late 19th century with the discoveries of Pasteur and Koch, supplanted the miasma theory of disease causation. For the miasmatists, as we have seen, disease is a product of local environment and, importantly, of "constitution." This allowance for local biological variability obtained its fullest expression in the colonies, where Europeans explained the apparent lower susceptibility of "natives" to tropical fevers as a result of their physical constitutions. Acclimatization became the *mot d'ordre* for Europeans, who were advised to "season" their bodies gradually to withstand the onslaught of tropical fevers. However, the discovery of the malarial parasite and its mosquito vector played an important part in solidifying the appeal of the germ theory and displacing ideas about the external causes of disease to simple, universal, biological agents. Once germ theory was recognized, the idea of "environment" became internalized and miniaturized in the form of invading entities; the key to medical success was now to exert control over body invaders. Thus, the door was opened to an understanding of human bodies as essentially the same everywhere, erasing notions of fundamental biological difference implied by individual "constitutions" and "acclimatization," bringing about further consolidation of biology as the standard measure of the human body.[49]

Until well into the 19th century use of the term normal was virtually limited to the fields of mathematics and physics. It was not until an internalizing approach to the body based on anatomy took hold in the early 19th century that arguments about the relationship between normal and abnormal biological states were seriously debated for the first time. Auguste Comte, writing in 1851, noted a major shift in conceptualization that had taken place when the physician Broussais argued in the 1820s that the phenomenon of disease is of essentially the same kind as that of health and, thus, health and disease differ from each other only in "intensity."[50] The internalizing and externalizing approaches of basic biomedicine and epidemiology today are both anchored by the idea of a universal somatic body where health and illness are conceived as opposite poles along a biological continuum. Application of epidemiological methods to the study of populations allows this continuum to be mapped and the results made use of in clinical settings, with the assumption that all human bodies are biologically equivalent. Conversely, clinical findings about individual bodily conditions such as those observed in clinical studies may be extrapolated using epidemiological techniques to entire human populations.

In epidemiology and biostatistics, the term "normal distribution" refers to a common pattern of variation around an average, commonly known as the Bell curve. Broussais postulated that normality should be understood as being on a continuum with pathology and, further, deviation must be understood in reference to a "normal" state.[51] This theme was taken up and expanded upon by several influential thinkers during the course of the 19th century, among them Auguste Comte and Claude Bernard. In the 1960s, Georges Canguilhem, in writing a synthesis of the work of the previous century in connection with normality, noted that "strictly speaking … there is no biological science of the normal. There is a science of biological situations and conditions called normal." Canguilhem concluded that normality can only be understood in context, "as situated in action," and moreover, diversity does not infer sickness, nor does "objective" pathology exist outside of the laboratories, clinics, and operating theaters where it is made visible.[52] Canguilhem's crucial argument, contra Broussais, was that the "normal" and the "pathological" are two fundamentally different states that cannot logically be placed on the same continuum. Their reconciliation along a biological continuum, Canguilhem argued, was in fact an artifact of the decontextualized clinical and laboratory methods used in biomedical research – a point to which we will return in chapter 7. "Normalization" can lead to the mistaken assumption that what is statistically "abnormal" is pathological, or that no pathology lies in what is statistically "normal."

Michel Foucault's work on the "archaeology of medical perception" illustrates how the rise of anatomical pathology in the 19th century helped create the standardized body of modern, scientific medicine.[53] Foucault, Canguilhem's student, has shown how representations of the body in premodern medicine were in effect "mute," a blank slate on which the timeless truth of disease was to be deciphered through a parsing of signs. Gradually, the truth of disease was displaced into the body: "Open up a few corpses" exhorted the great Parisian anatomist Bichat, "you will see dissipate at once the darkness that observation alone could not dissipate."[54] The body could now "speak," but only once the differences there observed could be understood as pathological deviations from a healthy norm. This marked a shift from the earlier notion that diseases are pure "essences" that mark the body from within.

Centuries of anatomical dissection supported the idea that the insides of bodies are basically similar in structure. However, with the rise of a statistical understanding of the norm, deviance from that norm became inherently linked to the idea of the pathological. As Foucault shows, it was then possible to "see" differences among abnormalities made visible when bodies were dissected. This variation was interpreted either as different diseases, or as different stages in the unfolding of the same disease, that could then be linked back to the signs and symptoms spoken about by patients, at times visible on the surface of their bodies. The anatomized body became an invariant, a standardized measure of disease mechanism. Extrapolating from the cadaver to ailing patients made it possible to imagine the symptoms that afflicted them as signifiers of invisible processes deep within the body.

Anatomical pathology and simple, descriptive statistics of clinical conditions represent early attempts to standardize bodily conditions, and gave birth to the notion of the "normal" as a principle for classifying previously disparate phenomena. Human difference was placed on a common grid of legibility that enabled standardization and classification in terms of deviance from a statistical average of findings derived from observation. As a classificatory and analytic scheme, normality was laid over earlier moral taxonomies that gradually faded even as their moralizing force lingered. Biomedicine became increasingly oriented toward bringing about the normal, confusing a statistical construct with actual wellbeing. Its power as an institution made these statistical constructs real and resulted in the "making up" of new kinds of people.

Intervention into the body became further standardized when surgery was slowly formalized through the application of routine protocols and procedures in the operating theater. Operating theaters are in effect laboratories where disease is isolated from the body of the patient and its broader social circumstances. The historian Thomas Schlich has pointed out the importance of surgery "for the transformation of hospitals from places of refuge for the indigent … into modern temples of medicine" in which surgical techniques that were initially physiological experiments conducted on animals became routinized as therapeutic interventions on humans.[55] As Stefan Hirschauer has argued, it is in the controlled setting of the theater, where drapes frame the aseptic "operating field," that anatomy learned from practicing dissection is operationalized by the surgeon's skill, and the "knowing how of making visible"[56] takes place. Surgical skills – dissecting, cutting, revealing – standardize the body, and allow surgeons to physically negotiate the many individual variations in human anatomy that they are confronted with surprisingly often. The ability to compare, measure, and extrapolate could only occur within the infrastructure of the modern hospital, which concentrates the bodies of the ill in one place and makes them available to observation in sickness and in death.

The philosopher Ian Hacking, in seeking to document the formation of the science of probability argues that our present understanding of the idea of normal is a key concept in what he labels "the taming of chance." Hacking notes that for a good number of years, use of the normal–pathological continuum postulated by Broussais with respect to the body was confined to medicine, but then toward the end of the 19th century, "it moved into the sphere of – almost everything. People, behavior, states of affairs, diplomatic relations, molecules: all these may be normal or abnormal."[57] Hacking argues that today we talk of "normal" people and, of even more importance, we often go on without a second thought to suggest that this is how things ought to be. Thus, the idea of normality is frequently used to close the gap between "is" and "ought," and so has a moral quality built into it. Hacking traces the present expanded understanding of normal directly back to Comte. He describes the way in which Comte, perhaps inspired by a personal brush with mental illness, moved normality out of the clinic into the political sphere, at which point "normal ceased to be the ordinary healthy state; it became the purified state to which we should strive, and to which our energies are tending. In short, progress and the normal state became inextricably linked"[58] and further, not only individuals, but also aggregates of individuals could be labeled as normal or otherwise.

Thus a fundamental tension was introduced into the idea of normal, in which it contains the meaning both of an existing average and a state of perfection toward which individuals or societies can strive – the idea of deviation by degree from a norm, and the idea of a perfect state, are encapsulated in the one term. Following the founder of sociology, Emile Durkheim, normal can be understood as that which is right and proper, and efforts to restore normality entail a return to a former equilibrium; to a status quo ante. But, taken further, normal can be interpreted as only average, and hence something to be improved upon. In its most extreme form, argues Hacking, this interpretation can lead all too easily to eugenics. Two ideas, therefore, are contained in the one concept of normal: one of preservation, the other of amelioration. As Hacking aptly puts it: "Words have profound memories that oil our shrill and squeaky rhetoric"; the normal now stands at once "indifferently" for what is typical, the "unenthusiastic objective average, but it also stands for what has been, good health, and for what shall be, our chosen destiny." Hacking concludes that this benign and sterile-sounding word, normal, has become one of the most powerful (ideological) tools of the 20th century.[59]

When Normal Does Not Exist

In recent years a good number of social scientists and certain psychiatrists have explicitly questioned the claims of epistemological neutrality embedded in the biomedical sciences. Specifically with respect to the idea of a norm Mishler et al., in tune with Canguilhem, made it clear long ago that there is no way to define a biological norm or deviations from that norm without reference to specific populations and their sociocultural characteristics.[60] They cite Redlich who insists that one must ask "normal for what?" and "normal for whom?" In other words, assertions about the normality of biological functioning, or about the normal structure of an organ, must be based on the relationship between the observed instance and its distribution in a specified population.[61] Further, implicit in any specified norm is a set of presupposed standard conditions with regard to when, how, and on whom measurements are made.

A major difficulty arises because the average value for a variable of some specified population may not correspond to an ideal standard, ensuring that "[s]pecific

government implemented a policy in the early 1980s whereby Inuit women were to be "evacuated" and flown south to give birth. This policy caused great unhappiness, not only because women were isolated from their families and made to eat "southern" food, but also because they were systematically subjected to technological interventions in hospitals in the Canadian south, where it became regular practice to slow down what were designated by medical experts as abnormal labor experiences. These practices led quickly to disputes and active resistance to the evacuation policy on the part of Inuit women.

What must be emphasized in the above account is not only the discrepancy between authoritative and subjective accounts about what constitutes a "normal" birth but, further, the assumption made on the part of the majority of obstetricians that their knowledge can be applied without modification to all births, regardless of marked cultural, socioeconomic, and even biological differences among pregnant women. This assumption persists even though there is considerable evidence to suggest that cultural and lifestyle factors influence pregnancy, the process of birth, and its outcomes.[69] Can this "boxification"[70] of birth based on a systematic setting aside of all apparent variation be justified, given that we have very little evidence as to what constitutes "normal" variation in the process of birth worldwide? Moreover, should the "average" Caucasian body be taken as the standard around which variation is established, whether in connection with birth or other health-related events?

In recent years, policy modifications have gradually been introduced so that evacuation only takes place when delivery is proving to be difficult. A birthing center was opened as a pilot project in the central Arctic region of Rankin Inlet, Nunavut, in 1993. By 1995 this project was recognized as an established birthing center comprising a small staff of certified non-Inuit midwives, supported by Inuit maternity care workers and a clerk interpreter. Between 70 and 80 women are cared for each year at the center, and there are plans to open other centers in more remote areas. Physicians do not attend births, but act as consultants when necessary, and attend weekly peri-natal committee meetings to discuss all cases. Local people characterize the center as culturally sensitive and the language used is Inuktitut, but a bureaucratic struggle remains in getting young Inuit women fully certified as midwives.[71] In 2007, the Midwives Association of Nunavut became a registered society, the purpose of which is to support and promote the reintroduction of Inuit midwifery to complement the biomedically based approach of the registered midwives currently practicing in Nunavut.

An audit study of the Rankin Inlet birthing center showed that of the more than 230 births that took place there between 1993 and 2004 not one maternal or neonatal death was recorded.[72] Rates of technical and pharmacological intervention in the birth process are very low indeed, and the overall number of deliveries has increased greatly in recent years as local women have come to trust the health care providers at the center. One obstacle is the relatively high number of pre-term deliveries, many of which have to be transferred to more technologically sophisticated centers. These premature births are thought to be due in large part to poverty, infections, anemia, poor nutrition, and high rates of smoking.[73] For those Inuit women whose pregnancies are considered to be "high risk," a flight of over 1,000 miles to the tertiary care hospitals of urban Canada for a technologically managed birth continues to be unavoidable.

Birthing centers also exist in Nunavik, a region of more than 500,000 square kilometers of tundra in the northern part of the province of Quebec. These centers, like the one in Rankin Inlet, make use of an interdisciplinary approach led by midwives. Over 3,000 women, 80 percent of all women who have given birth in Nunavik since the first center was opened in 1986, have been cared for in what has now become a string of widely distributed centers around the northeastern Hudson Bay and the Hudson Strait. These centers are linked by electronic and other forms of communication and are able to transfer patients when needed, weather permitting, to the principal center where there are some advanced technologies. Fifty per cent of the inhabitants of Nunavik are under the age of 20. The birth rate in this community is twice that of the Canadian population at large, and 25 percent of births are to women under the age of 20. Compared with the time when most women were evacuated, the records for these birth centers show very good outcomes and have a lower rate of intervention in the birth process than was formerly the case.[74]

Inuit involved with these centers argue that the establishment of birth centers has been fundamental for "community healing and marks a turning point for many families who suffered from family violence in Nunavik."[75] Male elders actively participate in ensuring the success of the centers. They believe that they contribute to community strength as a whole and, above all, compensate to some extent for the long-lasting damage to individuals and families created by forcible placement of Inuit children in residential schools run by religious organizations. This practice commenced in the 1870s and reached its peak in the 1930s to 1950s. The last federally funded school, designed expressly to solve the "Indian problem," that is, to stamp out "Indian" culture including languages, closed in 1996.

The midwifery practiced at these centers has been recognized as exemplary by the Society of Obstetricians and Gynecologists of Canada and has also been formerly praised by the WHO. However, the government of Quebec insists that Nunavik midwives should be sent to southern Canada for training, a demand that midwives strenuously resist, arguing that the integration of biomedical practices with the traditional knowledge that they uphold can only be learnt when training is carried out in the north with traditionally trained Inuit midwives present.

The above examples make clear that when clinical care is based solely on the management of objective criteria, diversity of human bodily variation may well be ignored to the detriment of good care.[76] Furthermore, biomedical interventions designed to "restore" the "normal" may go awry, because unexamined moral assumptions embedded in biomedicine often conflict with differing culturally embedded visions of individual and collective wellbeing. This is a theme to which we will return when we examine in depth in Part III the global implementation of several recently developed biomedical technologies.

Pathologizing the "Normal"

A further example of how statistical and moral conceptions of "normal" have become conflated resulting in an apparently neutral category defined solely in terms of deviation from an artificial "norm" is that of biomedical practice in connection with the end of menstruation. Medicalization of menopause commenced in the early part of the 19th century, but it was not until the 1930s, after the elucidation of the endocrine system, that menopause started to be thought of in North America and Europe as a disease-like state characterized by a deficiency of estrogen. In order to sustain this argument, it had to be assumed that the bodies of young premenopausal women would be the "normal" against which all female bodies should be compared. Postmenopausal, post-reproductive life was conceptualized as a deviation from the norm, and hence a pathological condition.

Experts supported this definition by drawing comparisons between middle-aged women and other female mammals living in the wild where postmenopausal life is highly unusual. The arguments of biological anthropologists that the presence of older women – of grandmothers – is biologically adaptive to the survival of highly dependant human infants and their mothers in early hominid life were ignored in creating this discourse of risk.[77] Furthermore, it was argued that women have lived past the age of 50 only since the turn of the 20th century, and that post-reproductive life is due entirely to improved medical care and living conditions, a second incorrect position.[78] These arguments reflected a widely shared ideology among medical professionals and women alike. The language of decrepitude and failure was pervasive in the literature about menopause throughout the 20th century.[79] The end of menstruation was described as ovarian failure, a deficiency disease, and it was asserted: "A progressive physical deterioration of climacteric women is scientifically established."[80]

This view of aging as a deficiency state, and the moral assumptions that underlay it, help to explain how until recently hormone replacement therapies of one kind and another have been the drugs of choice to treat the effects of menopause. Both the transitory symptoms, notably hot flashes and sweats associated with the end of menstruation, and the posited long-term effects of estrogen decline on many organs of the body are assumed to place women at increased risk for disease and death. Middle-aged women were initially eager to cooperate with this kind of risk management, and in the 1970s estrogen replacement therapies were among the top five most frequently prescribed drugs in the United States. However, a sharp decline in their prescription took place after 1975 when four studies were published in major medical journals linking ingestion of estrogen replacement medication to an increased risk for endometrial cancer. A protracted debate ensued as to how best to "protect" women from the postulated effects of reduced estrogen in the postmenopausal body without causing severe side effects.[81] Writers of these articles shared an assumption that the female body is unable to age in reasonably good health unless regularly fuelled with hormones, as the following quote exemplifies:

> Clinicians abound who believe that the menopause is a physiological event, a normal ageing process, therefore estrogen replacement therapy (ERT) is meddlesome and unnecessary. Presbyopia is a normal ageing process, but none will deny the need for spectacles. To do nothing other than offer sympathy and assurance that the menopause will pass, is tantamount to benign neglect.[82]

Due to concerns about endometrial cancer, from the early 1980s combined hormone replacement therapy (HRT), composed of estrogen and progesterone, replaced "unopposed estrogen" as the favored therapy, although women who had undergone hysterectomies, and were not therefore at increased risk for cancer, continued to be prescribed estrogen alone. Physicians were now expected to draw on abstract, epidemiological statistics to weigh up the "risks" and "benefits" of HRT prescription, on the basis of which, in consultation with "informed" patients, appropriate therapy would be selected. The rate of HRT prescriptions skyrocketed but, because no evidence existed about what might be the long-term effects of imbibing hormones for the 40 or more years of life remaining for middle-aged women, several clinical trials were approved, the most important of which is known as the Women's Health Initiative (WHI). This trial, designed to run for eight and a half years, recruited 16,608 postmenopausal women aged 50–79 years into the study, half of whom were taking HRT on a regular basis.

On May 31, 2002, more than three years before the trial was due to be completed, the data and safety monitoring board in charge of supervising the trial recommended that it be summarily stopped because the findings to date showed that an increased risk of breast cancer exceeded the expected benefits from HRT. It was agreed, on the basis of these and other findings, that HRT is not a suitable intervention for primary prevention of chronic diseases in women, in particular for coronary heart disease.[83] This decision caused something of a panic among the pharmaceutical industry, gynecologists, and women themselves. The North American Menopause Society (NAMS) published two position statements, one in 2002 and another in 2003. These comprehensive statements freely admit the lack of sound medical knowledge on which the promotion of HRT was based, and recommendations are made for use of HRT only on a short-term basis, at low dosages, to reduce hot flashes and other troublesome symptoms – in other words, a return to medical practice of the 1960s. Cause for additional shock became public in 2002 when it was reported that a trial conducted by the drug company Wyeth had shown that elderly women on HRT are at a doubled risk for dementia from 1 percent to 2 percent over five years.[84] Contrary to recognized protocol, the drug company secretly briefed a number of medical societies ahead of the public announcement of this finding in order to allow physicians to be ready to respond "knowledgeably to their constituents."[85]

In recent years, NAMS has supported controlled trials investigating the efficacy of complementary and herbal remedies to counter vasomotor symptoms, including black cohosh, primrose oil, and soy beans. The findings have been inconclusive to negative thus far (not surprising given that herbal remedies containing many active ingredients inevitably fare badly in clinical trials, something that is well known among pharmocognocists).[86] The expectation among medical professionals that all postmenopausal women should take HRT for their remaining years has been crushed, to be replaced by a much more cautious discourse about "natural" aging, best achieved with physician assistance. The dangers of smoking and the positive effects of exercise are prioritized; menopause is subsumed into the more encompassing phenomenon of aging, and medical monitoring of both women and men as they age is now considered essential to remain in good health.[87] At the time that the WHI trial was stopped, media coverage was extensive, and headlines such as "Hormone-use risk greater than benefit" and "Women warned to avoid hormone therapy" must have contributed greatly to the abrupt drop in requests for HRT prescriptions.

A recent report by the National Cancer Institute shows that breast cancer rates in the United States dropped abruptly in 2003, one year after many women stopped taking HRT. The sharpest drop was in the kind of tumors that are fuelled by estrogen.

Researchers at the Institute noted that these findings are "astounding," but one oncologist cautioned: "Epidemiology can never prove causality." Even so, he agreed that the use of HRT seemed to perfectly account for the data, and he and his colleagues "could find no other explanation."[88] Similar trends have been reported for Canada, New Zealand, Germany, France, Norway, and elsewhere.[89] A recent article in a leading British medical journal, *The Lancet*, presents findings that conclude that use of HRT must have "caused 1,000 deaths from ovarian cancer between 1991 and 2005,"[90] a situation in large part the result of the unabated "affair of the heart" of some gynecologists with estrogen – an affair fuelled by the drug companies.[91]

The case of HRT is just one rather dramatic example of routine medicalized monitoring that makes use of an array of technologies in which healthy people present themselves regularly for check-ups, including prostate specific antigen (PSA) testing for prostate cancer, mammography, Pap smears, and increasingly genetic testing of individuals and populations deemed at risk for specific diseases. Preventive monitoring is regarded as an essential part of health care in the developed world, particularly as costs for such tests come down with improvements in technology.[92] Some of these tests (such as mammography and Pap smears), when properly used, clearly save lives while others do not (as in the case of PSA screening).[93] All of these tests require making distinctions between values of normal and abnormal from scales representing estimates of risk based on large samples of so-called "normal" populations. These figures, frequently disputed and revised, vary from country to country, and point to the importance of what is at stake in defining the normal, and the consequences it entails for individual wellbeing.

Limitations to Biomedical "Objectivity"

In summary: it is claimed that biomedicine, because it is grounded in science, has a special technical status based on objectivity and standardization independent of society and culture. This rational, objective approach to the body is usually assumed by involved practitioners to be in striking contrast to other types of medical knowledge and practice, historical and contemporary.[94] Well-designed survey research will supply further objective insights about human health, but obtaining these findings is contingent on the ability to enrol "populations" of sufficient size to generate statistically significant findings – a task that has become increasingly problematic at a time when the majority of diseases of interest are multifactorial and difficult to observe in their "natural" state. This situation has arisen in large part because it is hard to find human populations today whose biology has not already been changed by previous biomedical interventions (chapter 7 will focus on how standardization has enabled clinical forms of experimentation). Furthermore, application of such objective methods and the logic of standardization that results are ill-equipped to capture the local context that affects the way in which health is understood and acted upon. Both these phenomena make an unreflective application of the concept of "normal" inappropriate, as Canguilhem remarked over 50 years ago. As the Inuit case above shows, the reality of "normal" biological variation very often falls outside what is deemed normal in biomedicine. Such variation is dependent upon the history of specific populations and the environments and social contexts in which people live.

The limitations of biomedicine's objective and standardized approach are evident in the recognition that "alternative" medical practices, often designated today as "complementary medicine," simply cannot be ignored, because people everywhere make extensive use of them.[95] However, the assumption on the part of policy-makers is that biomedicine should be the gold standard against which the worth of all other types of medical practice must be assessed, very often by subjecting their technologies to randomized controlled trials.[96] Moreover, it is assumed that the diagnostic categories of biomedicine alone, although they may be subject to further refinement, are the most reliable assessment of pathological changes in the body; this position can often be easily justified – for example, when a colonoscopy shows that there are no polyps in the intestinal tract, one can assume, aside from the occasional error, that this is indeed the case. For the majority of practitioners and the public alike, there is no denying that the present frontiers of biomedical knowledge represent the fruits of a long history of progress and scientific discovery, but the following chapters show repeatedly that biomedical knowledge and practice are culturally embedded,[97] so that the effects of their global dissemination are by no means straightforward.

The limitations of an approach based on a standardized body are further demonstrated by evidence from an unexpected quarter, namely molecular biology. A transformation in thinking about the human body has been gathering increasing momentum over the past two decades, described by some as revolutionary. This new approach is based on insights obtained from molecular genetics and the emergent sciences of genomics[98] in which genes and other molecular constituents of cells have become knowable entities and increasingly subject to human manipulation. One result of this new approach is that biological diversity can no longer be pushed to one side.

Better Than Well?

In addition to the assumption of a universal, decontextualized, body as the primary site for the production of medical knowledge and the management of disease, contemporary biomedicine is unusual in yet another way. Beginning in Paleolithic times, some evidence suggests that healers of the day may have made systematic use of plants with medicinal properties.[99] It is also evident that, until very recently, all medical traditions have directed their energies primarily toward prevention and healing. However, increasingly over the past quarter century, biomedicine strives not only to heal people, but to go further – to transcend nature and improve on bodies, minds, and even society, in a way that the early 20th-century eugenicists could never have dreamed of.[100] Recent advances in techno-scientific capacities, including developments in information technology, the creation of transnational collaborations, the ability to assemble subject populations worldwide for laboratory research and clinical trials, and emerging knowledge in molecular biology, together with numerous other innovations, have enabled this futuristic vision.

Certain aspects of biomedicine have recently morphed into practices in which the configurations of what were formerly thought to be unassailable boundaries between nature and culture are being actively transformed through technological manipulation. The result is previously unimaginable changes that are being brought about in human bodies. These technologies, often involving preparations of human organs, tissues, or cells – "human biologicals" – are rapidly spreading everywhere, bringing about surprising new alliances, and also divisions, among donors of biological materials of all kinds and recipients who are very often entirely unknown to each other. Reproductive technologies, organ transplants, genetic technologies, and stem cell technologies are dependent upon the use of human biologicals and therefore involve the commodification of body parts. This merging of nature with artifact, this shift from "representation to 'presentation,'"[101] is indeed a fundamental break with the past although, of course, continuities remain.

Even as biomedicine becomes increasingly occupied with moving to a point "after nature,"[102] it continues to share a temporal dimension with other medical traditions. A major concern in all medical traditions has always been about the causes of disease and affliction and hence inevitably with the past, whether biological or behavioral. These causes include individual genetic heritage; individual and group lifestyles; the anger or envy of neighbors or of the spirit world, caused by improper behavior; an "imbalanced" vital body, and so on. Our past, evolutionary, historic, and recent, comes back to haunt when we fall sick.

Health is no longer understood simply as an absence of disease in biomedicine, and wellbeing is sustained by improving on nature – an imagined state to be achieved by technologies of the present and the future. Epidemiological knowledge is used not only to identify risk factors for future diseases, but also to distinguish an increasing number of potential conditions that were until now considered part of "natural aging." We are all "patients-in-waiting."[103] The growing array of biomedical technologies used to modify these risk factors promises to annul the effects of the past in the present – the accumulated burden of life's "exposures" to noxious events, agents, and even genes. Pharmaceuticals can lower cholesterol, increase bone mass, and restore youthful hormone levels; they offer the possibility of enhancing life by targeting conditions previously thought to be unavoidable or irreversible. Medications such as Viagra or Cialis, initially marketed for erectile dysfunction in men, or antidepressants such as Prozac that are now marketed for a range of conditions including "social phobia disorder," have brought about the possibility of striving to become "better than normal." For the wealthy few who can afford such interventions, they provide a futuristic option of re-engineering bodies to an enhanced state of health.

In contrast, where biomedicine is not accessible or largely unavailable, the promise associated with it has become part of the local imaginary, with the result that many people go to great lengths and expend precious financial and social resources to obtain access to biomedical technologies.[104] Furthermore, pluralism – the resort by people to more than one kind of medical assistance, often for the same condition – is centuries old. As we will see in the next chapter, not only biomedicine, but also literate medical traditions (Chinese medicine, Ayurvedic medicine, Tibetan medicine) have attained a global reach. In various locales these mobile traditions interact and even hybridize with biomedicine and with indigenous, non-literate traditions in their many forms, to create diverse therapeutic economies. Yet even as it travels, biomedicine largely retains the coherent set of ideas and ideals discussed above that are exclusive to it. As we have seen, perhaps the most crucial distinction that differentiates biomedicine from other types of medical practice is its insistence that bodies can best be understood as standardized entities the world over. In contrast, virtually all other medical traditions pay careful attention to contingency when accounting for misfortune, often locating affliction in chains of previous events; local environments; the vicissitudes of various non-human actors including the spirit world, or an imbalance between individual bodies and the cosmos. For biomedicine, the laws of biology dispense with the need to search for local particularity; there is no ghost in the machine. This is the key to biomedicine's global reach, its universal claim to efficacy, and indeed its miraculous effects when technologies such as vaccinations, curative medication, and surgery are put to work. Biology alone is the standard that enables biomedicine to claim global purchase on achieving human health and wellbeing.

The sociologists Bowker and Star have defined a standard as "any set of agreed-upon rules for the production of … objects [that] spans more that one community of practice."[105] They add that "standards are deployed in making things work together over distance and heterogeneous metrics," citing the example of computer protocols for Internet communication.[106] Most significantly, they add that "there is no natural law that the best standard shall win – QWERTY, Lotus 123, DOS, and VHS are often cited as examples in this context."[107] Biology itself may be viewed as a standard: it is the set of rules that makes biomedicine, and more specifically biomedical technologies, work across vast distances and in highly different settings – whether these be different "communities of practice" (such as clinics or laboratories) or individual bodies. The next chapter shows how ethnography is a particularly useful strategy for revealing how biomedicine produces local and particularistic effects as it travels around the globe.

3

Anthropologies of Medicine

The two themes of "medical pluralism" and "medicalization" are set out in this chapter to illustrate how social scientists situate biomedical practice in the context of cultural, social, and political variables in their analyses. This historically and ethnographically grounded approach makes it clear how political and economic interests, prevailing moral concerns, and gender bias are often implicated in biomedicine. Furthermore, social science research makes it clear how the focus in clinical biomedicine on the material body, the assumption of a universal body, and the associated idea that illness is deviation about a standardized "norm," all contribute to the assertion of a moral position. This is so because it is a position that sets to one side the social and political origins of disease and illness and minimizes or even disregards local understandings about health and wellbeing. On the other hand, until recently, many social scientists, in common with the majority of scientists, have assumed that the "body proper"[1] falls fully into the domain of the natural sciences and is subject to biological laws. However, in contrast to medical scientists and biologists who pry open the material body to explicate the truths hidden therein, many social scientists prefer to leave the body "black-boxed." In the following chapter we will argue why the material body should not be set to one side, which would imply leaving in place an unexamined nature–culture dichotomy.

The Body Social

The assumption of a marked dichotomy between the "natural" and the "social" order so evident in European thinking since the Enlightenment is widely recognized as a product of Western metaphysics.[2] This stark separation of the social and intellectual life of humankind from the natural world – a separation assumed to be ordered by universal laws – facilitated the formation of the natural sciences as a discipline and also exerted a profound influence on social science theory from the early part of the 20th century. Emile Durkheim in *The Elementary Forms of Religious Life* wrote: "man is double"; in Durkheim's estimation a "higher" morally-imbued "socialized" body could be distinguished from the universal physical body common to us all. For Marcel

Mauss, Durkheim's nephew, and others who became a close-knit working group that published the journal founded by Durkheim, *L'Anneé Sociologique*, the corporeal body came to be conceptualized as a *tabula rasa* – the "first and most natural tool of man." Their position was that the body stimulates the human mind to model and represent the social world as being congruent with both the human body and the natural world.[3] Another pupil of Durkheim, Robert Hertz, wrote about the way in which the body is "good to think with"[4] and noted that the ready availability of the body as a referent "naturalizes" the social order. The idea of society itself, social taxonomies and categories, and embedded social hierarchies, were thus "naturalized" and made unquestionably real.

From the mid–1930s Mauss made a break with Durkheim when he explicitly argued for "a 'triple man,' one who is not only biological and social but in whom the psychological acts as mediator, bringing about the 'total man.'"[5] Mauss vividly demonstrated for the benefit of his lecture audiences how specific bodily techniques, some of which he learnt in the army, create physio-psycho-sociological assemblages of human action. In effect rejecting the position of Comte and Durkheim, Mauss posited the psychological as a mediating factor between the social and the biological, "thus creating a small space for the embodied individual as a wilful actor, with both the potential to resist the normative social order under certain conditions, and the capacity to display an irreducibly social character."[6] However, interest in Mauss' theories was not sustained, and throughout most of the 20th century, following the Durkheimian tradition, the material body was deliberately set to one side as a "black box," the contents of which were ruled inessential for sociological analysis. The philosopher Russell Keat commented on this phenomenon by pointing out that a good deal of time has been spent in the social sciences and humanities throughout the latter part of the 20th century in discussing the distinctiveness of human beings, while at the same time holding to an assumption about the non-distinctiveness of the human body.[7] Even as we write at the beginning of the twenty-first century, the interiority of the body remains notably absent from most social science literature, suggesting rather graphically that researchers continue to subscribe to a nature–culture dichotomy in which the material body, an assumed universal, is fully consigned to the domain of the biological sciences, where it most appropriately belongs.

Similarly, post-Enlightenment European and North American philosophers have attended more to the life of the mind than to the body itself.[8] There are, of course, notable exceptions, among them Karl Marx, Frederick Engels, and Walter Benjamin to name the best known. And Maurice Merleau-Ponty, in his *The Phenomenology of Perception*, set out deliberately to overcome mind–body dualism by taking bodily sensuous experience as primary. His phenomenological approach is a conscious rejection of the Kantian humanist tradition in which a transcendental ego claims to know the objective world using an abstracted, rational perspective. Merleau-Ponty argues instead that embodied, intentional selves interact with the world and that this interaction, largely mediated via perception, precedes all knowledge production. But Merleau-Ponty nonetheless directs attention to what he believes is universal individual behavior. His theory does little to overcome nature–culture or nature–society dualisms, and these categories were not themselves problematized by him. The assumption of a uniformly standardizable "body proper"[9] has survived with little substantial criticism for many years. Not surprisingly, perhaps, for many social scientists, philosophers, and bioethicists alike, the dominant understanding of the individual body from which societies are supposedly assembled continues to be thought of as "a skin-bounded, rights-bearing, communicating, experience-collecting, biomechanical entity."[10]

A recent turn once again toward materiality, notably in the field of cultural studies with its interest in the flesh and in body surfaces, has done little to relieve this situation.[11] However, several theorists, including Bruno Latour, Ian Hacking, Donna Haraway, and more recently Karen Barad, take a radically different stand from the majority of earlier writers. Each of these individuals has worked explicitly to set out new approaches to the human body in which the reality of the material is not denied for one moment but, equally, the biological body is not simply accepted as a universal entity that we are increasingly able to apprehend comprehensively by means of scientific investigation.

Our primary purpose here is to give readers, especially those with little or no experience of social science research, an introduction to the way in which such research has richly demonstrated how medical knowledge and practice of all kinds is deeply social. Emphasis has been given in anthropological research throughout the 20th century to knowledge production in connection with health, illness, healing, and related practices worldwide, showing conclusively that such knowledge cannot be fully comprehended in isolation from social, cultural, and political contexts. Initially the focus was on medical traditions other than biomedicine, but the way was paved for arguments claiming that biomedicine too should be analyzed in socio-cultural context, a position arrived at a little earlier by insightful sociologists.[12] Frequently buttressed by the work of Michel Foucault in which he considered the epistemological foundations of modern medicine, social scientists began in the 1970s to analyze the way in which the discourse and practices of biomedicine are permeated not only by political forces but also by social and cultural forces.[13] The work of historians discussed in the previous chapter, and that of social scientists to be discussed below, are in this respect largely complementary.

Allan Young, writing in the early 1980s, was perhaps the first medical anthropologist to assert that what is required is an "understanding of how medical facts are predetermined by the processes through which they are conventionally produced in clinics and research settings … the task at hand is to critically examine the social conditions of knowledge production."[14] Prior to this time, by far the majority of anthropologists had been content to research only "traditional" medicine on the assumption that biomedicine, being grounded in science, was of an entirely different order. After the publication of Young's work and that of several other social scientists, it became evident that biomedicine should be considered "symmetrically" to other medical traditions, that is, as an assemblage of knowledge and practices inextricably associated with political expediencies, social interests, and embedded values.

It is abundantly clear from much of what follows that ethnographic analyses of accounts and interpretations given by patients, families, community members, medical specialists, and other key informants provide indispensable insights as to the way in which medical knowledge and practice affect everyday life, often transforming it profoundly.

Contextualizing Medical Knowledge

As far as it can be ascertained, peoples everywhere have always amassed knowledge and instituted practices designed to preserve health and account for the incidence, etiology, and treatment of illness. Anthropologists started to record such knowledge from the latter part of the 19th century, but it wasn't until the 1920s that the physician/anthropologist W. H. R. Rivers, drawing on his experiences in New Guinea and Melanesia, argued that medicine in non-literate societies is not merely a random assortment of practices based on custom or superstition.[15] On the contrary, he insisted, medicine is an integral part of society at large. Building on this insight, anthropologists working in numerous societies have shown how medical knowledge and practices, of both experts and ordinary people as they go about daily life, are culturally and regionally informed and should be evaluated in context before judgment is made about their worth or lack thereof. Furthermore, professional medical knowledge in any society is systematized and has a logic to its practices that is transmitted to disciples, apprentices, and students.[16] The well-known British anthropologist, E. E. Evans-Pritchard, writing in the 1930s about witchcraft amongst the Azande, concluded that even this "exotic" practice could be construed, when examined in context, as a rational response to the apparent randomness of misfortune. Furthermore, he noted that Azande draw on multi-causal explanations for misfortune; quite often it is evident to everyone involved that social or morally related behavior accounts for a particular event, and it is then considered inappropriate to judge that witchcraft is involved.[17] Research that followed over the next half century in Africa, Asia, and among indigenous peoples of the Americas and Australia has made it clear that among non-literate medical traditions the idea is ubiquitous that, in general, the causes of disease and death are considered to be many. However, such causes comprise above all an "externalizing discourse,"[18] because they locate the origins of disease largely outside the human body and include references to human social relations, the environment, and the spiritual or cosmic order.[19] These external causes are not systematically linked to named anatomical pathology but bring about malaises of many kinds, depending on the circumstances of each case. Each illness episode is distinct. Furthermore, it is also clear that at times no reason is required to explain illness or accidents – they simply happen by chance.[20]

Among literate medical traditions, other than biomedicine, including Chinese medicine, Ayurveda, Yunnani, and the Galenic tradition, attention in medical practice is often paid to specific entities and changes on the surface of or inside the body believed to be signs of illness or imminent death, although internal signs can only be ascertained indirectly via pulse-taking and palpation, from sputum, and so on. Furthermore, the significance of such signs do not stand alone; they are made meaningful with reference to extra-corporeal events including social and physical environments, the behavior of the individual in question, and at times that of their relatives. Generalizations made about the physical condition of patients are not based on the assumption of a universal body, but rather on the basis of body types or constitutions shared in common with some people but not others, or else as the result of exposure to similar external conditions and events. A diagnosis may well be one of a cluster of diagnostic types, but rigorous standardization and systematization is not good practice – each illness episode has important qualities of its own.[21] Of course globalization and the spread of biomedical knowledge and technologies have affected – often dramatically – the knowledge, explanatory accounts, and practices of indigenous medical practitioners wherever they live. And similarly, ordinary people too are everywhere profoundly affected by these changes, a theme that recurs throughout this book.

As was made clear in the previous chapter, in contrast to medical systems that draw on an externalizing discourse, clinical biomedicine usually gives weight to an "internalizing" discourse, even when it is acknowledged that factors external to the body may well be at least in part contributory to the condition. In recent years this approach has become common even for the management of psychiatric disorder. Furthermore, biomedicine makes no allowance for misfortune or chance as an explanatory variable per se – a scientific approach to the "ordering of reality" does not permit this,[22] although unexplained conditions can be accounted for as being beyond the current state of scientific knowledge. With its assumption of a "body proper" given wholly by nature,[23] biomedicine is unique. Compared with other medical traditions biomedical explanations are, comparatively speaking, reductionistic, and focused primarily on the detection of named entities such as viruses, genes, biomarkers, or other signs internal to the body thought be directly implicated in malfunction or incipient malfunction, even when the habits, lifestyle, and at times the environment in which the patient is living may be taken into consideration. Furthermore, anatomy and surgery are two biomedical specialties that have not been developed in a consistent way in other medical traditions aside from a few remarkable exceptions such as trephination. These specialties together with germ theory, contributed greatly to a reductionistic, internalist approach that, until recently, has been the uncontested anchor for biomedicine and for the development of technologies that furnish representations of the inner body.

Medical Pluralism

Working for many years in Mysore State in India, anthropologist Alan Beals made the following comment over 30 years ago about the availability of medical practitioners in both urban and rural areas where he carried out his research:

> there are a wide range of practitioners including unpaid local healers, saints and religious figures, priests, drug and herb authorities [ayurvedic doctors], midwives, astrologers, government doctors, missionary doctors, private doctors, and foreign-returned doctors. Most of these practitioners are sincere men who believe in what they are doing and are trusted in return. A few practitioners in every category are insensitive, dishonest, or incompetent.[24]

Writing about the phenomenon of medical pluralism a few years later, Charles Leslie noted that the assumption on the part of the majority of health care planners at that time was that indigenous medical practices would soon die out, although some might be incorporated into a worldwide "cosmopolitan" medicine. Time has shown that this assumption was completely false. Aside from some notable exceptions where, due to major political upheavals or social disruptions, medical assistance of all kinds is virtually absent, nowhere has indigenous medicine simply faded away.[25] Beals listed several reasons why individuals select one type of practitioner rather than another – reasons that remain pertinent to this day. Among them are the kind of disease or affliction that needs attention; "folk" beliefs about the cause, cure, and appropriate curer for a specific problem; the economic and social status of the patient and her family, and the kinds of advice and information available at the time a particular strategy is adopted.[26]

The extent to which medical traditions other than those of biomedicine continue to flourish and the fact that people everywhere in the world frequently consult with more than one type of medical practitioner provide incontrovertible evidence that biomedicine alone is not sufficient to meet the needs of vast numbers of people.[27] Lack of economic resources nationally to build health care facilities, and the inability of some patients and families to pay for biomedical care account in part for thriving indigenous medical practices. But this tells only part of the story. Even where biomedicine is readily available, many people – wherever they live – use a pluralistic approach when dealing with illness and disability. Research makes it clear that patients and families often prefer to go to local healers even when a visit costs more than one to biomedical practitioners.[28] Furthermore, many governments actively support indigenous medicine, often for nationalistic reasons. In all the major cities of the world biomedicine is present but so too is a large array of Chinese and Ayurvedic facilities, among other complementary forms of health care in great abundance. Further, medications from an array of medical traditions are present in health food stores and pharmacies.

Japan has had a comprehensive socialized health care system since the 1930s and today boasts an abundance of technologically sophisticated biomedical facilities. Even so, while everyone routinely makes use of biomedicine for most of their health-related matters, the majority also make strategic choices at times among biomedical practitioners, acupuncturists, herbalists (who are trained MDs), masseuses, and traditional bone-setters, depending upon their ailments. With well over 100 years of exposure to biomedicine, the practice of East Asian medicine continues to flourish in Japan, most of it in a carefully monitored, standardized form. Furthermore, biomedical practitioners, notably those whose specialties are pediatrics, geriatrics, and obstetrics and gynecology, and those who work in pain clinics, refer their patients to East Asian medical practitioners and at times make use of traditional therapeutics themselves.[29]

Similarly, in Haiti, where the majority of people are pitifully short of resources, strategic decisions are made by people about visits to one or more of a range of possible healers, including biomedical practitioners, depending in part on the various therapeutic techniques on offer and the cost.[30] And in Bolivia it has been shown that resort to indigenous medicine sometimes constitutes a self-conscious challenge to the domineering attitudes with which biomedical practitioners can be associated[31] – since, for people living in Asia, Africa, and Latin America, biomedicine is at times associated with colonial oppression. However, there are times when the mixing of "traditional" beliefs with biomedicine can be dangerous. Research showed that the Mende living in Sierra Leone often made decisions about the use of the pharmaceuticals they had bought at the market on the basis of ideas associated with local medicines concerning an appropriate mix of color, consistency, taste, and so on. The researchers were rightly critical of the manufacturers for having assumed that there would be no local knowledge of any kind about medicinals that might affect the way their drugs would be used.[32]

In summary, the form taken by medical pluralism varies considerably depending upon geographical location, and the reasons for the choices that people make can only be fully appreciated in light of local histories and current conditions. Nowhere is biomedicine received into an environment devoid of ideas about illness causation and knowledge and practices relating to the body, and even when exposed to scientific knowledge people do not necessarily relinquish indigenous theories of disease causation, nor do they cease to use local "idioms of distress" to express their physical discomfort.[33] Furthermore, everywhere people have grown up with expectations about ideal family size and its composition, appropriate human social relations and mutual support, how to deal with birth, dying, and death, and so on, all of which can be profoundly affected by the introduction of biomedical knowledge and technologies that have the potential to challenge the accepted moral order.

The Modernization of "Traditional" Medicine

Traditional medical systems have long histories but they are neither static nor lacking in innovation. A considerable amount of integration, syncretism, and borrowing has taken place between indigenous and biomedical practitioners over the past century, and a large number of indigenous healers have adapted to the new global reality, often adding one or more biomedical technologies to their repertoire.[34] At times such adaptations are the result of pressures placed on healers directly or indirectly by governments to systematize and standardize their practices – to "biomedicalize" themselves.[35] Further, practitioners are not immune to the effects of a world where television and the Internet inform people everywhere about what is in their own best interest. The result is that "traditional" healers "modernize" their practices and package their wares to attract buyers. Although some have fallen by the wayside, many healers have proved, not surprisingly, to be innovative, flexible, and pragmatic.[36]

In some locations, where no money has been allocated to build biomedical health care facilities, indigenous practitioners continue to be the sole providers, sometimes after receiving basic training in biomedical principles of hygiene and contagion.[37] In many urban areas, the training of complementary practitioners is regulated, notably in East Asia, Europe, North America, and parts of South America, and extensive schooling in the principles of anatomy and physiology is commonly required, in addition to instruction in traditional knowledge and practice, the latter often in truncated form.[38] The result inevitably involves standardization and elimination of practices considered anomalous that cannot readily be "integrated" with a biomedical approach. Sometimes these changes are actively adopted by younger practitioners who wish to present themselves as offering modern, fully rational and scientifically grounded services.[39] In the case of non-literate traditions the possibilities for integration are, of course, much more limited, but this does not stop biomedicalization from taking place.[40]

Despite its undeniable efficacy in connection with many problems, indigenous or local medicine is often chosen preferentially over biomedicine and, as a result indigenous healers continue to flourish even where biomedicine is available. As Volker Scheid and others point out, today wherever biomedical and non-biomedical practices meet, arguments about legitimacy are inevitably grounded in the twin ideas of "tradition" and "modernity"[41] which help to explain the appeal of indigenous biomedicine. The Indonesian government, for example, has chosen to actively support indigenous medical practices for explicitly nationalistic reasons.[42] Biomedicine, associated with "Western" values, especially with what are believed to be American values, is perceived as a threat to the moral order, most clearly in connection with contraceptive use and other reproductive technologies.[43] Indigenous medicine, on the other hand, is strongly associated with positive family values thought to be under siege, and is therefore actively encouraged by the government. Similarly, biomedicine in India has long been understood as a "tool of empire," and the major revival and professionalization of Ayurvedic medicine that took place from the middle of the 20th century were fired by nationalistic sentiment.[44] Today the spread of HIV in India is regarded by some politicians as a "cultural invasion," as too is biomedicine by some. Ayurveda has been promoted as "an Indian weapon against this invasion."[45]

Medical Hybridization

When a decision was made in China at the time of the Cultural Revolution that the medical system should "walk on two legs," the government actively promoted both biomedicine and Chinese medicine, a trend that had already been fostered by the government since the 1930s. This was in part due to financial limitations and the enormous expense involved in adopting biomedicine wholesale, in such a populous and at that time economically deprived nation, but equally due to a firm belief in the efficacy of indigenous Chinese medicine coupled with nationalistic pride and a reluctance to succumb entirely to the values associated with the West. Although enormous pressure existed to "scientize" and rationalize the recognized schools of traditional medicine and their various approaches,[46] in contemporary China, the mingling of Chinese medicine and biomedicine has taken place to such an extent that Volker Scheid uses a metaphor taken from science and technology studies, a "mangle of practice,"[47] to describe the situation. He argues that pluralism is not adequate to capture the complexity, and points out that a great deal of genuine assimilation is evident in both discourse and practice, so that "synthesis" is a better descriptor.[48] Even so, it is evident that assimilation is not symmetrical, and that Chinese medicine has been transformed by biomedicine to a much greater extent than has biomedicine by Chinese medicine. Furthermore, institutionally, the buildings, organizations, personnel, schools, departments, books, journals, and ideologies of medicine and the body in contemporary China continue to be self-consciously bifurcated along "Chinese" and "Western" lines. And government financing of Chinese medicine is much less than for tertiary care biomedicine.[49]

The synthesis is, however, strikingly apparent from the point of view of patients. Everett Yuehong Zhang illustrates this when he shows how, among the Chinese men he studied, many deliberately switch back and forth between Chinese medicine and Viagra for problems of sexual dysfunction. Such switching comprises much more than simply a choice of medication; rather, differing types of what Zhang calls "an economy of potency" and an ethics of sexuality are involved – one involving "desire" and the other a traditional "cultivation of life" – both of which objectives these men hope to achieve.[50] Zhang demonstrates hybridization in the thinking of patients and practitioners between what is associated with tradition on the one hand and with modernity on the other.

Stacey Langwick, working in Tanzania, argues that it is inappropriate to think of biomedicine and non-biomedical therapies as being complementary strategies for dealing with different aspects of similar medical problems. She points out that use of a therapy does not necessarily mean that a patient has "faith" in either the therapy or the person administering it. She also shows how knowledge and practices involved in the diagnosis and treatment of malaria and in the condition known locally as *degedege* that has much in common with malaria are, in effect, "interdependent therapeutic ecologies rather than discrete differentiations of pluralist systems."[51] Langwick describes in detail how malaria and degedege become knowable in practice, informed by the very different ontological stances and epistemological propositions taken by biomedical practitioners and local healers with respect to these conditions. When patients resort to practitioners of both medical approaches for similar illness episodes, the result is one of both hybrid bodies and disease entities in the minds of patients.

Biodiversity and Indigenous Medical Knowledge

Global concern about the management of biodiversity has lent new support to indigenous practitioners in South and Southeast Asia, parts of Africa, and parts of Central and South America. The World Bank and the WHO have signed documents making it clear that these organizations are in support of the systematic utilization of plant, animal, and mineral products used by traditional healers for pharmaceutical research and possible drug development.[52] Traditional practitioners are encouraged to enter into agreements with biologists and conservationists eager to harvest and analyze plant materials of all kinds growing in isolated areas, about which indigenous herbalists know a great deal. Herbalists sometimes make arrangements with people running government- or NGO-supported projects for the preservation of biodiversity, on the understanding that in return they will have support for their local medical practice, be able to control access to medicinal plants, and even on occasion be able to obtain funding to build a clinic.[53] Formerly isolated healers are thus integrated into the global system of exchange, inevitably with the result that many begin to reconceptualize their understanding about the body, health, and illness.

One major difficulty that arises when traditional medical practitioners are incorporated into mainstream delivery of health care alongside biomedical practitioners is that their knowledge and practices are abruptly transformed due to the enforcement of standardization and conformity with practice regulations. The experienti of healers is devalued, and their personal approach to patients is replace textualized objectivity characteristic of biomedicine – thus the episten of traditional medical knowledge is seriously violated.[54] Market comm herbal medication exacerbates this situation. A good number of anthr written about the effects, mostly negative, of these transformations.[55]

of various kinds were overworked and spent less than a minute with patients. The powerful antibiotic tetracycline was prescribed routinely by virtually all practitioners for a range of symptoms including coughs, colds, and intermittent fever. Many patients could not afford to pay for the full prescription and so would buy only three days' worth. For chronic diseases such as TB only small amounts of medication were bought at any one time.

The ethnographic interviews carried out in the study by Das and Das showed convincingly that the experience of illness was punctuated by days when people had a small amount of money to consult a doctor (public hospitals are constantly over-flowing with patients, forcing people to seek out private care of one kind or another). On other days they could only afford to go to a drug outlet to buy medication, and on many days they were without money and pain simply had to be endured. Das and Das conclude that a conjunction of local medical practices, local concepts of disease, and household economies bring about a "medical environment" in poor Indian neighborhoods and that to accuse people of misusing medication is to fail to take account of the reality of everyday life and the complex ecology in which "self medica-tion" takes place.[63]

A Short History of Medicalization

Specialists in public health, epidemiologists, clinicians, and social scientists have directed their attention to the contribution of social and political conditions to disease causation since the late 19th century and to the unequal distribution of disease within any given society. However, until recently, these concerns have been dwarfed for the most part by biomedical interests working on the assumption that a therapeutic approach would eventually bring about the conquest of disease. In order to account for the growing importance of biomedicine in everyday life during the latter part of the 20th century, the sociologist Irving Zola argued that medicine had become an important institution of social control, supplanting the more "traditional" institutions of religion and law, with the result that many aspects of daily life were being "medi-calized" in order to "maintain" health. Zola made it clear that he was by no means totally opposed to the process he was documenting. Following Zola's lead, a genre of research appeared in which the word medicalization – "to make medical" – was adopted as a key concept.[64]

It can be argued that medicalization commenced many hundreds of years before Zola's observations, from the time that one or two people were first recognized as healers among certain human groups. Later, with the consolidation of the early literate medical traditions of Europe and Asia, between approximately 250 BCE and 600 CE, the first groups of healers to be professionalized made themselves available to deal with physical malfunctions and disease of all kinds, as well as with the exigencies of everyday life, including difficulties relating to the life course, notably infertility. Nevertheless it is usually assumed, notably in the sociological literature, that medicalization is a relatively recent phenomenon, one inextricably associated with modernization as it unfolded in the "West." For many commentators its origins lie with the professionalization of medicine and the emergence of medical specialties.

Commencing in the 17th century, European and North American modernization fostered what has been described as an "engineering mentality," one manifestation of which was a concerted effort to establish increased control over the vagaries of the natural world through the application of science. By the 18th century, legitimized by state support, the consolidation of medicine as a profession was taking place, together with the formation of medical specialties and the gradual accumulation, compilation, and distribution of new medical knowledge. As we saw in chapter 1, systematization of the medical domain was in turn part of a more general process of modernization to which industrial capitalism and technological production were central, both intimately associated with the bureaucratization and rationalization of everyday life. As part of this process, health began to be understood by numerous physicians and by the emerging middle classes alike as a valued commodity, and the physical body as something that could be improved upon.[65]

Professional medical interests expanded in several directions during the 18th and 19th centuries. First, there was an increased involvement in the management not only of individual pathology, but also of lifecycle events. For example, birth had been attended and assisted uniquely by women until the early 18th century in Europe and North America, at which time male birth attendants began to be trained and worked at the lying-in hospitals located in major urban centers to deliver the babies of well-off women. These accoucheurs later legitimized their right to practice through the formation of the profession of obstetrics.[66]

By the mid–19th century, other lifecycle transitions were medicalized, including adolescence, menopause, aging, and death, followed by infancy in the first years of the 20th century.[67] In practice, however, large segments of the population remained unaffected by these changes until the mid–20th century. A second aspect of medicalization involves standardization. With pervasive moves by the state, the law, and professional associations throughout the 19th century to increase standardization by means of the rational application of science to everyday life, medicine was gradually integrated into an extensive network of formal practices whose function was to regulate the health and moral behavior of entire populations. These "disciplines of surveillance" function in two ways.[68] First, everyday behaviors were normalized so that, for example, emotions and sexuality were made targets of medical technologies, with the result that human reproduction was brought largely under the purview of public health. Similarly, other activities, including breastfeeding, hygiene, exercise, deportment, and numerous other aspects of daily life became subject to surveillance – largely by means of public health initiatives and with the support of the popular media.

By the late 18th century the social consequences of medicalization were already visible. Those populations labeled as mentally ill, individuals designated as morally unsound, together with many individuals living in poverty were incarcerated in asylums and penitentiaries where they were subjected to what Foucault termed "panopticism." Inspired by Jeremy Bentham's plans for the perfect prison in which prisoners are in constant view of the authorities, the Panopticon was a mechanism of power reduced to its ideal form – an institution devoted to surveillance.[69]

These changes could not have taken place without several medical innovations. First, the consolidation of the anatomical pathological sciences whereby the older humoral pathology was all but eclipsed, so that belief in individualized pathologies was gradually abandoned in favor of a universal representation of the "normal" body from which sick bodies deviate. Second, was the introduction of the autopsy, enabling systematization of pathological science; and, third, the routinization of the physical examination and collection of case studies. Fourth was the creation by the state of the concept of "population" as a means to monitor and control the health of society at large, at which time disease started to be understood as at once individual pathology, and statistical deviation from a norm of "health." Treatment of pathology continued to be the core activity of clinical medicine, but the emergent epistemology of disease causation based on numeration gradually gained ground from the early part of the 18th century, resulting in a new discipline – public health – supported directly by the apparatus of the state, the key function of which was the oversight of populations.

Other related characteristics of medicalization, well established by the late 19th century and still evident today, can be summarized as "dividing practices," whereby sickness is distinguished from health; illness from crime; madness from sanity, and so on.[70] Using this type of reasoning, certain persons and populations are made into objects for medical attention and distinguished from others who were subjected to the attention of legal, religious, or educational authorities. In order to accomplish this end, various "assemblages" are deployed constituted by a combination of spaces, persons, and techniques. In the domain of medicine, these assemblages include hospitals, dispensaries, and clinics, in addition to which are government offices, the home, schools, the army, communities, and so on. Recognized medical experts function in these spaces, making use of instruments and technologies to assess and measure the condition of both body and mind. The stethoscope, invented in the early 19th century, was one such major innovation, the first of many technologies that permit indirect assess to the interior of the body, rendering the patient's subjective account of malaise secondary to the "truth" of science.

Several noted historians and social scientists argue that from the mid–19th century, with the hospitalization of citizens of all classes for the first time rather than only wealthy individuals, the medical profession was able to exert power over passive patients in a way never before possible. This transition, aided by the production of new technologies, has been described as medical "imperialism."[71] Many researchers limit use of the term medicalization to these particular changes, whereas other scholars insist that the development of hospitalized patient populations is just one aspect of a more pervasive process of medicalization, to which both major institutional and conceptual changes contribute. Included are fundamentally transformed ideas about the body, health, and illness, not only among experts, but also among populations at large.[72]

It is noteworthy that medical and public health management of everyday life was evident not only in Europe and North America, but also in 19th-century Japan and to a lesser extent in China. In India, Africa, Southeast Asia, and parts of Central and South America, medicalization was intimately associated with colonization, as will be explored in chapter 6. Activities of military doctors and medical missionaries, the establishment of tropical medicine departments and of public health initiatives, designed to protect the colonizers and to "civilize" the colonized rather than to ameliorate their health, were integral to colonizing regimes. As was the case everywhere, however, large segments of the population remained untouched by these activities until well into the 20th century.[73]

Opposition to Medicalization

In a review of the literature on medicalization, Peter Conrad argues that during the 1970s and 1980s the term was used by social scientists most often as a critique of inappropriate medical practice, rather than simply to convey the idea that something had been made medical.[74] Sociological and anthropological literature of this period argued uniformly that health professionals had become agents of social control. This position was influenced by the earlier publications of Thomas Szasz and R. D. Laing[75] in connection with psychiatry, where they insisted that the social determinants of irrational behavior were being neglected in favor of an approach dominated by a biologically deterministic medical model. Zola, Conrad, and others argued in turn that alcoholism, homosexuality, hyperactivity, and other behaviors were increasingly being "biologized" and labeled as diseases.

While in theory this move from "badness to sickness" relieved patients of culpability for their condition, it nevertheless permitted medical professionals to make judgments about the labeling and care of such patients that inevitably had profound moral repercussions with respect to how they should best be managed.[76] Medicalization of distress of all kinds has over the years become pervasive, a process described by Jacqueline Zita as "diagnostic bracket creep."[77] And media reporting keeps us all alert about conditions that we are informed are increasing dramatically, often explicitly linked to the ubiquitous stress thought to be associated with late modernity, including post-traumatic stress disorder (PTSD), attention deficit and hyperactivity disorder (ADHA), obesity, and so on.[78]

A reaction set in during the late 1970s against medicalization. Ivan Illich's stinging critique of scientific medicine entitled *Medical Nemesis* had the greatest effect on the public at large and on some health care professionals. Illich argued that due to over-medication, biomedicine may inadvertently produce disease, a process known as iatrogenesis. Illich asserted that biomedical treatment often creates negative, even serious side effects in the body (a position that is contradicted by no one today and is bolstered by incontrovertible epidemiological evidence that prescription drugs are a common cause of illness and death).[79] Illich went further and insisted that the autonomy of ordinary people in dealing with pain and illness is compromised by medicalization.

At the same time many feminists, among them anthropologists, publicly characterized medicine as a patriarchal institution because, in their estimation, the female body was increasingly being made into a site for technological intervention in connection with childbirth and other conditions associated with reproduction.[80] Similarly to what had happened in 18th-century Europe, medical anthropologists documented the ways in which midwifery throughout the world was being forcibly placed under the authoritative knowledge of governments and the medical profession.[81]

Other feminists have not critiqued medicalization per se, but have insisted instead that to cast women in a passive role with respect to medicalization is to perpetuate the very kind of assumptions that feminists have been trying to challenge. They note that an active resistance to medicalization contributed to the rise of the home-birth movement and to widespread use of alternative therapies and remedies of many kinds. But empirical research has also made it clear that the responses of individuals to biomedical technologies are pragmatic and based upon what is perceived to be in the best interests of women themselves, their families, and at times their communities.[82] The anthropologist Emily Martin's cultural analysis of reproduction was one of the first attempts to show how women are not simply victims of medical ascendancy, but rather exhibit resistance and create alternate meanings about the body and reproduction to those dominant among the medical profession.[83]

Today, the majority of women worldwide apparently continue to internalize the norm that their prime task in life is to reproduce a family of the ideal size and composition, that is, to contribute to reproduction of both the family and society, and that failure to do so will diminish them in the eyes of others. Under these circumstances it is not surprising that a pragmatic approach to medical technology and medical services is much more common than is outright resistance to technologies designed to assist with reproduction.

There has been a spate of recent publications on medicalization highlighting new concerns about this process. Unlike earlier social scientists, Conrad argues that the commercial and market aspects of medicalization and the associated direct-to-consumer advertising so pronounced in the United States must be taken into account.[84] Children as young as four years of age are being prescribed powerful psychotropic drugs to treat anxiety, attention deficit disorder, depression, and other problems.[85] On the other hand, Conrad insists, individuals today act increasingly as "consumers" of medical diagnoses, and actively seek medication out as legitimization for their distress. Many also search out "biomedical enhancements" such as human growth hormone or Viagra and clearly the Internet is highly influential in creating and sustaining this trend.

The sociologist Adele Clarke and her colleagues call for a recognition of "biomedicalization" directly associated with the ever-increasing practices of technoscience in medicine.[86] Kaufman and co-authors draw on this concept of biomedicalization to illustrate recent changes associated with aging in California, notably the way in which technological innovation permitting life-extension in connection with conditions such as cardiac procedures, kidney dialysis, and kidney transplants, has been routinized, resulting in significant moral and ethical concerns. The ethnographic findings of Kaufman et al. show that an imperative to treat, coupled with a discourse of hope that includes not only patients but also family members, outweigh the ideal of choice, including the possibility of stopping treatment. These authors conclude that the extension of medical jurisdiction over life itself "renders medical intervention natural and normal, especially in late life."[87] In summary then, medicalization desocializes illness and, further, "depoliticizes" what are fundamentally political questions revolving around the distribution of wealth and social justice.

The Social Construction of Illness and Disease

More than 30 years ago, when Susan Sontag contracted breast cancer, she warned us about the "punitive and sentimental fantasies" concocted in connection with certain illnesses. She was concerned about the way in which stereotypes and moralizing discourses are associated with so many illnesses. Sontag insisted that the "most truthful way of regarding illness – and the healthiest way of being ill – is the one

most purified of, most resistant to, metaphoric thinking." She was particularly concerned, not surprisingly, with some research current at that time in which a claim
was made for a statistically significant association between a given personality type
and increased risk for breast cancer.[88]

Sontag's exhortation to confine our interpretations about illness to the material
body is easily justifiable, it seems, as a means of eliminating inappropriate moralizing
and discrimination about specific diseases. She is not alone in this; many families
when confronted with, for example, psychiatric illness or biological conditions that
result in disability, seek out medical help with the hope of being given a neutral
professional label for the condition, thus relieving either the affected individual or
their family of responsibility. However, in taking this position, an assumption is made
that the causes of diseases can be fully explained and treated by confining attention
to the physical body alone. Moreover, it is also assumed that medical taxonomic
categories accurately reflect discrete, readily demarcated pathological conditions in
the body.[89] The following discussion shows just how difficult it is to sustain this
position.

In his work conducted in Iran in the 1970s, the anthropologist Byron Good
developed the concept of "semantic networks" in order to understand the complex
meanings embedded in language used to describe bodily distress and illness. His
interest at the time was in "popular" medical knowledge strongly influenced, in the
case of Iran, by the Galenic medical tradition and classical Islamic scholarship. Good's
argument is that the meaning of certain terms used in everyday language that refer
to bodily conditions do not specify merely a cluster of symptoms, but rather that
such categories are in effect a "syndrome" of common experiences – "a set of words,
experiences, and feelings which typically 'run together' for the members of a society"[90]
and which make physical sensations, moral order, and social events inseparable. Good
explores in detail the meanings associated with a common illness in Iran known as
"heart distress," the physical sensations consisting mainly of a pounding, irregular
heartbeat, or a squeezing of the heart, accompanied by anxiety. The illness is self-
diagnosed, and is most common in women and the elderly, who only visit a doctor
if the episode is judged as unusually severe, when they usually receive a prescription
of vitamins or occasionally a tranquilizer. Good establishes the complex semantic
networks associated with heart distress by carrying out extensive interviews; the most
common of these networks are first, problems with female sexuality, including concerns about the negative effects, physical and social, of taking the contraceptive pill,
and second, worries generated by the oppression of daily life. He concludes that heart
distress is not simply an individual matter but a public, collective project, recognized
as a legitimate expression of suffering.

Good's research, with its emphasis on the narrative representations of illness,
set off a train of research in which emphasis was given to the relationship among
language usage, physical symptoms, and social and cultural contexts. A decade later
Arthur Kleinman highlighted the way in which the experiences of illness and meanings attributed to it are inevitably situated in "local moral worlds"[91] – a concept that
is now used widely in medical anthropology and biomedical ethics. These researchers
alerted investigators to the inappropriateness of attempting to simply reduce or
"translate" the language of distress and suffering as equivalent to biomedical
categories.

For example, Robert Barrett has shown how the institutional practices of psychiatry first created in the 19th century made possible the production of a new category of knowledge – schizophrenia. Prior to institutionalization, the kind of "crazy" behavior involving disorders of cognition and perception that we now associate with schizophrenia would have elicited a range of responses, not all of them indicating that pathology is necessarily involved. Barrett, a psychiatrist and anthropologist, interprets schizophrenia as a "polysemic symbol" in which various meanings and values are condensed into a syndrome – stigma, weakness, inner degeneration, a diseased brain, and chronicity. He argues that without this associated constellation of meanings schizophrenia, as we understand it, would not exist.[92]

Barrett goes on to state that the individualistic concept of personhood so characteristic of Euro-America has contributed to our understanding of this disease. He shows how a theme of a divided, split, or disintegrated individual that runs through 19th-century psychiatric discourse was incorporated into the first descriptions of schizophrenia in the 1880s, and continues to the present day. Schizophrenia is not the only disease associated with splitting and dissociation, but it has become the prototypical example of such a condition. The loss of autonomy and boundedness characteristic of the condition are taken to be signs of the breakdown of the individual, and thus of the person. Further, in line with Ian Hacking's concept of looping, Barrett argues that the description, classification, and treatment of schizophrenic patients as broken people with "permeable ego boundaries" profoundly influence the subjective experience of the disease.[93]

Barrett insists that categorizing patients as schizophrenic implies a specific ideological stance that highlights, problematizes, and reinforces certain symptoms and experiences, such as, for example, auditory hallucinations, while paying little attention to others. Barrett's argument is not one merely about the social construction of disease – of schizophrenia as in effect a cultural myth – but a more subtle argument in which he does not dispute at all the reality of symptoms, or the horror of psychiatric disorder. He points out, however, that a careful review of cross-cultural literature indicates that some of the constitutional components of what we understand as schizophrenia may be virtually absent in non-Western settings:

> in some cultures, especially those that do not employ a concept of "mind" as opposed to "body," the closest equivalents to schizophrenia are not concerned with "mental experiences" at all, but employ criteria related to impairment in social functioning or persistent rule violation.[94]

Arguments similar to those of Barrett have been developed for clinical depression as it is currently defined, that is, as being a "psychiatric ethno-category" that implicates ideas about self and personhood characteristic of Euro-American society.[95]

The research of the anthropologist Junko Kitanaka on the relatively recent "rediscovery" of depression in Japan graphically demonstrates how specific histories and cultures inform the way in which ideas about the relationship between mind, body, and the social order come to be recognized as disease, and hence which conditions should no longer fall within the domain of families but should be attended to in the clinic.[96] Japanese psychiatrists have recognized depression formally as a disease since the late 19th century, but the Japanese public, although fully cognizant of "feeling down" and "being gloomy," continued to think that such sensations were simply part of everyday life. It was only from the 1990s that the public began to participate in the medicalization of depression. Kitanaka found that the medical management of suicidal tendencies became one significant aspect of this process of medicalization.

Suicide has long been understood in Japan as something that can be sub-classified into several types depending upon the context in which it takes place. One form, known as *kakugo no jisatsu* (suicide of resolve) is understood as an act of "free will." This type of suicide has for centuries been "estheticized," and continues to be so today in popular culture, the media, and even among many psychiatrists. Formerly, such acts of suicide were associated with the samurai class, but also included are people who believe that they have become a burden or have failed others in a profound way. Suicide rates in Japan (one of the ten countries in the world with the highest suicide rates) have remained at around 30,000 per year for more than a decade and approximately 100 people a day commit suicide. In an effort to stem this shocking situation Japanese psychiatrists appear regularly in the media stressing, as was formerly not the case, a link between suicide and depression. This biologized suicide is explicitly labeled as pathological – a disease that can be treated with medication.

However, Kitanaka argues that Japanese psychiatrists sometimes exhibit deep ambivalence about medicalization of suicidal patients; most continue to recognize "suicide of resolve," and in the clinic they actively draw on this distinction at times, notably with individuals who apparently have no pathology and who give rational narrative accounts about why their attempted suicide was "worthy." Psychiatrists strive to achieve a "minimum of shared understanding with patients about the biological nature of the 'mental illness,'" but at the same time deliberately avoid the realm of the existential, and do not actively explore the psychological aspects of the patient's distress.[97] Kitanaka argues that "instead of fundamentally destabilizing the cultural discourse, Japanese psychiatrists may well be complicit in reproducing cultural assumptions about suicide," in that they reinforce a moral hierarchy in which some suicides are estheticized as courageous, while others, although they may be sad and moving, are nevertheless thought of as simply mundane and pathological.[98] It is striking that this contemporary psychiatric practice, in which the psychological is set to one side, shows marked overlaps in practice in many of the clinics in Japan run by East Asian medical practitioners.[99] In both situations, although narratives about the intolerable life situations of patients are usually listened to with great sympathy, medical practitioners do not believe that they should "psychologize" and individualize the social suffering of the patient, nor do they make recommendations for change in the social lives of patients – rather, the task of the doctor is to ease "real" bodily pain in order to give patients the strength to deal with everyday life.

The ethnographic work of Lawrence Cohen in India furnishes a striking example of the move in that country to construct aging as a condition that should be recognized as needing professional attention on the part of the emerging specialty of social gerontologists. Cohen interviewed several activists working on behalf of the elderly in India who pointed out that they have had to promote the idea of "senior citizen" into local discourse because until recently there has been no awareness that aging could be anything other than an inevitable time of loss and decay. "The primary task of an Indian gerontology is ... not to study aging but to ... create it," one activist informed Cohen.[100] However, Cohen soon realized that the object of concern in the struggling field of academic and applied gerontology in India is pensioners living in the wealthier parts of cities, and that the majority of Indians are simply "erased" from this narrative. The gerontological world is dominated by a powerful story about the decline of the extended Indian family that formerly took care of all the needs of old people – a decline due to the advent of Westernization, modernization, industrialization, and urbanization. It is argued by activists that these old people are worthy of government support, but that such support should be made available to families who would then look after their aging relatives appropriately. In orchestrating this professional narrative, the diversity and reality of aging for most Indians, historically and in the present, in poverty and without supportive extended families living in spacious houses, is simply erased. Cohen's book includes heart-breaking descriptions of old people, especially women, living on the streets, many senile, who become local fixtures described by those around them as "crazy."

Among the many rich anecdotes that feature in Cohen's book is one about a middle-class family comprising a married couple and the husband's mother living together in a one-bedroom flat. The relationship between mother-in-law, Somita, and daughter-in-law, Sharmila, was always strained, and once the old lady became senile the situation deteriorated badly. The couple placed Somita in an old people's home but she was thrown out after three days, described as "crazy." Sharmila and her husband Mithun were accused of lying to the managers of the home and made to feel that they embodied the Bad Family described so often in the media and in professional literature. Somita was eventually diagnosed with Alzheimer's disease, but even then, although armed with a definitive biomedical diagnosis, no placement could be found for her for a very long time. Cohen spells out the advantages of receiving such a medical diagnosis in that blame is removed from the family, and Sharmila feels relief, although the theme of the Bad Family did not entirely dissipate in this particular case.[101]

This example makes it abundantly clear how paths to the social construction of the management of bodily conditions and their medicalization are not predictable, particularly in contexts where there are few facilities and universal health care is not available. It also highlights dramatically how efforts to modernize care are rarely directed equally at all segments of diverse populations – a situation that applies equally to the United States and elsewhere.

We have already discussed the "looping effect" in which, through the creation of specific conditions as diseases, populations to be managed are brought into existence. We turn now to a perspective brought to the fore as a result of anthropological research in connection with everyday life. This work highlights just how messy the process of medicalization can be, and demonstrates graphically the way in which biomedical diagnoses, by their very formulation, can work to eliminate the social, cultural, and political conditions that contribute to the causes of distress and disease.

The Politics of Medicalization

Medical anthropological literature is replete with further examples from many parts of the world that shows how the radically differing taxonomies of illness and disease generated by biomedicine, by other medical traditions, and in everyday discourse often cause disputes about the significance of symptoms, what counts as normal and abnormal, and how best distressful physical conditions should be managed.[102] For example, Aihwa Ong, working in Malaysia, argued that attacks of spirit possession on the shop-floors of multinational factories are expressions of complex, ambivalent responses of young women to violations of their gendered sense of self, difficult work conditions, and generalized stress associated with modernization. The psychologization and medicalization of these attacks by consultant medical professionals permitted a different moral interpretation of the problem by employers: one of "primitive minds" disrupting the creation of capital.[103]

Similarly, the refusal of many Japanese adolescents to go to school was thought for a decade or more by many psychiatrists in that country to be behavior that should be medicalized. In some instances the children (the majority of them boys) had undeniable major psychiatric disorders, but among the adolescents themselves, those who were articulate about their situation complained very often of manipulation by families and peers, and of other stresses associated with the competitive education system in Japan and of hours spent commuting on trains. Young people diagnosed with "school refusal syndrome" frequently remained essentially shut up in their homes for months on end, often in bed much of that time, their desperate parents unable to bring the crisis to an end. When medical help was sort out, often reluctantly because of feelings of shame, "family therapy" with the child's teacher present was usually suggested, although the father was often absent due to his obligations at work.[104] Children believed to be particularly vulnerable were those subjected to teasing by their peers; most often children who did not "fit" well into the classroom for a range of reasons including being "too clever" or "too stupid," obese, or having lived abroad for an extended period of time and hence being strange or otherwise "different." Japanese psychiatrists treating this condition attempted to take both the biomedical diagnosis and the socio-medical diagnosis seriously and to try to reconcile the two approaches.[105]

Since the late 1990s a new condition has been recognized in Japan, that of *hikikomori* (withdrawal), a condition characterized as a profound lack of interaction with other people. This term is now used much more commonly than is school refusal syndrome. *Hikikomori* is understood explicitly as a social and not a psychiatric problem, even by psychiatrists, who insist that most affected individuals are not depressed. Affected individuals usually shut themselves up in a room in the family home, eat alone, and spend a great deal of time using electronic devices of all kinds. It is estimated that about one million young people, a figure close to 1 percent of the entire population, ranging in age from teenagers to individuals in their late thirties, the majority of them young men, are affected by this condition. Efforts to deal with the problem are largely by means of support groups attended mostly by anguished parents rather than the affected individuals. The Japanese media has dubbed these and other efforts to deal with the problem as the "*hikikomori* industry."[106] Amy Bovery has argued that the origins of this condition are many and that social withdrawal is the end result in a society in which "the right to be different" is not widely acceptable.[107] The phenomenon of *hikikomori* shows once again how medicalization is not an inevitable response to social disorders, and warrants further investigation.

In China, Arthur and Joan Kleinman analyzed narratives about chronic pain as "normal" responses to the chaotic political changes of the latter part of the 20th century in that country. They argue that these political events were associated with "collective and personal delegitimation" of the daily life of millions of people, and that the subjective experience of physical malaise that resulted, when interpreted as and reduced to physical disorder in the clinical situation, fails to take account of – or even actively erases – the larger political picture.[108]

In a Brazilian shanty town, Nancy Scheper-Hughes interpreted an "epidemic of nervoso" as having multiple meanings: in part a response to the ongoing state of emergency in everyday life but also a refusal of men to continue demeaning and debilitating labor, and a response of women to a violent shock or tragedy (often the death of a child). The epidemic signals a nervous agitation, "a state of disequilibrium" – the only means of expressing dissent in *favela* (slum) society. Individuals are often very conscious of the injustice of their situation, but at the same time exhibit ambivalence, and describe their own bodies as "worthless" or "used up."[109] Scheper-Hughes concludes that the semi-willingness of people to participate in the medicalization of their bodies results from participation in the same moral world as their oppressors.[110]

In North America the condition known as "fetal alcohol syndrome" is a singular, complex example of the social construction of disease. Medical research suggests that excessive alcohol use, especially binge drinking, during pregnancy is associated with damage in the neurological development of the fetus, and hence with mental retardation. However, the methods used to diagnose fetal alcohol syndrome are questionable. It is clear that the condition has undergone "diagnostic creep," in that over the course of several decades an increasing number of signs and symptoms have become recognized as relevant, thus increasing the size of potential patient populations and simultaneously calling for greater moral regulation of the behavior of pregnant women to be supervised by social workers, legal experts, educators, and psychologists.[111]

Current estimates of the percentage of infants affected at birth (somewhere between 4 and 5 percent) are much smaller than had been previously estimated,[112] and today it is recognized by many that confounding factors, notably poor nutrition and other effects of poverty, are implicated, and not alcohol use alone.[113] Fetal alcohol syndrome and the related, less clearly defined, fetal alcohol spectrum disorder have distinctive political components and are thought of, particularly in Canada, as an "Indian problem," one associated with irresponsible and immature First Nations young women. The impoverished life of so many First Nations people, and the discrimination and racism that they continue to endure are left out of the equation in virtually all of the professional literature relating to this problem.[114] So too is systematic mention of alcohol use during pregnancy by large numbers of non-Indian women. The politics of race dictates the way in which knowledge about this disease is processed and transmitted, and the looping process is at work as First Nations communities themselves attempt to confront the problem and the negative image associated with their communities.

The psychologists Swartz and Levett point out that "psychological sequelae" have frequently been reported in connection with the impact of massive long-term political repression of children in South Africa. They go on to argue that psychologization is a too narrowly defined term to encapsulate the experience of the children – "the costs of generations of oppression of children cannot be offset simply by interventions of mental health workers."[115] Further, they argue: "it is a serious fallacy to assume that if something is wrong with … society, then this must necessarily be reflected in the *psychopathological* make-up of individuals."[116] In common with the other authors cited above, Swartz and Levett are concerned about the normalization and transformation of political and social repression and malaise into individualized pathology, and its management solely through medical intervention.

Beyond Medicalization?

Research such as that cited above is part of a large body of literature that highlights how medicalization contributes to masking significant historical, social, and political variables that contribute to illness and distress, while attention is directed toward the systematization and stabilization of diagnostic categories and the management of bodily conditions presumed to be an expression of underlying pathology. It is clear that at one end of the spectrum of probably all of these disorders, serious pathology is implicated and biomedical intervention might well be effective. However, it is also clear that a great deal of what in the biomedical world would be described as "somatized behavior" – evident in such cases as heart distress in Iran, *nervoso* in Brazil, and school refusal syndrome in Japan – is poorly managed by biomedicine. Even though individual medical practitioners are often sensitive to the contribution made by social and political factors to ill health, and many understand the dangers of applying medical labels to conditions when pathology is poorly understood, clinicians have no choice but to focus on the task at hand – care of the patient who, more often than not, is in serious distress.

Because the clinical encounter is one that favors an internalizing approach focused on the body, and the patient is seen in isolation from the context of his or her everyday life, a reductionistic, medicalized approach is virtually unavoidable and is indeed indirectly encouraged because biomedical diagnoses of bodily dysfunction are the levers by which the health care system is activated. At times, medicalization can be used to reassure patients and relieve them of guilt, but at other times medicalization oppresses them, as when the complaints of poor and minority patients are dismissed as due to bad or immoral behavior.[117] Equally pernicious are the subtle ways in which bias is built into the very diagnostic categories used by biomedical practitioners that force them to make marked distinctions between "normal" and "abnormal," and to use assigned categories of ethnicity or race to mark out those people assumed to be at differential risk for various conditions.

In summary, understanding medicalization primarily as enforced surveillance, as certain social scientists have done, is misleading. Individual citizens and even families frequently cooperate willingly with medical monitoring and management of bodily distress in the belief that they will benefit (although their assumptions about benefit may well not be realized). On the other hand, there is considerable resistance to the kind of enforced surveillance and medicalization of pregnancy of First Nations women, or monitoring of the workplace that takes place in Indonesian factories and elsewhere. There is also mounting evidence of resistance to genetic testing on the part of many people. Similarly, arguments restricted to a critique of the social construction of disease, at the expense of recognizing the very real, debilitating condition of individuals who seek out medical help, are also misleading. Ethnographic

investigation of the local effects of the economics of health care, available technological facilities, unexamined values embedded in biomedical discourse and practices, and
also in popular knowledge, all of which may promote or resist medicalization, give
considerable insight into the complexity at work.

In Pursuit of Health

The pursuit of individual health, an occupation taken very seriously by many people
all over the world today, is closely associated with the idea of self-governance.
Moreover, it is an activity fostered alike by all levels of government and the medical
profession. The very notion of health is, however, difficult to pin down. Despite
efforts to define it in contemporary health policy circles, as well as in medical and
popular literature, "health" takes on meaning primarily through the absence of physical disease. Such an interpretation tends to place it within the purview of the medical
profession, as something that is best sustained through systematic, technologically
sophisticated monitoring of individual bodies.

The assumption that health, like disease, is limited to the condition of individual
bodies and, further, that disease prevention automatically enhances health and is
primarily the responsibility of individuals, is a product of the social times in which
we live. Health is not a state or condition easily subjected to measurement – as public
health literature so often assumes[118] – and, while promotion of the rights of individuals with respect to health care is crucial, to focus on individual agency and responsibility disguises the social and political origins of disease and illness, together with
responsibilities of the state for promoting and maintaining wellbeing.

A tendency to view the preservation of health as an individual matter emerged
very early in Europe. It was among the elite living after the time of the highly influential physician Galen (200 CE) that the doctor was first thought of as the "manager"
of people's health, a condition having relatively little to do with either society or the
environment. Galen defined three types of health: the absence of dysfunction; a
minimalist definition of physical health; and a third, positive definition, in which
health was equated with happiness and an abundance of energy. Correct regimens
with respect to eating, drinking, sleep, wakefulness, sex, and the emotions were
spelled out in instruction manuals for both physicians and the literate minority. This
was in contrast to the classical East Asian medical system, for example, in which,
although a lifestyle regimen was strongly encouraged to promote wellbeing, the value
of sustaining health was understood primarily as being for the benefit of society at
large, above all in order to ensure successful reproduction and to produce a strong
workforce. In contrast, health in Europe from the time of Galen was valued as essential for individual wellbeing.[119]

At the time of the French Revolution, the right of individuals to state-supported
health care was first aired, an argument stimulated by the demand for healthy people
to be active participants in the modernization of society and in colonization.[120] A
triangulation of interests among the state, the medical profession, and individuals
became evident from the beginning of the 19th century with respect to the preservation of health and health care, at times in congruence with each other, but more
frequently partially at odds. Once government was implicated, the way was opened

up in the 19th century for promotion of the idea that good health is something owed to individuals by society – health became a right.[121] But it was not until the end of the 19th century that state support for public health and clinical care was widely recognized as integral to modernization, laying the foundations for the formation of national state-managed health care systems commencing in the early 20th century in most European countries, Japan, Canada, and Australasia, and then later in many other parts of the world, with the notable exception, of course, of the United States where state-managed care is available only to certain individuals including the elderly and the very poor although this *may* change in the near future. Furthermore, in 19th century Europe and North America a second trend emerged, and remains extremely powerful to this day, namely the idea that individual health and wellbeing can be improved upon, and is not simply finite and God-given.

In discussing what he understands as a remarkable expansion of the health sector over the past several decades, Robert Crawford situates the pursuit of health in a framework of political economy.[122] Writing about the United States, he notes that expansion of the medical sector in the 1950s and early 1960s went virtually unquestioned, the assumption at that time being that increased medical facilities would lead directly to improved health across society. This expansion was first challenged in terms of unequal access and a lack of equity, but it was the women's movement that provided a more stinging critique, pointing out the hegemony of medicine, and its role as an institution of social control.[123]

By the 1970s an about-turn in health policy took place, associated with fears about the burgeoning numbers of elderly in the population. It was now claimed that health care expenditures must be curbed, and political pressures were mobilized to cut costs at a time when citizens had come to think of health care not merely as a right in the abstract but as a personal entitlement. Crawford cites Robert Whalen, the Commissioner of the New York Department of Health, who asserted in the late 1970s that it was essential that people should assume "individual and moral responsibility" for their own health.[124] John Knowles, past president of the Rockefeller Foundation went further:

> The idea of individual responsibility has been submerged in individual rights – rights or demands to be guaranteed by Big Brother and delivered by public and private institutions. The cost of sloth, gluttony, alcoholic intemperance, reckless driving, sexual frenzy and smoking have now become a national, not an individual responsibility, and all justified as individual freedom. But one man's or woman's freedom in health is now another man's shackle in taxes and insurance premiums.[125]

Crawford argues that this victim-blaming ideology, well established before HIV/AIDS was recognized, justified a withdrawal from policies that smacked of entitlements to health care.[126] Leon Kass (later to become one of the primary bioethics advisers of President George W. Bush) even claimed that it is inappropriate that "excessive preoccupations" about cancer lead to government regulations that unreasonably restrict industrial activity.[127] Others argued in the 1970s, in the face of striking evidence to the contrary, that poverty was on the decline, and that further progress on this front would inevitably lead to improved health.[128]

These political moves designed to foster a sense of responsibility on the part of individuals came at a time when it was increasingly apparent to large segments of the public that people have no control over the polluted environments in which they live, the quality of food they are sold, and the safety of medicines they are prescribed. It was in this atmosphere that the "wellness as virtue" movement exploded,[129] a movement actively encouraged by governments, since in theory it would contribute to a decrease in health care expenditures.

As later chapters will show, an approach to "health maintenance" in which self-responsibility is a guiding norm, has a global reach today, often with unexpected consequences. But there are other ways to conceptualize wellbeing. Just one example must suffice here. Health, as it was understood by the majority of indigenous peoples of North America prior to colonization, was one in which the wellbeing of individuals is understood as being intimately related to the land. The anthropologist Naomi Adelson, carrying out ethnographic research among the Whapmagoostui Cree living in northern Quebec, analyzed the social ramifications of a key polysemic concept made wide use of in everyday life among the Cree – *miyupimaatisiium* ("being-alive-well").[130] The idea of "being-alive-well" is by no means limited to the physical condition of individuals; much more important are matters relating to the relationship among individuals and their social, spiritual, and natural worlds; the availability of sufficient food, in particular sufficient game (essential to avoid starvation until the latter part of the 20th century); active preservation of the Cree way of life amid non-native technologies including skidoos, SUVs, and firearms; and the continuity of Cree identity through a massive disruption brought about by the Quebec government's construction of the network of James Bay hydroelectric dams on Cree lands.

A plan, eventually abandoned, to build a second dam closer to the Whapmagoostui community site caused additional untold stress for a further decade. In recent years Cree activists and health care workers have self-consciously mobilized *miyupimaatisiium* in order to promote individual wellbeing, community solidarity, and autonomy from the South. At the same time, the improved biomedical services now available, staffed as much as possible by local people speaking Cree, are not rejected. Nevertheless the idea that the absence of disease is the best measure of health is alien to the majority.

In Summary

This brief overview of half a century of social science research on medical knowledge and practice shows how they are unfailingly rooted in a context that provides a logical framework within which illness and healing are interpreted and managed; this context is constituted by historical precedent, shared values, economics, and politics. The tension between internalizing and externalizing logics present in all medical knowledge and practice is linked to broader understandings of – and struggles over – ideas about the relationship among the physical body, individuals, families, communities, and nations with respect to disease causation and how best to alleviate sickness. Medical practices of all kinds have the potential to act simultaneously as modes of social control on the one hand, and as a release from pain and disease on the other.

As such they have the power to both subordinate and emancipate individuals and communities.

Biomedicine is exceptional among medical traditions because of its systematic approach to objectifying, classifying, and quantifying the human body, itself assumed to be derived from a universal template. This approach was entangled with the formation of the modern state and its concern to produce a fit workforce in order to enable the twin processes of modernization and colonization so central to the political economy of the 19th century. The modern state provided the infrastructure for applying statistical methods to vast populations and for increasingly sophisticated clinical and laboratory practices. Biomedicine, despite its grounding in science, is a site of struggle about control and the interpretation of what will count as legitimate truth claims with respect to body classification and management.

Even though the efficacy of many biomedical treatments is undeniable, disease taxonomies are inevitably socially constructed. This process is influenced in part by the difficulty encountered by medical practitioners in having certain conditions recognized as amenable to medical management and hence in receiving professional compensation for their services, and also by the ways in which language, culturally informed values, historical antecedents, social processes, and the material body itself contribute to the creation of categories through which illness is subjectively experienced and professionally recognized and managed.

Even though medical pluralism persists, and in some places flourishes, it is evident that biomedicine has proliferated over the previous century. This transformation has been due in part to the expansion of available medical services as a result of economic growth, and to a growing awareness by local peoples of what biomedicine has to offer. As a result, without doubt the health and wellbeing of much of the world's population have been improved, even though, on occasion, biomedical practitioners have actively promoted their wares, often backed by pharmaceutical companies, with negative consequences. Another pervasive change is that large numbers of people have come to internalize the idea that they are mainly responsible for their own health and wellbeing, and that medical practitioners can and should assist them in this endeavor. This has greatly contributed to the protean spread of biomedicine into just about every domain of life. Furthermore, among those who can afford it, many now make use of the apparatus of biomedicine to overcome their perceived physical deficiencies, frailties, and inadequacies.

Unanticipated difficulties arise with the globalization of biomedicine, notably where interventions are deployed in situations where the state does not have the means to generate reliable statistics. The result may be that what is locally considered important for good health care is at odds with what is being introduced from the top down – the Inuit case about birth is a good example of this phenomenon. Furthermore, there may be a lack of consensus at local sites about the value of biomedical technologies, particularly when their effects are perceived as a means of undermining the moral order. In addition, it is clear that very many people continue to be eclectic in their search for medical assistance for a variety of reasons ranging from perceived efficacy, cost, availability, convenience, trust, and, on occasion, what is believed to be morally appropriate.

4

Local Biologies and Human Difference

The previous chapters have situated biomedicine in historical and cultural contexts. As we have seen, when the human body became increasingly available for scrutiny, it was subject to inspection, classification, and ultimately "normalization" through statistical methods. "Normality" conflated matters mathematical and moral, and the growing power of biomedicine as an arbiter of human suffering became apparent in the "medicalization" of life and the mixed reactions it received and continues to receive. Social scientists have exposed moral assumptions underpinning biomedical interventions in their research, notably by demonstrating how a scientific understanding of health and disease is historically constructed and made "real" through biomedical practice, and how this approach often elides political and social realities implicated in the production of human suffering. Even so, an assumed biological universality of the human body has remained largely unquestioned – a position that we will challenge in this chapter.

We begin with a well-substantiated case about a universal biological phenomenon among women – the end of menstruation. This case shows how differences in individual bodily experience at the end of menstruation are not adequately explained as due to cultural "beliefs," but rather must be understood as local entanglements among historical and cultural activities, technoscientific interventions, and the biology of individual aging. We then introduce the concept of local biologies to draw attention to the way in which dynamic biological change is inevitably implicated in this ceaseless entanglement, resulting in patterned variation in subjective bodily experience, and also geographical differences in the distribution of disease and illness.

This is followed by a close look at the history of the fatal neurological disease, *kuru*, associated with the Fore of New Guinea, in order to illustrate biosocial differentiation in action and the local biologies that result. This account graphically demonstrates significant differences among the scientific interpretations and speculations about the cause of this disease and those given by the Fore themselves. It also demonstrates how an ethnographic approach in which historicized accounts about local practices are taken seriously furnishes the only plausible explanation as to how this terrifying disease suddenly appeared among the Fore and then just as suddenly died out.

The third illustration discussed in this chapter focuses on an epidemiologically demonstrated association between the experience of racism and low birth weights. This is followed by a short discussion of the relationship between microbes and humans. As everyone knows, the activities of microscopic biological organisms affect humans. Less often noted is the ability of micro-organisms to spread differentially among human populations, resulting in specific symptoms associated with the "kinds" of bodies the organisms infect. Reciprocally, microscopic organisms are profoundly modified by human activity.

We conclude with controversies about the origins of the HIV epidemic. These debates show the political and epistemological difficulties that arise when explanations remain wedded to a dichotomous distinction between nature and culture, and do not adequately engage with the way in which the emergence of diseases is historically and biosocially embedded.

On the basis of these illustrations we explore the extent to which human bodies everywhere are inescapably entangled with evolutionary change, history (global and local), environments (natural and social), as well as political events and culturally informed values. Our position is that the material body is a priori contextualized and subject to endless change with significant implications for human development and for health and wellbeing. Our position has much in common with that of the philosopher Bruno Latour who, in seeking to create a symmetrical account of what he describes as the co-production of nature/culture, called for recognition of a hybrid "object–discourse–nature–society" assembly, whose networks of entanglement demand analysis.[1]

The End of Menstruation

In the early 1880s, C. P. L. de Gardanne, a French physician, coined the word *ménopause* in order to do away with the term climacteric, fashionable all over Europe at that time, that he found too imprecise. De Gardanne wanted the end of menstruation alone to signify this lifecycle transition and not the numerous non-specific symptoms commonly associated with the climacteric. Since that time, in both the medical world and among women in Europe, North America, and increasingly elsewhere, the idea of menopause has been conflated with the end of menstruation. It has lost its former association with aging in general, and is no longer associated with both women and men, as was the case for the earlier concept of the climacteric.[2] Received wisdom has been that menopause is a difficult time for by far the majority of women, associated with unpleasant symptoms, physical and psychological.[3] In contrast, in many parts of the world, social changes associated with aging, such as becoming a grandmother, are regarded as more important than are individual biological changes that attract little or no attention. To think of the end of menstruation as *the* marker of female aging simply does not "fit" well with accounts about the meaning of growing old in many locations.[4]

The conflation of the concept of menopause with the end of menstrual cycling, combined with medical interest in the management of this lifecycle transition and interest of pharmaceutical companies in providing medication to counter menopausal symptoms, has meant that the dominant understanding of this midlife transition over the past 50 years in Europe, North America, and Australasia, has been one of a disease-like condition. Because the focus of medical attention is above all on declining estrogen levels, being postmenopausal has been likened to having a deficiency disease, similar to an insulin deficiency that results in diabetes.[5] This approach is supported by the mistaken idea that menopause is a recent phenomenon in human history. It has been suggested in many professional publications that because mean life expectancy for women until the turn of the 20th century was less than 50, virtually no women lived much past middle age until relatively recently. Postmenopausal life, it is often claimed, is a cultural artifact – the result of better health care and medical services.[6]

Such claims are very misleading. Until the first part of the 20th century infant mortality rates were high, and among those women who survived to reproductive age, many lost their lives in childbirth. If a woman lived through her own infancy and her reproductive years, then survival for several more decades was common. In order to take this effect into account when calculating age distribution in human populations, estimations of remaining life expectancy at 45 or 50 years of age are essential. These figures make it clear that living a long life is certainly not a recent phenomenon although, of course, more people survive to old age today than was formerly the case.[7] As we saw in chapter 2, the professional literature on menopause often makes a second point about the way in which the very existence of postmenopausal women goes against nature because in the wild virtually no mammals live past reproductive age. Accordingly, in the mid–20th century the interest in menopausal women by drug companies and the medical profession shifted away from the relief of menopausal symptoms per se, to the presumed negative effects of reduced estrogen levels believed to place all middle-aged women at "increased risk" in later life for a variety of diseases including osteoporosis, heart disease, and other conditions.

It should be noted that biomedical knowledge about menopause was initially created in large part on the basis of symptom reporting of small samples of women, virtually all of them living in Europe or North America, who presented themselves as patients in gynecological clinics. The majority of these women had gone to visit doctors because of physical or emotional distress, and a disproportionate number had undergone hysterectomies. As a result, medical knowledge on that topic has inevitably been biased – until recently.[8] Although data about increased risk for osteoporosis and heart disease in postmenopausal life were derived from more representative population sampling, only white women were sampled, even though WHO figures showed marked differences in the incidence of these diseases among countries. The belief in a standardized body led to the assumption that representative sampling of women everywhere was not necessary, although this assumption has recently been challenged with the introduction of the National Institutes of Health's Revitalization Act in 1993 that requires research samples to include an appropriate number of cases from the major ethnic and "racial" groups present in the United States.[9] Anthropological research into menopause prior to the 1980s was sparse, but it indicated that the meanings attributed to this experience varied cross-culturally and that negative associations were by no means always the case. In order to generate data on this midlife transition among non-clinical populations of middle-aged women, statistically comparable survey research was carried out in the mid-1980s with over 1,300 subjects in Canada, nearly 8,000 in the United States, and with over 1,300 in Japan.[10] The women in these studies were all aged between 45 and 55. The findings from this research indicated strongly that the menopausal transition is not a difficult time for the majority, whether in North America or Japan.[11]

The Japanese word *kônenki* is conventionally translated into English as menopause, but the meanings of these terms are not really equivalent. *Kônenki* is closer to the older European concept of the climacteric, in that it is understood as a long, gradual transition, part of the aging process of both women and men, to which the end of menstruation (confined, obviously, to women) is just one contributing factor. There was no specific term in Japanese to express the end of menstruation until Japanese physicians deliberately created the concept of *kônenki* at the beginning of the 20th century as a result of close contact with German colleagues. Most Japanese respondents in the study placed the timing of *kônenki* at aged 45 or even earlier, lasting until nearly age 60. One quarter of the questionnaire respondents who had ceased menstruation for over a year reported that they had no sign of *kônenki*. It is also of note that no word exists that refers *uniquely* to the hot flash in Japanese, even though this is a language in which very fine discriminations can be made in connection with bodily states.[12]

In the North American/Japanese study, women were asked to recall symptoms that they had experienced over the previous two weeks (research shows that longer periods of recall are inaccurate). Japanese reporting of hot flashes was low – approximately one third that of U.S. and Canadian women – and reporting of night sweats was extremely low, and not associated with menopausal status. Only 19 percent of Japanese women in this study had experienced a hot flash at some time in the past, and reporting of both frequency and intensity was much lower than amongst U.S. and Canadian respondents, nearly 60 percent of whom had experienced a hot flash. Reporting of sleep disturbance by Japanese women was also low, corroborating their reports about lack of severity of hot flashes.[13] Follow-up interviews suggested that, if anything, Japanese women over-reported symptoms in their eagerness to cooperate fully with the researcher.[14]

The majority, when asked in face-to-face interviews to describe their experience of *kônenki*, responded along the following lines:

> I've had no problems at all, no headaches or anything like that … I've heard from other women that their heads felt so heavy that they couldn't get up.

> The most common problems I've heard about are stiff shoulders, headaches, and aching joints.

> I get tired easily, that's *kônenki* for sure, and I get stiff shoulders.

A small number when interviewed, 12 out of 105, gave statements that sound much more familiar to North Americans and Europeans:

> The most noticeable thing was that I would suddenly feel hot; it happened every day, three times or so. I didn't go to the doctor or take any medication … I just thought it was my age.

Results of the survey research indicated that shoulder stiffness was the most common symptom reported by Japanese informants followed by headaches, and Japanese gynecologists noted that women when they came to see them complained most often of these symptoms.[15] Some physicians did not cite hot flashes at all when asked to describe the typical symptoms of *kônenki*. The biological anthropologist Melissa Melby has shown that Japanese men report many of these symptoms at the same rates or even higher than do Japanese women.[16]

The original research was done in the mid-1980s at a time when the end of menstruation was not medicalized in Japan. Since the 1990s articles about menopause started to appear very frequently in Japanese women's magazines, in which hot flashes are often described as the "typical" symptom of menopause (even though clinical encounters continue to indicate otherwise). A new phrase, *hotto furashu*, taken directly from English, is sometimes used to describe this symptom in both professional and popular literature, but among 50 Japanese women interviewed in 2005, most had not heard of it.[17]

Clearly Japanese doctors deal every day with middle-aged patients whose symptoms and experiences differ quite markedly from those that professional medical literature informs them are "normal" for menopause.[18] One or two doctors, when interviewed by Lock, asked why Western women have such a bad time at menopause. As a result of attending international conferences and reading professional gynecological journals, some Japanese gynecologists have come to believe that low symptom reporting in Japan is due to the fact that Japanese women simply do not pay "proper" attention to their bodies. Alternatively, they believe that their patients still behave stoically as was formerly expected of Japanese women. In contrast, many choose to hypothesize that a sufficiently marked biological difference – due perhaps to environment, diet, genetics, or some combination of all three – results in physical and subjective experiences at the end of menstruation for many (but not all) Japanese women that is markedly different from that commonly experienced by women in North America.

Recently, Melby conducted three years of research in Japan using survey research and qualitative methods compatible with Lock's earlier work and, in addition, she collected biological samples from 140 participants.[19] She found that hot flash prevalence was 22.1 percent.[20] This is nearly double that of 20 years earlier, but reporting of other symptoms had also gone up considerably, suggesting that these women may be in poorer health than those of the previous generation. It is also possible that they are now more adept at communicating with the medical profession than was formerly the case. Increased reporting of vasomotor symptoms is not surprising, given the extensive efforts at medicalization of middle-aged women by some prominent Japanese gynecologists, together with a great deal of media attention. There have also been significant dietary changes in Japan over the past two decades. Even so, this rate of symptom reporting continues to be strikingly lower than in North America.[21] Moreover, few of the women who report vasomotor symptoms (notably hot flashes) find them troubling, and the majority state that these symptoms disappear after a month or so. Melby's findings from the biological samples point strongly to the significance of a lifelong exposure to phytoestrogens (primarily soy bean) in the Japanese diet, resulting in very high levels of plasma phytoestrogens[22] that appear to be protective in many, but not all, women, at the end of menstruation.[23] Her conclusion is that this is only one among what are probably several contributing factors. She has also investigated the symptom of chilliness commonly reported by Japanese women at *kônenki*; her hypothesis is that there may be differences in the thermoregulatory system at work that in turn can be associated with several other variables, biological and cultural.[24]

Relatively few Japanese women seek out medication at *kônenki*, and the majority who do so prefer herbal medication.[25] Hormone replacement therapy (HRT) is not widely used, and relatively few gynecologists are eager to prescribe it, although there are some notable exceptions. When Lock talked to Japanese gynecologists in 2003, shortly after an important HRT trial (discussed in chapter 2) had been stopped in the United States, several of them stated that they did not intend to pay much attention to these trial results because the bodies of American and Japanese women are different, and therefore the findings are not relevant to their clinical practice.

Japanese accounts about the end of menstruation sound bizarre to most North Americans and Europeans and it is tempting to dismiss this discourse as an exotic anomaly. The danger, of course, is that the white Euro-American body remains the gold standard against which difference is seen either as statistical deviation or as due to cultural difference alone, leaving the medical model of a universal menopause intact. Among the considerable number of studies carried out in Hong Kong, Singapore, Taiwan, China, Korea, the Philippines, Thailand, Malaysia, and Indonesia, many reveal low reporting of hot flashes and night sweats.[26] Some of this research is methodologically weak, but the relative consistency of the results is nevertheless suggestive. Shea's work in China is particularly interesting because she found low reporting of hot flashes and sweats, similar to the Japanese study, but higher reporting of other symptoms that she attributed to stressful events the women had endured throughout their lives.[27] Beyene, in a comprehensive longitudinal study in the Yucatan, Mexico, found no reporting of the "typical" symptoms of menopause.[28] These differences are so far unexplained, and the phytoestrogen findings for Japan will not apply in all these locations. Similarly to Japan, no indigenous terms for the hot flash were found in Turkey, Indonesia, the Yucatan, and other locations. It is also of note that research in the Middle East suggests that symptom reporting may be similar to that assumed to be usual in the West, or perhaps a little higher.[29] It has been suggested that ambient temperature affects subjective experience and reporting of hot flashes, but that this only accounts partially for variation in hot flash frequency.[30]

In common with a few Japanese doctors, the response of some Western medical researchers has been to suggest that the women in these studies in effect bias the research findings. They claim that because individual responses to menopause are culturally dependent, inattention to hot flashes is essentially learned behavior. For example, on the basis of research in seven Southeast Asian countries,[31] Boulet and colleagues showed that headaches, dizziness, anxiety, irritability, and other non-specific symptoms were commonly associated with the menopausal transition by women recruited into their project. Symptom reporting was rather similar to that in Japan. Boulet and her associates argued that these symptoms should be understood as "a form of communication" on the part of women, and speculated that vasomotor distress may be "translated" by them into culturally meaningful non-specific symptoms associated with psychological distress. In making such an interpretation, the assumption is that when subjective reporting does not coincide with the findings anticipated by Western physicians based on experience with patients attending clinics in their home countries, then it must be the case that "exotic" women are, in effect, being duped by their language and culture.

Our opinion is that these findings suggest that it is not appropriate to conceptualize the end of menstruation as an invariant biological transformation subject only to superficial modification by social, cultural, and psychological variables layered over an unchanging biological base. The experience of the end of menstruation, in contrast to the first menstruation, can only be assessed retrospectively; nevertheless it is undeniably "real," and appears to be biologically programmed to take place in the majority of women between their late forties and mid-fifties; smoking and having no children apparently lowers the age somewhat.[32] Even so, despite its ubiquity, it is a process in which biology and culture mutually fashion each other, as the findings above make clear. Adding weight to this position, WHO population databases and other sources have shown convincingly that not all postmenopausal women are equally at increased risk for heart disease, osteoporosis, breast cancer, and other late-onset chronic diseases, and it is agreed that much of this variation depends upon lifestyle factors and cultural variations in diet.[33]

In a recent study with a sample of over 200 Mayan women whose average age at menopause was 44.3, endocrine changes at menopause were found to be very similar to those of American women of the same age, yet the Mayans, as noted above, reported no hot flashes (except very occasionally after migration to an urban environment).[34] It is known that plasma, urinary, and vaginal levels of estrogens do not correlate neatly with subjective reporting of hot flashes,[35] nor do measured rates of sweating, peripheral vasodilation, and deregulation of core body temperature.[36] Considerable mediation clearly takes place between measurable physiological changes, subjective experience, and the reporting of symptoms, some of which may be accounted for by as yet poorly understood biological pathways. It is reasonable to speculate, for example, that with urban migration and education women might experience hot flashes more frequently, perhaps as a result of dietary changes or due to a more sedentary lifestyle. From the perspective of women themselves, it must also be acknowledged that their primary concerns at midlife may be far removed from bodily symptoms (although this should not lead one to conclude that symptoms are simply ignored and therefore under-reported to researchers). For Japanese women, it is above all care of elderly relatives that occupies their attention at this stage of life, as well as such things as worries about their children, the current economic recession in Japan, and lack of job security.[37]

These findings about the end of menstruation make it abundantly clear that top-down interventions, driven by an assumption of a standardized body and designed to affect the health and quality of life of both individuals and specific populations, can lead to interventions with unexpected and at times harmful effects. There is now compelling epidemiological evidence, for example, that hormone replacement therapy may increase breast cancer rates.[38] Clearly, a precautionary approach should be taken to the introduction of new drugs and other technologies for global use; but further, we suggest, it is imperative to recognize the ways in which historical, environmental, and social processes are entangled locally with individual biologies.

Local Biologies

The example set out above strongly suggests that the embodied experience of physical sensations, including those of wellbeing, illness, disease, and so on, are informed in part by the physical body, itself contingent upon evolutionary, environmental, historical, cultural, medically induced, and individual variables. Embodied experience is also informed, of course, by language, culturally informed knowledge and expectations, social context, and so on.

Lock created the concept of local biologies to account for differences in symptom reporting at menopause.[39] This concept was not designed to draw attention to the way in which the categories created by the medical sciences are historically and culturally constructed,[40] although this is indeed the case, as the example of menopause demonstrates so clearly. Nor was it used to refer to measurable biological difference across human populations, although such findings contribute to the present argument. Rather, local biologies refers to the way in which biological and social processes are inseparably entangled over time, resulting in human biological difference – difference that may or may not be subjectively discernible by individuals. When subjectively experienced by patients and reported to doctors, manifestations of local biology are liable to be set to one side, or even dismissed, but they also appear in the laboratory, and today systematic attention to biological difference is taking place in laboratories carrying out research into molecular and population genetics. Such differences are, of course, published in medical journals, and frequently appear in the media.

The entanglement of biological and social processes is at times purposive, as when eugenics are put into practice, or attempts are made at public health engineering, but for the most part, it is incidental, devoid of any teleological aim, and is the result, for example, of agricultural practices or industrial pollution. We use the term "biosocial differentiation" to refer to the continual interactions of biological and social processes across time and space that eventually sediment into local biologies. In effect, then, local biologies are artifacts – snapshots frozen in time of ceaseless biosocial differentiation. However, the functioning of local biologies, whether as part of individual genomes, micro-organisms, cholesterol levels, or tumors, is not necessarily available to subjective assessment; usually the physical body carries on without our cognizance, its activities taken for granted until such time as they are made visible through medical assessment or produce discomfort and pathology.

Individual genomes and bodily functioning are, then, aspects of local biology, and reflect changes that have taken place over the course of both evolutionary time and during the *longue durée* of historical change. These transformations are the result of interactions among human genes and the environments in which people have lived, their economic and social arrangements, including marriage patterns and other factors that affect reproduction, local diets, and behavioral styles. Individual bodies represent a microcosm of these ceaseless interactions. But embodiment is also constituted by the way in which self and others represent the body, drawing upon local categories of knowledge and experience. If subjective bodily experience is to be made social, then history, politics, language, and local knowledge – including scientific knowledge to the extent that it is available – must inevitably be implicated. In practice this means that knowledge about the body is informed by social worlds and the social world is in turn informed by the reality of physical experience.

Today, the global reach of biomedical knowledge – disseminated by the media, markets, NGOs, and religions, as well as by governments – contributes to biosocial differentiation because individuals and collectivities increasingly resort to biomedicine to tame uncertainty and to better equip themselves to negotiate the future. The worldwide use of contraception, organ transplants, antibiotics, the training and practices of local health care professionals, and numerous other activities transform both the biological and the social aspects of these entanglements. Local biologies are thus inextricably situated in time and place, and emerge out of the ongoing dynamics of biosocial differentiation.

With the worldwide circulation and increasing adoption of biomedical knowledge, difficulties arise due to the largely unquestioned authority given to scientific knowledge. The example given above, of the effects of biosocial entanglement on the subjective experiences of the end of menstruation among women, does not correspond at all well to what is assumed in the medical world to be a universal event. Thus, although changes in ovarian and endocrine functioning are implicated in the mid-life transition of women everywhere, in consort with this biological reality, enormous complexity comes into play. This ranges from possible variations in endocrine functioning and the prevalence of osteoporosis across populations[41] to the language used to describe female aging – the result of attention being differentially directed to various bodily sensations, depending upon the culture and language in question. Certain languages emphasize clusters of symptoms that in other languages go unmarked, and vice versa.[42] Our argument is that such differences may in part be attributed to embodied experiences associated with local biologies, although it goes without saying that there is no simple relationship between biology and societies, nation states, ethnicity, communities, or even families.

Humans are unique with respect to both their genomes and their lived experience, and in this respect embodiment is personal. At another level of abstraction, many biological processes affect us all – pain, immunological responses to infection, the biological changes of aging, and so on.[43] However, individualized embodied experience of these processes is inevitably contingent, due to local biologies, language usage, and the social, environmental, and political contexts in which individuals live. Given the variables involved, inevitably certain of these experiences are relatively similar *across* groups of people living in shared environments, a good proportion of whom, until very recently, are likely to have shared biological ancestry – explaining why "race" is so often mistakenly confused with biological difference. Continuous migration from prehistoric times, accelerated dramatically today by globalization, ensures that people who have biological attributes in common are now widely dispersed, as was formerly not the case. Until the late 19th century, the majority of people, other than those living close to major historical trade routes, tended to live out their lives within a short distance of their birthplace.

Biological attributes are used by geneticists and others to ascribe people to populations that are, of course, not congruent with self-defined ethnic groups or communities. But the very fact that scientists are interested in documenting features of inclusion and exclusion based on biological attributes – formerly through anatomical taxonomies, blood typing, and so on, and now by means of DNA sampling – has made it relatively easy for prejudiced commentators to decontextualize the always provisional typologies of population biology and conflate them with social groupings to reproduce and naturalize a rhetoric grounded in the unexamined assumption of race as a biological fact.[44] Under the circumstances, it is not surprising that recognition of biological difference, and therefore of local biologies, has been anathema to many social scientists. However, given that molecular genetics and genomics are currently very much focused on demonstrating the significance of biological difference for disease susceptibility, it would be singularly unwise to go on doggedly ignoring these findings; more generally, recognition of local biologies strongly suggests that the black-boxing of the biological, human body and its marked separation from historical, social, and political events is inappropriate.

Systematic investigation exposed differences in symptom reporting at menopause; by taking these differences seriously it was possible to critique unexamined assumptions in the dominant medical discourse. This is not to argue, of course, that subjective accounts are more accurate reflections of an underlying bodily reality than are scientific or other accounts, but rather to insist that subjective accounts should be given attention in connection with individual care and, further, should be thought of as phenomena having potential epidemiological significance,[45] especially when similar subjective accounts come up repeatedly in any given group of people. Above all, local biologies should not be tinkered with inappropriately in order to force their phenotypic effects into biomedical taxonomies believed to be of universal applicability.

Rethinking Biology in the Midst of Life's Complexity

Two more important points about local biologies must be raised. The first is a critique by the eminent biologist Richard Lewontin of the common assumption that biology is determined by laws of nature, in much in the same way as Newtonian physics. He states that living organisms

> are composed of a number of parts with different properties that are in dynamic interaction with one another ... they change their shapes and properties during their lifetimes. ... In short: organisms are a changing nexus of a large number of weakly determining interacting forces.[46]

Lewontin wonders if biology is inevitably a story of different strokes for different folks, a collection of exquisitely detailed descriptions of diverse forms and functions down to the molecular level – or, from "this booming, buzzing confusion" can a biologist perhaps derive some general claims that are freed from the "dirty particulars" of each case? Not laws, of course, but at least some widely shared characteristics?[47] He agrees with the historian and philosopher of science Evelyn Fox Keller that both history and epistemology seem to speak against this, and that, as far as making sense of life – of biology – is concerned, all our models, metaphors, and machines, while they have contributed much to our understanding, provide neither unity nor completeness. On the contrary: facing up to complexity is the order of the day, although many obdurate problems continue to be studiously avoided and – troubling and potentially very exciting – much of what scientists assumed was settled, especially with respect to genetics, is gaping wide open again.

Richard Lewontin is well aware, of course, that not all biologists are comfortable with his emphasis on complexity and the "confusion" he associates with the functioning of living organisms. But it is becoming increasingly hard to ignore the fact that organisms of all kinds can and do adapt to new environments, toxic insults, and manipulations of various kinds with surprising rapidity. Whether it be the beak size of the finches studied by Charles Darwin on the Galapagos Islands,[48] the dramatic change in the reproductive life of cod in response to overfishing,[49] the development of resistance on the part of micro-organisms in response to antibiotics, or the effects of lifetime experiences and practices on health that are discussed in the examples that follow, it is no longer appropriate to think of biological change as inevitably a slow unfolding of events.

Is Biology Real?

Lewontin does not address the perplexing question of just how scientists have come to know about and are attempting to give accounts of this "buzzing" confusion, which brings us to a second point. If, as we are arguing, the idea of a universal biology is an illusion, then how can we take biological knowledge seriously? Our position, in agreement with Galison and Daston (chapter 2), is that the biological sciences produce real but partial pictures of what is under examination; in other words, biology is a partial rather than a universal theory. These "snapshots" are usually understood by involved scientists as different representations of the same ontological reality – the universal body in this instance. However, following our argument above for local biologies, we suggest that the snapshots are sometimes better understood as lenses onto a shifting and contingent reality. Insights from modern physics help make this point clear. Karen Barad, a physicist and philosopher, modeling her argument on quantum physics, argues that "realness" does not necessarily imply "thingness." What is real, she argues, "may not be an essence, an entity, or an independently existing object with inherent attributes."[50] Influenced by the physicist Neils Bohr, she states: "the primary ontological unit is not independent objects with independently determinate boundaries and properties but rather what Bohr terms 'phenomena.'"[51]

For Barad such "phenomena do not merely mark the epistemological inseparability of the observer and observed, or the results of measurements – phenomena are basic units of reality and not merely laboratory productions – they are "matter that matters."[52] Hence, it is not "things" about which we should be concerned but "phenomena."[53] Furthermore, insists Barad,

> apparatuses are not merely human-constructed laboratory instruments that tell us how the world is in accordance with our human-based conceptions. Rather, apparatuses are specific material configurations ... of the world that play a role in the production of phenomena.[54]

In other words, specific material practices (scientific practices) produce specific material phenomena, and this is accomplished by "agential intra-activity" – ongoing reconfigurations of non-isolable entanglements and relationalities in the world. Such ongoing reconfigurations are actually boundary-drawing practices that do not necessarily involve humans – it is "through such [dynamic] practices that differential boundaries between humans and nonhumans, culture and nature, science and the social, are constituted.[55] It is in this sense, then, that we understand biological knowledge to emerge from a broad range of "technophenomena" that result from the application of biomedical technologies ranging from gene sequencers and microscopes in laboratories to epidemiological studies of disease.

This can be illustrated by drawing on Barad's discussion of ultrasound scanning of the fetus. She argues that the construction of the fetus as a "self-contained, free-floating object under the watchful eye of scientific and medical surveillance" is the result of ever-refined imaging technologies. She also notes, as have other feminists, the absence of the pregnant woman in the discourse and debates produced about the subjectivity of this technologically revealed fetus and its legal status in the abortion debates so prominent in the United States. Barad argues that the fetus is not a "pre-existing object of investigation with inherent properties. Rather the fetus is a *phenomenon*, constituted and reconstituted out of historically and culturally specific intra-actions of material-discursive apparatuses of bodily production."[56] This does not mean, of course, that the fetus is not "real," nor that it has no "agency," but that its constitution as an autonomous entity with subjectivity is a specific form of reduction that precludes other ways of construing the situation, notably by deliberate exclusion of the pregnant woman, her body parts vital to pregnancy, her emotions, and the social context in which the pregnancy has arisen. Matter is not conceptualized as passive or inert in Barad's account, but she expressly notes that her position is not simply one of counter-posing the agency of the material world with that of the human world. Similarly, our position is that human biology is inevitably a social/material artifact because technologies designed to "tinker" with living matter are essential in its knowledge production. This situation is compounded because the material world is in a constant state of flux, and everyday human activities have always been a major contributor to this.

The case study of menopause is a telling example of such an intertwining in action. The end of menstruation is a "real" phenomenon that happens to every woman who lives to her late forties or early to mid-fifties; however, the way in which this phenomenon is produced and construed by the various involved actors – women, clinicians, epidemiologists, pharmaceutical manufacturers, anthropologists, and others – and how and by what means these various people come to "know" this particular happening are remarkably varied, with important social consequences.

We have attempted to show how local differences in biology are real phenomena that matter in concrete and important ways – for individuals, entire communities, and those who act as their stewards. As we have seen, mechanisms to explain the local biologies of menopause remain unclear. However, evidence is now growing from across the biomedical sciences as to how human biology comes to be situated in time and place. Below, we present four more cases, drawing on historical, anthropological, epidemiological, and basic science findings that begin to make clear a few of the mechanisms, specific situations, and social and political arrangements that produce human biological difference, giving a glimpse into how biosocial differentiation actually takes place.

Kuru and Endocannibalism[57]

For many years the mysterious neurological condition known as *kuru*, virtually confined to the Fore peoples in the eastern highlands of New Guinea, baffled local administrators and medical scientists alike. In recounting this history, Warwick Anderson makes it clear that the disease that was killing up to 10 percent of the population in some hamlets during the 1950s and 1960s signified very different things to the various involved parties: The Fore themselves explained the deaths as a result of sorcery; the young medical scientist, Carlton Gajdusek, who became deeply involved in an on-site investigation of *kuru*, believed that an infectious agent, most likely a virus, was implicated; among the anthropologists who became involved over the years, two believed the problem to be psychosomatic – the effects of extreme fear about sorcery; a biological anthropologist argued that nutritional toxins were probably implicated, while two more, Robert and Shirley Glasse (now Lindenbaum) postulated that endocannibalism (the consumption of parts of dead relatives by women and children for the wellbeing of self and society at large) was the cause.[58] The laboratory workers in Australia and the United States to whom Gajdusek sent specimens entertained yet more hypotheses about the causal entity. The Australian scientists for a long while favored a genetic explanation, but were puzzled because the speed with which this disease was coursing through the population certainly did not fit with the usual mechanisms of genetic transmission. Gajdusek conceded at first that a genetic mechanism might well be implicated but added: "ethnic-environmental variables are operating on the pathogenesis of *kuru* that have not been determined."[59]

Anderson documents the fierce disputes between the Australian scientists and those from the United States. He makes it very clear how high the stakes were in establishing the cause of *kuru* for these researchers, not merely in order to control the spread of the disease among the Fore and further afield (because Fore men had begun to leave the region in search of work) but perhaps, above all, for the achievement of scientific fame. In contrast to the scientists, Australians who administered that region of New Guinea simply regarded the condition as another impediment to order – they already had enough well-recognized diseases on their hands to manage without this mysterious condition that did not fit any recognized illness categories.

Carlton Gajdusek, who eventually was awarded a Nobel Prize for his work, found himself in an exceptionally delicate position in that he was dependent upon the Fore for their hospitality while living among them. He befriended many people, but at the same time desired to get access to the blood of families affected by *kuru*, and the brains of those who had died of the disease, in order to transform these materials into laboratory specimens for systematic investigation. As Anderson puts it: "Blood and brains, the germinal objects of [Gajdusek's] field research, were richly entangled in local community relations and global scientific networks."[60] Anderson shows clearly how the status of these key objects oscillated between gift and commodity, depending upon the circumstances and the people involved, with both the Fore and Gajdusek vacillating about whether or not such bodily materials should be treated as mere commodities.

When Gajdusek arrived in the region in 1957, in order to establish whether this neurological disease had an infectious, toxic, or genetic origin, he started to create charts that mapped the incidence of the disease, thus transforming "the bodies of the Fore, their social life and environment … [in]to a mobile archive of signs and numbers available for analysis at Okapa, Melbourne, Bethseda, or anywhere else."[61] Gajdusek had a mat-floor hospital built among the Fore hamlets where he attempted fruitlessly to treat patients. At the same time, after learning at a distance from experts in neuropathology in the United States how to prepare autopsy specimens, he then shipped them off to Australia and America for laboratory investigation. It was quickly suggested that the brain lesions of *kuru* victims resembled those of the rare lethal Creutzfeldt-Jakob disease found globally. Anderson comments that, suddenly, *kuru* was not just an affliction of the Fore: "Gajdusek had made it [*kuru*] essential to the understanding of neurological disease, whether local or global."[62] Descriptions of the Fore, people and place, and of *kuru* began to appear in the Western media. And, even as parts of the bodies of the Fore and bits of their environment began to circulate around the world, in exchange "bits of science and medicine circulated among the Fore."[63]

But the transmission of *kuru* remained elusive to everyone except the Fore, who knew that sorcery was at work. They also associated its spread with the increase of white men in the region. Over the years the majority of Fore became less and less receptive to the collection of specimens from their dead relatives. They wanted a cure for *kuru*, and were willing to cooperate with scientists to this end, even when sorcery was known to be at work, but many came to think that the scientists had let them down.

In the early 1960s the anthropologists Robert and Shirley Glasse started to apply themselves to the burning questions of how exactly *kuru* was spread from one person to another and why the epidemiology of its occurrence seemed to be confined largely to women, children, and adolescents, but did not occur in adult men. The Glasses immersed themselves in Fore life, establishing warm relations, quite unlike anything the Fore had ever experienced to date with respect to "white people." At first Robert Glasse worked primarily on kinship patterns, made confusing by impermanent and shifting alliances among the Fore, and the fact that they had little interest in their own lineages. The Fore told Glasse that the disease had come from the north a few generations earlier, and he was able to trace how deaths from *kuru* had spread from village to village, moving south; the more oral accounts Glasse collected, the more consistent and substantiated became the record of its spread. He concluded that the first case could probably be dated to the 1920s. The spread of the disease made it highly unlikely that genetic changes were causal.

While collecting these stories, Glasse became fascinated by other stories about the simultaneous spread of endocannibalism – a new fashion among the Fore dating from the early 20th century, that had also spread from the north at the same time as *kuru*. Fore women are responsible for the preparation of dead bodies that are roasted and then consumed, and corpses of *kuru* victims were not excluded from consumption. Only women and children partook of human flesh. Once a boy was initiated, he usually stopped this practice in the belief that it might make him weak. By the 1960s it was no longer possible to observe mortuary practices involving cannibalism; banned by the Australian government and by the missionaries, this behavior had died out everywhere except possibly in a few isolated hamlets.[64]

Gajdusek is known to have entertained the idea that cannibalism might be responsible for *kuru* transmission, but *kuru* brains showed no sign of any immune response to an infectious agent, and no autoimmune antibodies could be detected. Eventually, he pushed the idea out of his head as repugnant.[65] After reviewing all the literature, two biological anthropologists postulated that cannibalism could be involved; however, most scientists were not receptive, even when Glasse's findings became known. One geneticist was quietly converted after he learnt that the lethal neurological disease, scrapie, found in sheep, could be transmitted when goats and sheep were fed the brains of dead sheep.

Meantime, Shirley Glasse was investigating the devastating social effects of *kuru* on Fore families and communities.[66] And late in 1965, the infectious nature of *kuru* was established when it was shown that it could be transmitted in the laboratory to chimpanzees and that the resultant pathological changes in the brains of chimpanzees resembled that of human *kuru* brains. It was argued that a slow-acting virus with a long and varied incubation period must be the causal agent. Eventually, the extensive meticulous field observations, epidemiological and anthropological, began to mesh with the results of laboratory experiments being carried out in Washington. The fact that the prohibition of cannibalism coincided remarkably closely with a decline in new *kuru* cases was striking, allowing the Glasses together with another colleague to argue in *The Lancet* that "a *kuru*genic agent arose de novo in the Fore area from human, animal, or viral genetic material, and that its continued existence was ensured by cannibalism."[67] In 1968, 75 victims died of *kuru*, but all were older than 15 years of age (in striking contrast to earlier mortality patterns).

In the latter part of the 20th century interest among scientists in *kuru* lagged until the work of the maverick scientist Stanley Prusiner was finally recognized as significant. It was he who first argued that the "slow virus" was actually a misfolded protein, and not an infectious organism at all. The deadly protein is orally transmissible and causes a massive build up of amyloid, an abnormal protein, in the brains of *kuru* victims. Prusiner dubbed this protein a prion, a contraction for "proteinaceous" and "infectious." He, too, received a Nobel Prize, and went on to set up his own biotech company and then to become involved in several more, with the result, as Anderson notes, that human tissue was acquiring a different sort of social currency. Gajdusek had in effect been made into an "old timer"; he had been immersed in the gift-economy of earlier forms of commodification of biologicals, but by Prusiner's time molecularized material circulated as part of the highly networked and lucrative bio-industrial complex, and was no longer confined to small laboratories. Prions became a major cause of concern in the 1990s with the advent of new variant Creutzfeldt-Jakob Disease (nvCJD), a *kuru*-like illness also caused by prions. Cannibalism, in this case bovine cannibalism, was also implicated, as it emerged that humans had acquired the disease after eating meat from cows that had been given feed made up from the ground-up corpses of other cows contaminated with prions causing bovine spongiform encephalopathy (BSE), commonly known as "mad cow disease."

By the late 1990s genetic testing had shown that some individuals are at increased risk for particularly aggressive forms of *kuru* and nvCJD due to a specific polymorphism in their DNA. Genetic testing showed that *kuru* had exerted an undeniable selection pressure on the Fore because individuals homozygous for the amino acid methionine had been virtually eliminated from the population. The incubation time for the disease among these individuals was often as little as five years. Individuals heterozygous for polymorphism at codon 129 also proved to be vulnerable, but the incubation time is much longer, up to 40 years or more.[68] It is now accepted by virtually all involved scientists that endocannibalism was the mode of transmission of the prion among the Fore and, because this practice was stopped nearly half a century ago, it is assumed that it is very unlikely that any new cases will arise. *Kuru* is a dramatic example of a local biology resulting from the entanglement of social and biological phenomena. Not only did human behavior bring about a deadly disease, but it also resulted in significant genotypic changes among the Fore, thus rewriting their population biology.

Enormously important lessons have been learnt from the *kuru* epidemic, among them insights about the association between specific genotypes and the variable incubation times of prions. Following the outbreak of mad cow disease in the United Kingdom in which infected animals were first identified in 1989, more than 160 cases of nvCJD have been confirmed in humans as of 2009, the result, it is assumed, of ingesting products contaminated with BSE prions. Without exception, these patients tested homozygous for methionine on codon 129, as had Fore who succumbed quickly to the disease. It has been hypothesized that a second, bigger wave of nvCJD may be in the making in the U.K. that will manifest itself when, after an extensive incubation period, those people exposed to BSE prions who are heterozygotes for methionine on codon 129 become sick. Between 460,000 and 482,000 BSE-infected animals had entered the human food chain before controls on high-risk offal were introduced in 1989. Some estimates suggest that the incubation period can be as long as 34 to 50 years.[69] In the U.K., the practice of feeding the brains of their slaughtered companions to cows – forced bovine endocannibalism – has resulted in a deadly entanglement of social and biological phenomena, with striking resemblances to that among the Fore.

Racism and Birth Weight

Over the past two decades in the United States there have been concerted efforts to reduce the number of preterm deliveries and low birth-weight babies. Such births are the second leading cause of infant mortality across the population at large, and among African Americans the first cause. Furthermore, African American women are two to three times more likely than white women to deliver preterm. Although the overall number of preterm births has been reduced in the U.S., the gap appears to have widened because preterm births have declined faster among white than African American women. A large number of epidemiological studies have attempted to account for this disparity in terms of maternal age, education, lifestyle, and/or socio-economic position. However, the results make it clear that these variables account for only a small proportion of the difference. Moreover, college-educated black mothers are more likely to deliver very low birth-weight infants than are college-educated white mothers. And, further, it has been shown that women recently immigrated to the U.S. bear infants of higher birth weight than do women of the same race/ethnic category (as defined by the U.S. census) born and raised in the United

States, despite the frequency of lower socioeconomic status among the imm
Researchers involved with these studies argue that their findings "suggest that g
up as a woman of color in the U.S. is somehow toxic to pregnancy, and imply a
etiology for racial/ethnic disparities in prematurity that is not solely explain_ _ _y
economics or education."[70]

The epidemiologist Nancy Krieger points out that lately certain researchers have
been placing an increasing emphasis on the hypothesis that genetics, rather than social
variables, account for racial/ethnic disparities in infant mortality. She is highly critical
of these suggestions for two reasons: first, the overwhelming greater genetic variability within rather than between so-called "racial" groups; and, second, the many
changes that have happened in connection with the health of immigrant populations
have taken place far too quickly to be accounted for by genetics. Krieger argues that
what has to be investigated is "how people, as both biological organisms and social
beings, literally embody – via processes that necessarily involve gene expression – the
dynamic, social, material, and ecological contexts into which we are born, develop,
interact, and endeavor to live meaningful lives."[71] Krieger's thesis is that such an
approach raises questions about who and what can be held accountable for health
inequities, an argument she and her colleagues set out to demonstrate.

No other study to date has demonstrated the lifetime significance of the subjective experience of racism on pregnancy and its outcome. Regardless of their socioeconomic level, African Americans who reported the experience of racial discrimination
in three or more situations proved to be at more than three times the risk for
preterm delivery as compared to women who reported no experience of racism.
Further recent studies have supported this conceptual model set out by Krieger and
colleagues.[72] Krieger's conclusion is that "biologic expressions of race relations"
appear to be at work in accounting for the findings about low birth weight and she
goes on to caution that human biology should never be studied in the abstract.[73]
This example makes strikingly clear how individual women should not be held fully
accountable for the outcomes of pregnancies. In the United States, and elsewhere
too, no doubt, persistent experiences of racism in everyday life continue to take
their toll, despite dramatic political reforms throughout the latter part of the 20th
century.

Of Microbes and Humans

In their very make-up, micro-organisms can shed light on precisely how biology is
situated, on how humans transform the biological world in which they live and, in
so doing, change their own biological make-up. Evolutionary theory argues that
nature selects for the fittest – those who respond to the varied challenges posed by
diverse environments and reproduce most effectively; in other words, evolutionary
theory has made it clear how environments bring about biological changes. Humans
are unique in their ability to change the material world in which they live and most
environments are radically transformed by human activity or else are entirely man-
made – increasingly so today.[74] Human activity is thus an important factor in bringing
about a range of biological changes – climate change, genetically-engineered organisms, microbial evolution, and so on. However, because microbes "strike back" by

causing disease, they are a particularly informative example of the kinds of looping effects that show how biology is situated in time and place.

Of course, human intervention into the lives of microbes long predated microbiology: hygienic practices such as sterile surgical techniques (advanced by Joseph Lister in the late 19th century), were consciously used to prevent infections without an understanding that fevers were caused by micro-organisms, just as John Snow stymied cholera in 19th-century London. Such "a-microbiological" methods existed everywhere, and many people have long employed such practices, no doubt as a result of local observations that certain activities contain the threat of infection. In his magisterial study, John Ford documented how Africans prevented sleeping sickness through agricultural practices that isolated humans from tsetse flies, the carrier of the disease-causing trypanosome, thus breaking the cycle of infection.[75] And it is increasingly clear that ingestion of clay and certain plant materials by humans has functioned very effectively from the time of the emergence of *homo sapiens* to control infections of many kinds.[76]

No doubt the best-known example of how human behavior increased disease incidence, and in turn transformed human biology, is that of the sickle cell story. It has long been known that individuals who carry a mutation of the hemoglobin gene that causes it to "sickle" are more resistant to malaria caused by the *Plasmodium falciparum* parasite than are other people; and, not surprisingly, the gene has been found to be more prevalent in populations who have historically been heavily exposed to *falciparum*-carrying mosquitoes – peoples of Mediterranean, Indian, and African origin. Exposure was greatly exacerbated by the development of agriculture, including the introduction of irrigation that allowed increased opportunities for mosquitoes to breed in stagnant water pools close to human habitation. Individuals who inherit the sickle cell trait from both parents are prone to recurrent, painful, often debilitating crises. Where medical care is not available, as is so often the case in Africa, malaria is frequently fatal by adolescence. However, those individuals who are heterozygous, that is, inherit the trait from only one parent, usually manifest no symptoms, are able to lead a normal life unaffected by crises, and are resistant to malaria.

Another microbiological example shows how local conditions may change both the micro-organism and the disease it causes in humans. In the 19th century William Boog Leishman, a pathologist in the British medical corps in India, isolated a parasite from the spleen of a British soldier that he initially mistakenly believed to be the organism that causes sleeping sickness. The parasite was subsequently isolated from sores of "natives" in Delhi, from which it was established that it could cause both a mild skin condition, as was the case for the affected Indians, as well as a more serious visceral disease such as that of the British soldier. With further investigation, different strains of the parasite were correlated with different forms of the condition now known as leishmaniasis. The common sand fly is a vector for some strains of the parasite, while other strains are sustained in reservoirs by an intermediate rodent host, usually rats or mice. In this case, it is described as a "zoonotic" epidemic, whereas when it passes directly from human to human via the fly, it is described as an "anthroponotic" epidemic. The *Leishmania* parasite is classified into different strains associated with these different modes of transmission; in some cases, the disease targets the inner organs to cause "visceral leishmaniasis," whereas in others it remains confined to the skin, resulting in "cutaneous leishmaniasis," but both forms of these disease can result no matter the mode of transmission.

For almost a century after the parasite was described by Leishman, very little research was done on it, in large part because it was assumed that the disease affects only the poor, making it a neglected disease along with sleeping sickness, schistosomiasis, filariasis, onchocerciasis, dracunculiasis, and many other "tropical diseases."[77] As a result, no treatments at all exist for many of these diseases, while for others, including leishmaniasis, the only treatments available often date from colonial times. Furthermore, in the case of leishmaniasis, diagnostic methods have remained relatively crude, so that the simple 19th-century clinical distinction between "visceral" and "cutaneous" forms continues to inform its classification today. Recently, there has been a dramatic increase in leishmaniasis research, following the Iraq War as cutaneous leishmaniasis has become the leading infectious disease in the U.S. military.[78] While no therapeutic breakthroughs have yet been reported, advanced molecular techniques have been brought to bear on the disease, resulting in some intriguing observations.

There is now growing evidence that the same strains of the parasite actually cause different diseases in different parts of the world, or in different "types" of individuals. After the First Gulf War, American military physicians observed cases of visceral leishmaniasis in soldiers infected with the strain that usually causes cutaneous leishmaniasis in inhabitants of the Middle East. There is also evidence that the mode of transmission – zoonotic or anthroponotic – varies according to the condition of the host. In the West African city of Ouagadougou, a strain of leishmaniasis (the same as in Baghdad) that is usually transmitted through zoonotic vectors caused an anthroponotic epidemic, in all probability because a significant portion of the population was immunocompromised because of concurrent HIV infections. Because the Ouagadougou and Baghdad strains were shown to be genetically identical, this suggests that differences in diseases are due to local interactions among micro-organisms, host, and environment, pointing to the embeddedness of the body and how biology is situated.[79]

Another example concerns the mystery of the origins of syphilis. Yaws is a skin infection that was formerly common in children in the Caribbean, Central, and South America that has largely disappeared with the growing use of antibiotics (although pockets may still exist in remote areas). Yaws is spread by sores on exposed parts of the body (arms and legs) and is usually transmitted among children through play. While it has always been recognized that syphilis and yaws are related because of the similarities in the treponemal parasite that causes these conditions, molecular experiments carried out in 2007 on strains of the parasite isolated in Guyana suggest that yaws is in fact the ancestor of syphilis. This has led to speculation that yaws mutated into syphilis when it was brought from the Americas by sailors and other travelers returning to Europe, where its spread through sexual contact probably proved to be more effective than casual contact. What historians came to call the "Great Pox" killed nearly five million people in Europe. Similar explanations, positing the role of human behavior in the evolution of micro-organisms, have been advanced in one form or another for most infectious diseases.[80]

Antibiotics and Resistant Microbes

With the discovery of antibiotics, humans equipped themselves with a powerful technology for controlling infectious diseases. New antibiotics are produced ceaselessly
by pharmaceutical companies to combat mutant strains of micro-organisms for which
older antibiotics are ineffective. In addition to the mechanism of random mutation
that allows micro-organisms to acquire genetic traits and pass them on to their offspring, bacteria have also evolved highly efficient ways of spreading genes among
themselves that enable their resistance to antibiotics. These are mobile genes called
plasmids – usually small semi-circular, double-stranded rings of DNA – that can easily
be passed from one bacterium to another. But rapid transformations in micro-
organisms are also produced by the following: the availability of antibiotics; the
accessibility of physicians; local prescribing habits of medical practitioners; the ability
to pay for antibiotics; the capacity of health care systems to ensure accessibility and
monitoring; and the presence of antibiotics in the food chain.

Antibiotic-resistant bacteria have now emerged as a major public health hazard
worldwide. For example, *Staphylococcus aureus* is a bacterium commonly found on
the skin. So named because of its yellowish grape-like appearance in the Petri dish,
it is the bacterium most commonly found in skin infections where pus is produced,
resulting in boils and abscesses. A particular type of penicillin, methicillin, was formerly used to treat it until methicillin-resistant *Staphylococcus aureus* (MRSA) began
to make its appearance in first-world hospitals. Blame was put on widespread and
inappropriate antibiotic usage, as well as on advances in biomedical technologies
that resulted in increasingly ill and immuno-compromised patients being kept
alive, inadvertently creating an opportunity for the bacterium to evolve in its fragile
hosts who were being administered antibiotics. However MRSA has since spread
outside hospitals, and in some communities has evolved into a highly aggressive multi-
drug-resistant bacterium. There is no consensus as to how resistance has spread so
rapidly, although widespread antibiotic use in the community as well as opportunities
for transmission in athletic facilities have been implicated.

Drug-resistant tuberculosis is another example of how the social activities of
humans have brought about the emergence and spread of this bacterium. Tuberculosis
is a slow-growing, highly infectious bacterium that can easily become resistant if
antibiotics are not used correctly. Treatment with three or four antibiotics is the norm
today, with the shortest effective course being for six months, with proper antibiotic
usage ensured by "directly observed therapy" (DOTS). Successful treatment of tuberculosis thus requires a sophisticated public health infrastructure able to identify cases
of a difficult-to-diagnose condition and deliver and monitor complex treatment over
long periods of time. Breakdowns in public health services mean that there can be
interruptions in drug supplies to patients, who must turn to other means to treat
their disease.

Ethnographic research has shown how these breakdowns in public health, tied
to broader political decisions about health funding, actually breed epidemics of
multi-drug-resistant tuberculosis (MDRTB). When patients cannot obtain a regular
supply of these multiple drugs, inadequate treatment results and allows the tuberculosis to develop resistance to the antibiotics. Patients are often blamed for the

development of drug resistance on the assumption that they have not been taking the drugs properly and have therefore been "noncompliant." In reality, it is most often the health care system that is unable to supply drugs or counsel patients adequately, often leaving them on their own with little information and no resources in the face of a potentially fatal infection.[81] As described in the Introduction, culturalism is frequently embedded in public health practice in many parts of the world and ironically, it usually serves to worsen health care outcomes by antagonizing the very people who are in need of help.

The above examples make it clear how culture, politics, and economics, by structuring human activity and by altering human biology, can fundamentally transform micro-organisms. In addition, with the rise of biomedicine as a powerful technology for intervening in biology, biomedical technologies have indirectly become another force in the cultural shaping of biology. Because micro-organisms are not passive actors but respond to changing environments, sometimes very quickly indeed, they produce changes in both human biology and society in locally contingent ways.

Debates about the Origin of HIV

What is at stake in our insistence on situating biology in local histories, economies, and politics? How is the concept of "biosocial differentiation" relevant to global health today? As the medical anthropologists cited earlier have pointed out, using "culture" as the explanation for persistent poor health and non-compliance with biomedical regimens only worsens health inequalities and ultimately compromises individual and public health. Our argument goes further and suggests that reliance on a culturalist account fundamentally misrecognizes how human biology and society are co-produced, with lasting and damaging consequences for health worldwide. Nowhere is this clearer than in the heated public debates that surrounded the HIV epidemic – debates that went so far as to discredit a world leader and undermine a decade of public health programs.

If the discovery of the microbial origins of disease ushered in the "golden age of medicine," the HIV epidemic marked its close. The origin of the HIV epidemic remains a vexing question, still shrouded in accusation and blame, as Paul Farmer first pointed out in his ethnography of the emergence of HIV in a Haitian village in the late 1980s.[82] The several origin theories of HIV highlight, however, the importance of considering how the human body is situated within local ecologies in addition to the effects produced by history, politics, and economies.

Efforts to portray the way in which people seek to survive and reproduce human and social existence historically and in the present are often glossed as products of "culture." From there, it has been a short step to see culture as a monolithic force that determines peoples' identity and behavior. As we noted in the Introduction, doctors and public health professionals have often used the culture concept as the key in linking social factors and disease. Farmer chronicled how in Cange, a village in Haiti's remote Central Plateau, HIV was spread by a toxic combination of poverty, migration, and social inequality as local farmers, displaced by the building of a dam, were driven off their land and desperate young women who ended up in the city often had no choice but to sell sex to survive economically. Farmer indicted the culturalism of accounts in the scientific literature that instead blamed exotic cultural rituals, such as those associated with voodoo, and by implication, those who were assumed to subscribe to these cultural beliefs.[83] Such "scientific" racism was not directed only at Haitians, of course, as anthropologist Gilles Bibeau pointed out. "African sexuality" and other forms of "exotic" cultural practices were cited to explain the spread of HIV on that continent, buttressed by poorly executed statistics and selective readings of ethnographic anecdotes.[84] Once again, victims were blamed for their plight. Didier Fassin, who had worked in various parts of francophone Africa in the years of the emergence of HIV, denounced "culturalism" as a victim-blaming discourse while deflecting attention from the inability of public health to actually respond to the needs of those it was presumed to serve.[85]

The damage of scientific racism has been incalculable. It has been responsible for at least two decades of suspicion, accusation, and at times violent confrontation that have undermined efforts to combat the HIV epidemic. Those whose "culture" was blamed were understandably outraged, and many dismissed efforts to control the epidemic as yet another racist plot. Passions have cooled only to explode again over the years, the most internationally visible example being the controversy surrounding South African President Thabo Mbeki's assertion that the cause of the epidemic was not HIV but poverty and the legacy of racism. Writing about South Africa, Fassin has called this an "epidemic of disputes," but the term might as well apply to resentments that continue to smolder around the world and in the corridors of international organizations. The science journalist Helen Epstein, as well as former UNAIDS epidemiologist Elizabeth Pisani have suggested that, stunned by the virulence of these disputes, epidemiologists and public health officials may have ended up tip-toeing around difficult issues and hiding behind technocratic solutions, ignoring local efforts in which people were not afraid to address uncomfortable facts about sexuality. Former WHO HIV epidemiologist James Chin has called this situation the collision between epidemiology and political correctness.[86] One can only wonder whether, had we had the conceptual and research tools to properly situate the body and disease within history, the culture wars that erupted around the epidemic, and their undermining of the response to it, could have been avoided.

Theories of the origin of HIV highlight the way in which the body is situated in history, and the fact that culture is an always-evolving process informed by history and experience. The story of the origins of the HIV epidemic shows very clearly how the biology of the virus evolved in response to changing social conditions, and that these social conditions also modified the bodies of the human hosts of the virus – a classic example of biosocial differentiation.

There are currently three scientific hypotheses to explain the origins of the HIV epidemic. All start from the observation that HIV's most immediate ancestor is simian immunodeficiency virus of chimpanzees (SIVcpz), a retrovirus found in chimpanzees that inhabit the forests of west-central Africa. This observation is based on studies that have sampled retroviruses from humans and monkeys and sequenced key genes taken from them. Examination of genes using molecular methods can determine the genetic relatedness of retroviruses (as well as other organisms) by comparing the genetic sequence of a gene common to different viruses. The more the sequences resemble each other, the more related the viruses that harbor these genes are thought to be. In other words, the degree of molecular difference of the sequences measures the evolutionary time since they diverged from a common genetic ancestor. Biologists speak of a "molecular clock" to describe the sophisticated laboratory and statistical methods that are used to estimate the passage of time based on genetic divergences.

Existing HIV strains have been sampled in order to make clear that their most likely common ancestor was not a human virus but SIVcpz. HIV-2, a much more rare and less virulent strain found mainly in West Africa is believed to be descended from an SIV found in the sooty mangabey monkeys that live in West African jungles, accordingly named SIVsm. SIVcpz is believed to be an ancient virus, as it is found both in the *pan troglodytes troglodytes* and *schweinfurtheii* chimpanzee species that diverged from each other thousands of years ago. Thus, HIV, like most other infectious diseases of humans, is a zoonotic epidemic and chimpanzees were the primate reservoir from which HIV arose. The natural habitat of chimpanzees is the vast tropical forests of Central Africa that span the contemporary nations of Gabon and Cameroon to the west, Congo, the DRC, and the Central African Republic in the middle, and parts of Rwanda and Burundi to the east. The three origin hypotheses posit different explanations for how SIV was transmitted to humans and subsequently spawned an epidemic caused by mutating into the human virus, HIV. As we shall see, it is argued that changing social conditions provided optimal conditions for the spread of a blood and bodily fluid transmitted pathogen that drove this biological transformation.

What is known as the "natural transfer" theory hypothesizes that humans were contaminated by the chimpanzee virus through routine contact with their bodily fluids, most likely through the butchering and consumption of bushmeat. However humans and chimpanzees have shared the same habitat for eons, requiring that a historical change must have occurred to explain why HIV emerged at some point during the 20th century. In the Belgian Congo between World Wars I and II, forced labor practices implemented under colonial rule led to widespread migration and famines and, it is thought, intensified recourse to bushmeat to survive. At that time, both French and Belgian Congo were run as concessions, rented out to private companies that ruthlessly exploited native labor to build railroads and extract rubber and timber from the colonies. Epidemics of sleeping sickness, malaria, and other tropical diseases took a heavy toll, with astonishingly high mortality rates. It is estimated that during this period, up to a third of the African population of these colonies may have perished.[87] The natural transfer theory is supported by molecular studies that identify the period around 1931 as the most likely time the SIV began to diversify. Because diversification is a response to a changed environment, such as a new host, this suggests that around 1931 was when SIV "jumped species" into a human host.

Two other theories dispute the "natural transfer" theory's assertion that an exposure to chimpanzee blood through hunting was enough to trigger the epidemic.[88] One of them garnered widespread media attention after the publication of an extensively researched book by British science journalist Edward Hooper.[89] This theory argues that mass inoculation of over a million Africans with an experimental oral poliovirus vaccine (OPV) in the 1950s was responsible for contaminating a large number of humans with SIV. According to the OPV theory, this vaccine was contaminated with SIV because some batches were prepared using chimpanzee kidneys as a culture medium. Hooper found that the earliest recorded cases of HIV were

geographically clustered in areas where the experimental vaccine had been administered. Poor record-keeping on the part of the vaccine's developers has made it difficult
to counter Hooper's assertion.

Even so, the OPV theory has been vigorously contested. Hooper's proposed
timing (the 1950s) does not mesh well with that suggested by molecular studies,
which indicate that the HIV ancestor virus (aptly named the "Eve" virus) diversified
approximately 20 years earlier. However, these molecular studies do not indicate
whether this diversification occurred in humans or chimps and they do not, in and
of themselves, refute the OPV hypothesis. They imply that OPV would have had to
transmit a variety of genetically different strains of HIV. The vaccine's developers
have adamantly denied that chimpanzee cells were ever used in the manufacture of
the vaccine; furthermore, it appears that even if this had been the case, SIV would
not have survived the processes used to develop the vaccine.[90] Finally the geographic
correlation of early AIDS cases with vaccination sites could be an ecological fallacy,
a coincidence explained by the fact that whatever AIDS cases were present at the
time were more likely to have been reported by medical dispensaries that were also
used to administer the experimental vaccine.

A different theory has been advanced by the New York primatologist Preston
Marx, in collaboration with Ernest Drucker, an epidemiologist at the Einstein College
of Medicine in the Bronx. Marx's research has concentrated on another virus found
in monkeys – SIVsm. SIVsm appears to be the ancestor of HIV-2, a human retrovirus
found in West Africa that is both less infectious than HIV-1 and does not appear to
cause as severe disease in humans as does HIV-1. Marx and his collaborators found
that transmission of SIVsm was an extremely unusual occurrence amongst Africans
who had SIVsm-infected monkeys as pets despite their being often bitten;[91] the
"natural transfer" rate appeared to be too low to explain an epidemic. Marx, Alcabes,
and Drucker hypothesized that such rare cross-species infections could be amplified
by the serial passage of SIV to humans from an original monkey-infected human
through the reuse of needles. This is because, when a micro-organism passes from
host to host, it is the most aggressive or virulent form that is most likely to be transmitted onwards. Not only would serial passage explain how larger numbers of people
could be contaminated as reuse of needles was commonplace at the time, but it would
account for SIV's mutation into a more virulent HIV strain. In addition to widespread
anecdotal evidence that the reuse of needles was common throughout Africa in the
postcolonial period as late as the late 1980s, Marx and colleagues have collected data
showing that the exponential increase in the worldwide use of needles preceded the
decrease in the unit price to support their "reused needles" hypothesis.[92]

All three of these hypotheses – "natural transfer," OPV, and reused needles –
locate the origins of the epidemic in social changes occurring in Africa during the
colonial and postcolonial periods and the biological reconfigurations that resulted.
The natural transfer theory argues that migration and urbanization broadened and
intensified sexual networks sufficiently to trigger an epidemic that until then had
never reached a threshold of contamination that would have allowed it to spread
beyond the bush where hunters would have been exposed to SIVcpz. Both the OPV
and reused needles theories incriminate the dissemination of biomedical practices –
vaccine trials and increased use of injectable drugs – in the spread of the epidemic.

Shifts in disease ecology also play a role in all three hypotheses. Other sexually transmitted infections (STIs) – such as gonorrhea, chlamydia, genital herpes, and trichomonas – increase the transmissibility of HIV considerably. Malnutrition and the presence of chronic diseases such as sleeping sickness or tuberculosis are assumed to increase susceptibility to HIV. This may be an important explanation for why the poor are more susceptible to HIV than are other groups of people. In summary, all these are differing accounts of what we have called biosocial differentiation.

These biological factors were all concurrent with the social changes wrought by colonialism. Some STIs are believed to have been introduced by Europeans, and a concentration of male workers in work camps encouraged prostitution, furthering their spread. In addition, ecological changes caused by resettlement of villages and disruption of traditional agricultural patterns precipitated famines and epidemics of sleeping sickness.[93] Mobile public health campaigns reused needles both to diagnose and to attempt to treat the disease. It has been reported, for instance, that between 1917 and 1919 only six syringes were used to vaccinate up to 90,000 people in Ubangui-Chari (now the Central African Republic) and that UNICEF dispensed over 12 million injections of penicillin in a campaign to eradicate yaws between 1953 and 1957, when needles were still reused multiple times.[94] The OPV hypothesis, despite powerful circumstantial evidence, has been considerably weakened because of its biological implausibility (the inability of SIVcpz to survive the vaccine preparation process) and also by the molecular studies of the virus cited above that locate diversification of HIV prior to the OPV trials Hooper has argued as causal in the spread of the epidemic. The "natural transfer" theory has gained support in recent years, but does not eliminate the reuse of needles as playing a major part in the epidemic. Further molecular studies have identified a burst in the diversification of HIV in the 1950s and 1960s; this evidence would support both the OPV and reused needles hypotheses. Marx and collaborators collected reused needles in Cameroonian clinics to test out the serial passage hypothesis and found evidence to support the hypothesis that unsafe injections could have helped spread HIV.[95]

Despite the controversy over the origins of the HIV epidemic, there is a consensus about the complex interplay between the biological and social factors behind all three theories and the sophisticated scientific evidence marshaled to support them. All these theories discount individual sexual behavior as being the key to understanding the origins of the epidemic. This corroborates emerging epidemiological evidence that sexual behavior alone does not appear to explain differences in the spread of HIV epidemics. At the heart of these theories has been the inability of epidemiological-behavioral models of the epidemic to account for bio-socio-historical complexity and also the reluctance of many who reject these theories to acknowledge biology as deeply embedded in an ever-changing web of social relations. Explanations for differences in epidemic patterning continue to cite culture as causal while too often ignoring how specific historical events themselves also produce biological difference. Even when this is the case, however, a divide remains between the "biology" of HIV – viruses, co-factors, and host characteristics – and the "social" aspects of behavior, culture, and for that matter history, inevitably making it difficult to apprehend how biology and social relations are co-produced as local biologies and generate epidemics.

In Summary

The rise of the biological sciences as a powerful system for explaining and predicting illness has led to the assumption that bodies must everywhere be the same because biology is, in effect, a universal. In this chapter we have argued that biology is inevitably a snapshot, one situated in the time and space of a complex and shifting material reality, historically patterned by society, culture, economics, and politics. The end of menstruation, *kuru*, and low birth-weight babies are of course all real material events and things, and can be described in standard biological terms. As we have shown, however, these phenomena are the result of historical interactions between culture and biology – interactions usually left out of orthodox accounts about their happening – that assume a universal biological body as the substrate on which social factors act. We have also seen how micro-organisms are transformed by human activity and, surprisingly, how identical micro-organisms may cause different symptoms depending on the "kinds" of bodies they invade. Finally, historical and biological debates over the origins of the HIV epidemic that have brought about charges of scientific racism, political incompetence, and neo-colonialism show that what is at stake in being able to fully account for biosocial difference has enormous relevance not only for public health but for issues of global governance.

Understanding the body as contextually situated means that we attribute variations in biology to regularities produced by temporal processes rather than to statistical laws. This is significantly different from the biomedical understanding of bodily variation as governed by statistical rules and therefore manifest as a predictable, a-temporal, "normal" distribution. Regularities in bodily variation do apparently exist, but they are artifacts of the reduction of complex and varied biological and social processes to a decontextualized series of indicators. Serum hemoglobin levels are "normally" – in the statistical sense – distributed: 90 percent of the time they oscillate between 120 and 150 milligrams per liter of whole blood. A clinician will work to recontextualize this information when, for example, faced with a low hemoglobin in a vegetarian patient. It may certainly be possible to standardize hemoglobin for vegetarians or specific subpopulations, using what the sociologist Steven Epstein has called "niche standardization," but ultimately these are statistical operations on "thin" variables that do not capture the "thick" social dimensions of the production of biological difference.[96] The now irrefutable biomedical evidence of the multiple pathways by which poverty causes biological changes, for instance, points to how poverty is neither purely social nor biological.

In arguing for a situated body, one where biosocial differentiations may produce over time a local biology, we are of course refuting neither the value of biological knowledge nor the effectiveness of biomedicine. However, we suggest that there are limits to our ability to account for and predict illness on the basis of biology alone, as is all too evident from a consideration of contemporary developments in biomedicine, particularly with accumulating insights afforded by molecular biology and genetics. Indeed, these insights suggest a greater role for environmental and social factors than has been acknowledged previously when attempting to understand the material body in health and illness. Numerous environmental factors are themselves shaped by human actions: sanitation systems purify water of disease-causing germs even as factories release toxins into the atmosphere with long-lasting effects on human biology and disease. Such actions are patterned by communal practice and socio-political systems.

Molecular biology is providing increasing insight into how the human body cannot be viewed separately from the material, historical, and social circumstances that produced it. In effect, this undermines the notion of biology as a universal standard against which human difference may be adequately accounted for. This account of human difference points to the necessity to read the emerging molecular biological sciences, as well as more established findings from epidemiology, against the grain, so that the local and the particular may be given the attention they require by drawing on ethnographic research to make visible the interstices between universal taxonomies and local practices. Reading for the local and the particular – rather than for the universal and standard – gives insight into how history and environments condition the body in sickness and health.

Biological facts are "true," at least to the extent that they offer a reliable and agreed upon way of knowing, but they are technophenomena that constitute only a partial view of reality. Biomedical knowledge is itself inevitably situated in the circumstances that dictate what questions get asked (and by whom), and how answers are to be interpreted (and by whom), rather than emerging from the standpoint of a dispassionate observer able to achieve universal knowledge. Epistemological questions – how we come to know the world – and also matters that are profoundly political are at stake. Acknowledging, for instance, that economic inequality and "structural violence" produce not only health inequalities, but also even different bodies indicates that more biomedicine alone will not be enough to eradicate a given situation, and that a far more radical and far-reaching solution will inevitably be required.

Part II
The Biological Standard

5

The Right Population

The power of population is so superior to the power of the earth to produce subsist-
ence for man, that premature death must in some shape or other visit the human
race. The vices of mankind are active and able ministers of depopulation. They are
the precursors in the great army of destruction, and often finish the dreadful work
themselves. But should they fail in this war of extermination, sickly seasons, epidem-
ics, pestilence, and plague advance in terrific array, and sweep off their thousands
and tens of thousands. Should success be still incomplete, gigantic inevitable famine
stalks in the rear, and with one mighty blow levels the population with the food of
the world. (Thomas Robert Malthus)[1]

In Part I of this book, we explored the historical and social context within which
biomedicine emerged. As we have seen, beginning in the 18th century, methods for
objectifying the body by means of technologies of numeration became the basis for
a systematic approach in the clinic to describing and classifying symptoms in order
to situate them as part of disease taxonomies. Once clinical observations were subjected to such statistical analyses, it became possible to arrive at a quantitative understanding of human diseases as bodily states that could best be interpreted as deviations
from the "normal" body. Such a quantitative approach necessitates the aggregation
of data about populations as a whole against which the condition of individual bodies
is then assessed, as several of the case studies discussed in earlier chapters have illustrated. But populations do not exist in nature, rather they are technophenomena – the
result of the way in which clusters of people are formally defined by colonial powers,
nation states, and local government as specific entities for a variety of purposes,
including the statistical establishment of bodily norms, promotion of health and
wellbeing, development of medications by means of clinical trials, and so on.

In this chapter and the two that follow it, we use three very different examples
to show how specific populations have been named, ordered, manipulated, and
experimented upon. Each chapter includes both historical and contemporary perspectives that highlight how relationships of power and moral judgements are inevitably
implicated in the management of populations. However, these chapters also show
how targeted groups of people exert agency and actively engage with biomedical

interventions that are made available to them in order to bring about their own objectives and desire for wellbeing.

Foucault created the concept of "governmentality" in order to illustrate the way in which particular forms of classificatory thought that came to the fore in the 18th and 19th centuries in the natural sciences were transformed by counting and transforming aggregates of numbers into "facts" to be classified and managed by government. Central to this form of biopower, exemplary of the modern state, is the idea that a "population" is a living object, "an aggregate of bodies that exists unproblematically in nature,"[2] and that estimating the vital attributes of populations, above all, fertility and mortality, is of fundamental importance to the welfare of modern societies. Today, even in those countries bereft of the functional apparatus of the modern state, enormous efforts are made to regulate populations by outside forces, notably international aid agencies, NGOs, and humanitarian organizations, whose stated objective is to "save lives."

In considering the concept of population in this chapter, and in particular the governance of reproduction, we show how efforts have been made from the early part of the 20th century to create populations of the right size and composition. Central to this endeavor is the belief that both size and the "quality" of human populations can be controlled through the systematic application of biomedical technologies alone, in preference to economic inducements and other social approaches. Tracing this history makes clear how the problematic of population enabled biology to emerge as a standard for measuring and intervening in the name of health, and in so doing created a space for intervention in the lives of millions of people using biomedical technologies. It also shows how standardizing the body, and the resulting blindness to the contingency of the body, can have unintended consequences.

Everywhere, people have long made use of indigenous technologies to regulate fertility according to culturally informed expectations.[3] However, the introduction of manufactured bio-contraceptives has improved the lot of many women because they are able to practice fertility regulation with greater reliability than is usually possible with local products. With condom use women are also protected against HIV. Nevertheless, the distribution of bio-contraceptive devices under the aegis of top-down family planning programs that originate in the West has very often brought about unanticipated consequences – for example, when women make use of birth-control pills to increase their fertility,[4] or when broad-based maternal and child health programs already in place are abandoned in favor of programs that focus on family planning alone.[5] A possible increase in domestic violence has also been documented in association with the promotion of family planning and population control programs. Furthermore, the widespread use of ultrasound technology makes it possible to carry out what is sometimes termed "family balancing" – the termination of pregnancies on the basis of sex alone. The skewed sex ratios that have resulted in some parts of the world have significant long-term social consequences. In summary, reproductive technologies bring about radical societal transformations, often improving the lot of women, but at times reinforcing inequities of long standing – notably of gender and class.

Emphasis is given throughout this chapter to the relationship among the technological manipulation of populations, the politics of modernization, economic modes of production, and gender. It is evident that the "fit" between the disciplinary poles of population and the individualized anatomopolitics conceptualized by Foucault is often very poor indeed, resulting at times in severe distress and abuses of human rights among targeted populations and quite often, in poorer countries, in a reduction in the provision of comprehensive health care in favor of targeted objectives.[6] The illustrative examples set out below also make clear the way in which biomedical technologies associated with reproduction, although sometimes adopted wholeheartedly by individuals, families, and communities in their everyday lives, at other times are roundly resisted, or else co-opted and made use of pragmatically to bring about family aspirations that may well counter governmental objectives. Furthermore, in some situations local government is actively opposed to outside interference into reproduction.[7] The matter is further complicated because family members can be at odds with each other about reproductive practices, and both individuals and families as a unit may well have objectives that differ from those of family planning programs driven by demographic goals designed simply to reduce population size.

The Origins of Population as a "Problem"

Demography is defined as the statistical study of populations, and Thomas Malthus (1766–1834) is recognized today as the father of modern demography. His most famous essay on the principles of population caused an enormous stir at the time of its original publication in 1798 – including many hostile reactions – and the essay was somewhat modified over time with the publication of five subsequent editions. Malthus was writing in response to several influential thinkers of his day, among them the Marquis de Condorcet who argued that humans should be able to perfect themselves through the application of reason and will power. Malthus' position was that "most people" – by which he meant the lower social classes – were not capable of such will power. Moreover, he argued, human populations increase at a geometric rate, whereas the means of subsistence increase arithmetically, so that inevitably life will be destroyed. Malthus was not the first to declare that poverty is a "natural" condition, but his concern was above all that the pressures that large numbers of people place on resources result in human misery.

Initially, Malthus envisioned that war, famine, and disease were the only "positive checks" by which population could be controlled, but in the 1803 edition of his essay he added "moral restraint" as a further check, thus acknowledging that human behavior could result in population reduction through abstinence and the postponement of marriage – activities recommended specifically for the poor. Paradoxically, Malthus described the use of contraception, notably coitus interruptus, as a "vice" and an "improper act."[8] His argument, then, was not simply one about the size of a population; built into it were eugenic ideas directed at specific segments of society. He disagreed strongly with several economists of his time who assumed that a growing population would mean greater productivity, and his published materials effectively blocked increased relief destined for the poor in England.

Malthus clearly chose to ignore the economic reality of life for the poorer segments of society during his time. By the end of the 18th century, industrialization had advanced to such an extent in England that machinery was replacing male workers, creating widespread unemployment. At the same time women and children came to be valued as labor because of their supposed dexterity in the cotton mills and other kinds of factories. Tuberculosis and typhoid took an enormous toll, and needy families responded by giving birth to more children, whose paltry incomes were crucial to the survival of their families.[9] This situation was exacerbated by the enclosure of common land – a space where people had formerly been free to raise their own food and keep a cow – for the production of crops on a large scale by wealthy landowners. At the same time prices for basic staples increased when the Corn Laws (tariffs designed to stave off cheaper North American imports made available by colonization) were implemented to protect English crops. These changes made the lives of the poor increasingly untenable and contributed enormously to the move of many to the cities where they resided in slum conditions. The visibility of the poor in the cities contributed to the idea that "population control" had to be implemented. When the Corn Laws were eventually repealed in 1846, food prices in England decreased again, opening the way for the realization of world trade in agricultural products still in place today. The entanglement of concerns about population size, economic development, agricultural practices, the changing world order, and indifference to the reality of the lives of those primarily targeted for population control, so visible in this English example, was to be repeated in country after country throughout the world in the years to come, and is still visible today.

Malthus' essay had a profound effect on both Herbert Spencer and Charles Darwin, inspiring Spencer to formulate his social theory about the "survival of the fittest," that was to become a central concept in Darwin's theory of evolution. The essay also stimulated the creation of the apparatus necessary to conduct national population censuses, thus creating a new object of knowledge for intervention by the state. The first mandated census was carried out in America in 1790, followed by Great Britain in 1801 and then by other northern European countries. When, in 1957, the first Director-General of UNESCO, evolutionist and humanist Julian Huxley, called for a "World Population Policy,"[10] Malthus' thinking was evident in his pronouncement and in those that followed shortly thereafter. Even though food productivity increased enormously during the course of the 20th century, Paul R. Ehrlich, a founder of modern microbiology and a member of the American Association of the Advancement of Science, predicted in the late 1960s in his book *The Population Bomb*, that hundreds of millions would die from a looming population-crisis.[11] The highly influential Club of Rome reiterated this theme in the book *The Limits to Growth* published in 1972. Ehrlich, clearly a neo-Malthusian, argued that population growth would outpace agricultural growth unless controlled. In contrast to Malthus, Ehrlich saw no means of avoiding the disaster, although he proposed a goal of zero population growth:

> The battle to feed all of humanity is over. In the 1970s and 1980s hundreds of millions of people will starve to death in spite of any crash programs embarked upon now. At this late date nothing can prevent a substantial increase in the world death rate.[12]

The famines predicted by Ehrlich did not come about, but even so this apocalyptic literature written by him and others was enormously influential, and perpetuated Malthus' unfounded assumption of the inability of the poor to control their own sexuality, in contrast to peoples presumed to be more "civilized." Like Malthus, these mid–20th-century prophets set to one side social, cultural, and gendered contingencies inevitably implicated in human reproduction, while creating a climate in which population control was considered to be a matter of the utmost urgency.

Addressing the "Problem" of Population

We turn next to an overview of the science of eugenics, entirely discredited by virtually everyone today, that profoundly influenced the history of family planning and its implementation and, more broadly, global programs for population control. This is followed by a detailed account of the introduction of technologies of population control in India and China expressly designed to manage "excess fertility" in which not only government officials but also health care professionals are deeply implicated. The focus of our attention is on the effects brought about by these programs locally, notably on their unintended consequences, particularly that of sex selection.[13] This chapter closes with an ethnographic case study concerning the reproductive strategies made use of by Palestinian women living in Israel. These latter research findings contrast with those of India and China because Palestinian women live in a situation of ongoing political conflict in which their ethnicity is the most important variable taken into account by the government of Israel in formulating reproductive policy. For their part, Palestinian women are divided among themselves as to how reproduction and individual family size may best assist them with economic survival and the very survival of their communities.

The Palestinian case is a striking example of how population growth can be perceived as an enormous political threat, and not simply an economic burden, due to the potential for increased block voting power, and hence the possibility for radical societal transformation, unwanted by those in power. In India similar concerns are at work, but grounded primarily in divisions based on affiliation by caste, even though official efforts to abolish that system were begun in 1950 and by 1976 it was generally assumed that its abolition was being reliably enforced. However, in retrospect this has not been the case and there is evidence to this day of some aspects of the caste system still at work. Concerns about the aggregation of power by burgeoning numbers of poor and ethnic minorities are particularly apparent in national and local discourses that highlight the urgency of population reduction. Such concerns are exacerbated by a voluntary reduction in population size associated with a middle-class lifestyle and particularly with the education of women, the result of social and economic development. However, political concerns are inseparable from and often made essentially invisible by the economic arguments put out by global enterprises and organizations, and equally by national governments, about the supposed burden imposed by the simple existence of too many people. The effects of neo-liberal economies that have brought about increased poverty and very often dramatically reduced social security make the situation all the more fraught with concern.

A final introductory note: although governance designed to encourage reduced fertility is highlighted in this chapter, in certain situations, notably at times of war and under totalitarian regimes, population increase is frequently demanded and tracked by national statistics. As with population reduction, members of the medical profession and other health care professionals very often enforce government mandates for population increase. A case in point is that of Nicolae Ceaușescu's Romania where, from the mid-1960s to 1989, great pressure was placed on women to have four or five children in order to enlarge the labor force for the socialist state. This was a time of great economic hardship, making it difficult to raise large families. Women had very limited access to birth control, and in any case most were unfamiliar with the idea of contraception. Despite a realistic fear about heavy penalties for themselves and their doctors if they sought out illegal abortions, many desperate women did so.[14]

The inordinate power of enumeration, especially when humans are the units that are counted – whether their numbers are too great or too few – informs many of the most dramatic social transformations that have been brought about over the past 100 years.

Improving the Stock of Nations

In the late 19th century, Francis Galton, a first cousin of Charles Darwin, set himself the task of investigating the origins of "natural ability." He gave the name "eugenics," meaning "good in birth," or "noble in heredity," to the program he devised, the ultimate objective of which was human improvement. Among the first investigators to apply mathematical enumeration to human characteristics and considered a founder of modern statistics, Galton was attracted to the newly found concept of "normal distribution" known today as the Bell curve, originally developed by Carl Friedrich Gauss to explain planetary positions in astronomy. Galton was particularly interested in deviation about the mean of the curve, and devised experiments in order to demonstrate how statistics could be used to advance understanding of human heredity. He established an anthropometric laboratory in London and was joined by Arthur Pearson, described by one of his colleagues as "a lump of ice," whose function was to transform the study of biology into something resembling a hard science that would therefore establish it as the standard for understanding population phenomena. Pearson was the first to describe a theory of correlation that he then applied to numerical data he had collected, on the basis of which he declared: "We are forced, I think literally forced, to the general conclusion that the physical and psychical characters in man are inherited within broad lines in the same manner, and with the same intensity."[15] In giving the 1903 Huxley lecture to the Anthropological Institute in London, Pearson argued: "No training or education can create [intelligence], you must breed it," a statement that delighted Galton.[16]

Galton had already proposed that the human race might be actively improved along the lines of animal and plant breeding that had long prevailed in husbandry. "Undesirables" would be eliminated, and efforts would be made to permit the multiplication of "desirables" – approaches that he labeled negative and positive eugenics respectively. The only means available to achieve such objectives in Galton's day was to enact policies in which the state was assigned control over the reproductive lives of individuals designated as a burden to society. Sterilization of women, almost all of it involuntary, was the method by which this was usually accomplished. Much less was done to actively implement positive eugenics, although several government initiatives in the United States and Europe encouraged people to emulate those families in the public eye who were deemed by officials to be particularly healthy in mind and body because of their exemplary way of life.

The practice of eugenics was first firmly consolidated in the United States. As Daniel Kevles puts it: "Eugenics was British by invention and American by legislative enactment."[17] Charles Davenport, an American biologist well versed in the science of his day, devoted his time to the creation and collection of family pedigrees. Among other things, he observed that "pauperism," "criminality," and especially "feeble-mindedness" were, in his estimation, heritable. On the basis of these observations Davenport argued that individuals with such traits should be prohibited from reproducing so that defective protoplasm might be eliminated from the gene pool. In 1912 Davenport proclaimed: "Prevent the feeble minded, drunkards, paupers, sex offenders, and criminalistic from marrying their like or cousins or any person belonging to a neuropathic strain. Then the crop of defectives will be reduced to practically nothing."[18]

The Harvard geneticist E. M. East went further than most of his colleagues and argued that the biggest challenge lay hidden in the population of heterozygotes – the unaffected carriers of just one of the supposedly defective genes. This biological concept underlay his recommendation to put whole families under surveillance – a matter of urgency he claimed, because "civilized" societies permit the numbers of "defective" people to increase by means of medicine and charities that interfere with natural selection and keep them alive.[19] Comments such as these were well publicized, and thousands of Americans gave financial support to the activities of the Eugenics Record Office in Cold Spring Harbor, of which Davenport was the director. Eugenics was transformed rapidly in the early part of the 20th century from a rather obscure science formed around Francis Galton and his colleagues into a major political movement.

The link between biology and politics was, from the mid–19th to the early years of the 20th century, driven by the concept of "degeneracy," initially set out in the mid–19th century by Herbert Spencer when formulating his ideas about social evolution.[20] A pervasive fear of the time – the product of Malthusian ideas about the "natural laws" of poverty – was that the quality of populations, and hence the vitality of nations, was under threat because people who had inherited weak constitutions and were lacking in energy and of low intelligence were likely to "breed" faster than others, thus diluting the "germ plasm" of the nation. Applied eugenics could purge the population of this unwanted degeneracy.

It is sometimes forgotten that many staunch supporters of eugenics in the early part of the 20th century were progressive-minded socialists. Arthur Pearson was one, as were prominent public figures such as Emma Goldman, George Bernard Shaw, H. G. Wells, John Maynard Keynes, Margaret Sanger, Theodore Roosevelt, and Emile Zola. Among these writers and activists, the eugenics movement was recognized not only as a means to improve the biological stock of nations but, even more important, as a foundation for social reform. Margaret Sanger wrote that "Those least fit to carry on the race are increasing most rapidly … Funds that should be used to raise the standard of our civilization are diverted to maintenance of those who should never have been born."[21]

The eugenics movement, supported by many geneticists, grew stronger during the Great Depression[22] and research into diabetes, epilepsy, syphilis, feeble-mindedness, and other diseases was motivated not merely by an interest in the mechanism of the diseases, but by a concern about the resulting financial burden to society, contributing to the growing role of biology as the reference for addressing population problems. In the United States, it is estimated that something like 50,000 individuals were forcibly sterilized during the first half of the 20th century. This practice was replicated in Canada, South Africa, and across northern Europe, including the socialist countries of Scandinavia, with Germany being by far the most extreme example. Lawsuits continue to the present day in connection with these practices that persisted in all these countries until the 1970s. Similar programs were developed in Japan and China where, as in Europe, intellectuals were deeply involved in devising eugenic programs.[23] An upsurge of nationalism and militarism and concern about racial inferiority with respect to the West drove these programs in Asia. However, in both China and Japan emphasis was given to improvement of the quality of the population. In Japan measures were taken to ameliorate public health and environmental conditions with a view to elevating the health of the nation as a whole; above all, improvements in the health and education of women of reproductive age, rather than sterilization of those labeled as unfit, were the chosen methods.[24] This approach to eugenics reflects longstanding East Asian medical assumptions that, with the exception of certain extreme conditions, the health and behavior of peoples are formed primarily by early socialization and social interactions throughout life, rather than being biologically determined.

The historian Diane Paul raises an important question in connection with the eugenics movement in Europe and North America. She asks: "Did eugenics rest on an elementary mistake?"[25] Eugenicists in the early part of the 20th century argued explicitly that mental defects are linked to a recessive Mendelian factor (in today's language, an allele), leading some commentators to suggest that eugenicists were in error if they believed that by sterilizing only those individuals thought to be "defective," the "factor" for defectiveness would thereby be eliminated from the population. Paul notes that the eugenics movement expanded after the time when the mistaken beliefs of some early eugenicists had been thoroughly exposed. After reviewing the literature of the day, she came to the conclusion that the majority of eugenicists were satisfied that eugenic sterilization, even though they knew it would not eliminate the defective "factor" from the population as a whole, would nevertheless slow down deterioration, making sterilization highly worthwhile.[26] In other words, rather than rigorous scientific argument, the prevalent ideology of degeneracy, shared by very many influential people of the day, prevailed, and justified the widespread implementation of government-supported sterilization.

The development of technologies that targeted the female hormone cycle in order to regulate fertility – bio-contraceptive technologies – had the potential to manipulate reproduction successfully on a population-wide basis. The effectiveness of these bio-contraceptive technologies made it clear that biology not only could be a powerful standard for developing technological solutions for medical problems but also could address political and social concerns about reproduction that had previously been the object of economic and social reforms. The early birth control movement strongly supported Margaret Sanger's eugenicist views, and a 1940 joint meeting of the Birth Control Federation of America and the Citizens' Committee for Planned Parenthood was entitled "Race Building in a Democracy." It is not by chance that family planning in the United States initially targeted African Americans living in East Coast inner cities.[27]

The idea of global population control came to dominate thinking from the 1950s, no doubt spurred on by concerns about the obvious unrest associated with decolonization and the ambition to engineer "development" through social and economic "modernization." Whereas many influential thinkers in the early birth control movement, including Sanger, emphasized sexual freedom and women's rights when referring to people such as herself (although in her opinion such freedoms did not apply to the less well off[28]), a neo-Malthusian position is clearly visible in post-eugenic family planning discourse. It was argued that a nation's prosperity and stability could not be considered apart from reproductive behavior in all families. This position was not simply taken with respect to domestic policy but, of even more importance, became part of foreign policy.[29] A sensibility began to emerge in connection with birth control about "a moderate, restrained 'us' and the teeming, profligate 'them.' "[30] In postwar London in the early 1950s, in full knowledge of Nazi eugenic practices, the International Planned Parenthood Association rented its offices free of charge from the English Eugenics Society. And in North America Planned Parenthood–World Population took on as its main objective to "sell" the importance of international population control to the American public.[31]

The increasing availability of birth control devices based on the manipulation of human biology raised anxieties, because the assumption was that the middle classes would avail themselves of such technologies, whereas the poor would not do so. One of the most outspoken critics of the day was Garrett Hardin who published an article in *Science* entitled "The Tragedy of the Commons." Hardin's assumption was that family planning would not stop the population growth of the poor, who would both destroy the environment and reduce the caliber of American society.[32] But comments such as those of Hardin did not stop moves already under way in the 1960s to link global economic development to the implementation of population control, and being a recipient of non-military foreign aid was tied to the implementation of population control programs. In 1965, Lyndon Johnson, then president of the United States, officially backed family planning, linking its importance to the "global war on poverty."[33] As Helen Epstein notes: "Suddenly population control was the leading edge of development ... and the fate of the planet seemed to hinge upon the rapid expansion of family planning programs, especially in Asia."[34]

These programs, not surprisingly, were top-down in design with little if any local input, and were part of the Cold War climate in which it was feared that communism would spread throughout the "population powder kegs" of the Third World, enabling the enemy to take over the world.[35] A fear of the "other," very evident in strategies for population control, created a backlash that profoundly influenced the way in which population planning was implemented in non-Western countries. Critics in Asia, Latin America, and the United States argued in refutation of these policies that such neo-Malthusian ideas were both incorrect and dangerous. They insisted, contrary to Malthus, that population growth was not causal of poverty and inequality, but that the reverse was the case. The history of family planning programs in Haiti, the poorest country in the Western hemisphere, starkly illustrates this claim.

Life expectancy in Haiti has decreased over the past decade to 49 years of age, during which time the cost of living has nearly quadrupled. In the large slum community called Cité Soleil, a five-square-kilometer infamous slum in Port-au-Prince, the medical anthropologist Catherine Maternowska researched a family planning program and talked with women who said there are only two diseases to contend with – "hunger sickness" and sexually transmitted diseases. While some of the earliest clinical trials of oral bio-contraceptives were conducted by Americans in Haiti in 1957,[36] as early as 1964 Haitian-designed strategies for family planning were implemented in several Haitian villages as part of a broad primary health care initiative that tackled matters directly relating not only to public health but also to literacy and food production. Notably, these strategies did not view reproduction in strictly biological terms but rather as a broader social issue. At the end of the first two years, 40 percent of the adult population in three villages were practicing family planning in their reproductive years. Maternowska notes: "contraceptive levels in Haiti have never been recorded at such high levels since,"[37] even though surveys over the past decades have shown repeatedly that women in Haiti desire fewer children. Using both a historical approach to document the origins of the mind-numbing conditions in which the majority of people in Haiti try to exist today, as well as intense long-term ethnographic investigation, Maternowska describes what she terms a "political economy of reproduction." She documents the way in which the current United States Agency for International Development (USAID) funded top-down, privately run, family planning programs in Cité Soleil and was allowed to usurp attempts by the Haitian government to provide family planning as part of a broader primary health care initiative.

The USAID program in Haiti is focused solely on bio-contraceptive technologies, including injections, implants, and the pill. Program records make it all too evident that very poor patient–provider interaction takes place, and the part-time elite Haitian doctors and certain of the nurses explicitly treat clients as both inferior and stupid. Sexually transmitted diseases are rarely dealt with, because the program's objectives are limited to the dissemination of birth control. Clients must pay a "small cost" consisting of initial and follow-up fees – it is assumed that the service will not be valued unless people are made to pay for it. Women wait minimally for over an hour to be seen (during which time they could be working) and are then granted a minute or two by the doctor, unless it is the first visit when an internal exam is required. It is not explained to women why such an examination is necessary. People who are placed on injectable contraceptives must buy their own syringe – the equivalent of a small can of tomato paste – and they must also pay for any test that is ordered. Maternowska argues:

> Weighed against the urgent need to pay rent or prepare a meal for a hungry family, the long-term "benefits" of family planning quickly lose their value. Poverty in Cité Soleil reduces choices to the short term. The costs and benefits of seeking treatment are weighed scrupulously against other immediate competing needs, including water and food.[38]

The distribution of bio-contraceptive technologies, the *raison d'être* for most family planning programs, is embedded today in the global neo-liberal economy in which population reduction is the sole objective of reducing family size among the poor, wherever they reside. One reason why these programs receive a great deal of funding is because "population" is a highly naturalized category, one that "operates as a vast field of power, with its own imaginaries, discourses, institutional apparatuses, political technologies, and social effects."[39] The case studies that follow richly illustrate, as does the Haitian situation set out above, that although mobilization of the category of population and the perceived need for its control are framed by distinct, historical, political, and culturally informed ways in local contexts, biology is the standard that enables technical intervention.

Alternative Modernity and Indian Family Planning

Interest in Malthusian and eugenicist ideas was evident in India from the late 19th century where discussion about population size took place among both colonists and Indian nationalists. In the early 20th century Margaret Sanger was invited to India to encourage the use of birth control. Later, following a national inquiry after the Bengal famine of 1945, a program of population policy was called for, and in 1952 the Indian state became the first in the world to initiate a population control program that, as a matter of course, framed intervention in terms of human biology. This program, integral to the nationalist development agenda, was at once an appropriation of and a resistance to a Western conception of the modern.[40] The Rockefeller Foundation, Ford Foundation, USAID, the United Nations, and the World Bank, all concerned at the time about the "excess" population in India, invested in the population control movement, and gave funds to train local administrators and front-line workers. However, these contributions have never exceeded 25 percent of the total funding for family planning, allowing the Indian state to pursue its objective of implementing population control as part of its larger plan of "domesticating modernity."[41] There is evidence that many Indian families were voluntarily attempting to reduce their family size before family planning was made government policy, but this depended a great deal on the occupation and source of income of the involved families.[42]

Mahmood Mamdani has written about a well-known birth control program designed expressly to deal with "overpopulation" that was implemented in 1954 in rural Khanna in the Punjab. This program, described categorically by Mamdani as a failure, was kept going at great expense until 1960. When interviewing participants with large families who had been given contraceptive tablets by the program organizers, Mamdani was told that it would have been rude to refuse the pills when health workers came expressly to their door to distribute them. The pills were politely accepted and stored away or used as decorative objects. Mamdani shows graphically how the Jats in Khanna, the agricultural classes, were quick to adopt other types of technologies related to their work, thus achieving a measure of independence from the powerful Brahmins that controlled their lives. But even introduction of tractors into the community, that reduced to some extent the need for manual labor, did not mean that these farmers were prepared to reduce the size of their families. Only a great deal more mechanization could have supplanted the indispensable labor in the fields of all the family members, including women and children. Only a very small percentage of government employees, teachers, and other administrators were amenable to family planning – about 5 percent of the entire population. When asked, it was clear that the majority believed strongly that small families and, worse still, infertility, caused poverty, and not the other way around. The villagers argued vociferously that economic and family security were both entirely dependent on large families. They could not believe, even six years after its implementation, that the goal of the Khanna program was solely to limit the size of their families; they assumed that there was some other much darker objective, perhaps involving a take-over once again by "foreigners."[43]

At the national level other problems arose. In its nationwide advertising campaigns associated with family planning from the 1960s on, the Indian state is unambiguous that a small family is the means to material prosperity and that technology can substitute for human labor in rural India. However, Nilanjana Chatterjee argues that changes in the West associated with effective family planning, particularly in connection with the reproductive rights of women, went against the grain of an emerging postcolonial Indian nationalism. In part this response by nationalists was a reaction to the former imperial regime that had roundly criticized "overpopulation," but some Indian leaders also questioned the morality associated with contraceptive use and, further, a threat to patriarchy was explicitly of concern.[44] Indian women figured at the center of nationalist reformist agendas, and were portrayed as embodiments of that which is spiritually unique and morally upright in society.

Not surprisingly, in this climate, a program that focused on increasing the availability of information about contraception and motivating individuals, specifically women, to adopt family planning strategies, failed to produce a decline of any magnitude in the birth rate. The government was already well aware that in some locations it had been shown convincingly that voluntary reduction in family size was only effective when financial and old age security, food security, land reform, and improved education were dealt with reasonably satisfactorily and female discrimination was lessened.[45] There was nevertheless a pervasive sense among government officials that India could not afford to wait until such time as these matters of gigantic proportion were taken care of, and bio-contraception offered an apparently quick and easy solution. The focus was instead to be one of motivating individuals, resulting inevitably in a confrontation with deeply embedded values supported by nationalists.

As had happened at the time of the Bengal famine, once again in the 1960s widespread flooding and accompanying food shortages made reduction of the population size an urgent matter, and a "target and incentive driven population control program" was put in place, in which the government actively promoted the use of birth control. In 1975 the then Prime Minister, Indira Gandhi, proclaimed a state of emergency, in effect giving herself the power to rule by decree because of what she perceived to be enormous political unrest. This announcement was followed by 19 months of tightly implemented state control, during which time various policies were implemented with "brutal efficiency,"[46] among them coercive sterilization programs, overseen by Gandhi's son Sanjay Gandhi, the effects of which are still evident today. Over eight million sterilizations, frequently carried out in unhygienic conditions and often accompanied by violence, were performed in one year alone, for which the involved health care workers received monetary rewards when they achieved a prescribed number. People living in urban slums from the lowest socioeconomic strata who were occupying what were termed "unauthorized dwellings" were primarily targeted.

The anthropologist Emma Tarlo documents how, in Delhi, a growing market arose involving "bodies and space" during the "sterilization time" as it is now known, the objective of which was to stop people reproducing further, once they had two children. Incentives were given to employers who met targets for sterilization among their employees, and employers were not above withholding salaries until there was proof that sterilization had been carried out.[47] Tarlo documents a "hierarchy of motivation" that was informally established with the result that those at the lowest economic levels were disproportionately sterilized. Making matters worse, in Delhi a city ruling tied proof of sterilization to the right to have government-supported housing and government loans. For many, the choice was one between homelessness or sterilization, their previous dwellings having already been torn down. A black market in certificates of proof of sterilization came into existence, and the poorest of the poor were bribed, often by hired brokers, to submit themselves to sterilization, and then to hand the certificates over to the "professional motivators."[48] The bribes – cans of ghee, clocks, radios, and in some places rickshaw licenses – had to exceed the value of government incentives to undergo sterilization. As Tarlo notes, sterilization had much more to do with property rights than with family planning. When she interviewed people about the "sterilization time" several likened what had happened to the exploitative organ trade today; blame was frequently laid with petty bureaucrats and brokers who directly exploited the vulnerable, rather than with the central government. For many, human frailty was perceived as the real cause of this "critical event"[49] in Indian history.

Over the years, the family planning program in India has changed a great deal, in large part as a result of the growth of women's groups and the emergence of a substantial urban middle class. Both fertility and mortality rates have declined overall, but great variation exists among the states. In absolute terms, an increase in the population, currently standing at well over one billion, steadily persists. Tamil Nadu is a state that has been successful in reducing its fertility rate, and family planning practices are not as draconian as they were formerly, although a target system remains in place in the health care sector. Anthropologist Cecilia Van Hollen has documented the way in which monetary incentives continued to be provided in hospitals in Tamil Nadu throughout the 1990s for "motivation" of men and women to accept sterilization and insertion of intrauterine devices (IUDs), small coils placed in the uterus to prevent pregnancy.[50] The routinization of IUD insertion in Tamil Nadu has caused distress among a good number of women, many of whom say that they did not select this contraceptive method or that they had no idea that it had been inserted. A large number complain of discomfort and side effects, and serious complications can arise in those who are not carefully screened for infections before insertion of the device.

Following the 1994 UN conference on population held in Cairo, these bio-contraceptive practices in Tamil Nadu and elsewhere in India were challenged from the highest levels. NGOs documented human rights abuses associated with the target approach and also criticized clinical trials of Depo-Provera and Norplant, both contraceptives, in Northern India. As a result, in Tamil Nadu it was announced in 1995 that the target program would be stopped, and in 1996 a national "target-free" reproductive health care (RHC) program was inaugurated supported by the World Bank, USAID, UNICEF, and other international organizations. However, Van

Hollen argues that although this new program was decentralized and reorganized at district levels, and although in theory targeting was to be stopped, in practice, it continued to be encouraged. Van Hollen also found that although sterilization and IUD insertion were no longer to be required of people seeking abortions, implementation of this policy was very uneven.[51] She notes that from the mid-1990s women often willingly wanted to make use of contraception for economic reasons but, even so, coercive attitudes persisted in many hospitals. A modified authoritarian, top-down model remained in place at the local level, one that focused heavily on the medical control of sexuality of the "masses" by means of family planning, abortion services, and control of sexually transmitted infections, without paying attention to the concerns of individual women, or the broader economic, social, and cultural factors that have been shown repeatedly to contribute to the voluntary adoption of birth control.

Following the tsunami in 2004, Tamil Nadu has been offering survivors who lost all their children reversals of tubal ligation free of cost at government-run hospitals. Over 2,300 children under the age of 18 died as a result of the tsunami, and many others were left as orphans. In some families where the sons died but the girls remain alive, it has been reported that parents are desperate to be given assistance with the use of ultrasound to give birth to a boy. Local family planning experts argue that the failure of the Indian government to promote easily reversible contraceptive methods, including the pill, IUDs, and condoms, had led to this situation, and that far too many women had been coerced into undergoing permanent sterilization in order to meet population targets.[52] Social activists are concerned that the high-profile sterilization reversal program feeds into broad cultural biases that validate women only if they bear and raise children, especially boys, to adulthood. Concerns are also being raised because the operation does not guarantee a healthy pregnancy. One public hospital in Chennai (formerly Madras), Tamil Nadu's capital, reports that just 47 percent of its re-canalization patients have given birth. It has also been noted that initially no one was willing to adopt an orphan but, perhaps, in cases where tubal ligation reversal is not successful, this may change.[53]

The Indian example attests to how framing the population "problem" in apparently neutral biological terms allowed it to be harnessed to political projects, such as Indian modernization, that were vastly different from the political vision apparent in eugenicist population control programs. The emergence of biology as a standard also enabled the application of biomedical technologies to human reproduction on a large scale. The far-reaching, often unforeseen consequences of such high-profile, government-sponsored reproductive interventions point to the perils of standardizing human bodies and behavior through biology.

Following is another brief example of the paradoxical effects of biologically standardized attempts to regulate human reproduction. In a landmark study, anthropologist Caroline Bledsoe, working in the West African nation of the Gambia, documented how women use contraception to increase their fertility. Bledsoe came upon this contradictory finding in her analysis of the data from a larger, demographic project.[54] For many Western women, and for family planning programs, contraception is promoted to encourage "birth spacing" as a way of reducing total number of births. This approach assumes that a woman's reproductive years are biologically invariable and, therefore, the further apart births are, the fewer children will be born. However this ostensibly sensible biological standard contains, as Bledsoe and others have

shown, a number of unexamined assumptions. The first is that births in
produce healthy living children. This is clearly not the case for most wome
Saharan Africa, where as many as one in five children do not survive to age five. 1..
second assumption is that for all women there is a "natural" limit to fertility (that is,
the end of ovulation). The third is that an ability to bear children is unaffected by
life events. Bledsoe shows how women in the Gambia have an understanding of
fertility that is at times radically different from these hidden assumptions. Gambian
women understand their bodies, and their ability to bear children, as profoundly
affected by life events – including previous pregnancies – that may "tire" the body
and deplete it of reproductive potential. Moreover, the ability to bear a child that
survives at least to childhood is conditioned on a host of factors, as Bledsoe points
out. By allowing pregnancies to occur at a propitious time – for instance, when the
body has had time to rest or when food is readily available – contraceptives actually
work to increase fertility, understood as the number of surviving children.[55]

The One-Child Policy

Since the founding of the People's Republic of China (PRC) in 1949, the size of the
Chinese population, standing today at over 1.3 billion, has been of abiding concern
to consecutive governments. It is often assumed that the fertility decline in China
over the past 30 years, the fastest ever recorded to below replacement level, is due
entirely to the infamous one-child policy with the result that internationally, "the
PRC has been both acclaimed for its responsible slowing of population growth and
denounced for its repression of reproductive rights."[56] However, it is impossible to
distinguish, after the fact, between the separate effects of education, provision of
contraceptives, socioeconomic development, and the coercive component of the one-
child policy that make China distinct from other parts of the world.[57] For one thing,
the most dramatic decrease in fertility rate, from 5.9 to 2.9, occurred between 1970
and 1979, strongly suggesting that economic changes, and not biomedical intervention, were more powerful determinants of fertility. After the one-child policy was
introduced and implemented from 1980 on, the rate fell more gradually, and since
1995 has stabilized at around 1.7. It is quite possible, therefore, that China's total
fertility rate would have decreased very significantly without the one-child policy.[58]

The apparatus needed to bring about a nationwide orchestration of reproduction
was set in place in about 1975 (the exact date remains unclear), and the one-child
policy was launched in 1979–1980. This policy came about in large part as the result
of a "fetishization of numbers" on the part of Chinese demographers in which an
"ideology of population reduction" was adopted in order to catapult the entire
country into a modernized economy.[59] Mao Zedong was the "father" of birth planning in China. He was convinced, especially when confronted by the famine associated with the Great Leap Forward, that even in rural areas population growth had
to be slowed down, but the assumption was that this should be both gradual and
voluntary. Mao, in common with many other socialists, did not in principle accept
Malthusian arguments, but he nevertheless acknowledged a "socialist birth problem"[60]
because it had become clear to him that one result of the subsidies made available as
part of the socialization process of both urban and rural populations was an increase

in family size. Mao never explicitly conceded that China had too many people or that socialism could not support them; instead he began to argue that planning births would be the rational and scientific thing to do.[61]

Susan Greenhalgh, an anthropologist and demographer, has kept track of policy-making over the past 20 years in connection with birth planning in China, and in her recent book, based largely on numerous interviews conducted both in the past and the present with Chinese scientists and policy-makers, she sets out a rich account of the crucial years of the late 1970s and early 1980s in connection with what she calls "population science" in China. Her objective in this book is to expose a brief historical trajectory of the "messy intertanglings of science and technology with politics, policy, and power."[62] Greenhalgh points out that over most of the history of the PRC, science has been subordinated to the Chinese Communist Party (CPR) with the result that many practices labeled as "science" are informed by party politics. She also notes that Marxian social science has always counted as a basic science, and matters relating to population fell into this domain. However, during the 27 years of Maoist domination from 1949 to 1976, social science research was virtually abolished and natural science research was also suppressed. Significantly, "defense science," promoted to ensure national security, remained relatively untouched and the idea that this type of science could be a panacea for the huge social and economic problems that China faced, especially in the early Maoist era, was very popular. Under these conditions, "scientism" and its twin "technicism" flourished, and in the Deng era, when the one-child policy was put in place, they had become virtually official ideologies about how best to deal with all social and economic matters.[63]

In the 1960s, in the waning years of Mao's rule, his premier, Zhou Enlai, succeeded in placing the idea of birth planning on the political agenda. Arguments were put forward for later marriages, contraceptive use, and for sterilization after the birth of two children. However, Malthus' thesis continued to be thought of as having no relevance to China because of its association with capitalist economies.[64] The idea of specific targets for reduction in population size was first introduced into policy-making circles in the late 1970s after the death of Mao and the arrest of the Gang of Four. Deng Xiaoping brought about a shift in the nation's agenda to one of rapid modernization, and it was in this newly emerging climate that it became possible to openly discuss population control. At this time three distinctively Marxist-inspired Chinese sciences of population – one grounded in statistics, a second that made use of a Chinese school of population cybernetics, and a third group composed of so-called "humanists" (who were directly concerned about the impact of targeted reductions on the peasant population) – vied to have their respective policies officially implemented.

Close analysis by Greenhalgh of the micro-politics of this struggle reveals how the population cybernetics group, constituted by scientists who had formerly worked on missile science and who were extremely adept with mathematical formulations, won the day. This group was the only one to be influenced by recommendations being made by the powerful Club of Rome in connection with population management, and by Western population science. The cybernetics group regarded "population" as a biological phenomenon "subject to universally applicable models in which local culture, politics, and society did not matter."[65] An endorsement of biology as the standard for addressing the population "problem" is clear in their forceful argument put before the Chinese government for the application of science to eliminate igno-rance and superstitious beliefs. Drawing on ideas, images, and numbers from the Club of Rome and from China's own strategic military doctrines, the Chinese cyber-neticists created a narrative about a population crisis that was ruining the country's chance of becoming by century's end a rich, powerful, modern nation.[66] On the basis of predictions depicted by means of tables and graphs showing an exponential increase in population size if left unmanaged, in contrast to the statisticians and the humanists, the cyberneticists insisted that if a "one child for all" policy was not enacted right away China simply could not modernize.

The use of military metaphors by the cybernetic group reinforced their position that an assumed "optimal population" of 650–700 million appropriate for 100 years in the future was a target that must be met. This estimated demographic "carrying capacity" is a population roughly two-thirds the size of China's 1980 population. As Greenhalgh points out, the Chinese cybernetic scientists suffered from the same dif-ficulties as Western demographers, namely, that despite a claim to scientific precision, the complex economic, ecological, social, and demographic data needed to make these calculations were simply not available. The cyberneticist's projections amounted to rhetoric and nothing more, but the "apparent truth" of the measurements pre-sented to policy-makers was sufficient to impress those in the highest realms of power. Many obstacles remained, and a great deal of resistance persisted about the imple-mentation of a one-child policy, but it was an era of excitement as China began to embrace ideas and technologies from the West that would eventually come to inform population policies, although no foreigners were privy to internal government discus-sion. Greenhalgh notes that, in contrast to India, China openly set out to "embrace the global narrative of the West's scientific and technological superiority and sought to selectively adopt Western science and technology to achieve its own nationalistic goals."[67]

When the government first adopted the idea of a one-child family, it was stated that such a policy was to be a short-term measure and that it would be replaced in the near future by a "voluntary small-family culture."[68] A slogan proclaiming that "best is one, at most two; eliminate third births" was put out by the government in 1978. This was followed in September 1980 by a formally codified policy extolling "one for all" after extensive efforts to educate the public on the importance of limit-ing family size for the survival of the country as a whole. Between 1980 and 1984 a strict process of "one-childization" (*yutaihua*) was enforced,[69] during which time, with Deng Xiaoping's encouragement, persuasion of citizens could be legally sup-plemented by coercion. Administration and monitoring of reproductive practices was decentralized at this time and local cadres and health workers were made responsible for enforcement of policies. People with more than one child were subject to punitive fines, and by the mid-1980s there was a widespread peasant backlash to the nation-wide sterilization campaign under way for families with two children.[70]

In the early 1980s the Chinese government made contact with the International Planned Parenthood Federation, and during this time the PRC began for the first time to receive support from the United Nations to implement population control, including funds to improve the quality of contraceptives and training for demogra-phers and census-takers. Perhaps due to encouragement from these outside agencies, as early as 1984 modifications of a strict one-child policy began to be implemented, modifications that in effect remain in place today. Approximately 30 percent of the Chinese population lives in urban areas where the one-child policy has always been strictly enforced. Among the 70 percent rural population, in some areas 40 percent of couples are allowed a second child if the firstborn is a girl. In other rural areas a second child is commonly allowed five years after the birth of the first child, but only if the first child is a girl, or if the family has undergone great hardship. These policies tacitly support an ideology of son preference among rural families. A third child is allowed in Tibet and other relatively sparsely populated remote rural areas populated by ethnic minorities. The effectiveness of this policy is entirely dependent on essentially universal access to bio-contraception and abortion. By far the most commonly used bio-contraceptive techniques are IUDs and sterilization and research suggests that 80 percent or more of women have no choice about what contraceptive technique they use.[71]

Further policy changes took place during the 1990s when China began to move toward "a socialist market economy." Planning and management of production and reproduction were linked together to further modernization. Improvement of supervision over reproduction was introduced, designed in large part to limit corruption on the part of local officials, some of whom were extorting money from families with more than one child, destroying the houses of non-compliant people, and locking up others. By the mid-1990s figures showed a steady reduction in the birth rate toward the goal of 1.2 billion by the turn of the twenty-first century, and at this time too, China started to receive substantial assistance from the Ford Foundation, the Rockefeller Foundation, and the Japanese Organization for International Cooperation in Family Planning. China's participation in the groundbreaking 1994 Cairo Conference on Population and Development was crucial to further policy modifications.

Over the past decade China's economic reforms have moved further from socialism to embrace a neo-liberal market ideology. It is evident that the population has internalized the idea of family controlled limited reproduction through "discipline",[72] and recent surveys in urban areas and the better off rural areas reveal that 50 percent of respondents claim that they have no preference for a son.[73] The government, now relatively safe in the knowledge that the ideology of population control is entrenched in many of its peoples, is itself beginning to acknowledge some of the damage that was done over the past decades, and an explicit move has been made toward "client centered approaches" to population control rather than simply enforced bio-contraceptive use.[74]

Some discussion is under way today to consider a two-child policy. This would not solve the age- and sex-structure imbalances that have resulted from the one-child policy, but in the years to come it could ease the unavoidable social crises that are now taking place. Greenhalgh argues that the human costs of "one-childization" have been enormous and, further, that these costs are distributed unevenly across the country, with rural women, infant girls, and unborn females being the most severely affected. She insists that the "cultural injury to people's subjectivity ... and to their moral equanimity" is inestimable and that the "peasant" population, tagged "large in quantity and low in quality" has for two decades been targeted for coercive control, thus heightening rural–urban inequalities.[75] The impact of forced sterilization of women was perhaps the most damaging procedure, closely resembling in the minds of local people the spaying of animals.[76] Increased female morbidity, particularly in rural areas, is associated with the one-child policy because those women who choose to go ahead with a pregnancy after they already have one child do so in secret and without any health care. Abortion, when carried out, is not infrequently at a late stage of pregnancy.[77] Among local village cadres who must enforce the draconian version of the policy, many resisted, falsified numbers, and resigned their post, all the while dealing with entreaties and curses from their fellow villagers.[78] Trafficking of children, in particular young boys, is a burgeoning problem.[79] And in the near future, a lack of support for the elderly, very few of whom have any social security, will be an enormous predicament.

Although in the early part of the 19th century China had emulated Europe and adopted eugenics as a means of improving the race, as we have seen, in the Maoist era eugenics was rejected outright as a tool of imperialism. However, discussion about the "quality" of the population, to be achieved through the use of nurturance and education to which, in theory, all Chinese have equal access, became prevalent again in the latter part of the 20th century. The anthropologist Ann Anagnost was struck in the 1990s by the way in which an official rhetoric about quality had become extensively elaborated not only as part of the party line, but also in everyday life in China. Moreover, quality had become a central metaphor for overcoming a perceived backwardness in comparison to the West or Japan. Anagnost, while doing research in China, encountered people who, after admiring her son, would declare that the "quality" of Western children was higher than that in China – Western bodies being larger, more supple, and with a glow of health.[80] Lock encountered similar comments about her children when carrying out research in Japan in the early 1970s, and it appears that comments about the superiority of Western children could be heard in Japan from the end of the 19th century.[81] First in Japan and then in China, investment in a healthy population of biological quality – a potential wealth in the form of bodies that labor, produce, and consume – is thought of as essential to successful modernization. In theory, if not always in practice, no one is expressly excluded from this project, and efforts to bring about this quality in the entire population are, in effect, a form of "positive" rather than "negative eugenics."

We turn now to the troubling problem of an imbalance in the sex ratio at birth in favor of males that has been so widely reported in both India and China. These imbalances are undeniably associated with government policies in connection with population control resulting in an enforced reduction in family size. Government policies exacerbate a situation of son preference that results primarily from social and cultural mores, local legal practices, and, above all, a lack of economic and social security if sons are not born into the family. This situation demands thoughtful contextualization before hasty judgment is passed or a label of neo-eugenics is affixed to these practices, as some have done.[82] It should be noted at the outset that a careful perusal of comparative population statistics by two economic demographers has shown that females "go missing" at times other than at conception. They have shown that in India the lives of many women come to an abrupt end throughout the lifecycle, many from violence, some of which is self-inflicted.[83] In sub-Saharan Africa there is a disproportionately high rate of loss of female life from early childhood, one that peaks in the childbearing years and is associated with childbirth and with malnutrition. The absolute number of missing women in sub-Saharan Africa is comparable with India and China. These researchers also cite historical data showing that at the start of the 20th century in the United States a disproportionate number of women went missing. Taken together these data suggest very strongly, above all else, that ingrained gender discrimination is at work in accounting for missing women,[84] a phenomenon even more insidious and much less easily rectified than practices of government sponsored eugenics.

Biomedical Technology and Sex Selection

Infanticide and selective neglect of young children have very long histories and are very widespread.[85] Such practices had little, if anything, to do with individual desire, nor with state orchestrated decrees, but were most often carried out in efforts to benefit the welfare, continuity, and economy of extended families. In Japan, for example, records suggest that infanticide has been practiced since the 12th century. The idea of something akin to family planning, including selective reduction in family size, commenced in the 18th century.[86] The Japanese word for infanticide – *mabiki* – is a euphemism, the prime referent of which is to rice cultivation and the thinning of spindly, weak seedlings; the midwife was the one usually enjoined to carry out *mabiki* shortly after birth, but such practices were contrary to state edicts and had to be carried out in the utmost secrecy. There is no strong evidence for son preference historically in Japan and this is certainly not the case today,[87] however, research over the past two decades has made it clear that in many countries female fetuses and infants are most likely to be disposed of,[88] and "son preference" is particularly evident in India, China, and Taiwan and, until recently, in South Korea.[89]

It should be noted that agreement does not exist among population experts as to what exactly is the "natural" sex ratio at birth, and whether or not this ratio is universally distributed. A book entitled *The Descent of Human Sex Ratio at Birth* documents the genealogy of the idea of a "natural" sex ratio commencing from the latter part of the 19th century, in which a dialogue began involving two different conceptual approaches among mathematicians, biologists, and sociologists about the most appropriate methods of assessing the sex ratio at birth. The authors of this book argue that what is today accepted as the "natural" sex ratio at birth has never been adequately proven, earlier arguments should be revisited, and further research is called for making use of a "stochastic hypothesis developed through the calculus of probabilities."[90] The presently accepted ratio is commonly assumed to be 105 boys to 100 girls (often expressed as "a ratio of 105"). This figure may eventually prove to be wrong, and more evidence may demonstrate that the assumed "natural" sex ratio at birth is not a universal. However, as we will see shortly, there is considerable historical evidence and even more so in recent years that, in certain geographical locations the sex ratio at birth and, in some places, the ratio of boys to girls among infants, is significantly skewed toward males, strongly suggesting human intervention in the survival of fetuses and infants.

Ultrasound screening (sonography) for pregnant women to ensure that pregnancies are "normal" became routine in Europe and the United States in the 1960s, making it possible to inform women about the sex of the fetus they are carrying. This relatively simple piece of technology is available today in very many parts of the world, allowing people to practice what is described euphemistically by some experts as "family balancing,"[91] that is, the termination of pregnancies on the basis of the sex of the fetus alone in a medical environment where no questions are asked. Although these practices are illegal virtually everywhere, statistics show a rapid change in sex ratios in favor of boys over a short period of time that corresponds closely with the introduction in India and China of ultrasound technology that makes it possible to assess the status of a fetus during pregnancy. This technology was introduced not long after policies of population control in which reduction in family size was strongly recommended (as in India), or began to be legally enforced (in China's case).[92] Ultrasound technology is the agent that makes these practices possible, but demand for its use to enable sex-selected abortions is embedded in the respective political, social, and cultural contexts of these two countries.

Sonar technology was first developed by the British and French navies to detect icebergs and submarines under water. It was later adapted for several uses in medicine among which fetal sonography has been extremely successful. Physicians quickly realized that the fetus, until then invisible and secreted inside the body of a woman, could be made "visible" and managed as a patient, one whose development could be normalized by means of ultrasound technology.[93]

Sonographic images are, of course, representations of fetuses. As Rayna Rapp notes, "Such uterine *baby pictures* are resources for intense parental speculation and pleasure, for they make the pregnancy *real* ... weeks before kicks and bulges protrude into the outside world. The real-time fetus is a social fetus, available for public viewing and commentary" (emphasis in the original).[94] Rapp notes that the fetal image indexes women's obligations, responsibilities, and choices. The machine monitors the health of the fetus, but it also enables what is expected, and indeed demanded, with respect to reproduction.[95] Clearly, when enormous social pressure exists to give birth to a male child, sonography can bring about either intense pleasure or misery.

Remarkable improvements in sonographic machines today produce screen-wide images that create, in the words of Karen Barad, "a phenomenon constituted in the intra-action of the 'object' (commonly referred to as the 'fetus') and the agencies of observation."[96] We previously referred to Barad in chapter 4 to point out that the fetus can be viewed as a technophenomenon: in other words, the machine does not simply create constraints on what one can see; it helps produce and is itself part of the body it images. Importantly, biology is a standard that enables the global circulation of fetal ultrasound machines and the production of these technophenomena. The images that appear once snapped by the ultrasound technician are not straightforward "pictures." Sonographers interpret them in terms of biological standards to determine developmental abnormalities, growth rate, and, at times, sex, but these images are subject to competing, at times disputed, interpretations. "Standardizing the body" thus allows fetal ultrasounds to work, paradoxically producing objects that may take on a life of their own, outside the clinic or the examining room, and profoundly altering the structure of human populations potentially for generations.

Contextualizing Sex Selection: India and "Family Balancing"

No government condones sex selection. India made it illegal in 1994 to carry out this practice in fertility clinics, either before or after conception. Even so, despite the establishment of supervisory boards, monitoring of the situation at local and national levels, demands that medical records be available for inspection, potential and on occasion actual punishment of practitioners who break the law, and media campaigns against sex selection, the practice continues unabated. It is reported to be on the increase,[97] and is actively encouraged by widespread advertising. To date approximately 300 doctors have been prosecuted for aborting fetuses on the basis of sex, but only a handful have been convicted, and even fewer jailed.[98] It is estimated that 1 out of every 25 female fetuses is aborted each year in India, resulting in a total loss of 500,000.[99] This phenomenon is particularly prevalent among well-off people. High-caste families in the Punjab have just 300 girls for every 1,000 boys, and in south Delhi about 832 girls are born per 1,000 boys.[100]

Numerous reports suggest that fertility clinics in India discreetly generate a multi-million dollar black market through sex selection practices, and it is thought that doctors, together with many women activists who believe, no doubt rightly, that women will be subject to abuse if they produce several daughters and no sons, work together in ensuring that such clinics continue their practices. Despite a cost of about $15,000, the demand for ultrasound is apparently enormous including in villages with no running water. Two physicians who run an infertility clinic in Mumbai state that their use of the technology is limited to "family balancing," thus enabling women to have children of both sexes in a timely manner; they insist that it is patronizing to point a finger at Indian practices when reproductive technologies are widely used in the West.[101] In contrast, some feminist groups in India argue that the government is complicit in the increase of sex selection practices by withholding tariffs on the importation of ultrasound and *in vitro* fertilization (IVF) technologies.

Social science research makes it clear that sex selection in India is much more complex than the simple availability of reproductive technologies, profitability, and poorly enforced government policies. Ultrasound technology makes it possible for people to achieve less crudely what has long been established practice in some parts of India, notably in the northern and western provinces, but the practice appears to be spreading south as well.[102] Prior to the 1990s, over and above infanticide, selective neglect and abuse of female children of all ages resulting in malnutrition and high mortality rates accounted for the more than "100 million missing women" Amartya Sen documented in India and China in the early 1990s.[103] Today the number is estimated to be 101 million for the world as a whole. Sen points out that data suggests that the sex bias in mortality has dropped, but in its place a newer form of sex bias has become visible, that of "sex natality," in which female fetuses are preferentially aborted in India, China, and elsewhere.[104] In India these practices are particularly evident in regions where entrenched patriarchy persists; certain family obligations and rituals can only be performed by the eldest son; a large gender gap exists in literacy rates; there is low participation by women in the labor force; there is a customary neglect of female children of long standing, and a dramatic separation of women from their natal families occurs after marriage.[105]

Research links increasing evidence for son preference to an overall reduction in family size that commenced in the 1930s, culminating in the sterilization of millions in the 1970s, described above. The Green Revolution of 1945, followed more recently by further economic and land reforms in which considerably less human labor is required in the agricultural sector, have also contributed substantially to a reduction in family size in rural areas.[106] These changes have resulted in added pressure to ensure family continuity and security in old age by the survival of at least one boy and preferably two to adulthood in the new, small family units. After ultrasound scanning of the fetus commenced in India in 1979, evidence for increased sex selection became apparent in the national statistics a short time later. Recent research also shows that a daughter is often welcomed into a family, especially where boys are present, but that second and third daughters are likely to suffer from neglect, in large part because they are thought of as a drain on the family economy as dowry payments continue to be made at marriage. However, more than 50 percent of surveyed families report that they think of boys and girls as equal, and 63.9 percent would like to have one daughter. It has been shown that education of women and exposure to media coverage about sex selection and related topics have the biggest influence on bringing about a change in attitudes but even so discrimination against women continues to be very evident and reports of polyandry and sex slavery are frequent.[107]

Despite serious efforts from before the time of Partition 40 years ago to integrate Indian women fully into mainstream public life, including the establishment of female suffrage, results have been, at best, mixed.[108] With respect to education and health, elite segments of society have been successful in diverting money away from the poor, exacerbating already existing disparities. Laws passed to improve the status of women, including the banning of infanticide and child marriage, have not brought about significant changes in practice. Drèze and Sen conclude that, in contrast to many other countries where lowered mortality rates resulted in an improved status for women, anti-female discrimination has if anything actually increased in India with declining mortality.[109] Bandyopadhyay, a sociologist working in villages in West Bengal, encountered flat denial among women and midwives, whether Hindu, Muslim, or tribal peoples living in these villages, that sex-selective abortions were being performed. However, she concluded on the basis of statistics on sex ratios at birth that in these villages the practice was undeniably taking place in the easily accessible private clinics. She also noted that in nearly half of the families in these villages senior women or men decide and enforce what should be the ideal family size and composition.[110] Prenatal sex selection using ultrasound is thought of as scientific and neutral by many people – a practice performed by professionals – thus relieving all but the very poor, who cannot afford it, of direct responsibility for their actions.

In Bijnor, a town in northern India of just over 100,000 people, the sociologist Patricia Jeffrey finds that son preference is very evident among Hindu families, and that with consumerism there has been an escalation in dowry expectations, making daughters an ever greater financial liability. Over 20 kiosks and clinics offer ultrasound in Bijnor. Most of the owners of these clinics proclaim that they do not practice sex selection, but they often state that their neighbors do so.[111] In contrast to the enforced sterilization campaigns of the 1970s, the government remains at arms' length from private medical clinics, making only desultory efforts to rectify matters by enforcing the law.

It is abundantly clear that the forces of modernization per se do not necessarily bring about changes in gender discrimination and that in parts of India, for structural, cultural, and economic reasons, women and female children are subordinated to males in many families, one result of which is female feticide. There is a perceived urgency by many, including members of the Indian government, to bring about an end to these practices that ultrasound enables so efficiently. Research accumulated over years strongly suggests that significant change will only be accomplished when policy changes at local and national levels result in social security in old age, changes in inheritance patterns, an end to illegal dowry practices, and increased education of and respect for women. Meantime, the government gives cash payments and other incentives to parents when a girl is born.

On the basis of recent interviews with Indian families residing around San Francisco, physician and anthropologist Sunita Puri found that negative sentiment and even outright discrimination toward female children persists among a good number of immigrant families, a situation of enormous concern to local pediatricians.[112] Clearly further research is needed; however, precisely because biomedical technologies do work, the effects and significance of the social, cultural, and economic contexts within which they are put to use need to be documented.

Contextualizing Sex Selection: Disappeared Girls in China

In contrast to India, in China state involvement in population control has a long history from before the time of Mao, and sterilization eugenics were systematically practiced from early in the 20th century on disabled and other individuals labeled as burdens on society, because it was believed that they contributed to the "degeneracy" of the race, a practice that continued in parts of China until a decade ago and sporadically persists to the present day.[113] However, as noted above, Chinese socialism was actively opposed to Galtonian eugenics, although under the "hard" regime of the one-child family, sterilization was made use of widely.

From its earliest days, the Chinese Communist Party explicitly made women the equal of men in law and later, in the early 1990s, female infanticide, abandonment, and mistreatment of children were outlawed. At the same time, measures were taken to rectify an undeniable sex ratio imbalance by institutionalizing a national program to subsidize school fees for girls; providing housing and employment privileges to one-daughter families; waiving the one-child policy in several locations; and making use of pro-daughter media campaigns. Despite these changes, nationwide the sex imbalance at birth continued to rise to 121 boys to 100 girls before starting to drop a little in the latter part of the 1990s. Greenhalgh points out that what this means is that every year "roughly a million infant girls vanish from the statistics, abandoned, killed, adopted, or aborted *in utero*."[114] A large number end up as part of the "unplanned floating population" associated with urban areas. Greenhalgh notes that for political reasons it has been impossible for the Chinese government to publicly acknowledge this situation until very recently, because the need for drastic population control was assumed to be a national emergency of the greatest order, so that the fate of a subpopulation of illegal baby girls is, Greenhalgh argues, in the minds of government officials by comparison "quite trivial."[115]

In her examination of the discourse used in Chinese documents, Greenhalgh shows how, partly in response to criticism from the West, the government claimed expressly that the one-child policy would in the end be beneficial to Chinese women, particularly those living in rural areas. However, she points out how sexuality had long been understood as a site for political control in socialist China, something to be regulated as integral to economic development and national building. The human rights language associated with birth control in the West did not become part of the official Chinese birth control program. Instead, such discourse drew on classical Chinese medical discourse in turn embedded in Confucian culture, in which disciplinary practice in connection with sex was deemed essential for good health, not simply of individuals, but for society as a whole. The material effects of this government-generated discourse brought about the desired fertility decline but, just as it did in India, resulted in unintended consequences – the disappearance of females, mostly as a result of sex-selected abortions, and the creation of a large population of legal non-persons from those who went missing after birth.[116]

At the time that the one-child policy was implemented, it was assumed that due to decades of socialist egalitarian education, "outmoded" cultural beliefs would quickly die out. The persistence of a strong desire for boy children, particularly in rural areas, came as a surprise to many population policy-makers, whose initial reaction was to ridicule it as a remnant of "feudal culture." Their approach was initially to solve this problem by "ideological exhortation of the masses" and by the good example set by those in power,[117] but in the late 1980s the approach changed to one of accommodation. The central government chose to adjust its policy rather than deal head on with the economic realities that rural families face if they are unable to give birth to at least one son, in order to manage the land allotted to rural families as a result of post-Mao reforms, and also to provide security in old age. The "actual difficulties" of rural couples were implicitly recognized, but the obvious reasons for persistent son preference were never openly acknowledged.

Greenhalgh suggests that the family division of labor by gender was

apparently either too self-evident (because biologically based) or too unchangeable (because deeply rooted in peasant tradition) to be overtly noted, let alone challenged. The effect of this silence was to naturalize the gendered division of work, taking gender off the agenda for policy intervention.[118]

There were also explicit concerns that if the one-child rule were to be enforced too literally, many families would actually drown their daughters if they were firstborn. The government recognized that single-son households experienced difficulties but that in single-daughter households the social disruption was more acute. Thus, argues Greenhalgh, gender inequality was built into the regulations enforced in the majority of Chinese provinces.[119] In 1988, rather than provide substantial welfare benefits, the Deng government decided to allow rural families whose first child proved to be a girl to have a second child. The lives of baby girls were saved, but their social inequality was reinscribed into law.

Throughout the time of the one-child policy, many political cadres, doctors, and families colluded to circumvent the sex selection that was indirectly encouraged. Baby girls were often quietly hidden after birth, never registered, placed in orphanages, or passed along to childless couples.[120] Greenhalgh's many years of documenting the Chinese system of "birth planning by the state" clearly reveals the existence of an enormous "caste" of "unplanned persons" – approximately 10 percent of the entire population – who exist on the margins of the state, the majority of whom are girls and women. Very little is known about the lives of these people whose very existence is blotted out of official statistics. Practice varies in rural and urban areas, but the majority of this "black population" (in Chinese parlance) is comprised of those who are not registered at birth and therefore have grown up without any basic rights and without access to schooling, health care, or other benefits. Most end up as drifters, forming the core of what is known as the "floating population" of many millions plus who "disappear" into the cities of China.[121] Very little indeed has been written about this disturbing problem of massive proportions. Greenhalgh speculates, no doubt rightly, that the profound impact of being illegitimate and regarded as unimportant relative to one's siblings, and as a serious burden to one's family, must be exceptionally debilitating and have a major impact on the sense of self worth of these individuals.[122] Greenhalgh and Winckler conclude: "birth planning, in conjunction with China's male-centered culture and market economy, has masculinized the social order, making a large gender-gap ... a constitutive feature of Chinese modernity."[123] It has also been noted that the policy designed to assist China in its rise to become one of the two greatest economic powers in the world is likely to lead to a decline in the growth rate as a result of a rapidly shrinking working population in the coming years.[124]

Vanessa Fong, an anthropologist who has investigated ethnographically what it is like to be a "little Emperor" – one of the generation of male singletons who has grown up in China over the past two decades – finds that these teenagers are frustrated by their parents' low incomes and the scarcity of educational and professional opportunities. Many are not destined to get the prestigious and high-paying jobs that they have been led to believe they deserve.[125] It seems that even members of the "right" population may be paying a price.

Paradoxically, having no children and being labeled as infertile is heavily stigmatized and not regarded as a hidden asset in dealing with China's population "problem." Social benefits are not available for childless women, and, since the 1990s, female infertility, particularly in urban areas, is often characterized as a "disorder of civilization and modern living" for which women themselves may be held culpable. It is assumed that women who do not become pregnant have in effect violated cultural norms about gendered behavior by being overly preoccupied with "intellectual pursuits," or exhibiting inappropriate sexual behavior. Assisted reproductive technologies are available at a price for middle-class families where infertility has been diagnosed. Increasingly, however, some urban women, whether fertile or not, decide against having children. More so than infertility, this is regarded as "deviant" behavior that challenges the ideal of motherhood as natural and inevitable for all women, an ideal that persists in spite of "excess" births in China.[126]

Recently laws have been enacted in China against sex selection based on the results of sonographic screening, but at the same time it has been reiterated by the government that a woman has a right to know the sex of her unborn child, and ultrasound machines, introduced to China in the mid-1980s, are present in even the smallest rural clinics. As in other countries, a Chinese woman can go to one clinic for an ultrasound and, when informed that the fetus is female, present herself at another clinic for an abortion with no questions asked. Despite efforts on the part of the government to remedy the situation, it is clear that the sex ratio continues to worsen, although the degree to which this happens today varies greatly depending upon geographical location. It has been shown that the single greatest contributor to "missing" girls is fetal sex selection, which has become a thoroughly normalized practice. However other practices also contribute but less so than fetal sex selection:

putting girls up for adoption, not reporting their birth, or abandoning them. Infanticide is virtually non-existent.[127]

Based on ethnographic research carried out in rural central China at the turn of this century, Junhong Chu and a team of researchers found a strong persistence of son preference. Local family planning managers reported that many women are eager to use prenatal sex determination in order to produce sons, but it is also evident that abortions often take place very late in pregnancy, sometimes as late as the fifth month of gestation. Some women believe that late abortions are a small price to pay if they are able to give birth to a son.[128] If a family has one daughter and is permitted another child, and if the second pregnancy proves to be that of a female, then abortion is highly likely, even though many women reported that "destroying life" is wrong. Some report that pressure from their husbands or in-laws leaves them with no choice, but it was also clear that the women themselves were usually eager to comply. The availability of prenatal sex determination suits many women who argue that they can now achieve the family they want without violating the family planning policy, hiding a child, or paying heavy fines. However, women also report that in public medical facilities, because abortion based on sex selection is illegal, some of them are lied to and told that they are carrying a boy when this is not the case. The only way to circumvent this problem is to go to a private clinic and, to be certain of an accurate test result, to bribe the doctors, in addition to paying the relatively expensive fee.[129]

Evidence for a growing sex ratio imbalance in both rural and urban areas is undeniable. A 2007 report in *China Daily* notes that in the city Lianyungang in Jiangsu province the ratio currently stands at 163.5 boys to 100 girls, and a total of 99 cities have sex ratios higher than 125.[130] A professor cited in the report states that the sex imbalance will affect "stability and harmony."[131] In an article published in the *British Medical Journal*, researchers report that as of 2005 there are more than 32 million "excess" males under the age of 20 in China. It is pointed out that this imbalance in the male to female ratio in the reproductive age group will worsen over the next two decades and only begin to modify once the one-child policy is dropped.[132] Evidence is accumulating in both India and China that the sex imbalance is contributing to an increased demand for the services of sex workers and a further spread of HIV/AIDS. Rising violence against women is also documented[133] as is trafficking in women and girls,[134] showing the enormity of long-term societal consequences.

Sex Selection in a Global Context

Das Gupta et al.[135] have noted strong commonalities among China, northern India, and the Republic of Korea with respect to powerful, patriarchal, lineage-based systems of kinship and inheritance patterns. The Korean case is of great interest because census data suggests that throughout the early 1990s an imbalanced sex ratio in favor of males was even more pronounced in South Korea than in either China or India. This situation also came about as a result of a state-sponsored program for population control implemented in the 1960s designed to reduce overall family size. This program was set up during a time of rapid urbanization and a marked rise in overall wealth, accompanied by easy access to ultrasound and a widespread desire for at least one son.

Between 1995 and 2005 a rather dramatic change then took place, bringing about a declining trend in the sex ratio at birth and returning it to what is assumed to be the "natural" range. The figures make it clear that in the latter part of the 1990s, sex selection was practiced almost exclusively in connection with second daughters, and that by 2005 this practice had essentially ceased altogether.[136] During this time, new laws and policies were implemented so that women could become household heads (a change in part spurred on by a rising divorce rate and a tendency for the courts to award custody of children to women). Educational policies became less discriminatory toward women than they were formerly; gender equality in the work place increased, and use of ultrasound to determine the sex of fetuses was banned. Clearly, structural changes, including recognition of the substantial economic contribution of women to households, were central to restoration of the sex ratio imbalance, and policies making indiscriminate use of ultrasound illegal would not alone have had the same effect.[137]

The governments of India and China have both actively attempted to bring about similar changes, but thus far are thwarted by their respective chequered histories in connection with population management, national and local, and especially by a "persistence of the local."[138] In certain regions in India, discriminatory practices against women of very long standing appear to be particularly deeply embedded among some families. Most troubling is the increased incidence of sex selection for sons among urbanized middle-class families in India, and the documentation of the persistence of these practices among both Chinese and Indian families after immigration. Today, wealthy Chinese and Indians have the freedom to travel to clinics in the United States to achieve their desire for boy babies in privacy, making use of pre-implantation genetic testing (PGD) technologies, thus making it possible to select the sex of one's child without recourse to abortion. The most famous of these clinics in Las Vegas receives over 140,000 hits a month from China on its Internet site[139] and over 12,000 hits per month from India inquiring about PGD.[140] A sperm-sorting technique is also gaining popularity. For a cost of $23,000 couples can send a semen sample to one of a small number of clinics in the United States from anywhere in the world to select for male producing sperm, although the success rate is not as yet highly reliable. These technologies are now available in India.

Although the media widely reports the practice of sex selection in Asia, less well known is the fact that surveys of clinics in the United States have shown that "non-medical sex selection" is practiced in that country as well. One survey has shown that among reproductive medicine clinics surveyed in the U.S., 42 percent offer sex selection when a client requests it.[141] Researchers believe that they have uncovered the tip of an iceberg and note that there is little government support for adopting regulations. In contrast, they found that among IVF clinic practitioners there is strong support for professional guidelines, although not legalized regulations. In other countries where sex selection is clearly prohibited, it may well be that "family balancing" is at work as well. In Canada, for example, where sex selection is illegal and abortion on demand is a woman's right with no questions asked, it is likely that some women are in fact undergoing sex-linked abortions to bring about their desired family balance. It is virtually impossible to investigate these practices due to the way in which statistics are collected. One specialist at a U.S. clinic reports that his clients come from all over the world, the largest numbers being from Canada followed by China.[142]

The anthropologist Marcia Inhorn reports that non-medical sex selection for males is increasingly taking place in the Middle East, where not only are local clients served, but efforts are made to encourage a reproductive tourism industry designed to suit South Asian customers.[143] The demographer Caroline Bledsoe has recently found a possible discrepancy in Spain in the sex ratio at birth among Chinese immigrants living there,[144] suggesting that such practices are carried out in Europe as well and a recent article in the *New York Times* reports that there is a "hint" of a similar bias among Asians living in the United States.[145] These findings about sex selection imply that structural changes and economic wellbeing alone will not be sufficient to stop such practices. Unexamined stereotyped assumptions about female inferiority are proving to be extraordinarily resilient among certain populations, despite legislation to the contrary. In part lack of enforcement of laws is to blame, and on occasion doctors are complicit, but this is clearly not the whole story. Social and cultural factors that persist after immigration involving persistent discrimination against women, even in countries where their rights are strongly upheld, appear to be at work. No amount of regulation of ultrasound technology will resolve this problem.

Although there is widespread condemnation by both internal and external commentators about the extent to which sex selection appears to be taking place, the shortcomings of the biomedical technologies used to this effect are rarely noted. On the basis of ethnographic work with physicians living in California whose specialty is reproductive medicine, Sunita Puri notes that there is agreement among her medical informants that the sex of a fetus cannot be determined by ultrasound with unfailing accuracy in the early states of gestation.[146] Ultrasound specialists with whom we have spoken in Montreal concur that only from about 17 weeks can the sex be determined with reasonable confidence, although in some cases it can never be achieved due to the position of the fetus *in utero*. These specialists are aware of cases referred from other clinics where the sex had been wrongly interpreted from sonographic images. It is probable then, that some women in India and China are opting for abortions based on inaccurate ultrasound information and at times may be aborting male fetuses. On occasion too, it must be that they give birth to female babies when a male was expected, and the ethnographic data from China suggests that this is indeed the case. It is highly likely that many women are having late, sometimes very late, abortions after the sex can be determined with reasonable accuracy; once again the Chinese findings indicate that this is indeed the case.[147] Such abortions are very traumatic, can result in injury and other complications, and on occasion in death, and are likely to interfere with future reproductive success. A question arises as to why these technological uncertainties are so little addressed by medical people, national and local politicians, social scientists, feminists, and involved women and their families, when the health and very lives of women are at stake.

More than any other kind of biomedical technology, those that affect reproduction bring to the fore an inherent tension among individual desire, perceived family interests, and that which is deemed appropriate for the nation, and indeed the world as a whole. These tensions are rife today because, as individuals and families are pressured to reduce their family size to conform with efforts to standardize the "population problem," a global circulation of ultrasound technology has permitted families to take a certain amount of control with respect to the sex of their offspring. As genetic engineering, including germ-line manipulations, advanced stem-cell technologies and other innovations become available, these tensions will be exacerbated yet further, particularly when discussion turns to future generations and to what extent we are willing to create our descendents by means of technological assistance. The looming question is one of governance, and whether this will be accomplished – and if so, how – in an era with a heightened sensitivity about individual rights, particularly when matters relating to health are increasingly managed as part of the globalized market. Given this situation, should genetic manipulations of all kinds, including sex selection, be made into a public health matter that is strictly monitored and controlled? The findings presented above suggest that such an approach is unlikely to bring about extensive change unless accompanied by serious efforts to reduce gender inequality in the family – efforts that need to be directed above all at expectations about the place of young wives in the family. Persistent society-wide discrimination against women as a whole, evident in some countries more than others, contributes greatly to this problem.

We turn now to a strikingly different example of population politics, one in which economic, rural–urban and, above all else, ethnic differences figure prominently in the management of reproduction in a nation in ceaseless internal dispute and turmoil.

Reproducing Nationalism

The following account of reproduction among Palestinian women is taken from *Birthing the Nation: Strategies of Palestinian Women in Israel* written by the anthropologist Rhoda Ann Kanaaneh who herself grew up in Galilee. Kanaaneh's ethnography shows graphically how reproductive technologies are not "value-neutral"; rather they are inextricably tied up in local political struggles with surprising consequences at times. From the outset Kanaaneh stresses the striking difference in reproductive practices between urban and rural Palestinians living in Israel, reflecting regional ideas about the worth of children. Sometimes, competing ideas are evident, even within single families. Although much of her ethnography is focused on the region of Galilee, Kanaaneh is acutely sensitive about the porosity of this boundary and the mobility of its population. Palestinians who live inside the borders of Israel created after the 1948 war are citizens of Israel, numbering 23 percent of all Palestinians, and 20 percent of Israel's population, of whom about half live in northern Galilee. Galilee is imagined both by Palestinians themselves and by the Israeli state and many of the Jewish population as a "wild frontier to be settled and Judaized."[148]

Following Ginzburg and Rapp's lead,[149] Kanaaneh demonstrates how family planning has emerged as a matter for contestation in Galilee – more specifically how new forms of social stratification and changing gender relations are articulated and contested making use of local discourse and practices associated with reproduction, nationalism, economic transformations, and medical regulation. She argues: "Reproduction has been politicized and maternity nationalized." Women's bodies are deeply inscribed as reproducers of the nation, whether they bear many or few children.[150] As is the case in India and China, it is as a result of the technology of census-taking that this politicization has largely been accomplished.

Drawing on historical records, Kanaaneh documents the ways in which strategies of nationalist homogenization have been practiced in Israel since its inception. She is quick to note that Israel is not unique in this respect, but she shows how, in Israel's case, what she calls "political arithmetic" feeds into a nationalistic politics, one goal of which is "de-Arabization," while simultaneously bringing about "Judaization."[151] Many strategies are designed to consolidate the nation of Israel as Jewish, including marriage and adoption laws, welfare and immigration policies, regulations about land holding, and identification cards. Perhaps the primary purpose of manipulated population statistics, made use of by both sides, is as fodder for the endless dispute about land, resulting in "fetishized maps of warring demographically imagined nations."[152] The building of numerous small Jewish settlements in areas such as Galilee where the Palestinian population is strong has been actively encouraged as part of the process of Judaization.

The Palestinian population in Israel was from the outset characterized as a "problem population" by the authorities, one that was likely to burgeon out of control – but so too were Jews of African or Asian origin regarded as problems. Furthermore, the notion that distinct categories of "Arab" and "Jew" could be made based on essentialized biological difference was clearly problematic due to numerous cases of intermarriage. Even so, by 1965 all residents of the state had to be registered with both "nation" and "religion" specified, as a means of clarifying who counted as first-class citizens. Benefits were given to Jewish families with more than three children with an explicit goal of increasing the Jewish population, and family planning programs were cautiously promoted in Jewish communities. In contrast, by the 1980s many family planning programs had been opened in the "Arab sector," even in areas where comprehensive health care was not available. It is notable that the infant mortality rate among Palestinians today is twice as high as it is among Israeli Jews and increasing privatization of health care services has brought about greater inequities in recent years.[153]

Despite the existence of a "selective population policy" of many years' duration, the growth rate of the Israeli Palestinian population is twice as high as that of the Jewish population, and in the West Bank and the Gaza Strip it is even higher.[154] Kanaaneh argues that the discriminatory policies of Israel have worked over the years to fire up Palestinian nationalism – a sentiment that unites Palestinians wherever they reside. One aspect of this nationalism is manifest as an ethnic-based "political arithmetic" that counts all Palestinians as a single unit of 4.5 million, wherever they live – a ploy that Edward Said argued was a deliberate act of "political self-realization."[155] Of course, this strategy essentializes who will count as a Palestinian. Kanaaneh notes that the effect among Palestinians in responding to the Israeli fear of an "Arab time bomb" has been to resist efforts to reduce their population, going so far in some instances as to give up on the use of contraceptives. Both the Palestine Liberation Organization and the Palestinian Authority support a pro-natal policy, and the Palestinian press openly celebrates high fertility.

There is, however, a second position, popular in leftist Palestinian circles, which argues that in order to bring about economic stability, to improve education levels, and to further modernize, the Palestinian fertility rate must be lowered for the good of the population as a whole. In her research, Kanaaneh finds that many informants who consider themselves "modern" are deeply involved in this economic rationality in which the idea of investing well in a few children is central. These families identify themselves as consumers with middle-class values, and contrast themselves explicitly with "backward" Palestinians whom they regard as primitive, dirty, and having too many children. This is a dramatically different version of reproduction as a nationalistic endeavor, but it is also explicitly set out in opposition to the Israeli position and equally politicizes the bodies of women. These competing discourses encourage debate among Israeli Palestinian women, and permit individual and family flexibility in reproductive decision-making. Differences between urban and rural Palestinians and upper and lower classes are often articulated on the basis of reproductive practices. In addition to the modern–traditional divide, religious distinctions among Christians, Druze, and Muslims are at times mobilized to heighten sensitivities about the politics of reproduction, intertwined with the most prominent ever-present distinction of Palestinian and Jew and its associated ideological, economic, and topological discourse.

Despite these many differences, both self-defined "modern" and "traditional" Palestinians make gendered distinctions with respect to reproduction. Boys are regarded by virtually everyone as the "backbone of the nation,"[156] although son preference can at times be subjected to contested discourse. While some people believe that it is essential to produce sons for nationalistic reasons to protect the "besieged homeland," others argue on a more personal note that one needs a balanced family of both sexes, and yet others claim, rather extravagantly, that the "whole world prefers boys."[157] Some families are concerned that their sons are likely to die young, and argue that giving birth to several boys is important. For many others, family continuity achievable only through patriliny is of prime concern. Yet others declare that a preference for sons is an authentic part of being Arab. Various folk methods are made use of to try to ensure the birth of a boy, and IVF is available for those who can afford it, including semen-sorting technologies.

These discourses about reproduction are in practice flexible; even so, the culturally informed ideology that results creates a tension between ideas about modernity and backwardness that color daily life to a high degree.[158] Many Palestinian women believe that part of being modern is to embrace medical technologies to enhance health, beauty, and fertility. However, ambivalence is also evident about such technologies, often characterized as "artificial" and "invasive." Even so, Kanaaneh found that perceived control over one's life brought about by contraceptive use is thought of by many as a means to "escape marginality, negotiate identity, and attain progress."[159]

Kanaaneh points out that the ideal of a large family, associated by many in Galilee with backwardness, continues to dominate in many parts of the Gaza Strip and the West Bank. For Palestinians living in the Occupied Territories, experience of everyday life is one of a colonized people whose agency is severely circumscribed and dictated by those in power, a situation that also applies to Palestinians living in Israel but less coercively. In the Occupied Territories where death is a daily occurrence, it is not surprising that a much more pronounced resistance to family planning is evident, justified in the name of survival.

In Summary

Producing the "right population" emerged as a central preoccupation with the rise of the modern state in the 19th century and, as Foucault explained, was crucial for the exercise of "biopower." The right population was understood as one whose "quality" could be assured by inciting the "right" kinds of people to reproduce, and one that was rid of undesirable elements. The latter were increasingly defined in biological terms during the course of the first half of the 20th century, and biology furnished a set of standards for comparing bodies and potentially charting their reproductive course. This explicitly eugenic impulse has faded away, but its legacy can be seen in the standardization of the reproductive body in biological terms, and in associated reproductive biomedical technologies.

The application of numerical approaches and statistical analyses to large groups of individuals, including the idea of the "normal" – in the sense of average – individual, is essential if a concept of "population" is to have political applicability. In this chapter we underline two more aspects of the "problematization" of population that have received relatively little critical attention: the use of biology as a standard for enabling powerful forms of intervention worldwide, and the resulting adoption of bio-contraceptive technologies that bring about political ends, sometimes forcibly imposed. The result is that these technologies are the most commonly used of all biomedical technologies, utilized by billions of people worldwide. When adopted voluntarily, they are viewed as emancipatory by many, women in particular. However, their use may have unforeseen, deleterious consequences, due to the ease with which these highly portable technologies that work anywhere readily escape government and legal controls, as the complex matter of sex-selection attests.[160] This particular example dramatically highlights the competing interests and aspirations of involved individuals, families, health care professionals, governments, and policy-makers in connection with the implementation of biomedical technologies.

6

Colonial Disease and
Biological Commensurability

By the late 20th century, biomedicine had achieved an unprecedented global dominance, even in parts of the world where other medical traditions remained vigorous. The result is that biomedical technologies are today virtually ubiquitous, and often avidly sought-after – even by those who cannot afford them. This chapter sets out the ways in which this situation came about, emphasizing changes that took place in the early part of the 20th century.

In the late 19th century a theory of human biological equivalence gradually emerged. This occurred as new microbiological theories of disease causation were put into practice in a piecemeal fashion. Their success led to microbiology becoming defined as a standard for intervention into individual bodies and populations in the European colonies. This helped to displace the common existing assumption among scientists and academics of all kinds that human bodies are biologically incompatible due to racial differences and variation brought about by environment. As we will see below, these new biological approaches were first used to deal with "critical events" that took place during the first half of the 20th century in many parts of the colonized world. The apparent success of these approaches provided what appeared to be convincing evidence of the existence of biological commensurability to medical people and colonial administrators. Thus the groundwork was laid for recognition of a universal human biology, enabling the means for using standardized interventions on human bodies wherever they reside, up to the present day.

The account set out in this chapter challenges a common unexamined assumption, namely, that biomedicine was and is made in the "West" and then exported to the "rest." In other words, that biomedicine is a singularly Euro-American achievement that can be "applied" without modification anywhere to rid people of disease and improve the health and wellbeing of populations. It has often been the case however that medical practices have became widely accepted only after their implementation and standardization in colonial settings at which time they were transported back to Europe.

An Anthropological Perspective on Global Biomedicine

The anthropologist Veena Das introduced the term "critical events" to refer to historical moments when both individual existence and social order are at stake. Her widely acclaimed ethnographic study of contemporary India focused on the 1947 Partition of India and Pakistan and the 1984 Bhopal industrial disaster, and showed how "critical events" generate new social categories and forms of action.[1] In our consideration of the global circulation of biomedical technologies, we draw on Das's concept to frame epidemics, infertility and childbirth, and famines as "critical events" that linked global and local realities, crystallized new forms of knowledge and action, and realigned social relations in historically significant ways.

Epidemics have of course been a regular occurrence throughout human history; however, in the context of the struggle to assert colonial dominion, they became a battleground where both European political supremacy and the lives of colonial armies and settlers were at stake. Once biomedical approaches to epidemics were proven to be reasonably successful, they were mobilized to address other problems at the intersection of individual experience and the social order. Two of the more important examples concern control of fertility and birthing, and nutrition. At these vital nodes where individual and collective wellbeing intersect, biology emerged as a standard for intervening on bodies and populations. Epidemics, infertility, and famines did not have to be "problematized" as a matter of "population," even though the threat to collective and individual vitality was all too clear. Given that these phenomena often result in devastating social consequences, they were experienced as "critical events" in which the demonstration of the power of biology alone as a standard for calibrating interventions into individual bodies weighed heavily in favor of a biomedical approach. The apparently effective application of biomedical technologies helped to discredit miasmatic theories current at the time that linked climate, constitution, and race in a medical geography that followed a logic of difference, rather than one of similarity.

Effective though they appeared to be, biomedical approaches were nonetheless freighted with moral assumptions of European superiority including, at times, eugenicist ideas of improving the "quality" of the "native races." However, once several epidemics appeared to have been brought under control, fertility rates appeared to improve, and famines had apparently waned, biological equivalence and moral superiority were reconciled in the ultimate goal of producing healthy colonial populations, in order to bring about the colonists' objectives of the extraction of wealth. This apparent success ensured that, once the crises passed, biomedical approaches remained in place, resulting in the medicalization of key aspects of human and social life. We show in this chapter how medicalization has complex and locally varied histories, and that struggles over how these critical events are to be defined and managed continue to this day. As a consequence, the power of the standard of biology continues to be evident in the contemporary imperative to save biological lives and the mobilization of medical humanitarian interventions.

The rise of a scientific and systematic approach to human health in Europe was from the outset entangled with European experiences of exploration and the resistance they encountered. Accordingly, the full flowering of biomedicine can be divided into four phases. In the first phase, throughout the 19th and early part of the 20th century, biomedicine and its associated technologies were used primarily beyond the borders of Europe and North America as a tool of empire, to protect the health of settlers and soldiers. During this "imperial phase" attention was focused on the debilitating and often fatal fevers that afflicted Europeans in the tropics, usually glossed as "malaria."[2] The second period was marked by the idea that "natives" and Europeans were, in contrast to earlier thinking, biologically commensurate. This phase took hold after World War I, when "native" labor became increasingly indispensable to colonial economies, and biomedicine was called upon to contain the threat of epidemics. In many parts of the world, the period between the two world wars was the first time large populations of people were exposed to biomedicine, when an imperial logic of conquest gave way to a colonial approach to government. At this time, biomedical techniques came to be used increasingly to manage the health of subject populations rather than being reserved solely for settlers and conquering armies.[3] The 1960s ushered in a third phase when biomedicine began to be used as an emblem of nation-building and modernization by newly independent states in Africa, Asia, and Europe (although in many countries this move was combined with revived or revitalized traditional medical practices). This "golden era" of nationalist health care systems quickly passed when most states found that they were unable to afford tertiary care for all but a wealthy few, and structural adjustment programs eroded public health care services and infrastructure in poor countries. The stage was thus set for the ongoing fourth and longer wave of biomedical globalization, carried out by development agencies, NGOs, and other humanitarian efforts to improve the health of the global poor. A nascent global biomedical technology market that provides services and goods to those who can afford to pay for them also promotes this last phase. These phases can be glossed as imperial (prior to 1920), colonial (1920–60), nationalist (1960–80), and non-governmental (from 1980 to the present).

Biomedicine as a Tool of Empire

From the earliest times of European settlement in Africa in the 17th century, high rates of illness and untimely death led to the reputation of the tropics as "the White Man's grave," engraining European thinking with images of pestilence and death. The application of biomedicine became explicitly hitched to imperial ambitions when biomedicine gained institutional prominence and credibility as a result of mounting evidence of successes in disease control after hygiene measures were implemented in the capitals of 19th-century Europe. Biomedicine came to be understood as the key to preserving the health of imperial armies and settlers in the face of the onslaught of tropical diseases they would face.[4]

The entanglement of biomedicine with imperialism was initially driven, therefore, by purely instrumental goals, and was limited almost entirely to a military enterprise concerned with the health of conquering armies left behind after the first European colonists had moved on. The first battle in this early campaign was waged against tropical fevers, thought at the time to be due to bad air (hence "malaria," from the Italian *mala* + *aria*); and the battle was eventually won with the use of quinine derived from the bark of the cinchona tree native to the Andes. The bark of the cinchona tree was recognized by Peruvian Indians in the 17th century to have anti-malarial effects,[5] and was first brought back to Europe by Jesuits. Once the active ingredient, quinine, was extracted in 1820, it began to be used successfully by military physicians to prevent and treat malaria, contributing to success in colonial wars. This experience led historian Daniel Headrick to speak of European medicine as a "tool of Empire" in his influential book by the same name.[6]

It would be simplistic to attribute imperial expansion to quinine alone; indeed, it has been argued that the decrease in deaths due to malaria was the result (and not the cause) of successful empire building.[7] For example, in his study of the impact of anti-malarial measures in British campaigns in South and Southeast Asia, the historian Mark Harrison argues that these only became effective once a particular culture of military command was in place; one that integrated military strategizing with a "bio-medical managerial ethos" that implemented improved hygiene.[8] The success of biomedical intervention was clearly dependent upon a series of political and social conditions, rather than simply on the application of a biomedical technology. The global reduction in malaria – at least to the extent that it was brought under control so that the benefits of colonization outweighed the risks for European settlers – relied as much on colonial social practices as on the biological efficacy of quinine. But even so it was chalked up as proof that biomedicine and its drugs were useful, even in the hostile climes of the tropics.

Acclimatization and Racial Difference

Although from the mid–19th century a new, systematic approach to disease was emerging in the operating theaters and hospitals of Paris and other European capitals, in the colonies miasma theory continued to hold sway. Most tropical fevers are exotic in their florid symptomatology, and the epidemics that punctuated colonial rule were largely unfamiliar to European doctors.[9] The exception was cholera, but after John Snow's discovery and the development of urban waterworks, cholera had become a distant memory. The tropical diseases posed an immediate and pressing problem: "Could the white races colonize the topics?"[10] Or would they be unable to do so because of the hostile environment?

The question was both political and medical. Miasma theory was widely adhered to in the colonies where Europeans in large numbers first encountered tropical cli-mates and exotic diseases. These ideas had first become popular in the Middle Ages and persisted within a broader understanding of nature that emerged with the post-Enlightenment objectification of the natural world as described in chapter 2. From the 16th century onwards, as Europeans began to travel and encounter strik-ingly different landscapes, flora, fauna, and peoples, this diversity in nature would gradually come to be explained by the notion of "acclimatization" from the late 18th century. The "Acclimatization Societies" that were founded in the mid–19th century in France reflected increasing colonial exposure and were largely concerned with improvement of agriculture and the domestication of exotic animals. In Paris, the Jardin d'Acclimatation was established in 1860 as a zoo where "acclimatization" served as the scientific pretext for exhibiting exotic animals and humans culled from

African "tribes" for curious Parisians; today it is an amusement park. Acclimatization was a powerful idea that linked climate, environment, constitution, and temperament through the trope of "adaptation." At the time, the term was devoid of any biological mechanism or understanding, although that would gradually emerge of course in the wake of Darwin's theory of natural selection.[11] The white races therefore could colonize the tropics even if their "humoural sensibilities were naturally adapted to more temperate zones"[12] – it was a matter of acclimatizing or "seasoning" themselves.

Acclimatization was also a powerful theory of racial difference. A common view was that the races resulted from adaptation to a given climate. The strength of this position can be seen in the belief of many that moving members of a race to another region would cause them to degenerate, like a plant transplanted to a foreign soil. European settlement of tropical lands was fraught not only with the immediate threat of death from fever, but with the more pernicious decay of degeneration that would soften, emasculate, and enfeeble Europeans caught in a tropical spell. This view coexisted with a somewhat contradictory set of beliefs that affirmed "natives" to be acclimatized to tropical climes and therefore "immune" to the tropical afflictions of Europeans, while evidence of "native" ill-health, "feebleness," and "indolence" were taken as signs of racial decay.[13] This understanding of racial difference as "constitutional" was not "biological" in the sense we understand biology today, because a scientized biology did not yet exist. As the historian Worboys notes when writing about tuberculosis in the 19th century: "there was ambivalence about whether acclimatization could be achieved to a sufficient level in a matter of years by the 'seasoning' of individuals, or whether it would take many generations and need to be 'fixed in the blood.'"[14]

At the time a far more convincing standard by which difference could be evaluated was the science of climate. Meteorology standardized acclimatization through precise measurements of temperature, air, and soil. The influence of acclimatization on medical thinking was also visible in 19th-century epidemiology, which, in the manner of Snow's "cartography" of cholera, compared disease rates in different locales and sought to link them to climate. Theories of acclimatization legitimated indifference, if not fatalism, to the health of "natives." Acclimatization and miasma theories coexisted with pre-microbiological ideas that disease could be spread from person to person through contagion that informed practices of quarantine during epidemics. This medical pluralism led to selective application of quarantine measures to control epidemics. When quarantine threatened to disrupt trade, colonial administrators did not hesitate to attribute epidemics to climate and constitution rather than contagion as, for example, during a cholera epidemic in India in 1867–69, when medical statistics were used to "smother" contagionist arguments for quarantine.[15] Medical theories – miasmatic or contagionist – were used by political and economic actors to legitimate their preferred course of action.

By the end of the 19th century, however, a new theory of disease had emerged to rival the miasmatic ideas that linked disease to climate, adaptation, and bodily humors. Louis Pasteur, working in Paris, had made convincing demonstrations of the microbial origins of diseases by definitively proving the efficacy of vaccines against anthrax and rabies based on his germ theory and, in Berlin, Robert Koch had identified the micro-organism responsible for tuberculosis. Germ theory challenged beliefs about environmental causation, and the colonies were set to become the global stage where new microbiological theories could be applied and tested, and where convincing demonstrations of efficacy could be obtained using "native" populations as subjects.

Colonial Epidemics: Microbial Theories Prove Their Worth

The 1900 epidemic of sleeping sickness that devastated British Northern Uganda was a "critical event" that, in retrospect, inaugurated a global deployment of biomedicine. The epidemic spread with breathtaking speed and caused a staggering loss of life of over a quarter of a million in the Ugandan Protectorate alone by 1905, according to one official estimate.[16] Although the disease had previously been described by European travelers to Africa for at least the past 200 years, its emergence with epidemic ferocity in Uganda that summer caused a near panic in London, as colonial officials contemplated the threat to their empire. The disease was widely feared; its victims initially complained of headaches and muscle pains before becoming increasingly drowsy, hence the name "sleeping sickness," until they finally succumbed. While we now know that sleeping sickness is caused by a parasite that infects humans through the bite of the tsetse fly, at the time this was not yet known, making the epidemic even more terrifying.

At the turn of the 20th century the British Empire was at its zenith and contributing greatly to the growth of the biomedical sciences: over 2,000 medical personnel were stationed overseas to care for colonial administrators, and "nearly a fifth of [all British] medical practitioners served or derived their income from the empire by the end of the century."[17] Many physicians signed up to work in the colonies because such positions offered better job security than at home and, for the adventurous, the chance of making a name for oneself as a discoverer of the tropics. As concerns mounted in London and other European capitals about the devastating effect of a tropical environment on the health of the colonists, Patrick Manson and other entrepreneurial medical scientists set about mobilizing the powers that be, in the names of Empire and Science, to back a series of expeditions that would pave the way for the discovery of the microbial origins of malaria, sleeping sickness, and a variety of other tropical diseases. Imperial rivalries between the French, the Germans, the Dutch, and the British were intense, and these rivalries would help to drive biomedical research, as scientists from the imperial capitals raced to be the first to discover the causes of exotic, terrifying, tropical diseases, and thus imbue the campaigns with geopolitical significance.

In France, the Pastorians were not part of the elite medical establishment, a situation that led them to seek opportunities outside the traditional academic path. The historian Ann-Marie Moulin notes: "Pasteur's disciples gathered around the master and, emboldened by the early successes of anthrax and rabies [vaccinations], firmly believed in the dawn of a new medical era." Long before the program had achieved any replicable results, they assumed that a scientific paradigm of medicine would be universally applicable.[18] When sleeping sickness epidemics hit the previously unaffected protectorate of Cameroon (wrested from the Germans by the French in World War I) and other territories of French West Africa, the stage was set for Pastorians to intervene, unfettered by Parisian medical politics. Eugène Jamot headed up a major campaign with military precision, commencing in 1926, against an epidemic of sleeping sickness. Jamot was a French military physician who had led the military campaign to take Cameroon from the Germans in World War I, and he subsequently became head of the Pasteur Institute in Brazzaville, the capital of French Central Africa. Special teams moved methodically to quarantine affected areas until all inhabitants had been screened and treated. This involved lining up the entire population and palpating their necks to search for swollen lymph nodes. When these were found, a needle would be inserted to withdraw the lymph that was then examined in the field under a microscope. Those individuals in whom the parasite was found were identified with a large "T" (for trypanosomiasis) painted on the forehead or chest and subjected to treatment.[19] The treatment was not very effective, and also highly toxic, often causing visual disturbances, and even permanent eye damage or death. Nonetheless Jamot's campaign achieved remarkable results, stopping the epidemic in its tracks – in all probability because confirmed cases of the disease were quarantined, and restricted travel was applied to everyone, rather than because of the "treatment."

This campaign was a powerful demonstration that Pastorian approaches, properly applied, could be used to stamp out tropical epidemics and, further, convincing evidence that there were no significant biological differences between Europeans and their colonial subjects. The strategy was replicated across Belgian and British Africa, and became the model on which infectious-disease eradication campaigns would thereafter be based. Pastorians were not unanimously welcomed everywhere. French colonial authorities resented accusations by Pastorians that colonial policies exacerbated epidemics by encouraging labor migrations (thus allowing germs to spread), tolerating lax supervision of population movements, and encouraging agricultural policies that required specialization in specific crops for export. Colonial administrators thought that the Pastorians were meddlesome know-alls who rode roughshod over established policies in the name of science – in short, that they were arrogant cowboys.[20]

However, the growing economic importance of the African colonies for France made it increasingly difficult to resist Pastorian campaigns on purely ideological grounds because the need for preservation of the health of local laborers was clearly essential. For example, the historian Rita Headrick has shown how colonial authorities panicked when they became aware of the astronomically high mortality rate amongst laborers who had been conscripted to lay the track for the Congo–Océan railroad from Brazzaville to Pointe-Noire in the 1930s. The railroad was a cornerstone of colonial efforts to tap into world markets through the exportation of timber and rubber harvested in the interior by conscripted labor. In response, the authorities brought in colonial physicians who applied biomedicine of the day to bring about a substantial decrease in the mortality of African laborers.[21] France was not alone in being increasingly tied to its colonies and the expansion of trade in general led to fears that diseases of the topics could spread, ship-borne, to Europe and America, as was the case with the global plague epidemic of the late 19th century.[22]

Moulin reminds us that "the germ theory of disease had been the matrix of the Pasteurian doctrine ... the official view had eclipsed consideration of the secondary factors which could amplify or even trigger infection and account for the explosion of collective evils." She cites what she describes as Pasteur's brazen statement that signified the mood of the new hygiene: "whatever the poverty, never will it breed disease."[23] For the Pastorians, social conditions could be simply reduced to their impact on the circulation of germs. The apparent effectiveness of campaigns premised on microbiological methods of control thus confirmed Pastorian ideas, and by extension the biological equivalence of bodies through which microbes circulated.

Sleeping sickness epidemics were later attributed to colonial disruptions of local cultural and economic systems that had until that time kept parasite and man apart. These local ecologies were understood as fragile and the massive migrations forced by colonial economic policies meant that epidemics spread like wildfire.[24] Paradoxically, Pastorians recognized the importance of these local ecologies even as they espoused the idea that human biology was universal.[25] Their solution, however, was not to pay attention to specific ecological niches and nurse them back to health, but to impose a top-down program to break the cycle of infection, the success of which was touted as evidence of universal biology. This was brought about by the ability of the Pastorians to enforce control measures on a pliant colonial society to stop the transmission of infection.

Other epidemics targeted by international campaigns at the time included hookworm in the American South and Latin America, yellow fever in Africa and Latin America, and dengue fever in Asia and Latin America. In addition to their adherence to a microbial theory of disease causation, the campaigns all exhibited a military-like organization in their implementation. In the absence of treatment for the diseases in question, these were classic public health campaigns aimed at quarantining cases and destroying insect vectors that spread the disease. While not completely successful, the campaigns nonetheless were a powerful demonstration, not only to the involved scientists but also to the general public that learned of them through press reports, that biomedicine could work everywhere. The effectiveness of the techniques used to eradicate infectious diseases validated the new biomedical theories about the microbial causes of epidemics. These campaigns, as noted above, were successful in part because of the introduction of the microscope that was brought from imperial centers to colonial field sites where the campaigns were staged. In the words of a pioneer of British colonial medicine, Dr J. L. Todd, "the future of imperialism lay with the microscope."[26] Deployed in colonial sites the world over, the microscope transformed understanding of local fevers as microbial pathogens were given form under its lens.

Resistance to the Biomedicalization of Epidemics

Historians have documented the local impact of the introduction of new biomedical approaches and the associated public health campaigns to which Africans were subjected. For example, Luise White has shown how epidemics of vampire rumors that swept East Africa were a powerful local commentary on colonialism whose vivid imagery of blood-sucking Europeans was in fact literally, and not just metaphorically, correct (recall how campaigners inserted needles into the necks of colonial subjects in order to sample lymph fluid!). These practices fed into widespread beliefs that Europeans were cannibals and that they used substances retrieved during biomedical procedures – blood, lymph and other body parts – to perform macabre experiments.[27] Lyons and Cloarec, recounting the history of sleeping sickness campaigns in the

Belgian Congo and Côte-d'Ivoire respectively, report that Africans would not only flee into the bush to escape the eradication campaigns, but would even persuade traditional physicians to remove their lymph nodes so that they would not be subjected to the dreaded needles, no doubt making them more susceptible to other diseases.[28]

From the turn of the 20th century, malaria, yellow fever, hookworm, sleeping sickness, and onchocerciasis were just a few of the epidemics that were confronted using the new biologically based medicine by carrying out colonial expeditions, building new research institutes, and undertaking philanthropic endeavors in Asia, Africa, and Latin America. But this was achieved with some difficulty, because in many parts of the world the deployment of biomedicine was thought of as part of an oppressive colonial apparatus, and was often met with incomprehension, suspicion, or even outright resistance. While colonial perceptions of biomedicine as a colonial tool to be avoided or resisted would gradually be overcome in many communities around the world, in others a legacy of mistrust of biomedicine as a "Western science" remains.[29] A vaccination campaign against yellow fever in Rio de Janeiro in 1904 led to riots,[30] and the legacy of these campaigns lives on today manifest in widespread wariness of biomedical research and recurring reports that contemporary public health campaigns are viewed with apprehension and often suspected to be forms of experimentation carried out on unwitting participants. Paradoxically, the very success of the early epidemic eradication campaigns has in some locales left a mute resistance to subsequent measures to improve public health among postcolonial peoples.[31]

Echoes of this legacy can be found in some of the circulating theories of the origins of HIV discussed at the end of chapter 4, and in widespread rumors that circulated throughout northern Nigeria in 2004 that the campaign to eradicate polio through universal vaccination was a Western plot to sterilize Muslim women – rumors that stymied the campaign there. Subsequent outbreaks of polio in northern Nigeria only served to confirm local beliefs that it was not a real anti-polio vaccine that was being injected into people, but a contraceptive.

In summary, throughout colonization, growing evidence that biomedicine could "work," even for natives heretofore assumed to be immune to tropical ailments, opened a door for biomedicine to be used as an ideological tool, a way of winning "hearts and minds" and showing what colonial authorities believed to be the beneficial effects of colonialism. Not only was biomedicine good for colonialism because it kept colonial labor productive and reasonably healthy, it also justified the colonial enterprise as a kind of hygienic enlightenment, whereby colonial powers could be seen as bringing progress – in the form of improved hygiene, proper etiquette, and an improved lifestyle to its "backward" colonial subjects who were assumed to be unwashed and unhealthy. The distant audience for this endeavor was a skeptical metropolitan public back home that remained unconvinced that the economic and human costs of colonialism were worthwhile.[32] Increasingly, natives and settlers found themselves placed on the same biological plane.

Microbiology as a Global Standard

Colonial campaigns to control epidemics became paradigmatic cases of biomedical globalization whose legacy remains visible today in international infectious disease control efforts. But these encounters in foreign lands "struck back" as engagements at the peripheries of empire worked their way back into metropolitan biomedicine. The microscope was a powerful tool, an "obligatory point of passage,"[33] that established the micro-organism as the standard for understanding and controlling epidemics worldwide. By the end of World War II many administrators and medical people assumed that infectious diseases, wherever they occurred, would be brought under control through the continued advance of biomedical science, and the discovery of effective antibiotics and vaccines went ahead at a steady rate. Beyond the industrialized world, infectious diseases still caused significant morbidity and mortality, but there was an expectation that "the rapid pace of medical and scientific progress"[34] would eventually make epidemics a thing of the past everywhere and the development of therapeutic agents after World War II fuelled this expectation. The war accelerated the development of a pharmaceutical industry in France, Switzerland, the United Kingdom, and the U.S.A. when Allied powers were cut off from the necessary raw material provided by the German chemicals industry. The pharmaceutical industry rapidly took on a global reach after the war, when it began to produce and market antibiotics and vaccines to combat infectious diseases, and a growing biomedical corps throughout the world prescribed them to patients.

The legacy of colonial infectious-disease eradication lived on in campaigns to control a variety of infectious diseases in many locations. The best known example is the eradication of smallpox in 1977 through a worldwide vaccination campaign; moreover, many developing nations also successfully controlled infectious diseases without outside help through a range of biomedical and hygiene measures: for example, China dealt with schistosomiasis, Cuba with dengue fever, several West African nations with onchocerciasis.[35] Although the claims that epidemic disease would be completely conquered are often thought of today as hubris, these victories transformed the lives of hundreds of millions of people for the better, and provided concrete evidence that biomedicine could be harnessed to achieve important national and international goals.

Evidence that micro-organisms could cross borders heralded an age of international biomedical cooperation under the aegis of microbiology. International cooperation to combat infectious disease was initially orchestrated through the League of Nations Health Office, and diplomatic cooperation amongst the world's nation-states was formalized in 1948 with the creation of the World Health Organization.[36] The eradication of smallpox in 1977 is still celebrated as a triumph of international cooperation and of the ability of biomedicine to bring nations together. The notion that health should be managed by nation-states, with occasional international collaboration on specific issues, has been superseded by a belief that health "threats" must be viewed in a dynamic, global perspective, and that the principal political and administrative actors of the last century are no longer able to contain rapidly evolving biomedically related phenomena. Writing about the SARS epidemic, referring to the 1648 century Treaty of Westphalia that recognized states' sovereignty within their own borders, Fidler has argued that we have moved to a "post-Westphalian" era in biomedicine when states can no longer claim sovereignty over health issues within their borders. Talk of "global health" has superseded "international health," reflecting both the increasingly transnational character of health threats that operate irrespective of national boundaries and the global nature of the response they entail.[37] The new "global health" paradigm that has emerged out of the worldwide

dissemination of biomedicine can be viewed as a successor to the discipline of tropical medicine that was so important during colonial times. The perception of global
biomedicine that today holds sway, supported by a powerful alliance of international
institutions, industry, philanthropy, and NGOs, reflects the success of proponents
of germ theory and the technologies they utilized in establishing microbiology as
the standard by which these critical events were to be managed.

This is particularly evident in the case of AIDS, the first time since the global
influenza pandemic of 1918 that the whole world has been confronted with an infectious disease that afflicts rich and poor alike. AIDS began and continues to be multiple
epidemics, as was recognized in an early epidemiological classification that distinguished a "pattern 1" epidemic affecting mainly gay men in industrialized nations, a
"pattern 2" epidemic affecting mainly intravenous drug users in southern Europe and
parts of South America, and a "pattern 3" form that is a generalized, heterosexually
spread epidemic in Africa. Differences between epidemics are widely attributed to
"social" factors such as poverty, inequality, and racism while the virus is taken as the
biologically invariant final cause.[38] Microbiology continues to serve as a standard,
allowing technological interventions to be developed with confidence in their universal application. This is most visible in the focus on technologies that target the
virus itself, namely anti-HIV drugs and diagnostic technologies.

As a result of the standardization of multiple epidemics in terms of a single, causative agent (HIV), a fundamental inequity was made glaringly visible, as the treatment
for the virus (anti-retroviral drugs) was unaffordable in most poor nations. International
agencies, led by the WHO, insisted that treatment was not "cost-effective" in low-
income countries, where prevention and palliative care were to be stressed. But in an
era of globalized biomedicine, and as health increasingly came to be framed as a
human right, a two-track view of the epidemic could not be sustained, and collapsed
in 2000, at which time the WHO made a remarkable about-face and belatedly began
to champion universal access to treatment for HIV, culminating in the highly visible
"3 by 5" campaign announced in 2003 that aimed –and failed – to treat three million
people with the HIV drugs by 2005.[39] AIDS had become a humanitarian emergency,
calling for the same kind of muscular intervention as an earthquake or a tidal wave.

As a result, global control of infectious diseases essentially came full circle, conju-
gating colonial humanitarianism with a new round of vertical campaigns to test and
treat entire populations according to a microbiological standard. It marked a victory
for the Pastorian paradigm over one that emphasized social factors including poverty
and economic inequality as the principal drivers of HIV epidemics. Such a "social"
approach was caricatured in the widely publicized views of the former South African
President Thabo Mbeki who expressed skepticism that HIV caused AIDS, indicting
poverty and racism as causal instead. While Mbeki strayed far from scientific orthodoxy by associating with "AIDS dissidents," the notion that poverty and inequality
were significant social determinants of epidemics had nonetheless long been a mainstream notion widely accepted by epidemiologists and clinicians. Juggernaut AIDS
treatment programs, with their focus on saving individual lives through treatment,
have effectively moved the response away from an emphasis on addressing social
determinants and even away from prevention programs to focus on biology alone.

The global circulation of microscopes, syringes, and fumigation nozzles characteristic of colonial campaigns has given way to the circulation of anti-retrovirals,

polymerase chain reaction (PCR) technologies, rapid diagnostic tests and, of course, condoms, all calibrated by biology alone as the standard for addressing epidemics. What is at stake is the control of an affliction that threatens the vitality of individuals and entire populations. These technologies are mobile and powerful, but run into technical problems when they encounter local biologies. Early colonial biomedical technologies, as we have seen, were caught up in webs of local interpretation and practice: needles used to aspirate cerebrospinal fluid or lymph fluid from the neck triggered widespread rumors that Europeans were vampires. Today, misunderstandings and unanticipated consequences arise in connection with the dissemination of facts and practices associated with the distribution of condoms and anti-retrovirals. Condoms may be used to prevent unwanted pregnancies and to protect from sexually transmitted infections, but their use can also signify a lack of trust in a partner, or be taken as evidence of infidelity. Anti-retrovirals are effective in reducing the quantity of HIV in the blood by blocking its replication, but they can cause rare toxicities, including fatal ones – leading to rumors that they are actually poisons sent to sicken unwitting victims.[40] Malnutrition makes it more likely that individuals will suffer from toxic side effects when using these drugs, and different individuals metabolize the drugs differently, leading to different drug levels in their bodies – a crucial example of the importance of taking account of both individual narratives of ill health and of how individual biology is situated.

Infertility and Childbirth as Critical Events

An ability to master infectious diseases that have devastated humans from time immemorial is without doubt the major 20th-century achievement of biomedicine, one that increased life expectancy for millions, rid the world of the scourges of polio and smallpox and of many other infectious diseases through the development of vaccinations, and in so doing transformed what it means to be healthy. Most deaths from infectious diseases occur in the young – primarily in infants but also in young adults. Once the majority of individuals who were born began to survive into adulthood due to the availability of vaccination and antibiotics, the event that now claimed the most lives became childbirth. In the absence of basic obstetrical care, women in some parts of the world still face a lifetime chance as high as one in four of dying during childbirth. Birthing is perilous, an event filled with danger because obstructed labor and other obstetrical complications can, and often do, kill. Birth is not merely a biological event, of course, as it is also a key event in the reproduction of society; concomitantly, obstetrical pathology and infertility may threaten both individual and collective survival. Recognition of this can be seen the world over and informs anthropological interpretations of birthing practices as being located in a "liminal" zone, outside of ordinary social life.[41] As was the case for colonial epidemics, we now explore how birth also became a critical event that facilitated the introduction of biomedical technologies predicated on a standard biology to the colonies.

The global biomedicalization of childbirth began when a wave of concerns about fertility, birthing, and the rearing of children swept much of the world after World War I. Birth rates became a standard measure of the health of nations after plummeting in the wake of World War I when millions of young men were killed, and many more died in the great influenza pandemic of 1918. Policies aimed at increasing birth rates were put in place in many countries, and this pro-natalism often resulted in increasing medicalization of childbirth that had up until then taken place largely outside of clinical settings.[42] Pro-natalism and a growing concern for child health contributed to the rise of eugenicist ideas discussed in the previous chapter that framed the "problem of population."

A link between getting the "right population" and reproduction in the first half of the 20th century came about when giving birth was moved from the home into the hospital and increasingly put under the care of physicians. But this global bio-medicalization of childbirth differed in scope from the infectious disease eradication campaigns, because it introduced technologies and invasive obstetrical procedures directed at a specific population, that of potential mothers, that changed the way this private, intimate event was subjectively experienced everywhere it was adopted.

Birthing in the Belgian Congo

In the 1920s, low birth rates were observed not only in what is now the former Belgian Congo but also in the British protectorates to the east, and French Equatorial Africa to the north. This phenomenon raised the specter of a Central African "infertility belt" that has received considerable attention from that time to the present. Worried about the impact of declining fertility on the availability of colonial labor, colonial authorities, missions, and some benevolent European women's associations – occasionally working together but more often independently of each other – encouraged African women to have more children. Breastfeeding was discouraged in favor of canned milk, because it is more difficult to conceive while breastfeeding. The concern with fertility drew attention to the high rates of obstetrical complications and infant mortality, spurring colonial officials to experiment with maternal health clinics and lying-in hospitals. These facilities introduced European obstetrical practices current at the time: forceps for difficult deliveries, and in the case of obstructed labor, craniotomies, and embryotomies – practices performed to save the life of the mother that involve evacuating the obstructed fetus by destroying it. The use of these technologies would not decrease until after World War II when, with the advent of antibiotics, cesarean sections became safer.

The Belgian Congo was notable for aggressive pro-natalist policies, stimulated by a colonially induced panic about plunging birth rates and reports of an epidemic of infertility. Low birth rates in the Belgian Congo during the interwar period prompted dire warnings in the Belgian media of a "dying race" and dramatic accounts of childless villages, aimed at a Belgian public that was beginning to come to grips with the brutality of King Leopold's concessionary rule over the colony. Millions died of starvation and disease as local populations were displaced and ruthlessly exploited to harvest rubber, the most infamous atrocity being the cutting off of the hands of Congolese workers who tried to flee the work camps.[43] In a setting of such misery, miscarriages were legion.

One of the most richly textured accounts of the introduction of bio-obstetrical technologies into local worlds comes from Hunt's historical ethnography of a mission hospital in the Belgian Congo that retraces the history of this hospital, drawing on archival material as well as interviews with surviving Congolese, Britons, and Belgians who had spent time there.[44] The hospital was a microcosm of the global biomedicalization of childbirth and the misunderstandings that occurred with the introduction of new technologies. Hunt recounts the arrival of a British missionary and physician, Dr Chesterton, at the Yakusu Baptist Hospital in 1920. After the first surgical operation Chesterton performed at the mission that December "when he set his surgical gloves to boil in the cookhouse fire, two of his domestic servants saw a boiling soup of black human hands and imagined that the doctor was going to eat them."[45] The servants were about to run away, but their curiosity got the better of them and they stayed to watch the next surgery. Chesterton's "work of the knife" in fact resonated with local practices of healing involving scarification, and eventually helped to establish his legitimacy as a healer.

Until the interwar period, the tropics were widely viewed as unsuitable for European women; however, concerns over European men taking up with "native" women led many colonial powers to encourage settlement by white women with the result that more comprehensive maternal health programs were developed for the wives of Europeans. These programs became a model for maternal and child health programs, and helped to spur the implementation of such programs in colonial homelands, showing how bio-obstetrical technologies were sufficiently standardized to enable colonial experience to leverage obstetrical reform in Europe. Hunt notes:

> by the 1950s, infant mortality was lower among Belgian infants in the colony than in the metropole, indicating how well developed this infrastructure had become. Most women living in Belgium continued to have home births, attended by professional midwives or doctors, until after World War II. Indeed, lying-in hospitals, long associated with indigent and unwed mothers, did not become the norm in Belgium until … postwar health insurance legislation effected a sudden and rapid hospitalization of child-bearing.[46]

The circulation of obstetrical and health-promotion technologies between the colonial periphery and metropolitan heartland laid the foundations of a global maternal and child health apparatus. The use of biomedical technologies in these settings allowed entry into different moral worlds where concerns about bodies, fertility, and birthing were tied up in local therapeutic economies and systems of meaning. The colonial biomedicalization of childbirth comforted colonial powers in their view of themselves as bringing "civilization" to their colonial charges, as Hunt and others have shown, and although the latter viewed the strange new technologies with apprehension and suspicion, local women often pragmatically appropriated them to their own ends.[47]

The effectiveness of these technologies was acknowledged by pregnant women, colonial health care authorities, and the colonizing European governments, helping to legitimate the application of these technologies to childbirth, particularly after the quantification of birth rates as standardized statistical measures of fertility began to be associated with national prowess.

A Global Practice of Fertility Control

By the 1960s the majority of former colonial lands had become independent nations, eager to modernize and take their full place on the world stage. Biomedicine was emblematic of modernization, and newly independent states rushed to build hospitals and provide modern health care. Pro-natalism was gradually replaced with a concern to limit births and produce "modern" nuclear families. Once biology emerged as the standard for calibrating measures to address the "population problem," obstetric interventions such as forceps delivery, and the promotion of canned milk for new-borns were replaced by sterilization surgery, the birth-control pill, the IUD, and contraceptive implants and injections. "Family planning" gained global prominence pushed by foundations and governments in the North worried about a "population time-bomb."

Human reproduction continues to attract intensive efforts to intervene biomedi-cally the world over and, indeed, for many women fertility control is the only contact that they have with either biomedicine or the modern state. For even the poorest women, family planning programs channelled through NGOs such as the International Planned Parenthood Federation offer access to contraception. It is in the realm of fertility control that the global reach of biomedicine has been the greatest. Efforts to manage reproduction are predicated on a biologically standardized body. As we have seen in chapter 2, the normalized "Friedman curves" central to the obstetrical dogma of "active management of labor" are made use of everywhere, with inappropriate outcomes, as the Inuit case makes clear (see pp. 48–50). Likewise, fetal growth curves used to estimate gestational dates using ultrasound prove unreliable when ultrasound technologies travel to places such as Ghana, as Müller-Rockstroh points out, where fetuses grow at different rates.[48] The biological standardization of reproduction also enabled the first clinical trials of birth-control pills to be conducted in Puerto Rico, Mexico, and Haiti in the late 1950s when they could not be conducted in the U.S.A. where the birth-control pill was invented, due to anti-birth-control restrictions. Research findings and lessons learnt from the implementation of population control programs continue to flow from South to North and vice versa in a circulation of biomedical technologies across geographical terrain enabled by the use of biology alone as a standard that has contributed to the constitution of a global practice of fertility control.

Intimate Colonialism: The Biomedicalization of Domesticity

The biomedicalization of childbirth and childrearing was a pervasive phenomenon, a beachhead from which biomedical technologies could colonize the intimate domestic sphere. In Africa the biomedicalization of reproduction reflected concerns over the availability of the African labor pool and a "demographic panic" over declining birth rates in Europe that raised anxieties about the sustainability of empire, mirroring the eugenic thinking prevalent in Europe after World War I. These moral concerns encouraged forms of domesticity in what historians have called an "intimate coloni-alism."[49] In both British East Africa and Belgian Africa, the perceived infertility "epidemic" was blamed on racist assumptions about the "loose sexual mores" of African women and informed a sophisticated and extensive response to address the "root cause" of infertility. This response concentrated on women, seeking to transform them through the dissemination of Western practices of childbirth and childrearing. This strategy was justified by the idea that African women would be more accepting of these campaigns once they saw the beneficial effects of such Western practices, even though some colonial commentators attributed the problem precisely to the fact that African women did not have an innate sense of motherhood.[50] At stake were conflicting visions of motherhood: one that conceived of motherhood as the domain of individual women, and another that located mothering within a nexus of social relations.[51] Ultimately the creation of a network of maternal and child health centers tipped the balance in favor of the former – motherhood as an individual attribute – and in so doing created forms of domesticity familiar in the West.

Obstetrical practice was linked to campaigns that sought to teach women in the ways of "proper" and "hygienic" motherhood, introducing a normative view of how children were to be raised and the body cared for. In writing a history of cleanliness in Zimbabwe, Tim Burke showed how companies seeking to create new markets for hygiene products such as Lifebuoy soap rapidly exploited colonists' concerns about hygiene. In the 1920s colonial administrators, worried that "native women" were teaching their children "unhygienic" traditional practices, resolved to teach indigenous peoples proper cleanliness. They deployed a small army of "Jeanes teachers," so named after an American philanthropist who funded the domestic educators, and these emissaries set about cleaning homes, instructing women in the proper way to clean their baby's bodies, and even building latrines. These domestic teachers met with considerable resistance, and were viewed as busybodies who had no right to poke their noses into the personal affairs of others, or for that matter into their homes. Gradually, however, many of these practices took hold, actively encouraged both by younger Africans who sought to affirm their modern identities in opposition to their more conservative parents, and by the makers of Lifebuoy and Lux soap. These programs and others successfully linked obstetrical practice to the creation of an African domesticity.[52]

New colonial domesticities were modeled on a normative, European household that became known when contact with Europeans increased after growing numbers settled in Africa. Initially European domestic space was limited to the households of missionaries.[53] This increased in importance when health conditions improved in the 1920s and women came to join their settler husbands, constituting a growing class of European settler households. The settler household was an expanding point of contact between "native" servants and settler domesticity with its European rituals of childrearing, cleaning, and cooking. Some of these servants would go on to become the first generation of nurses and physicians' assistants. For the rest, their competence in the care of the European body – with its rituals and routines structured around colonial notions of hygiene – formed a vanguard for new forms of domesticity anchored by biomedical notions of hygiene, particularly in the realm of childbirth and childrearing. In other words, the care of the settler body, learned as an exotic trade and dependent on the growing proficiency of "natives" with the unfamiliar, provided a site for fashioning colonial subjects into health care workers and moral evangelists.[54] The colonial preoccupation with proper childrearing radiated outward from obstetrical care and the model European household, transmitting practices and technologies that placed women at the heart of a sanitized domestic sphere organized around childbearing and childrearing. The biomedicalization of childbirth and the encroachment of ideas and practices of hygiene into the domestic sphere were motivated by apparently neutral concerns to conform to biological standards of hygiene. Nonetheless, as these accounts show, this "intimate colonialism" reflected prevailing moral assumptions. Nowhere was this more visible than in the medicalization of evangelism.

Biomedicine, Evangelism, and Consciousness

The historical entanglement of biomedicine and domesticity can be traced to the encounter between settler bodies and "native" servants. In medical evangelism, however, the original encounter was between "native" bodies and colonial missionaries, and the historical trajectory moved from a paradigm of proselytization and conversion to one of religious self-transformation and self-fashioning that merged biomedicine with the care of the self. The occasion of illness was a privileged moment for converting the suffering soul. In the colonial world, missionary work – that of saving souls – and medicine – the curing of bodies – were mechanically linked. Missionaries ministered to the ill and the dying in the service of the Lord. Ultimately it did not matter whether illness was explicitly attributed to sin, because care and, occasionally, cure could serve as powerful demonstrations of the superiority of Christian faith as both a spiritual and a material doctrine.[55] Missionary medicine helped to link domesticity and "hygiene" with spiritual notions of purity.

Historians and anthropologists have argued that evangelization did more than "convert" individuals to Christianity. Evangelization, when allied to bodily healing practices, generated new forms of historical consciousness, political agency, and presumably, subjectivity. In her historical ethnography of an African healing church in contemporary Botswana, the noted anthropologist Jean Comaroff showed how bodily practices of healing were a form of social therapy, a salve that borrowed biomedical ideas and practices to heal the psychic wounds of political repression that could only be expressed in the language of bodily affliction.[56] Comaroff's insight is important because it is an early example of how biomedical practices "traveled" out of the clinic and into other sites including churches, where they were, and still are, used to deal with afflictions that do not correspond to biomedical disease entities.

Of course, affliction is not always political. People experience real aches and pains, which may or may not be linked to social circumstances. Biomedical interventions can excise certain kinds of pain, effecting a powerful demonstration that the source of suffering is within the body. Writing about the pulling of teeth in early 20th-century Southern Africa, Landau notes that even though the reason for toothache was likely due to poor oral hygiene as a result of increased sugar consumption afforded by the colonial economy, "as missionaries localized pain to the individual, they also localized the linkage between pain and wrongdoing to the individual."[57] Surgical dentistry, like other biomedical practices, was developed as a technique to address affliction in terms of a decontextualized body standardized in anatomical, pathological, and biological terms. Landau's study of "surgical evangelism" in colonial Southern Africa takes an apparently mundane practice – pulling teeth – and shows how it upset

> experiential relationships that, epitomized by the ancestors, defined and united persons within their community. In contrast, missionaries' therapeutic practice tended to disrupt this prior community and substitute the idea of the individual as enclosing the relevant field of sickness/wellness.[58]

Biomedical technologies introduced strange objects and rituals (forceps and sterilization, for instance) in times of crisis, spreading knowledge about their effects. Mobilized together with the missionary project of evangelization, these technological interventions were agents for transforming consciousness and powerfully inscribing a moral discourse into bodily experience.

The Biological Standardization of Hunger

In this section, we explore another facet of the rise of global biomedicine: famines as critical events that led to the standardization of hunger in biological terms. The biomedicalization of famines is particularly significant because it lies at the origins of modern humanitarianism. The famines that ravaged Eastern Europe and the Soviet Union in the 1920s spurred massive humanitarian relief efforts aimed, for the first time, at providing succor to civilian populations outside of wartime. These efforts helped create the first international NGOs (such as Oxford Famine Relief, now known as Oxfam, founded in 1942). The Ethiopian famine of 1984–85 spawned the Live Aid concert and a tradition of celebrity advocacy, heralding a highly mediatized form of global humanitarianism and led to the consolidation of cooperative efforts that today constitute a veritable disaster relief industry.[59]

Today, many take for granted the biological standardization of hunger and the forms of intervention that deploy biomedical technologies in both the food and famine industries. Global agribusiness and food conglomerates work hand in hand with nutrition science to produce "healthy" foods based on which food group is currently fashionable – such as "heart-healthy" packaged foods in the U.S.A. – to help the wealthy lose weight, while relief agencies provide nutritional supplements to malnourished people based on evidence garnered from clinical trials. Diet however has been an arena for the globalization of biomedicine since colonial times. In the British colonies, and to a lesser extent in their French and Belgian counterparts, variation in both diet and social conditions created a natural laboratory where dietary practices could be linked to health. The colonial discovery of malnutrition was a scientific breakthrough, and through the lens of biology previously disparate phenomena were brought into sharp focus. Matters of appetite, consumption, preparation, tradition, and cultivation, to name a few, were boiled down to the elemental question of diet. The biomedicalization of diet is today so ubiquitous as to be in effect invisible, so thoroughly do many of us now take for granted standardized food measurements and the link between diet and our biological futures. This was not always the case, and the advent of a scientific approach to nutrition as a way to improve the vitality of populations marked yet another facet of the biological standardization of the body.

Just as the medicalization of fertility has shifted between concerns about over- and under-fertility according to time and place, so too has the medicalization of diet been concerned with over- and under-nutrition in different times and places. For the average North American consumer, the question of what to eat has become heavily invested with biomedical understandings of risk for disease. For the diligent consumer who is anxious about his cholesterol or weight, a trip to the supermarket requires navigating a forest of nutritional health claims and consulting tiny charts that count calories, sodium, lipids, types of fats, and carbohydrates. These anxieties emerge from decades of actuarial and epidemiological research that has shown how the common health problems of affluent North Americans are linked to overweight and an inappropriate diet. Nutritional science, working from within the paradigm of biomedicine, carried out research into diet by reducing it to its elemental ingredients, reflected in our current obsession with fats, sugar, and carbohydrates. The dietary omens we read on food labels today trace their origin back to the "colonial discovery of malnutrition."

The Colonial Discovery of Malnutrition

Historian Michael Worboys notes that

> the problem of malnutrition in third world countries, then colonial territories, was first "discovered" between the wars ... there had been some awareness of nutritional problems before then, not least with regard to famines, but it was only then that the matter was constructed as an imperial problem and put on the world political agenda.[60]

As in the case of fertility, colonial concerns with nutrition began in the 1920s as a result of the "key colonial need for able-bodied labourers."[61] Surveys carried out in Kenya and India showed that malnutrition had pernicious effects even when epidemics and famines were apparently on the decrease.[62]

During that period, key discoveries were made linking various diseases, such as pellagra, to dietary deficiencies in vitamins and minerals. These findings followed the careful observation of geographical and social differences in particular diseases and the linking of these to differences in diet. Scurvy, which had been known to occur in diets poor in citrus fruits since the 18th century, was linked to vitamin C deficiency in 1932. The colonies, particularly India, furnished an ideal laboratory for studying the impact of diet on nutrition because of the variety of diets that could be found there. In India, the "Sikh diet" of meat and wheat was considered superior to vegetarian diets with rice as a staple. The discovery of the link between macrocytic anemia (a lack of red blood cells in which those that remain are swollen) and folate (a water-soluble form of vitamin B) was first made in India in 1928, when the British scientist Lucy Wills traveled to Bombay to work with "Mohammedan women" who were commonly found to have this particular form of anemia during pregnancy.[63] Wills showed that a diet supplemented with the popular British savory spread Marmite reversed the condition. Marmite, an acquired taste, is made from yeast extract and the "Wills Factor" was eventually identified as folate or folic acid, recommended universally today for pregnant women.

The historian Jennifer Stanton[64] has documented how, in another British colony, the Gold Coast (today Ghana) in West Africa, colonial concerns over infant mortality emerged after a survey, undertaken in the wake of a partial census, showed that over half of newborns died in the first year of life.[65] In the wake of the survey, infant welfare clinics were set up in the main towns and were well attended. In 1929, a young Jamaican-born British physician, Dr Cicely Williams, was appointed Woman Medical Officer and one of her responsibilities was overseeing the clinics. Women physicians were unusual in the colonies, and Williams also stood out by linking her clinical practice to an understanding of local language and custom – a closeness that would hinder acceptance by others of her important nutritional discovery. Williams treated over 100,000 malnourished infants and observed that the weaning crisis that occurred between ages two and four with the birth of the next child was associated with a syndrome not described in the medical textbooks of the time. Affected children were stricken with edema (swelling due to leakage of fluid into tissues), were lethargic and irritable, and had darkening and peeling of the skin at flexion points. She named the disease "kwashiorkor" that in a Ghanaian language means "displaced child," and she suspected it was due to a protein deficiency at weaning and transition to a protein-poor diet.

Williams' colleagues rejected her hypothesis out of hand, saying what she was seeing was a form of pellagra, a skin disease that had begun to reach epidemic proportions in the American South and was associated with a maize (corn) diet. Pellagra was later found to be caused by a deficiency in the vitamin niacin and the amino-acid tryptophan. In maize, these nutrients are present but in a form that is difficult to digest, explaining why diets where maize is a staple may lead to deficiency. Indigenous Americans, for whom maize is a staple, had, hundreds of years earlier, learned to treat corn with lime, which creates a chemical reaction that makes niacin and tryptophan more easily digestible, but this traditional treatment was forgotten with urbanization in the South of the United States. Williams doubted that she was dealing with pellagra, as she knew that in Ghana maize was fermented before being eaten, and because she showed that Marmite did not cure the condition, she demonstrated that it was not macrocytic anemia.

Despite initial skepticism, the confirmation of Williams' hypothesis vindicated her and confirmed the power of a biological understanding of disease to link disparate diseases within a universal framework that offered the possibility of effective intervention. Her outspokenness had by then led to her transfer by the British Colonial Office to Indonesia where she was jailed by the Japanese during World War II. After the war, she went on to become the first head of the WHO's maternal child health division. There, she launched a survey of kwashiorkor throughout sub-Saharan Africa in 1950. Stanton quotes the survey's conclusion that the disease was "the most serious and widespread nutritional disorder known to medical and nutritional science."[66]

Kwashiorkor is now recognized as being due to a protein deficiency that manifests itself even in the presence of adequate caloric intake, and is clinically distinguished from other forms of malnutrition by muscle wasting in the presence of normal or even increased body fat – the effect of a diet rich in calories but poor in protein. An important sign of kwashiorkor is the swelling of the abdomen which was found to be due to decreased levels of a critical protein, albumin, in the blood. Albumin attracts water and holds it in the blood vessels (much like salt). When it is insufficient, fluid seeps into the surrounding tissues causing edema. Blood albumin levels have since become the standard biological measure of malnutrition. However, it was early on established that in the case of severe malnourishment, albumin alone was not a replacement for feeding, as it does not by itself nourish the body.

Albumin's role in preventing water from leaking out of the blood vessels and into surrounding tissue led to interest in the protein as a blood volume expander for patients who were in hypovolemic shock, when their blood volume was critically decreased from hemorrhage. During World War II, the benefits of albumin for injured soldiers were widely touted. Battlefield injuries resulted in blood loss and shock, and albumin promised to be a more practical therapy than blood transfusions. Albumin infusions did not require that blood type between donor and recipient match, and could be stored more easily than blood. After its World War II debut, albumin began to be widely used in critical care medicine, where it was employed to treat different kinds of hypovolemic shock – a condition that occurs when there is a significant blood loss, but can also occur when severe infections or inflammations cause blood vessels to become "leaky." Albumin became a popular volume expander in these conditions and was a staple in intensive care units around the world.

Human albumin is a blood product that is not manufactured but collected from blood donors, whose plasma is pooled and "fractionated" to cream off the valuable protein. For many years it was the most widely used of all biopharmaceutical solutions (as an intravenous drug), with several hundred tonnes being produced and administered annually.[67] After being establishing as a biological standard, albumin embarked on a second career as a treatment: by the mid-1990s, albumin had become a multibillion-dollar global market.

Albumin as Surplus

Albumin fell out of favor starting in the late 1990s when the *British Medical Journal* published a synthesis of several epidemiological studies that suggested that albumin was not in fact of clinical benefit for patients suffering from hypovolemia, and might even increase mortality.[68] This meta-analysis dealt a massive blow to the global albumin industry. However the treatment had by then become popular in many parts of the world. In China the popularity of albumin was rooted in local practices, as the anthropologist Jing Shao documents in an interview with a physician who practiced in Henan, where Jing Shao did his fieldwork:

> Dr. S had only learned of albumin in the 1950s and still remembered the few instances in his own practice when he first used it in the 1970s, when imported albumin became available in his hospital. The patients who received albumin injections before or after surgery were all important local officials: a deputy chief of the prefecture, a chief of the organization division of a county's Communist Party committee, and the head of the Communist Party branch in his hospital. At the time it was prohibitively expensive … This luxury of albumin treatment with vague clinical benefits was offered to officials not for the purpose of making money, Dr. S insisted, but, rather, in the context of the informal gift economy of the socialist era, to appeal to their sense of privilege in the hope of drawing favors from them in the future.[69]

China's blood products industry, in existence since the 1950s, received a major boost in the 1980s after importation of blood products was banned as a measure to keep HIV out of the country. Economic reforms further stimulated the blood products industry. The technology on which the industry was based collected blood from donors, extracted the plasma, and returned blood cells to the donors. The vigorous domestic market for albumin fed the plasma fractionation industry particularly since albumin production requires no additional equipment and minimal extra cost when whole blood is used to produce other blood products such as red blood cells for transfusions or immunoglobulins. Marketing albumin was therefore a very profitable sideline for the blood products industry, spurring ruthless competition between blood firms and unscrupulous "blood heads" – brokers paid to recruit and transport blood donors. Collection stations proliferated across the country, and as Jing Shao notes:

> Most collection stations were set up in county towns, primarily because of their proximity to rural areas where donors could be more easily recruited. They were operated mostly by local public health facilities such as local disease-control stations and health centers for women and children and by the less profitable hospitals in the health care market, including small county hospitals, hospitals of Chinese medicine, and clinics funded by failing state enterprises and the military. Profits from plasma collection provided a much welcomed sideline income.[70]

In China albumin was, erroneously, marketed as a "nutritional drug" and proponents of the plasma fractionation industry argued that China was an albumin-starved nation. Development was linked to albumin consumption: "from the industry's perspective, it seems that the nation's gross domestic albumin consumption has somehow acquired a GDP-like quality, capable of measuring the nation's health and wealth at the same time."[71]

As is now well known, shoddy collection practices – notably, the reuse of needles – helped fuel an HIV epidemic amongst blood donors. The majority of these were poor peasants whose farming activities were no longer profitable as a result of the same economic reforms that were driving the blood industry. Unable to live off the land, these peasants sold their blood, and when they sickened with HIV, purchased nutritional albumin shots.[72] The link between the albumin industry in China, blood collection, and a biomedicalized approach to understanding nutrition is a cautionary tale. After the colonial discovery of malnutrition, albumin became the biological standard for the measurement of malnutrition. The biologization of hunger led to its measurement becoming confused with the treatment when albumin started to be used to treat malnutrition. Albumin, plasma fractionation, and blood banks are strikingly portable technologies and we have seen the unexpected consequences – in this case tragic ones – that may result when they are taken up in a local therapeutic economy.

This example shows how, after World War II and in the heyday of nationalist biomedical projects around the world, the question of nutrition and diet came to be viewed as a technical problem. The need to develop life-saving interventions for malnourished populations, whether victims of natural and man-made disasters or the severely ill, continued to be a focus of attention within biomedical research and

practice. The biological standardization of hunger, subsequent to the colonial discovery of malnutrition, led to its formulation as a clinical problem. In addition, and
consistent with the nationalist problematic of population, the biological standardization of hunger provided a standard for calibrating development and agricultural
policy. Despite progress in agricultural methods – such as the much-heralded "Green
Revolution" that dramatically increased food production through the use of high-
yielding varieties of such staple crops as maize, wheat, and rice – malnutrition did
not disappear because, as is now widely acknowledged in the wake of work by Nobel-
prize winning economist Amartya Sen, famines are not due to food shortages but to
social and economic disruptions.

The Biologization of Salvation

Famines were also critical to the development of modern humanitarianism. Already
in the early 20th century, media reports made the widespread suffering and death of
faraway strangers cause consternation in Western Europe, and the first NGOs were
founded in the 1920s in response to the famines that ravaged Eastern Europe at the
time. Also, as noted earlier, these organized efforts to provide famine relief to civilian
populations in foreign countries created a historical precedent. A science of famine
relief has since emerged. Large-scale clinical studies of malnutrition were conducted
from the 1960s, mainly done with children in poor countries as well as in refugee
camps that concentrate large pools of malnourished individuals. Studies conducted
in Iraq, India, Nigeria, Uganda, Zambia, and other countries contributed to the
production of a standardized definition of malnutrition.[73] Considerable work was
done to validate such measures as body mass index, upper arm circumference, skin
fold thickness, hip-to-waist ratio; no mean feat given the range of variation in body
size and type across the world (a new permutation of earlier concerns of physical
anthropologists with measuring human heads to quantify racial differences). The
standardization of bodily measurement laid the groundwork for clinical trials to
evaluate the impact of nutritional interventions to improve nutritional status. The
"biologization" of famine pursued the colonial discovery of malnutrition, further
standardizing the body in nutritional terms.

The biologization of famine united the culture of rescue that girds humanitarian
operations and biomedicine, and is still visible in the medical humanitarian industry
that has resulted. The convergence was both pragmatic and ideological: famine relief
is intertwined with providing biomedical assistance to populations because the conditions associated with famine – droughts, wars, and economic turmoil – often occur
where public health infrastructure is poor, if present at all. One cannot save lives
without providing both food and medical care. Famine and disease go together; thus,
famine relief must be provided alongside biomedical assistance to populations, usually
through a common operational infrastructure. Modern medical humanitarianism was
born of the violence of the Biafran civil war in Nigeria in the late 1960s.[74] A small
group of French doctors, led by Bernard Kouchner (who at the time of writing is
the French Foreign Minister) founded Médecins sans frontières (MSF), an NGO
dedicated to bringing medical care to the forgotten victims of conflict. MSF broke
with what had until then been a tradition of political neutrality in humanitarian relief

operations. Organizations such as the Red Cross had historically been required to adhere to strict neutrality in order to gain access to military and civilian populations in need of help. MSF and other medical NGOs such as Médecins du Monde that followed in its wake, argued for the "right to intervene" and adopted a policy of explicitly denouncing perpetrators of violence against civilians, ushering in the era of "witnessing" as a human rights practice.[75] The positions advocated by the medical humanitarians from the 1970s, including a right to health, have now become ortho-dox – since the 1990s, even military operations comprise a "humanitarian" element. The paradox of bombing-while-treating underscores the central tension in humani-tarian aid between the urgency of saving biological lives and the need to address the circumstances that put those lives in peril in the first place. Considerable ambivalence exists, even amongst those in need of "saving," about the stripped-down notion of standardized biological life operative in many humanitarian missions.[76]

The developing world is often viewed through the lens of deprivation, poverty, and hunger. These are vital issues for our times, and they index the deeply troubling inequalities that characterize the global situation. These inequalities, however, do not only manifest themselves as deprivation. Dramatically increasing rates of overweight – even among the poor – have been attributed to the widespread availability of "cheap calories" produced by global agribusiness, conjugated with increasingly urban and sedentary lifestyles and a corresponding shift away from "traditional" diets. Another important factor is the economic changes in countries such as China and India where marginal gains in real income by the poor translate into greater caloric consumption.[77] The health consequences of these "epidemics" have yet to be fully recognized, but ominous signs include skyrocketing rates of diabetes, heart disease, and other "chronic" ailments previously thought to be "diseases of civilization" only present in more affluent countries. The changing epidemiology of chronic diseases worldwide heralds a growing biomedicalization of even the world's poor, a situation that augurs well for the pharmaceutical industry, that has already seen burgeoning sales of anti-diabetic and anti-hypertensive drugs in the developing world.

As these chronic diseases increasingly afflict the poor and the not-quite-poor in the developing world, these individuals turn to biomedicine for treatment. Veena Das has conducted extensive ethnographic research in slum neighborhoods of Delhi and has shown how even poor residents increasingly afflicted with diabetes and hypertension spend a large portion of their meager income on pharmaceuticals. Those faced with kidney failure, a common outcome of diabetes and poorly controlled hypertension, borrow, scrimp, and save for a desperately needed kidney transplant.[78] Ironically, malnutrition is brought on by a complex interaction of global economic forces affecting the food and agricultural industries with changing local standards of living and ideas about the good life. The resulting epidemic of obesity-related health conditions promises a far more intense biomedicalization of the poor than afforded by earlier generations of famine relief and primary health care efforts.

The biomedical problematization of diet has thus moved from colonial anxieties about maintaining an able work force to concerns about rising rates of metabolic and cardiovascular diseases in both affluent nations and those striving to achieve affluence, as well as interventions conducted on populations in conditions of famine and war by NGOs and development agencies. A reductionistic approach has prevailed through-out these interventions, limited to a decontextualized understanding of the influence of diet as being limited to the quantifiable actions of specific types of substances: vitamins, carbohydrates, sugars, fats. Dietary surveys, anthropometry, and biological markers such as albumin and hemoglobin are examples of how biology has become the standard by which hunger is to be understood and managed. The resulting discoveries that have shaped nutritional science and intervention are evidence of the power of biology as a standard to influence not only what we eat but also the bodies we have. In America, industrialized food production used a reductionistic approach to diet – what Pollan calls "nutritionism" – to improve health, paradoxically leading to even worse health as Americans eat ever more "low-fat" foods rich in sugars and carbohydrates.[79] Famines are now managed through food aid programs administered via humanitarian relief agencies that rely on the latest nutritional science. And in China, the growth of a blood products industry conjugated with economic reforms resulted in the circulation of albumin in ways that would trigger an HIV epidemic. Together, these examples point to how the biological standardization of the link between diet and individual and collective vitality has made it amenable to biomedical intervention with at times tragic consequences when biomedical technologies are taken up out of the contexts in which they were developed to specific ends. The link between diet and vitality is no doubt recognized across all the cultures of the world. However, in stark contrast to most indigenous ideas about diet, biomedicine associates vitality with diet by, on one hand, reductionism (disaggregating food into its constitutive elements) and, on the other hand, decontextualization (food is isolated from the broader context of its production and preparation).

Madness

As we have seen, fevers, birthing, and diet were increasingly subject to scrutiny and intervention as biological standardization leveraged the global deployment of biomedical technologies between World War I and World War II. In contrast to infectious epidemics, fertility, and hunger, madness remained outside the realm of biological understanding until after the end of the colonial era; no biological standard was available. Bereft of effective tools, or even a coherent paradigm to manage mental illness, colonial psychiatrists struggled with an apparently bewildering array of pathologies that did not correspond to those they had been trained to diagnose and treat in the West.

Our brief discussion here focuses on two contrasting attempts to standardize psychiatry in the face of the enormous differences in symptoms exhibited by individuals and the apparent profound influence of cultural mores on their manifestation around the globe. The first example shows how, in the absence of a biological standard for addressing mental illness, psychiatrists in colonial settings experimented with prevailing local models of the psyche to understand and treat madness. With the discovery of neuroleptic drugs to treat schizophrenia in the 1950s, biological psychiatry began to encroach onto a domain until then dominated by psychoanalysis. The growth of a global psychopharmaceuticals industry is the context for our second example, which shows the difficulties that arise in the absence of an agreed-upon standard for therapeutic intervention. This discussion makes clear how the global circulation of biomedical technologies requires "standards" to work, and that in the absence of the "gold standard" afforded by an assumed universal biology, other forms of st[...]zation are required.

Histories of colonial psychiatry have stressed the coercive and downright cruel treatment reserved for those suffering from mental illness in colonial regimes.[80] Frantz Fanon is widely cited as a counter-example for his innovative and humane treatment of the insane in a violent colonial situation. A black Frenchman born and raised in Martinique, Fanon first experienced racism when he moved to metropolitan France to pursue his medical studies. He completed his training in psychiatry which, at the time, was dominated by the psychoanalytic approach to mental illness fathered by Sigmund Freud 50 years earlier. This approach stressed the role played by an individual's development and life experiences in the structuring of the self (we return to this point in chapter 11). In this view, universal psychic processes, such as the resolution of the Oedipus complex described below, were held to structure the human self. Mental illness was however clearly the result of contextualized personal experience, and could only be understood and treated using highly individualized methods.

After completing his medical specialization Fanon was deployed to an asylum in Algeria in the service of the French colonial administration. At the time, a nascent Algerian independence movement was being brutally repressed by the French. In Algeria, Fanon confronted the barbaric conditions in which psychiatric inmates were held. He experimented with a form of "social therapy" by integrating patients into a semblance of normal life, and he drew on psychoanalytic and existential theories prevalent at the time to justify this approach, and to refute racist ideas that colonial subjects were somehow different or childlike versions of more fully realized Europeans. Fanon would eventually move beyond a patient-centered orientation to espouse a radical political approach to healing the wounds of colonialism that would take the form of a revolutionary, anti-imperialist struggle. Indeed, Fanon is best known for his powerful denunciation of colonialism that appeared in two books he wrote as a young man, evidence of his remarkable insight into how racial violence damaged the psyches of both colonizer and colonized. Fanon subsequently joined the Algerian Liberation Movement to which he remained faithful until his untimely death of leukaemia at age 32.

The idea of a universal psyche came under a challenge in the 1960s in French West Africa. Dakar is a bustling metropolis set on the very Western tip of Africa, its slaving fort a site often visited by politicians and tourists. As the capital of French West Africa, Dakar has long been a cosmopolitan city, where a substantial French population included many Africans who, as residents of the original "four colonies," that made up French West Africa, were entitled to French citizenship. The city was the hub of a literary and cultural scene, and its future President, Leopold Sédar Senghor, a poet and cultural theorist who later would be the first African appointed to the prestigious Académie française, became a prime spokesman for negritude, the cultural movement celebrating African roots. It was in Dakar that a remarkable experiment in cultural psychiatry took place in the 1960s.

Henri Collomb was a French military psychiatrist who had served throughout the colonies in Somaliland, Indochina, and Djibouti when he was appointed as Chair of Neuropsychiatry at the Faculty of Medicine of Dakar, still today a leading African medical school. Like Fanon, Collomb rejected the repressive asylum model of biomedical care afforded psychiatric patients. However, Collomb, unlike Fanon, did not believe that European theories of mental illness should be mechanically applied to understand psychiatric disturbance in non-European contexts. He was not so much a cultural relativist as suspicious of an assumed universalism. Collomb set up an integrated clinical research, treatment, and training unit bringing together French and African researchers, physicians, anthropologists, and psychoanalysts to attempt to understand and treat mental illness in what came to be called the Dakar School. This school publishes the prestigious journal *Psychopathologie africaine* in which a range of scientific papers investigated the phenomenology, epidemiology, culture, and the course of mental illness, in a wide range of African contexts. Although little known outside the French-speaking world, the ideas put forward by the Dakar School profoundly influenced psychiatry and contributed greatly to contemporary "cross-cultural" or "ethnopsychiatry."[81]

Edmond and Marie-Cécile Ortigues, both psychoanalysts, were part of Collomb's team and set out to delineate the contours of the Oedipus complex in their African patients. In so doing, they were influenced by the work of the rising Parisian star in psychoanalytic circles, Jacques Lacan. Lacan, at that time a psychiatrist in the Parisian asylum of Ste-Anne, proposed a bold and revolutionary rereading of Freud, including of the Oedipus complex, based on the structuralist and linguistic theories prevalent at the time. Freud understood the Oedipus complex as rooted in the male child's unconscious desire to kill his father in order to be reunited with his mother. Lacan interpreted the complex metaphorically, arguing that the child's psychic conflicts were structured by the painful transition from the sensuous binary relation between child and mother to a tripolar world constituted by an emerging contact with language and the force of the paternal law. The child's identity is forged as much by its arduous entry into language and culture as by its primary relationships. The Ortigues rejected a mechanistic, universalizing view of the Oedipus complex, of the sort that had been popularized by anthropologists of the day. This mechanistic reading of the Oedipus complex was often used to justify racist assertions of cultural superiority, and continues to be used at times to pigeonhole individuals. Rather, they argued that

> human existence demands a minimal social setting (of three people) and the ability to locate oneself within this setting (that is, the ability to use and understand the pronouns "I," "you" and "he"/"she") precludes the possibility that whole societies could live in a state of pre-Oedipal development.[82]

For the Ortigues the Oedipus complex was a partial theory, not a universal one; it could be used to guide psychoanalytic practice with individual patients, but not to ground the idea of a universal psyche.

Lacking a robust explanation to account for what appeared in practice to be enormous variation in the forms taken by mental illness, global psychiatry continued to be confronted for many years by the problem of how best to account for the apparent pervasive influence of culture. The Dakar School had its corollary in the North in the transcultural psychiatry movement, a branch of psychiatry that began to attend to the relationship between culture, migration, and mental illness. Psychological and psychiatric anthropology have also made major contributions to this literature much of which emphasizes the cultural construction of categories of "madness" and the way in which culture informs the experience of mental illness.[83]

Transcultural psychiatry was an attempt to deal with the lack of a universally accepted theory of psychopathology. As the Ortigues' experience showed, even Freudian theory had to be stripped down to its barest structural formulation in order to give a convincing account of a universal psychic structure in the face of manifest cultural differences in the presentation of and language used to describe mental illness. In contrast to the body, the mind, undeniably embedded in social life, resisted standardization. Medicalization of madness was not evident in most parts of the world until substantially after the colonial era when psychiatry became a global hub for the circulation of individualizing and population technologies of the sort seen earlier with infectious diseases, birthing, and nutrition. Two developments augured the global medicalization of madness in the 1980s. The first was the adoption of an "a-theoretical" phenomenological classification of mental disorders, starting with the third edition of *The Diagnostic and Statistical Manual of Mental Disorders* (DSM-III) published by the American Psychiatric Association in 1980. The second was the rise in production of psychopharmaceuticals; together they mark an attempt to develop for mental illness the kind of global standard furnished by biology for non-psychiatric illness.

While the first psychoactive drug, chlorpromazine, was discovered in France in 1954 and used for the treatment of psychotic patients, psychopharmaceuticals did not begin to be used widely until the so-called "Prozac" revolution in the 1990s, when a new class of antidepressant, the selective serotonin reuptake inhibitors (or SSRIs), was marketed. Lacking the side effects of earlier tricyclic antidepressants, SSRIs were thus more easily prescribed and rapidly became a cultural phenomenon when books, films, and confessional accounts about the drug poured forth.[84] Andrew Lakoff, a medical anthropologist who conducted research in Argentina, has written about the complex negotiations that had to be undertaken to convince the Argentine psychiatric milieu to adopt the diagnostic categories of the third edition of the American Psychiatric Association's *Diagnostic and Statistical Manual of Mental Disorders* (DSM-III). Argentinian psychiatry remained under the sway of Lacanian philosophy and was deeply mistrustful of standardized approaches necessitated by the adoption of the DSM-III. Without the diagnostic equivalence afforded by these standardized categories – what Lakoff calls "liquidity," drawing on a metaphor from economics – not only would it be difficult to market drugs specifically indicated to treat disorders as defined by the DSM, but it would also be difficult to participate in global psychiatric research.[85] In urban Bengal, Stefan Ecks has documented the difficulties encountered by pharmaceutical firms as they sought to medicalize depression in order to sell drugs. The concept of depression did not translate into local understanding of sadness, which was not seen as a medical problem, but rather as something to be addressed through the strengthening of one's social networks and, most importantly, engaging in practices to "focus the mind."[86]

Thus, while "madness" long resisted biological explanations, the DSM-III brought about a new form of universal for dealing with mental illness across different contexts around the globe. This newly discovered universal is an a-theoretical and phenomenological approach to classification. The DSM functions as a standardizing technique, one that could with apparent success be "translated" across different cultural contexts and localities, as the Argentine and Indian examples show. Once local idioms of distress are made commensurable, two kinds of biomedical technologies can be readily disseminated: psychopharmaceuticals and psychotherapies. Evidence that anti-depressants and antipsychotics can relieve symptoms in different parts of the world is used to argue post facto for an underlying biological basis to mental illness, although this argument is challenged among psychiatrists themselves.[87]

In Summary

This chapter has explored how epidemics, fertility, and hunger came to be standard-ized in biological terms. This occurred in piecemeal fashion as biomedical technolo-gies were deployed in response to critical events that threatened individual and collective survival. Colonial epidemics were eventually controlled by campaigns that mobilized microbiology and microscopes, and to this day epidemics the world over are seen as local manifestations of the activities of specific micro-organisms on their biological hosts, human and animal. In response to moral panics about colonial infertility, childbirth was medicalized and programs experimented with to introduce obstetrical care, laying the groundwork for maternal and child health programs around the world today. Fnally, the colonial discovery of malnutrition linked up everyday dietary practices with theories about good nutrition in biological terms. The legacy of this biologization of hunger remains with us today, not only in what we eat but also in unanticipated sequelae in the form of inappropriate use of albumin in China, for example. More broadly, the biologization of life spawned an important geopolitical force in the form of medical humanitarianism. An important exception is the management of madness, for no biological standard has yet emerged for the care of mental illness. The difficulty of making biomedical technologies "work" when no biological standard exists is visible in successive attempts at standardization in the domain of psychiatry where no unified biological theory has been able to account for mental illness.

Global biomedicine still bears the legacy of its originating, colonial moment of globalization. Many medical schools were founded in the colonial period and some still maintain a colonial culture of hierarchy that continues to powerfully shape the clinical encounter even in the postcolonial context. The lessons of colonial microbial disease control – the "hit hard" approach of "vertical" campaigns targeting single diseases – are still deeply entrenched in the design and implementation of health programs, buoyed by the success of the campaign to eradicate smallpox in the 1970s. A focus on infectious diseases, and the goal of eradication that informs a military planning ethos in global public health – has been difficult to dislodge, even in the face of evidence that mental illness, accidents, and chronic heart, lung, and metabolic diseases driven by changes in lifestyle (such as smoking and high-calorie diets) are becoming major causes of morbidity and mortality in the developing world. This is in part due to the HIV epidemic and the continued crippling impact of malaria and other infectious diseases in developing countries.

Tracking the circulation of biomedical technologies shows how biomedical effec-tiveness is embedded in social, cultural, economic, and political processes. In an era of soaring health inequalities, it might seem heretical to question the dissemination of life-saving biomedical practices. But the hidden agendas and implicit assumptions that travel with biomedicine can at times be counter-productive. What this chapter and others in this book show is that improving global health is unlikely to succeed if it is simply assumed that making more medicines and health services available to more people is purely a technical or logistical matter. It is already widely recognized that "health" is powerfully affected by social, political, and economic conditions. Moreover, when take up by local therapeutic economies, biomedical technologies may be used on bodies that are literally materially different in some respects from those the techniques were developed for, and also for different ends than they were intended; furthermore, the kind of social and economic infrastructure to ensure appropriate application of biomedicine may well not exist. Improving global health thus requires taking difference seriously – in bodies and in social, political, and economic situations.

7

Grounds for Comparison: Biology and Human Experiments

A belief in the universality of biology does not make all bodies the same; rather, it establishes a set of agreed-upon rules about how the body is assumed to work, and furnishes a series of hypothetical equivalences, for example, that a liver, a stem cell or a chromosome is biologically equivalent in all human bodies. Human biology becomes, then, a yardstick that can be used to measure difference in terms of variation about a norm, and in this way bodies are made commensurable. Our focus of attention in this chapter is on experimental medicine and above all on the development of the enterprise of clinical trials and their globalization, for which an assumption of biological commensurability is indispensable.

The idea of biological commensurability allows people to be sorted into standardized groups and populations because their biology is assumed to be the same. This provides the grounds for meaningful comparisons to be made among them. Comparing apples from different orchards generates a more precise form of knowledge – about orchards, soils, farmers, or varieties – than, say, comparing apples and oranges. Such comparisons are the basis of modern, scientific biomedicine. We will discuss in this chapter the rise of statistical methods to establish proof, the ability to encompass variability and difference within the framework of the "natural experiment," and the acceptance of the randomized controlled trial as the gold standard of evidence for improving collective wellbeing. Recent work by anthropologists that documents how these human experiments play out in the lives of researchers and subjects while highlighting the social and political circumstances that are a precondition of these experiments and trials will then be presented. Our argument throughout is not to deny that biology is "real" nor to say that biomedical experiments are flawed. Rather, drawing on ethnographic illustrations that make use of the concepts of local biologies and biosocial differentiation, we wish to underscore how such knowledge is necessarily partial, to caution against unexamined assumptions of universality, and to draw attention to how biomedical comparisons can have significant political, social, and health implications, increasingly of a global order.

The Laboratory as the Site of Comparison

The rise of the "experiment" in biomedicine is associated with the objectification of nature, and hence of the body, that emerged after the Enlightenment. Internal pathology began to be made visible through the routinization of autopsies, and by the 19th century a systematic approach to the investigation and naming of diseases based on autopsy findings was in place. These findings were complemented by a quantitative approach to studying the distribution of illness in the clinic that, as we shall see, was increasingly applied to entire populations beyond the clinic.

Claude Bernard's *Introduction to Experimental Medicine* published in 1865 is recognized as having made a major contribution to initiating the era of modern experimental medicine. The assumption that much can be learnt about the structure and function of human bodies from studies using animals has a very long history; however, Bernard argued for the application of scientific methods to the understanding of disease through the implementation of laboratory experiments on animals. These experiments were designed to discern the chemical processes that maintain health in all living bodies and established that animals could serve as "models" of human physiological processes. For Bernard, the basis of science, and of the experiment, was the method of comparison between, for example, what one might expect to see and what one actually sees as a result of experimentation in any given case or among cases.[1] Prior to the introduction of animal models, comparison could usually only take place in the mind of the physician on the basis of his experience, although at times direct comparison became possible in the clinic when two patients with the same disease presented themselves at more or less the same time. In the laboratory, however, controlled manipulation of animals offered the possibility of deliberately creating the circumstances in which comparisons might be made. Laboratory research began with systematic, replicable investigations on physiological mechanisms, cellular pathology, and bacterial action, largely conducted on animals and designed above all to obtain "proof" of a mechanism or of therapeutic efficacy. When Pasteur famously inoculated cows with cowpox and sheep with anthrax to demonstrate the effectiveness of his vaccine, he showed that the laboratory need not be hidden away in a hospital or university, and that powerful comparisons could be made in the real world for all to see.[2]

Despite its initial successes experimental medicine was nonetheless fraught with problems from the outset. People argued about the questionable validity of animal models and the importance of inter-species variation. Research with *Vibrio cholerae* is a classic example of the difficulties, because simple introduction of the germ into animals failed to produce cholera-like symptoms, creating arguments about the worth of a model that could only be induced to produce certain changes in research animals after the subjects had been extensively and viciously manipulated.[3] Nonetheless, by the early years of the 20th century, the laboratory was playing an increasingly important role in elucidating disease processes and developing effective treatments. By the time World War II broke out, the laboratory had become a site where therapeutics were systematically developed and tested using experimental approaches that made use of animal models, and it was gradually accepted that animals are sufficiently biologically similar to humans to stand in for them as experimental models.[4] The sites of laboratory research had also begun to expand from their original places in the

European heartland and the chemical factories along the Rhine to the outermost reaches of the European empire, where field laboratories used to study exotic tropical diseases that afflicted settlers resulted in networks of research institutes dotted throughout Africa, Asia, and Latin America.

The Colonial Laboratory

Although in the mid–19th century Louis Pasteur provided powerful evidence of the microbial origin of disease with his famous anthrax experiment, Pastorian theories – and biomedical practices, notably vaccination, for which they provided justification – were initially met with lively resistance in France by medical doctors and the public health establishment. Only after World War I was the French establishment slowly convinced of Pasteur's findings, as has been detailed by the historian and sociologist of science Bruno Latour in his aptly named book *The Pasteurization of France*.[5] Latour shows how the germ theory of disease slowly gained traction in France, effectively granting micro-organisms the power to reshape society, when the displacement of older miasmatic ideas by germ theory transformed practices of sanitation and hygiene as well as government policy. Germ theory even brought about changes in how the relationship between nature and society was viewed and acted upon;[6] in the colonies, Pastorian ideas drew colonial attention away from climate and geography, where it had been directed by miasma theory, to indigenous populations now seen to be reservoirs of disease. In colonial societies, those "reservoirs" of "native hosts" were neither able to speak nor to resist endemic disease eradication campaigns informed by the novel Pastorian ideas. The political context of colonialism thus afforded even greater traction to germ theory.[7]

   With military precision, Pastorian campaigns mapped and segmented colonial territory, and developed a sophisticated and centralized apparatus that methodically applied testing and treatment to the populations residing within. The success of colonial infectious disease eradication campaigns led by Pastorians that were discussed in the previous chapter, such as those conducted by Jamot against the *grandes endémies* (major endemics) did not go unnoticed. Indeed these campaigns set the stage for later "vertical" disease eradication approaches such as those that (successfully) targeted smallpox in the 1970s and (somewhat less successfully) polio in the 1990s.

   A global network of Pasteur Institutes tested and consolidated Pastorian theory (today called microbiology) and trained generations of key colonial officials.[8] The Instituts Pasteur became the vanguard of tropical disease research, initially financed largely by philanthropy. Along with the Instituts Pasteur in French Indochina, Tunisia, and Senegal, the Rockefeller Institute in New York, the Wellcome Trust in London, and the Fundación Oswaldo Cruz in Brazil established research laboratories that together girdled the earth. In the capitals of the colonial powers, training institutes such as the London School of Hygiene and Tropical Medicine, the Antwerp Institute for Tropical Medicine, and the Royal Tropical Medicine Institute in the Netherlands produced the next generation of global researchers. Their findings demonstrated the microbial origins of many diseases found around the world, thus demonstrating the stability of biological phenomena across heterogeneous environments and cultures. This was the first step toward a global epidemiology that would later become established in association with the international institutions that began to collect and compare health statistics across nations. These institutions laid the ground-work for the foundation of the World Health Organization.[9]

Latour refers to Pasteur's pedagogy as a "theater of proof."[10] As discussed in the previous chapter, while the medicalization of fertility and nutrition showed the generalizability of biological approaches to human vitality, it was germ theory that most convincingly demonstrated the biological commensurability of humans, making the colonies available to act as a theater of proof. The Pastorian shift toward a microbial theory of disease causation structured a powerful imaginary of the colonies as vast laboratories where the enactment of hygienic measures could be tested, and the results compared across time and space. On the colonial stage, the proofs of efficacy that gradually accumulated confirmed the underlying doctrine of biological commensurability, allowing colonial lessons to be repatriated to Europe as tried-and-true practice rather than simply as theory. Extrapolation of findings from colonial sites to other colonies and even to the heartlands of Europe was not confined to questions purely of health; many techniques of modern government – urban planning, taking fingerprints, identity documents and so on – were first tried out in the colonies before being implemented in imperial homelands.[11] Implementation of new technologies of government and disease control in colonial settings was not limited to Britain or France, as the historian Warwick Anderson has pointed out in his writing on American hygiene in the Philippines.[12] The majority of these practices sought to manage space and people in terms of conceptions of hosts, reservoirs, and infectious pathogens – key concepts in microbiology. In other words, the social and political conditions in the colonies where colonial powers were not constrained in the implementation of new policies made them a testing ground from which proven policies could be repatriated.

Population health practices in the colonies were not, however, grounded in the kind of statistical comparisons with which they are associated today. Statistics, a technology of the state, emerged as a formal practice for counting and sorting populations by European governments in the 19th century. However, such quantification was not systematically applied to the colonies until well into the 20th century. In the absence of the apparatus of a quantifying, modern state, with its capillary tentacles of power distributed throughout the nation, colonial administrators had but a patchy view of the populations they subjugated who, in any case, could only be systematically counted by rounding them up by force. The numerical demonstration of biomedical efficacy was therefore confined to military forces in the colonies and, increasingly, to those populations who could be enrolled into an experimental apparatus and thus counted – a practice that is expanding exponentially today.

Experimental Bodies

Infamous examples abound of what such an experimental apparatus looked like. In the United States, the notorious "Tuskegee Study of Untreated Syphilis in the Negro Male" was conducted on African American men in the town of the same name in Alabama. Carried out over 40 years between 1932 and 1972 by the U.S. Public Health Service, poor African American men with syphilis – 399 in all – were recruited and observed in order to characterize the "natural history" of syphilis. Even when effective treatment with penicillin became available, the study subjects were not treated; 28 died of syphilis, another hundred from complications due to the infection, and 40 wives and 19 children were infected. The history of this experiment has been the subject of several books and many scholarly papers and is often cited as the reason why to this day many African Americans are suspicious of clinical trials and indeed of biomedical practice in general.[13] In wartime, experiments conducted in Nazi Germany by individuals such as Dr Josef Mengele resulted in the formulation of the Nuremberg code of research ethics in 1947, although this code came too late to affect the treatment of the Tuskegee men. Japan also conducted human experiments during its occupation of China during World War II, and low-key and less controversial experiments were conducted across the colonial world, largely to find treatments for tropical diseases.

"Experimental bodies," notes the medical historian Ilana Löwy "are entities which can be substituted for patients' bodies in order to investigate diseases and look for treatments."[14] Colonial and, more infamously, Nazi and Japanese experiments point to how political circumstances contribute to the production of "experimental bodies," most often the bodies of marginalized, stigmatized, or oppressed populations who "stand in" for the bodies of everyone else. However, even though confinement and other forms of social control may have made these bodies easily available to medical researchers, racist assumptions of essential biological difference at times limited their use for experimental purposes even before the knowledge generated by such experiments came to be viewed as ethically compromised.

As Löwy points out, most of the work on experimental bodies takes place in laboratories, with the notable exception of clinical trials that make use of large, statistically valid samples of research subjects. Live laboratory animals; their organs and tissues; human tissues, cells, and genetic material, as well human subjects, all fall under the rubric of experimental bodies used to facilitate quantification, comparison, and replication of results. Löwy notes the way in which experimental bodies are "easier to control" than real-life bodies, creating remarkably homogenous laboratory entities ranging from genetically modified animals to tumors suitable for experimentation.[15] By the 1950s, it had become possible to genetically manipulate laboratory animals on a large scale, often designed according to researchers' specifications, and more recently to engineer human genes into animal bodies, in effect standardizing experimental animals. Karen Rader has written the history of the genetic standardization of the laboratory mouse, the most famous example being the OncoMouse® patented in the United States after a long legal struggle.[16] While it is possible to standardize and in effect make the same bodies out of laboratory animals this, of course, could not be the case with humans. Generating scientifically credible knowledge about human bodies required another approach, one that had to grapple with the ethical impossibility of manipulating human bodies to make them the same.

Rise of the Clinical Trial

John Snow's analysis of the cholera epidemic in London is considered by epidemiologists to be one of the first "natural experiments." "Natural experiments" refer to spontaneously occurring variations in circumstances that can be observed in order to deduce their potential effect(s) on an outcome of interest. Such experiments are called "natural" because the administration or withholding of the intervention is not performed by researchers, but occurs in the real world as part of variation in different geographical locales, usually behavioral or environmental, that permit comparison. Strategies have been developed to observe populations and analyze the effects of specific factors on them, among which are "cohort" studies used to observe groups over time and track how exposures to various factors influence the health of such groups. Case control studies compare individuals suffering from a disease (the "cases") to those without the disease (the "controls") to search for factors associated with the disease. The link between smoking and lung cancer was established by such studies, initially in Nazi Germany in the 1930s and subsequently in Britain and the U.S. in the 1950s.[17]

The reality of human difference is a fundamental challenge to the interpretation of findings of these natural experiments. Are the phenomena observed in certain people due to the specific factors under study, or might they be due to biological differences among the involved people? To combat this difficulty large numbers of subjects are included in the study and geographic, social, and even "racial" diversity is ensured. Large numbers allow statistical calculations to prune out the "noise" of human variation, establish a "quantitative average," and hence the biological norm it is assumed to represent.

Take, for example, the observation that heart disease is less common in southern than northern Europe. This observation triggered a search for putative causes that were quickly narrowed down to differences in diet, notably a greater use of olive oil and red wine in southern Europe that was correlated with low blood cholesterol levels and other biological factors. The rest of the story is well known: rare is the individual who has not been exhorted to eat a Mediterranean diet or has not drunk a glass of red wine relieved of guilt by its supposed positive health effects.[18] Yet a lingering question remains: is it really the red wine and olive oil that lead to Mediterranean longevity? Or might a more fundamental difference at the biological level not reducible to culturally patterned ways of life be implicated? The answers to this question are likely to lie in explanations that take into account processes of biosocial differentiation that have unfolded over long periods of time, yet such processes are statistically tuned out or ignored.

While evidence from "natural experiments" have long suggested potential factors that may well contribute to disease, it was in the laboratory that the actual biological mechanisms of disease causation first began to be revealed and where biologically effective agents were developed, such as the diphtheria anti-toxin introduced in 1894 after preliminary work had been carried out with animal models. However, laboratory evidence could not *prove* that administering a vaccine such as the diphtheria anti-toxin would actually work effectively and without danger in human bodies, raising once again the specter of difference – this time between what happens in the laboratory and what might happen in the real world of clinical practice. The central problem of biomedical research remained then as now: how to transform findings from laboratory research, the task of which is to identify potential therapeutic agents making use of test-tubes, animal models, and biochemical manipulations, for safe and effective use in clinical practice on patients. By the 1950s, as the historian Harry Marks puts it:

few physicians doubted that laboratory scientists could produce potent and effective therapeutic agents. The production of reliable therapeutic *knowledge* was another matter. Laboratory scientists challenged the physician's traditional reliance on clinical experience. It took correspondingly little time for clinicians to question the relevance of laboratory studies to human disease.[19]

This inherent tension between laboratory scientists and clinicians stimulated the development of a rigorous means for evaluating therapeutic agents before their introduction into the clinic. The growth in the development of new remedies and biomedical technologies and growing public anxiety about the potential toxicities of quack remedies provided a further impetus to introduce regulation of therapeutic interventions. After the nefarious consequences of improperly tested technologies and use of drugs on human populations began to come to light (including the use of high oxygen therapy for premature babies and prescriptions of thalidomide for nausea in pregnant women in the late 1950s), rigorous testing of medical interventions intended for use on humans began in earnest. To achieve a controlled standard it became apparent that carefully controlled comparisons between treated and non-treated subjects were necessary in experimental settings. The full effect of interventions could then be observed objectively while eliminating the bias introduced at times by overly optimistic interpretations of treatment results by researchers, or by "stacking the deck" with ideal patients.

Carrying out experiments on humans added another complication not present in animal studies, namely the placebo effect, the significance of which came to be appreciated early on in clinical research following a convincing experiment. In the 1950s it was believed that for patients with heart disease who suffered chest pain because of inadequate blood flow to the heart due to blockages in the coronary arteries, tying off another artery in the chest (the mammary artery) would drive more blood to the heart and decrease symptoms. In a famous experiment conducted in 1959, patients in the control group received a sham surgery that included cutting open the chest and exposing the artery – but not tying it off. Thirty-two percent of the patients who were given the real surgery got better – compared to 43 percent who received the sham surgery![20]

In summary, the maintenance of objectivity was accomplished by developing methods to eliminate bias that continue to be made use of today: carefully selected control groups to ensure a good comparison; randomization to eliminate bias in the selection of patients for testing (see below); "blinding" to ensure researchers do not know who among the subjects receive the intervention and are therefore unbiased in their observations; and administering a placebo to those who do not receive the intervention so that the "pure" effect of the intervention can be distinguished from the placebo effect brought about by believing one has received an intervention. However, researchers continue to be bedeviled with another problem, namely that random events can introduce an unknown or unforeseeable factor that may influence the outcome, thereby confounding the comparison. So-called confounding factors, of which there are many, including biosocial difference that results from "local biologies," are not controlled for, precisely because they are unknown and unrecognized.

Taming Difference by Chance

The British geneticist R. A. Fisher, known for developing common statistical methods such as the "exact T-test," is credited by Harry Marks with "embracing" chance by exploiting an until-then unknown advantage using the mechanism of randomization.[21] Prior to Fisher's publications in the 1920s, researchers could only control for factors influencing outcomes that they knew about beforehand. Researchers today, testing a drug to prevent heart attacks, can make sure that known risk factors for heart attacks – such as high cholesterol, smoking, or hypertension – are equally distributed in both the experimental and control groups; however, clearly they cannot do this for factors that are unknown. Randomization distributes unknown confounding factors equally in groups to be compared, but there is still a chance that random allocation would stack the deck in favor of one side or the other. Fisher realized that the probability of this happening could be quantified.

A powerful new technology was now added to the basic experimental strategies – mathematical methods for detecting and eliminating bias *due to chance alone*. This is perhaps most familiar in the calculation of the "margin of error" in political polls that predict, for instance the popularity of a political leader (60 percent) within a range (plus or minus 5 percent) nine times out of ten. The uncertainty introduced by confounding factors (including biosocial differences) could be mastered, and expressed as a probability value, the one time out of ten when the results would not hold. Such methods were not strictly speaking new in the world of science as they had existed since the early 20th century, but had been discredited because of their use by eugenicists. However by the 1930s a small number of British physician-mathematicians began to apply these mathematical methods to the study of disease rather than to the quality of populations, leading to their acceptance in clinical settings.[22] The growing power of mathematical methods to "control" for chance gave fresh relevance to the repeated observations of real-world variations among human bodies, effectively taming the "wild card" of biosocial difference and laying the groundwork for the emergence of a new form of human experimentation guaranteed, it was argued, to give ironclad evidence.

The new experimental method of the randomized controlled trial (RCT) became the pinnacle of biomedical research design because, by incorporating technologies of randomization, placebo-control, and blinding, it appeared to be impervious to bias, and the most objective of clinical research methods to date. In RCTs, the intervention to be studied is allocated to one group to which a control group is compared. To eliminate the placebo effect, the control group receives a proxy for the intervention: if it is a drug that is being evaluated, individuals who are controls receive a pill (the placebo) that appears identical to the drug under investigation but contains a biologically inert substance. When a surgical technique is being evaluated, the placebo may even include "sham" surgery. Randomization ensures that any biological variation in bodies is equally distributed across experimental arms; indeed, this is why evidence from RCTs is considered to be the most valid, because the effects produced by therapeutic agents can be rigorously separated from the background "noise" of placebo effects, biased observers and subjects, and chance events. The RCT has become the gold standard for proving that a new drug or intervention is indeed effective. As a result it is now accepted that it is statistically possible to "prove" the efficacy of an intervention *even without having any a priori knowledge or understanding of the biological mechanism involved.*

The Alchemy of the Randomized Controlled Trial

Clinicians are all too aware that clinical trials are interlinked with drug marketing and that drug companies frame research questions in such a way that the answers will contribute to the marketability of their drug. While the introduction of the randomized controlled trial has tempered precipitous marketing of inadequately tested drugs, current controversies around drugs that have been recalled belie this, and have led to demands for ever more stringent testing. Given the expense of randomized controlled trials, and indeed of the entire drug development process, it is not surprising that biomedical research funded by the pharmaceutical industry is skewed toward producing drugs that will grab a share in wealthy markets. In psychiatry trials have been designed expressly to produce results that can allow antidepressants to be marketed for anxiety.[23] Similarly, clinical trials to support new indications for existing drugs (or even drugs that have "failed" a clinical trial) in order to expand their market share have been conducted for drugs of all therapeutic classes.[24]

However, in addition, a more subtle form of manipulation exists: tinkering with the actual research design of trials, including the criteria by which patients are selected. For example, rather than compare a new drug directly to its most powerful competitor, a pharmaceutical company may decide to use a clinical trial to show that their new drug is better than a weaker competitor. This process is the equivalent of rigging the World Cup so that a new team is consistently matched with the weakest team during play-off rounds, allowing it to progress to the following rounds relatively unchallenged. This can buy valuable time for a challenger drug to build a market share, with the hope meanwhile that the market leader will falter because of unexpected side effects. Since the statistical methods used to compare treatments are engineered to detect a superior treatment, another strategy has been to devise alternative statistical methods to demonstrate "non-inferiority."[25] These examples show that, however accurate statistical methodologies are, the playing field where they are used is not a level one. Considerable attention has been drawn to the way in which the results of such trials are manipulated – for example through the non-publication of unfavorable results, or the suppression of evidence of drugs' toxicity or ineffectiveness once they are marketed.[26] Sociologist of science Catherine Wills refers to these practices as the "'alchemy of the RCT,' characterized by the ritual invocation of randomization and control as tools to transform … imperfect materials into the stuff of certainty."[27]

The Problem of Generalizability

Clinical trials are used to compare the effects of two different interventions – a vaccine versus a placebo, or a newer drug against an established drug for the treatment of a disease. However, a clinical trial cannot measure the effect of the clinical trial apparatus *itself*, to which both experimental and control groups are subject. The effect of the clinical trial can be due to a number of factors, including the highly selective recruitment and enrolment processes trial participants must go through before they are included. Such recruitment processes are designed to ensure a necessary level of clinical homogeneity and sufficient cooperation to follow the rigorous biomedical regime they will receive. After a biomedical intervention is "proven" in a clinical trial, it must be moved out into the real world and put to use on patients who, inevitably, have not been carefully selected, where medical care is less intense, and the effects of the intervention cannot be so rigorously monitored. In other words, the intervention must eventually be implemented without the clinical trial technology, with the result that clinicians, epidemiologists, and medical scientists must constantly struggle with the problem of generalizability, or "external validity" as this hiatus is called, when making sense of clinical trial results and judging their relevance to the problems at hand in busy health care settings.

Among the difficulties that arise are the following: patients who decide to enrol in RCTs – the research subjects – are known to be more motivated than those who decide not to do so, making it potentially problematic to generalize results obtained from these subjects. More "work" is required of research subjects than of regular patients who need only attend routine doctors' appointments, because numerous visits at specific times are demanded of research subjects and more blood tests are required. This means that research subjects have to be highly motivated to be in a clinical trial and to value the meager compensation – perhaps a free meal or bus fare – that is offered for volunteers.[28] Not surprisingly, research subjects are considered to be unrepresentative of patients who appear in regular clinics that take all-comers. Moreover, the follow-up of research subjects is better than in ordinary clinics due to the importance of collecting accurate, unbiased, and timely data. Considerable effort is spent on tracking and following research subjects once the trial has ended, so research sites tend to be much better equipped and offer better medical care than do regular clinics. This trial infrastructure inevitably has an indirect impact on the care received by research subjects in trials but also, as we shall see below, on their communities that indirectly may benefit from this infrastructure.

Biomedical practitioners, epidemiologists, and health activists recognize that results from trials may have limited generalizability or "external validity" – even when the experiment is rigorously conducted and has recognized "internal validity," because the subjects "inside" the experiment are not representative of people "outside" in the real world. The assumption that people who become subjects in RCTs represent the general population is based largely on the idea of biological equivalence and designers of clinical trials assume that local contingencies can be statistically modeled away when subject populations are assembled across diverse sites. Epidemiologists acknowledge this is not always the case when they distinguish between efficacy – the effect of an intervention demonstrated in a clinical trial – and effectiveness, that is, its real-world effect that is often less than would have been expected.

It is well known that differences between the controlled environment of a clinical trial and the settings of ordinary clinics have an important impact on therapy. Most important, ordinary patients, by definition, are not vetted as are trial participants; they may be more ill or likely to have other diseases, take medications of various kinds that interact with one another, or be less disciplined in taking their medication. In addition, in many parts of the world health care facilities cannot deliver medications properly and, occasionally explicitly acknowledged, there may be local biological variation that affects outcomes. These can include host factors such as nutritional or immunological status or genetic predispositions, or culturally informed expectations about the body in health and illness.

Common medications used in the treatment of arthritis and diabetes have recently been subject to controversy after showing more harmful side effects when used in the general population than those detected in the clinical trials, in all probability because patients were more ill than were subjects in the trials.[29] Learning from what happens *after* interventions have been implemented has become an important extension of RCTs. In phase IV clinical research, or post-marketing surveillance, as it is known, data on the effects of drugs are gathered after the drugs have been approved and put into regular use. The importance of post-marketing surveillance lies in its ability to detect significant side effects or toxicities not visible in a clinical trial in an effort designed explicitly to bridge the world of experimentation and that of the clinic. Drug recall is now recognized as an unavoidable outcome of the marketing of certain drugs with enormous loss of profits to the pharmaceutical companies involved.

As is recognized the world over, it is undeniable that biomedicine works well in curing numerous acute, time-limited conditions that are essentially everywhere the same – broken bones, cataracts, or acute infections – in which culture and environment play a relatively minor role in when and how the condition manifests itself. However, biomedicine works less well for those conditions that exhibit significant variation in how they materialize and, when they do so, tend to be chronic (mental health problems of all kinds, numerous complex multifactorial diseases, psychosocial problems, allergies, skin conditions, and many infectious diseases). The numerous conditions that fall into this second group offer a challenge to the idea of a standardizable universal body, and the very range of these conditions suggests it is important to recognize the limitations of assumptions of biological equivalence.[30]

We have already discussed how colonialism and the rise of the state enabled the generation of biomedical knowledge because, in the management and ordering of social and political arrangements, a healthy economy was explicitly linked to the promotion of the physical health of involved populations. The creation of groups of people that are made into subjects in natural laboratories is a further example of a biopolitical activity out of which biomedical knowledge is generated, and the mechanics of that knowledge generation today increasingly takes the form of clinical trials. As we have seen, the clinical trial is itself not a neutral, context-free technology of knowledge generation. Furthermore, as will be made clear below, its very conditions of possibility lie in the inter-relationship of the geography of human illness, the political economy of care, and attempts to improve population health. However, the health promotional activities of colonial governments and the state are strikingly different from what takes place in RCTs because no *direct* link is made between the health promotion of subjects in RCTs and the wellbeing of the economy as a whole. On the contrary, human subjects are simply intermediaries who assist in the production of biomedical knowledge that will eventually, it is hoped, be profitable, have global application, and cure disease.

Medical Standardization and Contested Evidence

The power of the RCT is reflected in the strengthening belief that biomedical practice must be informed by "evidence" derived from RCTs or related scientific studies, a belief that gave rise to the evidence-based medicine (EBM) movement. While the RCT originated with awareness that some biomedical technologies are in fact harmful and a perceived need to prevent this, EBM resulted from observations that improper application of well-recognized and widely used biomedical technologies can also cause great harm, and this incited growing discomfort with the concentration of therapeutic power invested in specialist "experts." A recognized need for evidence-based medicine also acknowledges the limitations of the RCT discussed above. As the anthropologist Helen Lambert notes:

> not all diseases and clinical interventions have been or can be studied by an RCT. The uneven availability of such research "evidence" can give rise to bias within biomedical policy and rationing decisions by favouring those types of clinical interventions for which the best RCT data exist. By their design, complex and population-based interventions (such as nutritional supplements for pre-school children from low-income families) are less likely to be substantiated by evidence from clinical trials than simple, individual treatments (such as a new drug).[31]

The rise of EBM over the past 20 years is based on the assumption that this approach would improve the rational and efficient care of patients, and give support to governments and health care insurers eager to contain medical costs. As the British sociologist of medicine David Armstrong explains,

> Proponents of EBM took the logic of the clinical trial and promoted it further. Essentially, supporters of EBM identified and traced the passage of medical evidence from the scientific experiment to clinical practice. This involved not only the trials that produced evidence of effectiveness but also synthesis of this knowledge.[32]

Evidence-based medicine marshals facts – the results of RCTs, observations from epidemiological studies of cohorts, clinical expertise – into hierarchies, and synthesizes them into "practice guidelines" in the form of algorithms and rules by which actual biomedical practice comes to be grounded in scientific evidence and systematized. Not surprisingly, EBM has been criticized by many, including doctors who argue for the importance of the art of medical practice and contest the devaluing of clinical experience.[33] The ability of EBM to improve individual health has also been challenged by those who argue that the problem is not a lack of evidence, but the unwillingness or inability to apply evidence-based results due to political, economic, and/or social reasons. For example, reluctance to abandon the use of the fetal heart monitor during labor,[34] over-prescription of drugs, and resistance to hand-washing are just three of the examples where biomedical practice remains stubbornly resistant to change, despite strong evidence that such changes are needed. The growth of "operations research" that uses epidemiological methods to identify why evidence is not put into clinical practice shows that a concern about an apparent resistance to change in various aspects of medical care has recently gained currency in the biomedical research community. EBM is also contested by those who question why only certain forms of evidence (that is quantitative and not qualitative findings) count, and these critics point to the limitations of kinds of evidence that is made use of, as we have seen above in the case of RCTs.

Our argument for the recognition of biosocial differentiation, local biologies, and lived embodiment is consonant with these critiques of EBM in that these factors are automatically ruled out as valid evidence. First, we suggest that differences exist not only between people "inside" and "outside" clinical trials, cohort studies, and other sites of clinical research, but also among people in different locales – in other words, that human biology and hence human bodies are inevitably *situated* in evolutionary, historical, environmental, and social contexts. Second, as will be made clear in what follows, biomedical knowledge-making is increasingly dependent on social processes that inadvertently make populations available for observation and experimentation. These processes are exemplars of biosocial differentiation. In other words, *what makes clinical trials possible are the very conditions that make comparison between those inside the trials and those outside increasingly difficult to sustain.*

Globalizing Clinical Research

Biomedical research infrastructure, located in universities and laboratories, is no longer confined to the former imperial capitals and a few colonial outposts, but can be found throughout the world. The United States continues to furnish the bulk of research funding, by means of public and private funding, as has been the case since the mid–20th century, but the global infrastructure now makes it possible to conduct research far from funding sources. In many instances, it is today cheaper and easier to conduct such research "offshore," where the "right kind" of human subjects can be recruited faster and with less effort than in the U.S. or Europe, and where overhead costs of labor, use of facilities, and so on, may be several orders of magnitude less than in the industrialized West.[35] In a related development a global medical tourism industry has flourished that provides offshore biomedical services at low cost. Finally, the growth of massive global health programs executed in infrastructure-poor developing countries by local governments, NGOs, and relief organizations has created a massive demand for the identification of the most effective therapeutic interventions in such situations.

The growing appetite for evidence of the effectiveness of new biomedical products has brought about a remarkable situation in which global health inequalities make participation in research often the only way to obtain access to medical care in poorer parts of the world. Clinical and intervention trials increasingly conducted in Africa and South Asia constitute populations of impoverished subjects as part of experimental laboratories. Another, less evident aspect of this practice, is the production of biomedical knowledge from populations whose life circumstances – and, we would argue, whose biology – are significantly different from those who will benefit from the resultant knowledge. Testing of biomedical technologies on populations removed from those that will use them constitutes yet another kind of experiment. Pharmaceuticals are a critical nexus in these practices. As medical anthropologist Adriana Petryna notes, this demands "innovative empirical work that is required to convey the moral and ethical realities of emergent global drug markets."[36]

Anthropologists have recently begun to investigate the gap between the ideal world of the clinical trial and the real world in which they are put into practice as a way to examine one particular aspect of the contemporary global economy. Petryna has focused attention on the globalization of clinical trials, increasingly conducted offshore from the major pharmaceuticals markets where the drugs being tested are to be sold. She notes how she first became interested in this phenomenon during her research on the effects of the Chernobyl nuclear disaster in the Ukraine, where she noticed an astounding growth of clinical trials. Petryna points to how this worldwide expansion has been driven by a number of factors, including regulatory frameworks that require randomized controlled trial data to license drugs, the growing difficulty of recruiting "naïve" patients in North America and Europe (that is, those who have not previously been treated with medications for the condition under study), and the relative financial savings made by setting up clinical trials outside the major industrialized economies. Being treatment-naïve means, for instance, that a hypertensive research subject has never before been treated with hypertension drugs. The disease is therefore assumed to exist in a "pure" and untampered state, more readily standardized than in treatment-experienced patients whose hypertension has been adulterated by previous drug therapy, making the "noise" of these prior interventions difficult to isolate from the "signal" of the drug under study. Originally focused on the "second world" countries of post-socialist Eastern Europe, where Petryna did her initial fieldwork, the geography of clinical trials is expanding globally, particularly to developing nations with sufficient biomedical infrastructure to support them such as Latin America, South Africa, India, and Thailand.

In many places, enrolment in a clinical trial ensures real or perceived improved access to health care on the part of research subjects, and may be the only way to obtain medical care for many people.[37] This situation makes it clear that the belief that research subjects who consent to participate in trials do so in a disinterested or uncoerced manner is a fiction. Petryna refers to this matter as "ethical variability" to underline how the outsourcing of clinical trials relies on these landscapes of constraint that are not taken into account.[38] She points out that a globalizing political economy has created a terrain in which the bodies of poor populations are made available for clinical experimentation, and although those who participate benefit by receiving health care while part of the trial, they are unlikely to be wealthy enough to afford the drugs that are eventually marketed having successfully passed through trials. While arguably in the real world of clinics and doctor's offices there is always a degree of "ethical variability," Petryna points to the paradox of arguing that clinical trials are a social good because they allow those who otherwise would not to obtain medical treatment, even though recruitment of subjects rests on the assumption that participation must be voluntary and altruistic for clinical trials to be ethical. Her work forces consideration of the broader social forces that alter the foundations on which the rules of ethical research are constructed and, we argue, also undermines the grounds of biological comparison on which biomedical research is based.[39]

Creating Markets for Biomedical Technologies in Developing Countries

"Offshoring" clinical trials refers to how drugs that will be sold mainly in wealthy markets of North America, Western Europe, Australasia, or Japan may be trialed in South America, Eastern Europe, South Africa, or India, raising the issue of "ethical variability." Today, however, growing numbers of clinical trials are conducted to identify interventions that will be used by populations of developing countries, whether rich or poor, with the result that many clinical trials conducted in the developing world are no longer that far offshore. The first reason for this is that global pharmaceutical firms turn to developing countries, and their growing middle classes, as a source of new markets. In the emerging markets of India, Latin America, and Asia, the chronic diseases of affluence – including diabetes and heart disease – are on the rise, making available to pharmaceuticals firms populations of "naïve" patients (in the sense that they have not previously been treated). However in these emerging markets chronic infectious diseases – including tuberculosis, hepatitis B, and HIV – remain prevalent. This situation is often compounded by malnutrition and exposure to tropical diseases. These markets therefore pose a challenge: unlike in Europe or America, the common chronic diseases of wealthy countries are often associated with infectious diseases and their sequelae (for instance, hepatitis B and liver cancer). Marketing drugs in these emerging economies requires conducting clinical trials designed to test novel formulations of drugs to address these bio-historical specificities.[40] The second reason clinical trials among the world's poor are no longer so far "offshore" is because of the growth in a humanitarian market for biomedical technologies developed for the poor. Global health inequities in access to biomedical care are therefore a powerful driving force behind the globalization of clinical trials.

Medical anthropologists and health activists have long decried the global health inequity that divides the world's population into two groups: the populations of the wealthy industrialized nations who benefit from biomedical resources while those of the developing world are largely excluded.[41] Poverty makes it difficult to afford protection from environments where parasites proliferate and the appropriate treatments are unaffordable. For instance, living in shanty towns or in war-damaged buildings increases exposure to parasites transmitted by fly-bites and vermin and the diseases that result, such as Chagas disease in Latin America or leishmaniasis in the Middle East and Africa; parasites such as those that cause schistosomiasis or onchocerciasis (river blindness) that thrive in stagnant pools of water are difficult to avoid for those who must work in muddy fields barefoot; and of course air-conditioned offices and homes and even mosquito nets are an unimaginable luxury to the poor for whom malaria is an everyday threat. Such diseases are therefore largely confined to the poor in developing countries. The pharmaceutical and biotech industries have had until recently little incentive to invest in developing drugs and other biomedical technologies to address diseases that largely afflict people who cannot pay for them. No new drugs, for instance, had been developed since the 1950s for the "neglected diseases" just mentioned, and the ones that exist are produced in limited quantities, prohibitively expensive as a result, and often toxic to boot.[42]

Since the turn of the century, there has been acknowledgment by industry and governments alike of these growing health disparities and the failure of the market to address global health needs. A phrase – "global health" – is today often used to mark the arrival of a new approach to the health problems of the world's poor. "Global health" signals a break from the "international health" of old, coordinated by nation-states through such organizations as the UN. In contrast, "global health" is broadly characterized by its recognition of the increasingly transnationalized nature of health threats, initially viewed through the lens of U.S. national security,[43] and an embrace of NGO and private-sector approaches.[44] Faced with the challenge of treating these neglected diseases of the poor, global philanthropists, NGOs, and wealthy governments have devised mechanisms to spur development of new biomedical technologies – drugs, vaccines, diagnostic tests, and so on – for these diseases. Funds have been established to capitalize start-up of drug and vaccine development, to purchase newly developed drugs and vaccines for diseases common among the poor, and to deliver health care that targets specific diseases causing particular hardship including HIV, tuberculosis, and malaria. Underlying this approach is a market rationale, inciting biotech firms to compete for funds and, eventually, profits. Upstream, they provide a boost to biotech and pharmaceuticals investment in research and development of these technologies. Downstream, they ensure that there will be buyers for new vaccines or drugs for these neglected diseases of the poor – in this case, governments and organizations that are committed to purchasing these technologies on behalf of populations that cannot afford them. The end result has been the creation of a growing humanitarian market for biomedical technologies to address diseases that disproportionately affect the world's poor.

The International AIDS Vaccine Initiative (IAVI), for instance, is a prime example of this kind of new global health assemblage – funded by governments and foundations, IAVI funds research but more importantly works to ensure that there will be a market for any AIDS vaccine that may eventually materialize. Public–private partnerships have become the new orthodoxy of global health, ostensibly combining the best of both worlds: private sector efficiency and responsiveness to market conditions, and public sector resources and stewardship. However, the increasing weight in global health of the private sector, particularly of corporate philanthropy, has not been without its critics. The Gates Foundation, for instance, is now the world's leading funder of global health, dwarfing many governments, and critics have voiced concern about the disproportionate impact such actors have on setting the agenda for global public health.[45]

In addition to this humanitarian market, biomedical technologies may become more available to the world's poor because some segments of the pharmaceutical industry are responding to criticisms that they are indifferent to global health inequities. Following the denunciation by global AIDS activists of the prohibitive price of AIDS drugs that makes them out of reach for the vast majority of the population suffering from this disease wherever they live, certain pharmaceutical companies have shifted their business models, deeply discounting drugs in developing country markets. Differential pricing is advanced as a humanitarian gesture by these companies, who claim that they sell at a loss in poorer markets. Of course, high prices in wealthy countries help to ensure a profit, and the tax benefits such "donations" inevitably accrue help cushion the blow. Thus, even the poorest of the poor, who cannot afford to pay for medicines, have become a new kind of market for drug companies, a "humanitarian" or social market.[46]

Testing Biomedical Interventions for the World's Poor

The development of drugs targeted to respond to the health conditions of affluent populations in poor countries, or even of the poor, requires the same kind of rigorous testing that other biomedical technologies must undergo, including laboratory studies and clinical trials. Clinical trials of interventions targeting these conditions, notably HIV, are increasing among the global poor, although such trials are most often conducted by NGOs and research institutes rather than the contract research organizations hired by pharmaceutical companies for "offshore" trials. In Petryna's term, these trials raise questions of "ethical variability." The sheer scale of human suffering caused by disease amongst those who do not have access to basic sanitation and medical care creates a "state of emergency" that, even though efforts may be made to retain elementary ethical practices of informed consent, produces research conditions that can be questioned on other ethical grounds, as will be discussed below. The following examples underscore Petryna's point that social, political, and economic conditions constitute a variable terrain that shifts the relationship among so-called autonomous research subjects, informed consent, and disinterested researchers that forms the basis of biomedical ethics. She notes that

> in "zones of crisis," protection and safety considerations are weighed against immediate health benefits or the knowledge to be gained. Ethics and methods are modified to fit the local context and experimental data required … "ethical variability" becomes a core value and a presumed course of action.[47]

This "ethical variability" challenges the way biomedical ethics is supposed to work by drawing attention to the broader political economy that shapes the conditions that make certain research questions viable, or helps to make participation in research an attractive proposition. We argue that ethical variability is linked to the biological variability that is equally an outcome of these conditions. We now turn to ethnographic examples to explore, first, how the global geography of economic and health inequalities fundamentally structures *which* research questions get asked, and second, *how* they are answered, and hence the production of biomedical knowledge itself. These examples reveal otherwise unexamined moral assumptions in global biomedical research and the political and economic circumstances that make certain kinds of "evidence" possible while other forms are discarded. We then turn to ethnographic considerations of biomedical research that stress the moral economies that tie researchers and subjects together and, further, how access to biomedicine afforded within that moral economy is a fertile terrain for biosocial differentiation, as vulnerable bodies are partially exposed to powerful biomedical technologies.

Disputes over Perinatal HIV Transmission Trials

Trials conducted in the late 1990s in Uganda compared the anti-retroviral drug AZT to a placebo as a prevention of mother-to-child transmission of HIV. The trial generated controversy because another, more complicated AZT regimen (involving longer treatment with the drug and its intravenous administration during labor) had already been proven, in a Franco-U.S. study, to decrease HIV transmission from mothers to children during birth. This meant that the women receiving the placebo in the Ugandan trial would be deprived of a proven, effective treatment. Marcia Angell, the editor of the *New England Journal of Medicine* at the time, went so far as to compare the Ugandan trial with the infamous Tuskegee experiments conducted on African American men through the 1930s.[48] Supporters of the trial argued that the simpler regimen being tested needed to be proven against the "standard of care" in the developing world – that, at the time, was nothing because HIV-positive pregnant women did not get any treatment as part of prenatal care. This argument rehearses the "state of emergency" justification, where conduct of trials that would not be acceptable in industrialized nations appears legitimate in local conditions characterized by poor health, lack of access to health care, and steep economic inequalities. The trial went ahead, and the simplified AZT regimen was shown to be superior to placebo, although not as good as the longer and more complicated regimen used in industrialized nations.

Physician and medical anthropologist Claire Wendland followed this debate firsthand from Malawi, a southern African country with a severe AIDS epidemic where she practiced obstetrics. She points to an issue overlooked in the debate:

> whereas different standards of research are seen as egregious exploitation of the poor, different standards of therapy are seen as regrettable but necessary due to the realities of economic heterogeneity. Why have research and therapy come to be seen in this way as subject to different ethical codes? Research is not inherently more dangerous than therapy.[49]

The point was underscored by subsequent trials conducted in Uganda to test another anti-retroviral drug, nevirapine, for prevention of mother-to-child transmission. Nevirapine has an important advantage over AZT: because of its pharmacokinetic properties (it is more quickly absorbed and stays longer in the body than does AZT), it need be given only once to achieve the equivalent anti-HIV effects of those of AZT, which has to be administered over several weeks. This biological phenomenon – giving only one pill once labor has started, rather than beginning a treatment at 32 weeks of pregnancy – provides a great advantage in developing countries, where few women have access to prenatal care and the resources required to monitor even a simplified four-week course of AZT are practically nonexistent.

In other words, nevirapine was a "game-changer," a potential magic bullet that could make a huge difference in developing countries where the AZT regimen – even the simplified one that was ultimately proven to be effective against placebo in the Ugandan trial – was complicated and expensive to administer. The U.S.-funded clinical trial of nevirapine was not placebo-controlled, since the "standard of care" was the simple AZT regimen already proven in the controversial trial just discussed. Nevirapine was shown to reduce transmission of HIV from mother to child more effectively than does AZT, to which it was compared (8.2 percent of mothers receiving nevirapine as opposed to 10.4 percent receiving AZT transmitted HIV to their offspring). The relevance of conducting such a trial was conditioned by nevirapine's practical advantages over AZT – advantages that were overwhelming in the context of an HIV epidemic in a continent with minimal health care infrastructure. The results were also briefly applicable in industrialized nations, until more effective strategies emerged that involved putting pregnant women on a three-drug cocktail of anti-retroviral drugs – the standard strategy by 1996 for *treating* people with HIV but, until that time, not for *preventing* its transmission.

The Ugandan nevirapine trial caused considerable controversy after it emerged that shoddy practices had been used in the management of the data from the trial, raising questions about the actual validity of the results.[50] These irregularities were denounced by a physician, Dr Jonathan Fishbein, at the U.S. National Institutes of Health. He aired concerns about poor data management and raised a red flag about data showing that the women who received the drug subsequently developed resistance to it, making them more difficult to treat.[51] For women whose HIV became resistant to nevirapine, given to *prevent* transmission during pregnancy, subsequent *treatment* with a standard three-drug cocktail would not be as effective. It was claimed that the concern with the potential for single-dose nevirapine to cause drug resistance had been downplayed when the trial had been designed because, at that time, in the late 1990s, efforts in the developing world were directed toward *preventing* HIV, not *treating* it. This strategy was not to change until 2000, but by then nevirapine had been accepted as the standard strategy for preventing mother-to-child transmission of HIV, and the drug continues to be widely used as a single dose, although considerable efforts are now being made to deploy the three-drug cocktail preventive regimen worldwide.

Both the AZT and nevirapine trials show how framing a problem as a public health emergency can suspend some of the normal criteria by which biomedical efficacy is judged. In this case, the emergency was the risk that millions of women worldwide – the vast majority of whom live in Africa – could transmit HIV to their children. Nevirapine showed considerable promise as a panacea, leading to the rapid implementation of a clinical trial to prove its efficacy. Left unexamined was the risk that the drug posed to the long-term survival of the women to whom it was administered – a risk that would only emerge if the prospect of offering treatment was envisaged which, at the time, it clearly was not. Moreover, because the trials were randomized, researchers did not need to engage with the fact that poverty, malnutrition, and environmental factors may make poor women in developing countries react differently to drugs than those in wealthy countries. Research design ensured that such confounding factors would have been distributed evenly between experimental and control groups of African women in the trial. Even so, evidence from these and other trials suggest that the toxicities of these drugs are more significant in these contexts than in the subjects that participated in trials in wealthy countries.

Further trials have since generated yet more controversy. The anti-retroviral drug tenofovir is currently being tested as a pre-exposure prophylaxis, or PrEP, for HIV – a kind of "evening before" pill that would protect individuals from acquiring HIV. Initial trials, sponsored by the large American NGO, Family Health International (FHI), planned to recruit sex workers in Cambodia, Cameroon, Malawi, and Nigeria in 2004 and 2005. The sex workers would have been randomized to receive either placebo or the drug, and tested regularly to see if this would lead to any difference in HIV infections between the two groups. All women were to be given condoms and prevention counseling. A row arose after Cambodian sex workers and French AIDS activists protested that the trials were unethical because they did not offer guarantees that women who were infected with HIV during the trials would subsequently be treated for their infection with anti-retroviral therapy. Furthermore, the women did not receive enough information on the risks they were facing, including the risk that, should the drug not work and they were to become infected, the virus could have become resistant to the drug. The trials were never completed, because pressure by international sex workers and HIV activists drew media attention to them. A demonstration at the 2004 Bangkok International AIDS Conference led to the Cambodian Prime Minister shutting down the Phnom Penh trial and subsequently, as a result of a French documentary, in February 2005 the Cameroonian Ministry of Health halted the trial in that country.[52] Later that same year, FHI stopped the Nigerian trial, and in October 2005, the Malawian Ministry of Health stopped the only remaining trial in that country. By 2007, however, new trials of tenofovir were under way at other sites. Behind the controversies over the tenofovir trials also lay unease with the assumption that it was acceptable to observe women at continued high risk of HIV without addressing the financial circumstances that may have driven them to sex work.

The AZT and nevirapine trials generated important and statistically robust evidence about the drugs they tested. The controversies that surrounded these trials indicate how facts are conditioned by political and economic conditions and moral assumptions. It was assumed to be relatively more important to "rescue" children from potential contamination by HIV than to treat their mothers so that the children could survive (indeed, the assumption that children are more important than their mothers has run as a thread throughout biomedicine's colonial and global engagements). In the case of AZT and nevirapine, the moral assumption that children were more important than their mothers was quickly overturned, in no small measure due to feminist activists hardened by earlier battles designed to bring attention to the "M" in mother and child health programs. Once it was acknowledged that mothers should receive treatment, these trials – and the interventions they spawned – became obsolete. Nonetheless, economic realities and political and institutional inertia meant that single-dose nevirapine continued to be given, posing ongoing risks to women to whom it was administered, despite updated guidelines and new "evidence" contradicting its use. Wendland closes on this note:

> The historically created split between research and therapy worked in the First World's favor … the self-appointed guardians of medical morality, envisioning themselves as members of a world community, set moral standards based on Western philosophical constructs. But when it came time for the concrete realization of these standards – that is, when the findings of research needed to be made available in the form of therapies – the boundaries of community shrank to the borders of the nation-state. Third World peoples were left pinned between an unreachable standard and an inadequate set of resources. Researching the second-best is unethical, American bioethicists said to African doctors, nurses, patients, and policymakers; but paying for the best is up to you. It is this maneuvering, I would argue, and not the use of a placebo control group, that was the most serious ethical violation in the perinatal AZT controversy, and it remains a tragically underexamined problem in bioethics today.[53]

What Should Count as Significant Evidence?

After many years of isolation, in the mid-1990s the Chinese government began to remove obstacles to international development aid in the Tibetan autonomous region (TAR). Vincanne Adams, a medical anthropologist who had worked in Tibet for more than a decade at the time, was asked by Tibetans to join a team of doctors, nurses, and midwives from the United States to develop a program for training rural health care workers in "safe motherhood."[54] The local government, very aware that maternal death in childbirth was taking a heavy toll, was eager to obtain whatever assistance they could to improve the situation. The group of Americans planned to introduce a midwife-training program and sought out funding to do so. In order to obtain support, Adams and colleagues were obliged to develop a "statistically robust" project that would be comparable with data being collected from projects in other countries. They were told in no uncertain terms that they could not use maternal mortality as a measure in this research because "not enough women die in Tibet to get a good power calculation."[55]

This criticism could not be dismissed simply as heartless by Adams and colleagues, because evidence-based guidelines demand that maternal mortality aggregates be made on the basis of death per 100,000 live births – something that would never be possible given the size of the Tibetan population. Adams asks rhetorically, what "sort of epistemic imperative" could possibly turn a statement about not enough maternal deaths into a "true fact"? She adds, this statement "felt like a lie," given that proportionally 40 times as many women die in childbirth in Tibet as compared to the United States.[56] Adams' group was told that they should instead look at infant mortality, given that the deaths of newborns were high enough to get "good statistics."

The project was also charged with not being able to find a reliable control group. Because all rural health workers meet at the country headquarters of the research project every few months for training and a review of skills, it was argued by potential funders that there would be "cross-contamination" and interventions would "leak" over into those communities designated as controls, and therefore not slated for special care. As Adams puts it: "the desire for scientific rigor in our project, in effect, aroused a need to reproduce a laboratory-like situation in which we could designate a 'study-population' and treat it as if it were stripped of all features that did not pertain to the discrete variables we were measuring."[57] Adams takes issue with the assumption that careful project design would result in the bodies of women being decontextualized so that they could then reliably be treated as non-dependent variables. In Adams' estimation, this production of "facts" out of context[58] led to the "erasure" of a population of people that desperately needed good medical help.

This particular case also illustrates another difficulty in the globalization of biomedical experiments – that of problems with enumeration at the local level. Tibetan women made clear to Adams that villagers were very cautious about divulging information because they were well aware that their local beliefs about the part the spirit world plays in successful pregnancies and birth were not compatible with those of the health care workers. This discrepancy made "truth-finding" a complicated process. The research team, which included educated Tibetans, was convinced that such beliefs block the way to a more appropriate, biomedically based understanding on the part of Tibetan women about maternal death and infant morbidity. These beliefs, health care workers argued, prevent women from seeking out good prenatal hospital-based care and are, in effect, simply lies that women tell themselves. The research team, in their certainty about their own truth-claims based on numbers (with their own moral orientation), could not appreciate that local beliefs are not arbitrary, but equally "embedded in a moral terrain."[59] For the targeted Tibetan women, the "instruments of modernity" designed to force them to let go of "outmoded beliefs" would strip them of morality. Ultimately this situation is, once again, a question of moral economy and what will count as truth and shows how misunderstandings arise at the intersection of the moral economy of the biomedical experiments and that of the communities where these are performed, even when such research addresses problems of unquestionable importance, such as maternal mortality in Tibet. We turn now to examine this intersection in greater detail.

Living with Vampires: Perceptions of Research

Medical research in developing countries necessarily often involves exchanges of blood and bodily substances for medical care. The social relationships that develop and sustain such medical research are therefore often viewed by participants and even researchers as a kind of economy, as the following quote obtained by anthropologists working in the West African country of the Gambia shows:

> The Medical Research Council takes blood from healthy people and sells it …

> When one joins the … study, they will take much blood and if you are not lucky the child may die.[60]

Fairhead, Leach, and Small were investigating a clinical trial of a vaccine to protect against pneumonia that had been conducted in this poor West African country by the U.K.'s Medical Research Council, which has research stations in seven Gambian towns. The MRC has conducted research in the Gambia for over 60 years, and its base in Fajara is an impressive complex that houses a hospital, gleaming laboratories, a computer center, as well as offices, training rooms, and housing. In the course of their study, Fairhead and colleagues observed how the research practices of MRC workers intersected with local understandings of blood and vitality – what the authors called an "economy of blood."[61] Their reports echo similar observations reported by other researchers – medical and anthropological – in many other parts of the world. Writing about East Africa, historian Luise White noted "vampire rumors" that locate Western origin biomedical practices within a broader economy of extraction and exploitation.[62] As we see shortly, a veritable global economy in blood and body parts does indeed exist, making such rumors even more trenchant – and is a potentially powerful influence on the way biomedical technologies are perceived and ultimately used.

In the Gambia, what Fairhead and colleagues showed, however, is that these observations are just surface manifestations of a more fundamental way of life, whereby entire communities have settled into an uneasy coexistence with a research apparatus that gives jobs and economic incentives even as it takes blood and other bodily samples. The MRC complex is dedicated to the study of tropical diseases such as malaria as well as non-tropical diseases that are found in the Gambia – most notably HIV. Its base in Fajara is a gleaming icon of modernity in a desperately poor country, the whole secured by a barbed wire fence and top-level security. While the rest of the town is often plunged into darkness because of a tenuous power supply, even in the middle of the night the research complex glows brightly. In this respect, the MRC complex resembles other research facilities that constitute far-flung outposts of biomedical research and public health agencies and universities. It must be under-lined that such research has made, and continues to make, significant progress in understanding diseases of the poor, and that critical ethnographic studies – such as that of Fairhead and colleagues – are often embraced by these research institutes and agencies whose staff are all too aware of the ethical challenges posed by research in developing countries.[63] Research institutes pass unnoticed in wealthier countries where the ambient poverty is not as striking; however, in places like Fajara the contrast can at first glance be unsettling.

Fairhead, Leach, and Small were among the first to make use of ethnography to examine the impact of this medical research apparatus on the lives of those with whom it interacts. They interviewed research subjects and field-staff of malaria research programs and vaccine trials, as well as those who live in the communities from which research subjects were recruited. The MRC was widely appreciated for the quality of the health care it provided. This was not surprising because the contrast between MRC medicine and local facilities was as starkly visible as that between the brightly lit facility and the surrounding villages. The MRC facility was older than most of those who were interviewed and, in many ways, provided them with more services than does the Gambian government. While the scientists at the center came and went, as did the trials and experiments, the facilities stayed. Only that of the church exceeds the temporal stability of the MRC, and it is established as a fixture of life in these communities. Fairhead et al. describe how "being with MRC"[64] anchors a set of pragmatic calculations by which local people weigh the dangers of participating in the blood economy of the researchers against the benefits that could accrue from letting one's blood be taken and presumably sold to strangers in faraway places.

Fairhead and Leach's colleagues Molyneux and Geissler studied a malaria vaccine trial conducted by the MRC in the Gambia. In this trial, field staff were drawn from the same communities where research subjects – called "volunteers" in this experi-ment – were recruited. Two aspects of the trial stood out in the minds of those associated with the trial: the requirement to carry out regular blood-drawing to check for malarial parasites, and the provision of free medical care to all the volunteers. Moreover, "if the volunteer was young and unmarried, his parents were entitled to share his benefits, whereas if he was married, his wife and children were," a situation where Geissler's informants described the regular provision of blood samples as "a high but necessary price for family health care" with the result that "the exchange of blood specimens and medicines was the defining feature of research" for these "volunteers."[65]

Research staff referred to research subjects as "brothers" or "sisters" to express the sense of relatedness that grew during the two-year-long study, constituting what Geissler called a "trial community." This idiom of kinship ended up being crucial to the trial's remarkable success at recruiting and retaining research subjects. Geissler notes that "staff and villagers ... underlined this kinship to underscore that no harmful or selfish intentions could enter the trial community, e.g. to counter the suspicion that the MRC represented Europeans' interests."[66] Staff were able to draw on the metaphor of kinship to reassure villagers they could be trusted, and by extension the foreign researchers with whom the staff worked. Kinship also played an important function in deciding how to allocate health care, a complicated process:

> Because the biogenetic rules of entitlement mixed kinship and economic transactions in ways that did not always coincide with villagers' lives and understandings of kinship, fieldworkers found it difficult to apply them. Distributing medicines broadly, irrespective of the sick people's link to the trial, quickly exhausted scarce resources; yet, limiting benefits to active volunteers caused conflicts with the communities. Fieldworkers had to balance their diverging responsibilities towards the people they lived with and the trial management. They took decisions in face-to-face interactions, responding to particular requests rather than realizing formal prescriptions, and variously made and erased boundaries and emphasized or ignored connections in more fluid ways than the rules of health care entitlement, even after their field-based adaptations, foresaw.[67]

These ethnographic studies point to another paradox associated with this kind of human experimentation. While the authority of the evidence that accrues from clinical trials derives from procedures to ensure "objectivity" (such as blinding and randomization), creating such conditions is not possible without a tissue of social ties, reciprocal obligations, and material and symbolic exchanges already in place. Two apparently irreconcilable moral economies intersect during such trials: that of science and the objectivity that it prizes, and that of "trial communities" that recognize both commodified and noncommodified forms of exchange.

For many people, such as poor Gambians, the existence of ethical variability by the standards of medical research conducted in the West in local research protocols is the lesser of two evils – the choice is no medical care at all or medical care that comes by being part of a clinical trial. Neither altruistic nor brute exploitation, these trials are simply another form of exchange between the powerful, their intermediaries, and the powerless. Anthropologist Kris Peterson argues that ethical practice requires recognition that trials may have important social consequences that transform the lives of both research subjects *and* those around them, and that researchers should act accordingly.[68] But such consequences are often "misrecognized" because they occur long after the trial has ended, and outside the frame within which the research is conducted. The Gambian example shows that the global apparatus of biomedical research, particularly clinical trials and other experiments that enrol populations, relies on highly localized social relations that enable an economy of the gifting of blood specimens necessary to the production of evidence, and these social relations persist long after experiments end. Importantly these relations condition access to biomedical care and other resources that may in fact produce biological differences between those they enfold and those they exclude. "Being with MRC" refers to an ongoing process of biosocial differentiation as these ethnographies show. In the case of the Gambia, for instance, decades of research conducted in poor communities has resulted in improved access to health care and jobs that have helped to actually transform the biology of surrounding communities. As producers of biosocial differentiation then, clinical trials result in the creation of local biologies and local economies.

This shows how research subjects may be biologically and socially different from those to whom the evidence from the trial is to be applied. This is most visible when evidence from trials in, say India, is used to prescribe drugs in Sweden, but occurs even when they are in the same geographic locale, for instance, when results from MRC studies in the Gambia are applied to populations that have not had the benefit of growing up under the MRC's benevolent health stewardship. We turn now to further examples of how clinical experiments may produce biosocial differences, transforming individual bodies and social groups as they gain access to powerful medicines.

Experimental Communities: Social Relations

In the 1920s a leper colony was established by the French colonial physician Emile Marchoux on the outskirts of Bamako in the colony of French West Africa. Marchoux was one of the Pastorians described in the previous chapter, having trained in the emerging science of microbiology at the Institut Pasteur of Indochina. Subsequently, he was charged with founding the first African microbiology laboratory in Saint-Louis, in what is today Senegal. His interests eventually turned to leprosy and he founded the Institut central de la Lèpre some 20 kilometers from Bamako, capital of the French Sudan. Marchoux was a humanist, and did not seek to control the ravages of leprosy by forcibly rounding up and quarantining lepers. Rather, he sought to attract lepers to the *lazaret*, as leper colonies were called, with the promise of humane treatment. Marchoux's approach was a successful one, drawing in many who had been ostracized from their communities. However, treatment at the time was largely ineffective, and those who flocked to the Institute for relief became a willing group of experimental subjects when the Institute's scientists tried out new treatments in a quest for a cure for the stigmatized disease. The leprosarium was renamed the Institut Marchoux in 1935, and continued to experiment with new agents as possible treatments. The historian Eric Silla has chronicled how a community of lepers and their families grew up around the Institut when patients intermarried and settled around the grounds of the facility. Gradually this community became the small town of Djikoroni, which has since been swallowed up by sprawling Bamako, becoming one neighborhood among many in the city, but distinguished by this particular, biomedical history.[69]

Seventy years later in the same part of West Africa, in the mid-1990s, two large clinical trials of AZT for the prevention of mother-to-child transmission of HIV were carried out, one sponsored by the French national AIDS research agency (ANRS), and the other by the rival American Centers for Disease Control (CDC). Even though these trials were placebo-controlled, they did not attract the same scrutiny as the Ugandan trial, probably because they took place in French-speaking countries. The French study tested 14,385 women in Bobo-Dioulasso (Burkina Faso) and Abidjan (Côte d'Ivoire), while the American study tested 12,668 women in Abidjan. All the women received state-of-the-art pre-test counseling in connection with HIV. Of the total of over 27,000 women tested, 3,424 were found to be positive. However, in the American study 618 HIV positive women never returned for their results and the post-test counseling; in the French study the figure was 648. Researchers told Nguyen that the rate of drop-out was lower in HIV negative women, suggesting that women suspected their diagnosis and decided not to return for results. Of the HIV positive women who returned for their results, only 711 were included in the actual trials, the remaining 1,447 women were either excluded for reasons described below, or simply did not consent.[70]

The trials had an enormous impact in shaping the early response by the local population to the epidemic – simply because of the sheer number tested at a time when HIV testing was not routinely offered elsewhere. Based on Nguyen's fieldwork with HIV prevention and care programs in both countries in the mid-1990s, the majority of people who knew their HIV status had found this out by having been recruited into the trials.[71] Of course, only a small minority of women were actually enrolled in the trials, although a very large number had been screened to have a significant pool from which to enrol a necessarily smaller number of eligible study subjects. There were numerous reasons that disqualified women, most usually not presenting themselves early enough in pregnancy to receive AZT, or suffering from anemia, that could be dangerously worsened if they received AZT. Women who had tested positive but were not eligible to enrol in the trials complained bitterly that they had been "discarded." They resented lack of access to what they perceived to be a panoply of services for women who had been included in the trials, and therefore had been randomized to receive either placebo or AZT.

Indeed, the women who were included in the trial did receive medical care and social services that were not available to others. After having been tested, many of them found their way into community groups in search of material and social support; some even set up organizations for their fellow would-be trial subjects. The ethical requirements that informed the inclusion criteria that determined who was accepted into the trial generated a perception of injustice that ironically laid the groundwork for a shared solidarity that, over time, would resurface when women enrolled in the trials were prioritized to receive anti-retroviral drugs in the French government's first HIV treatment program in Africa. Nonetheless, over time, as drug access broadened and health returned to the women, the groups that grew out of the trial flourished. Some of the widows remarried, and many of the younger women went on to find husbands – some of whom they met in the groups – and to have children. Like the Bamako leper colony that became a village that later on would blend into an expanding city, these clinical trials spawned community groups whose members' access to treatment has kept illness at bay, attenuating many of the differences that set them apart from the expanding cities in which they now live their lives unnoticed.

This work shows that these globalized efforts to produce biomedical knowledge have a number of unforeseen consequences. The first is that biomedical experiments – clinical trials and cohort studies, in this case – produce novel forms of social relations. These forms of sociality are particularly salient in settings where they are directly linked to fundamental individual and collective vitality, notably in settings where nonexistent public health infrastructure and poverty means that participating in research becomes a survival strategy. The resulting trial communities should be viewed as sites of production of local biology. Anthropologist Paul Rabinow first proposed the idea of "biosociality" – new forms of social relations organized on the basis of biological conditions or common genetic make-up – over a decade ago.[72] Today, we see a kind of research-driven sociality as people gather together with intent to participate in clinical trials. The consequences of such forms of sociality will be a crucial field site for future medical anthropological investigation that will need to address the biosocial differentiation of those who are included and those who are excluded from clinical research.

In Summary

A cornerstone of scientific biomedicine, the ability to compare populations under controlled conditions, was built on the assumption that human biology could be used as a standard for comparison. Comparison requires experiment – a virtual or deliberate creation of the conditions of comparison. Biomedicine is unique compared to other laboratory sciences in that it must experiment, at some point, on humans, and, because there are severe limits to what one can do to experimental subjects, comparison *must* be grounded in the assumption that humans are biologically similar. Today, evidence of biomedicine's effectiveness is increasingly derived from vast experiments that enrol subject populations worldwide.[73]

These experimental populations are contemporary "theaters of proof" where statistical technologies choreograph the performance. Prevailing moral assumptions and political and economic imperatives, however, leave many questions unaddressed by this experimental apparatus and uncomfortable answers are suppressed. The political and economic imperatives that drive research and that also weave culture, history, and power into biological reality described in the ethnographic examples in this chapter remain hidden from view. However, what is "proven" in these studies determines the medications we take, the diagnoses we are given, and even the policies of governments and other large institutions.

The kinds of people who make themselves available for experimentation, however, are likely to be biologically different from those who have no pressing need to subject themselves to clinical trials, undermining the grounds of comparison that would enable the generalization of such evidence. Based on data from trials, interventions are being rolled out across the world and entire populations made subject to interventions even though the real-world setting in which these interventions are carried out is completely different from the laboratory of the clinical trial: this too is an experiment.

Part III

Moral Boundaries and Human Transformations

8

Who Owns the Body?

It is as clear as noon-day, that man, by his industry, changes the forms of the materials furnished by Nature, in such a way as to make them useful to him. (Karl Marx)[1]

We are in an era in which the processing of human cells, tissues, and organs into therapeutic tools and pharmacological agents has burgeoned into a globalized industry, with the potential to create enormous wealth, especially for drug and other biotechnology companies. Articles about the commodification of human eggs, sperm, blood, cells, and organs appear frequently in the media. The language of individual rights, privacy, and dignity is often appended to such articles, and sometimes discussion about the appropriate disposal of body parts is included, couched in the language of property. But debate about the broader social implications of commodification of tissues and organs is less common – notably about new forms of inequity and equally, at times, new forms of social solidarity that are emerging as a result of these technologies.

These debates and changes will be discussed in this chapter and the two that follow it. Furthermore, the "social life" of human body parts, to paraphrase the anthropologist Igor Kopytoff,[2] and their ambiguity as signifiers, together with the social ramifications of the moral economy associated with this new form of exchange will be considered. When human body parts can readily be disaggregated and redistributed for use as therapeutic material in other people, or else as research material, what does this entail for our sense of relatedness to one another? Medical use of human and animal bodies has long been justified in terms of saving lives and enhancing medical knowledge, and obviously biomedical knowledge should not stagnate, but irresolvable contradictions persist when human body parts and human experimentation are the principal means to this end.

Disputes may arise in the social exchange of virtually all kinds of objects, but the commodification of human cells, tissues, and organs is of particular concern because boundaries assumed to be natural and inviolable are inevitably transgressed through technological manipulation. Debates about what constitutes "self" and "other" also arise when organs, for example, are transplanted from one person to another. Or, when people provide bodily fluids or tissue for research, arguments take place about where the line should be drawn between individual interest and privacy and possible financial gain, as opposed to the gifting of biological material for the greater good of humankind. Disagreements are not simply about ownership, property rights, intellectual property, or even about alienability, but also result from a profound angst about possible violations of the moral order. This chapter, and those that follow it, are about techno/biologicals of one kind and another and, above all, about the social repercussions of their creation, supply, and application in practice.

Commodification of Human Biologicals

The specter of body parts being illicitly sold and bought worldwide is upon us, in large part because of increasing exposure in both the media and in movies. However, the sensationalistic treatment often given this topic misses much of the complexity involved, including the very idea of what constitutes commodification. In its original meaning a commodity was understood as something of use, advantage, or value. Commodification can be thought of, therefore, as the production or conversion of ideas, knowledge, and objects into items that are considered useful and/or have exchange value. In contemporary society this implies more often than not that these items will have monetary value, but this is not necessarily the case. Thus, despite rigorous opposition to the sale of organs and certain tissues in many countries today, the reality is that bodies are inevitably commodified when body parts are donated or procured for purposes of exchange, but the market is not necessarily involved. Highly colored, shocking accounts about the sale of organs tend to deflect attention away from the routinized activities of exchange in the transplant world, as though there is nothing out of the ordinary about these activities. Recycling of human parts has become an everyday matter, newsworthy only when criminal activity is involved, or else a plane carrying organs for transplant crashes, losing all human life on board and the lungs they were transporting in order to save yet another life.[3]

The transformation of biologicals of all kinds into commodified artifacts has a long history, often accompanied by unsavory tales that raise social and moral issues. Human corpses and body parts procured from the living and the dead have had value as trophies of war, religious relics, items for ritual performances, anatomical specimens, therapeutic materials, and medicinals for peoples everywhere for many hundreds of years. In Europe, the commodification of human bodies for medical purposes, even though it fell largely into the domain of the Church until the 17th century, was more often than not associated with violence due in large part to the importance given to anatomical knowledge and hence the need to practice dissection.

When the philosopher Jean Baudrillard states baldly: "for medicine, the body of reference is the corpse," he has in mind "Western" medicine.[4] In no other literate medical tradition, whether it be East Asian medicine, Ayurvedic medicine of South Asia, or the Unani tradition of the Islamic world, has anatomy been held in such high regard as the key means of knowledge about the body. In Europe, an interest in anatomy is well documented in Greek medicine after the time of Hippocrates. It is perhaps fair to suggest that anatomical thinking was consolidated as a result of the practices of Aristotle who performed anatomical dissection and vivisection on animals, but it was the vivisection of humans and animals by Herophilus in fourth-century CE Alexandria that earned him a lasting reputation as the "father of scientific anatomy."[5]

In church precincts in thirteenth-century Italy, anatomists performed dissections of corpses of criminals and vagrants in public.[6] Vesalius is reported to have taken a beating heart out of an individual involved in an accident, and by his own admission he and his students desecrated graves, stole corpses, and ransacked ossuaria to obtain the human material they so dearly wanted; they were particularly keen to get their hands on the bodies of women.[7] Public dissections continued until the early 19th century in civic anatomy theaters built in many parts of Europe. This practice ensured that the bodies of individuals on the margins of society accrued enormous medical value, and Ruth Richardson argues that by the 17th century in Europe, as already was the case for human relics, the human corpse was bought and sold like any other commodity. The urgent medical "need" for dead bodies made the practice of robbing graves in Europe and North America both tempting and lucrative.[8]

According to Linebaugh, increase in the trade in corpses in early modern Europe is evidence of a significant change in attitudes toward the dead body:

> The corpse becomes a commodity with all the attributes of a property. It could be owned privately. It could be bought and sold. A value, not measured by the grace of heaven nor the fires of hell, but rather quantifiably expressed in the magic of the price list was placed upon the corpse.[9]

The fact that popular opposition to dissection was beginning to be heard in the 19th century caused certain members of the medical profession to turn increasingly to "body snatchers" for assistance. The poor were understood quite literally to be more valuable dead than alive, and several notorious murderers were eventually brought to justice in England, the most famous pair of whom, Burke and Hare, regularly plied their victims with whisky before smothering them. The bodies were then sold promptly to London hospitals of good repute, with no questions asked.[10]

The Anatomy Act, designed to prohibit the sale of dead bodies in the United Kingdom, was signed in 1831, later adopted with some minor modifications by the commonwealth nations and those American states in existence at the time, and it continues to be the foundation of modern law in connection with these matters. Prior to the passing of this Act, one could not be prosecuted for "stealing" a dead body, either before or after burial. Even after the Act, workhouses and other institutions that housed the poor, including hospitals, were defined as "lawfully in possession of the dead." Due to the quasi-property status of the corpse, these institutions were able to confiscate the bodies of those who died when no claimant came forward or when no money was available to pay for a funeral, and make use of them as they wished.[11] Richardson remarks that to die without provision for burial was the key indicator of social failure, and the Victorian poor did everything they could to avoid such a fate. Friends and neighbors would make collections to pay for funerals, corpses were hidden at home, or more than one body was placed in a single coffin.[12]

In the interests of medicine, consequently, the plundered bodies of the poor, and in North America, in addition, the bodies of African Americans, First Nations peoples, and new immigrants, were effectively assigned to a "state of exception";[13] their bodies were not due the respect given to the rest of society. It was not until the end of the

19th century that significant public outcry against such practices brought them to a halt. However, at that time corpses, regardless of their social status while living, began to be conceptualized as biological objects, as wholly part of nature and therefore without cultural baggage, and it became relatively easy, in the minds of medical men at least, to strip bodies of social, moral, and religious worth, not just those already designated while alive as beyond the pale. Commodification for the benefit of scientific advancement became both legal and laudable.[14] Even so, for families, the bodies of deceased relatives were not so easily divested of social meanings,[15] a situation that continues to the present day.

Clearly, commodification of the human corpse is not, then, a feature associated solely with the globalized economy of modernity, as many apparently believe. The use of human bodies as slaves and for labor of all kinds, including sex and child labor, has a long and tortuous history, and many of the same legal and ethical questions in connection with exploitative economies of labor are at issue in the commodification of body parts. But it is only recently that the human body has attained medical and commercial value as a mine for spare parts and research, and as a therapeutic tool.[16] Until well into the 20th century the biotechnology industry has not had the technological know how to capitalize on isolated organs and tissues.

Objects of Worth and Their Alienation

Although body commodification is of long standing, there is no doubt that the global dissemination of capitalism that commenced in the16th century, and currently takes the form of extraction of wealth by multinationals from the "developing" world, has exacerbated the situation. A foreshadowing of the form that commodification of body parts takes today is evident in the way that human labor was exploited in colonized countries.

The anthropologist Michael Taussig, writing about the effects of capitalist relations of production among indigenous miners in Colombia and Bolivia, draws on the classic work of Marcel Mauss about modes of exchange in premodern societies where markets do not exist. Mauss' thesis was that the "gift exchange" practiced routinely in very many such societies resulted in vital bonds of reciprocity forged between involved parties. Such bonds were of supreme importance because it was understood that individuals give away a modicum of their "essence" with a gift that must be returned in kind.[17]

Taussig points out that the practice of the modern market system strives to deny this "metaphysics of persons and things reflected in social exchange" and to replace the type of fetishism described by Mauss with the commodity fetishism of capitalism discussed by Marx. Whereas the former derives from the "organic unity" understood to exist among persons and the things they produce and exchange, the latter – commodity fetishism – has its origin in the alienation that arises among persons and the things that they produce and exchange.[18] As David Harvey put it: "the grapes that sit on the supermarket shelves are mute, we cannot see the fingerprints of exploitation upon them."[19]

Taussig's later research into terror and healing elaborates on the many forms of commodification of the colonized body, not simply as a source of labor, but as an object for exoticism and prurient desire. He shows how, repeatedly, different regimes of value attributed to the native body by exploiter and the exploited result in disorder and the disruption of the conventional meanings assigned to human bodies by both parties.[20]

The Wealth of Inalienable Goods

One dilemma with which Marcel Mauss never came to grips when writing about pre-capitalistic exchange, was the difficulty of explaining the accumulation of wealth – of gain – even in non-modern societies. Like the majority of theorists who followed him, he attributed a natural autonomy to the workings of reciprocity, and assumed that an egalitarian, timeless condition prevailed. Annette Weiner, in her meticulous reworking of anthropological theory about exchange, argues that many investigators, including Mauss, failed to observe how hierarchy and relationships of power function in all societies. She focused on "inalienable possessions," on things that people never trade, or trade only when reduced to dire straits. Inalienable possessions, whether in the form of land, property, or valued objects, signify difference, and ownership of such possessions tends, Weiner argues, to attract other kinds of wealth. They are imbued with affective qualities – expressions of the value an object has when it is kept by its owners and inherited within the same family or descent group.[21]

Clearly body tissues, organs, and even fluids are in theory regarded as inalienable and different from all other materials; the body and body parts represent life itself, individual, familial, and communal – past, present, and future – and these meanings continue to adhere to them even in death. However, as the above discussion about the commodification of corpses in medieval Europe suggests, a universal taboo against the commodification of body parts has never in practice prevailed; the commodity status of body parts is contestable, negotiable, and mutable. It is well documented, for example, that detachable, disposable body parts including nails, sputum, menstrual blood, and hair were, and continue to be, commodified as objects that have the potential to both harm and heal, depending upon context.[22] The boundaries between sorcery and healing are blurred, and bodily objects, especially "surplus" tissues and body appendages, take on different meanings and have changeable value depending upon how and when they are put to use.[23]

New possibilities for improving one's status and accumulating potential wealth have come about now that techno/biologicals have become indispensable to the biotechnology industry. In recent years, several indigenous groups have negotiated contracts with drug companies whereby they will be reimbursed for donation of their blood for DNA analysis, but many contracts state that reimbursement will only take place if the company in question successfully produces a new drug from the genetic material. Although such exchanges have the potential to create wealth for indigenous populations, to date no drug development has been successful in making use of venture capital biologicals obtained from humans and local populations have not benefited.[24] Alienation of body parts can also result in a more dramatic loss and diminished status when impoverished people who sell a kidney in the hope of improving their life or that of their family all too often actually worsen their situation by becoming infected or chronically debilitated (see chapter 9).[25]

A Bioeconomy of Human Biologicals

All forms of commodification lie at the complex intersection of temporal, cultural, social, and political factors and, further, the "commodity candidacy" of things is contingent, but inevitably this process is fluid and open to dispute both within and between localized systems of meanings and exchange.[26] With increasing globalization, the circulation of commodities, including that of human labor, sex work, cadavers, and body parts, transcends local meanings and regulations. Production and consumption are often spatially at a great remove from each other, and linked by means of a string of intermediaries all with their own interests, leaving the original providers of goods and services subject to exploitation – a situation glaringly evident in connection with the sale of organs for paltry sums of money by live donors, very many of whom live in abject poverty.[27] Today, the scale and extent of commodification is vast, and the forms it takes are many. Waldby and Mitchell note: "Tissue sourced from one person may be distributed in altered forms along complex pathways to multiple recipients at different times and at different locations throughout the world,"[28] although inevitably technological limitations remain. It has only recently become possible to freeze unfertilized human eggs for a great length of time using liquid nitrogen[29] and, although techniques for preservation of solid organs outside the human body have improved, the time they remain of use for transplantation is limited, particularly in the case of livers, hearts, and lungs.

Arjun Appadurai argues that commodities should not be understood "as one kind of thing rather than another." An item is not necessarily always a commodity, and may not originally have been created or produced for that purpose. Transformation into a commodity may be one phase in the life of some things;[30] commodities, therefore, have a social life – a life history of sorts.[31] Clearly when fulfilling their original function, body parts are not commodities, but in one phase of their "life" they may become commodified. For example, only after the technology was refined and transplants routinized did vital organs rapidly acquire immense value to interested parties other than the individuals in whom they reside: physicians, transplant coordinating organizations, dying patients and their families. But for an organ to achieve worth to these third parties, it must first be made into an object, a thing-in-itself, entirely differentiated from the person from whom it is procured; its previous social history must be made anonymous, and its value assessed solely in terms of quality for transplant – is it fatty, aged, diseased, or is it vital and healthy, and has it been well cared for during and after the harvest? Linda Hogle has discussed the way in which, over the years, the procurement of organs has been increasingly standardized in order that the resultant "product" is of good quality.[32] Only then is an organ readied to enter the world of exchange. Similarly, before semen can be made use of for insemination by donor, it must be prepared and transformed into "technosemen."

The social lives of products are intimately related to relationships of power. Sale of kidneys is virtually limited to those who feel obliged to do so through economic need, or who are coerced into it.[33] On the other hand, women who sell their eggs may not be in dire straits; they may believe that this is a relatively easy means to earn money to put themselves through college or they may be genuinely altruistically motivated. Furthermore, gendered or symbolic meanings attributed to objects available for commodification crucially affect their value (moral disputes about stem cells obtained from aborted or donated fetuses have made this abundantly clear). The commodity candidacy of "things" must be examined in context and, more often than not, is contestable and subject to revision.[34]

The fetishism associated with biologicals as a result of their reduction to objects potentially destroys the possibility for human affiliation as a result of exchange. This is particularly striking with solid organs because they are "scarce commodities," and cannot be acquired fast enough to meet the ever growing "need" of waiting patients (see chapter 9). The inherent contradiction between gifting what is usually thought of as inalienable and of supreme value, and the reification of procured organs as therapeutic objects, is damped down by an insistence on the part of the transplant world of the anonymity of organ donors, justified in terms of their right to privacy. By extension, donor families cannot usually track the trajectories taken by the organs of their deceased relatives after donation. Families are not informed about who has become the recipients of their "gifts," in order, it is argued, to prevent them seeking out any form of material compensation. However, as we will see in the following chapter, this stark separation of donors and recipients is being overtly challenged in some places by citizen-organized activities. Similarly, the anonymity of sperm donors is rigorously maintained in part, no doubt, so that they are not subjected to monetary demands for the upkeep and education of their biological offspring, although some sperm banks today make it possible for adult children to trace their fathers.

Who Owns the Body?

One special feature associated with human biologicals, as Linebaugh intimates in his historical discussion, is the question of ownership, posed by the relationship of physical bodies and of body parts to individuals.[35] Property rights in almost all European countries and in North America are invested in living individuals, following John Locke, who argued forcefully that every man is the "proprietor of his own person."[36] However, capitalizing on the dead raises a dilemma for property law. Moreover, the vision of families auctioning off parts of their relatives even as they die appears ghoulish to most of us. In connection with organ transfer, elaborate networks have been set up in most countries where organ transplants from brain-dead bodies are routinely carried out in order that procurement and dispersal of organs can be rigorously monitored, not only for quality, but also for fair play. These networks depend on organs that are freely donated by family members without any expectation of recompense other than gratitude. Even in those 20 European countries where, as of 2002, the state has the legal authority to take organs regardless of the wishes of deceased individuals or their families, organs are rarely, if ever, taken without family cooperation, although clearly the expectation is that families should be willing to give.[37]

Similarly, in most parts of the world, solid organs procured from living donors must be "gifted" on the assumption that donors and recipients are vulnerable to exploitation when a market model is in place (although this position is contested by some ethicists in the United States and elsewhere).[38] Outright sales of solid organs are illegal in most countries, although in certain countries, including India, Egypt, and Iran, the law is regularly flouted, and on-line sales of human organs are one means by which this takes place.

This situation is in contrast to renewable human biologicals or those believed to be surplus to requirements when, aside from gifts to relatives, payment is usually made, as is the case of eggs and sperm. Lesley Sharp notes that today, with respect to both dead and living bodies, "the human body is a treasure-trove of reusable parts,"[39] and the legal market for body parts in the United States alone is currently around $600 million annually.[40] Corpses are worth somewhere between $100,000 and $230,000 on the open market.[41] But, not surprisingly, the value of specific bodies and body parts depends upon their geographical origin. A kidney procured from a living donor can be purchased for anything from about $250 to $30,000 depending upon where the transaction takes place.[42]

Since the mid-1950s the metaphor of the "gift of life" has been used with considerable success to promote organ donation in both Europe and North America.[43] But what kind of a "gift" is a donation of human tissue and organs? Richard Titmuss, writing about blood donation when transplant technology was still at the experimental stage, posed a fundamental question: "Why give to strangers?" Categorically opposed to the sale of blood, Titmuss' argument is profoundly political, namely that contemporary society is strengthened when individuals have the right to exercise the moral choice to give to strangers in non-monetary form; in his estimation, social policies concerned with blood donation should always be designed to encourage this form of social solidarity.[44]

When considering donation of blood and organs, the majority of commentators, Titmuss included, return to the seminal work of Marcel Mauss who himself believed that his theory of the gift, a discourse about a fundamental form of human solidarity, has relevance for contemporary society. Commenting on social security systems taking shape in France and Great Britain in the first half of the 20th century, Mauss ventured to suggest that "the themes of the gift, of the freedom and the obligation inherent in the gift, of generosity and self-interest that are linked in giving, are reappearing in society, as a dominant motif too long forgotten."[45] Generous donation of blood to the troops during and after World War II suggests that Mauss was right about this type of community solidarity and, similarly, Waldby and Mitchell suggest that, after the terrorist attacks of 9/11, the "excessive desire to give blood" on the part of American citizens was perhaps driven in part by a sense that the body politic was itself wounded by these attacks.[46]

Even when body materials are freely donated for medical research, problems can arise because, once "gifted" to a medical institution, the material becomes the property of that institution, and the "gift" cannot be reversed. As Waldby and Mitchell point out, "the informed consent procedure acts as a kind of surrogate property contract." Body matter that is "gifted" is made into a "covert form of property" because informed consent is, in effect, already based on property rights – those of the recipient.[47]

One result of increasing mobilization of biologicals is that, in most instances, donation of organs and tissues cannot be thought of as simple acts of civic responsibility. As a result of biotechnological processing, what formerly were limitations of space and time are transcended – national boundaries are rendered highly permeable, and techno/biologicals can be "immortalized," sometimes for years on end.[48] This means that substances such as sperm, fetal cells, and suspensions of DNA circulate in an arena over which national governance and legal restraints hold no sway, making debate and implementation of guidelines and laws about the global distribution of techno/biologicals and control over contaminated or damaged materials a matter of urgency.[49] Several commentators have argued that what we are currently witnessing is the capitalization of "life itself."[50] And Charis Thompson notes that virtually the whole of the "biotech mode of (re)production" is today embedded in a world of "promissory" or venture capital.[51] With the exception of those techno/biologicals that cannot be preserved well enough to travel for hours on end, body parts, apparently donated altruistically, "gifted" with the social good in mind, are likely to rapidly become part of capital accumulation. Alternatively, they are simply stolen and then entered into the lucrative illegal trade that includes human, drug and small arms trafficking, smuggling of exotic animals and prized animal parts, and the illicit procurement of human body parts.

Despite increasing media reporting to the contrary, massive denial about the trafficking of humans and the marketing of corpses and body parts for enormous profit has dulled public sensibilities in the West, although there are signs that this is changing as outrageous and exploitative cases are increasingly being reported.[52] A recent incident concerning the trafficking of body parts centered on a New York tissue recovery company run by a former dentist who had created unscrupulous ties with several funeral homes. It came to light that body parts had been "harvested" from numerous bodies at these homes, perhaps up to a thousand, and permission of the next of kin had been falsified. Among those whose bodies were violated was that of the revered radio commentator Alistair Cooke. He had died at aged 95 of lung cancer that had spread to his bones. His bones had been ground up and added to those of others for use in reconstructive surgery and tooth implants.[53] In addition to the illegality involved, procurement of biological material from very elderly people is not recommended, use of cancerous bone material violates the United States Food and Drug Administration Regulations. Trust in the medical profession and its business associates is left in tatters when stories such as this come to light.

The Commodification of Eggs and Sperm

Advancements in cryo-preservation technologies during the mid–20th century made it possible to store semen indefinitely and the first commercial human semen bank opened in 1972 in the United States.[54] Since that time sperm banking has become a multi-million dollar industry in many parts of the world, the vast majority of such banks owned and operated by physicians. Eggs began to be commodified later in the 1970s when IVF technology was developed. The sale of eggs and sperm results in a market for genetic material, a situation that appears to be much better controlled than is the market of material taken from corpses, but it is an enterprise that has been remarkably under-studied. In the case of egg donation, a biological match of donor and recipient has first to be confirmed. Once achieved, the donor takes hormones for about six weeks to synchronize her menstrual cycle with that of the potential recipient and to stimulate egg production.[55] Outpatient surgery is carried out to remove the eggs, that are then mixed with sperm and, if fertilization occurs, the resultant embryos are implanted into the recipient. Compensation to the donor for this procedure varies according to agency and region, but in the United States the national average is around $4,200.[56]

Egg donation requires a physically invasive procedure for retrieval that is not, of course, the case for sperm. However, as the sociologist René Almeling notes, sperm donation restricts the activity of donors for a much longer period of time: "Men sign a contract and agree to produce sperm samples once or twice a week for at least a year, and each visit must be preceded by two days of abstinence from sexual activity."[57] If selected as donors, men must also return six months after they stop donating for an HIV test. In contrast to women, who are paid regardless of how many eggs they produce at one procedure, men are paid only for samples deemed acceptable based on sperm count and quality, both of which can be negatively effect by stress, sickness, or not abstaining from sex. Sperm donors are usually paid between $50 and $100 per sample.

Donors, both men and women, are recruited through advertising and network referrals, and many more women than men wish to become donors. Staff interview and select "good" donors. They are likely to accept women who seem to be upright and caring people, who should also be good looking because their photograph will be made available to potential recipients. Male donors, on the other hand, are expected to exhibit responsibility, because they must appear regularly at the clinic for many months, and financial motivation is not a disadvantage to their selection; on the contrary, they are strongly encouraged to think of regular donation as a job.[58] Their physical appearance matters little because photographs are not routinely made available, although racial, ethnic, and religious backgrounds are monitored for both male and female donors to assure diversity. Today, some men agree to release identifying information to offspring at later dates. Medical personnel physically screen potential donors who must also prepare detailed family medical histories going back three generations. The vast majority of potential donors are not accepted. Over 80 percent of women who apply are rejected, partly because they volunteer in such great numbers. Over 90 percent of male applicants are refused because of the need for exceptionally high sperm counts. Once selected, donor profiles designed to appeal to buyers are prepared that will be used to bring about matches.

Women are strongly discouraged from becoming "professional" donors, and men are prevented from being the biological parents of too many offspring. Despite payment, egg donors are treated as though they are providing a gift, and recipients are encouraged to send thank you notes, thus conflating the transaction into a mixed economy of gift and commodified exchange. Sperm donors are sometimes treated rather like regular employees by the staff at sperm banks, with the result that some men apparently virtually lose sight of the fact that this employment will result in pregnancies, for which they are indirectly responsible.[59] Almeling notes that the commodification of male and female genetic material is, not surprisingly, informed by anatomical and biological difference. Furthermore, her empirical investigation shows how stereotyped gender roles are reinscribed into the commodification of genetic materials resulting in "economic valuations" that "intertwine with cultural norms in specific structural contexts."[60]

Whereas eggs, being easily damaged, undergo the minimum of technomanipulation during procurement and transfer, sperm are much more amenable to technically managed improvement. Schmidt and Moore define "technosemen" as the new and improved bodily product about which semen banks create information that is then presented to potential clients in great detail.[61] Semen analysis includes counts of sperm samples and often involves, in addition, morphological and motility assessments. Digital imaging devices and electron microscopy are used to accomplish these ends. A so-called penetration assay, using hamsters, is used to determine if semen are capable of penetrating an egg, and genetic testing and screening for diseases, blood type, and other procedures are also carried out. Sperm are then subjected to several special washes and sometimes to centrifuging to enhance their motility, and they may also be separated out according to whether they are X or Y chromosome bearers, with the intent of increasing the numbers of either one in a sample designed to enable sex selection (the effectiveness of this last procedure is debatable, see also chapter 10). Men whose sperm do not fare well in these kinds of manipulations are rejected as regular donors, and agencies are not above implying that the sperm that successfully survive this onslaught are superior and therefore likely to produce the ideal, powerful men of the future.[62] At the same time natural "unprocessed" sperm is described as "irrational, dirty, and unpredictable";[63] such sperm, it is claimed, can produce genetic defects, cause sexually transmitted diseases, and fail to create pregnancies. The result, Schmidt and Moore argue, is that technosemen is presented by involved companies less as an option, than as an imperative necessary for a successful (immaculate (!)) conception.[64]

Commodification of human biological material is not limited to body parts. One other aspect of the "biosocial relations of production"[65] is that of "medical tourism," a practice that exploits the massive global health inequities so blatantly obvious today. The burgeoning market in health services permits prospective patients (including a good number of the 46 million uninsured Americans) to receive care that they are not able to afford in their own countries in the favored sites for medical tourism including India, Thailand, Cuba, Singapore, and Mexico. Conversely, elite medical facilities in the United States, and to a lesser extent in the United Kingdom and elsewhere, attract wealthy patients from Saudi Arabia, the United Arab Emirates, Argentina, Brazil, and other countries. At all these sites, medical tourists are charged a great deal more than are local people, resulting in enormous profits. One result is that public health care in countries such as India, Thailand, and elsewhere is being undermined, and there is an increasing hemorrhage of doctors and medical personnel to private facilities and to well-paying public facilities in "developed" countries. In the words of the bioethicist Leigh Turner, "Health care, for so long that most local of activities, is now 'de-territorialized' as patients fly great distances in search of treatments they can afford to purchase."[66] This subject will be taken up again in chapter 9 with a discussion of medical tourism involving the sale of human organs.

The second part of this chapter is devoted to two specific examples of biomedical commodification. The first is illustrative of the way in which the biosciences attempt to capitalize on local biologies to advance their interests. Our purpose is not simply to illustrate glaringly obvious ethical issues that arise because of the unequal power relationships at work, but to make it clear how accounts limited to discussion of domination and subordination are not adequate to elucidate the complexities involved in the confrontation of radically different regimes of value with respect to bodily commodification. The second example, that of the establishment of national genetic databases, an activity that today implicates people worldwide, makes it clear that the scale of the commodification of human biologicals is truly global, and that the question of property in the body remains far from resolved.

Immortalized Cell Lines

Technological developments in molecular genetics have in recent years made human DNA into a highly valuable resource, and very many thousands of human cell lines are now maintained in laboratories around the world. The origin of these cell lines may be from patients, healthy research subjects, "exotic" peoples, aborted fetuses, cadavers, or ordinary citizens whose blood has been taken for routine medical tests – every one of us is a potential source of "biologicals." The most famous cell line is known as HeLa, named after the African American Henrietta Lacks, from whom some virulent cancer cells were originally obtained. These cells have been cloned repeatedly and are stored worldwide in laboratories so that, in the words of Anne Enright, "there is more of her [Henrietta Lacks] now, in terms of biomass, than there ever was when she was alive."[67]

Hannah Landecker, in her superb book *Culturing Life: How Cells Became Technologies*, sets out to tell one of the most important stories of 20th-century science, namely how "living things may be radically altered in the way they live in space and time and thus may be harnessed to human intention."[68] She writes about the excitement among scientists in the early part of the 20th century when they discovered for the first time the ability of cells and tissue to grow independently of the bodies that they constitute (a finding also key to the development of the organ transplant enterprise). This "novel biotechnical object" – the immortalized cell line – was destined to have significant effects on the development of molecular biology, most notably in the 1970s on the creation of recombinant DNA, thus paving the way for the genetic biotechnologies in use today.

This process of "culturing life" was formalized by mid-century when human cells began to be understood as "factories whose productive and reproductive capacities could be harnessed to make large volumes of cells and biological molecules."[69] Thus cells began to be mass-produced, at first in order to replicate viruses, but shortly thereafter as a means of reproducing and storing many kinds of tissue for research purposes. Eventually cell lines began to be used routinely as a research tool for the development and testing of therapeutic materials and vaccines of all kinds. Cell lines may be cultured for a short time only as "proxy diagnostic bodies for the patients from whom they have been extracted."[70] Alternatively, they can be cultured long term as immortalized cell lines, thus creating self-replicating *in vitro* populations, achieved through finely orchestrated technological assistance in the form of a medium in which the objects being cultured can thrive.[71] Landecker notes that the laboratory practices that create living cell lines "make it increasingly difficult to say where the body is bounded in time, space, or form,"[72] a phenomenon that has both biological and social repercussions.

Some cell lines are patented and others are not, with remarkably different consequences. Patenting makes it particularly difficult to separate out the several use values implicated in keeping replicating cell lines "immortalized," among which are overarching values including the goals of the scientific inquiry, the hope for scientific progress, and the desire for profit. Not surprisingly, sight is easily lost of the contribution made by the cell donors, without whom no immortalized lines would exist.

Of course, on many occasions people are all too happy to be rid of a body part when it takes the form of a cancerous organ. But even so, as in the now infamous Californian case of John Moore's cancerous spleen, donors may become litigious when they realize that profit is being made out of their body parts without their knowledge or consent, no matter how repellent is the removed mass.[73] Material taken from Moore's spleen became the origin of the "Mo" cell line that was patented by his own doctor and a research assistant. The doctor did not think that it was necessary to inform his patient about this matter, and once investigation of the case was under way it became clear that this was not the first time that he had taken out patents on material obtained from his patients.

In 1984 John Moore brought a lawsuit against his doctor, the Regents of the University of California at Los Angeles, and the pharmaceutical companies that licensed the Mo cell line. The case raises novel issues with potentially far-reaching consequences:

> Did John Moore's doctor wrongfully take and profit from a part of John's body? Was Moore informed enough to have given informed consent for the removal and subsequent use of his spleen cells? Did John Moore deserve a fair share of the potential multi-million dollar profits from the products and research resulting from his cell line? What would happen to science if the court recognized John Moore's property rights?[74]

As Beth Burrows notes, the legal contest became a media circus, in which proceedings went from trial court to the appeals court and then to the Supreme Court of the state of California, by which time John Moore had been labeled as "a greedy bastard out to destroy the progress of medical science" and also as a "biological freak."[75]

In the end the Supreme Court ruled that the doctor should have revealed what he planned to do with the cells, but they denied John Moore's claim to ownership on the grounds that medical research could be hindered. Human rights lawyer George Annas comments: "in the court's flowery words, recognizing [Moore's property claim] would threaten to destroy the economic incentive to conduct important medical research." Annas is unequivocal that patenting of human cells, genes, and gene fragments should be prohibited. Time has proven that arguments about patents being necessary in order that scientific progress not be slowed down are erroneous.[76] It is abundantly clear that once material is patented, the majority of patent owners do not share their material or their provisional findings with potential competitors, at times bringing the scientific endeavor to a grinding halt. This is so despite industry claims about "a reverence for life" and the assertion of one company president that "the next generation of new drugs for human physical suffering depends on the critical relationship between gene patents and progress toward treatments and cures."[77] A counter-argument has been put forward in which it is posited that in a situation of too many claims to property rights in a commodity, a "tragedy of anticommons" can come about, with the result that a resource is underused because competing "owners" block one other.[78]

It is not only pathological specimens that are of interest to the biotech industry. When people have blood drawn as part of a regular health check-up, many are never made aware that their sample may be converted into a cell line from which profit might be made. In order to procure patents on biologicals, it must be shown that through the "process of their production" the "natural" object has been transformed into an "invention."[79] It is the hybrid condition of the cultured cells – their ambiguity as being at once both natural and cultural – that makes such claims possible. DNA processed this way is no longer a discovery taken from nature but rather material that is "gifted" following ethical guidelines for procurement of bodily materials. With "informed consent," donors relinquish all rights of control over what happens to their body parts, as the Moore case makes abundantly clear. Unless certain limitations are set out when consent is given, it is assumed that individuals no longer have an "interest" in their body parts, and cell lines become the intellectual property of their inventors.

James Boyle argues that individual rights and private property have for a long time been given privileged places in the English-speaking world. We are, in his words, "driven to confer property rights in information on those who come closest to the image of the romantic author, those whose contributions to information production are most easily seen as original and transformative."[80] Boyle opposes this tendency because it leads us, he argues, to have "too many intellectual property rights, to confer them on the wrong people, and to dramatically undervalue the interests of both the sources of and the audiences for the information we commodify."[81]

Arguments have been put forward that the authors of intellectual property – those who take out patents, including bench scientists and their employers – can readily ignore the public interest. Our bodies, dead or alive, as well as all other types of biological material, provide the raw materials out of which information is created and privatized with a view to profit.[82] Yet even within the biotech world, disputes have begun to appear suggesting that the current form that intellectual property takes is so broad that it actually slows the rate of innovation.

The Exotic Other

When Isidro Acosta, lawyer and President of the Guaymi General Congress of the Guaymi peoples who live in a remote corner of Panama, met in 1993 with Adrian Otten in Geneva it was in connection with the collection of blood drawn from indigenous peoples by certain drug companies to be made into immortalized cell lines. At the time, Otten was the senior official responsible for negotiations in connection with trade-related intellectual property rights (TRIPS), destined to become one facet of the international General Agreement on Trade and Tariffs (GATT). Acosta's concern was to try to have human genetic material excluded from patenting under this agreement, but his trip to Geneva was to no avail, with the result that the United States Patent and Trademark Office has for years had an enormous backlog of requests to ratify patent claims on human genetic material.

Acosta felt a sense of urgency when he undertook the trip to Europe because he had learned only weeks before that the U.S. government's Secretary of Commerce had laid patent claim to a cell line created from a blood sample procured from a

26-year-old Guaymi mother of two. The cell line contained unusual viral material and "it was hoped that it would be of use in the search for vaccines and therapeutics possibly for both HIV/AIDS and leukemia." If granted, the patent would have given the U.S. government the exclusive right to decide who could use this cell line, and at what cost.[83] The Guaymi General Congress had already made a request to the U.S. government that the specific claim be dropped, but Acosta went to Geneva to try to ensure that this new form of neo-colonialism be abandoned completely. As far as the Guaymi whom he represented were concerned, bio-prospecting resulting in the private ownership by pharmaceutical companies of the very essence of human life was absolutely unacceptable.

In the end, this particular claim to patent was dropped, because the cell line did not prove to be as valuable as the prospectors had thought it might be. Similar patent claims made about the same time on cell lines, one procured from a Hagahai of New Guinea, and another from an individual in the Solomon Islands, also created a public furor. The Solomon Islanders were from the outset opposed to patenting and to profiteering from the manipulation of human tissue. In contrast, it is claimed that the Hagahai as a group had agreed to the creation of the cell line and to its patenting. The hope was to create a vaccine against leukemia from Hagahai DNA because it appeared that many Hagahai had immunity to the retrovirus that causes this particular form of leukemia. An agreement was reached that, should money result from the vaccine, then the Hagahai peoples would receive half the proceeds.[84] Given that this particular group of people had only been "discovered" in the 1980s, and dubbed at the time as a "Stone Age tribe," it seems unlikely that the majority understood the full import of what was involved, even though Carol Jenkins, an anthropologist who had been working among the Hagahai on and off since 1985, acted as the principal mediator in making the monetary arrangement. In the event, both the Hagahai and Solomon Island patents were dropped when it was evident that the cell lines were not, after all, going to be of use in producing a vaccine and were not, therefore, profitable.

The current procurement of human tissue to make cell lines, of which the above cases were early examples, was fostered by two legally binding international agreements that in effect globalize intellectual property laws. The first, the Convention on Biological Diversity, was adopted at the Earth Summit in Rio de Janeiro in 1992, and the second, the GATT TRIPs agreement, was signed in June 1994. These two agreements ensure that virtually all GATT signatories, with the exception of only a few very small countries, must implement intellectual property provisions.[85] The legal practices of North America, Europe, and Japan, countries in which human, plant, and animal genetic material may be patented as immortalized cell lines, set the standard for the entire world.

In effect, gene prospecting sets up "exotic" bodies as a scarce resource, the essence of which can be extracted to transcend time and space to join the never-ending circulation of commodities that drives the engines of late modernity. The concerns of the individuals whose cells are taken are primarily about the continued indifference concerning their everyday life on the part of the dominant world order. The political activist Aroha Te Pareake Mead, Foreign Policy Convenor and Deputy Convenor of the Maori Congress in Aotearoa in the 1990s, has responded to this indifference with insightful barbs. She says that all human genetic research must be viewed in the context of colonial history: "Human genes are being treated by science in the same way that indigenous 'artifacts' were gathered by museums; collected, stored, immortalized, reproduced, engineered – all for the sake of humanity and public education, or so we were asked to believe."[86] Mead, a past chair of the Commission on Environmental, Economic and Social Policy (CEESP) associated with an NGO called the International Union for the Preservation of Nature, insisted in the mid–1990s that a gene and combinations of genes are not the sole property of individuals, rather "[t]hey are part of the heritage of families, communities, clans, tribes, and entire indigenous nations";[87] she adds that the survival of indigenous cultures will not come about through gene banks, but through an observance of fundamental human rights. As far as Mead is concerned, patenting is not a tool of humanitarian research. She claims, moreover, that talk of ethics is simply deception, and she argues that "informed" consent among peoples such as the still largely non-literate Hagahai to draw their blood was probably originally established by using sign language. Mead insists that the burden of proof should be on researchers to demonstrate how their project will benefit indigenous communities. Paul Ndebele and Rosemary Musesengwa, writing about rapidly increasing genetic research in southern Africa, make the same point.[88]

Potential for the accumulation of scientific knowledge from the creation of immortalized cell lines, together with the enormous profit incentive associated with it in the form of a futures market, must be weighed against inalienable possessions – body tissues that represent for many indigenous peoples their history, genealogy, and their very survival. But increasingly groups of people everywhere, in the hope of long-term health benefits, are willing to contribute to the activities of the medical-industrial complex, sometimes with very little to show for it.

We have come a long way from the time in the 17th century when the British East India Trading Company, the Dutch East India Company, the Danish East India Trading Company, and their various rival companies were importing hundreds of thousands of sacks of peppers and spices from East and Southeast Asia. These luxury items, incredibly profitable, filled the holds of merchant ships so that the sailors had to wade up to their knees through the cargo. Spices had their culinary uses but, above all, they had medicinal properties, and these ships were in effect floating medicine chests.[89] Nutmeg, cinnamon, cassia, cloves, pepper, camphor, and numerous other spices were treasured for their healing properties. It is not now necessary, as was formerly the case, to import enormous quantities of raw materials for conversion into medicinals. Today only a small number of samples are needed, because DNA is extracted, active ingredients are identified, immortalized cell lines are created, and intellectual property rights are then established by means of patenting, whether the material is of plant, animal, or human origin. Biotechnology makes it possible to "harvest" a minimum of materials in the wild and procure just a few DNA samples from which enormous profits may possibly be made, thus deftly disguising the linked matters of inalienable wealth, property rights, and potential exploitation.

Biological Databases

From the latter part of the 1990s, plans were laid in several countries for the creation of large national or regional genetic databases, touted by many as the obvious next step forward once the human genome was mapped. The development of technical capability to procure and rapidly process, store, and retrieve massive amounts of DNA-derived information enabled the formation of research platforms comprising the manipulation of genetic material from entire populations. Located in Iceland, the United Kingdom, Quebec, Estonia, Sweden, Taiwan, Tonga, the Gambia, Mexico, and other places, these databases (known as biobanks, DNA banks, biomedical databases, among other designations) are distinctive in that they not only are the storage sites for DNA samples from many thousands of people but have the facilities to link this genomic information with individual medical records and, in some cases, with genealogical records.[90] The anthropologist Gísli Pálsson regards the formation of large-scale biomedical projects such as DNA data banks (one of the earliest being that of the United States military, in operation since 1992[91]) as an "extension and intensification of governance and the biomedical gaze."[92] Furthermore, it was not clear, notes Pálsson, whether such banks should be located primarily in the public or private sector, or whether they should be recognized as a hybrid techno-science production – a consortium of both.[93]

Databases comprised of linked DNA and health records are believed to be the key to developing a much improved scientific understanding of the contribution of genes to the common major disorders found worldwide, including diabetes, heart disease, cancer, and obesity. Such databases are also believed to be necessary to help understand why all individuals do not respond to drugs in a similar way and also to advance what is known as "personalized medicine," through which it is hoped that drugs will be tailored, to a degree at least, for individual bodies. Clearly, the establishment of these databases raises numerous ethical questions many of which have been aired in the media and the professional literature over the past few years. The greatest potential for harm arises when stored DNA is linked to individual medical records that could be made public, inadvertently or otherwise. More generally, genetic databases are assemblages that raise concern because they result in a form of hybridization – in this instance of bodily tissue with electronic data – a condition compounded by the ambiguity in people's minds about what exactly informed consent really entails in such a complex situation.[94] Pálsson argues: "the critical issue has become the use and control of the information that can be derived from body components, rather than the components themselves."[95] Sarah Franklin states that such developments make a distinction between substance and information analytically obsolete.[96] In contrast to the material that constitutes immortalized cell lines, much of which was obtained over a good number of years without informed consent, DNA stored in biobanks has up to now usually been obtained making use of an opt-out system. Alternatively DNA has been collected on the basis of informed consent that can at times be renegotiated if the scientists find that they want to change or add to the uses to which the DNA will be put.

Information resulting from these databases is, in effect, permanent and highly mobile; it can be used for multiple research purposes and by many different researchers and has a global reach. Access to the data by third parties willing to pay a fee is often permissible, rendering the usual approach to informed consent inadequate. Clearly, because the material is genetic, privacy questions arise not only for individuals but also for families and communities. But such concerns have been countered by arguments about the value that people make to society when donating tissue to biobanks; such individuals are being responsible citizens while at the same time retaining, in theory, autonomous control over the future of their tissue. Although a few donors or their offspring may possibly benefit from drug development as a result of DNA donation in the years to come, many argue that, even so, the limits of the idea of consent "freely given" are exceeded in this instance, and a real danger exists for exploitation of individuals.[97] Above all, in an age when governments are bent on national security, information that will increasingly become available through these data banks presents an enormous challenge to the very idea of privacy.[98]

The commercialization of human tissue, similarly to language used in connection with organ donation, is steeped in the linked ideas of "the gift" and "gift relationships." Use of such language immediately frames the procurement of human tissue in the same way as it does that of organ donation, namely that the commodification of human body parts is undesirable.[99] It is assumed that individuals are motivated by altruism when contributing their bodies or bodily substances for research. In examining documents put out by the Nuffield Council and the Medical Research Council in the United Kingdom, the sociologist Richard Tutton points out that these organizations are explicit that an appropriately moral and ethical relationship is established by forming a "gift relationship" between research participants and involved scientists, a relationship thought to foster feelings of trust on the part of the public. In trying to ensure that this relationship is not sullied, it has been argued by the MRC that it is best if institutions rather than individual scientists are made the custodians of sample collections.[100]

But, it is clear that this argument does not reveal everything that is at stake. Difficulties remain because of the ambiguous question of whether or not property exists in human tissue. Clearly, if individuals are required to give up rights of ownership at the time of donation, then property in human tissue is recognized, but recent guidelines as well as rulings for researchers working in public institutions make it clear that such individuals do not, in turn, become entitled to ownership. Donor and researcher are both expected to exhibit altruism for the greater good of society. As Tutton notes, this language deflects attention away from "the significant scientific and commercial interests that are at play," because once products are produced from donated samples they have the potential to become exceedingly valuable, at times priceless, property.[101] In the United Kingdom, where there is no relevant law, ethical debate is rife in connection with the U.K. Biobank, and efforts are regularly made to modify the guidelines. Recent arguments have been in favor of donors who would be able to withdraw their samples at any time, suggesting, argues Tutton, that people "loan" rather than "gift" their DNA to databanks. However, once the researchers have secured intellectual property claims, then withdrawal would no longer be an option.[102] A second change being considered is that certain members of the public may in the future be asked to form part of the group that has principal oversight for the management of data banks.

The first national genetic database was formed in Iceland in 1998 with much media fanfare. At the time, the Icelandic government was eager to diversify its economy, particularly because its prime staple of cod fishing was faltering badly, and it appeared that the country as a whole might well benefit from its "unique" genes and the extensive well-kept genealogical records in its possession. In 1996 Kári Stefánsson, an Icelander working at the time at Harvard University, and his former student, Jeff Gulcher, both physicians, founded a genetics company, deCODE. The company, funded by U.S. venture capital, is U.S. owned and registered, and is situated on the campus of the University of Iceland in Reykjavik, the nation's capital. deCODE was awarded a 12-year exclusive monopoly license by the Icelandic government, strengthened by a second arrangement with the pharmaceutical giant Hoffman LaRoche, with the result that the Iceland biobank was from the outset handsomely backed by "biocapital."[103]

At the time of the merger with Hoffman LaRoche, it was agreed that deCODE would focus primarily on the genetics of 12 common diseases. Pálsson notes that for deCODE, Iceland appeared to provide the ideal context for the production of bio-value because of its history colored from the outset by geographical isolation, and its highly literate, small population of 300,000. A supposition was made by involved scientists that the citizens of Iceland are, in effect, genetically "pure," and hence very attractive candidates for research.[104] The sociologist Hilary Rose argues: "the most powerful element in the highly successful sales pitch of deCODE was the claimed uniqueness of Viking genes. This worked as a self-flattering image to the Icelanders and to venture capitalists. It brilliantly mixed romance with market appeal."[105]

The project was made all the more enticing because carefully documented genealogies of Icelandic families commencing from approximately the 12th century are readily available for inspection. These genealogies, initially recorded and preserved primarily to justify land claims, incorporate oral history from the ninth century on into their records. Over the years other records useful to the deCODE endeavor had been created by Icelanders including the family sagas, church registers, administrative records, and so on. Added to this, throughout the 20th century, medical records of the entire population have been kept in good order. In the 1990s a genealogical database was constructed involving all Icelanders, based initially on three censuses that had been taken in 1703, 1801, and 1910, covering the entire country.[106] Later, 12 more censuses, carried out between 1703 and 1930, were added, expanding this database, now known as the Book of Icelanders, which is also the name of a valued medieval text. Pálsson has likened this remarkable database to "a machine that establishes and generates connections and relationships among people."[107] A total of 700,000 people appear in the Book – the majority of them born in Iceland since the first Norse settlement in the ninth century. This database is, of course, invaluable for establishing family pedigrees. However, Pálsson comments on its "empty spaces," notably in connection with paternity, a problem that is more marked the further back in time one goes. It is also clear that at times families have "purified" their records. And, without doubt, there was also some inaccurate recall of the past. Despite doctoring, the record is remarkable, although the founder of the Book of Icelanders has likened his task to "working out a puzzle the size of a football stadium, with half of the pieces missing and the rest damaged and randomly scattered."[108]

One version of the Book is available only to researchers at deCODE. No personal names are attached to this data that is encrypted and subject to close surveillance. Once combined with genetic and medical data information, the genealogical database was expected to provide invaluable insights into the causes of several common diseases, but this objective has fallen far short of expectations, in large part due to the complexity involved because environmental variables are also profoundly implicated in disease causation. A second version of the Book of Icelanders, one that includes the actual names of individuals, was made available to the public in 2000 by Kári

Stefánsson. The year 2000 is a significant year for Icelanders who were celebrating 1,000 years of Christianity in their nation, the establishment of which religion represented a significant break with Nordic animism. And in 2003 the Book of Icelanders was put on the Worldwide Web. Anyone with an Icelandic social security number can access this website, although it is only possible to trace one's own relations and not those of other Icelanders. Pálsson documents the overwhelming response to this website that enabled a major Icelandic hobby of tracing family genealogies to become a concerted national endeavor. He notes: "Icelandic society has been celebrating itself digitally."[109] However, this "imagined genetic community" caused many people in Iceland – a country that just over 60 years ago gained full independence after 700 years of colonial rule, first by Norway and then by Denmark – to worry about an another form of colonialism in which the genetic heritage of the country, in effect communal property, was being sold off. Responses on the part of the medical community and in some of the media strongly reinforced people's misgivings.[110]

Paradoxically, DNA analysis has debunked the "purity" of Iceland's population. It is now evident that more than 60 percent of the female population originally came, many of them as concubines or slaves, from northern Scotland, the Hebrides, and the west coast of Ireland. They were not, therefore, of Viking but rather of Celtic origin, people who migrated from the Iberian peninsula around 1000 CE.[111] A further problem was that the purported appeal of Icelandic isolation actually served to cramp the objectives of deCODE, especially once the company was remade under Hoffman LaRoche. It is true that isolated populations subject to "genetic drift" are excellent research subjects when the diseases being investigated follow Mendelian inheritance patterns. However, in the case of complex, common diseases in which numerous genes are implicated, none of which individually has great explanatory value, a small isolated population is not the best research site because data from 300,000 subjects is simply not large enough for the task at hand.

In addition to scientific limitations, a good number of Icelanders reacted very negatively from the outset when a proposal to construct what was to be called the Health Sector Database of the entire population was abruptly announced in parliament with a demand for urgent action. The move, initiated by deCODE Genetics, met with criticism because of concerns about privacy and how the database would be managed. Given that there was no existing model on which to draw to deal with these concerns, the bill was withdrawn. When reintroduced and passed the second time round, the bill had clear specifications about a payment that must be made of approximately one million dollars by deCODE for a license to collect the DNA, the money to be used by the Icelandic government to further medical research and development.[112] Furthermore, the Icelandic state would receive 6 percent of any profits that accrued from the database. Even after the passage of this bill, debates about methods of data collection and the protection of privacy persisted.

The Health Sector Database was to be organized on an opt-out basis, but intense opposition steadily increased, notably from health care professionals, who resisted the accession of their patient information by deCODE scientists. This was so effective that the database was never constructed as planned, and a legal judgment from the Iceland Supreme Court in 2003 effectively blocked it for the foreseeable future. The company has insisted that it can continue to identify disease-related genes without such a database and has articles published in the prestigious journal *Nature*.[113] However, deCODE revealed in 2008, even prior to the financial meltdown of the global market, that its net losses were in excess of $530 million, and that the company had never turned a profit. Their website stated: "If we continue to incur operating losses longer than anticipated, or in amounts greater than anticipated, we may be unable to continue our operations."[114] It is also the case that deCODE is involved in a lawsuit against former employees for computer fraud and disclosure of confidential information.

On November 16, 2007, deCODE launched the program called deCODEme™. In order to promote this program in which individuals can pay to learn about their own genome, deCODE promoted itself as "The company that has led in the discovery of genes that confer risk of common diseases is empowering individuals to explore their own genome." The website states:

> Through your subscription to deCODEme™, you can learn what your DNA says about your ancestry, your body – traits such as hair and eye color – as well as whether you may have genetic variants that have been associated with higher or lower than average risk of a range of common diseases.[115]

The website also informs readers that the introductory cost of having one's genome analyzed is $985. Clearly, deCODE was trying to recover some of its losses, but the current collapse in global markets, which affected Iceland particularly badly, did not bode well for the company. In November 2009 deCODE Genetics filed for bankruptcy.[116]

The anthropologist Gilles Bibeau has researched the Cart@gène biobank project in Quebec, inspired by initiatives such as deCODE and similar databases in the Baltic states. The initial objective of Cart@gène was to map the "Quebec genome" and correlate DNA samples taken from citizens of Quebec with health records maintained by the Quebec Health Insurance Board and also with detailed demographic records stored in the Balsac database that covers the population of eastern Quebec. Bibeau followed the debates about who would "own" such a database and any of the discoveries derived from its use, as well as the predictable concerns over privacy that slowed down funding of the project.

Overlooked in these debates, Bibeau argues, are a number of suppositions that he shows to be problematic. The first, as in the Icelandic case, is the "myth" of the existence of a pure genetic pool. Bibeau shows how both historical records and the detailed demography available for Quebec do not support a belief in the persistence of a homogenous genetic pool. Even in the 17th and 18th centuries, shortly after New France was founded, intermarriage occurred very frequently with settlers from England, Ireland, and Scotland, and with the indigenous Amerindian population.[117] However, because the original band of settlers who came to America from France in the 17th century were few in number, a reduction in genetic variation among them due to the small pool of marriage partners in the very early days of settlement inevitably took place, resulting in what is known in population genetics as a "founder effect." One consequence has been "genetic drift," so that rare mutations are disproportionately present in the modern population of Quebec, as indeed they are in similar environments thinly peopled for hundreds of years.

Bibeau critiques an implicit "genetic nationalism" that he argues animates Cart@gène: "the insistence on the founder effect and genetic drift" he writes, "is but the avatar of a quest for 'souche.' "[118] The term *de souche* (meaning "of the cradle") is a politically freighted term that in Quebec harks back to the idea of an original, founding people and serves, in certain contexts, to exclude to the present day all people thought of as outsiders. Bibeau argues that the predicaments raised by genetic projects should not be understood solely in scientific and ethical terms, but must be construed in the political, economic, and cultural circumstances in which they arise.

Cart@gène ran into difficulties from the outset in recruiting enough subjects to power its research. Moreover, a growing awareness among many of the involved scientists about the complexity of gene–environment interactions has replaced the competitiveness formerly evident among population genetics research platforms largely by one of collaboration, in the hopes of assembling ever-larger meta-databases to tease out the elusive genetic contribution to human disease. A Montreal-based international consortium, the Public Population Project in Genomics (P³G), designed to develop and manage "a multidisciplinary infrastructure for comparing and merging results from population genomic studies," was created expressly to enable "the international research community to deliver more effective health care strategies aimed at disease prevention, and at tailoring medicines and other treatment regimens to individuals, families, and communities."[119] Cart@gène was one of the three founding Charter members of P³G that today includes 18 Charter members comprising biobanks situated all over the world. The consortium claims that it now has a critical mass to confront the enormous task of eliciting the distribution and function of genes that contribute to complex disease.

Concluding Comments

Until recently the assumption has been that people are willing to contribute to medical research or to donate their blood and organs out of altruism, and for this reason they agree to gift their cells, tissues, and organs to medical and research establishments. Today it is abundantly clear to many people that these freely given items have enormous potential wealth that is at times in fact realized, resulting in large profits, usually for biotech companies, but sometimes for groups of researchers.[120] This situation has apparently persisted for so long because, when challenged, it has been argued that research is "for the good of humanity" and therefore donation should be altruistic.[121]

In response to criticisms about the form that donation takes, the notion of benefit-sharing is often raised as a method of ensuring that donors and gift-givers of tissue and body parts receive something in return – an approach supported by the ethics committee of HUGO the Human Genome Organization (HUGO). Setting off from a position in which the "co-production" of bioscience and politics is recognized,[122] Cori Hayden takes up an argument for the politics, rather than the ethics, of benefit-sharing. She notes that an ethics of benefit-sharing starts out from a position of "inclusion" in that those who donate or who become research subjects are made active participants in the research process, the dissemination of knowledge, and resultant wealth, should it accrue. The assumption by most ethical commentators today is that some form of "giving-back" is required. However, in order to avoid an unconstrained market model, arguments are made by these commentators for benefits to be shared with donor and/or research communities.

But Hayden points out that the idea of "collectivization" must be used advisedly. She argues that efforts to counter outright commercialization and market commodification of human biologicals drives the idea of benefit-sharing. She tracks discussions by lawyers, politicians, and bioethicists in recent years. These discussions make it clear, Hayden argues, that "property rights for each of us in our own DNA and organs; an open market in kidneys and spleen tissue; the prospect of indigenous patents or copyright; even plant collection as a commodity transaction," are all positions that those concerned about the commodification of techno/biologicals abhor.[123] This is particularly so following the John Moore case. But clearly, if these positions are to be ruled as unethical, autonomous individuals can no longer be treated as the "sovereign ethical subject." In their place the "collectivity" is put forward as a unit for benefit-sharing,[124] together with the argument that communities should be "protected." Suggestions of this kind first arose in connection with the ill-fated Human Genome Diversity Project.[125]

Hayden argues that "in efforts to re-authorize bioscience participation as an act that exceeds the gift but that cannot proceed, unleashed and unchaperoned, directly to the market, benefit-sharing proposals ... *need something like 'community'*" (emphasis added).[126] However, few groups of people, including so-called indigenous groups, continue to be constituted as clearly bounded communities, but are dispersed in urban and rural settings; many, in fact, are globally distributed. Ethicists suggest that to counter this difficulty, individuals should form advocacy groups[127] designed to negotiate benefits and mobilize the distributive process. However, such a suggestion is not efficacious, given the reality of the everyday lives of the majority of people whose bodies and body parts are increasingly subject to commodification. Hayden notes that there are several ways of constituting collectives other than by creating advocacy groups, including the creation of charitable trusts that have been present for some time in the United Kingdom, and that act as custodians of body organs and tissue rather than as brokers. She concludes that it is important to mark that "in the proliferation of calls for a new ethic of benefit-sharing, we can see ways in which political legitimacies [new forms of biopolitics] are being configured in some ways and not others, in the name of a science that can and must give back."[128]

The account in the previous chapter about the globalization of randomized controlled trials and in the following chapters about organ commodification, *in vitro* fertilization, and molecular genetics, make it all too clear that in the global context people who coalesce around activities related to body commodification are very unlikely to mobilize themselves as a benefit-sharing community. The desperation that drives so many people to sell parts of their bodies or else make their bodies available for scientific research is such that they are forced to enter into deals that are clearly unsavory and provide very minimal, if any, benefits to keep, let alone share. The following chapter about organ commodification makes this situation dramatically clear.

In closing, we return briefly to a discussion about promissory capital. Eugene Thacker argues:

> Marx's conditions of labor power have been rewritten by the biotech industry. Instead of a human worker, who views his or her labor power as property to sell, exchange, and circulate we now have a nonhuman biological network of cell lines, tissue cultures, and genomic databases. Labor is not, then, real-time labor of the physical body; instead it is the archival labor of cell cultures, databases, and plasmid libraries.[129]

There can be no argument that such biological collections produce value as a result of orchestrated human intervention. But to insist that human cells and tissue, deliberately decontextualized from the human body, actually labor as they reproduce, is to reify such material products in much the same way as do those scientists who insist that organs and tissue can be technologically transformed into objectified objects that retain no metaphoric meaning or emotional ties. These arguments lose sight of the alienation and estrangement that by far the majority of people feel when reduced through poverty to selling body parts. Even when organs are freely donated to save the lives of others, or somatic cells are sold or donated in order that others can bear offspring, experiences of estrangement are not uncommon (see chapters 9 and 10). Furthermore, the very act of being encouraged or forced to part with a body organ or tissue can cause people to reflect in new ways on what constitutes self and other, insider and outsider, what is alienable and what should not be put into circulation. Such a situation should perhaps be viewed as an estrangement, not of labor, but of life itself.

9

The Social Life of Organs

Our focus of attention in this chapter is primarily on the vital technology of organ transfer, that is, the location of "donors," procurement of solid organs, such as hearts and kidneys, and their transplant into ailing recipients. Solid organs do not regenerate (liver and lungs are partial exceptions in this respect if only small biopsies are removed), and regulations about organ procurement are very stringent in most countries. Moreover, technologies that allow the integrity of solid organs to be maintained outside the human body for long periods of time do not exist, adding to the material limitations of these practices. Organs for transplant – that is, solid organs that are alive – cannot be fractionated or cloned, and so have a limited social life involving, with a few exceptions, just two human bodies. The result is that, in marked contrast to technologies involving the use of sperm and human cells, there are finite limits to the number of organ transplants that can be carried out, creating what is called a "shortage of organs" by people involved with the transplant enterprise.

Emphasis will be given in what follows to the way in which technologies of organ transfer, probably more than any other type of biomedical technology, are frequently associated with exploitation of disadvantaged peoples, above all in situations where organ sales are commonplace, where social inequity and poverty are widespread, where no socialized health care system exists, and where state regulation is inefficient or, worse, chronically corrupt. But there is also a potential for transplant technologies to bring about new forms of social solidarity among donors and recipients, although this possibility is more often than not actively suppressed by organ procurement agencies in North America, Europe, and elsewhere, for fear that donor families might pressure recipients into reciprocating in some way for their "gift." We will also consider how transporting body parts from one person to another has the potential to bring about profound changes in subjectivity in both donors (if they are living) and in recipients. Above all, transplantation inevitably calls into question normative, culturally agreed-upon categories about what constitutes life and death, self and other, gift and commodity.

Organ sales in non-Western settings will be considered first in the discussion that follows, in part because it is all too easy for many people to imagine that these practices have nothing to do with the organ transplant enterprise as it is routinely carried out in the West, even though, as noted in chapter 8, medical tourism is on the increase. It is currently estimated by WHO that one fifth of the 70,000 kidneys transplanted worldwide every year come from the black market.[1] Furthermore, due to what is known in the transplant world as a "shortage of organs," pressures are increasing in the West, notably in the United States, to consider financial repayments in exchange for organs that can be of use in the transplant enterprise, making it all the more urgent to discuss the effects on human relations of organ sales in countries where this presently takes place, whether they be illegal, semi-legal, or legal.

Bioavailability – Who Becomes a Donor?

The sale of solid organs was made illegal in India in 1994 following extended debate in which numerous scandals figured prominently. Recommendations followed to limit donors to three classes of people: patients diagnosed as brain dead, living related donors, and a third category of "exceptional" cases that could be authorized by special medical-bureaucratic committees. In writing about the situation in India, the anthropologist Lawrence Cohen notes that after organ sales were outlawed, in a very short period of time, by making use of the third category of the exception, it actually became easier for clinics and brokers to negotiate kidney sales than had formerly been the case. Cohen documents the reasons for this situation, among which is reluctance on the part of potential recipients to put someone in their family at risk if it is possible to arrange to buy a kidney.[2] Although potential recipients are concerned about the sacrifice of their family member should they become a donor, it appears that they are rather easily able to erase all thought of the sacrifice made by a kidney seller. Sellers are beyond the pale, outside the network of relations where consideration is due and, what is more, not in a position to demand any further form of repayment in the future for their beneficence, as might a family member. But, of course, as Cohen makes clear, people who sell their kidneys do so with the intention of supporting their families – their sacrifice is one born of desperation. That this goes largely unnoticed by the recipient makes the transfer all the more poignant.

Once the immunosuppressant drug cyclosporine was put on the market in the later 1970s it became possible to transplant organs without paying close attention to the immunological matching of donors and recipients as had previously been essential, although the compatibility of blood groups continues to be important. Because biological constraints were largely transcended by cyclosporine, populations of potential donors were created as a result of this new technology, willing to sell their organs on the basis of economic need alone. Cohen, asking who becomes organ donors and why, created the concept of "bioavailability" to encompass a range of harmful bodily exchanges, among them organ transplants. Not surprisingly, above all else it is poverty that drives bioavailability.[3]

Cohen undertook ethnographic research in Chennai, India, resulting in some troubling findings. The women with whom he spoke had all been informed that if they were going to sell a kidney then, for health reasons, they must first undergo tubal ligation. In fact, every one of them had already had "that operation." In much the same way as Malthus had viewed the habits of the English peasantry in the 18th century, Indian bureaucrats, notes Cohen, believe that poor women, both rural and slum dwellers, are so given over to passion and unreason that their sexuality must be controlled – in the Indian case through sterilization. A "logic of operability" takes over, and a form of governmentality is enacted to transform such women into citizens who behave in a correct manner for modern India – individuals who are rational and controlled, albeit, in this case, through enforced control of their reproductive lives. By selling a kidney, these same women are performing what they believe is in their own best interest as Indian citizens, that is, the hope of securing the future of their families. Their men folk do not like to sell their organs – they are "unmanned" by the operation, and they must work; but so too do the women have to work. Cohen found that most of the money that results from sale of an organ in Chennai, about $1,200 for a kidney in the late 1990s, was used to repay high interest loans – "debt bondage in which money passes from the patient to the donor, and to the moneylender and other creditors."[4] If any is left over, it is used for schooling, dowries, and other family matters. Inevitably families get into debt again, with only the scar as a troubling reminder of the sacrifice that can never be repeated. On the other hand, Cohen found that in rural India men are more "bioavailable" as organ sellers than are women. Debt in agricultural areas usually results from crop failure, price collapse, and so on. Farmers are willing to sell a kidney if it is going to get them through the emergency of crop failure; they simply go to Delhi, perhaps without much reflection, and sell a kidney, although many live to regret it later. In urban Chennai, by contrast, women are on the spot and no money needs to be spent on travel – they are the organ sellers of choice for families in which debt is chronic and constantly mounting.[5]

Very few of the individuals in India who sell organs are given any medical follow-up, although they are often malnourished and living in polluted environments,[6] making them particularly vulnerable to subsequent illness. But this is only half the story. The majority of people with end-stage renal disease in India die without a transplant because they cannot afford to go to the private clinics where organs are available for purchase. Cohen notes with irony that in India, due to economic constraints, there is a shortage of recipients, and not of donors. Among those people who have a transplant, many quickly find that they cannot afford the medications that they must take, almost certainly for the rest of their life, in order to avoid organ rejection. The corruption and scandals associated with virtually all of the high-end, privatized medical clinics in India where transplants take place is part of a larger environment in which facilities for privatized medical care became sites of investment and monetary exchange in the 1990s. These "public–private assemblages" link "medical institutions and political influence to various sources of capital – liquor, armaments, pharmaceuticals, and 'black money.'"[7] Individuals who must sell their organs in order to live become pawns in this neo-liberal economy of self-sacrifice, but all too often their sacrifice is doubly in vain – the lives of both seller and buyer are usually improved only for a short time, or not at all.

Aslihan Sanal's research in Turkey graphically depicts the difficulty of sustaining a satisfactory transplant program in a country beset with insurmountable difficulties that work against it.[8] Transplants were first practiced in that country in the mid-1970s and soon received government support. Despite a collective effort in the following years to pass a transplant law and create an organ-sharing network, leading to the founding of the Turkish transplant society in 1990, the program has not been a success. Among the many factors contributing to this situation, Sanal documents the following: divisions among the transplant surgeons themselves, including an unwillingness to have organs distributed equitably via the network; the creation of government-supported private hospitals from early in the 21st century that specialize in transplants and cater to the Turkish middle classes, thus exacerbating the inequities already present in the system; a lack of public understanding about brain death and a strong resistance to mutilating a dead body, resulting in very low rates of cadaver donation; the clandestine sale of organs among living related donors, although this is illegal; and the documented trafficking of organs among people in Turkey, Russia, India, and Iraq, in which wealthy Turks travel abroad to become recipients and wealthy foreigners come to Turkey to receive organs. Furthermore, there has been inflammatory media reporting about the Turkish transplant world in which one doctor involved in so-called "organ sales with consent" is described as the "organ Mafia doctor" and is explicitly associated with the criminal underworld and with widespread corruption throughout the Middle East. Although some aspects of this story amount to nothing more than rumor, this doctor was caught *in flagrante* transplanting kidneys from two Palestinian donors into two Israeli recipients each of whom declared emphatically that these were voluntary donations untainted by the exchange of money. Sanal also documents the sources of most cadaver organs in Turkey: bodies of people confined in asylums, those who have committed suicide, and those who die in catastrophes such as major earthquakes. Similar to Cohen's work in India, this research in Turkey makes it abundantly clear just how difficult it is to run an equitable transplant program in countries whose health care systems are chronically underfunded; where national and regional stability cannot be taken for granted; where enormous inequities exist within the country, and corruption is commonplace. Even so, there are many medical professionals in such countries who struggle to provide good, equitable medical practice, usually with relatively little reward for their dedication.

An article in the *Clinical Journal of the American Society of Nephrology* describes an Iranian model of paid kidney donation using donors unrelated to the recipient.[9] This program was adopted in 1988 with the result that by 1999 the long waiting-list for kidney transplants in that country was eliminated. The Dialysis and Transplant Patients' Association (DATPA) in Iran controls all transactions, and no brokers or other intermediate agencies are involved. Transplants can only take place at specified university hospitals, the expenses are fully paid by the government, and involved doctors receive no incentives of any kind. Once the donation is complete, the donor receives a monetary reward of about $1,200 and free health insurance paid by the government. Most donors also receive a "gift" of money from their recipient, but donors and recipients cannot make independent arrangements prior to the donation and the transaction of the "gift" takes place under the auspices of the DATPA. If the recipient is poor, then the donor will receive a monetary gift from a charitable organization in addition to being paid for the actual organ. The government subsidizes the cost of immunosuppressant medication for recipients. Foreigners are not allowed to participate in this program, although refugees from Afghanistan living in Iran can receive organs from Afghan donors.

Statistics cited in this article indicate that both donors and recipients come from all walks of life. Recipients who cannot pay for transplants are fully supported by the government and charity, and no potential recipient is turned down for economic reasons. Only 6 percent of donors are illiterate and more than 63 percent have a high-school education or more. There is no discussion about what exactly motivates donors. However, it is argued that since the implementation of a system of paid unrelated donors, the coercion commonly reported in families when related donors had to be found has been considerably reduced. A law was passed in 2000 enabling donation from brain-dead bodies, and today about 12 percent of all kidney transplants make use of such organs. The authors of this article do not claim that the system is without faults, but they argue that it is strictly regulated and that the former illegal trade in kidneys has now been eliminated in Iran.[10] Presumably, given that the number of dialysis patients has gone down, the Iranian government has made considerable savings in the overall health care budget.

The anthropologist Nancy Scheper-Hughes has written about "transplant tourism" undertaken by potential buyers who cannot obtain organs in their home country and are desperate to buy one.[11] These tourists come from parts of the world where waiting-lists are long, notably North America, Europe, Japan, and the Middle East, including Israel, a country where most people are opposed or reluctant to donate organs from brain-dead relatives.[12] The majority of vendors live in India, Southeast Asia, and Eastern Europe.[13] Commodified kidneys are the primary currency in this form of exchange and, as does Lawrence Cohen, Nancy Scheper-Hughes sets out to made visible the clandestine side of this activity, above all the "living 'suppliers" who participate in this particular form of bio-exchange. Wherever she goes to investigate this trade in various parts of the world, ranging from Turkey to the Philippines, Scheper-Hughes finds that the kidney is used as a "collateral against debt and penury."[14] What is also striking is the failure, the "intentional oversight" on the part of governments, law-enforcement agencies, the respective medical professions, and ministries of health in the involved countries, to halt these activities.

Scheper-Hughes' argument is that discussion about altruism, autonomy, social justice, and the good society that runs through bioethical discourse as it has evolved in the West in connection with organ transplants is entirely inappropriate in situations where great poverty exists. Her point is that to imagine that the global procurement of organs and their sale can be dealt with through careful regulation is at best naive; this will not happen any more than successful regulation of drug peddling or trafficking of humans she insists, because these activities are inextricably entangled in the criminal world, no doubt accounting in large part for why so little is done to prevent the exploitation of organ sellers. Similarly, Das[15] is critical of the way in which a form of bioethics grounded in the language of rights is increasingly applied globally. She argues that a language of rights masks the politics of violence and suffering involved in organ procurement, particularly where gross inequalities are present, and where bribery and corruption are embedded in daily life and in government circles.

The procurement of blood is equally problematic in some parts of the world. Richard Titmuss' concerns about the sale of blood have, in the time of HIV/AIDS, proved prophetic.[16] In rural Henan province, China, beginning in the early 1990s, "military units, cash-strapped provincial health bureaus, and other interested parties created business ventures to procure and resell blood plasma for both urban and international markets."[17] The donors, 60 percent of whom were women, were paid between $2.40 and $24.00 per donation. Many donated twice a week and some perhaps daily. The blood was not tested for HIV, and at many of the collection centers it was pooled by type; plasma and blood cells were then separated – the plasma being harvested for resale and the blood cells reinjected into donors in order to keep them healthy for the next round of plasma donation. These practices, combined with poor sterilization techniques, led in some villages to HIV infection rates of between 60 percent and 80 percent among adults, leaving shortly thereafter thousands of orphans in need of care. Not until 1998 did the Chinese government outlaw for-profit blood centers and finally, following an international outcry, make some efforts to enforce the law. Kathleen Erwin highlights the inequity at work in blood donation in China. She notes that the "iron rice bowl," the social safety-net that was in place throughout China until just a few years ago, is no longer in existence, leaving desperate villagers unable to meet their basic needs. Blood, long thought of as a vital, almost sacred essence in China, is not something that is easily relinquished and would, under better circumstances, be inalienable.[18]

Accounts such as these, in which the sale of tissue and organs necessarily only occurs in the black market and cannot be disassociated from poverty, appear to be at a far remove from the voluntary donation of blood that most of us do from time to time, or from the signing of a driver's license to state that one is willing to donate organs. But boundaries of many kinds dissolve in the application of biomedical technologies, especially with globalization, and what is routinized and regulated in the West cannot be dissected out cleanly from the global economy of exchange. As medical tourism steadily increases, the interdependence of North and South is laid bare, as is the way in which neo-liberal economies exacerbate inequities within democracies and among countries whatever their form of government.

A Shortage of Organs

The idea of organ transplants, a pervasive fantasy from mythological times, became a viable possibility only after Alexis Carrol, the 1913 Nobel Prize winner for medicine, showed that not only could cells and tissues be kept in suspended animation but they could also be made to function and reproduce independently of the donor body.[19] Experience derived from treating badly wounded bodies in World War I provided further technological insights but, even so, in the first half of the 20th century successful transplantation was limited to autografts (self-grafts). Attempts at allografts, from one individual to another, or xenografts (cross species), were doomed to failure until the 1950s, despite a considerable amount of experimentation. In addition to technological deficiencies, numerous philosophical and ethical issues were raised about these practices until well into the middle of the 20th century. In both Paris and Boston, where transplant technology was strongly promoted, it was argued that organ transplants "transcended the laws of nature"[20] and desecrated the human body. Drawing on the results of extensive animal experimentation, in 1954 the first successful kidney transplant was carried out between identical twins. Animal experimentation also increased knowledge about the immune system and recognition of the importance of long-term immunosuppression of the recipient's body by means of medication. However, throughout the 1960s immunosuppressant use had mixed success, and only after the development of cyclosporine in 1978 was it possible to routinize organ transplant technology.

The practice of transplant technology is entirely dependent in Europe, North America, Australasia, Japan, South America, and in many other countries upon voluntary donations, and everywhere human organs are thought of as scarce commodities. A metaphor of a "shortage" of organs, firmly embedded in transplant discourse, is so powerful that it affects both the market value of human body parts and the globalization of the enterprise. Indeed, today the claim is often made that there is a growing shortage of organs for transplant. The assumption behind this claim is that voluntary donation rates have declined in recent years. There is no doubt that waiting-lists for organs, especially kidneys, are long and growing,[21] however, this state of affairs can be accounted for in other ways than public reluctance to donate. First, there are fewer car accidents than was the case 20 years ago, due to better automobile safety devices. Second, trauma units are much more effective in preventing patients with traumatized brains from becoming brain dead, and therefore candidates for organ donation. Third, as is well documented, the population of technologically advanced societies is aging rapidly. These changes mean that the potential donor pool has steadily declined over the past two decades.

On the other side of the equation, the demand for organs has increased because the population is aging. Moreover, mounting cases of end-stage kidney and liver disease are due not only to an aging population, but to complications associated with increasing rates of diabetes and hepatitis C among younger people (the latter being largely as a result of drug injections). These are diseases associated with poverty and social inequality, many of which could be prevented. Furthermore, the number of patients deemed eligible to become transplant recipients has increased exponentially over the past decades. This situation is a direct consequence of decisions made by committees constituted by transplant communities and, increasingly, of public expectations. The result is that making transplants available for tiny infants, for individuals over 80, and for patients with co-morbidities is now taken for granted. Furthermore, second or third transplants are routinely carried out when earlier ones fail. In other words, the transplant world has broadened its sights, and has itself increased the "need," at a time when there are many fewer potential donors. This discrepancy goes virtually unnoticed in the official discourse about transplantation.[22] One result of the growing "need" for organs is that, whereas until recently organs were procured primarily from brain-dead donors, in the United States, as of 2001, more than 50 percent of organs are acquired from living donors and it has been shown that they function much better than do those taken from brain-dead bodies. A second result is that desperate patients are increasingly likely to consider transplant tourism.

Running through debates about an organ shortage are several assumptions: First, organs go to waste if not donated, and every citizen should be willing to contribute to their use in the transplant enterprise. Second, and associated with the first assumption, is the belief that organs are simply mechanical entities whose worth is entirely without symbolic or affective meaning. Third, is that making a diagnosis of brain death is straightforward and easily accepted as human death by everyone involved and, moreover, families should be willing to interrupt the grieving process for up to 24 hours while organs are procured. A further presumption is that donation, being eminently worthwhile, is likely to assist families in the mourning process. One way of thinking about these assumptions is that, imbedded in them, are moral positions that it is presumed are shared by all – in other words, an unexamined hegemony about the value of organs and their alienability is at work. And from the point of view of potential recipients and their close relatives these assumptions add up for many to a sense of entitlement.[23]

Sharon Kaufman and co-authors argue that the shortage of organs and the increase in the number of organs obtained from living donors have opened up "new dimensions" to intergenerational relationships.[24] The clinic, patient, and patient's family together bring about a bond between biological identity and human worth, "a demand for an old age marked by somatic pliability and renewability, and a claim of responsibility that merges the 'right to live' and 'making live.'"[25] Expectations for a long life facilitated by medical assistance if necessary are firmly entrenched in American middle-class society today. One expression of this is that the number of kidneys transplanted into people aged 65 and over in the United States from both live and cadaver donors has increased steadily during the past two decades.[26] As a result of ethnographic research, Kaufman and colleagues found that many middle-aged people believe that donating a kidney can actualize their love for a parent or another senior relative. Donation is the "natural" thing to do, and it is simply not acceptable in an age of transplant technology to sit by watching a parent die and do nothing. Among the seniors themselves, once the possibility of a transplant is aired by their relatives, for many, but not all, the idea of a transplant becomes eminently thinkable.[27] This research, carried out in California at major hospital centers, leaves readers wondering if this new "ethical field" is distributed equally across the United States and among all kinds of people. One thing is evident from the statistics in the United States and elsewhere, women become donors much more often than do men.[28] The findings of Kaufman et al. clearly illustrate one reason why there is a "growing" shortage of organs, and leave readers in no doubt that the moral economy associated with health care and aging is heavily weighted toward life extension regardless of cost, at least for patients who are conscious and whose "personhood" is in no doubt to family members. A next step would be to follow up on elderly organ recipients and find out what happens when they experience organ rejection. Do recipients then start to think more along the lines taken by many recipients in Japan, Mexico, and elsewhere (as we will see below), that is, to feel intense guilt for having unnecessarily damaged the healthy body of the donor, whether parent, sibling, or adult child? Before continuing this line of discussion we will consider the concept of "brain death."

In most countries where voluntary donation of organs is the norm, organs are procured from both living donors and from what are known as "brain-dead" donors, although the respective proportion of living and brain-dead donors varies considerably from country to country. In the following section we turn to a consideration of brain death – a new death invented in the latter part of the last century in order that organs, already thought of 40 years ago as a scarce resource, can be procured legally for transplant.

Inventing a New Death

With modernity, ideas about life and death and associated beliefs of transcendence were disentangled from the realm of the sacred. As part of this transition, from the middle of the 19th century, death and its legal determination were made into a medical matter. The pronouncement of death by a physician signaled the simultaneous demise of body and person for all but the pious, and biological death became, *ipso facto*, the end of all life. But it has been argued that this secular vision opened up a frightening void, for in theory life no longer had any meaning other than the achievement of mundane, earthly, satisfactions. Freud,[29] Heidegger,[30] Ernest Becker,[31] and other late 19th- and early 20th-century intellectuals posited that, with secularization, keeping death at bay became a source of meaning in life – that ideas about transcendence were internalized and individualized, and the "soul" was displaced by the self-reflective, rational mind so characteristic of modern society in the West. Another change brought about by secularization was that the life course of individuals began to be conceptualized as a finite unit of biological time, rather than, as was formerly the case, as contributing primarily to transcendental intergenerational ties linking the living and the dead.

With the development of intensive care and trauma units replete with batteries of technological devices, the relationship among life, death, and transcendence, assumed to have been thoroughly compartmentalized and secularized, became confused. Whereas for a century or more, making a distinction in the medical world between a living individual and the finality of death had usually been unambiguous (but not inevitably so), with the development of certain new technologies this was no longer the case. Among them, a technology that came into routine use from the middle of the 20th century is the artificial ventilator, a device that enables patients to breathe when they can no longer do so independently. The presence of this machine means that intensive care unit (ICU) specialists are often dealing with entities suspended between life and death. These "living cadavers," as they were known when first formally recognized in the medical world, are usually labeled today as "brain dead." With technological support, the bodily organs of such cyborgs function close to "normal," but their minds have suffered an "irreversible loss of consciousness" leaving the former patient with no awareness or possibility for continued bodily functioning independent of a machine.[32]

In 1967 the flamboyant South African surgeon, Christiaan Barnard took the world by storm when he performed what was touted as the world's first human transplant. It was immediately clear to involved medical specialists that if transplants were to become part of regular clinical care, then organs would have to be made routinely available, and clearly they could not come from ordinary cadavers in which the material body was no longer functioning effectively. Almost overnight, the organs of patients diagnosed as "irreversibly comatose" became targets for procurement, but before this could be accomplished a new, legally recognized death had to be invented.

A complex conjunction of events and technologies must intersect in the creation of "living cadavers." First, an "accident" must take place – an automobile or a plane crash; a drowning; a conflagration causing smoke inhalation; a major blow to the head; or a "cerebral accident" in which the brain suddenly floods with blood. These accidents frequently result, some of them inevitably so, in major trauma to the brain. Brain trauma is also caused by other accident-like events, among which gunshot wounds to the head or suicide attempts are the most common. More often than not victims of such severe trauma, because they can no longer breathe for themselves, cannot survive without the aid of an array of technologies, among which the artificial ventilator is indispensable.

The ventilator, together with the responsible ICU staff, becomes, in effect, a simulacrum for the functioning of the lower brain stem, and takes over the involuntary task of breathing for patients who are no longer able to cope independently. Certain of these individuals will make a partial or complete recovery, but the hearts of others stop beating, or their blood pressure drops irrevocably, and their bodies then die in spite of the ventilator. For a third class of patients, resuscitative measures are only a "partial success,"[33] so that with the assistance of the ventilator, the heart and lungs of such patients can be made to continue to function, but the brain becomes irreversibly damaged resulting in a permanent loss of consciousness.[34] Creation of the concept of "irreversible coma" in 1969, later modified to "whole brain death" in 1981 by the Uniform Determination of Death Act in the United States, permitted the procurement of organs for transplant from patients in this condition on the grounds that they are dead. Similar laws have been passed in other countries where brain death is recognized as the end of human life.[35]

Making sure that death has taken place, and that individuals are not simply undergoing temporary soul loss or the like, has long been a concern – so much so that in many medieval European societies individuals were thought of as dead only when putrefaction had set in. Once the medical world wrested the pronouncement of death from the religious domain and insisted on the infallibility of their methods of assessing biological death, public concerns about wrongful determination of death and premature burial, very common in the 19th century, diminished (but did not disappear entirely).[36] The creation of ventilator-dependent brain-dead bodies elevated similar concerns once again, because a pressure of time comes into play if organs are to be procured from the brain dead. For transplants to be successful, organs must be perfused with appropriate fluids to keep them "normal" as soon as is expedient after the declaration of death, and family permission to take organs has been granted. In order to achieve a timely, legal, death, whole brain death is pronounced when, on the basis of neurological and other tests, it can be determined with certainty that a patient will never recover consciousness, even though, with the aid of the ventilator, the heart continues to beat. This clinically established moment is located as early as possible along a recognizable continuum of dying.

Procurement of organs from the brain dead and their transplantation into dying patients is a quintessentially modern, utilitarian exercise, in which the living bodies of dead persons are commodified for therapeutic purposes. Once legally recognized as the end of human life, brain-dead bodies at once became a scarce resource, rigorously monitored and managed by the international medical community – a bioavailable population of invaluable entities for the transplant endeavor, on occasion also used for experimental purposes.[37] Use of living kidney donors has increased exponentially in Europe and North America in recent years, but procurement of organs from brain-dead donors has also become indispensable to the success of the transplant world, particularly in connection with hearts, livers, and lungs, but also for kidneys, and for other organs less often transplanted.

The Good-as-Dead

Brain death constitutes a radically new form of soul loss, not a temporary phenomenon but a permanent loss of what is usually understood as the person from their living body. This betwixt and between condition creates discomfort for many involved health care workers and families alike, and is not what most individuals would intuitively recognize as death, because the brain dead are warm, have a good color, urinate and defecate, have a pulse, and continue to breathe. Due in part to the ambiguous condition of the brain-dead, it is customary to soften the reality of this technologically orchestrated death and to draw on premodern tropes to encourage donation, including the idea that donors may "live on" in the bodies of recipients. Even so, nearly 50 years after the recognition of brain death as a diagnostic category, a good number of families refuse to agree to the donation of the organs of their brain-dead relatives because they simply do not believe that the person lying in front of them, giving every appearance of being asleep, is indeed irreversibly unconscious and entirely beyond hope.[38] Only 50 percent of families approached to donate organs in the United States agree to do so.[39] Furthermore, corpses continue to generate feelings of awe, respect, and often dread in the minds of many people. Surveys in Sweden, Japan, and the United States have shown that a good number of individuals refuse permission for autopsies and for donation of organs because they do not want their relatives to suffer any further pain or indignity. And some people fear a form of retribution should the living-dead be defiled.[40] It is not easy to become inured to the hybrid of the brain-dead body as being no longer fully human, and research suggests that, even among those in the general population who support organ donation, a good number may think of the brain-death condition as "good-as-dead" rather than truly dead.[41] Along this line, Don Joralemon has argued that the failure of numerous public education efforts to substantially increase organ donation rates in the United States suggests a tacit rejection of the idea that brain death truly is death.[42]

Perhaps more surprising is that some medical professionals who work most closely with brain-dead patients, when asked, make it clear just how difficult it is to equate brain death with the end of human life. For one thing, all intensivists (specialists who work in intensive care units) agree that the body is alive – it must be if organs are to be taken for transplant – but they also agree that the condition of brain death is irreversible and that the patient has suffered an irreversible loss of consciousness.[43] When interviewed, intensivists in North America stated that they talk to families in the following way: "The things that make her her are not there any more," or, "He's not going to recover. Death is inevitable." One doctor, who, in common with many of his colleagues, chooses not to say directly that the patient is dead, because he personally does not believe this is the case, tells the family firmly that the patient is "brain-dead" and that there is "absolutely no doubt but that things will get worse." Another physician pointed out that it is difficult to assess what is best to say to the family, because in most cases it is not known whether they have religious beliefs:

> I believe that a "humanistic" death happens at the same time as brain death. If I didn't
> believe this, then I couldn't take care of these patients and permit them to become organ

donors. For me the child has gone to heaven or wherever, and I'm dealing with an organism, respectfully, of course, but that child's soul, or whatever you want to call it, is no longer there. I don't know, of course, whether the family believes in souls or not, although sometimes I can make a good guess. So I simply have to say that "Johnny" is no longer here.[44]

On the other hand, several doctors agreed that it is essential to take control to some extent when discussing brain death with families. They suggested that families often find it difficult to accept that there is no chance of a reversal, and this is where the doctor cannot afford to appear diffident or to equivocate. However, as one intensivist noted: "You can't go back to the family and say that their relative is brain-dead, you've got to say that they're dead – you could be arrested for messing up on this." This doctor recalled that during his training he had described a patient as "basically dead" to his supervisor who had abruptly responded by insisting: "He's dead. That's what you mean, basically." The task for intensivists, then, is to convince the family, even though their relative appears to be sleeping, that he or she is, in fact, no longer alive; what remains is an organism or vessel that has suffered a mortal blow.

On the basis of ethnographic work in the United States, Lesley Sharp points out that the origins of organs taken from the brain dead for transplant are deliberately dehumanized and sanitized in order to make conversations with families more comfortable when donation is being considered.[45] She notes that many donor kin cannot accept the "fact" of a technologically diagnosed death and entertain ideas about more than one death. It is commonly believed among them that when brain death is declared, the patient, having entered a condition of an irreversible loss of consciousness is, in effect, "socially dead." This knowledge permits families to cooperate with donation. But they also believe that the private, individualized self continues to exist until the body can be clearly identified as a cadaver.

All of the doctors and nurses working in ICUs at various sites in Canada and America agreed, when interviewed by Lock, that once brain dead, a sensate, suffering individual has ceased to exist because his or her mind no longer functions. However, some nurses continue to talk to brain-dead patients as they care for their bodies in preparation for organ procurement.[46] Although ICU practitioners rarely have serious second thoughts about reversibility, it is also evident that many of them continue to harbor some doubts about the condition of a recently declared brain-dead patient, and it is often those with the longest experience who are willing to exhibit the most misgivings. An intensivist with over 15 years of experience said that he often lies in bed at night after sending a brain-dead body for organ procurement and asks himself, "Was that patient really dead? It is irreversible – I know that, and the clinical tests are infallible. My rational mind is sure, but some nagging, irrational doubt seeps in."[47] These doubts, whether on the part of ICU practitioners or families, are rarely publicly acknowledged, and procurement of organs from the brain dead is a largely unchallenged part of routine medical practice in the West.

Although from the time that brain death was first recognized, assertions were made that it did not constitute a radical break with the usual medical death signified by the demise of the cardio-pulmonary system,[48] time has shown that such claims are equivocal. Apart from anything else, one or two patients diagnosed as brain-dead have existed on ventilator support for over a year, forcing some neurologists to demand how such a condition can possibly be equated with the end of life.[49] Furthermore, although the ventilator does not determine how patients who are hooked up to it should be diagnosed, represented, or treated, without its existence this new death could not have been invented.

The hybrid of the brain-dead body is worrying. As we have seen, many medical personnel, although they may well suppress their feelings, do in fact struggle, not with the concept or the validity of the diagnostic measures, but with the condition of the patient, someone whose appearance is not quite dead but whose gift of life must be expediently procured. Inevitably, anguished families too are filled with ambivalence; many do not easily share the moral economy dominant in biomedicine, that brain death is the end of human life, and some have real doubts about the validity of the concept, making them unwilling to donate organs. Behind their backs, families such as these may be thought of as ungenerous and irrational by the transplant community, the majority of whom believe firmly that organ transplants are an unquestionable good, but any feeling person who has witnessed parents sobbing over their child killed by a drunken driver may not be able to accept such an unreflective argument.

Over the years, refinements in neurological diagnostic categories brought about the recognition of other conditions in which a loss or partial loss of consciousness is involved, with the result that a growing number of patients are thought of as good-as-dead.[50] This category now includes not only those who become brain dead, but also many thousands more individuals in any given year, including people in a "permanent vegetative state," those with "minimal consciousness," and the severely demented. Common to all these conditions is that consciousness is fatally impaired and, at a minimum, tube feeding and constant care is required. However, in contrast to the brain dead, the majority of these patients breathe without assistance, and a few, even among those deemed as hopeless cases, make partial or even full recoveries.[51] Such comatose bodies are no longer self-regulating, so that "normalcy must be both produced and regulated by detailed and ongoing surveillance."[52]

Sharon Kaufman has written about the way in which the existence of such patients is hedged by the specter of litigation, of talk of rights, and obligations to "choose," according to whose best interest is at stake. Other factors that come into play are a desire for some control over the impossible situation, an awareness of a time pressure, and debates among professionals and family members about whether or not further treatment should be classed as "futile." A cluster of rhetorical devices used in connection with comatose bodies makes it possible to consider such patients as either living or dying.[53] Given that a "shortage" of organs plagues the transplant world, the logical next step of visualizing patients with extreme neurological damage as potential organ donors – as bioavailable – is regularly aired today in both the medical world and that of bioethics.[54]

Struggling for National Consensus

Research in several different geographical locations highlights how the linked networks of organ donation, procurement, and transplant can be blocked or facilitated in a variety of ways. At issue is not primarily an absence of technical know-how or expertise, although a lack of facilities is certainly an impediment, as we will see shortly.

But perhaps of even more significance are cultural and political considerations. Although the term "brain death" is used as a diagnostic category in medical practice around the world, cross-cultural research has revealed that the meanings with which it is imbued, its significance in determining the end of human life, and the actions that it authorizes, are not everywhere the same.

The diagnosis of brain death does not always signify the death of a person, in the way that the Harvard committee originally intended, nor even is it necessarily associated with the end of all hope of recovery. Evidence of these cultural differences became apparent when several countries, among them Sweden, Germany, Denmark, Japan, and Israel, had protracted public discussions commencing from the late 1960s as to whether or not declaration of brain death could be legally recognized as the end of human life.[55] This is in striking contrast to North America, the United Kingdom, and some other European countries where the overwhelming focus, particularly in the media, has been on life-affirming stories of organ recipients whose lives were saved as a result of a transplant. In these countries little or no public consideration has been given to the invention of a new death.

In Japan, in striking contrast, a vituperative debate persisted for over 30 years among lawyers, medical professionals, intellectuals, and members of the public in professional forums and the media as to whether or not brain death could count as the end of human life, a debate that far outstripped public discussion about any other bioethical matter. In contrast to the attention given in North America and elsewhere to organ recipients, the Japanese debate, known as *nôshi no mondai* (the brain death problem), has centered on the vulnerability of potential donors and the many possibilities for abuse of the dying and the dead.[56]

Numerous national opinion polls were carried out during this time, the results of which are confusing and make clear that there is no consensus on the matter. The present Japanese law on the subject, enacted only in 1997, places medical interests second to family concerns, and recognizes brain death as the end of human life only when the diagnosed patient has given prior notice of a willingness to donate organs and the family has co-signed the official donor card. A brain-dead individual who has not signed a donor card, or whose family has not co-signed the card, remains attached to the ventilator, and is not recognized as medically dead. As of mid-2008, it is reported that 44 percent of the population has signed donor cards; however, organs have been procured from only just over 80 brain-dead donors since the late 1990s.[57]

Several factors have contributed to this impasse, perhaps the most important being that a murder charge was laid against the first doctor who carried out a heart transplant in Japan – a procedure that virtually everyone concluded involved, without doubt, malpractice. A series of 19 other murder charges were laid against doctors who procured organs from brain-dead bodies in the years before the legalization of recognition of brain death as the end of human life, all of which were in the end dropped. Other factors that aggravated the situation include the following phenomena: a lack of trust on the part of the public in the medical profession that has over the years been involved in several major scandals (although people often trust their family doctor, they do not extend that trust to the profession as a whole);[58] a conservative legal profession opposed to the recognition of brain death as the end of human life; widespread publicity in connection with the opinions of some well-known Japanese doctors opposed to the recognition of brain death; extensive media criticism of hospital practices, particularly in connection with efforts to procure organs; and the mobilization of citizen groups to block the recognition of brain death as anything other than a clinical condition. Equally important are culturally informed practices in connection with death, notably the importance of the family in making end of life decisions;[59] a widely shared understanding that death is a process and not an event; a reluctance on the part of many Japanese doctors to firmly declare that there is no hope of recovery once brain death has been declared; a concern on the part of many people about the commodification of the bodies of their deceased relatives; and a strong resistance to "gifting" body parts to strangers.

Japanese participate extensively in reciprocal formalized gift exchange to promote social solidarity among networks of people known to each other, somewhat reminiscent of the situation described by Marcel Mauss for premodern societies. Until recently, gift giving entirely free of obligations and networks of reciprocity has not been common in Japan, and the idea of receiving an anonymously donated organ with no expectation of or possibility for reciprocation smacks of selfishness to some. There are also fears, as is the case in other countries, that a brain-dead body, exhibiting virtually all the features of biological life, is not dead. Certain key commentators in Japan, opposed to the recognition of brain death as the end of human life, have argued that brain-dead bodies are murdered when taken off ventilators. However, religious organizations have not been outspoken in these debates,[60] rather, such reservations arise from what are assumed by many Japanese to be rational, common-sense responses to an extraordinary technology that appears to threaten fundamental moral order and basic human relations.

Of course, by no means do all Japanese respond in the same way, hence the extensive public debates and demonstrations, but the dominant ideology has in effect prevailed until very recently, even after the law made organ procurement legal.[61] Japanese neurologists working in ICUs – even though they themselves are for the most part adamant that brain death has an undeniable finality indicating that the person no longer exists – believe that few Japanese can accept this reality.[62] Their doubts stem from their belief that numerous Japanese draw a distinction between social and physical death in which it is commonly thought that the social self persists after declaration of biological death.[63] As a result, the Japanese medical profession, exceptionally proficient with technological interventions of many kinds, has been forced to put most of its energies into transplants that make use of living related organ donors. When no living related donor is to be found, Japanese patients sometimes opt to go abroad to buy organs at great expense. These are organs taken from brain-dead donors designated as "surplus" or unusable in the United States, Australia, or elsewhere. Others buy organs illegally in China or Southeast Asia, to the disapproval of the Japanese government and many of their fellow citizens.

In July 2009 the Law on Organ Transplantation was rather suddenly revised and will start to take effect in 2010. It will now be possible for Japanese individuals, regardless of their age, to donate organs (until this time it has been impossible in Japan to procure organs from children under 15 years of age even with parental permission). Only those individuals who have actively refused to become donors ahead of time will not be considered as donors, and agreement of family members to donation continues to be necessary.[64] The Japanese press points out that the push to revise the law probably gained momentum after the World Health Organization proposed in 2007 a restriction on patients seeking transplants abroad.[65] Added incentive for change may have arisen because some countries, such as Germany, have actively refused to consider Japanese patients for transplants in their country.[66] It will be of great interest to see if the number of organ transplants carried out in Japan (a total of 345 ever from brain-dead donors) increases as a result of a change in the law, and begins to approach the rate of many thousands a year carried out in the European Union and the United States.

People associated with the far right of the political spectrum in Japan are among those who over the years have vociferously countered the legal recognition of brain death. This type of dissent feeds off nationalistic, anti-Western sentiments, in which the uniqueness of Japanese values is emphasized. Similarly, Hogle shows how disputes in Germany about the commodification of human body parts and their use as therapeutic tools are powerfully influenced by the history of National Socialism in that country and its practices of eugenics.[67] Revulsion about the history of Nazi experimentation makes many people reluctant to cooperate with the transplant enterprise. Moreover, beliefs derived from the medieval period about the diffusion of the essence of life throughout the entire human body, including a concept of "cellular memory," are influential in resisting the transformation of body parts into technological artifacts.[68] Rather than conceptualizing organs as essentially machine-like interchangeable parts, in Germany a dominant ideology is one in which the particularity of individual organs is stressed. It is important to preserve procured organs in as fresh and unchanged manner as is possible in order to retain their unique, essential qualities. The ideas of "solidarity" (a powerful metaphor from the former East Germany) and Christian "charity" are both made use of publicly to encourage organ donation, but Hogle argues that in multi-cultural Germany, largely for historical and cultural reasons, making organ donation into a social good in which everyone can participate is fraught with difficulties.[69]

The Social Life of Human Organs

In order for body parts to be made alienable they must first be visualized as thing-like, and detachable from the body, dead or alive. The mystical essence everywhere associated with body fluids, organs, and tissues must be dissipated, and these entities can then be reconceptualized as objects available for commodification. This process of reification and fragmentation, so characteristic of biomedical practice, has been criticized repeatedly as a dehumanizing move.[70] The assumption behind much of this criticism has been that patients and their families participate in this process of reification unwillingly, but a careful reading of the literature on medicalization has revealed that individuals are sometimes happy to relinquish the dense social, cultural, and mystical associations inevitably associated with body parts, because these are moralized discourses that bring an accompanying burden of responsibility and more often than not, of blame for sickness and dysfunction.[71]

Mixed metaphors associated with human organs encourage confusion about their worth. The language of medicine insists that human body parts are material entities, devoid entirely of identity, whether located in donors or recipients. However, in order to promote donation in many parts of the world, organs procured from brain-dead bodies are often actively animated with a life force by medical professionals, and donor families are not discouraged from the belief that their relatives "live on" in the bodies of recipients, or even that they will be "reborn."[72] Organ donation is commonly understood as creating meaning out of senseless, accidental, deaths – a technological path to transcendence,[73] although in non-Christian settings such metaphors have considerably less leverage.

Research has also shown that due to the enforced anonymity that surrounds donated organs, large numbers of recipients experience a frustrated sense of obligation about the need to repay the family of the donor for the extraordinary act of benevolence that has brought them back from the brink of death.[74] The "tyranny of the gift" is well documented in the transplant world,[75] but it is not merely a desire to try to settle accounts that is at work when people want to know more about the donor. It is abundantly clear that donated organs very often represent much more than mere biological body parts; the life with which they are animated is experienced by recipients as personified with an agency that manifests itself in some surprising ways, and profoundly influences the recipient's sense of self.

A few years ago a Montreal heart surgeon was responding to stories that had been circulating for some time in several U.S. states about whether prisoners on death row should have the option of donating organs for transplant before they are put to death. This surgeon was uncomfortable about organ donation from these death row prisoners, because he was concerned not about the highly questionable ethics, but about receiving a heart that had been taken out of the body of a murderer. He said, with some embarrassment, "I wouldn't like to have a murderer's heart put into my body," then he added hastily, trying to make a joke out of the situation, "I might find myself starting to change."[76]

A good number of organ recipients worry about the gender, ethnicity, skin color, personality, and the social status of their donors, and many believe that their mode of being-in-the-world is radically changed after a transplant, thanks to the power and vitality diffusing from the organ they have received. That certain of their surgeons also think this way suggests that fetishism is doubly at work, even in the materially oriented world of biomedicine – the fetishism of objectivity postulated by Marx, and the mystical fetishism described by Marcel Mauss. Body parts remain infused with life and even personality, and cannot be stripped casually of their human attributes. Contradictions are rife. Once an organ is procured and transplanted, the recipient is severely reprimanded – even thought of as exhibiting pathology – if she attributes animistic qualities to this "life-saving" organ.[77] Human organs imbued with living qualities, as the anthropologist Nicholas Thomas argues with respect to commodified objects in general, are "promiscuous"; they are at once things-in-themselves, and diffused with a life force and exhibit an agency that is manifestly social.[78]

The anthropologist Lesley Sharp argues that receiving an organ is a personally transformative experience that may affect how recipients assess their own social worth.[79] She suggests that this transformation takes place at two levels – first, subjectively, so that a recipient's sense of self may be extended to include qualities attributed to the donor, and second, through interactions with family, communities, and the medical profession. Sharp notes, as does Hogle,[80] how the language used in connection with organ procurement depersonalizes bodies and body parts, but that many recipients repersonalize organs through the creation of narratives about their rebirth. The organ takes on a biography of its own, independent of the person in whom it resides.[81] The result is that, despite the force exerted by the medical profession to work against the animation of organs by patients, and the flat rejection by them of the possibility of identity transformation, it is evident that many patients, at least in Canada and the United States, believe themselves to be "reborn" after a transplant. This response on the part of recipients may in part be due to the availability of the same culturally tinctured language of transcendence resorted to by transplant coordinators when they animate organs in order to encourage donation.

Interviews carried out with organ recipients living in Montreal reveal that just under half are very matter-of-fact about the organs they have received. These individuals insist that after an interim period of a few months they ceased to be concerned about the source of the new organ encased in their bodies, and resumed their lives as best they could unchanged in any profound way save for a massive daily medication regime. The responses of the remaining recipients were different: although they knew very little about their donors, they produced emotionally charged accounts about them; about the particular organ they had received, and often about their transformed identities.

Stefan Rivet falls into the first group. He is a 41-year-old kidney recipient, doing well when interviewed five years after the transplant. He says:

> I heard about the donor, even though I wasn't supposed to. It was a woman between 20 and 25. She was in a car accident ... I wrote a letter to them, it must have been a terrible time for them, and I wanted to thank them.
>
> Did you find it hard to write that letter?
>
> No, no, it wasn't hard for me. Like saying "thank you" to someone if they do something for you, that's just the way it was.
>
> Did you feel at all strange because it was a woman's kidney?
>
> No. At first you wonder how could a female kidney work in a man ... But once the doctor tells you that it works exactly the same in men and women you don't question things any more. I have my kidney, and I can live, that's all you really worry about.[82]

In contrast, many other recipients undergo a rather dramatic transformative experience.[83] One such was Katherine White who first received a kidney transplant and then, ten years later, after the kidney failed and her own liver was also in jeopardy, received a double transplant of liver and kidney. Six months after the second surgery she had this to say:

> I have no idea who the donor was, all I know is that both the kidney and liver came from one person because you can't survive if they put organs from two different people into you at once – your body would never be able to deal with it. I wrote a thank you note right away that I gave to the nurse. But they don't like you to know who it is, sometimes people feel that their child has been reborn in you and they want to make close contact. That could lead to problems. I still think of it as a different person inside me ... It's not all of me, and it's not all this person either. Actually, I might like some contact with the donor family ...

You know, I never liked cheese and stuff like that ... but all of a sudden I couldn't stop eating Kraft slices – that was after the first kidney. This time around, the first thing I did was to eat chocolate. It's driving me crazy because I'm not a chocolate fanatic. So maybe this person who gave me the liver was a chocaholic?! ... Some of the doctors say it's the drugs that do things to you.

... sometimes I feel as if I'm pregnant, as if I'm giving birth to somebody. I don't know what it is really, but there's another life inside of me, and I'm actually storing this life, and it makes me feel fantastic. It's weird, I constantly think of that other person, the donor ... but I know a lot of people who receive organs don't think about the donors at all.

A while ago I saw a TV program about Russia and it seemed as though they were actually killing children in orphanages to take out their eyes and other organs. This disturbed me no end. I hope to God it's not really like that. My parents and my uncles all thought I shouldn't have a transplant, they said you can't be sure that the patient is really dead. Brain dead is not dead, they said. But I know that's not right. In a way I wish I could have a pig's liver or kidney – it would be much simpler then.[84]

Katherine is unlikely to have informed her doctor in any detail about her transformed self; she knows full well that he would chide her for harboring such ideas. The public and private faces of transplantation are held apart, and the inherent contradictions present in both professional and public language are smoothed out of existence.[85]

When donors are living and related to the recipient, accounts given by recipients about their experiences are less dramatic but no less moving than those given by individuals whose transplanted organs come from brain-dead bodies,. The majority of recipients in Japan obtain organs from close kin, and thus, rather than being concerned about fundamental changes to identity and embodiment – as is apparently often the case in North America – recipients focus above all on the intense, enmeshed everyday relationship that develops between the relative who donated the organ, usually their mother, and themselves. These recipients dwell above all on feelings of gratitude for the "treasure" that can never be repaid[86] and worry about the harm that they may have caused to their relative whose healthy body was cut apart on their behalf. When an organ is rejected, as inevitably happens at times, feelings of guilt and shame are overwhelming, and the possibility for a second transplant from another relative, if indeed it is a possibility, cannot be contemplated.

In the course of many years of researching the U.S. transplant enterprise, Sharp observed how social relationships between brain-dead donors and recipients have been transformed from one based entirely on imagination, due to enforced anonymity, to something that can be celebrated in the public sphere. For example, donor families today can attend the Transplant Olympics in which organ recipients participate. It is common to build edifices as donor memorials and to hold public gatherings in which donors and recipients come together as groups to celebrate the past lives of donors. The leitmotiv of such gatherings is one of loss and redemption, and speakers are organ recipients who quite often know very well who was their donor.[87]

These gatherings are reminiscent of meetings of 12-step programs such as Alcoholics Anonymous in which individuals give testimony about their spiritual death and rebirth (in the case of transplants, donors and recipients in effect simultaneously die and are reborn). The result is a profound transformation, often involving significant reforms in the daily lives of recipients. Metaphors derived from Christianity are drawn on liberally, and testimonies are delivered in a manner similar to those used in Pentecostal churches, even though organ recipients are not necessarily believers. Sharp points out that both donor kin and organ recipients quickly learn how to narrate their stories appropriately in public. The contents are self-sanctioned so that the untimely, often brutal death of the donor is never mentioned. Also passed over in silence are the roller-coaster rides of potential organ rejection that numerous recipients experience, the side effects of the regime of endless medication, and the economic hardships that many must endure due to the exorbitant cost of medication. With professional urging, the telling of such disturbing, sometime gruesome "details" is reserved for private spaces, because they are likely to have a negative effect on the transplant world as a whole. Sharp discusses how bonds created between donor families and recipients – in the cases where they do eventually meet – ensure that organs continue to be anthropomorphized and animated. She notes that, in her experience, such bonds only very rarely go badly wrong.[88]

When Resources Are Short

In Mexico organ donations from brain-dead donors are relatively rare, and so transplant programs, as in Japan, depend on living donors, the majority of whom are close relatives of the recipients. Reasons for low rates of cadaveric organ donation are complex, and include religious beliefs including lay Catholic interpretations of resurrection that requires an "intact" body. A belief in miracles as an ever-present possibility also makes some Mexicans – among them both patient families and medical staff – reluctant to accept a diagnosis of brain death as truly signifying the end of all hope for recovery.[89] However, research reveals that most at issue is not rejection of the brain death concept per se, but rather dimensions of the political economy of health care. This makes the diagnosis and support of brain-dead patients difficult in practice and it is hard for families to place their trust in the procedures.[90] Substantial infrastructural limitations exist that make identifying and maintaining brain-dead patients in Mexico challenging, including the scarcity of tertiary level hospitals, ventilators, and medical staff with expertise in diagnosing and managing brain death. Further complicating matters is deep-rooted skepticism – bred by the long history of corrupt single-party rule in Mexico – with which many Mexicans view both medical professionals and the (largely state-run) health care institutions where they work. In such an environment, fears about the inappropriate diagnosis of brain death and/or the potential for profiteering from donated organs are not uncommon, and form substantial barriers to the routine adoption and implementation of the brain death concept. Furthermore, a sentiment common among Mexicans, including their political leaders, is that procurement of organs from brain-dead bodies is not humane, and is an activity in which only a country such as the United States would actively participate (a feeling shared by many Japanese). These findings from Mexico highlight the way in which political and economic factors can cripple national transplant programs; without concerted investment in the coordination of such programs that include considerable economic and educational input, such programs are unlikely to be a success, particularly when obvious cultural constraints are also present.[91]

On the basis of extensive ethnographic research, the anthropologist Megan Crowley-Matoka argues that the family in Mexico, the core of social and moral life, is regarded as both a "national" and a "natural" resource for organs.[92] Organs exchanged as transplants "are often experienced neither as objectified parts, nor as wholly other, they contain the self of the donor, yet are also always already connected to the self of the recipient through familial relatedness."[93] Above all, it is mothers who are expected to donate – their sacrifice is part of their prime role as nurturer of the household, and ultimately their bodies are thought of as more expendable than those of working men. Donation patterns "fit" with the brutal reality of an impoverished life and the accepted division of labor in Mexican households. Sharing among families of both biological and social substance is explicit. At times, analogies are made between giving birth and organ donation; notably, a symbolic association is made between the penetration that must take place to procure a donor organ, sexuality, associated loss of purity in women, and a resultant birth. Not surprisingly, then, mothers are thought of as the best donor candidates. With the exception of young unmarried men, donation by males is associated with negative sexual connotations. In actual practice, these cultural constraints are by no means always observed but, even so, Crowley-Matoka argues, the dominant discourse is evidence of a "hegemony of deeply embedded [national] values," where a religiously infused idea of the suffering, nurturing woman remains dominant.[94]

Crowley-Matoka has carried out one of the very few studies anywhere in which organ recipients have been interviewed some time after receiving a transplant. Repeatedly the people to whom she talked made statements along the following lines: "I thought everything would change, once I got my kidney. And it has – but not always like I thought it would … I thought I would be healthy again, and normal, but really I'm just a different kind of patient now."[95] Crowley-Matoka finds that, rather than achieving the promise of health and a new life held out by the medical world, recipients live in a "persistent liminality."

Many Mexican kidney patients spent years trying to get their condition recognized as real, in part because symptoms of renal failure can be hard to diagnose outside of specialty clinics. Some patients are eventually referred for dialysis, but the mortality rate while on dialysis is unacceptably high, and related at least in part to malnutrition, the presence of other illnesses, length of time before diagnosis, and other factors. Enormous barriers exist in the health care infrastructure that put constraints on transplant programs, and relatively few people end up on waiting-lists. Most Mexicans do not think of a transplant as a realistic possibility – this technology is high-end medicine for movie stars and the rich. In contrast to the North American situation, potential recipients must often be convinced by medical professionals that a transplant is not only a realistic, but a desirable, goal; for many, their names will not be put down on a waiting-list until a relative or special benefactor has come forward who is clearly willing to act as the donor.

Crowley-Matoka notes that reticence is such that a "demand" for transplants had to be created by the staff in the large center in Guadalajara where she worked, and this was usually achieved by telling patients that they will be restored to a "normal" life by undergoing a transplant. However a normal life does not simply imply regaining individual health in Mexico, but rather a return to "productivity and reproductivity";

when people decide to undergo transplants it is because they have been convinced that they will be able to work, have children, and live to raise them.[96] On return to daily life, most organ recipients were confronted with a harsh reality – one of bodily side effects, some very serious; persistent threats of organ rejection; constant concern about an inability to pay for the expensive medications; an inability to return to work in factories or agricultural settings where they would be exposed to kidney-damaging chemicals; and discrimination by employers who assume that people who have had transplants will be sick all the time. There are also concerns among men who have had transplants about a loss of sexual potency – of being like a gelding or a half-woman; divorces sometimes result because wives become fearful about their partners; many are concerned about an inability to bear children; and certain young people who have had transplants fear or develop an inability to form lasting relationships.

It is highly unlikely that Mexico is unique with respect to these experiences. Crowley-Matoka's research highlights the discrepancy between the rhetoric of the transplant world and the reality of everyday life for many people. This is not to suggest that organ transplants should not be done, but the social ramifications and life-long effects of this remarkable technology, especially when it is put into practice in countries that are short of high-tech resources, are systematically ignored or else presented in biased form simply as numbers of lives saved.[97]

In closing this section we turn briefly to the Egyptian situation. The research of anthropologist Sherine Hamdy graphically demonstrates the social, political, and economic dimensions of the technological assemblage associated with organ transplants.[98] Approximately 700 to 800 kidney transplants making use of living donors are performed each year in Egypt; however it is striking that, although sale of organs is strictly illegal, the majority of donors are not related to the recipients and sell their kidneys to unrelated recipients while transplant doctors turn a blind eye. Donors, whose desperate stories occasionally appear in the newspapers, usually receive somewhere between $4,000 and $6,000. Wealthy Egyptians in need of a transplant sometimes choose to go abroad, taking a family member as a donor, for what they assume will be better care. Procurement of organs from patients declared brain dead is illegal in Egypt, thus creating a great demand for living donors.

During the course of extensive fieldwork Hamdy interviewed some of the 30,000 patients in Egypt with end-stage kidney failure who, in order to survive, are tethered for hours several times a week to dialysis machines. Transplants are carried out in both public and private hospitals in Egypt, but the vast majority of patients on dialysis cannot contemplate a transplant because they are unable to find the necessary resources to pay for the medical services, the prohibitive cost of the kidney itself, and the cost after surgery of life-long medication. Furthermore, the people interviewed were unconvinced that a transplant would in the end be of benefit to them. Above all, when considering receiving an organ from a living related donor, patients were concerned about the sacrifice of the donor and their probable loss of health. In addition, the investment in a transplant would inevitably effect substantially the economic wellbeing of the family as a whole, and in any case the majority of potential recipients believed that their own post-transplant lives would in all probability not be improved enough to justify the costs involved.[99]

The reasons that Egyptian dialysis patients come to such conclusions are in large part because they are all too well aware of the gradual collapse of socialized health care in Egypt over the past decades, and many have personal experience of widely publicized substandard care. They are also well aware from television, radio, and word of mouth reports of corruption in the medical profession. But beyond these concerns, Egyptians are today apprised of what is described as the improper use of the nation's natural resources and of what undeniably are extensive health-related problems believed by the public and medical professionals to result from excess pesticide usage and improper handling of toxic waste. In Hamdy's words, Egyptian dialysis patients often appeal to what they regard as "local biology" that in effect renders organ transplantation inefficacious due to a contaminated environment, endemic parasitic infections, poverty, the intake of poisonous food, an inappropriate use of pharmaceuticals, and medical mistreatment.[100]

There is documented evidence that the numbers of individuals with kidney failure and liver disease are on the increase in Egypt.[101] When interviewed, nephrologists noted that the kidney diseases they see today are more aggressive than formerly and increasingly difficult to treat. Several of these specialists, like their patients, insisted that this situation is the result of environmental degradation and the ingestion of toxins. Among other things, formaldehydes are used to preserve milk, hormone-pumped chickens are imported rather than using local "country" chickens, and pesticides rejected in the West as unsafe are dumped on Egypt. Some doctors pointed out that today, as a result of U.S. "aid" packages and other political arrangements in the Middle East, people eat bread made from imported U.S. wheat that, after storage in the hot and humid conditions of Egypt, produces a fungus that is linked to kidney and liver toxicity, and cancer. There is substantial scientific evidence to support these claims,[102] and there are additional difficulties with pesticide residues in the local crops.

In classical times Egypt was the breadbasket for the Roman Empire and, even though later on there were on occasion bad harvests, malnutrition, and corrupt regimes in which the grain was not equitably distributed, until recently Egypt has been largely self-sufficient in grain production. The building of the Aswan dam, completed in 1971, ruined many hundreds of acres of fertile soil, but even so, the country continued to be able to sustain itself. In recent years the situation has changed completely. Since the 1970s, a combination of extensive U.S. subsidies, placing Egypt under pressure to import U.S. grain, together with the transformation of locally produced coarse grains that formerly nourished the majority of Egyptians into animal food, has left the vast majority of Egypt's population in difficult straits. The meat products that result from the use of grain to feed animals now feed tourists, resident foreigners, and wealthy Egyptians, but not the majority of the population.[103]

Since the 1990s there has been a proliferation of dialysis clinics, and many patients argue explicitly that what they regard as a failed Egyptian state is complicit in the production of failed Egyptian bodies. Currently government expenditure on health care amounts to 2 percent of the total GDP[104] and the cost of health care for Egyptians is increasing rapidly. Given the expense and justified concerns about toxins, many patients conclude that having a transplant will change their lives little, for the new kidney too, will soon be damaged. And clearly under these circumstances donors too, no matter how well intentioned they be, will be unable to survive on one kidney, no matter what the medical profession claims. No human organs can be "spare" in this kind of polluted environment, and the majority of needy recipients turn their energies toward cultivating steadfastness.[105]

Altruism, Entitlement, and Commodification

Organ donation has long been associated with altruism, but if this is the case, body parts cannot be thought of as mere material things, detritus from the dead or spare parts from the living made available for recycling; social value must inevitably be attached to them. Altruism is, in effect, charity made modern. Auguste Comte created the concept of altruism at the end of the 19th century, and posed it in opposition to egoism, a condition that he feared would destroy the tattered remnants of social solidarity in urbanized, modernizing society. Deliberately stripped of any religious connotation, altruism is a thoroughly secularized form of charity from which no direct reciprocity to givers is anticipated. But an expectation exists that society as a whole will benefit from such acts. Even though the 1968 law in the United States regularizing organ donation was named the Uniform Anatomical Gift Act, it was nevertheless assumed from the outset that gifts of organs would be "free," that is, they would be charitable altruistic donations, as is the case in by far the majority of the countries that participate in this particular technology, even when sales take place clandestinely in a few of them.[106]

However, use of the "gift" metaphor has the effect of individualizing donation, of making the act into a personal choice – one that "fits" with a dominant ideology in North America of having the right to dispose of one's body as one would wish. From the outset some potential donors assumed that they would be able to "direct" their donations – that is, to name, if not an individual, then at least the ethnic group to which the organ should be donated. But altruism, in contrast to gifts that are handed to specific individuals, is expected to benefit society at large, and constitutes a form of fellowship that cements people together in modernity. Confusion can multiply because, where bodies do not "belong" to individuals, as is the case in Japan, the question arises as to whether individuals have the "right" to choose donation of their own bodies. This is why families have been legally able to veto donation until recently in Japan.

Whereas donation from brain-dead bodies to a well-regulated donor pool that enforces anonymity and practices an egalitarian distribution of organs can no doubt be thought of as altruistic, the same cannot be said for the procurement of organs from living donors, whether for payment or for direct donation to a relative. The Mexican and Egyptian situations make it abundantly clear that matters are by no means always as clear-cut as they seem. Donation within families does not preclude a moral economy to which monetary values contribute. Although it is not always the case, the decision to donate a kidney "may be born of a brutal calculus in which one family member is driven to provide a kidney to another to safeguard the economic survival of the family as a whole."[107] More often than not this means that wives donate to husbands, and some describe the decision explicitly as being driven by economics. In other instances cars, real estate, travel, and so on may be traded among family members for an organ. Cases of non-related donations also came to light in Mexico in which organs were traded for land that resulted in positive long-term fictive kin relationships. Mixing of market values with human body parts is clearly not uncommon where live donors are involved, but it does not *necessarily* involve blatant exploitation.

Clearly, globally, there is no "norm" as far as transplantation is concerned. But, as we have seen, the very success of the technology, together with demographic changes that have resulted in the aging of populations, have brought about a "shortage" of organs that diminishes the worth of altruistic donation and encourages extensive commodification, some of it highly exploitative. When a moral economy exists that supports the saving of life at all costs, as is apparently supported by certain medical professionals and involved families in the wealthier parts of the world, the shortage is exacerbated. Even national decisions that reject brain death as the end of human life inevitably result in medical tourism by patients in search of organs. At the same time, efforts to outlaw the sale of organs in certain places mean that people with money simply travel elsewhere to obtain what they so desperately need.[108] To think of this enterprise as anything other than globally networked is a grave mistake. The Egyptian case lays bare another form of global networking, one that is produced by efforts at development under a globalized neo-liberal economy, with tragic consequences for the health of poor populations, not only in Egypt but equally in many other countries. The increasing poverty that results from such development strategies, bringing about, among many other things, basic dietary changes that in the Egyptian case actually have toxic effects, has far-reaching consequences as a recipe for widespread organ failure. Similarly to the discussion in chapter 5 in connection with the use of the ultrasound scan for sex selection of a fetus, the impact of transplant technologies on the everyday lives of people who are directly involved with this enterprise is context dependent, and the social-political-economic environments in which they take place demand attention.

Ethnographic research in connection with technological practices promotes a reconsideration of assumptions about governance and the basic social contract. In the case of organ transplants, and reproductive technologies (to be discussed in the following chapter), the following issues need attention: the relation between self and other; assumed boundaries between nature and culture, and life and death; new forms of kinship; and the relationship among commodities, gifts, and altruistic donations. The discussion provoked by use of these technologies acts as a touchstone for extensive political debates about nationalism, modernization, development, and progress, the present global neo-liberal economy, inequality, poverty, graft, and, above all, whose lives are valuable, and whose can be sacrificed.

We cannot now go back, and few would want to; but to complain about an organ shortage and to count the success of the organ transplant enterprise solely in terms of the number of years of survival after a graft is hopelessly inadequate. Meanwhile, in the United States, the average wait time for a kidney is expected to increase to 10 years by 2010. In China, two out of three transplants rely on organs removed from condemned prisoners.

10

Kinship, Infertility, and Assisted Reproduction

A substantial literature has documented that women worldwide bear the major burden of infertility. Of course, an inability to produce a child may well be due to a failing on the part of the involved male, but until recently in many parts of the world this state of affairs has gone largely unrecognized or, quite simply, has been flatly denied as possible. "Barren" or "sterile" women are made responsible for a failure to reproduce, and are liable to suffer marital duress, divorce, or abandonment.[1] Worldwide, medicines, potions, and rituals are available to relieve this unwanted condition, and in many places, notably parts of Africa, adoption or fostering of children is common, a practice that solidifies social networks and compensates families who are not able to have their own biological offspring. Infertility and its management are the subject matter of this chapter. It is this topic, perhaps more than any other, that highlights a great divide between those who live in perpetual poverty and have little or no access to health care and those who are better off.

It is argued that the first successful *in vitro* conception resulting in a live birth in the United Kingdom in 1978 brought about the "invention" of infertility as a biomedical problem.[2] Between 1978 and 1985 the World Health Organization (WHO) conducted a worldwide epidemiological study in order to standardize the investigation of infertility. In that study, couples were defined as infertile if they had not conceived after more than one year of unprotected sexual activity.[3] It is now well established that many couples, although apparently infertile after one year, go on to achieve conception without any treatment.[4] In a report published in 1991 the WHO revised its position and defined a woman (rather than a couple) as having "primary infertility" if she has been "exposed to pregnancy for two years" but has not conceived. When a couple has already produced a child but then is seemingly unable to have more children, the condition is described as "secondary infertility."[5] This situation arises most frequently when a sexually transmitted infection (STI) is present, and is usually resolved once the infection is cured. On the other hand, primary infertility – due to anatomical malfunctioning, post-abortion damage, or rare genetic abnormalities – is much less tractable. Largely as a result of the ever-increasing medicalization of infertility in many countries over the past 30 years, it is now more generally accepted that either or both partners may have contributed to an inability to reproduce, and WHO records indicate that approximately half of diagnosed cases of primary infertility are due to male sexual dysfunction of one kind or another,[6] making both men and women potential subjects of medicalization. In all, it is estimated that between 50 and 80 million people worldwide are infertile (although these figures can only be a guideline) and approximately 8–10 percent of couples experience primary infertility but, inevitably, this figure varies somewhat from region to region. Today it is possible for those people with sufficient means to try to overcome their apparent inability to reproduce by resort to one or more of a wide array of reproductive technologies.

Assisted Reproductive Technologies

Assisted reproductive technologies (ARTs) inevitably intervene dramatically into domestic life, with the result that regulations have been enacted about the limitations of their acceptable use in many places where these technologies are available – the United States being one notable exception. In the majority of countries, regulations, sometimes legally enforced, carefully delimit use of ART in order that the ideal of the "natural" procreative family will not be violated, as the Egyptian example cited below illustrates. In striking contrast, in the United States, ART users are recognized as customers or consumers, and have considerable liberty to choose how their own reproduction will be accomplished. For very different reasons, in those countries where increased reproduction is regarded as a matter of national importance and not merely the product of individual desire, laws bearing on ARTs are similarly not stringent, and use of the gametes of strangers and resort to gestational mothers are supported, if such techniques are necessary to bring about reproduction. The case of Israel, the most striking example of a country where every encouragement is given to women to produce offspring by all means possible, will also be discussed below.

Clearly, debate about assisted reproduction exposes deeply held values – political, cultural, familial, and religious – as to what should be the appropriate forms and means of reproduction and, further, what constitutes kinship. Tensions between government control and free enterprise about what will count in any given nation as "natural" and acceptable methods of reproduction are readily apparent in the social science literature dealing with ARTs, as this chapter makes clear. In common with organ transfer, ARTs are applied (by no means always with success) to overcome bodily failings, and in so doing normative boundaries between culture and nature are challenged, with value-laden consequences for human social relations. The focus in this chapter will be on the perceived benefits and challenges to social relations posed by ARTs by highlighting the different forms and objectives this technology takes in several geographical locations.

Case studies show graphically that the actual technological manipulation of conception is not per se of primary concern to most involved parties, with the exception of certain representatives of religious organizations – the Vatican, for example, is concerned about the destruction of embryonic life that is inevitable with ART practice. However, at issue everywhere are the implications of such manipulations for the contribution made by genetics or in a more diffuse way by bodily substance during gestation to the creation of kin. This raises concerns about what counts as parenthood, who are siblings, and who are more distantly related kin or simply unknown others. Fears about adultery and incest also surface in connection with ART use, as do, in some instances, debates about identity, ethnicity, and the citizenship of children created by means of ARTs.

Before turning to ethnographic accounts about reproductive technologies, we first consider infertility in sub-Saharan Africa, a region where ARTs are largely absent, and where, in a good number of countries, secondary infertility is disproportionately high due to sexually transmitted infections (STIs) and other infections. Today, despite this situation, the majority of health care practitioners and people working for NGOs in Africa systematically dismiss infertility as a major health problem in this region, even though most cases are eminently treatable. This apparent lack of concern for infertile individuals living in sub-Saharan Africa is in striking contrast to the situation in other countries today where, even for poorer segments of the population, antibiotics are usually available, and encouragement is given to middle-class couples who have reproductive difficulties to make use of ARTs, including couples living in China and India where overpopulation is a top priority.

Problematizing Infertility Figures

Creating standardized estimates of infertility rates poses major difficulties, and this is particularly apparent with respect to the situation in Africa, although it is by no means limited to Africa. Clinical establishment of infertility in most countries is based on a mechanistic model of what are thought to be deviations from "normal" physiological processes presumed to occur under "natural fertility" conditions.[7] Fertility outcomes based on this model are understood as being the result of various "intermediate variables or proximate determinants including, among others, factors such as contraceptive use and effectiveness, the prevalence of induced abortion, the duration of postpartum infecundability, and the frequency of intercourse."[8] For clinicians, early treatment is advantageous and so, in contrast to WHO guidelines, most still work on the assumption that one year of "exposure to pregnancy" without success is sufficient time to diagnose infertility.

Epidemiologists doing community surveys and demographers using census surveys both make use of quantitative approaches designed to estimate the prevalence of infertility in various geographical sites. Like clinicians, demographers have settled on a definition of infertility different from that used by the WHO, but for a different reason. They define infertility as the inability of a non-contracepting, sexually active woman to have a live birth.[9] Demographers have shifted the end-point of investigation from conception to live births, and this is because it is thought, especially when using large population-based samples, often based on secondary data, that while one can establish birth histories, it is virtually impossible to get information on abortions, miscarriages, and still-births. For this reason it is recommended that demographers use much longer time spans of up to seven years to establish estimates of infertility.[10]

It is evident that the results of comparative studies of infertility are biased by the use of different definitions of infertility, and it has been shown that, depending upon the definition used, the estimated prevalence rates of infertility as well as the sociodemographic characteristics of the women labeled as infertile vary markedly.[11] For example, a major difficulty is likely to arise when only non-contracepting women married for the past five years are included in research samples designed to estimate infertility. In many parts of the world, a woman may well have been abandoned or divorced before five years have passed, for the very reason that her partner and his family have long since declared her infertile. If the goal is to find out about infertility prevalence, whether worldwide or in a specific population, then clearly it should not be assumed that it is only married women who attempt to become pregnant; nor should divorced or widowed women be omitted from research samples. Furthermore, indigenous methods of contraception, ideas about birth-spacing and ideal family size, long separation of cohabitants due to work migration patterns, and so on, should all be taken into consideration. But there are further very serious problems with research carried out in Africa, notably with what has come to be known as "the infertility belt," stretching across sub-Saharan Africa, to which we will now turn.

From Underfertility to Overfertility

As we noted in chapter 6, historical research into infertility in colonized Africa documented how, in the 1930s and 1940s, unsubstantiated rumors circulated about events described as "racial suicide, dying races, empty villages and self-aborting women."[12] At a time when the colonizers wanted the local population to serve as a fit and active labor force, it was claimed that "native women" were inducing their own abortions, "detribalized women" were avoiding maternity, and "the psychological shocks of colonialism and modernity vitiated the desire to procreate."[13] It was believed that such women, traumatized by the effects of colonization on themselves and their societies, were refusing to reproduce. In contrast to this moral panic, the historian Nancy Hunt draws on the published materials of Anne Retel-Laurentin who worked in the Central African Republic in the middle of the last century. Retel-Laurentin was trained as a doctor but also had considerable exposure to ethnological methods. By the end of the 1960s, she had written an extraordinary social epidemiology of Nzakara sub-fertility. In contrast to other colonists who insisted that the infertility of African women was due to their loose behavior and self-administered abortions, as well as local "lazy" men, Retel-Laurentin argued that miscarriages played a major role in the infertility of women.[14] Hunt notes that Retel-Laurentin made it her business to understand and participate in local life and she paid serious attention to indigenous explanations of infertility, while at the same time recognizing the importance of clinical care. Retel-Laurentin took note of the effects of polygyny on reproduction and on the transmission of STIs; she tracked the circulation of women, as well as the colonial forms of sex work, and she paid attention to the way in which recognition of infertility among local people intensified distrust and sorcery accusations.

Throughout the late colonial period in the early part of the 20th century, theories persisted about the cause of low fertility rates in sub-Saharan Africa, including poor hygiene, nutritional deficiencies, endemic disease of various kinds, alcoholism, an excessive number of abortions, and widespread apathy in the face of European demands for labor. However, by the 1970s, and partly under the influence of

Retel-Laurentin's work and a few others like her, it became accepted that STIs probably accounted for most cases of infertility or sub-fertility in Africa. This position was consolidated by a WHO survey carried out between 1979 and 1984 using standardized protocols to investigate infertility involving 25 countries including four in sub-Saharan Africa. The findings made it clear that, compared with women in other parts of the world, those experiencing infertility in the African countries were more likely to report histories of an STI or pregnancy complications, or to have bilateral tubal occlusion causing infertility.

Nevertheless, as a result of investigation of Retel-Laurentin's work and that of a second researcher, a pharmacist and botanist working in the former Belgian Congo, Hunt is driven to question whether a sub-Saharan infertility belt actually exists, at least as presently understood and represented. "Statistics have effects" she insists, but they are inevitably artifacts. Hunt's argument is not that low fertility rates do not exist in this region, nor that STIs are not heavily implicated, but that two specific regions with high infertility rates – the Belgian Congo and the Central African Republic – rapidly came to be thought of as representative of the whole of sub-Saharan Africa. To lump together such a vast territory that has had significantly different experiences of colonization and widely varying social and political organizations is gravely mistaken.[15]

An article published in the *International Journal of Epidemiology* presenting a comprehensive reassessment of research into primary and secondary infertility in sub-Saharan Africa over the past 30 years provides strong support for Hunt's argument. Findings from 28 countries collected from among the general population as part of Demographic and Health Surveys and World Fertility Surveys conducted in sub-Saharan Africa from the late 1970s through to the late 1990s are revisited and modified in this meta-analysis.[16] The original response rates were apparently very high in each of the surveys, the designs of which were reasonably comparable; however, to remedy some of the inevitable shortcomings, only data on ever-married, childless women who entered their first marriage at least seven years before the date of censoring were included in the study.

Some very interesting trends emerge in the meta-analysis, although obviously research of this kind, even with careful modifications, has unavoidable weaknesses. Primary infertility is relatively low in all the countries surveyed and exceeds 3 percent in less than one third of them; however, two countries, Cameroon and the Central African Republic, where Retel-Laurentin did her work, are particularly high, at 6 percent. The prevalence of secondary infertility varies enormously from country to country. Once again Cameroon and the Central African Republic rank very high, as do Lesotho, Mozambique, and Mauritania, all with ranges of 20 to 25 percent for women aged 20–44, whereas in Togo secondary infertility stands at 5 percent and in Burundi and Rwanda at 7 percent. The other countries range between these extremes. The author of the meta-analysis, Ulla Larsen, points out that the remarkable geographical variability with respect to infertility demonstrated by this study needs to be accounted for, and that further research is needed into differential access to health care, midwifery care, and untreated medical problems (notably STIs), among yet other variables.[17]

The anthropologist Pamela Feldman-Savelsberg has carried out ethnographic research into infertility in Cameroon, a country that exhibits enormous linguistic and geographical diversity. Among the 250 ethnic groups living in the country, where the official languages are both French and English, it is abundantly evident that successful childbearing is highly valued; however, as noted above, fertility is highly compromised. It has been suggested that this part of Central Africa may have the highest infertility rate in the world. Even so, "hyperfertility" is officially recognized as causing a "population problem," leading Feldman-Savelsberg to note that, despite the shocking infertility figures, scant attention is given to this public health problem.[18] Clearly this is an instance of "barrenness amidst plenty."[19] Cameroon is a country that captures the attention of demographers because it has not entered what is known as "the demographic transition," a widely documented shift in reproductive behavior in which national birth rates drop as a result of improved social conditions.[20] It is the continued high fertility rate that receives attention in Cameroon, and not the suffering of those who are infertile.

Feldman-Savelsberg worked among the Bamiléké, who make up roughly 25 percent of the entire Cameroon population, and are recognized by Cameroonians for their high birth rates and relatively low female sterility compared to other peoples living in Cameroon. Even so, infertility is feared among the Bamiléké, and for good reasons. As part of rural polygynous households, infertile women are likely to fall into disfavor and be given less land and material resources crucial to their wellbeing. Worse still, they may be divorced because they have not produced children essential for the continuity of the dual-descent kinship system in which both the matrilineal and patrilineal lines are important.

In pre-colonial Cameroon, the area was divided into sacred kingdoms in which the paramount chiefs and ritual specialists had a dual responsibility for the fertility of both the people and the land. Fertility was and is a sign of and the basis for "economic, political, and spiritual strength."[21] Labor-recruitment and the spread of STIs during the colonial period caused major disruptions, and colonial reports of the time express repeated concerns about the need for "reproductive strength," with the result that government attention in the early 20th century was directed toward infertility. At the same time, missionary medicine strove to replace local birth attendants with hospital-based birthing carried out by midwives. In postcolonial years, the government of Cameroon argued for some years that the country continued to be "underpopulated" and encouraged appropriate birth spacing but no birth control. Cameroon was at the time unique in sub-Saharan Africa when an infertility clinic was opened there in 1972.

The ethnographic work carried out by Feldman-Savelsberg reveals an "ethnodemography" created out of local theories about procreation that include scientifically recognized factors such as how often a couple has sex and the suggestion that something may be anatomically "wrong." However, anatomical problems may result from witchcraft, what are regarded as "improper" emotions, and other factors external to the body. Broader factors are also implicated including the spiritual, physical, and political condition of the local leader; the goodwill of ancestors; and kinship relations. In other words, this ethnodemography can be understood as a kind of problem of "public health."[22] In contrast, the Cameroon government is today concerned with political survival and with receiving outside aid as a result of an economic crisis lasting for over a decade. It has been informed in no uncertain terms that it must deal with its excessive rate of reproduction, and infertility has disappeared into the shadows.

Feldman-Savelsberg argues that under the circumstances it is likely that infertility is on the increase as a result of the degradation of public health services and the unchecked spread of STIs, but she insists that this situation should not be interpreted simply as one of differing "belief systems." She concludes that in this multi-ethnic state, relations between local politics and central government are crucial and adds, "the current climate of mistrust has already had dramatic effects on public health projects in Cameroon," particularly among the Bamiléké living in the highland grass-fields region, who are suspicious that public health projects that emphasize contraception and population reduction are threatening what they, the Bamiléké perceive as their most precious cultural resource – human fertility.[23]

In the 1990s Karina Kielmann, an anthropologist, undertook an ethnographic study that involved research in local clinics about the experience of infertility in Pemba, an island with a population of about 70,000 that is part of Tanzania. The resident Irish midwife with whom she spoke thought Kielmann was wasting her time, and described infertility as a "blessing in disguise." Kielmann soon realized that this kind of comment was not unusual when she found an entry made in a hospital logbook: "many women come to the hospital complaining of infertility, but it is not something we should devote our efforts to given the high fertility rate."[24] The total fertility rate in Pemba, that is, the average number of children born to a woman over her lifetime, is approximately 7.9 and family planning services are widely accessible. However, as is the case elsewhere in Africa, these services are separated from facilities that provide advice about and medication for STIs, as well as from maternal and child health facilities. Kielmann observed that STI clinics in Pemba are severely underfunded, and tend to be highly stigmatized by local populations. At the time she did her research, posters produced by the Ministry of Health referred to STIs as "diseases of sexual promiscuity."[25] Not surprisingly, infertility is not easily talked about, in biomedical settings at least, where what is considered as an excessively high fertility rate is of prime concern. Expatriate health workers in the clinics made little effort to understand local idioms of distress used by women to narrate the causes of infertility. This was the case even though, as Kielmann notes, women are exceedingly articulate about the location of the pain they experience and the reasons for their inability to bear children, including the possible involvement of spirits and jealous co-wives.

Local people working at primary health care units in Pemba frequently refer women who appear to be infertile to traditional healers of various kinds, including traditional birth attendants. But many women are in turn actively encouraged by healers to consult with biomedical doctors once the healer is satisfied that he can be of no assistance with the physical aspects of the problem.[26] The case studies Kielmann collected reveal clearly that local understanding of infertility and its management simultaneously entertains multiple possible explanations for why a woman is unable to bear a child. Such narratives allow affected women and their families some room to negotiate how their condition will be managed:

> Halima, 22 years old, has been married to her first husband for eight years. Her husband has another wife who has five children. [Halima] says that her infertility is due to a problem … inside her uterus. She first went to see a mkunga [a traditional birth attend-ant] who, after examining her, said that she had a ruined abdomen … She then consulted

a Chinese doctor at Mkoani Hospital, who examined her and gave her drugs to stimulate ovulation. She "conceived" for one month, but then started to bleed. [Halima's] husband accompanied her to see a mganga [a specialist in spirit possession] who said that she was possessed by land spirits ... The mganga ... staged a ceremony ... to expel the spirits.

At this juncture Halima went together with her sister to see a maternal and child care aid who told her to go to Wete Hospital, where she was examined by the Swedish doctor resident at the time. He told her it was a case of primary infertility and recommended that she have a "tubal blow."[27]

Clearly a multifaced, pluralistic discourse that ranges between internalizing and externalizing explanations for the management of infertility was present in the public domain in Pemba when Kielmann did her research. Kielmann argues: "The simultaneous logic of greedy spirits and faulty organs objectifies the meaning of infertility, thus deflecting blame from individual women and encouraging them to persist in their search for treatment and therapy."[28] Even so, little if anything is achieved by any of the healers, including the biomedical doctor, to overcome the problem. The biomedical doctors whom Kielmann talked to made it clear that they are acutely aware that infertility could be tragic for the women who came to them, but pointed out that they simply did not have the resources or trained personnel to deal with the problem effectively.

Kielmann chose to base her study largely in clinical settings where inevitably the physical tragedy of infertility is made very visible. Based on years of research experience in mainland Tanzania, the historian Steven Feierman brings another perspective to the problem. He writes about how the way in which women relate the condition of their bodies, healthy or otherwise, depends in large part on the state of complex extended family relationships.[29] Feierman points out that in the village of Ghaambo, where he worked, the concept of fertility has profound social meaning and is understood in a much broader sense than simply that of disease or pathology. For Ghaambo women, or indeed women elsewhere in Africa, fertility is the capacity to bring life to the next generation of the extended family network. Conception and giving birth to a living child is, Feierman argues, only a part of the Ghaambo fertility story. Women's narratives about fertility recount a whole range of conditions, social and biological, that make it possible for infants to be born and, even more important, to survive. These conditions include family support, the capacity to provide food, local economies, and personal factors including jealousy and anger. In other words, fertility is by no means simply a biological matter, but is intimately associated with social relations, social status, and power.

Feierman's argument is not designed simply to elucidate local concepts; he goes further and argues that this social approach to fertility makes great sense in a world of poverty where infant mortality rates are high. Well-cultivated networks of relatives are essential in a world where there are no effective public institutions for support – no public safety-nets for life crises of all kinds. Feierman notes:

Husbands can be good or bad, supportive or scornful, but unless a husband is very wealthy, and almost none are, a husband's help is not enough. The small and constricted world of a husband and a wife and their children is never large enough, or robust enough, to get people through crises. In the wider network, some are better off, some poorer. If everyone helps others, the chances of survival for the poor are much better, and people are well aware of that.[30]

The health insurance network is, in effect, a "social insurance network" – the web of relationships on which women depend. It has been shown repeatedly, Feierman adds, "that people across eastern and central Africa rely on these networks of relatives to consult diviners, provide food and nursing care in hospitals, to pay for antibiotics when prescribed but not provided, to bring firewood and water when a woman is ill, and to do a thousand other things."[31] He concludes that the women he has talked to are correct when they insist that their health depends upon their social networks.

This situation does not mean that medications, herbal or biomedicine, are not understood by the Ghaambo to have a direct effect on "the body-as-mechanism," although for some conditions ritual or social therapy is also required. Healing acts are "complex interventions in social, moral, and material relations" and uncertainty and skepticism about healers and the efficacy of their therapeutic methods are everywhere evident. Moreover, efficacy is judged not only in narrow materialistic terms, but also with respect to social healing.[32] If women in sub-Saharan Africa are to survive the ordeal that infertility precipitates, then support from the social network is essential, even to obtain the antibiotics indispensable to treatment for STIs. But the situation is becoming increasingly bleak because resources have been steadily diminishing over the past decade in the entire region, a situation exacerbated by external demands to reduce population size, often tied overtly to economic aid.

One method frequently made use of in Africa to overcome the social repercussions of infertility deserves mention, the widespread practice of fostering. In households where there are insufficient means to raise all the children, offering a child to a childless female relative is common practice. This practice often benefits not only the fostering parent but also the child who may receive better food and more schooling than would have been the case in their natal family. Women who cannot bear their own children and who foster children often receive enormous solace from this practice but, even so, they rarely escape the stigma of infertility.[33]

The Danish political scientist Lisa Ann Richey sums up the big picture in connection with fertility management in sub-Saharan Africa with reference to Tanzania.[34] Since 1994, as in virtually all other African countries, national public expenditure for reproductive health has steadily declined in Tanzania, and the funds that remain available have been devoted almost exclusively to clinics handing out contraceptives. This decline has taken place in spite of a general agreement arrived at in 1994 at the Cairo International Conference on Population and Development that emphasis should be given to the overall improvement of women's reproductive health as a key goal in strategies for economic development. Richey points out that, commencing in 1995, the Tanzanian government came under stringent pressures to carry out "structural adjustment" by Tanzania's donors and lenders, integral to which was a demand to bring about fertility decline as rapidly as possible, with a narrow focus on birth control rather than more generally on overall reproductive health.

Once the economic recession associated with the structural adjustments imposed by the World Bank began to take its toll in the 1980s, Tanzanians reported that they were deliberately reducing the size of their families because of increasing poverty, with the result that the total fertility rate dropped quite significantly.[35] One effect of the recession proved to be that the Tanzanian National Family Planning Program was heralded as a success by outside observers. However, fieldwork in the Kilimanjaro region made it clear to Richey that medical services were abysmal, and the health of both men and women was in decline. Health workers complained to Richey about a chronic shortage of even the most basic supplies including sterile gloves, syringes, and gauze. They were unable to insert IUDs but, even more importantly, they had no access to antibiotics because this type of medication was not considered necessary in family planning clinics, and infections were going untreated.[36] From the mid-1990s local doctors documented that as a result of untreated infections infertility rose quite dramatically, as did high-risk births. They also noted that, rather than coming to the family planning clinics, people preferred to treat themselves with bush medicine.[37] Richey points out that Tanzanian women had more access to reproductive health care in the 1970s than they do at the present time. In Tanzania today, 35–45 percent of all deaths in adult women are due to HIV/AIDS, but integration of care for HIV into the Family Planning Program has not even started, with the result that the majority of women have nowhere to turn when they attempt to avoid this disease or to get treatment for it.

Richey is scathingly critical of top-down donor-reliant initiatives that promote use of contraceptives alone, in preference to providing comprehensive reproductive health care. Under outside pressure, the Tanzanian government has steadily withdrawn funding from the health care sector, with the single exception of those clinics that provide family planning; even so their approach is praised internationally as a model for other countries. For example, the former British Secretary of State for International Development is on record as stating: "Tanzania's achievements in economic reform and improvements in health and education are very impressive."[38] And yet Richey found that nearly half of the residents in one of Tanzania's wealthiest rural areas have no access to formal health care at all.[39]

Because policy-makers assume that sub-Saharan Africa is now in a chronic state of emergency as a result of the HIV/AIDS epidemic (and now, in addition, resistant TB), reproductive health, including infertility is increasingly given short shrift. This problem is compounded because young married women are strongly encouraged by health care workers never to have unprotected sex and therefore, presumably, never to produce children. And yet children are essential, not simply as a source of pride and for the continuity of the lineage, but for their contribution to the family income and, once older, as part of the social networks that provide the only form of health and social security for their extended families. Because general health care is essentially non-existent in Tanzania today, the basic tasks of women as laborers, money earners, and household managers are put into jeopardy should they become sick. Furthermore, with migration to the city, access to good nutrition has declined and diabetes rates have soared. Added to this, the structures of the family and of social networks have changed dramatically due to the deadly effects of HIV/AIDS, leaving middle-aged and older people, especially women, as the only source of care and support for young children. This is indeed an urgent human rights issue, one that traditional forms of social security, the ubiquitous social networks of Africa, are not able to combat at all effectively without outside support and reliable basic medical care.

The discussion that follows, about the way in which infertility among the middle classes and the wealthy is handled by means of ART technologies, is in striking contrast to the situation in much of sub-Saharan Africa. However, one thing is common, namely that until very recently infertility has been coupled just about eve-rywhere with stigma and shame. As we will see below, the practices associated with the medicalization of infertility raise some very serious problems indeed, medical, social, and moral. However, understanding the causes of infertility solely as a medical problem – as a condition of potentially treatable physical abnormalities and patholo-gies – has certain advantages in the right kind of medical setting. The condition can and should be decoupled from a moralizing discourse in clinics, making a neutral space for patients to confront both their physical problem and the broader social ramifications of the situation on their own terms. However, while certain interna-tional organizations, NGOs, and African governments strongly discourage the treat-ment of infertility as a serious medical problem in Africa, the small amount of under-financed and short-supplied assistance given by harried biomedical practition-ers to infertile women will not bring about lasting change. Even teaching local popu-lations that the proximate causes of secondary infertility, STIs, are infectious diseases that can be treated effectively using antibiotics is unlikely to take place, and even if it does take place, the medication is unlikely to be available.

The research of Feierman, Kielmann, and others makes it clear that women who believe that they are infertile do not simply succumb to their situation; they are not passive victims of structural violence. Even so, given the paucity of medical resources set aside to assist them, the scarcity of biomedical and increasingly indigenous healers, and the dearth of good research designed to ask why infertility rates vary so much from one geographical space to another even within the same country, the everyday lives of the majority of women who cannot bear children will continue to be very hard indeed. We turn now to medically assisted reproduction, the practice of which stands in striking contrast to the African situation where so little attention is paid to infertility. Another point of note is that the perpetuation of kin and social continuity figures prominently in narratives about infertility everywhere, although among many middle-class families, wherever they live, such narratives are colored by an emphasis on individual desire.

Reproducing Culture

Early in the 1990s Marilyn Strathern pointed out the capacity of ARTs to challenge a fundamental unexamined assumption in Euro-American culture, one in which a conflation is made between what are thought of as the "natural facts" of reproduction and what is often described today as "social parenthood." Strathern, a British social anthropologist, draws on a lifetime of research in New Guinea to create a compara-tive, reflexive argument in connection with Euro-American assumptions about kinship:

> By kinship I understand not just the ways in which relatives interact with another, but how relationships as such are held to be constituted. Having sex, transmitting genes, giving birth: these facts of life were once taken as the basis for those relations between spouses, siblings, parents and children which were, in turn taken as the basis of kin rela-tions. Incorporated into such a reproductive model were suppositions about the con-nection between natural facts and social constructions. These ideas about kinship offered

a theory, if you like, about the relationship of human society to the natural world. They also incorporated certain ideas about the passage of time, relations between generations and, above all, about the future.[40]

Strathern analyzed official debates about assisted conception in the United Kingdom. She focused on how, when an emphasis is given to the individual in the representation of persons, it displaces other possible ways of understanding human relationships in connection with reproduction. An approach that takes the idea of a collective of individuals (as is common in the West) rather than families or larger groupings as the basis for understanding human social arrangements is in striking contrast to other parts of the world, as generations of anthropologists have shown.[41] Perhaps not surprisingly, in contemporary Western society overcoming infertility, whether male or female, is a matter of individual choice. Individuals become consumers of human gametes and fertilized embryos that are market-enhanced through technological manipulation, advertising, and promotions.[42] These medicalized objects are packaged as products available for consumption as part of contemporary enterprise culture. Strathern argues that above all else, because the new technologies "enable" rather than simply produce objects for consumption, they carry the connotations of service. Moreover, such technologies collapse a stark distinction between body and machine formerly believed to be unassailable, as do harvested organs for transplant and stored DNA collections, resulting in hybrids of nature and culture.[43]

Strathern argues that discussion about ARTs inevitably exposes the way in which the concept of kinship is constructed. To talk about kinship in the context of the nuclear family is to naturalize social relationships in a specific cultural milieu; human kinship in Euro-America is regarded as a "fact of society rooted in facts of nature," argues Strathern.[44] This is so because the nuclear family and intergenerational ties of blood are in theory understood as "natural," indisputable, and prior to everything else. However, persons recognized as kin are divided into two types, those related by blood and those related by marriage, that is, "the outcome of or in prospect of procreation."[45] The effect is that "*kinship thus connects the two domains*" of the social and the natural (emphasis in the original).[46] In contrast to many other parts of the world where social relations, often regardless of whether or not blood or marital ties are involved, are given priority over biological connections in establishing kin,[47] in Europe and North America, from the end of the 19th century, the idea of nature has increasingly become biologized, reinforcing and molecularizing, by means of genetics, a belief in "natural" kinship as primary. However, technological innovation forces us to consider, usually with mixed feelings of anxiety and hope, what is now made visible – entirely new conjunctions of bodies and machines.

Sarah Franklin, like Marilyn Strathern, creates an account of assisted conception to reflect on the concept of kinship and procreation. In addition she produces a critical account of the discourse associated with assisted conception.[48] Franklin shows how medical, media, and popular representations about reproductive technologies partially inform the subjective knowledge and experience of consumers. She argues that IVF is portrayed as a "hope technology," and notes that both failure (as high as 75 percent in many clinics) and success rates are continually subject to redefinition. Failures may be portrayed as a "relative success" under certain circumstances. Retaining hope and "hope management" are keys to the practice of this technology.[49]

Assisted Reproduction in the United States

In her comprehensive research into assisted reproduction in the United States, Charis Thompson combines science and technology studies and feminist theory with ethnographic research to discuss what she describes as "culture in the making."[50] Thompson characterizes the "dynamic coordination of the technical, scientific, kinship, gender, emotional, legal, political, and financial aspects of ART clinics" as an "ontological choreography," because these various domains, usually conceptualized as being of different kinds – part nature, part self, and part society – are made to engage with each other.[51] It is only by coordinating these elements that the clinic can function successfully:

Thus, for example, at specific moments a body part and surgical instruments must stand in a specific relationship, at other times a legal decision can disambiguate kinship in countless subsequent procedures, and at other times a bureaucratic accounting form can protect the sanctity of the human embryo or allow certain embryos to be discarded. Although choreography between different kinds of things goes on to some extent in all spheres of human activity, it is especially striking in ART clinics. They are intensely technical and intensely personal and political.[52]

Thompson points out that in order to carry out her investigation she must document not only the choreography of associations, but also "ontological separations" that at certain junctures in ART procedures are deliberately maintained between things. For example, the desire to be a parent is not discussed in the clinic and is deliberately kept apart from the actual biomedical procedure in clinic discourse.

Thompson argues that the undeniable high rates of failure in ART clinics associated by some commentators, notably certain feminists, with exploitation and even danger, are not inherently due to the formation of numerous hybridities – the component parts of the ontological choreography. Nor is exploitation due to the inevitable moments of reductionism and objectification. Rather, she argues, it is the moments when the choreography goes wrong for one reason or another – for example, as a result of a poor legal decision that leaves a child without a good home, or the fact that the cost of ART cannot be borne by most people, or the awareness that procedures are badly conducted – that gives rise to exploitation. When successful, when new forms of reproduction and new ways of making parents and children are the end result, then ontological innovation has taken place – the choreography has worked; infertility has been transcended to be replaced by parenthood.

In creating an ethnography of the clinic Thompson highlights four key elements of ontological choreography: normalization, gender, naturalization and socialization, and agency. One of the most striking features of normalization, she argues, is the way in which access to ART clinics is controlled. In the United States, despite the availability of clinics to everyone in principle, given the expense involved, patients at the clinics are overwhelmingly from white, middle- or upper-income families. Although exceptions are increasingly evident,[53] patients are not only well off but are usually heterosexual and in a stable relationship. The comportment of potential patients and their partners is also a feature of normalization and the perceived ability of potential consumers to comply with the demanding medical regimen is openly discussed at staff meetings before patients are accepted.[54] Given that a successful outcome, in the form of the birth of a child, is essential to the reputation of the clinic, potential parents must be vetted before being accepted as patients.

Thompson suggests that such normalizing procedures, though value-laden, are not surprising. She documents dissent among staff about normalization practices. She also notes that while she was carrying out this project, a time came when the clinics had a capacity to treat more patients than were coming forward for treatment, in other words, supply began to outstrip demand, with the result that the appropriateness of patients became less of an issue – the ethical frame moved away from one of social interventionism to that of a respect for privacy, accompanied by the adoption of biological rather than social norms. The change was in part made possible by experience with the technology. It became increasingly possible to predict on the basis of biological tests which patients would likely be success stories – who would in all probability have an appropriate "ovarian response" to treatment cycles. Even so, once access to the clinic had been achieved, appropriate patient and partner comportment continued to be important if the treatment was to be completed; if the couple failed in this respect, then some medical personnel felt obliged to suggest strongly that the course of treatment be terminated.[55] All procedures are, of course, fully documented, and the production of statistics is integral to the regulation and calibration that takes place – to the normative "epistemic culture" of the clinic.[56]

Drawing on the work of Judith Butler and Ann Fausto-Sterling, Thompson's position is that gender is "performative" even in the predominantly "heteronormative" sites of ART clinics. The usual ways of comprehending gendered life-course and social roles are compromised by infertility, and the experience of coming to terms with this difficulty is often associated with frustration, despair, and, especially in the case of men, with stigma and demasculinization. In the clinic men may simply be reduced to an "ejaculatory role," potentially compounding their compromised sense of self. However, Thompson finds that use of ribald humor and efforts to convince men about their hypermasculinity – of their high sperm counts, when relevant; virility; ability to masturbate effectively, and so on – apparently serve to restore the male partner to his allotted position with respect to reproduction. Thompson concludes that the performance and reproduction of gendered stereotypes in the clinic are important in "bringing order to these novel sociotechnical settings."[57]

In turning to the question of naturalization, Thompson argues that use of ARTs makes it clear that motherhood is becoming "partial." In other words, it is now possible to "do" kinship rather than simply fulfill an ascribed role, so that biological elements assumed to be relevant to kinship and socially meaningful kinship categories are now underdetermined, in particular when use is made of gestational surrogacy and IVF with ovum donation. Both surrogate motherhood and the use of ovum donation for IVF draw on substance (the uterus or ovum) as natural resources for making parents and children, as well as genes, but they distribute the elements of identity and personhood differently.[58] Furthermore, it is possible to argue that shared substance is a much more intimate biological connection than are shared genetics. Shared substance, that is, what is shared between the future mother and the fetus she gestates, is confined to becoming a mother. Genes, on the other hand, are shared among many different kinds of relations.

During the course of her research Thompson encountered 51-year-old Flora, who had gestated embryos that resulted from *in vitro* fertilization of the eggs of one of her daughters with the sperm of her second husband. Flora and her second husband will be the legal parents of the child once born, and Flora's daughter, who already has children of her own, will be the baby's half-sister and not its mother. Flora, a well-off Mexican, who crossed the border to California for the procedure, already has five children but wants to "give" her new young husband a child of his own. Thompson notes that Flora did not seem to be particularly perturbed by the inter-generational confusion that would result from the birth of the child – a child that will be genetically related to both her first and second husband; that Flora, as gesta-tional mother, will give birth to her own grandchild, and Flora's daughter, as a result of donating an egg, will be both the progenitor and sister of Flora's daughter! However, Flora's daughter was not especially happy with the situation. As a result of treatment she had produced an exceptional 65 eggs that were all inseminated with the sperm of Flora's husband. Forty-five eggs became fertilized and five fresh embryos were transferred to Flora's uterus. After three cycles Flora became pregnant, leaving a good number of embryos unused and stored in a freezer. Flora's daughter was uncomfortable about these stored embryos fertilized by her stepfather's semen. They are technically owned by Flora and her husband, but for Flora's daughter they create anxiety and smack of something close to incest.[59] This case study, as do others spelt out by Thompson, makes clear the value of conducting ethnographic research on a topic as unfamiliar as the social ramifications of ART. Even more important, perhaps, but hard to do, would be to follow these new families as the children evolve beyond infancy and become independent actors in their own right.

Nature and culture are without doubt co-produced in ART clinics, and Thompson's work demonstrates how this interaction, unstable and shifting though it may be, responds to cultural categories, in this instance those of the United States, and to normative values about reproduction and the wellbeing of children. However, as a result of ART technology, there is more than one possible answer to the question: who is mother? And, equally, who is father? Thompson concludes that technological change and cultural conservatism go hand in hand, and that the usual assumption that a lag exists between technological innovation and cultural reaction is not always the case.[60]

In turning to the final core feature that Thompson considers, that of agency, her position is that, although bodily objectification is unavoidable during many of the procedures in the clinic, women nevertheless are cooperative with these procedures and do not find the experience demeaning. The synecdochal aspects of diagnosis, in which parts of the body – eggs, fallopian tubes – come to stand in for the woman as a whole, do not appear to affect the subjective experience of women undergoing ART. Thompson's interviews suggest that although figuratively speaking "the woman is rendered into multiple body parts many times during a treatment cycle," neverthe-less "the patient orients herself as an object of study and intervention and willingly complies with treatment."[61] The authority of clinic personnel is enforced in the way in which they limit and circumscribe information that they give to patients; and yet, Thompson argues, even under these conditions women freely exert agency by actively participating in procedures. Only if and when treatment proves to be a failure, do women then experience considerable alienation.

Given that, in the best of infertility clinics, procreation is only about 25 percent successful, it must be the case that many couples come away from treatment sessions of many months feeling frustrated, no doubt angry, and out of pocket. Women who have undergone many rounds of hormone stimulation treatments should also feel concerned about possible long-term side effects on their health. Thompson does not deal with these important matters, but Gay Becker's work[62] makes it clear how the staggering array of medical options now available to women and men have profound financial and emotional impacts on consumers of ART technologies. She argues that many Americans, when they believe themselves to be infertile, embody the idea that they have a disability, thus allowing them to resort to technology to overcome the problem. At the same time, they resist the way in which the medical world transforms their whole life into a problem of infertility. Her interviews with hundreds of infertile people in the United States reveal that the majority question the claims made for the technologies and how they are put into practice; in fact, patients become "vigilantes" as they act out their ideals of informed choice and autonomy.

Becker concludes, as does Thompson, that most couples undergoing assisted reproduction strive to achieve what they think of as normalcy – the ideal of a hetero-sexual family as the reproductive unit, and Ellen Lewin has shown how lesbian couples also fulfill these ideals to a degree.[63] Lewin points out that when lesbians make use of ART technologies, they in effect disengage sexuality from procreation, as is indeed the case for all ART conceptions; but in the case of a lesbian couple, if a child is born, then the usual assumption that gay couples cannot contribute to family forma-tion breaks down. Following interviews with lesbian mothers, Lewin concludes that many lesbians resort to ARTs in order to strengthen a feminine identity that they value, and such claims are further reinforced by formalized marriage that serves to accommodate normative ideas about kinship and reproduction. Extended family members may be invited to the weddings of lesbians with the intent of fostering integration of the couple into a wider family and community that is not exclusively gay. Lewin, Thompson, and Becker all come to similar conclusions. As Becker puts it: "technology as a template of culture is one arena in which normalcy is both resisted and reaffirmed and through which the enactment and transformation of cultural practice occurs."[64] This is particularly so with ART technologies and applies equally to the use of this technology outside of North America.

Assisted Reproduction in Egypt

For nearly two decades Marcia Inhorn has worked on the topic of infertility in Egypt and elsewhere in the Middle East. As a result she has been able to carefully track the repercussions of the introduction of new IVF technologies[65] over the years into the clinics that cater to middle- and upper-class infertile couples living in this part of the world. Her basic point has remained the same during this time, namely, in marked contrast to North America and Europe, the lives of infertile patients in IVF clinics in Egypt, and more generally in the Middle East, are very often marked by stigma, silence, and suffering. Moreover, Inhorn notes that this suffering is rarely compre-hended in the West because of the widespread assumption that in the "less developed world" overpopulation is a problem that must at all costs be combated. Although today IVF centers flourish in most urban capitals of the Middle East, as Inhorn points out, "the reproductive technologies themselves – representing for the infertile, the potential bounty of globalization – are often either inaccessible or unhelpful in over-coming intractable infertility."[66]

Inhorn's ethnography highlights the way in which local use of reproductive tech-nologies in Egypt is put into practice in light of culturally informed values and structural and economic forces. Reciprocally, she argues, the IVF clinics refashion local culture in various ways. For example, the notion of women producing "eggs" for *in vitro* fertilization is rejected in Egypt and, further, Sunni Islamic prohibitions exist in connection with the use of third-party donation (of sperm, eggs, embryos, or uteruses). Such prohibitions are common elsewhere, of course, but in Egypt reli-gion and government work closely in tandem to uphold these prohibitions. There are further differences with practices common in the West, among them, local short-ages of hormonal medications leading to "suitcase trading" of IVF pharmaceuticals across borders. Severe moral stigma associated with the use of IVF also exists, with the result that few if any support groups exist, and many involved couples keep their activities secret from extended family and friends. Inhorn documents how, increasingly, wealthy Egyptians become part of a transnational flow of medical migrants in search of relief from infertility, often motivated by the belief that they will get better medical care in the West. Some have one or two trials at IVF in Egypt, but plan to go abroad for a third round if necessary. Others go directly to clinics in Europe and America, but some return having had one or more unsuccessful trials and then try again in Egypt. A few women Inhorn interviewed had spent up to $30,000 to try to get pregnant. A single trial in Egypt, where prices are considerably cheaper than in the U.S., can run to about $1,700.

Inhorn uses empirical data to illustrate eight "constraints" in the practice of IVF in Egypt that graphically demonstrate the consequences, often unintended, of the global transfer of this particular technology. The first constraint is that of class. IVF clinics, by far the majority of them private, are inaccessible for the majority of Egyptian couples, thus exemplifying what Ginsberg and Rapp have described as the "euphemized violence of stratified reproduction."[67] This is also the case elsewhere in the world, but in Egypt it is estimated that about half of the population now live in dire poverty or on the margins of poverty, and many people designated as middle class also cannot afford IVF, or at best only one round of it. Furthermore, although a few well-off women attending IVF clinics in Cairo felt sorry for those who could not afford treatment, many others hinted strongly that poor women do not deserve to become mothers.[68] In a country where motherhood is, as Inhorn puts it, "cultur-ally compulsory," such sentiments are particularly crass and stigmatizing.

A second constraint arises as a result of a lack of knowledge or understanding about what exactly is involved with IVF, a constraint that inevitably affects the poor and non-literate population of Egypt more than those people who have had formal education. A major difficulty is that among many Egyptians local knowledge has it that procreation is "monogenetic," a term first used by Carol Delaney with reference to her work in Turkey.[69] The belief is that men, and men alone, bring life into the world, making them the only true blood relatives of their offspring, resulting in what is commonly called "patrilineal kinship." The assumption is that preformed fetuses are present in sperm, and that the woman's role in procreation is simply one of nur-turance of the homunculus once it is transferred to her body. Inhorn notes that when British and French medical practitioners arrived in Egypt in the early 19th century as part of colonization they may well have reinforced the theory of homunculism because many of them too supported this theory, and it was not until the mid–19th century that the function of the sperm and ovum were better understood in European medicine.

Gradually, recognition of the indispensable genetic role played by the egg has gained ground but, even so, discourse about infertility among non-literate Egyptians tends to lay blame on the woman because she is thought not to be receptive to her partner's sperm. Men may well have "sperm weakness" at times, but even when this is acknowledged, it is usually assumed that the woman's contribution to infertility is less tractable than that of men. Inhorn found that people undergoing IVF treatment in clinics in Egypt are virtually all literate, and they have internalized with considerable accuracy the scientific account of human reproduction, and therefore have overcome this particular constraint that leads so many couples to eschew this technology. She also notes that both the media and key Islamic leaders have given public support to IVF, although they also point out how such technologies can be abused, and what transpires in laboratories also worries many Egyptians. Certain men are particularly concerned because they believe that their "weak" sperm may be mixed with that of other men, with the result that if a child is born it will be the product of adultery.

The third constraint is that of religion. A relevant fatwa explains clearly what is acceptable and what is forbidden with respect to IVF. Most importantly, in Sunni Islam no third party may be involved in donation of eggs, sperm, or embryos, or be made use of as a surrogate uterus. Recently Shi'a Islam has permitted some modifications to this law. Inhorn argues strongly for a growing influence of religion in Egypt in connection with the use of IVF among not only Muslims but also Copts. Many people whom she interviewed regarded donation of sperm and ova as outright immoral, and a form of adultery.[70] They worried about the possibility of incest being committed, even if entirely unknowingly, because a "child of sin" would never be accepted by its social father. Given that adoption is also prohibited in Egypt, this leaves many people who cannot afford IVF in a dismal position. Even so, a good number of individuals in discussion with Inhorn compared the United States unfavorably with their own country where they believe morals remain important.[71] However, it is also clear that some desperate Sunni Muslims are now traveling to Iran and elsewhere to get treatment from Shi'ite Muslim doctors who are willing to use donated gametes if this proves necessary. For the majority, religion continues to act as a major constraint, with the result that the normative patriarchal family with a "pure" lineage is the only family than can be reproduced in IVF clinics.

Medical practitioners and their skills are the fourth constraint discussed by Inhorn. The three founders of IVF in Egypt comment on poor quality control in many centers, as well as arrogance on the part of doctors who are not sufficiently concerned about their patients. These founder doctors are critical of the expense involved in setting up private clinics with imported technology and of the overall shift toward private health care in Egypt. They argue that public health care should be much better supported and that money would be better spent on primary prevention of infertility.[72] Despite claims to success and a discourse that "sells hope," the success rate in Egyptian IVF clinics is poor, making for yet another constraint on this technology. Between 70 and 80 percent of patients in the clinics never become pregnant, and the "take home baby rate" in Inhorn's study was 7 out of 77 trials (including repeat trials). Inhorn describes how success rates are deliberately inflated in many clinics, and she explains that this is possible because a uniform standard for calculating success rates has not yet been established in Egypt.[73]

In a discussion about the sixth constraint, that of gender, Inhorn points out that infertility in an Egyptian man results in a form of "double emasculation" because it strips him of "both his masculinity and his patriarchal power."[74] Men in Inhorn's study respond in a variety of ways to this identity crisis: denial, avoidance of diagnosis and treatment, or overt or covert wife-blaming. Others become resigned to what is assumed to be God's will. Alternatively, an endless quest for treatments can be undertaken with a wife who, as she approaches 40, becomes an increasingly bad candidate for IVF. Another way of dealing with the matter is to take a new, fecund wife and resort to intra cytoplasmic sperm injection (ICSI) technology to assist "weak" sperm. ICSI, with relatively high success rates, represents a revolution in the treatment of infertile men in Egypt, but it can be a catastrophe for aging first wives who face divorce. Gender, then, becomes yet another a constraint, and ICSI is at once "a blessing and a curse."

Inhorn found that stigma and the fear of stigma presented an enormous difficulty for many families, in particular about what to tell their child or children. One woman said to Inhorn:

> I will not tell my baby he is from ICSI when he grows up. I wouldn't like it at all to tell him that I and my husband had to do something which is not the "natural pregnancy way." It might affect his psychology ... The children around might give him a psychological complex.[75]

Another source of stigma is that IVF is itself a questionable technology – one associated with illicit sex, illegitimate offspring, and enduring sin. Hence many couples resort to elaborate cover-ups, even with close family members, making for a seventh constraint to the use of IVF.

The final constraint Inhorn discusses is named by her "embodiment." She describes the "tortured body history" of many of the women who end up in IVF clinics, very often after years of futile searching for a successful treatment for infertility. Even when infertility is diagnosed as due to the male partner, the woman must "put herself on the line" and go through hormone stimulation treatment if she is to attain a pregnancy. Among the 66 couples that Inhorn interviewed, nearly three quarters of the husbands suffered from infertility, and in nearly half the cases they proved to be the sole cause of infertility for the couple. In Egyptian ICSI centers the range of male infertility is commonly between 70 and 75 percent, but the underlying causes of most cases are unknown.

One laboratory director with whom Inhorn talked suggested that the semen samples of many men coming to the clinic had apparently deteriorated over the previous years to levels that are considered not acceptable for IVF treatments.[76] Clearly the most intractable cases of male infertility appear in clinics where ICSI is being used, but it is not known why male infertility is so widespread and apparently on the increase. Theories abound, including environmental pollution, especially DDT; occupational exposures to arsenic, lead, and other heavy metals and pesticides;

"ambient lead pollution" – a recognized problem in many cities of the Middle East, and lifestyle factors including heavy smoking and caffeine consumption. Various other medically related factors are also associated with male infertility in Egypt, including high levels of diabetes, sexually transmitted infections, schistosomiasis, and the adverse effects of mumps on the testes among individuals who have never been vaccinated. Inhorn suggests that this situation should be thought of as a manifestation of local biology. Notably, many of these variables are reminiscent of those commonly associated with increased rates of kidney failure in Egypt discussed in chapter 9. Whatever the cause or causes turn out to be, it is clear that a standardized biomedical explanation about low sperm counts and poor sperm motility is not adequate to address the troubling question of high prevalence of male infertility that appears to be on the increase.

When Egyptian men present themselves to IVF clinics for treatment, they are subjected to hormone treatments, in the same way as are women, very often with devastating side effects.[77] Several of the men interviewed by Inhorn showed the signs of flabbiness, pudginess, and weight gain associated with this kind of treatment – medication that many had been willingly taking for years even though they come to believe that it is useless. Paradoxically, these men are emasculated in the name of bringing about virility. Thus both men and women in IVF clinics live with tragic bodily histories.

It is evident that Thompson's four key elements associated with ART clinics – normalization, gender, naturalization and socialization, and agency – are to a degree relevant, although they are realized in entirely different ways in a resource-poor country such as Egypt where family dynamics, religious-based values, and class structure differ greatly from those of the United States. The physical histories of individuals in Egypt, including frequent exposure to infectious and parasitic disease, toxic environments, lack of consistent vaccination programs, and the inadequate, even iatrogenic treatment that people receive quite often in badly run IVF clinics, add another dimension to the story, making it clear that infertility is embedded in local histories and economies. The condition of infertility is ubiquitous, but it is nevertheless virtually ignored by the medical worlds in sub-Saharan Africa for two reasons: a lack of medical resources and a belief that excessive reproduction is a chronic problem. In contrast, virtually everywhere else, those who can afford it are actively encouraged to seek out treatment, although with very different outcomes depending on where they obtain medical care. We turn now to another case that highlights how politics are deeply implicated in ART use.

Assisted Reproduction in Israel

Susan Kahn, an American anthropologist, opens her book *Reproducing Jews*, about the use of ARTs in Israel, with an anecdote that is in striking contrast to the situation in Egypt and very many other parts of the world:

> A Jewish baby is born to a woman on the outskirts of Jerusalem. The baby is healthy, the mother is happy, guests bring gifts, and the child is welcomed into the world. The birth is remarkable because the mother conceived the child without having sexual intercourse and the baby has no identifiable father.[78]

Kahn points out that such births occur regularly in Israel "as part of a small but growing trend among unmarried Jewish women who give birth to children they have conceived with anonymous Jewish donor sperm."[79] She goes on to explain that an unusual confluence of social, legal, and rabbinic forces has enabled the birth of these children. Many Israelis, including unmarried but fertile women, have actively embraced new reproductive technologies as an acceptable path to pregnancy. The Israeli medical community has given full support to the use of these technologies and its researchers are world leaders in the field; Israeli legislators have drafted regulations to provide broad-based access to the technologies. Orthodox rabbis have ensured that resort to them is commensurate with traditional understanding of Jewishness and relatedness that includes unmarried Jewish women who have ready access to the technologies in order to become pregnant. As a result of ART use a new conceptual space has been created in Israel in which ideas about both a normative family and the Jewish collectivity are undergoing a radical transformation.[80] But this space has historical precedent, in that an imperative for Jewish women to reproduce has been reinforced by various state policies since the 1950s.

Israel has more fertility clinics per capita than any other country in the world. and they attract patients from all over the Middle East and Europe. Further, in marked contrast to virtually all other countries, these new reproductive technologies, including those involving third-party donation, are subsidized by the Israeli health insurance plan. In theory, until two live children have been born, every Israeli can have access to unlimited rounds of infertility treatment. Furthermore, Israel was the first country in the world to legally recognize surrogacy treatments. Recognition of a full range of ART services is in striking contrast to the fact that family planning facilities in Israel do not receive state support, and are funded only on a charitable basis. Moreover, contraception is not provided as part of basic health care services and abortion, although legal, is only exceptionally subsidized.

Kahn describes Israel as a deeply pronatalist society, one with an "overwhelming desire to produce Jewish babies, a place where a barren woman is an archetype of suffering."[81] She argues that childlessness is regarded as tragic not only for Jewish women, but for Jewish men who are commanded to procreate according to Jewish law. However, it is not difficult to detect that there are other imperatives at work as well, among them, that certain people believe that they must counter what is perceived to be a demographic threat as a result of Palestinian and Arab birth rates. Other influences focus on the necessity of producing soldiers (of both sexes) to defend the state, while yet others think that the horrific loss of six million Jews in the Holocaust must be compensated. Kahn notes the complex social divisions among Israeli Jews that cut across Jewish ethnicity, religious affiliation, and class background, so that responses to ART are not of one kind, and she attends to these differences in writing her ethnography.

On the basis of her ethnographic findings, Kahn argues, contrary to many other researchers reporting about ARTs, that use of these technologies does not necessarily mean that biogenetic relatedness takes on overwhelming importance, as it appears to in Egypt, for example, thus diminishing other socially based forms of kin-making. Quite the contrary, in Israel ART use has resulted in new, diverse, and legally recognized ways of creating relatedness, and this has come about because the government, in contrast to very many other countries, freely permits third-party involvement in conception. Kahn's research focuses on unmarried women who are heterosexual (many cohabiting with male partners) as well as lesbians and divorcees. She notes that a high proportion of these women are former immigrants from the Soviet Union. All such unmarried women, once they have a child, receive good social support, including subsidized housing and tax exemptions. But Kahn also stresses that these women do not think of themselves as consumers picking out goods from the reproductive marketplace; rather their consent to artificial insemination suggests that they understand themselves to be participating in a "communal process of reproduction and they make every effort to integrate the children they bear into existing family networks."[82]

The unmarried but fertile women with whom Kahn talks make it clear that for them artificial insemination is the best way to become pregnant. This method is regarded as clean, safe, efficient, and honest (because "a mother can tell the child the truth: he does not have a father").[83] Clinic staff are very supportive of unmarried women and reject candidates only when they detect what they believe to be major psychological problems. In theory, women can choose among sperm donors only with respect to whether they are Ashkenazi or Sephardi Jews, and whether the donor has dark or light skin – thus perpetuating a distinction among Jews of European and North African origin. Sperm are routinely screened for HIV and for Tay-Sachs genes. Children born from this standardized artificial insemination procedure are regarded by all concerned, including the state, as "ours," and rather than being considered as products of individual choice, the children are automatically thought of as belonging to a family. But Kahn's ethnography makes it clear that some mothers are troubled when their child confronts them with the question of who is their father, although others show few signs of worry: "I'm going to tell him that I really wanted a baby, so I went to the clinic, where a very generous man gave his sperm specially so I could have him."[84]

A striking finding by Kahn is that statistics about procreation success rates are not available either at the clinics or elsewhere. Doctors quietly justify this by stating that they do not want to attract conservative rabbinical attention to their practices, particularly because a few patients are religiously observant women. Several features of the clinics are notable, one being the "kosher conditions" that are created in tending to infertile orthodox Jews. Another is the close links established between fertility specialists and moderate rabbis; rabbinical provisos and concerns about ART use are translated into medical language equivalents thereby ensuring that "rabbinic theory turns into medical practice."[85] It comes as a surprise to learn that at times even gentile sperm are made use of in the clinics.

Many rabbis follow the reasoning that adultery takes place when forbidden sexual relations take place, but argue that the creation of a conceptus cannot be adultery. In order to justify this position they draw on a widely circulated myth about a maiden in a bathtub who becomes pregnant because a man had discharged semen into the bath. The woman remains a virgin even though sperm enters her womb. By analogy, because sexual intercourse has not actually taken place in ART procedures, introduction of semen from a man who is not married to the woman undergoing treatment is not adulterous. Not surprisingly, some rabbis dissent strongly from this position.

The use of non-Jewish sperm also incites rabbinical arguments. Masturbation is not permitted according to Halakhic principles; however, in cases of severe male sexual dysfunction a donor is required if conception is to take place, and masturbation is the only method of obtaining sperm. Resort to non-Jewish sperm overcomes this religious prohibition and, if a child is born, because Jewishness is conferred matrilineally, the child will be both a Jew and an Israeli citizen. Non-Jewish sperm has a particular value because it assists with procreation but does not "produce." In other words, a gentile has no paternity claim of any kind over the child. Even so, for some rabbi such sperm is understood as polluting Jewish kinship, and should not be used. Kahn uses her interviews with rabbis to demonstrate how symbolic meaning is ascribed to bodily substance in their imaginations, and she succeeds in making it clear just how flexible and debatable such meanings can be among the religious experts.[86] Israeli sperm banks also exhibit this flexibility. Europeans, many of whom have been volunteers in kibbutzim – including some Germans – are in the majority as donors to some banks. Other banks import frozen sperm from the United States. However, some banks will not accept Palestinian donations claiming there is no demand for such sperm, while in other banks donors of all denominations are accepted, including Muslims.

Kahn carried out research in connection with ovum transfer in a clinic attended almost exclusively by ultra-orthodox Jews and religious Muslims, although some secular Jews and Christian Palestinians were also patients. Use of egg donation also poses a challenge to Halakhic principles. If an egg is to be removed from one woman's womb and transferred to another woman then normative ideas about motherhood are severely tested. Is maternity located in the genetic substance of the egg, the gestational environment of the womb, or perhaps in both? Rabbis take one of three positions on this matter. Some argue that maternity is established at birth, and therefore whoever carries the child to term is the mother; others argue that the child should be understood to have two mothers; and yet others insist that such a child has no mother at all.[87] Kahn points out that rabbinic disagreements about the status of the mother in connection with ovum donation have "not slowed the rush to create regulations that legislate the appropriate uses of ovum donation. Nor have these disagreements and Halakhic ambiguities prevented Israeli Jews, religious and secular, from using the eggs of non-Jewish women to create Jewish babies."[88] Kahn cites one disagreement among a group of rabbis who argue that a child born of a non-Jewish egg simply needs to be converted to "sanctify the people of Israel."[89] It is illegal in Israel for women to sell eggs, and so the only sources of ova for infertile women are "spare" eggs, that is, those eggs "left over" once a couple has conceived. Women involved in infertility treatment are routinely asked if they will donate eggs, and this includes women from Turkey, Europe, the United States and elsewhere who have been patients in Israeli clinics.

A prominent Jerusalem lawyer informed Kahn that the "critical shortage of ova" is one reason why unmarried women – whether single, divorced, or widowed – are encouraged to make use of the services of infertility clinics, but they can only do so on the understanding that they will donate "spare eggs."[90] Kahn points out that according to rabbinical thinking, formerly married women can freely donate ova because, no longer being in a marital union, there will be no adulterous union of egg and sperm. She concludes that technologies involving ovum donation bring fundamental questions of kinship into sharp relief, including "where do mothers come from?" In the case of Israel this inevitably raises a second question: "where does Jewish identity, the primary substance of Israeli kinship come from?" Is this identity embedded in bodily substance? Or is it created in the gestational environment? Furthermore, can the incorporation of non-Jewish gametes into Jewish bodies change the meaning of what it is to be an Israeli?[91]

Unmarried women are the only people legally allowed to become surrogate mothers in Israel, but the practice is shielded from media exposure after reports about a "rent-a-womb" enterprise caused a stir. Surrogate mothers in Israel are most often women in tight economic straits who frequently have children of their own whom they are desperate to feed and raise as well as possible. A divorced woman puts it as follows:

> My first motivation was financial; I have to worry about the future of my children, I want to give them a good education and a warm home, and I don't have the means … after I met Tova (the contracting mother), I immediately agreed. Afterward we became friends and now I'm doing it with all my heart.[92]

Kahn found that unmarried women who are recruited as surrogate mothers and those who make use of infertility clinics to become pregnant could be differentiated in Israel according to their economic situation. This is the case in most countries where the practice of surrogacy is allowed. However, in Israel, in addition, it is the case that unmarried women, regardless of their income, are actively encouraged by the state to assist in the reproduction of Jews and therefore of Jewish citizens. Kahn concludes that "the advent of new reproductive technologies, and the attendant fragmentation of maternity into commodifiable components" may well shortly lead to major legal battles that will "pit orthodox rabbis and possibly some feminists against secular lawyers in a drama over conflicting ideologies of the origins of relatedness."[93] Meantime, what is being accomplished in IVF clinics is the political or religious reproduction of legitimate Israeli citizens whose existence depends upon the unfolding of a complex, internally contradictory discourse about what will count as bona fide reproduction in the absence of sexual intercourse.

ART in Global Perspective

Each of the extended cases cited above about infertility clinics in the United States, Egypt, and Israel reveals in no uncertain terms how "natural facts" are reproduced by means of the technological conjoining of human gametes. This is carried out with the objective of producing offspring who are legally recognized, and who are products of neither incestuous nor adulterous relationships, in whatever ways these are locally defined. The sociotechnical networks that permit these activities are inevitably constrained by the human gametes and human organs that they are designed to manipulate.[94] However, within these constraints there remains a large degree of flexibility for discursive interpretation, both professional and popular, as well as medical, political, religious, and legal maneuvering about how gametes should be used and how gestation can and should be brought about. Much of this jockeying revolves around local normative understanding about the relationship among symbolically loaded sex gametes, the act of procreation, and the constitution of parental kin and kin relations.

Research from other parts of the world affirms that stratified reproduction is, almost without exception, associated with ARTs wherever they are put into use. Economically deprived women simply do not have access to these technologies except as egg donors or surrogate mothers, and they are subject to exploitation because they are willing to make use of their bodies in order to improve their lot and that of their children. It is quite possible, as Kahn's work suggests, that at times positive connections are made across class differences, but what little work has been done on this topic indicates that this is unusual.

The ontological choreography described by Thompson in American ART clinics cannot be readily transposed to clinics everywhere, even though the basic technologically facilitated practices are essentially the same. In contrast to both Israel and the United States, the majority of non-Western countries ensure continued "normalcy" in family life by means of highly regulated government control of ARTs. In Japan, for example, a country with a history of several hundred years of a "planned family,"[95] the implementation of reproductive technologies, carried out under government-enforced medical guidelines, shows continuities with the past, and only reproduction of what is understood as the "natural" biological family is permitted in ART clinics. Use of surrogate mothers and sperm donors is prohibited except under very exceptional circumstances when close "biological relatives" are usually made use of as substitutes. Formerly, adoption, usually of grown children or young adults, was common in Japan, often undertaken to economically benefit the family enterprise. Today, adoption, whether of infants or older children, is unusual, and many women claim that such a practice smacks of the not-so-distant past when the samurai class kept mistresses and formally adopted children from these unions into their households and family lines.[96]

Liza Handwerker's research on ART use in China demonstrates that, despite the draconian restrictions of the one child per family policy, middle-class women who find they are infertile turn to both traditional Chinese medicine and technologically assisted reproduction if they can afford it. As noted in chapter 5, stigma associated with infertility persists, even when population reduction is of overriding government concern. Government surveillance of female fertility has been achieved over the years through the charting of menstrual cycles by health care workers, distribution of free contraceptives, and tracking pregnancies. Paradoxically, this technology of normalization has made visible those women who are childless and presumably infertile. Handwerker cites one of the 100 interviews she completed on the subject in the early 1990s:

> I am sure the pressure to have children is greater than in any other country. I especially feel a lot of pressure from my work unit ... I feel so much pressure because of the mandatory birth certificate which provides me with permission to have a child. I have had to turn in my certificate the last three years because I couldn't have a child. I felt terrible ... they give you permission and then you can't even give birth. I feel so humiliated to have to get a new certificate each year.[97]

Doctors in China justify the use of aggressive measures to assist infertile women for humanitarian and scientific reasons. These medical specialists perceive that they are fulfilling a social need. While some are in the business to make a profit, others argue that the reason they offer these services is to ensure the continuity of the patrilineal line, thus releasing women from being held culpable for failing in their duty.[98] Surrogacy and gamete donation is also made use of to a limited extent in China, with only small rewards for the donors.[99]

In Sri Lanka, Bob Simpson found that the enthusiastic embrace of things Western, including ART, concealed an undercurrent about concerns for "traditional" kinship values.[100] Simpson recounts how doctors and the general population alike are keen to highlight the role that local understanding of kinship plays in the uses to which ART is put. The practice of polyandry (two brothers sharing one wife), was common in Sri Lanka, formerly Ceylon. This practice, outlawed in the mid–19th century, continued in some parts of the country for another hundred years. Polyandry is associated with fraternal solidarity and also with the frugal management of land, and traces of that sentiment persist.

When family solidarity and continuity could not be achieved in any other way, adoption between families was formerly common in Sri Lanka. Today the passing of gametes and embryos among extended family members attending ART clinics is understood as an "adoptive process," hence use of donor sperm is not regarded as ethically problematic except among some Christian patients. On the contrary, several of the people with whom Simpson talked suggested that intra-family donation would in all likelihood minimize jealousy and anxiety on the part of the husband, whereas anonymous donation might be considerably more problematic.

The link between a desire for intra-familial sperm donation and the vestiges of polyandry suggests to some people involved with ART in Sri Lanka that this is a culturally appropriate way to deal with these technologies, particularly at a time of declining fertility rates. Simpson concludes: "In short, the new technologies are given overwhelming endorsement in contemporary Sri Lankan society, not simply because they address the personal tragedy of involuntary childlessness, but because they carry a collective and much weightier symbolic load."[101] These technologies help to make a brighter future for Sri Lanka at a time of ongoing violence in which so many young people lose their lives.

Similarly to Simpson's research, that of Aditya Bharadwaj considers how in India clinicians and infertile consumers assimilate the techno-science of conception developed by the former colonizing West.[102] Based on substantial ethnographic work in India's five major cities, Bharadwaj's argument is that, once the "Western" science of conception is assimilated into the universe of the Hindu faith, it becomes evident to both local specialists and patients that this science of conception is incomplete. A "clinical theodicy" emerges, one in which practitioners actively draw on what is thought of as the "parallel sciences" of India that contain a great number of religious elements to assist in making sense of intractable infertility. This is in part accomplished by attempting to counter the uncertainties associated with causality, about why a specific patient is cursed with infertility. In biomedical clinics in the West such questions are simply not discussed in terms other than the material body itself. ARTs are not the only biomedical practice that is being "indigenized"[103] in India, and the new "science of conception" is part of an all-encompassing larger cultural process in which "[t]he so-called 'Western' and 'modern' emerge embedded in the traditional: a process that connects the imagined past to the present, and the present to an imagined future."[104]

Elizabeth Roberts reminds us that Catholicism is the only major religion in the world that has banned ARTs outright on the grounds that destruction of embryos is involved and also because humans are seen to be interfering with a process that should remain within God's dominion. In the implementation of these technologies in Ecuador, Roberts finds that involved medical professionals and basic scientists set themselves up against the Church by proclaiming in effect that they have the spiritual power to manipulate clinical outcomes in laboratories and clinics. Such practitioners consider themselves to be eminently modern scientists, but the introduction of spirituality into their practice is not regarded as anomalous. Roberts is quick to point out that the production of IVF babies in Ecuador is not in any way a religious-nationalistic project, and she argues that being a Catholic is more aptly characterized as a personal identity rather than an institutional or national affiliation. When Ecuadorian doctors include religious rituals in their practice – "when God is in the laboratory" – they are challenging the Catholic Church and not, as in India or some Muslim countries, demonstrating ambivalence about Western-derived biomedicine. The Ecuadorian practitioners are explicit that modernity is not always about the emergence of the secular and does not imply the total "banishment of enchantment from the realm of natural law."[105]

Although normalization is at work in ART practice everywhere, it is clear that cultural, religious, and political interests and values are implicated as powerful forces constituting and repetitively reinscribing what is normal, including that of gendered relations at local sites. Inevitably, ART practices make both motherhood and fatherhood partial, in that bodily substance and genes are technologically separated and, when third-party donors are involved, this separation persists beyond the moment of conception. Anthropological research has shown for a century or more that even though the act of sex and procreation could not literally be separated prior to technological intervention, separation of biological and social parenthood is highly valued in many societies in producing solidarity. As Rayna Rapp notes, nothing familiar is necessarily lost by turning to ARTs: "the challenges that scientific reason and practice might offer can, instead, be comfortably integrated into cosmological ways of knowing,"[106] and also, one might add, into the conduct of everyday life. However, because of their cost, these technologies inevitably reinscribe hierarchical differences within and among societies, and for the majority of individuals worldwide they are out of reach. For such people fostering and adoption remain as the only means to ensure some form of economic support and social security in old age.

Part IV
Elusive Agents and Moral Disruptions

manifestations easily be explained away as a kind of madness, as they might well strike people who otherwise appeared normal and led unremarkable lives.

Because these curious illnesses seemed to affect largely women, they were classified as "hysteria," a term adapted from the Greek word for uterus. Attending the lectures of the famous neurologist Charcot, in Paris, Freud was fascinated by Charcot's ability to trigger, and then stop, attacks of hysteria using hypnosis and other unconventional techniques. Returning to his neurological practice in Vienna, Freud treated his hysterical patients using the new techniques, and gradually came to believe that the symptoms were the result of painful memories that had been repressed and forgotten. As the anthropologist Allan Young summarizes:

> As far back as we know, people have been tormented by memories that filled them with feelings of sadness and remorse, the sense of irreparable loss, and sensations of fright and horror. During the 19th century, a new kind of painful memory emerged. It was unlike the memories of earlier times in that it originated in a previously unidentified psychological state, called "traumatic," and was linked to previously unknown kinds of forgetting, called "repression" and "dissociation."[8]

Young goes on: "This new conception was based on the idea that intensely frightening or disturbing experiences could produce memories that are concealed in automatic behaviors, repetitive acts over which the affected person exercised no conscious control."[9]

Unlocking the Pathogenic Secret

Freud discovered the key to unlocking these hidden memories. With his patients lying on a couch facing away from him, he encouraged them to speak whatever came to mind, a technique he called "free association," and tell him their dreams. Freud discovered that skilful listening was a valuable tool, giving clues that could be used to probe the patient and allow painful memories of past events to emerge. Such memories had remained unconscious – too painful to remember; they had been repressed only to re-emerge as the mysterious symptoms that Freud sought to treat. Free association and dream recall loosened the mechanisms that had kept these secrets under lock and key, tricking the mind to reveal its secrets by diverting consciousness elsewhere.

Freud came to realize that even though the strange symptoms of hysteria had no anatomical-pathological explanation, they had a basis for the patient through their symbolic link to the pathogenic event. Freud believed that everyone suffers from primordial conflicts relating to the infantile processes of individuation; that apparently innocuous events could trigger symptoms and these symptoms were traces of earlier traumatic events that had been repressed but that could nevertheless resurface in fragmentary or symbolic form as the symptoms. Linking the symptoms and the patient's narrative required careful analysis and interpretation and, importantly, being able to find the clues in the emotions the patient projected onto the invisible therapist sitting behind her, emotions that often mirrored the structure and force of previous

\ships. Debilitating pain on swallowing could be the trace of a childhood insult
"difficult to swallow," or a girl's chronic nervous cough might be the residue
 traumatic sexual encounter. The "transference" of ways of relating with significant others onto the therapist provided a powerful mechanism by which the therapist
might come to understand the patient.

Freud developed the technique of psychoanalysis in his clinical practice but also
on himself, analyzing his own dreams and interpreting them through rigorous introspection. Gradually, he realized his own reactions to a patient were an important
guide to understanding the significance of the patient's words, and that it was as
important to analyze his reaction to the patient as the patient herself. The analyst's
response to the patient was termed "counter-transference," and understanding it
required that the therapist be able to analyze his counter-transference in terms of his
own past and the difficult issues it raised. The psychoanalyst therefore would himself
have to be psychoanalyzed initially in order that he gain the self-awareness and skills
to listen, with a "third ear," to both his inner world and the patient lying on the
couch beside him.

The Pathogenic Secret as a Technology of the Self

The Freudian account of the self and how it might be known defined therapeutic
practice for a wide variety of afflictions. The legacy of Freud is visible in the vast
family of diagnostic and therapeutic practices that can be glossed under the label
of "psychotherapy" and that seek to treat patients by linking present suffering with
past experiences. These experiences – events or ideas that have been repressed
beyond consciousness – are assumed to be at the origin of symptoms that result in
disabling pathology and have therefore been described as "pathogenic secrets."[10]
Notably, it is not the event itself that is thought to be pathological, but the way it
is managed by the mind. The "talking cure" of psychotherapy requires a particular
kind of dialogue between patient and therapist that seeks to recover painful memories and mobilize emotional and intellectual awareness. This is done through the
application of what can be called "technologies of the pathogenic secret," that range
from Freud's classical "free association" on the couch and the interpretation of
dreams to more pragmatic approaches for eliciting narratives and analyzing their
meaning.

The language of psychotherapy is today so commonplace that it has entered the
vernacular of Western societies and everyday understanding as "Freudian slips,"
repressed memories, "neurotic" behavior, and so on. The popularization of these
Freudian concepts would likely have made Freud shudder, because the psychological
common-sense they express runs counter to the psychoanalytic approach that suspects
common-sense and "just-so" stories of hiding a deeper, more painful truth. Freud,
and the psychotherapeutic techniques that have proliferated in his wake, incite individuals to talk, and more importantly to remember, directing therapeutic action to
release pathogenic secrets. As painful memories are coaxed into consciousness and
spun into words, patients come to experience themselves in specific ways, as subjects
of an Unconscious from under whose sway, without expert intervention, it is
not possible to emerge. Psychotherapeutic techniques constitute a broad family of

price to be paid (letting perpetrators go free) is small compared to the greater good that is achieved: reconciliation and collective healing.

Writing about South Africa's Truth and Reconciliation Commission (TRC), historian Deborah Posel notes how the therapeutic disclosure of painful memories was transformed into a public confessional:

> the public declaration, acknowledgment, and scrutiny of some sort of inner damage – whether pain, trauma, or guilt – regulated by the listening and questioning role of those experts to whom the confession was made, and with the offer of some sort of transcendence. The pervasiveness of this confessional impulse throughout the TRC's hearings derived directly from the fundamental ethical premise of the national reconciliation process.

This premise was, she explains, that:

> in the aftermath of apartheid, therefore, all were damaged; there could be no position of absolute moral purity or innocence. Nor was victimhood a position of passivity; the damage could be repaired, not as a matter of external reparation alone, but also – indeed, primarily – through the interior work of rehabilitation, rooted in the act of speaking out and in the capacity for compassion for those responsible for the suffering. The TRC's public hearings performed this mutuality of damage, and hence the shared need to be healed. When victims wept in the retelling of past traumas, or their mothers telling their stories wept, the message to the TRC's audience was that these victims needed healing too, as did the perpetrators of horrendous acts of brutalization.[14]

The technology of the pathogenic secret, then, enabled a "performed mutuality of respect, compassion, and dignity" which was as much about healing the self as healing a divided nation, in the process blurring the boundary between self and collectivity. Posel's account of the TRC is another example of how the linkage between trauma, confession, and healing making use of the concept of the pathogenic secret may be used as a moral leveler, this time outside the clinical encounter.

The Practitioner-Self

We have seen how Freud's concept of counter-transference allowed the development of a therapeutic expertise anchored by the practitioner's self-awareness, and the corresponding ability of the therapist to "read" her own reactions to the patient to tailor her treatment. The concept of counter-transference and the way it is used in practice make the self of the therapist available as an instrument for diagnosing and calibrating intervention in the therapeutic encounter. Counter-transference is the most explicit example of how mastery of biomedical technologies requires self-fashioning by the practitioner, underlining how biomedical technologies of the self transform both the patient and practitioner.

Careful training of the practitioner-self has not been limited to psychotherapists, however, and in the latter half of the 20th century it came to be standardized in the teaching of biomedical practitioners in order to impart diagnostic and therapeutic skills applicable to all biomedical conditions. The skills required to dissect cadavers and perform surgery, interpret microscopic images, or interview patients, to name a few, require practitioners to mobilize their own embodied experience to learn how to "feel" their way around a patient's body or narrative and "see" patterns meaningful for diagnosis and treatment. Byron Good's ethnography of medical students at Harvard University shows how "the first two years of medical education provide a powerful interpretation of reality, anchored in the experience of the student,"[15] and illuminates how the self must be transformed in order to make biomedical techniques "work." Good notes evidence of this transformation:

> One of the most shocking moments in anatomy lab was the day we entered to find the body prepared for dissecting the genitalia, the body sawn in half above the waist, then bisected between the legs. Students described their shock not at close examination of the genitalia, nor simply at the body being taken apart, but rather at the dismemberment, and a dismemberment that crossed natural boundaries. Dissection follows planes of tissue. Here the plane that cut the body was straight and hard, cutting across natural layers of tissue in an unnatural fashion. The majority of the time is spent trying to separate natural surfaces, to distinguish the boundaries of gross forms to identify tiny nerves, veins, lymph glands, and to match these to the anatomical atlas.[16]

Stefan Hirschauer vividly describes how the skills first imparted in the anatomy lab of the medical school come to be embodied in the surgeon:

> hands remain the most important instruments for viewing. Bare hands can, for example, make something out and then stretch some tissue to make it more transparent, or they identify nerves by way of their tensile strength. "Blunt" dissection involves stretching, tearing or shifting tissue with one's fingers, during "sharp" dissection hands serve as holders for the scalpel, scissors or the electric cauterizer. Vessels, skin, tissue and bones are tackled differently depending on the way in which they resist: the skin is treated with the scalpel, the yellow layer of fat and the peritoneum with scissors, muscles with the cauterizer ... dissection, which is the precision work of making objects visible, is at the same time classifying work.[17]

That "becoming a doctor" – or therapist or nurse – is a transformative experience for those who undergo it has been a common theme of literature, film, and autobiographical works. Most of this literature focuses on the limits to empathy, the human dramas, the ethical dilemmas, and the personal trials that result when a (usually) young and naïve practitioner is exposed to the suffering of patients and the cynicism of hardened colleagues. Good, Hirschauer, and others demonstrate a more subtle point. They clearly show how learning to master biomedical technologies and then using them requires self-mastery and the ability to "use" the self as an instrument.

The Sources of Therapeutic Efficacy

The therapeutic instrument of the (practitioner) self can only work once it is embedded in a specific context, or assemblage, that brings together clinicians and patients. The practice of biomedicine occurs in hospitals, universities, and clinics, supervised by regulatory bodies and accrediting authorities ultimately governed through legislation. Therapeutic power is most visible in how the practitioner asserts "control" over the patient. Critics of medicalization have attacked this form of domination that originates in political processes that designate who may practice medicine and accordingly decide which forms of embodied expertise are authorized to diagnose and treat in a given society. In addition to mastery of biomedical technologies therefore, practitioner-selfhood encompasses the political and social processes that confer therapeutic legitimacy. The power to heal is not only a result of individual prowess, but the social relations that accrue to those endowed with therapeutic authority. Indeed, these social relations may be as important as a practitioner's individual skills in the process of healing, if not more so.

In a moving account, Janice Boddy, an anthropologist working in the northern Sudan, recalls the death in the mid-1980s of her Sudanese friend. Amal was pregnant, but there were warning signs the pregnancy was not going well; Amal appeared ill and thin, and complained frequently of stomach pains. Yet she was refractory to the urgings of her husband and her anthropologist friend to see a physician in the next town: "she confided in me that she could not bear the thought of being examined by strangers, all of them men." Boddy adds:

> So we went for Miriam, the busy district midwife who questioned Amal and examined her eyes and mouth but was not alarmed. When the pains returned I suggested we call for Sheffa, the midwife from a neighboring district, who had impressed me with her cool professionalism and kindly, no-nonsense approach. Sheffa was a qualified nurse's aide – well beyond Miriam's achievements. She had a confidence Miriam lacked, and a bedside manner that would, I was sure, convince Amal to seek the medical help she clearly required. But the family objected that Miriam would take offense, placing their good relations with her, hence the welfare of all its women, in jeopardy. Midwives are powerful people; their prompt response can mean life rather than death for mothers and infants alike.[18]

Boddy left the Sudan shortly thereafter and, a few months later, Amal died. This poignant account encapsulates how therapeutic power is real – a matter of life and death – and how it flows from both biological and social efficacy, as Amal's family clearly recognized. Mastering biomedical technologies requires self-fashioning, but practitioner-selves, who can feel their way around the body, navigate the perils of obstructed labor, or, as we shall see next, shepherd a patient through a painful loss, draw their power from the social relations that recognize their efficacy.

The fact that, in most countries of the world, therapeutic legitimacy is largely restricted to biomedically trained practitioners reflects the hegemony of Western, "modern" biomedicine. Practitioners and patients have contested this therapeutic monopoly, and have advocated for recognition of other forms of healing, often subsumed under the categories of "alternative" or "traditional" medicine. While these efforts have incurred only modest success, a vibrant "parallel" therapeutic economy nonetheless exists everywhere, evidence that medical pluralism is alive and well today. Political disputes over who can heal are often framed in terms of efficacy and the supposed primacy of "biology." These are also disputes over which kinds of expertise are to be granted the social powers that come with official recognition and, we argue, about how the self may be mobilized to heal.

The Self's Therapeutic Powers

A staple of anthropology has been the study of exotic rituals such as spirit possession, shamanism, and various other forms of healing. Despite the temptation to focus on the "cultural" in these non-Western forms of healing, anthropologists have highlighted the role of the individual healer and demonstrated how therapeutic efficacy lies in the person of the healer as much as in collective belief. In 1949 Claude Lévi-Strauss suggested that shamanistic healing lay in "symbolic efficacy," that is, the ability of the shaman to offer a spectacle that was a re-enactment of his own illness and cure. Symbols can be effective in very powerful and real ways, Lévi-Strauss argued – much as placebos can cure, or collective beliefs can spawn "hysterical" epidemics. What is symbolic – or cultural – can also be biological, as Lévi-Strauss was at pains to point out.[19]

Luc de Heusch, in an essay first published in 1964, built on Lévi-Strauss's work to advance a typology of therapeutic action.[20] Drawing on ethnographic accounts, he argued that illness is a crisis that threatens both the afflicted individual and the social order, and that healing requires the transformation of self. Shamanism can be contrasted with spirit possession by the location of the handling of this crisis: in the former, it is the healer who becomes possessed while in the latter it is the patient. In the case of shamanism, the healer must be transformed in order to heal the patient, while in the cases of spirit possession it is the patient who must be dramatically transformed. Shamans heal those afflicted through passage to a spirit world in order to recover lost souls or placate offended spirits, while spirit possession can only be cured through the mediation of a healer able to negotiate directly with the offending spirit and so transform the self of the sufferer. We turn now to an ethnographic example to explore how the self is mobilized to heal in spirit possession.

Amongst those who claim Wolof or Lebou ancestry in Senegal, *rab* denotes ancestral spirits often held responsible for unexplained events, curious coincidences, and mysterious afflictions. Spirit possession, and other forms of supernatural illness causation are common the world over and have been extensively studied by anthropologists. Spirit possession in Senegal was studied in the 1960s by András Zempléni, a noted French anthropologist working with the Dakar School of Ethnopsychiatry described in chapter 6. Zempléni documented how afflictions attributable to spirit possession vary along a continuum. At one end, spirit possession is total: there is no more "self," only the spirit: these cases are evidenced by the birth of deformed children and serious illnesses that transform the body such as kwashiorkor, a serious form of malnutrition. A prescient child is evidence of a powerful spirit, that "amuses itself by dominating its little companion."[21] In most cases however, illness is caused by intermittent possession by the spirit, a state that requires active management by a healer, with the goal of accomplishing a *modus vivendi* with the possessing spirit who has "colonized" the self of the patient.

Therapeutic intervention (the *ndöp* ceremony) is multi-staged, culminating in the naming of the offending spirit and ritualized possession and initiation of the patient into a therapeutic order.[22] Importantly, a familial consensus around the nature of the illness must take place before the healer is sought out: the family's interpretation of the symptoms will determine which therapist will be resorted to. Consultation with the therapist is remarkable for the fact that the experience of the patient is relatively unimportant, as compared to the taking of the history from the family. The consultation deploys a variety of methods: dream interpretation and divinatory techniques are used by the therapist to access the spirit world in his capacity as mediator between the social and the world of the disease. This preliminary phase of care leads to the "interrogation" of the patient, during which process the spirit is hailed, teased, and cajoled in order to prepare for the naming of its identity. The type of aggression of which the patient has been made victim is diagnosed, as well as some general features of the offending spirit. This lends coherence to the patient's symptoms, allows the prescription of symptomatic treatment, and sets the stage for the curative intervention of the naming of the *rab* and the possession ritual.

Zempléni notes that two parallel processes are engaged throughout the diagnostic phase of the *ndöpkat*. The patient's symptoms are "translated" by the healer into symptoms of a longer family drama that continues to play out between deceased ancestors in the spirit world and the living. And in parallel, the family's concerns are reformulated as an entreaty to the spirits, requiring their recognition that the illness of the individual is a collective symptom. This social mobilization is a prerequisite for cure, and the agility of the therapist lies in his capacity to ensure that the patient's family adheres to the treatment. Adherence requires investment, materialized in the tithe required of family members in order that the *ndöpkat* be paid.

The next phase of the therapeutic process is marked by the "mothering" of the patient: tactile intimacy with the therapist mirrors discursive attempts to display a welcoming spiritual community in order to encourage the spirit to declare himself. The patient's reaction to this therapeutic experience, the symbolic system of the family, and its mediation through the dream experience of the therapist are all used to identify the offending spirit and reassemble the components of the patient's self. This is followed by the ceremony in which the spirit is named and a series of rites by which the components of the patient's self are "measured" by the healer in order to be able to manipulate them subsequently. The naming of the spirit is equivalent to the recovery of the key that will make everything else fall into place and provide the beginning of closure, much in the way that an interpretation offered during a psychotherapy session may trigger crucial insight by the patient into his symptoms, or a particular detail unlocks the meaning of the plot in a *roman à clef*. Consultation with the *ndöpkat* demands a coherent collective undertaking by the family, and is designed to help in the repair of damaged familial relationships.

With the naming of the spirit, the subsequent phases of the ceremony re-enact the patient's possession and depossession by the spirit. The patient is symbolically buried, evoking death and rebirth of the patient-initiate; subsequently, the patient clutches an animal while it is sacrificed, with instructions not to let go until the last twitches have died out and the spirit has left. The ritual possession that follows the naming of the spirit, and that will take place repeatedly throughout the life of the patient, functions as a symbol for the central event, the sacrifice, and for the patient's bodily experience of this healing event. Zempléni points out that the naming of the *rab* is a diagnostic maneuver that must precede this powerful therapeutic act of extraversion, which transforms the symptom from an internalized and continuous distress to an externalized and periodic possession state.[23]

Zempléni's account shows how the self is mobilized and transformed to gain therapeutic efficacy. Naming of the spirit permits the transformation of a fantasmatic being, only known to the patient by the symptoms he provokes, into an element of

the collective symbolic system, legitimated by the group present during the ceremony. The illness is collectivized, not by being interpreted collectively but by being
made available as a collective symptom. In other words, naming the *rab* places the
patient's symptoms within a series of other "symptoms" (those other events by which
the presence of the *rab* are manifest in the lives and history of the family), allowing
them to acquire contextual meaning in a collective field of signification. But efficacy
is more than symbolic:

> what counts maybe as much is this real, warm and permissive presence of family, neigh-
> borhood and acquaintances. Interpersonal exchanges are renewed, communication re-
> established, relations partially readjusted, aggressivity expressed. That the ceremony is
> decentered from the patient and that she is accorded a great deal of liberty favorizes the
> resocialization.[24]

This leads to a second recasting of the experience into a collective one, marked by
the public nature of the closing ritualized possession. Healing is a collective activity,
with the therapist mediating between family, patient, and ancestral world.

Zempléni documented the case of Khady Fall, a woman whose life had been
indelibly marked by loss: a stillborn child, then a daughter who died, and her own
subsequent sterility. Many years after these events, whose pain still haunted Khady
and was exacerbated by a bitter familial conflict between the in-laws, Khady was
possessed by a spirit. Zempléni shows how spirit possession established a delicate,
complicated and life-spanning equilibrium between Khady's paternal and maternal
lineages. But more significantly, this equilibrium, and the spirit possession idiom
through which it was accomplished, extended the therapeutic effect beyond Khady's
personal misfortune. Zempléni shows how her powers derived from her possession
by a spirit. This allowed her to resolve the seemingly intractable and bitter rivalries
that surrounded her and transcend painful losses that threatened to leave her bereft.
The *ndöpkat* healing ritual initiated her into a therapeutic journey that eventually
transformed her into a healer.[25] Khady's personal journey shows an indirect therapeutic effect of spirit possession: while the *ndöpkat* ritual may allow individual and
group psychotherapeutic effects, reintegrating illness within a collectively manageable
and intelligible system, it also creates healers whose personal illness and its transcendence confers on them therapeutic legitimacy as healers.

In non-biomedical healing traditions, the self is clearly a powerful therapeutic
agent, whose mobilization through ritualized practice achieves tangible diagnostic
and therapeutic effects, mirroring the way in which psychoanalysts must themselves
undergo treatment in order that they may master their own counter-transference to
achieve therapeutic effect for others. In contrast, the fashioning of the biomedical
practitioner-self does not require the transformation of personal suffering into healing
power. The above examples show how social relations and their skilful reworking are
explicitly acknowledged as integral to healing: the successful healer must enlist families and indeed entire communities to "own" the symptom collectively in order that
the illness can be cured.

Although the healing expertise of biomedicine is often viewed as objective and
therefore "scientific," the subjective dimension of biomedical healing is acknowledged in a concern for good bedside manner, empathy, and so on. These attributes

are seen as strictly personal, while the ways in which political and social status may amplify the therapeutic power of the biomedical clinician are rarely discussed. The consistent appearance of the "self" as integral to healing in biomedicine and non-biomedical traditions challenges distinctions between the "objective" approach of biomedicine and the purportedly "subjective" basis of traditional medicine; more-over, it requires us to seriously reconsider the division between self and body and its corollary, culture and biology.

Technologies of Health Promotion

Whether the self is a repository of pathogenic secrets, an instrument for "reading" the patient, or charged with healing powers, the examples above show how treatment of both patient and therapist requires a self, or several selves, to be acted upon, mobilized, and transformed in various ways. Biomedical techniques, be they the probing questions of the psychotherapist, the manual dexterity of a surgeon's fingers, or the sharp gaze of the radiologist, act as technologies of the self by fashioning subjective forms of expertise: this is the "art" of biomedicine. Such procedures and processes challenge the demarcation of biomedicine as objective, in contrast to more "subjective" and "traditional" forms of healing. We now consider how attempts to generate empowerment and self-help in the name of promoting health constitute another technology of the self.

The notion of "empowerment" in biomedicine dates to the 1970s, a direct con-sequence of epidemiological studies that increasingly linked unhealthy lifestyles to subsequent disease. The "new public health" initiated by the widely influential Canadian Lalonde Report in 1974 drew attention to social determinants of health and the limitations of biomedicine in achieving healthy populations. This approach to public health, enshrined in the Ottawa Charter for Health Promotion increasingly saw empowerment as an important strategy for promoting health by enabling people to change unhealthy behaviors (such as smoking and overeating), "take control" of their lives, and foster communities to "enhance self-help and social support."[26] Empowerment and self-help came together as two strands of contemporary public health practice that, no longer overtaxed by needing to react to epidemics or ensure public hygiene, sought to intervene directly on individuals and groups in the name of health promotion.

The idea of empowerment was a reflection of the times. The 1960s and 1970s had spawned social movements in North America, as African Americans, feminists, and gays and lesbians demanded equality and recognition. These were new social movements, no longer constrained by the boundaries of economic class, and they espoused new approaches to political mobilization that stressed self-awareness, pride, and organizing communities as a direct form of political mobilization. In doing so they drew from a repertoire of techniques that in 1960s America were widely used to "raise consciousness" and expand human potential. The history of these techniques can be traced to interwar Germany, where Freudian ideas, existentialist philosophy, and a heady climate of cultural experimentation led to the development of novel approaches blending psychotherapy and dramatic expression – "psychodrama" – whereby individuals could "act out" their psychic conflicts.[27]

In the 1930s, a young Jewish psychologist named Kurt Lewin fled Nazi Germany for the U.S. Lewin is considered the founder of social psychology, and he was deeply influenced by the ideas of both Freud and Marx that, in Germany, were synthesized by the famous philosophers of the Frankfurt School, as well as the emerging field of psychodrama. In the U.S., he began his career with a series of experiments designed to examine the influence of leadership style on the functioning of small groups – a concern clearly informed by the rise of fascism in Germany, that was also visible in the Frankfurt School's investigations into the "authoritarian personality."

When World War II broke out, Lewin was hired by the American Army. The war effort enlisted psychologists mainly out of a concern that shellshock and other psychological disturbances resulting from the battlefield might compromise troop numbers, as had been the case in World War I. Army psychologists argued that shellshock was a normal human reaction to the experience of war, rather than a disease, and therefore should be "managed" by strengthening healthy psychological coping mechanisms. The historian Laura Kim Lee has examined how Lewin concentrated on devising methods to improve cohesion in the small groups that were increasingly important to the conduct of the war and that, it was believed, could form a psychological bulwark.[28] After World War II, Lewin continued his research in Connecticut, where he renewed his focus on fostering democratic group functioning. This had become an important concern in post-war America as it began to grapple with the issue of ethnic and, to some extent, racial integration.

Technologies of Empowerment

In Connecticut Lewin convened workshops to study small group functioning. Volunteers from surrounding communities were brought together to discuss and role-play incidents in their lives, under the watchful eyes of researchers, until a fateful evening in 1946. Until that time the experiments had a predictable format: the group would gather in the morning, participants would raise the matter of their relationships at home or at work, and discussion was enlivened by psychodrama exercises. In the evening, the researchers would meet privately and debrief by going over the data they had collected while observing the group that day. On the day in question in 1946, the other group members demanded they be allowed to attend, arguing that restricting the debriefing to the facilitators was undemocratic. Lewin acquiesced, and, as Laura Kim Lee reports, "when the participants were unexpectedly allowed to take part in the interpretation of their own behaviour, the electrifying result was recognized as a fortuitous discovery."[29] In his account of that discovery, Anderson recalls

> the few participants who attended the first of these evening sessions soon tired of sitting quietly and listening to a bunch of professors and graduate students talk about what had happened ... [they] challenged the reports ... and offered their own version ... There were some tense, heated confrontations, yet there was a growing sense of exhilaration ... they had accidentally stumbled upon a powerful method of human relations training [in which both participants and researchers had been "empowered"].[30]

This discovery has been credited as the birth of participatory action research, where research subjects participate in the interpretation and analysis of the research data that, in this case, included observations of themselves. Such methods were to become enormously influential not only in social psychology, but also in education and management. The focus of the groups shifted from the "there and then" of the events that occurred outside the groups to the immediacy of interactions and feelings within the groups, whose instant feedback functioned as a kind of mirror where one was revealed to one's self through the perceptions and reactions of others. These technologies of the self differed from those oriented to recovering a pathogenic secret in one crucial aspect: they focused attention on the "here and now" of the group process, turning it into a laboratory for learning and a tool for self-transformation. Such groups were initially called "T-Groups," in which T stood for training, before becoming more widely disseminated under the moniker of "sensitivity training."

The impact was broad. As Anderson recounts,

> Sensitivity training became popular with many businesses and governmental organizations in the 1950s. It was the great psychological assembly line that helped produce people who were adept at perceiving the emotional undercurrents of a situation and smoothing off the rough corners of interpersonal communication.[31]

The potentially subversive heritage of the groups, with their roots in continental philosophy, Freudianism, and Marxism, was "given a crew cut and a white shirt and transformed into boot camp for legions of Eisenhower-era organization men and women."[32] It was not until the 1960s that this approach, comprised of techniques and exercises developed in the U.S. Army, research labs, and management schools, would migrate to the population at large to become known as the "counter-culture movement." Parsed in the language of humanistic psychology, "encounter groups" formed the cornerstone of the "human potential movement" that sought to empower individuals through group processes and the magic of "encounter." The new social movements of the 1970s – feminism, Black Power, Gay Liberation – drew on these techniques in the name of consciousness-raising and empowerment, and are still used today in management, community organizing, and self-help groups. Detox programs require that substance abusers live together, sharing menial chores and personal experiences as part of group sessions. Political movements such as the 2008 election campaign for U.S. President Barack Obama encouraged volunteers to talk about why they wanted to volunteer for the candidate in order to build a grassroots political movement.

Technologies of Self-Help

Freudian ideas and social psychology were also applied to achieve explicitly therapeutic goals, as a complement to biomedical therapy for those suffering largely from psychiatric afflictions. The model of a "therapeutic community" was developed in England after World War II as an alternative to the asylum for psychiatric casualties of the battlefield. At Northfield Military Hospital in Birmingham, in 1945 two psychiatrists, John Rickman and Wilfred Bion, performed an experiment. Rather than maintain the strict hierarchies that separated patients, nurses, and doctors, they installed a flattened, democratic structure, recognizing that all could be thought of as playing a significant role; moreover, these democratic responsibilities were extended to patients who were also expected to take on a therapeutic role. Most British psychiatrists at the time were trained in psychoanalysis, and Rickman and Bion shared their interest in applying psychoanalytic techniques to groups. They went a step further, however, in extending group therapy to the level of the "therapeutic community" that institutionalized self-help in its very organization.[33] The therapeutic outcomes were remarkable, and the success of the experiment contributed to the community psychiatry movement. Therapeutic communities remain current today, particularly for rehabilitation of those suffering from drug and alcohol addiction. The anthropologist João Biehl, for instance, has documented such a therapeutic community in Brazil.[34]

The idea of self-help also drew on powerful Christian notions of sin, confession, and redemption to inform practices aimed at collective healing. The archetype was Alcoholics Anonymous (AA), whose "Twelve-Step Program" uses public "confessions" to bind sufferers together and enable recovery from harmful dependencies. Carole Cain's ethnography of AA explores its origins in Christian groups in Oxford in the 1930s, and the conception of alcoholism not as a sin but as a disease of the self: "The AA member comes to see not only his drinking as alcoholic, but his self as alcoholic. The disease is a part of one's self." Cain describes how recovery requires transforming the self, and assuming the "identity" of an alcoholic in AA meetings. This identify is constituted by introducing oneself as an alcoholic every time one speaks, and is solidified through the use of colored chips to signify the length of abstinence.[35]

Practices designed to bring about empowerment and self-help use specific techniques for presenting one's self, talking about one's self, and examining one's self in public. As Cain shows, these are powerful technologies that produce new forms of identity, new forms of belonging, and new social relations. Technologies of self-help and empowerment migrated effortlessly from social movements that sought to expand human potential to groups organized around a shared affliction. By equating alcoholism with disease, biology was used as a metaphor to create social ties and produce a community of alcoholics. We turn now to an example of how biology is used in the literal sense to create social ties and produce communities amongst individuals who suffer from a common biological condition.

Confessional Technologies

In the years between 1994 and 2000, international donors concerned about the AIDS epidemic began to stress "empowerment" of people living with HIV as a human-rights based response to the epidemic. Empowerment required disclosure: being able to be "out" and talk about being HIV positive. This was a difficult step for many, for disclosure could lead to blame, violence, and even being disowned by family. This reluctance was addressed by a wave of empowerment training workshops that coursed across Africa after 1995, that Nguyen studied ethnographically as both participant and observer. The workshops trained Africans to give testimonials about being HIV positive, using the kind of experiential and active listening techniques pioneered in T-groups, sensitivity training, and "encounter" episodes, by mirroring the posture of their interlocutors, asking open-ended questions, and practicing active listening. The technologies used in the African setting became popular – some participants reported to Nguyen putting them into practice in everyday life immediately after finishing the workshops and being delighted with the effects. Many set up discussion groups to encourage other people with HIV to talk about their affliction in order that they might be "empowered." Nguyen attended these groups regularly from the moment of their inception in 1998. However, in Côte-d'Ivoire and Burkina Faso, in the first few years, the groups did not seem to foster the kind of environment of spontaneous sharing, caring, and self-help desired by their organizers, despite participants' eagerness to embrace the techniques. Very few men attended. Attempts to get participants talking were at first met by silence and, eventually, by halting attempts at self-expression that more often than not were a litany of complaints that seemed devoid of affective content. But over time, the dynamic in the groups started to change. After awkward, embarrassed beginnings a more convivial atmosphere began to prevail. Previously laconic participants became voluble and animated. Gradually, the charismatic side of some of the participants emerged.

Although the testimonials given in the groups were not scripted to the extent that Cain describes for AA groups, the process of being diagnosed with HIV was often recounted as a form of spiritual conversion, the first step on a road that led to greater enlightenment and the adoption of a more responsible, moral life. These declarations were inevitably followed by exhortations to the audience to get itself tested. Nguyen observed how the religious tone disturbed many of the Western aid workers employed by the agencies that funded these efforts. The workers had come to international AIDS work through AIDS activism in the North, and many were from the gay community. For them, the moralizing tone of the messages conflicted with aid workers' personal values that stressed empowerment, sexual openness, and acceptance.

Initially, Nguyen suspected that these evangelical narratives were a readily available idiom for speaking about the difficult experience of being HIV positive, a reflection of the growing popularity of Pentecostal churches in West Africa. Nguyen spent considerable time interviewing volunteers and adepts in religious organizations. Some of these organizations were responding directly to the epidemic in various ways: volunteering at the hospital, holding prayer services, providing emotional and material support; others were not so directly involved with the epidemic but concerned with affliction more broadly understood. Some of his informants spoke of volunteering to work with the ill and dying as a religious experience, while others expressed the desire to offer solace to those afflicted. From these interviews it emerged that the idiom of conversion was a way of expressing how being diagnosed with HIV reframed moral dilemmas and required a transformation in response.

Being diagnosed with HIV foretold disease and death, and for those who live in poverty and have minimal access to health care there is little in the way of resources to confront the threat. Above all, it became clear to Nguyen that what was at stake were the ethical implications of being diagnosed with a disease associated with sexual immorality. Talk of "conversion" and atoning for past errors was not necessarily a statement of religious faith, but recognition of the predicament posed by the paradox of being encouraged in community groups to disclose a "shameful" diagnosis in public. How could self-disclosure help when it led to being stigmatized or, worse, being disowned by family and friends when they were the only source of material support and, with it, resources to pay for health care?

In the groups, many told Nguyen privately that they felt odd talking about their sickness because speaking publicly of any disease in a context where "everyone suffers" (from poverty, hunger, and the ailments that accompany them daily: malaria, gastro-intestinal diseases, rashes, and so on) smacked of selfishness. To do so about a "shameful sickness" was brazen at best, or even antisocial: flaunting the fact that "one doesn't care what others think!" These concerns, which were only expressed *sotto voce*, echoed the vocal discomfort the Western AIDS activists voiced when they heard the implication that HIV was a consequence of immoral behavior.

Yet the community groups, and the Western activists, might also bring material help – food, medicines, perhaps more – and *they* were the ones encouraging disclosure. As one woman in a group said, "How can I live a good life now?" The question of how to live a good life, and in this case how one might stay alive, was an ethical question; not about moral behavior, but about deciding between difficult choices. Poverty meant group members had little to work with – in fact, they had only themselves. Weighing the risks and benefits of disclosure required painful readjustments about what relationships one valued and whom one trusted: was it worth "coming out" about being HIV positive? Could strangers with whom one shared only a disease really be counted upon when one needed them for survival, more so than one's own family? For many, publicly speaking about being HIV positive required them to see themselves differently. As the fragile ties that bound the groups strengthened through the months and years, as participants called on each other in times of illness and came to view each other as friends, disclosure revealed itself as an unexpected resource. Talking about one's self could lead to new social relations; and it was precisely this notion of self that charged talk with a powerful social valence.

These testimonials therefore were not an act staged by the NGOs – although when the first public testimonials took place on television and radio, Nguyen often heard people say the testifiers were "just doing it for the money." The testimonials were evidence of genuine conversions, because they were made by people who did not usually talk about themselves in this manner. As confessional technologies gradually became woven into the lives and talk of people with HIV, they made available a particular narrative of the self that could then be used in everyday life. More significantly, perhaps, they created a tissue of social relations brought about through shared disclosure. And, unexpectedly, Nguyen documented how proficiency in these narrative techniques helped to broker access to life-saving anti-HIV medications when these slowly trickled into West Africa in the mid-1990s, in effect separating out those who would live from those who would die. "Empowerment" of people living with HIV in Africa, and the self-help technologies mobilized to bring empowerment about, drove gradients of access to treatment and as a result biological differentiation. Many therapeutic pioneers only got inadequate treatment with one or two drugs that nonetheless helped them to survive. The legacy of this biological differentiation lives on today in the form of viral resistance to drugs acquired as a result of inadequate treatment in the past.

Thus when, by the mid-2000s, the years of empowerment were finally replaced by mass treatment programs, those who had only been partially treated could not benefit fully from the expanded access international programs now offered to full treatment. Those whose HIV has become resistant face a future less certain than those whose virus is susceptible to the anti-retroviral cocktails. The life-giving force of the drugs is today visible as HIV group members marry and bear children with partners they met through the groups.

Practices that seek to manage affliction through talking about one's self assume that this is an interior reality that is experienced and, when shared, can be cathartic. Moreover, these practices often become entangled with biomedical practice. The formalization of these practices in the form of confessional technologies that train people to talk about the self, whether in self-help groups or in the psychiatrist's office, is a biomedical technology that links the clinic to many other sites where the self is elicited through talk and can indeed produce biological transformation – blurring the boundaries between the psychological and the biological self in practice.

Conclusion

When biomedical technologies redefine death, move organs from one body into another, or read our genetic make-up to unlock the past and predict the future, they confront assumed biological and cultural boundaries; yet, as we have seen, whether these boundaries are biological or cultural, they are not predetermined or stable. Practices such as spirit possession and shamanism disrupt the boundary between self and other, challenging a particular notion of the self as bounded by the body, and as individualized and ahistorical.

The assumption that there is such a thing as a "self" or "person" that is everywhere the same has long been contested by anthropologists, even as the body continues to be viewed as invariant by them.[36] As we have argued from the outset, a duality of mind and body should not be taken for granted; nor should the assumption that the self varies across cultures leave unexamined a belief that the body is, in effect, constant. When psychiatry is comprehended as a technology of the self, it not longer appears so different to the "exotic" practices of spirit possession and shamanism that similarly function to restore alienated selves. Biomedical efficacy is revealed as a subjective performance, that is, a result of the mastery embodied in the practitioner, rather than an objective ability to carry out standardized skill. And while the self emerges as a surprisingly material entity across these varied forms of healing, the boundary between self and other – individual and group – becomes increasingly difficult to locate.

Most biomedical technologies do not require that a "self" be made available, of course, because their substrate of action is the biological body. It has been rightly pointed out, however, that many biomedical technologies – such as pharmaceuticals – are nonetheless individualizing, not only in that they target an individual body, but also because they bring about effects largely independently of social context. Women can control their fertility unbeknownst to their husbands; college students and their professors can boost their concentration with psychostimulants ("cosmetic neuropharmacology"), and even the blues can be smoothed over with antidepressants. In an ongoing ethnographic project that focuses on how the urban poor in India seek to better their health, Das and Das show that seeking to quell aches and starve fevers using antibiotics and anti-inflammatories highlights this individualizing power of biomedicine. They argue that the ethic of self-care visible in the packages of medicines, syringes, and treatment cards that can be seen even in the poorest neighborhoods constitutes a kind of self-fashioning.[37]

Biomedical technologies can work on the self without requiring any kind of public mobilization of selfhood – they work to transform the body directly according to local conceptions of the normal and the pathological body, grounded in economic conditions, as Das and others have shown. Whether or not a self is called to testify (as in the above example of "confessional technologies" and self-help for people living with HIV in Africa), biomedical technologies assist in the production of local biological differences. What these ethnographic accounts demonstrate, however, is that it is precisely their power to transform the body, and the experiences that result, that produce a pragmatic self as both subject and object of therapeutic action. Taking medication requires an ethic of self-care and helps to produce over time a therapeutic subjectivity. This is reinforced by the experience of the biological changes (such as the relief of symptoms) that result. The ways in which individuals change their biology through the use of biomedical technologies, and the effects of those changes as they become experienced, discussed, and acted upon, point to the difficulty of attributing human embodied difference solely to variation in cultural "selves," and to the importance of local biologies.

12

Genes as Embodied Risk

In the remaining three chapters of this book we turn to a discussion of molecular genetics and genomics. This is an explosive field in which new technologies are proliferating incrementally resulting in phenomenal amounts of data that present an unprecedented challenge with respect to storage, retrieval, and, above all else, interpretation. In this chapter, we confine our attention to two technologies that have already been made use of in medical settings for several decades – genetic testing and genetic screening. The remarkable worlds of genomics and postgenomics are discussed in the next chapter, including the possibility that a paradigm shift is under way with enormous repercussions for the biological sciences and for society at large. In the final chapter we turn to human difference.

The function of genetic testing and screening is not simply to be able to name one or more of the genes that an individual carries but, above all else, to be able to make predictions about the future, in particular about the health of individuals, and by extension certain of their family members, based on their shared genetic heritage. This means that genetic testing and screening are inextricably entwined with technologies of risk assessment and with the knowledge that carriers of a given gene are by definition predisposed to a specific disease or diseases associated with the presence of one or more copies of the gene in question. When confronted with what are today often called "Mendelian disorders," that is, conditions in which Mendel's laws are assumed to apply, making predictions about future disease based on the results of genetic tests is for the most part reliable. However, many uncertainties remain even after the presence of a specific genetic mutation is known, and such predictions by no means make it easy to come to decisions about which course of action to follow, as we will see below. However, in the human population as a whole, Mendelian disorders are rare, and the activity of most genes are either not highly predictable or are simply not understood at all; this makes the question of genetic testing and what health care professionals, individuals, and families can or should do with information about their genotype highly problematic – a topic to be considered in the following chapter.

This chapter opens with a discussion about the idea of embodied risk followed by a necessarily brief discussion of the gradual shift from 18th-century ideas about generativity to a position in which life came to be conceptualized as propagated by means of genes. Next is a short foray into the literature so prominent in the latter part of the 20th century in which genetic hype and the supposed promise of genetic engineering were highly visible, only to recede somewhat into the background over the past several years, once the enormity of what confronted us in attempting to understand and manipulate the world of postgenomics became undeniable.

Gradual expansion of genetic testing and screening in the clinic over the past two decades has been accompanied by publication of a body of literature in the social sciences and bioethics about the anticipated impact on everyday life of the dissemination of knowledge concerning embodied genetic risk. A discussion of this literature follows, including findings about the biopolitics of genetic testing and screening with particular emphasis on "genetic citizenship" and "biosociality."[1] Consideration of these new social science concepts inevitably involves the question of subjectivity and to what extent individuals may experience themselves as profoundly changed on the basis of knowledge about the genetic self.

The position of several involved researchers is that it is necessary to move beyond an assumption of an inevitable conflation of knowledge and power initially proposed by Michel Foucault to a position that highlights the agency and, above all else, the heterogenous responses to genetic technologies of individuals, families, and labeled populations. In common with the sociologist Paolo Palladino, we insist that a theoretical bifurcation of knowledge and practice results in a false dichotomy that obscures the multiple ways in which actors of all kinds often jockey for power when they engage with the possibilities and uncertainties of emerging knowledge in genetics, including being confronted with risk estimations made by experts.[2]

Genetic screening is discussed in the second half of this chapter. In contrast to genetic testing, genetic screening is by definition applied to selected populations, and consideration of this technology inevitably raises the possibility of eugenics, returning us to concerns discussed in chapter 5 in connection with sex selection. The concluding section of the present chapter, in which the implementation of the technology of preimplantation genetic diagnosis (PGD) is discussed, also raises troubling ethical dilemmas. However, such dilemmas should be confronted, we argue, not merely as moral matters but equally as expressions of social and political interests in need of dissection. Furthermore, similarly to discussion in preceding chapters about other biomedical technologies, genetic technologies are constantly subject to adjustment and modification, resulting in unstable and shifting expert knowledge best thought of as perennially knowledge-in-the-making. The result is that the boundaries of nature and culture, including those involving the human body itself, are not only technologically mediated and inextricably entangled, but subject to constant remaking and revision and hence to ongoing debate.

From Hazard to Embodied Risk

The idea of being "predisposed" to an illness stems from the 18th century (some would argue much earlier than that) when discussion among medical professionals and lay people alike about individual "constitution" and its contribution to disease vulnerability became apparent.[3] However François Ewald, a political scientist, argues that the "philosophy of risk" as we understand it today is very much a product of contemporary society – a radical epistemological transformation involving a "muta-tion" in attitudes toward justice, responsibility, time, causality, destiny, and even providence.[4] This transformation is a product of a secularized approach to life where "the ills that befall us lose their old providential meaning." In a world without God, control of events is left entirely in human hands – a logical outcome when life is transformed into a rational enterprise.[5]

The anthropologist Mary Douglas argued that use of the word "risk" in this restricted sense, rather than its former usage as a synonym for "danger" or "hazard," has the rhetorical effect of creating an aura of neutrality, of cloaking the concept in scientific legitimacy. Paradoxically, this permits statements about risk to be readily associated with moral approbation. Danger, reworded as risk, is removed from the sphere of the unpredictable, the supernatural, the divine, and is placed squarely at the feet of responsible individuals. Risk, in Douglas's words, becomes "a forensic resource" whereby people can be held accountable.[6] As the French sociologist Robert Castel puts it, mobilization of the concept of risk becomes a novel mode of surveil-lance – self-surveillance – in other words a component of the micro-physics of power that Foucault noted with reference to emerging neo-liberal society. Castel warns that such "hyper-rationalism" comes with a cost and that there may be "iatrogenic aspects" to this new form of prevention among which chronic anxiety could be prominent.[7]

Because it is not possible to willfully control the presence or activity of genes, it would seem that the idea of genetically "embodied risk"[8] should be understood as significantly different from the calculations of risk conferred by high cholesterol levels or high blood pressure, in which it is usually assumed that prudent behavior may well rectify the matter. Furthermore, a widely shared understanding of genes persists today as one of genetic essentialism,[9] that is, a belief that genes are the essence of life itself and make us what we are. Conceptualizing them as inherently risky is potentially anxiety provoking even though everyone knows all too well that genetic mutations can cause serious illness, physical damage, and death. Furthermore, by focusing exces-sively on genetics, the danger is that other factors that contribute to disease are largely eclipsed, in effect leaving the cause of diseases as solely due to misfortune in the form of "bad blood."

More than a quarter of a century ago, when commenting on plans by health policy planners to make genetic testing widely available in the near future, Edward Yoxen argued that a shift in public perception would likely take place so that genes would come to be thought of as "quasi-pathogens."[10] Media reporting and profes-sional publications since that time suggest that public concern about genetically driven risk predictions has indeed proliferated in contemporary society,[11] but perhaps not to the extent that certain social scientists thought would be the case. Given that individual responsibility for "risk management" is strongly promoted by many gov-ernments and medical practitioners, it is reasonable to assume that individuals may want to try to predict and hence prevent whatever ill health may be in store as a result of their genetic heritage, with the result that genetic testing may well be eagerly accepted when offered. However, to date, the responses of individuals to having themselves genetically tested are decidedly mixed (see below), including among people who come from families in which rare, deadly, single gene disorders are present.

It seems that a good proportion of the public are not as enamored with the idea that we will soon be able to solve the ills of the world on the basis of accumulating knowledge about genes as a few outspoken biologists would have us believe. Although gene talk is everywhere,[12] and a large number of people today send money to companies offering ancestry testing to find out about their purported genealogy, it is clear that the majority are not preoccupied with the idea of embodied risk, although at certain times this is the case, especially in families affected by lethal childhood disorders when they are making decisions about reproduction.

Three other introductory points are of note in connection with genetics. First, activities designed to assist with the avoidance of misfortune and danger are ubiquitous in the history of humankind, but the idea of being "at risk" in its technical, epidemiological meaning is a construct of modernity.[13] In theory morally neutral, the notion of risk provides a means whereby experts can minimize direct intervention into people's lives, employing instead the agency of subjects in their own self-regulation through "risk-management."[14] Second, the effect of genetic testing is in striking contrast to that of the assisted reproductive technologies considered in chapter 10, in which the idea of the normative family and its reproduction is challenged, with the result that the assumed "relationships between the biological 'facts' of conception and the social categories of kinship"[15] are in effect weakened. Molecular genetics, in contrast, has the potential to "strengthen the conventional categories of reproduction and biological relatedness"[16] by bringing to light exactly which segments of DNA have been transmitted to the next generation and by which parent. Third, again in contrast to both assisted reproduction technologies (ARTs) and organ transplants, with the development of new "high throughput" technologies that can process a great deal of data very quickly indeed, the cost of genetic testing is steadily decreasing, so that pressures are beginning to mount to shortly incorporate such testing into routine clinical care.

From Generation to Rewriting Life

Prior to the 18th century, similarities and differences between offspring and their parents were thought about in very general terms under the rubric of "generation." It was not until the mid–18th century that the idea of heredity was seriously considered in biological terms, leading shortly thereafter to the insights of Gregor Mendel and Charles Darwin. Following an interval of many years the New Biology, indebted to Mendel's insights, took practical form between the 1940s and 1970s. The result was a molecularized vision of "life itself" made possible by technologies that facilitated experimentation with and manipulation of the internal environment of cells in entirely new ways – these technologies became what Bruno Latour would call the "ways and means" of bringing about a potential paradigm shift.[17] The philosopher of science Hans-Jörg Rheinberger argues that to persist in conceptualizing "nature" and "culture" as being in opposition to one another became entirely inappropriate as a result of these developments.[18] Calculated, radical manipulation of nature was now the order of the day – the beginnings of an ever-deeper invasion into the molecular universe, one contemporary outcome of which is known as synthetic biology or "extreme genetic engineering."[19] Furthermore, Rheinberger notes, this molecularized vision resulted in a reconceptualization of the fundamental processes of life as now being based upon "the storage, transmission, change, accumulation, and expression of genetic information."[20] In other words, "genetically enshrined instruction" began to be understood as the driving force not only for life itself, but also for the development of organisms and deviation from accepted norms.

This molecular approach became the "central dogma" of molecular biology, first explicitly formulated by Francis Crick in 1958 and encapsulated as a "super-slogan" that was beyond dispute: DNA makes RNA, RNA makes protein. Thus, the "genetic code" became conceptualized as the primary driving force for life, development, health, and disease. Within a time span of fewer than 20 years, molecular geneticists learned not only to understand the language of genes in principle, but also to spell it: "they had learned to read, to write, to copy and to edit that language in a goal-directed manner."[21] However, as Rheinberger is quick to note, this language is entirely metaphorical. Even so, it enabled practical innovation so that by the early 1970s a group of technologies was created, known as "recombinant DNA technologies," designed to create precise functional equivalents of DNA in the laboratory. These so-called "soft" technologies – "a kit of purified enzymes and molecules"[22] – had themselves been evolving for billions of years in the real world when they were appropriated by scientists and transformed into tools for investigating and providing novel instructions to intracellular environments.

Rheinberger sums up the situation thus: "With gene technology, informational molecules are constructed according to an extracellular [deliberately created] environment and are subsequently implanted into the intracellular environment" for observation, thus enabling the natural.[23] This deliberate "rewriting" of life, radically different from anything that had gone before it, was also the beginning of an era of euphoric genetic essentialism, culminating in the announcement of the mapping of the human genome in 2001 (even though the map was not entirely complete at that time). Rheinberger notes that these changes came about as the result of shifting "assemblages"[24] or "conjunctures"[25] bringing about new insights into the workings of molecular biology based largely on genetic engineering, that also resulted in an accompanying shift in social climate.

The principal result of these changes was the birth of the discipline of molecular biotechnology that straddles the corporate world and that of academic research centers, a field to which both entrepreneurs and academic scientists today contribute.[26] In the second half of the 20th century, two related "products" that resulted from this new approach to molecular biology were the technologies of genetic testing and screening, now in widespread use. It is of note that predictions about future risk based on testing for Mendelian genes is rarely confined to individuals; ideally, with family cooperation, test results are extended to blood relatives, and "medical pedigrees" are then created that make visible tiny parts of the genetic body and are of significant use for research purposes in addition to informing family members of their fate.[27] In contrast to other forms of risk, then, embodied genetic risk is inevitably distributed among family networks with enormous potential repercussions for family divisiveness or, alternatively, bonding.[28]

Genomic Hype

It is undeniable that biology is increasingly malleable in our hands, and for some advocates this newfound ability to tinker with the basic building blocks of life itself has kindled a vision of the transformation of both the human body and society for the better. However, the startling promise made when the mapping of the human genome was first embarked upon will certainly not be kept, namely that the sequencing of the human genome will tell us what makes us uniquely human.[29] True enough, it is increasingly becoming clear which genes humans alone possess – but to imply that genes inform humanness is a grave mistake. Furthermore, the assumption was made that we would soon be able to tinker effectively with genes to radically improve humankind and free ourselves from our bonds to nature.

Along these lines the United States Office of Technology Assessment made the claim over 15 years ago that the new genetic information coming down the pipeline would ensure that each one of us in the near future would have "a paramount right to be born with a *normal*, adequate, hereditary endowment."[30] And Daniel Koshland, a molecular biologist and past editor of *Science*, went on record in 1989 as saying that: "no one will profit more from the current research into genetics than the poor." He made it clear that "weak" and "anti-social" genes would slowly be "sifted out" of the population.[31] In 1995 James Watson, the co-discoverer of DNA, argued: "the genetic dice will continue to inflict cruel fates on all too many individuals and their families who do not deserve this damnation. Decency demands that someone must rescue them from genetic hells." He went on to ask: "If we don't play God, who will?"[32] A newspaper report from 2000 confirmed that James Watson continues to support his earlier position in favor of an unfettered genetic engineering: "if we could make better human beings by knowing how to add genes, why shouldn't we do it?"[33]

Most people, including the majority of scientists, have always thrown up their hands at such outrageous claims, and it is disturbing to read how this hype is taken up by two bioethicists who insist that global health inequities can best be dealt with through the "harnessing" of genomics. They justify their position by arguing that the emergence of a "health genomics divide" should be avoided, and that investment is needed to ensure that the developing world is not left out, as is already the case with information technology and agricultural biotechnology.[34] It is indeed possible that the kind of investment suggested by these bioethicists might in the future have some value in the management of, for example, malaria, but even if such a technology in itself does not prove ecologically disruptive, as many experts fear, it is in any case bound to fail unless it goes hand in hand with the provision of clean water and sewage disposal; adequate food supply; concerted efforts to reduce global warming; substantial economic aid that is actually realized, coupled with debt relief; and ready access to basic health care. Co-option of incoming assistance of whatever kind by local governments notorious for corruption and infamy will worsen the situation. The problem with genomic hype is that it ignores local biologies; local, regional, and global politics; environmental variables; the reality of social arrangements and worsening poverty; and it makes the assumption that technological innovation, in and of itself, is always for the good.

Francis Collins, the Director of the National Human Genome Research Institute, made his position clear when interviewed in 2003 for *Time* magazine. He predicted that low-cost genome sequencing for all will allow us to have "individualized, preventive medical care based on our own predicted risk of disease" and would generate a "new breed of designer drugs" tailored to serve these needs.[35]

Collins assumes the existence of sound public health, good nutrition, and the absence of major infectious and parasitic diseases when making this comment (a position not justified even with respect to the United States). But over and above this, research findings make it clear that molecular biology is a long way from personalized cures for the kinds of diseases Collins has in mind – heart disease, diabetes, asthma, obesity, dementia, and so on – although cancer research looks more promising. The head of GlaxoSmithKline's genetics research arm, Lon Cardon, stated at a 2009 symposium that the terms pharmacogenetics and personalized medicine should not be used. He made it clear that although huge advances are being made into documenting human genetic variation, the idea that treatment will eventually be personalized is simply not possible.[36] The persistent hype by certain scientists, no doubt exploited to acquire yet more funding, is troubling, and so too is the narrowness of vision, with the result that the situation with respect to health that prevails in most of the world is ignored.

The existence of these massive global health inequities should not lead to outright dismissal of the potential benefits of advances in genetics. On a much more modest level, two researchers argue forcefully that congenital disorders associated with the effects of deprivation, including food shortages, maternal infections, and toxic exposures of fetuses that have a lifelong impact after birth, are much more frequent in "lower-resource countries" than elsewhere, and cause an inordinate loss of life and suffering.[37] Christianson and Modell argue that the health burden of these conditions is consistently underestimated and even ignored. Their estimate, on the basis of WHO statistics, is that one third of the current 10.8 million per year early-childhood deaths are associated with common, treatable congenital disorders. They make a strong plea that local primary care practitioners, usually well respected in their communities, should be trained to assist with such problems as a routine part of maternal and child health care, and that with simple, relatively cheap technologies,[38] a great deal can be accomplished. These researchers go on to point out that Westernized bioethics, with its emphasis on autonomy and individual rights, cannot be adequate for addressing the crying health needs in such settings. To be ethical "these services must be equitable and accessible and provide simultaneously for the care and prevention of congenital disorders."[39] Without attention to prevention, health care costs will spiral out of control, they argue. They explicitly conclude that advances in genomics cannot on their own improve world health, as has been suggested in a recent WHO report;[40] rather a radical approach to public health is called for, in which the massive impact of congenital abnormalities is squarely confronted.

Many simple, inexpensive technologies exist that can prevent illness, but are inadequately implemented; for example, numerous women die in childbirth because they cannot obtain basic life-saving obstetrical care when they need it. In areas where malaria is endemic, prevention of malaria with mosquito nets and anti-malarial drugs – interventions that significantly improve child survival – have not been systematically made use of. Low weight at birth is considered one of the most preventable causes of illness in children. Dietary supplementation and prenatal care to protect a future mother's health are simple biomedical interventions that dramatically decrease low birth weight, but they too are implemented unevenly. Common congenital abnormalities, such as congenital hypothyroidism, saturnism (lead poisoning), and congenital syphilis are easily prevented. While they have been largely eradicated from wealthy countries, they continue to afflict newborns in the developing world, despite the existence of simple screening tests that can identify hypothyroidism, high lead levels, and syphilis infection.

What follows are accounts taken from research carried out in settings with high resources available for health care (although, of course, such resources are not always equitably distributed). Many of these findings sound a cautionary note that will become of global relevance when the technologies of genetics and genomics become more widely distributed.

Geneticization

In the early 1990s the epidemiologist Abby Lippman coined the term "geneticization" to gloss what she perceived to be a new form of medical surveillance. Lippman characterized geneticization as a process "in which differences between individuals are reduced to their DNA codes."[41] Above all, she was concerned about the possibilities of an indirect reinforcement of racism, social inequalities, and discrimination against those with disabilities, the result of a rekindled conflation between social realities and an essentialized biology grounded in small differences in DNA sequences.[42]

Adam Hedgecoe, a sociologist, insists that the application of genetic knowledge and technologies is just the latest in a long line of attempts to advance our understanding of the body at the molecular level.[43] He is less inclined than he believes Lippman to be to see geneticization as "an opportunistic tactic employed by doctors to gain power over patients."[44] Hedgecoe argues for recognition of a concept of "enlightened geneticization." His point is that even though the contribution of environmental and other factors is today widely accepted in scientific discourse about disease causation, genetic explanations are nevertheless very often prioritized and subtly divert attention away from non-genetic factors.[45] Hedgecoe has shown how this type of discourse is reproduced in contemporary psychiatric medical literature.[46] More subtly than was formerly the case, genetic reductionism, rather than outright genetic determinism, is at work, but it is also clear that geneticization has some positive attributes, as does medicalization more generally. For example, it is apparent that once a disease is medically recognized, particularly when behavioral changes are involved, social stigma and allocation of individual and family responsibility for the occurrence of such conditions are reduced.[47] What is more, many families take comfort in being told that a disabling condition is the result of faulty genetics and therefore, by implication, moral or behavioral shortcomings in the family are not implicated.[48]

Nikolas Rose approaches emerging genetic technologies from the perspective of Foucaultian biopolitics. He suggests that in advanced liberal democracies where life is "construed as a project," values such as autonomy, self-actualization, prudence, responsibility, and choice are integral to "work on the self." Rose argues that genetic forms of thought have become "intertwined" into this project, and the merged language of genetics and risk "increasingly supplies a grid of perception that informs decisions on how to conduct one's life, have children, get married, or pursue a career."[49] Life potentially becomes one of "optimization." But Rose is quick to add that there is little evidence to date that someone labeled as genetically at risk is reduced to a "passive body-machine that is merely to be the object of a dominating medical expertise."[50]

The discussion that follows illustrates the way in which the desire for and the realization of genetic knowledge have the potential to restructure individual subjectivity, family relationships, and the biopolitics of medical activism. At least one publication in a technical journal encourages its readers to believe that the public is pushing scientists down a path of increased testing and screening,[51] but it is evident that resistance to genetic testing exists on the part of very many people, no doubt because they anticipate some of the possible social consequences of this particular technology. It is estimated that only between 15 and 20 percent of adults designated at risk for a named genetic disease, or for carrying a fetus believed to be at risk for a genetic disease, have been willing thus far to undergo genetic testing, a finding that has held for over 10 years (these numbers vary from country to country and differ according to the disease in question).[52] It has also been shown that a good number of people, when tested, ignore or challenge the results.[53] No doubt this situation exists because uncertainty, disbelief, doubt, and kinship concerns color people's responses to test results in connection with the majority of Mendelian disorders that are caused by a mutation in a single gene. But worry about social discrimination of many kinds, including stigma, insurance coverage, and possible employment difficulties, also contribute to the reluctance of people to consider testing.[54] Further concerns arise because the material effects of genetic mutations are so varied. Responses to the possibility of undergoing genetic testing depend upon the age of onset of the disease in question and whether or not reproductive decision-making is implicated. Furthermore, testing cannot predict the severity of many conditions or even if symptoms will manifest themselves at all, and for by far the majority of single gene disorders, such as Tay-Sachs disease or polycystic kidney disease, there are few if any preventive measures to be taken, and no treatments available.

Genetic Testing and Human Contingency

Rayna Rapp's classic ethnography about the social impact of amniocentesis exposes many of the problems associated with genetic testing that continue to be of fundamental concern today. Amniocentesis is a technology used primarily to detect Down syndrome and also certain single gene disorders in which the involved genes function according to a Mendelian pattern of inheritance. Genetic counselors are required to counsel clients before they proceed to genetic testing. Rapp shows graphically how, despite a firm policy of non-directive counseling and a resolute belief that they are "information brokers" of "rational" knowledge, American genetic counselors convey information to women in a variety of ways that frequently depend upon the declared ethnicity of the individuals receiving the results.[55] They often encourage, apparently inadvertently, "stratified reproduction," in which "some categories of people are empowered to nurture and reproduce, while others are disempowered."[56] Rapp's ethnography also makes it clear that many women, when confronted with the possibility of genetic testing, are non-cooperative, and frequently reinterpret or resist the generalized risk information they are given before making a decision about whether or not to agree to undergo a test. Counseled women and their partners must inevitably confront "the gap" created among statistical estimations of risk, their concerns about undergoing the actual test, and their doubts about the meaning of results.

Several women interviewed by Rapp, including some who were well educated, misunderstood what they had been told; however, even when the import of counseling was correctly internalized, making a "rational" decision about termination of a wanted pregnancy raised an array of difficulties. Some people expressed disbelief about the accuracy of the testing; others were concerned because amniocentesis can induce pregnancy loss; some believe that Down syndrome is not a reason to abort a fetus and, among these people, several are particularly concerned because the test tells them nothing about the severity of the phenotype. Yet others, believing that they themselves have a healthy lifestyle, do not accept that their fetus is at risk for disease. Religious beliefs also play a part in decision-making, as do family economics, the reproductive experiences of extended family members, and attitudes to disability in general. In some families, the pregnant woman is made to feel responsible for the "problem" having arisen in the first place.

Rapp describes the women who have been tested as "moral pioneers" because they and their partners are expected to make rational decisions about abortion of wanted pregnancies, when in reality they are confronted with complex, heart-rending decisions. As one woman put it: "I'm so sick of being a statistic."[57] Rapp concludes that all the women whom she interviewed were "participating in an impromptu and large-scale social experiment,"[58] forcing them to bring to consciousness and tussle with values embedded in the private domains of their everyday lives. Virtually all of the interviewees made it clear that making a decision about selective abortion was extraordinarily difficult, and that decisions had to be contextualized in the reality of family situations. Strategies for family survival under the increased economic pressure that a child with a serious health problem would bring were uppermost in many narratives, especially those given by working-class women, as this account by a postal worker makes clear:

> With my other two, Lionel worked nights, I'm on days, we managed with a little help from my mother. When Eliza was 3, my mother passed on, then my sister, she helped out as much as she could. With this one, we're planning to ask for help from a neighbor who takes in a few kids. I couldn't keep a baby with health problems. Who would baby-sit?[59]

Carole Browner's work among Mexicans living in America has shown how the presence of male partners during genetic counseling sessions can have a profound effect on decision-making. With few exceptions, the husband's role in decision-making was understood by both partners as supportive, and facilitating of the decision that the woman herself had chosen. However, Browner found that when women appeared to be uncertain and vacillating about having a test, clinicians tended to forge alliances with the male partner who they assumed would be more able to "see reason."[60]

Several researchers, including Rapp and Browner, have shown that when genetic information is incorporated into accounts about illness causation, such knowledge supplements rather than replaces previously held notions about kinship, heredity, and health. For example, writing about Huntington's disease, a single gene disorder with adult onset (on occasion very late in life) that affects approximately 1 in 10,000 people, and for which there is no known treatment, the sociologists Cox and McKellin make it clear that lay understandings of heredity conflict with Mendelian genetics, because the scientific account does not assuage the feelings of families dealing with the lived experience of genetic risk.[61] Similarly to Rapp, these authors argue on the basis of empirical findings: "theories of Mendelian inheritance frame risk in static, objective terms. They abstract risk from the messiness of human contingency and biography."[62] The conclusion is that test candidates and their families jointly engage in a "complex social calculus of risk" that is fluid, contingent and inter-subjective.[63]

People who come from families with Huntington's disease vacillate about testing, sometimes for many years, in part as a result of the uncertainties involved about age of onset, and because no treatment exists for this condition.[64] Moreover, increased knowledge about molecular genetics complicates estimations of future risk, sometimes making "educated choices" about testing problematic. For example, since the time that the gene associated with Huntington's disease (known as the Huntingtin gene) was mapped in 1993, it has become clear that estimations of risk that certain people had previously been given, based on linkage studies[65] prior to the time that gene mapping commenced, were incorrect, sometimes wildly so. The result was that these people had to be given new estimates, on occasion entirely different from earlier information, with enormous social repercussions.[66]

Furthermore, it is now known that there is no straightforward, unequivocal link between the presence of a Huntingtin gene and the expression of the actual disease, as was formerly believed to be the case. It has been shown that the cause of the mutation is due to an expanded number of "repeats" of a trinucleotide that is part of the gene. Ordinarily individuals have approximately 11 to 30 repeats, but those with Huntington's disease have more than 38 of these triplets. Those people whose number of repeats fall between these two ranges are known as "sporadic cases" and it cannot be predicted through testing whether or not they will manifest the disease. When individuals from Huntington families are tested they are given one among three possible results on the basis of the number of repeats that they have: "No, you won't get the disease," "Yes you will get the disease, but we cannot be sure at what age it will start to affect you, although we can give you some idea" or, to a small number of tested people: "We simply don't know. You may or you may not get the disease."[67] The present situation of uncertainty about what were formerly thought to be uncontroversial predictions about future disease applies to several other single gene disorders, and is the direct result of newly emerging burgeoning knowledge in molecular genetics. The biopolitics of genetic risk is currently riddled with problematic estimations that gloss over the uncertainties embedded in rapidly changing scientific knowledge.

The anthropologist Monica Konrad, also drawing on ethnographic research, sets out to describe "the making of the 'pre-symptomatic person.'"[68] She too uses Huntington's disease as an illustrative example, and is at pains to emphasize what happens in families where some people choose to be tested and others refuse. Inspired in part by anthropological research into divination, Konrad explores the "prophetic realities" unfolding in contemporary society as a result of genetic technologies. Like Rapp, Konrad is concerned with "moral decision-making" and her emphasis is on how, when bodies are made into oracles, the resultant "moral systems of foreknowledge" are enacted both within and across generations. Her work, like virtually all the other social science research on genetic testing, makes it abundantly clear that the idea associated with bioethics of a "right to know," and an assumption of individual autonomy with respect to decision-making in connection with genetics is extremely problematic. Konrad discusses at length the "pragmatics of uncertainty" that infuse the everyday lives of people living with genetic foreknowledge and, further, the new forms of "relational identity" that testing brings about – how and when to inform one's children of your own test results; whether to be entirely "truthful" or not, or whether to say nothing at all; and should the children be tested, and if so, when? Value is associated with the idea of kinship, the very ties of which are medicalized as a result of genetic testing, thus accounting for the reason that "affectively charged kinship talk" consistently dominates gene talk.[69]

When the sociologist Nina Hallowell interviewed women in the United Kingdom who come from families where cancer is very common and who were undergoing testing at a specialty clinic for BRCA genes associated with increased risk for breast cancer, without exception she found that these women believed that it was their duty to themselves and to their children to undergo testing. Moreover, many women who had already borne children believed themselves to be responsible for having unknowingly put their children at risk.[70] On the basis of these findings, Hallowell argued that women, more so than men, are likely to develop feelings of "genetic responsibility," that is, experience an obligation to undergo testing and reveal the results to kin. As one woman put it:

> A large proportion of my concern is a responsibility to my daughter. And I think also it's sort of a helplessness … I've passed on the gene to my daughter. I must make sure now that I alert her to what might be in store for her, because I have that responsibility.[71]

Most women interviewed by Hallowell were frightened of undergoing the test, scared that it might affect their employment or health insurance, but nevertheless they went through with it. Sometimes women were pushed to do so by their spouses or sisters:

> I said to my husband that I didn't want to know. I said, if I'm going to get cancer then I'm just going to get it. I don't want to go for this test. And my husband, he kept saying … you know, you should, because it's not just for you, but for the kids.[72]

Mutations of BRCA genes are not involved in by far the majority of cases of breast cancer, being implicated in only approximately 5–10 percent of cases. Even when these mutations are found, this by no means determines that an individual will get breast cancer, though inheritance of a single copy of these genes from either parent puts individuals at increased risk. It is estimated that, on average, BRCA mutations, particularly common among Ashkenazi populations, place people at an increased lifetime risk of somewhere between 60 and 80 percent compared to the population at large. However, a recent study shows that lifetime risk for breast cancer among Ashkenazi women has apparently increased over time. Breast cancer risk by age 50 among mutation carriers born before 1940 was 24 percent, whereas among those born after 1940 is 67 percent.[73] These striking results strongly suggest that environmental factors are implicated. Furthermore, in contrast to Huntington's disease, regular surveillance can be used to detect breast cancer very early and treat it, in the majority of cases, with success. Preventive medicine in the form of invasive prophylactic surgery can also be resorted to. Even so, the result of the extent to which the media and public activism have been effective in broadcasting information about breast cancer and the BRCA genes,[74] combined with the symbolic significance given to the breast, has resulted in a burning anxiety about the disease among women, even though breast cancer mortality has declined considerably in recent years.[75]

The above discussion shows how knowledge about genes can initiate or else inhibit action, and increase or reduce anxiety. Inevitably the future is brought into the present, and family relationships are transformed. But does such knowledge result in what might be called a genetic subjectivity? Is there a tight looping effect,[76] between genetic disclosure and a radical transformation in sense of self? Are people consumed by the idea that they are their genes? Or is genetic knowledge usually absorbed into pre-existing beliefs about risk to self and family as several of the above researchers have suggested? We return to these questions later in this chapter.

Genetic Citizenship and Future Promise in America

Rayna Rapp and her associates have documented how networks of families increasingly coalesce as a result of shared knowledge about the rare single gene disorders that afflict their children. Such groups provide mutual social support and lobby the United States Congress for improved research funding (and similar activities happen in many other countries). These activists are painfully aware that only rarely will drug companies invest in research into these kinds of diseases because there is no profit to be had in researching the so-called "orphan diseases," over 1,500 of which are distributed across a mere 2 percent of the world's population. Lobbying for public funding is deemed essential, much of it directed initially at locating the relevant mutations on the human genome. These practices often have direct links to biocapital, and the state is involved only in so far as political lobbying for recognition of the disease and funding for it is indispensable.[77] Such alliances constitute "genetic citizenship" in action, and involve not only mobilization of affected people, but new ways of envisioning the future, when gene therapy may possibly become a realistic option.[78]

One of the citizen support groups investigated by Taussig and her colleagues is LPA (Little People of America) founded in 1957. These researchers graphically demonstrate, now that biotechnology presents a possibility for normalization, the irresolvable tension that exists for people who frequently endure stigmatism in their daily lives as a result of their physical condition. Taussig et al. characterize this tension as "flexible eugenics," a situation that arises when "long-standing biases against atypical bodies meet both the perils and the possibilities that spring from genetic technologies."[79] The idea of the "natural" is thus subject to continuous renegotiation resulting in "flexible bodies." Members of the LPA take different subject positions with respect to the choices now available to them in connection with treatment, such as limb lengthening, and also about genetic testing. Many LPA members fear genetic testing may be used inappropriately, and that pressure will be brought to bear on couples to undergo abortions when testing is positive for dwarfing. Furthermore, when LP couples opt to undergo genetic testing, "choice" is inevitably compounded by uncertainty, because several dwarfing conditions exist in which different genes are implicated, but there is virtually no knowledge, other than the isolated experiences of some families, about how these genes are likely to interact during reproduction and with what phenotypic effects.[80] Research of this kind shows how, even among politically active groups, concerns about persisting uncertainties and the outcomes and possible unwanted consequences of technological interventions are dominant and, further, that within activist groups people are by no means of one mind.

It is also evident from this research that the assumption of a marked distinction between lay and professional expertise is not appropriate; new forms of "entanglements" among patients, families, health care professionals, and politicians are apparent, as is the wide circulation of "expert" knowledge in many domains.[81] Powerful activist movements emerge around certain conditions, but there is also the danger that people, in their eagerness to help in the advance of medical knowledge, inappropriately transform themselves all too readily into experimental subjects.[82]

Biosociality and the Affiliation of Genes

In putting forward the concept of biosociality, the anthropologist Paul Rabinow cited the geneticist Neil Holtzman, writing in 1989, who argued that early detection of genetic susceptibility and predispositions would shortly become routine. Rabinow chose to give particular emphasis to only one of the many issues raised by Holtzman: "the likely formation of new group and individual identities and practices arising out of these new truths."[83] Rabinow is careful to note that groups formed on the basis of individual experiences with rare diseases were already in existence some time before genotyping became available, and will clearly continue to function with respect to "pastoral" and political activities.[84] But he nevertheless suggests that new congeries of people will emerge as a result of knowledge founded in molecular genetics: "it is not hard to imagine groups formed around chromosome 17, locus 16,256, site 654,376 allele variant, with a guanine substitution."[85] Such groups will have "medical specialists, laboratories, narrative traditions, and a heavy panoply of pastoral keepers to help them experience, share, intervene, and 'understand' their fate."[86]

At the time when Rabinow first introduced the concept of biosociality the idea of groups literally coming together on the basis of a specified chromosomal abnormality as Rabinow suggested (with a touch of irony one assumes) seemed far-fetched to many. In retrospect his insight has proved to be prescient in some respects. An article in the *New York Times* in late December 2007 discusses the experiences of certain families with extremely rare genetic mutations who, as a result of a new diagnostic technology, learn about the DNA mutation that has affected one or more of their children and, with access to email and the Internet, have made contact with similarly affected families.[87] The two disorders discussed in this article are usually diagnosed under the rubric of autism and/or mental retardation: however, by making use of

DNA microarray analyses, newly identified chromosomal disorders that are apparently fully determined by aberrations in specific segments of DNA can readily be spotted at a current cost of $3,000. So far only six children have been diagnosed with the congenital disorder known as 16p11.2, a condition that is not inherited. The other condition discussed in the *New York Times*, 7q11.23, has been found in 11 children worldwide. Without doubt further cases will emerge, as microarray analysis becomes more widely used. The making up of these "new" diseases is a powerful example of how certain syndromes and behavioral disorders are increasingly likely to be reclassified as genetic or congenital disorders, once the molecularized body is rendered more visible. However, the question of what conjunction of variables brought about these chromosomal aberrations in the first place remains unaddressed.

The search by the parents of two children diagnosed with these new disorders forms the import of the article in the *Times*. In both cases, the parents experienced considerable comfort and hope for the future as a result of talking with families where children had been given the same diagnosis as that of their own child. One parent complained that the diagnosis of autism they had previously been given did not mean anything because, quite simply, it is "too non-specific." He and his wife rejoiced because the genetic diagnosis relieved them of guilt and offered a glimmer of hope for treatment in the future.[88]

It has been asked by the anthropologists Kelly Raspberry and Debra Skinner whether increasing use of genetic information and technologies will bring about a paradigm shift in the "knowable body" and in everyday conceptions of health. Is biomedicine moving toward a single notion of "body as text" – an informatics notion of the body? Alternatively, will genetic information simply "deepen" understanding of the conventional biomedical body?[89] The findings of these researchers, from a study carried out with ethnically diverse families in the southeastern United States in which a child had been diagnosed with a genetic disorder, showed that, in most instances, genetic information was simply incorporated to provide "another piece of the puzzle" in determining what was wrong with the child. Further, similar to the findings reported in the *Times*, these authors found that a genetic diagnosis frequently gives legitimacy to a disorder as "truly" biological, and allows families to escape from catch-all "soft" diagnostic categories such as autism and ADHD (attention deficit and hyperactivity disorder), thus offering some hope for a "cure" in the not-too-distant future by means of genetic engineering. Nevertheless, a "hybrid notion of causality" is maintained in the minds of these families – one in which it is undeniable that chromosomal deletions bring about very real bodily changes. Inevitably, questions about the range of phenotypic expression, severity, and individual compensatory capabilities are always uppermost in the minds of affected families. The genetic body made knowable through technology requires, then, family interpretations about the meaning of identified genes to be continually modified as a result of lived experience and ongoing uncertainties. Knowledge about genetic reality rarely transcends or precludes the ever-present uncertainty, hope, wishful thinking, and sometimes despair that constitutes everyday life when a genetic disorder or chromosomal abnormality has been identified.

A decade on, Rabinow admits limitations to the concept of biosociality, even though it has been made extensive use of by numerous researchers.[90] He notes that already there is a shift in the time horizon that he formerly considered, brought about in large part by a redefinition of what is a gene and of genetic action[91] – a shift that we will expand upon in the next chapter. On the other hand, it is clear that, with respect to biopolitical activism in connection with single gene disorders, biosociality is a reality, although this was in fact also the case to a considerable extent before genetic testing became possible.

A great deal more research is needed before questions about the possibility of a radically transformed subjectivity as a result of knowledge about one's genotype can be answered. The findings to date, some of which are set out above, suggest that usually it is above all family dynamics and kin relations that influence the way people respond to the results of genetic testing for a disease that causes havoc in their family and with which they are already all too familiar from early childhood. Survey research suggests that, among those relatively few people who choose to be tested, many experience a sense of relief once they come to terms with what they have learnt, whether their results are positive or negative.[92] Tested individuals often report that they are better able to make plans for marriage, reproduction, informing children of their risks, planning a career, and so on.[93] But it remains an open question as to whether information about one's genotype, whether positive or negative, profoundly alters the subjectivity of the majority who are tested, even though a degree of certainty about individual futures may result. Recently, Browner and Preloran, in contrast to other researchers, interviewed individuals who are *already* ill, and who have difficult-to-diagnose neurological disorders. When, of their own choice, these people underwent genetic testing it was abundantly clear, as the research cited above also showed, that the majority of individuals and their families, rather than experiencing a radical identity transformation, absorbed knowledge about genes and their effects into the exigencies of their everyday lives.[94]

The book, *Mapping Fate*, by Alice Wexler draws outsiders into the life of a family where Huntington's disease is present in a way that thus far no ethnography has succeeded in doing. Alice, a historian, and her sister Nancy, a geneticist who first mapped the Huntington gene, come from a family where their mother and three brothers all died of the disease. The book weaves together a tale of family life with its struggles, secrets, and interludes of calm with accounts about the activist work of the Wexlers' physician father in forming various committees and foundations to combat Huntington's disease and promote research into it. Also recounted is the fascinating history of Nancy Wexler's work with a Venezuelan community where Huntington's is highly prevalent, and where a great deal of significant research has been carried out in connection with the genetics of this disease. Alice and Nancy both struggle with the question of whether or not to participate in the game Alice describes as Russian roulette, and have their genetically allotted "fate" tested. Fragments from Alice's diary reveal the real torment that the possibility of having the test precipitates:

> The immensity of it scares me shitless. The idea of really knowing – and what if it is positive? Or if Nancy is? Once we do know, there's no going back ...
> ... Alternately exhilarated, depressed, elated, overwhelmingly anxious, and frantic. I find it hard to think about the test at all. My mind tries to escape to other things. I only want to take this test to find out that I don't have the illness ...
> ... Now the plan is for us all to get together to talk about the test – get everything clear before we do it ... I'm not sure if Dad is really prepared for this.[95]

In trying to reach a decision, Alice talked with people who had taken the test and found, not surprisingly, a wide range of responses. One individual recounted the way her life had changed radically when she tested negative – she was now married and had changed her job, but she could not escape Huntington's disease because her two brothers tested positive. One man stated that he had lost his "creative terror" when he found he was negative for the disease, and then later had been arrested for writing bad checks. Several people who tested positive, contrary to the published findings of psychologists, argued that their uncertainty was not reduced. They now had the enormous worry of when the disease would strike, and many found this harder to bear than a generalized uncertainty about whether or not they would get the disease. Alice herself opted not to be tested. She concluded that she perhaps actually enjoys the ambiguity she settled for when she resisted "sharp categories and binary definitions."[96]

It is clear that we must avoid the temptation on the part of social scientists and others to create sweeping generalizations about profound changes in identity in connection with genetic testing. People interpret what fate has dealt them in the form of genes in numerous ways that are unpredictable and not wholly consistent or rational, even to themselves. An outsider who tries to generalize about such responses is, it seems, doomed to failure.

Genetic Screening

Research suggests that programs offering genetic screening for populations deemed to be at risk for specific single gene disorders have been welcomed among families habitually afflicted by them, with one or two notable exceptions (see below). The effects of many of these diseases commence *in utero*, cause great suffering from the time of birth, and result in early death. The success of screening programs is measured in terms of a reduction in the incidence of the disease in question, and not in terms of the removal of mutant genes from susceptible populations. The historians Keith Wailoo and Stephen Pemberton have pointed out that management of these diseases by means of screening programs has become "potent sites for debates about family planning, religious values, and state intervention in the shaping of ethnic, racial, and communal identity."[97] In the United States particularly, several of these diseases have become vehicles for solidifying categories of race and ethnicity. Tay-Sachs disease, for example, a deadly lipid storage pathology that affects brain neurons, has been described since the late 19th century as a "Jewish disease," although it is also found among French Canadians, Franco-Americans in New England, Cajuns, and Pennsylvania Dutch. Among Ashkenazi Jews, 1 in 25–30 is a carrier of the gene, and a similar number of French Canadians and Cajuns are affected, but it has been only among the Jewish population that "genetic citizenship" was actively mobilized to combat the disease perceived within the community to be a real threat to the Jewish population as a whole.[98] The affected genes are autosomally recessive so that if both parents are carriers then a fetus has a 1 in 4 chance of being homozygous[99] for the gene in question. Such infants will inevitably be born with the deadly disease, live for only a few years, and suffer a great deal while alive.

Beginning in the 1970s, screening programs to detect the Tay-Sachs mutation became available in several places in North America. In Montreal, for example, a program that has been operating for over 30 years screens teenagers from families known to be at risk as carriers of Tay-Sachs. The Montreal program is monitored at arms' length by the Quebec government, screening is voluntary, and individual informed consent is required after potential participants are given an educational session. Results are confidential, and not even the parents of the tested teenagers are informed of the genetic status of their children (although no doubt this does not stop many parents demanding that their children pass along the information). Individuals who have been screened in the past, now adults, state that without the program they would not have had children. When individuals who are carriers decide to marry and have a family, a decision about abortion only has to be made if, on testing, the fetus proves to be homozygous for the Tay-Sachs gene. Over the past 30 years not one infant with Tay-Sachs disease has been born in Montreal.[100] A similar program exists for β-thalassemia, also autosomally recessive, and only one infant has been born with this disease over the past 30 years. Plans to set up another program in Montreal for screening sickle cell anemia were firmly rejected from the outset by the targeted community, largely of Caribbean origin. Without wholehearted community support, screening programs are today entirely out of the question in most locations.[101]

The doctor who set up the programs in Montreal has been accused of practicing neo-eugenics, but such a position is one that interprets all voluntary abortions as eugenic. Furthermore, given that the genes in question are not eliminated from the population, this program falls far short in its implementation of the original "science" of eugenics (see chapter 4). Dr East, the Harvard doctor who called for monitoring of heterozygotes in the early 20th century, would have insisted that all detected carriers of unwanted genes be sterilized, thus slowly ridding the entire population of the gene.

From the outset, religious leaders and Jewish community groups have supported Tay-Sachs screening programs. The most famous program, Dor Yeshorim (meaning "upright generation"), was founded by Rabbi Ekstein and adapted so that orthodox Jews, among whom abortion is not permitted, could participate. Based initially in New York and Chicago, this program has tested hundreds of thousands of Jews in North America, Europe, and Israel. As was the case in Montreal, this program started out by testing adolescents, but individuals are not informed about their status as carriers for Tay-Sachs disease or for other single gene disorders for which testing became available in the 1990s. This practice is justified, it is argued, because of the considerable stigma associated with "genetic disease" among the Orthodox community. When a marriage is being arranged between two families, the potential couple is at liberty to contact the rabbi to learn about their genetic status for Tay-Sachs, but only as individuals, not as a couple. Tested individuals, or a designated proxy, are then informed as to whether the potential union is "genetically compatible," but the actual test results are never made available to tested individuals or their family members. Almost without exception, when it becomes clear that the potential union is not "compatible," plans for marriage are abandoned. The program, recognized by large segments of the Orthodox community as enormously successful, is designed expressly to facilitate religious observance in which procreation is obligatory and abortions can only be obtained when a mother's life is at risk. Prainsack and Siegal point out that Dor Yeshorim is based on "a notion of genetic couple-hood,"[102] and they insist that to argue that this program compromises individual choice is inappropriate.

The program has also been criticized as paternalistic,[103] and questions have been raised in connection with "perpetuation of noxious stereotypes about Jewish inbreeding and disease,"[104] and the way in which rabbis who actively encourage participation in the program are no longer available as a "source of independent guidance regarding ethically difficult choices."[105] Even so, Dor Yeshorim has been celebrated as an unqualified success, although debates have persisted about its application for diseases other than Tay-Sachs. Francis Collins, former director of the National Human Genome Research Institute, described the addition of testing for all but a few diseases other than Tay-Sachs as a "nightmare."[106] Gaucher's disease, for example, first recognized in 1980, is an adult onset disease in which the "penetrance" of the gene is not complete, so that symptoms vary considerably among affected individuals, and some of those with the genetic mutation do not exhibit symptoms at all. Collins and others are very concerned about a slippery slope in which people may attempt to "genetically design" their offspring.[107] Rabbi Ekstein agrees with this position and has placed a strict limit on which diseases can be tested.

A third program in operation for over 30 years is based in Cyprus where screening for β-thalassemia takes place. This program, initially sponsored by the WHO, is grounded in the idea of "collective risk management" and is compulsory for all residents of Cyprus who are of reproductive age.[108] One in seven Cypriots is a carrier of a gene for thalassemia, a group of inherited disorders characterized by reduced or absent amounts of hemoglobin, a rate that is said to be the highest in the world for inheritable single gene disorders. Ninety-three percent of the children born homozygous for the gene suffer from a lethal form of the disease. Prior to the institutionalization of the screening program, it was estimated that one in every 160 newborns in Cyprus had thalassemia and it was clear to medical personnel, both at WHO and in Cyprus, that the prevalence of this disease constituted a threat to the economy of the country and to its health care system. Thalassemia was until recently highly stigmatized in Cyprus, and its appearance in a newborn was associated with wrongdoing of one sort or another in the family. Affected children were liable to be hidden, some were suffocated, and parental divorce was common. Ethnographic research by Patricia Book in the 1970s showed clearly how great was the suffering of involved families.[109]

It became apparent to medical authorities in Cyprus that it was essential above all to combat the stigmatization associated with the disease and the idea that it is a retribution for past sins. With this in mind, thalassemia began to be publicized as a collective Cypriot problem, one for which compulsory screening would provide relief. Widespread education began to be carried out in schools and by the media, and patient-groups, politicians, international experts and, above all, leading clergy of the Greek Orthodox Church added their support to the idea that a screening program would assist families in making decisions about marriage and reproduction. It was evident from the outset that if screening was going to take place, then this must happen before young people became formally engaged.

Once the program was set up, the Cypriot Orthodox Church began to routinely require people to obtain a premarital certificate to testify that they had been screened and counseled before the marriage was performed (until recently, civil marriage was not possible in Cyprus). The Church does not prohibit carriers from marrying one another, and only 3 percent of potential couples in which both are shown to be carriers of the gene abandon plans for marriage, although many resort quietly to abortion if fetal testing is positive. Turkish Cypriots are also legally required to present a screening certificate before marriage. In other words, screening is an "obligatory passage point" for marriage in Cyprus.[110] The number of babies born in Cyprus affected with thalassemia has decreased to virtually zero since the inception of the program, but it has been criticized as unethical, on the grounds that Cypriots are not free to opt out, and that the principle of individual choice is over-ruled.[111] The program has also been criticized for being authoritarian and paternalistic, and some commentators are particularly disturbed because the Church is involved. Virtually all of the critical commentators live outside the country. By far the majority of Cypriots are at ease with the system and continue to use it even though certificates of screening are now no longer needed in order to have a marriage ceremony performed,[112] and Cypriot health care practitioners are proud of what they have accomplished. Thalassemia is treated unequivocally as a public health problem, one requiring systematic intervention. No one is required to terminate a pregnancy, nor is anyone sterilized. In Cyprus, similar to the Dor Yeshorim program, the approach is collectivist rather than individualistic.[113]

Beck and Niewhöner remind us that genetic testing of all kinds is "embedded in and contingent on material-discursive practices with their own specific historicity," and that genetic screening, especially, fosters a "memory politics" of a shared distant past.[114] These authors compare the testing of thalassemia in Cyprus with that for cystic fibrosis in Germany. The creation of the screening program in Cyprus allowed Cypriots to interpret the disease as a "collective 'ethnic' fate, to understand the gene pool as a 'tragic commons' that required collective management."[115] By contrast, genetic testing and screening in Germany are inevitably understood against the backdrop of Nazi-eugenics so that it has been virtually impossible to set up screening programs; those that exist are hedged with extraordinarily complex form-filling designed to cover every possible ethical eventuality related to the practice of screening. No recognition is made of the fact that people in Germany today come from diverse historical and ethnic backgrounds, knowledge about which is highly relevant for the effectiveness of screening practices.[116]

Inevitably, wherever they are set up, individuals exposed to screening programs come from families where sensitivity to the havoc that mutant genes can wreak has been fully internalized for centuries before screening programs became available. Relatively little ethnographic research has been carried out on screening programs for deadly childhood disorders, but it seems likely that the majority of tested individuals would generate accounts about relief from an enormous burden of uncertainty that the test results bring about when couples learn that only one or neither of them is a carrier. On the other hand, those few who find that both marriage partners are carriers are left to make a distressing choice. Community responses to these programs make it evident that side-stepping terrible suffering is acceptable to the majority and, further, that stigmatization of inherited conditions is markedly reduced.

Religious fundamentalists and a few bioethicists aside, virtually no one voices opposition to voluntary screening programs set up to detect lethal single gene disorders of infancy. Even disability rights activists who are very sensitive about possible misuses of genetic testing are rarely in opposition to a technologically induced reduction in the incidence of these conditions.[117] Rather the conception of fetuses whose destiny is clearly one of terrible suffering is avoided. The causative genes are not eliminated from the gene pool, so that those few who argue that clinicians are in danger of tinkering inappropriately with the human genome are left with no scientific justification for their position. However, a recent study on Gaucher's disease found that one quarter of fetuses homozygous for the gene were aborted over an eight-year period, even though a satisfactory treatment now exists for the problem, and half of the infants born never manifest any symptoms at all. A medical specialist commenting on this situation stated that genetic tests should not be given for diseases that are eminently treatable, and that shortly we will have the ability to screen for thousands of genes by analyzing one blood spot, but with little knowledge as to what exactly possession of these genes may mean for disease incidence. Others argue, in contrast, that couples have "the right to know" and should not be denied information.[118]

Clearly, the question of what counts as valid information and what might better be described as obfuscating and disinformation is at issue here. Equally important is how populations designated at risk are created, what genes are being screened, by whom, and for what purpose. Wailoo and Pemberton point out that "the pattern of expansively testing Jewish bodies created its own new dilemmas."[119] Tay-Sachs screening brought thousands of people into clinics for testing and their bloods furnished data that assisted greatly in the compilation of knowledge about other genetic diseases, then labeled by many as "Jewish diseases," although no evidence existed that such diseases are associated uniquely with the Jewish population. This labeling took place even when scientists went to great lengths in their communication with the media to avoid the public reaching such a conclusion.[120]

The political struggle over testing for sickle cell anemia, first recognized as a disease in the early part of the 20th century, stands in strong contrast to the Tay-Sachs story. From the outset, sickle cell was associated almost exclusively in the United States with African Americans among whom 1 in 10 people is a carrier, although individuals who come from India, the Middle East, and the circum-Mediterranean area, as well as the occasional Caucasian, can also be affected. In 1949 Linus Pauling, a chemist, demonstrated that the condition is one of a group of hemoglobinopathies, thalassemia being a second. Individuals with sickle cell anemia are homozygous for a genetic mutation, hemoglobin S, that causes red blood cells to assume a sickle shape, that in turn block blood vessels and reduce oxygen flow, resulting in damage to internal organs. Affected people experience severe crises of pain, and even with treatment are subject to various debilitating illnesses including strokes. Heterozygous individuals – carriers of one mutated gene – experience few if any symptoms. The heterozygous condition is highly adaptive in malarial infested regions because it confers considerable resistance to that disease.[121]

In 1968 Linus Pauling, by then a Nobel Laureate, proclaimed: "There should be tattooed on the forehead of every young person a symbol showing possession of the sickle-cell gene ... two young people carrying the same seriously defective gene in a single dose would recognize this situation at first sight, and would refrain from falling in love with one another."[122] In making this preposterous statement Pauling was deliberately ignoring the fact that symptoms vary a great deal among affected individuals and, even at that time, a large number of people with the disease lived well into middle age. The sociologist Troy Duster points out that by the mid-1970s, when genetic screening programs first became available, in complete contrast to programs for Tay-Sachs disease in which screening was voluntary, six states and the District of Columbia required by law that children be tested before they entered school.[123] This was the case even though no treatment was available. The Black Panthers had at first thought that screening programs might be a means whereby African Americans could assert some control over their own wellbeing, but it soon became clear that whites would be running the programs that would very quickly begin to resemble the methadone maintenance clinics located in black communities across the country.[124] Rebellion against these programs rapidly emerged in response to what were perceived to be coercive and racist maneuvers, at a time when information about the ongoing Tuskegee experiments was beginning to become widely known. The programs were quickly judged a failure by the government, and replaced in the early 1980s by neonatal screening for black infants – a practice that offered genuine assistance to affected families.[125] Duster describes the mandatory screening programs as a "back door to eugenics" because a specific ethnic group, African Americans, was targeted with the intent of actively encouraging disposal, not only of fetuses affected with the disease but also heterozygotes, who would in life manifest no symptoms of illness. This is an undeniable example of "stratified reproduction" in which power relations enable some categories of people to reproduce whereas others are actively disempowered.[126]

Testing for sickle cell disease is available in several non-Western countries including Nigeria and Pakistan, and the anthropologist Duana Fullwiley has carried out ethnographic research in connection with attitudes toward genetic testing in Senegal, West Africa. She notes that the physicians whom she interviewed, the majority of whom are trained in France, were frustrated with the effects of what Fullwiley describes as "discriminate biopower."[127] Although Senegal has one of the lowest rates of HIV in Africa, at a little over 1 percent of the population, and sickle cell disease affects 10 percent or more of the population, the funding provided by NGOs, following UN and WHO directives, is almost exclusively for HIV/AIDS, and not for sickle cell disease. Nor are there local campaigns to raise awareness about the disease, making physicians who specialize in genetic disease very frustrated indeed, especially because customary marriage patterns are usually with cross-cousins or other intrafamilial partners. The result of this "erratic" biopower is that no systematic attention is directed toward the prevention of sickle cell disease. Furthermore, physicians tend to have a paternalistic attitude toward their patients and assume that they fully understand why women and their husbands do not come forward for testing.

In the minds of physicians, Fullwiley notes, genetic testing and abortion are conflated; the belief is that if the fetus being carried proves to be homozygous and tests positive for sickle cell anemia, then an abortion is the only option for the pregnant woman. Their assumption is that women do not want to be tested for sickle cell because abortion is not acceptable to this Muslim population and, further, Wolof "tradition" is that women should have many children. Nevertheless, the doctors encouraged Fullwiley to talk with women. In conducting 42 open-ended interviews, she found that 40 women agreed that prenatal diagnosis would be a good thing and one third of them said that they would abort a fetus if it tested positive for sickle cell disease. It was clear that people's decisions – their "personal biopolitics" – were based largely on their ideas about the severity of the form of sickle cell that they were familiar with as a result of family experiences, and were not restricted by religious tenets.[128]

Fullwiley writes about the way in which the concept of "tradition" is not contrasted with an idea of "modernity" by most Senegalese. However, the foreign-trained physicians do indeed make this distinction, and associate "backwardness" with tradition. In Wolof discourse, tradition is not linked with the past so much as it is "associated with possibilities that humans 'create' over time." The term does not have an opposite and "encapsulates what we [in the West] would call the contemporary."[129] Fullwiley's work provides an important lesson about the value of ethnographic findings, and implicitly critiques a great deal of research in which it is assumed that "tradition" must be supplanted with the modern. She reminds us that research has shown that in the West very many people exhibit "amalgams" of belief involving fate, faith, and science. Similarly in Senegal she shows how pragmatic and judiciously selective people can be in assessing the potential worth of genetic testing to be followed by abortion if the test is positive.

Although the majority of women interviewed cited religion as a major influence on their thinking, Fullwiley found that, even among those opposed to abortion, some thought that testing would be helpful in order to know what the future had in store for them. Others thought testing of male partners might give women just cause to divorce unsympathetic or disagreeable husbands. Alternatively, reluctant young women might be able to avoid entering a marriage arranged by the family in which it was proven with testing that children could well be born with sickle cell. Among those women who agreed that selective abortion would be acceptable, Muslim teaching was cited in which it is argued that, prior to "ensoulment," embryos are simply "life." After a period of gestation (about the length of which there is some disagreement), once embryos become "human life" and not simply life, only then is abortion considered murder. In summary, Fullwiley found that the principal matters that families raise when discussing genetic testing or screening include "recent family history and present family character, spiritual conviction and religious interpretation, marital problems and familial pressure to resolve them, and the social obligation to raise healthy children."[130]

These convictions, although many are clearly local in kind, are strikingly similar to narratives created elsewhere in that, rather than being grounded in an overtly ethical discourse, it is the family, the wellbeing of its members, and the resolution of family discord, that are given priority in justifying genetic testing.[131]

Preimplantation Genetic Diagnosis

We turn in closing to preimplantation genetic diagnosis (PGD) – a technology raising considerable concern among those activists who believe we are entering an era of neo-eugenics. In 2006, the Human Fertilization and Embryology Authority of Great Britain passed a landmark ruling that permits thousands of women who carry the BRCA1 and BRCA2 genes associated with breast cancer to make use of PGD to avoid giving birth to an infant who carries one of these genes.[132] The ruling also applies to a third gene associated with bowel cancer. This announcement revived extensive discussion about the "cherry-picking" of embryos, and the production of designer babies.

To elaborate, a woman carrying a BRCA gene who wishes to become pregnant, even if she can do so in the usual way, deliberately chooses to make use of IVF technology. She first undergoes hyperstimulation of her reproductive system in a specialty clinic, and shortly thereafter up to 15 eggs are recovered and fertilized by her partner's sperm or that of a donor. If successful, several embryos will be formed, and a single cell is then removed from each embryo at a very early stage in development in order to test for the BRCA genes. Only those embryos that do not have the BRCA mutations are implanted into the woman's body for further development.

Genetic screening of pregnant women whose fetuses are assumed to be at high risk for disease was first institutionalized in the 1960s when the technique of amniocentesis became widely available. Initially it was used for detection of Down syndrome and shortly thereafter began to be used for diseases inherited in Mendelian fashion. But the U.K. recommendation drastically changes the picture. As noted above, mutations of BRCA genes are implicated in only 5–10 percent of cases of breast cancer and are not involved in by far the majority of cases. Even when the mutations are present, this by no means determines that an individual will get breast cancer. It is estimated that on average BRCA mutations put people at an increased lifetime risk, as compared to a so-called normal population, of somewhere between 60 and 80 percent. These risk estimates are not stable and have been reassessed at ever-lower percentages in recent years.

Patient groups involved with the breast cancer movement support the new recommendation; their argument is that affected families will now be able to avoid this disease altogether and, further, that the mutation may well disappear entirely from the population as a result of the routinization of PGD. Both these claims are erroneous. These advocates gloss over yet other difficulties: undergoing IVF treatment is not without risk, and it has still to be demonstrated convincingly that IVF children are not at increased risk for certain conditions in adult life. Recent research strongly indicates that the effects on an embryo of lying in a liquid medium in a Petri dish may have life-long repercussions in connection with gene expression.[133] Moreover, both failure to conceive, and multiple births (inevitably involving cesarean sections) are common with IVF. What is more, IVF and PGD are expensive, somewhere between $13,000 and $17,000, and are not covered by the basic health care system, so that many people will be hard pressed to make use of this technology, raising fundamental questions about equal access for potential clients. Turning to the larger picture, preventive measures can be taken against breast cancer and early detection and treatment have improved dramatically over the past two decades, substantially bringing down mortality rates.[134] And, of course, breast cancer is a condition that only occurs much later on in adulthood, and does not cause suffering or mortality in children or adolescents.

Now that PGD is available, women and their doctors can select "good" embryos for implantation and leave the "bad" ones in storage or donate them for research. Should this practice be understood as a form of neo-eugenics? With respect to bringing about an imbalance in human genetic variation, the answer is a definitive "no."

Nor can use of PGD as it is practiced in Europe and North America be described as state-enforced disposal of unwanted life. However regulations in connection with IVF vary considerably from country to country. There is no regulation of any kind by the United States government or in Italy, and virtually no monitoring of what happens in private clinics. Some U.S. practitioners want this to happen, and certain U.S. states have regulations. Limited regulation is present in Canada and stringent guidelines exist in Sweden, the United Kingdom, and France. In the United Kingdom and France only a very limited number of trained clinicians are allowed to carry out PGD. Among those countries with guidelines, there is considerable variation as to what conditions may be tested for, with the United Kingdom being the most flexible. Links among politics, local values, and private enterprise (notably in the United States) and the form that control (or lack of it) takes in connection with PGD are evident, resulting quite often in "reproductive tourism."[135]

In light of these varied government responses, it is not appropriate to posit that unfettered neo-liberal values are equally at work everywhere, enabling a laissez-faire eugenics; but can this cherry-picking of unwanted fetuses perhaps be described as a negative eugenics because coercion is involved? Research cited above suggests that concern is in order.[136] Clearly governments are not directly involved, but unequal power relationships are very often at work, and unexamined prejudices are implicated. Overt coercion is no doubt rare, but pressures, subtle and not so subtle, are exerted among families and in clinics, and indirectly via medical and government-supported guidelines.

Legitimate concerns about IVF and PGD do not stop here, however. Rapidly accumulating knowledge about molecular genomics makes it clear that there are reasons to consider if it is ever appropriate to abort a wanted pregnancy because a fetus is shown to carry a susceptibility gene for such complex disorders as breast cancer, heart disease, and Alzheimer's disease (see chapter 13). Probability estimates in connection with complex disorders are in effect guesstimates, and one cannot predict with any degree of certainty who among those carrying one or more suscep-tibility genes will eventually get the diseases in question.[137] Furthermore, and most important in calculating risk estimates, epigenetics are not taken into consideration – in other words, the significance of the relationship among macro environments both social and physical, the micro-environment of the body, and gene expression is bracketed out (this point will be elaborated on in the following chapter). In making individualized risk estimates for susceptibility genes, biostatisticians take very few variables into account, making such estimates highly questionable.[138] And yet it is now well known that knowledge of what brings about or inhibits gene expression in complex disorders is crucial, rather than the mere presence or absence of a gene – making the types of probabilistic risk modeling used in connection with single gene disorders inappropriate for complex multi-factorial conditions.[139]

Obviously if one's mother and several sisters have died of breast and/or ovarian cancer, PGD may well appear to be the best choice.[140] And ethnographic research conducted in the United Kingdom by Sarah Franklin and Cecilia Roberts makes it very clear that although most people are positive about the advantages of PGD over fetal testing accompanied by abortion, they nevertheless do not approach this technology lightly; many consult clinicians but then decide to go no further. Even involved doctors evidence considerable caution.[141] Creating "perfect," disease-free babies is simply not on the agenda in the clinics that carry out these technologies, in contrast to the rhetorical hype that appears all too often in the media. Furthermore, the reality of genomic complexity and the low success rates associated with IVF technologies are likely to hamstring all efforts at creating babies to order, perhaps indefinitely. This will be the situation even if the mapping of personal genomes comes down to $1,000 per individual, as promised by James Watson and Affymetrix.[142] If and when this happens, the uses to which PGD will be put will no doubt continue to be limited primarily to testing embryos for genes associated with specific lethal or highly debilitating diseases. In the United States, perhaps more so than in other countries, where there is aggressive direct-to-consumer advertising, combined with virtually no federal or state control over the application of reproductive technologies, consumers are no doubt particularly vulnerable to exploitation. However, these laissez-faire practices, with all the usual attendant problems of economic gain, duplicities, and inequities, are not capable of producing babies to order, or "breeding" a superior population of people.

There can be no argument that the application of biomedical technologies has the potential to profoundly affect "local moral worlds," in Arthur Kleinman's idiom.[143] However, the ethnographic work cited above makes clear that genetic testing and screening are being used almost exclusively to avert untold individual and family suffering. PGD, on the other hand, facilitates increased human intervention into reproduction by making it possible to choose among and, in effect, rank fertilized embryos. For families who can afford it, using this technology to avert the birth of a child with a deadly single gene disorder may well be more acceptable than resorting to abortion. However, the danger is that this technology will be used in order to select fertilized embryos out and deliberately discard them on the grounds that they are predisposed, but by no means destined, to get an unpleasant disease in the future. Michael Sandel, a philosopher, has voiced profound concerns that go beyond the need for regulation of these emerging technologies of reproduction. He argues that: "A Gattaca-like world, in which parents become accustomed to specifying the sex and genetic traits of their children, would be a world inhospitable to the unbidden, a gated community writ large."[144] Sandel believes that, by making use of enhancement technologies such as PGD, we are radically transforming our "moral landscape" and, as reproduction is less left to "chance" and rests more on "choice," parents may well "become responsible for choosing, or failing to choose, the right traits for their children."[145] What is more, suggests Sandel, human solidarity and humility are likely to be reduced as a result of these practices.

Even though it appears that to date the majority of involved health care practitioners, individuals, and families have shown restraint, despite some inappropriate advertising on the Internet, Sandel's concerns should be addressed, although technological limitations will continue to serve as a serious limiting factor on what can be accomplished by this technology. In the United States particularly, related problems may well arise because health insurance companies refuse to cover infants whose condition could have been predicted by genetic testing or screening and their births avoided, although some states have already blocked such activities.[146] And the question of governance looms large. Should the market be fettered and laissez-faire reproduction be controlled by the state? Is it possible to contain reproductive tourism in the current environment of global laissez-faire economies? And, perhaps the most contentious of matters, will perceived individual rights or the rights of couples in connection with reproduction be understood as overly constrained if increasingly government intervenes in the implementation of ARTs? Of course, for the millions of people who cannot entertain for one moment the possibility of availing themselves of these technologies, such discussion is entirely beside the point. But it must be noted that, indeed, "human solidarity," such as it is, may well be further reduced by medical interventions of this kind into the reproductive lives of the wealthy, leaving the impoverished to make do with highly troubling practices of long standing such as infanticide and severe neglect of unwanted children in order that others may survive.

We turn in the next chapter to the common complex disorders with which all families are confronted to one degree or another. It is clear that knowledge about the contribution of genes to disease causation is undergoing a radical reformulation, in turn affecting possibilities for the conceptualization of genetically embodied identities. This situation is in large part due to the fact that only rarely does a single gene or chromosomal abnormality "cause" a disease or disorder and, even then, as already noted, the severity of the problem is by no means always predictable. For by far the majority of diseases, numerous genes, protein products, other molecules, and environmental variables are involved in causation, disease course, and eventual outcomes. This situation does not dislodge the research findings set out above with reference to single gene disorders, but it makes the task of interpreting both the biological and social import of newly emerging postgenomic knowledge exceptionally challenging.

13

Genomics, Epigenomics, and Uncertain Futures

A man's future health and happiness depend on conditions that are already in existence and can be exposed by the oracles and altered. The future depends on the disposition of mystical forces that can be tackled here and now. Moreover, when the oracles announce that a man will fall sick ... his "condition" is therefore already bad, his future is already part of him. (E. E. Evans-Pritchard)[1]

Divination has been a preoccupation of humankind for many thousands of years and continues to exert a hold over what may well be a majority of the world's population. Whether its practice involves an examination of the entrails of sacrificed birds and animals, the patterning of cracks formed by heating animal bones, the alignment of yarrow stalks according to the rules of the I Ching (The Book of Changes), consultation with oracles in trance-like states, or sessions with any number of kinds of fortune-tellers, divination produces knowledge not readily available to ordinary people – knowledge that has the potential to incite action. Historical and anthropological research suggests that a primary concern during divinatory proceedings is explanations for what has already taken place, for it is in the reconstruction of past events that causes of misfortune are uncovered and moral responsibility is assigned, on the basis of which suitable action can be determined.[2]

However, divination does not simply link the past to the present. Omens for the future are also integral to divinatory practices. Research carried out in the 1990s by Nadia Seremetakis in Inner Mani, Greece, showed how interpretations or "warnings" by "gifted" women result in associations being made among events and people that are given meaning usually kept apart in people's minds; because dreams and divination do not comply with a linear temporality and events that may have taken place years apart are often conflated to bring about new significance. Furthermore, exactly where, when, and on whom future danger or misfortune will alight is not clearly foretold by the women when retelling their dreams, but even so they often speculate on who might be "targeted."[3]

With the rapid accumulation and dissemination of findings from molecular genetics and genomics[4] (the study of the genomes of cells and of whole organisms), a new divinatory space has arisen that has the possibility of creating a highly potent zone of anxiety about what the future may have in store for the health of individuals and indeed families. Moreover, this rapidly advancing ability to bring "potential futures into the present"[5] means that in theory each one of us is now constituted as part of a single population, that of the "pre-symptomatically ill,"[6] because we all are susceptible to one condition or another as a result of our genetic heritage. Having one's genes named by an expert would, one might think, bring about greater insight into future possibilities than do fables told by a fortune-teller; however, paradoxically, the more we learn about the world of molecular biology, gene–environment interactions, the activity of genomes as a whole, and developmental biology, it is increasingly clear that, on their own, genes – with relatively few exceptions – are associated with little predictive power. Even though at times genetic technologies permit us to speculate with much more precision than was formerly the case about who may be struck by bodily misfortune, a characteristic feature of all forms of divination nevertheless remains – namely that in seeking to take control of the future, new ambiguities and uncertainties inevitably arise, as ethnographic findings presented in the previous chapter made all too evident.[7] However, the discussion that follows in this chapter makes it clear that the emerging sciences of genomics and epigenomics (the study of cellular molecules that control the expression of genes and other molecules involved in heredity) are filled with uncertainties and surprises and, further, they are changing at an unprecedented speed, creating an unstable "logics of vitality."[8]

As this knowledge expands, several remarkable transformations have come about in scientific reasoning, among them increasing agreement that genes are in, effect, concepts and not biological facts per se – rather it is the genome and not the gene that can more readily be thought of as a material reality constituted by DNA.[9] This shift in reasoning means that research is focused on systems of interacting macromolecules rather than on discrete particles. Second, gene expression, or perhaps more appropriately, the activation and deactivation of specific segments of DNA, is dependent upon a large number of variables, so that genes cannot by themselves be thought of as the driving force of life. These insights and many others mean that making predictions about future risk for illness on the basis of classically defined protein coding genes alone has become extraordinarily problematic for all but the rare Mendelian mutations associated with single gene disorders, and even then, as we have seen, not all such predictions are conclusive.

It is abundantly clear that genomics and its associated technologies form the cornerstone of a vibrant new approach in the biological sciences, accompanied at times by hype about a utopian future shortly to materialize, at which time, it is claimed, we will be liberated from the deficiencies and deformities that nature persists in bestowing upon humankind. For the time being, however, genomic consortia are heavily occupied with a massive collection, systematization, and storage of material for research purposes, in particular of DNA samples. The U.K. Biobank, for example, is currently investigating the respective contributions of the "genetic predisposition and environmental exposure (including nutrition, lifestyle, medications etc.) to the development of disease."[10] This project, the largest of its kind in the world at present, is still in the process of enrolling half a million individuals willing to donate blood and other bodily materials for storage at the bank, to be linked with medical records and socioeconomic data. Thus far, about 100,000 people living in the U.K. have agreed to participate. Already, the challenge of locating specified samples for use in experiments has become so great that robots have been installed that are programmed to work all night lining up retrieved materials for scientists to make use of the next morning when they come into work. A phenomenal number of research findings are being made every day in connection with genomics at this particular biobank and at thousands of other sites around the world, but the task of interpretation, of what exactly these findings mean for human health and illness, is, in many respects, in its infancy.

In this chapter we take up three matters: the eclipse of the dogma of genetic determinism; the emergence of the field of epigenetics; and the contribution of "susceptibility genes" to complex disease, using Alzheimer's disease as an illustrative example. In the chapter that follows the question of biological difference among humans in light of molecular genetics and genomics will be discussed.

Dethroning the Gene?

Over the course of the past decade billions of dollars were invested in what came to be known as the "Holy Grail" of biology – the mapping of the human genome. The first rough maps that resulted – one created with public funding, the details about which appeared in *Nature*, and a second, carried out with private funding, published in *Science* – caused enormous excitement and a great deal of commentary about the big breakthroughs that lay just around the corner. However, knowledgeable commentators suggested at the time that these maps are equivalent to having a list of parts for a Boeing 747 but no idea as to how the parts go together and no knowledge of the principles of aeronautics.

It is now well known that while mapping the human genome involved scientists set aside approximately 98 percent of the DNA they had isolated, labeling it as "junk" because it did not code for the production of proteins and therefore did not conform with their idea of how the blueprint for life was assumed to work. In the years since the announcement in early 2001 that the Human Genome Project was relatively close to completion, the situation has changed dramatically, and "junk" DNA, thrust summarily to one side in order to focus on the task of mapping only those genes that code directly for proteins, is no longer ignored. A 2003 article in *Scientific American* states: "new evidence … contradicts conventional notions that genes … are the sole mainspring of heredity and the complete blueprint for all life. Much as dark matter influences the fate of galaxies, dark parts of the genome exert control over the development and the distinctive traits of all organisms, from bacteria to humans."[11] This article goes on to point out that it is now believed that what was formerly discarded as junk DNA without doubt makes a singular contribution to bringing about biological variation. Much junk DNA has, as yet, no known function, although some non-coding DNA is genetic "switches" that regulate the expression of genes, and at times it may be employed by proteins to assist their work. Furthermore non-coding DNA produces non-coding RNA,[12] the function of which is proving to be remarkable. Almost overnight we have entered an era in which the "dark" parts of the genome are beginning to fluoresce,[13] although much research remains focused on genes that code for proteins.

The activities of non-coding RNA (ncRNA) are understood today as comprising the most comprehensive regulatory system in complex organisms, a system that functions to create the "architecture" of organisms without which chaos would reign.[14] To this end, ncRNA has been shown to profoundly affect the timing of processes that occur during development, including stem cell maintenance, cell proliferation, apoptosis (programmed cell death), the occurrence of cancer, and other complex ailments.[15] Consequently the research interests of molecular geneticists are no longer confined largely to mapping the structure of genomes, but have expanded to unraveling the mechanisms of cell and organism function both in connection with individual growth and development and with respect to changes over evolutionary time. Central to this endeavor is to understand gene regulation – above all how, and under what circumstances, genes are expressed and modulated.[16] In this rapidly proliferating knowledge base, known as epigenetics, organized complexity is recognized, and activities of the cell, rather than that of genes or DNA alone, are the primary target of investigation. Effects of evolutionary, historical, and environmental variables on cellular activity, developmental processes, health, and disease are fully recognized; even so, a great deal of research remains focused at the molecular level.

This emerging knowledge has exploded the central dogma on which molecular genetics was founded. Metaphors associated with the mapping of the human genome – the Book of Life, the Code of Codes, the Holy Grail, and so on – no longer appear so apposite. And gene fetishism (never embraced wholeheartedly by all involved scientists[17]) is now on the wane among a good number of experts, although recognition of discontinuities and ruptures across knowledge domains is crucial in coming to grips with the current status of genomic knowledge. It is readily acknowledged that classical genetics was a highly productive time and that furthering knowledge about genomes continues to be of singular importance. However, genes are no longer conceptualized as deterministic by the majority of researchers, although this is not so across the board, and sweeping claims continue to be made, by evolutionary psychologists and evolutionary psychiatrists, among others, about direct causal relationships between genes and behavior.[18]

Eclipse of the Genotype–Phenotype Dogma

A critical review of the history of genetics shows clearly how struggles over what will count as authoritative knowledge have been the norm for over 100 years.[19] The form that these disputes take crystallized with the introduction at the beginning of the 20th century of the genotype–phenotype distinction, causing friction among the separate disciplinary fields of heredity, embryology, and developmental biology, each of which brought a particular orientation toward research in connection with the transmission of hereditable material from one generation to another. The eminent Danish scientist, Wilhelm Johannsen, eager to put theories about the biology of inheritance on a sound scientific footing, argued forcibly for the recognition of a distinction between structure (the genotype) and its expression (the phenotype). Johannsen insisted that earlier ideas about inheritance, described by him disparagingly as the "transmission conception of heredity," were not only outmoded, but clearly wrong. In making this claim, Johannsen set himself up as the founding father of the science of genetics, and set himself apart from his predecessors, among them Gregor Mendel, Francis Galton, and August Weismann, all of whom assumed that personal qualities and behaviors could be transmitted from generation to generation.[20]

Johannsen deliberately likened the new genetics to the "hard" science of chemistry. This hope was later reiterated by chemist H. E. Armstrong writing in the 1930s: "some day, perhaps, biography will be written almost in terms of structural chemistry, and the doctrine of descent stated in terms of the permutations and combinations affected between genes."[21] Thus was the stage gradually set for an era that came to be dominated by genetic determinism, consolidated, as everyone knows, by the mid–20th-century discovery of the structure of DNA – final evidence, it was assumed, of the units of inheritance. The Human Genome Project, designed explicitly to expose the structure of the sequence of the DNA base pairs in the human genome, was the culmination of this approach. Although some outspoken scientists, James Watson among them, apparently assumed that once we had this map in hand we would in effect have a full understanding of how genes work and of what makes us human, it was evident before the map was complete that some major surprises were in store. An ontological shift can be detected from about the 1970s in which a good number of researchers began to be more comfortable talking and writing about DNA rather than genes.[22] Concomitantly, the idea of the gene started to become disconcertingly fuzzy for many of them (although some clinical geneticists, focused on single gene disorders, are an exception).

Findings that resulted from mapping the human and other genomes forced considerable self-reflection in the world of genomics. Above all, the discovery that we humans have only approximately 30,000 genes, whereas some less complex organisms, notably some plants, have many more, was a great surprise – a cause for some humility, perhaps! Furthermore, it is now clear that many genes encode for more than one protein, and that these proteins can be used in many different contexts, while many others do not encode for proteins at all. A further remarkable insight made it evident that gene expression is by no means always a unidirectional process. Increasingly it has become clear that multiple factors, including events both internal and external to the body, enhance or inhibit gene activity throughout the lifecycle. Another surprise was the discovery of "retroviruses," such as HIV, composed of RNA that are able to "reverse transcribe" their genetic material into DNA to infect the host's genome. These and other crucial insights have, in effect, overthrown the central dogma of genetics that prevailed until the beginning of this century – that any one gene sets off a unidirectional flow of information from DNA to RNA to protein to phenotype. This model has proved inadequate to account for the molecular and cellular activity in the human body that is currently being made visible.

The molecularized universe clearly is very much more complicated and exciting than most people had imagined; entirely in consort with postmodernity, it is a landscape littered with a pastiche of shape-shifters – so-called smart genes, jumping genes or transposons, silent mutations, and so on – an environment of the unexpected, in which boundaries formerly thought to be stable are no longer so, with enormous implications for the routinization of genetic testing, as many involved with health care assume will shortly be the case.

Epigenetics: Beyond Genetic Determinism

The philosopher Lenny Moss has pointed out an enigma evident in the natural sciences that periodically comes into stark relief whenever conceptual ground begins to "shake or shift."[23] The problem is how to account for the "apparently 'purposive' nature of the living organism in the purely mechanistic terms of our post–17th-century understanding of nature."[24] Even more vexing, argues Moss, is the question of "how to locate ourselves – the purposive, flesh-and-blood investigators – within the conceptual framework of our biological inquiry."[25] Moss identifies a continuum along which strategies for coping with this enigma can, in theory, range. At one end lies full-blown preformationist theory in which the Creator determines all. René Descartes fell closer to the other end of the spectrum – one of pure epigenesis, in which "ostensibly purposive life-forms were spontaneously generated from inert matter,"[26] although many of Descartes' followers were unable to make the break with preformationism. Moss concludes that neither of these extremes has been of direct relevance for biological investigation over the past 100 years; investigators have come to an uneasy agreement that both genes themselves and levels of interaction greater than the gene are involved.

Along similar lines, philosopher Paul Griffiths notes:

> it is a truism that all traits are produced by the interaction of genetic and environmental factors [but] the almost universal acceptance of this view has done little to reduce the prevalence of genetic determinism – the tendency to ignore contextual effects on gene expression and the role of non-genetic factors in development.[27]

Moss agrees, noting that the idea that living matter can organize itself into a "self-sustaining, self-organizing, boundary-maintaining entity" has been difficult to establish in the face of the apparent attractiveness of genetic determinism. Demands that the door be opened to fundamentally different conceptions of the organism, in which the genome is situated in a living organism, have been repeatedly rebuffed.[28]

Those who work in this lively field of epigenetics are forging a new approach in which genetic determinism is abandoned. Space does not permit a detailed summary of current theories of epigenetics; suffice it to say that the very word epigenetics has more than one meaning[29] and that some claim that the discipline is not that new but came into being in the 1940s or earlier,[30] while others disagree vehemently with this position. Most current research into epigenetics focuses primarily on the expression and regulation of genes. Questions posed about the phenotype, for example, ask why monozygotic twins do not always manifest the same diseases and, when they do, why the age of onset can differ by up to two decades.[31] This narrowly conceptualized epigenetic approach immediately makes the limitations of genetic determinism patently evident.

A broader, more critical form of epigenetics, known by its adherents as "developmental systems theory" (DST), supported by a mix of philosophers and biologists, is currently gaining ground. Using this approach, it is argued that epigenetic phenomena should be recognized as having independence from the activity of genes.

The starting point is an ontological reversal of genetic determinism, and gives priority to dynamic interactions among very many variables, with numerous possible outcomes. Barnes and Dupré, sociologist and philosopher of science respectively, ask what this means for the usual assumption of geneticists that complex organisms grow from a single fertilized egg – the process known as ontogeny:

> The life sequence of an organism is a series of cell divisions, differentiations, and deaths. What does this imply about the nature of the organism? Is each organism produced anew by the process of ontogeny, or does an ever-present organism merely develop and change in the course of the process? The first formulation equates the organism with its final form. The second assumes that the organism is there throughout, present as whatever material object exists at any stage of development. This alternative recognizes organisms as constantly changing entities, not the outcomes of a line of development from A to B but entities traveling round an unending cycle of forms. On this view, organisms should be understood as life cycles.[32]

Barnes and Dupré note further "instead of being spoken about as independent atoms of hereditary material, genes, conceptualized as DNA, are now referred to as parts of the chemical/molecular systems within the cell, and specifically as sources of particular protein."[33] DNA is not simply involved, then, with heredity; one now has to ask what does DNA do "all the time," throughout the lifecycle?

The biologist Scott Gilbert argues by extension that the DST approach implies that "our 'self' becomes a permeable self. We are each a complex community, indeed, a collection of ecosystems."[34] Paul Griffiths argues that the DST approach encourages researchers

> to investigate how a trait actually develops, what resources its reliable development depends upon, whether there are many developmental routes to this outcome, or only one, over what range of parameters is this developmental outcome stable, and how the "environment" changes as a function of initial development differences that produce this trait.[35]

Contingency is the name of the game. It is now accepted by DST researchers, and many others working in genetics and genomics, that genes do not have clearly demarcated beginnings or ends; nor are they stable, and only very rarely indeed do they determine either individual phenotypes or the biological make-up of future generations. Quite simply, then, genes are not us, and the gene can no longer pass as the fundamental animating force of human life; it has been dethroned.

The question now being asked by Richard Strohman, a molecular biologist, is: "if the program for life is not in our genes, then where is it?" He notes that many of his colleagues have been arguing quietly for a long time that "there is no program in the sense of an inherited, pre-existing script waiting to be read." Rather, he argues, "there are regulatory networks of proteins that sense or measure changes in the cellular environment and interpret those signals so that the cell makes an appropriate response."[36] This regulatory system, a "dynamic-epigenetic network," has a life of its own, so to speak, with rules that are not specified by DNA.

Epigenomics

Systematic research into epigenetics is just beginning to take off and, although genetics and genomics play an indispensable role in this research, ultimately the objective is directed toward explaining what it is about inheritance, health, and illness that genetics alone cannot explain.[37] A widely cited example is provided by findings that have accumulated over the years in connection with what is known as the Dutch famine of 1944 that occurred in the western part of the Netherlands. Thirty thousand people died from starvation as a result of a food embargo imposed by the Germans in World War II that resulted in the complete breakdown of local food supplies, adding to the misery of an already harsh winter. Birth records collected since that time have shown that children born of women who were pregnant during the famine not only had low birth weights but also exhibited a range of developmental and adult disorders later in life including diabetes, coronary heart disease, breast, and other cancers. Furthermore, it has been shown that this second generation, even though prosperous and well nourished, themselves produced low birth weight children who inherited similar health problems.

These findings strongly suggest that expression of specific DNA sequences had been repressed due to radically reduced nutritional intake during pregnancy and that this effect persisted in ensuing generations. It is now known that these changes are the result of molecular processes that take place at specific sites at the cellular level, the best known of which is called methylation. It has been shown convincingly that environmental variables can alter this complex process and that the changes that result can be inherited independently of DNA. These findings are currently attracting a great deal of attention among researchers[38] and have opened the door to what is being described positively by some as neo-Lamarckianism. Increased knowledge about methylation and other key processes at the level of the cell are beginning to make clear some of the crucial mechanisms involved in dynamic epigenetics, and furthermore, making apparent compelling evidence about the indivisibility of nature and culture and the means by which extensive variation is produced over time.[39]

However, as Strohman makes clear, scientists are currently suspended between paradigms: genetic determinism is a failed paradigm he argues (although the majority of involved scientists quite possibly disagree with him), and research into dynamic epigenetics is only just taking shape – in short, we are betwixt and between, and the current generation of scientists, especially when they work in alliance with the corporate world, have, for the most part, been trained for and remain firmly embedded in a deterministic framework. And yet, even Craig Venter, who headed up a privately funded group that was one of two to first map the human genome, is on record as commenting that genes cannot possibly explain what makes us what we are; similarly, Strohman insists that while the Human Genome Project did indeed tell us a great deal about our genome, it told us nothing about who we are and how we got this way.[40]

Interpretations of this kind bring us firmly into the realms of anthropology and philosophy. The fundamental question becomes one of whether or not DNA has any "agency" or "activity" at all – concepts that Neumann-Held and Rehmann-Sutter argue are in any case thoroughly anthropomorphic.[41] From the societal perspective what, then, does it mean to assume, as biological determinists apparently do, that mapping the human genome actually configures human identity; that biology fully informs us about who we are? Can we indeed "know" ourselves on the basis of our genetic make-up? Although epigenomics moves the focus of inquiry clearly to the level of the cell, many researchers continue to focus on molecular activity as, in effect, the origin of agency. Research networks involving social scientists, social epidemiologists, and basic scientists – formations that might well incite radical change and insights – remain very rare indeed.

Gabriel Gudding argues that technologies that enable rapid DNA analysis permit a massive redeployment of agency and morality to the gene.[42] He reminds us that increasingly DNA evidence is used as the irrefutable mark of individual identity, whether as part of the rapidly increasing surveillance technology, as forensic evidence in the courtroom, as verification of the remains of people "disappeared" in the Argentinian Dirty War or Kosovo, for example, and in determining if a female athlete is "really" what she claims to be. By conflating sex, gender, and genes we assume that we can be "truthfully" informed on the basis of DNA testing about who among us are men and who are women. Our biographies are written today, at least in part, in terms of structural chemistry, as many of the early geneticists had envisioned. Genotype does not fully determine phenotype, but traces of DNA can determine, almost with irrefutable certainty, whether someone was present or not when a particular event took place. But this is only one very limited aspect of embodied identity, a decontextualized glimpse of a chemical identity, leaving the dynamics of individual growth and change, self-reflection, the effects of early nurturance, social and environmental interactions of all kinds and local biologies entirely out of the picture.

In her book *The Century of the Gene*, Evelyn Fox Keller sums up where she believes we now stand:

> Genes have had a glorious run in the 20th century, and they have inspired incomparable and astonishing advances in our understanding of living systems. Indeed, they have carried us to the edge of a new era in biology, one that holds out the promise of even more astonishing advances. But these very advances will necessitate the introduction of other concepts, other terms, and other ways of thinking about biological organization, thereby loosening the grip that genes have had on the imagination of the life sciences these many decades.[43]

Keller, while she is clear that the concept of the gene is "good enough" for many experimental purposes, concludes that it is time to think about adopting new concepts to bring about more appropriate insights into the workings of living systems. Gelbart insists that the term "gene" may have become a hindrance to many biologists in their attempts to understand the molecular world[44] and Keller adds that this problem is no doubt even more marked among "lay readers."[45] However, the empirical findings set out below suggest that, in the context of complex disease, people from affected families are by no means wedded to the idea of the gene as a powerful deterministic force.

The APOE Gene and Alzheimer's Disease

The case of the APOE gene is a compelling example of how attempts to forecast the future based on the function of so-called "susceptibility" genes are fraught. Increasingly, we can test for genes associated with specific complex diseases, but it is exceptionally difficult to make meaningful estimates of how and under what circumstances such genes place individuals at increased risk. In light of rapidly accumulating research findings, many researchers argue that we will never be in a position to make reliable estimates of risk for most complex conditions. Even in the case of the Mendelian genes, it is frequently not possible to predict age of onset or severity for many of these disorders, as we have seen, and ongoing research shows just how complex are these so-called, single gene disorders. The cystic fibrosis gene, for example, is not a simple material object at all: any one of over a thousand DNA sequences can code for functionally defective variants of the implicated protein, all of which are characterized as the cystic fibrosis gene.

When it comes to the common diseases that affect people from all walks of life, wherever they live – heart disease, cancer, dementia, asthma, obesity, and so on – all thought of accurate predictions about future disorder based on genetic testing alone is severely compromised by the complexity confronting researchers and the public. This is so for four reasons: first, the questionable accuracy of representation of the population databases on which estimates of increased risk are calculated; second, the insurmountable difficulty of converting increased risk estimates created from these databases into individualized predictions; third, knowledge about molecular genetics is subject to constant modification and will continue to be in flux for the foreseeable future; and, fourth, genes involved in all but the single gene disorders are susceptibility genes. In other words, such genes do not have high penetrance[46] in the language of genetics, cannot on their own account for the disease in question, and inevitably function in concert with many other variables including other genes, in addition to the microenvironment of cells and macroenvironments external to cells and to bodies. These difficulties are, of course, inextricably intertwined, with the result that estimates of risk based on calculations of probability in connection with susceptibility genes alone have, almost without exception, little explanatory power, and in any case are constantly being revised, usually downward, as further knowledge comes to light.

The DNA that constitutes the APOE gene, implicated in both heart disease and late-onset Alzheimer's disease (AD), was mapped very early, in 1993, and although a remarkable amount of work has been carried out on this gene, its lifelong activity in the human body remains elusive. In what follows we will focus on the relationship of APOE to risk for late-onset Alzheimer's disease.

Alois Alzheimer originally observed a case of what is now known as early-onset Alzheimer's disease. This rare form of dementia occurs in approximately 170 extended families worldwide, has long been thought of as a genetic disease, and is associated with three specific mutations each of which has been mapped.[47] It is not strictly true to claim that the gene determines even this autosomal dominant form of the disease, because the age of onset for identical twins can vary by as much as a decade.[48] Early-onset AD usually (but not inevitably) manifests itself somewhere between the ages of 35 and 60, progresses relatively quickly to death, and accounts for between 2 and 5 percent of all diagnosed cases of the disease. Research into this Mendelian form of the disease continues and contributes greatly in efforts to better understand what is commonly known today as late-onset Alzheimer's disease.

The search for a genetic basis to late-onset AD, the common form of this disease, has thrown open a Pandora's box. The first publication on this topic appeared in 1993 and explicitly made an association between a variation of the gene known as APOE and increased risk for the common, late-onset form of AD.[49] This finding forced some revisions of the received wisdom of the time, namely that Alzheimer's disease in older people is "sporadic," and does not "run in families." The APOE gene is located in humans on chromosome 19, is present in all mammals, and is essential for lipid and cholesterol metabolism. The gene almost without exception comes in three universally distributed forms APOEε2, APOEε3, and APOEε4, and evidence from over 100 laboratories has shown that it is the APOEε4 allele that puts individuals at increased risk for AD. Between 14 and 16 percent of so-called Caucasian populations (the most extensively studied population) carry at least one ε4 allele; however, it is unanimously agreed that the presence of the allele is neither necessary nor sufficient to cause the disease for reasons that are as yet very poorly understood. In other words, the ε4 allele is an example of a susceptibility gene, one that contributes to disease causation only under certain circumstances.

It is estimated that at least 50 percent of ε4 carriers never get Alzheimer's disease,[50] so and research in connection with the allele shows that when it is implicated in AD, exactly the same final biological pathway is involved as that set in motion by the autosomal dominant genes associated with the early onset form of the disease. However, the biological changes in which APOEε4 in its homozygous form is implicated become manifest later in life, usually between the ages of 65 and 75.[51] For individuals who are heterozygous and have only one ε4 allele, the age of onset is usually later. Given that somewhere between 30 and 60 percent of patients diagnosed with late-onset AD do not have the ε4 allele, there must be at least one other, and probably several more, pathways to Alzheimer's disease.[52] Involved scientists assume that such pathways are constituted by mutually interactive genes, non-coding DNA and other macromolecules, in conjunction with environmental factors, internal and/ or external to the body. The effects of these alternative pathways become apparent late in life, usually after age 70 or later.

Despite broad-based consensus in the dementia research community about these findings, it is at the same time agreed that the allele alone determines nothing with respect to the incidence of AD. This segment of DNA is neither necessary nor sufficient to cause the disease. Major problems inherent to research design are among the many causes of confusion about estimations of genetic risk for AD. Many studies do not represent a named population at large, instead they are often based on clinical samples. When general population samples are made use of, the relationship between APOEε4 and AD appears to be significantly weaker than is commonly suggested.[53]

There is another very important factor that must be noted. Throughout the history of AD, it has been shown repeatedly, since the time of Alois Alzheimer, that the diagnosis of this condition is not robust. In general terms, there is no argument about the broader taxonomy of symptoms of dementia; however, of the various conditions subsumed into that category, Alzheimer's disease, by far the most commonly diagnosed of these conditions, is the waste-basket category – the one made use of when other types of dementia have been ruled out. When this condition is diagnosed, doctors are required to write on the chart "probable Alzheimer's disease." Arguments persist as to whether Alzheimer's is merely a phenomenon of aging – simply the signs of senility evident in us all if we live long enough,[54] or is it indeed a disease? If a disease, then what exactly are its distinctive pathological features?

Several other conditions exhibit what are assumed to be the defining pathological signs of the AD brain, including Parkinson's disease, Down syndrome, various toxic conditions, and so on. And the behavioral features considered characteristic of AD do not "fit" well with changes in the brain when it is autopsied. Some afflicted people have many of the plaques and tangles associated with AD but have exhibited few if any behavioral changes in life and, conversely, a few people who exhibit significant signs of dementia while alive have few plaques and tangles at autopsy.[55] In other words, Alzheimer's is neither a biological fact nor a firm taxonomic category and is best thought of as a concept – a gloss for an undeniably devastating condition. This uncertainty has enormous repercussions for creating estimations of risk for AD based on population studies. The stark reality is that neither the genotype nor the phenotype for the condition is robust.

An over-emphasis on the contribution believed to be made by APOEε4 to the genetics of AD obscures the fact that many other risk factors have been associated with AD, some of them well established, including toxic environments, head trauma, education levels, chronic stress, prions, and so on. Furthermore, APOEε4 has been shown to work in unexpected ways in certain locations. For instance, among Pygmies, and other populations whose subsistence economy was until relatively recently predominantly that of hunting and gathering, APOEε4 apparently protects against AD, a finding that holds when controlled for age.[56] Rigorous epidemiological studies have reported low rates of AD in parts of Nigeria, and the presence of an APOEε4 allele does not appear to be implicated when it does occur. On the other hand, APOEε4 is significantly associated with AD among African Americans, although less so than in white populations.[57] It is argued that risk-reducing factors (in Africa) and risk-enhancing factors (in North America) must be implicated including, no doubt, other genes that are selectively switched on or off in association with diet, stress, environment, and so on.

Clearly, as a result of both methodological inconsistencies and the complexity involved, the contribution of APOEε4 to AD is far from being fully understood, and the association continues to be just that – an association. Despite 15 years of research, no one knows how and under what circumstances the ε4 allele functions to initiate the pathology that develops into AD. Nor is it known what it is that protects the numerous people with this particular allele who never become demented. The current situation has been summarized by two neurogeneticists as follows: "First, and most importantly, the heritability of AD is high … this had been demonstrated in various studies … over the past decades." But, these experts go on to note, "most of the research currently being done has faulty methodology, lacks replication, and is inattentive to haplotype[58] structure."[59] Using the citation index PubMed, Bertram and Tanzi show that in 2003 alone a total of 1,037 studies were carried out on the genetics of AD, out of which 55 analyzed genes were reported to have a positive association with increased risk for the disease, while 68 tested negative. Candidate genes have been examined on every single chromosome and mitochondrial DNA has also been investigated. These authors conclude with a caveat: "while the genetic association per se [of APOEε4 with AD] has been extremely well established … there is no consensus as to how this association translates pathophysiologically," nor how it functions in conjunction with the other numerous candidate genes.[60]

It is evident that basic science and epidemiological findings about late-onset Alzheimer's disease are subject to continual revision and are far from conclusive. In order to try to improve this situation, a publicly available, continuously updated database has been created known as Alzgene. This database comprehensively catalogs all genetic association studies in the field of Alzheimer's disease with the result that more than a dozen susceptibility genes have been picked out as the most significant contributors to AD, although none have statistical significance to anywhere near the degree that does the APOE gene. What is more, the rank ordering of these candidate genes changes month by month.[61] A new technology known as genome wide association studies (GWAS) has recently become available in which up to 20,000 samples of DNA are placed on gene chips capable of scanning a million single nucleotide polymorphisms (SNPs) at a time, that are then converted into readable information by means of high-speed computational analysis of enormous power. The current assumption among involved scientists is that GWAS research may provide some answers about the combined function of multiple genes in the incidence of AD. However, because this research is not "hypothesis driven" – that is, informed by a specific research question – some describe it as a search for several tiny needles in a gigantic haystack.[62]

The APOE gene is an exemplar of unpredictability; the activities of this segment of DNA make it patently clear that when dealing with the genetics of complex disease, recognition of the co-construction of the material and the social is indispensable. In other words, estimates about future risk and the effects on an individual of being informed about such risk, together with possible associated transformations in embodied identity and practices of self-governance, cannot be assessed independently of the "non-human actor"[63] – the DNA segment itself – and the environment in which it is functioning.

As Paul Rabinow has pointed out, people learn about genetics from a number of sources: the medical world, advocacy groups, the media, direct-to-consumer advertising, friends, relatives, public forums, and on the street.[64] They usually have time to reflect on what they have heard, are not pressed into taking immediate action and, more often than not, are particularly interested in gleaning information about one or more specific diseases that they believe "run" in their families. Given that knowledge in molecular biology is very often unstable and inconclusive, people's decisions about testing will be influenced by how knowledge is imparted to them and exactly what it is. Questions that arise immediately in connection with susceptibility genes are whether or not families have been made aware of the molecular complexity involved, and also of the inability, in many cases, of experts to predict the severity of the disease, or if the condition will occur at all. It is no surprise, then, that current guidelines about genetic testing for the APOE gene do not support its routinization in clinical care, particularly because there is no known treatment for the disease but it is possible that this may change in the not-too-distant future.

Genetic Testing for Late-Onset Alzheimer's Disease

Even though official guidelines are currently opposed to routine testing for the APOE gene, several private companies offer testing (the U.S. based Athena diagnostics holds the patent for APOE testing), and an "Early Alert Alzheimer's Home Screening Test" kit is marketed directly to consumers.[65] Furthermore, a strong argument is being made among certain neurologists that individuals who show some memory impairment and are diagnosed with mild cognitive impairment (MCI – believed to be a sign of incipient Alzheimer's disease) should be routinely tested for their APOE status. Recent research suggests that although by no means everyone diagnosed with MCI "converts" to AD, those diagnosed individuals who also have the ε4 allele are at much greater risk for conversion, and should be identified as early as possible.[66] In addition to testing carried out in these settings, an NIH-approved randomized controlled trial involving APOE testing that goes under the name of REVEAL (Risk Evaluation and Education for Alzheimer's disease) has recently been carried out at four research sites in the United States.[67]

The 442 subjects for this study are young or middle-aged and healthy, but come from families where one or more members have been diagnosed with Alzheimer's disease. The educational level of these individuals is high – a mean of 17 years at three research sites, and of 15 years at one other. As a group, participants are given a lengthy PowerPoint education session about the genetics of AD. If they then decide to participate in the project, blood is drawn, and a few weeks later individuals are informed in private which of the APOE alleles they carry. This "disclosure session" is followed by 12 months of follow-up monitoring during which time the research subjects respond to three rounds of structured interviews. The hope is to find out what impact knowledge about the APOE genotype has had on anxiety levels, sense of wellbeing, changes in health care coverage, and other variables, all of which are assessed using standardized scales.

Open-ended interviews were carried out by anthropologists with a sub-sample of 79 of the REVEAL subjects at all four sites, 12 months or more after REVEAL participants had initially received their genotype.[68] To the surprise of these researchers, nearly 75 percent of the participants had forgotten, mixed up, or were confused about their genotype and the associated risk estimates for AD that they had been given. This finding is noteworthy because 91 percent of the informants stated that "wanting to know" their genotype was a major motivation for participation in the REVEAL study, although making a contribution to research was of greater importance to most people. Even though the majority could not recall their risk estimates accurately, nearly half had retained the gist of the information, and were able to recall, reasonably accurately, whether or not they have a "good" or "bad" gene.

Among the four people found to be homozygous for ε4 who were given the highest risk estimates – an increased risk over a baseline population of approaching 60 percent by age 85 – three were able to recall their ε4/4 genotype accurately. The fourth recalled that she has the "bad genes" but added: "I'm still totally confused, although I do know I have two of them, whatever those bad things are." The single African American who is homozygous for ε4 has only one affected relative, her mother. Pearl is able to recall her genotype, and has a rough idea of her increased risk over the coming years; however, she says that she knew about this risk anyway because of her "blood" (her family history) and adds, "really, it's all up to God, you know." She is pleased she was tested, and angry with her sisters because they simply "brushed off" her result, as she puts it. Pearl was hoping REVEAL would "prove" that she will not get AD, but now she is back in God's hands. She says she was anxious while going through the study, but that this anxiety let up quite quickly once she had completed all the interviews. As a result of the project, she has reduced the fats in her diet and is thinking about changing her health insurance, but cannot really afford to do this. Other than her immediate family, Pearl has not told anyone about her result, not even her family doctor. She believes that what counts more than anything else is a positive attitude coupled with faith.

Of those who found out that their genotype is ε3/3 (the majority of participants), one of them (Adele) had the following to say:

> According to that test, I don't have the risk, okay? So, technically I should feel better. But I don't believe it, given that there are four people in my family with the disease.

Of course, it could be that Adele's family members are also ε3/3, because, as noted above, at least half of all patients diagnosed with AD do not have ε4 alleles. Furthermore, Adele has been taught as part of the REVEAL education session that she does indeed have increased risk, whatever her genotype, because her relatives have the disease, but she has apparently not fully grasped (or perhaps forgotten) what she was taught. Other informants clearly express their confusion about the test results:

> From one meeting to the next I would come in and I couldn't remember what my risk was. And to this day, I'm not 100 percent sure. But I know that it's elevated.

A second said:

> I don't remember much ... to be truthful, not much. I'm sure I have it [my risk estimate] somewhere, but I don't remember where.

A third responded as follows:

> Is it the 3/4 that's the least likely to get it? I don't even remember. But it was good news. Whatever it was.

Some people were explicit about their frustration with the project:

> Well, I know where I am at, where I stand. I can let my kids know where we stand. You know, I mean, maybe get it, maybe not.

And for others subjective experiences about memory loss appear to cause more anxiety than does genotyping results:

> I can say that I've always felt all my life that I've had some memory issues ... so I have that little question, whether it's something that you actually had in some way even when you were very young ...

The psychologist Martin Richards created the concept of "blended inheritance" some years ago to account for a prevalent understanding he documented among the British public in which a mixing or blending of influences from each parent is thought to be the way in which inheritance works, rather than by means of a Mendelian transmission of genes.[69] Such ideas stem from a long tradition of such reasoning evident as early as classical times.[70]

The REVEAL qualitative findings made it clear that among many respondents there is a tendency to identify a family member who in some way resembles the afflicted person as the individual most likely to be at risk for developing Alzheimer's. For example, Katherine said:

> I showed you the picture of me and my dad. We look like clones, practically, physically. And nobody's really said – I don't know whether or not that makes a difference, a person's physical appearance. But I have a suspicion that it does.

Robert commented:

> Do I think I have a higher than normal chance? Yes. Heredity. And also I'm so much like my mother, who had Alzheimer's. There's a very high likelihood that one or more of her children will have a predisposition toward it. And I would say I'm front-runner because of so many other characteristics that are very much like my mother's.

It is perhaps not surprising that when the REVEAL interviewees discussed theories of causation, multi-causal explanations were common, and genetics did not dominate the exchanges. Even though the REVEAL project was about genetic testing everyone had been carefully taught that APOEε4 does not *cause* AD. When asked what caused her father's illness Caroline responded: "I can't pinpoint any one thing." Another participant replied:

> I think [genetics] play a part, but I don't think that's all. I'm sure that a lot of the diet, and the health, and the exercise that we do today will prolong life and mental acuity.

It appears that the REVEAL education sessions worked to reinforce a concept of multi-causality already in the minds of many participants prior to the study, knowledge that is reinforced by family physicians and other medical professionals, the media, and Alzheimer support groups, each source arguing that multiple factors undoubtedly contribute to the causation of Alzheimer's disease.[71]

Interpretations of Risk Estimates

Results from the follow up questionnaires indicate that tested individuals do not experience increased anxiety levels that extend much beyond the time of actually receiving their result.[72] When open-ended interviews were carried out more than 12 months after being told of their estimated risks, the majority of participants had transformed the information they had been given into accounts that "fit" with their experience of being related to someone with Alzheimer's disease, personal assessments of their own family history, and the accumulated knowledge about the disease that they had gathered from a variety of sources. In other words, in a manner reminiscent of individuals responding to testing for single gene disorders, risk estimates provided in the REVEAL study rarely displace "lay knowledge" that participants bring with them to the project about who in their family is particularly at risk. Rather, this "scientific" information is either nested into pre-existing knowledge – woven into what Arthur Kleinman would call an "illness narrative" that encompasses past experience and family stories[73] – or else it is simply forgotten, or actively rejected. Anne Kerr and colleagues commented some years ago that, in effect, individuals act as their own authority about the interpretation of genetic information.[74]

All the REVEAL participants seemed particularly receptive to what they had been taught about the uncertainty of how exactly genes contribute to AD. The education sessions that everyone was required to attend in all probability worked to reinforce the concept of blended inheritance already in the minds of the majority of participants prior to the study. No doubt this was because it was repeatedly emphasized that the APOEε4 allele does not determine disease occurrence but, rather, only puts individuals at increased risk. It is also evident that many individuals who believed they are at 100 percent risk for AD because of their family history were reassured that this is not the case.[75] There is, of course, a possibility that some of these people now believe they will not get AD, but the education session was designed to avoid this misunderstanding.

Given the current state of knowledge about the APOE gene, the validity of the individualized risk curves and increased risk estimates that have been handed out to the REVEAL research subjects have to be questioned. But, in any case, responses of the REVEAL participants suggest that few, if any, significant changes resulting directly from the test results take place with respect to subjectivity, behavior, and anxiety about what the future holds in store. Individuals do not apparently believe their futures to be profoundly changed from what they had already envisioned but, rather, hold firm to ideas already internalized about what "runs in the family," the power of family resemblances as predictors of future disease, a belief in AD multicausality, and the impossibility of ever being sure about the future when a stubborn disease such as AD is at issue.

Many, perhaps the majority of researchers in the Alzheimer world believe that family history continues to have more predictive power about what the future has in store than does the APOE gene. Furthermore, current research directions are likely to show that combinations of genes, environments, lifestyles, and other macrovariables provide information that will, in effect, contextualize the activities of the APOE gene. It is quite possible, then, that the DNA segment known as APOEε4 is unlikely ever to amass sufficient power, scientific or symbolic, as a potent signifier of dementia. Clearly this gene does not captivate people, as do the BRCA genes. This situation may well change if and when medication is found that acts differentially on the three basic APOE alleles and proves to be effective in blocking the molecular path to dementia. At such time a concerted push to routinely test individuals for the APOE gene may well come about. Even so, the APOEε4 polymorphism will persist in being unpredictable in its actions in individual bodies and inherently elusive. At present, public activism in connection with Alzheimer's disease continues to take place in connection with well-established forms of biosociality that have no bearing at all on genetics or genetic testing. These activities include contributing financially and as research subjects to the search for medications; lobbying for better care of AD patients and, above all, for improved support for home care.

Advances in molecular genetics have certainly brought about a reproblematization of life itself as we have seen, but the reign of the gene as the supreme icon of this transformation is undergoing an eclipse brought about by genomic and epigenomic insights that are neither deterministic nor stable, making predictions about future encounters with complex disease highly questionable.

Learning (Again) to Live with Uncertainty

The hubris associated with the Human Genome Project was always entirely out of place. Most involved scientists knew from the outset that mapping the genome was a relatively straightforward step toward a second challenge of a much bigger order, namely, understanding how genes function *in vivo*. As the extent of the complexity of functional genomics became increasingly apparent, it was glaringly evident that there were going to be few, if any, straightforward answers. Progress has been made in mapping a good number of the single gene disorders, but little alleviation and no preventive measures or outright cures have been found as yet, and gene therapy is proving to be exceptionally difficult to execute. As technoscience produces an increasingly large deluge of findings in the world of genomics and epigenomics, it is undeniable that DNA is just one actor among very many others in the molecular world, and as such, with only one or two exceptions, it cannot stand alone as a reliable signifier for individual futures.

As members of society, we have been schooled to take responsibility for health and illness – to practice risk avoidance and exert prudence. It was pointed out long ago that such an individualized, depoliticized approach to disease causation permits governments to rescind responsibility for toxic environments and reinforces societal inequities, making the poor particularly vulnerable to ill health and shortened life expectancies. Globally, this situation is unconscionable. It is claimed that in the not-too-distant future individuals will be informed routinely about their personal genome profile as part of basic clinical care,[76] and hundreds of DNA tests for identifying genes associated with specific disorders are already available.[77] However, it must be emphasized that a gradual routinization of genetic testing has the potential to reinforce the current individualistic approach to health and illness.

Nevertheless, knowledge about DNA often incites action, bringing about social, and political as well as individual activities. With epigenetics gaining ground, and the entanglement of nature and culture ever more apparent, emerging insights may in part influence the form that political activity takes in connection with disease prevention, challenging the primary allocation of responsibility for health and illness as entirely that of individuals and families, and arguing instead for an extensive recentering of public accountability in the domains of society and politics.

14

Human Difference Revisited

In closing this book we take up, all too briefly, the troubling question of biological difference among humankind. As noted in chapter 4, by far the majority of cultural anthropologists have for the past half century been adamantly opposed to the division of humans into racial categories, primarily because of a justified concern about the deadly conflation so often made between visible biological difference and an essentialized discrimination. The ordering and classification of the world about us – the creation of taxonomies – is a fundamental, indispensable, human activity,[1] but the classification of specific objects and events has a history and implications. As we have seen, the consolidation of statistics in the 19th century became the pre-eminent means by which human groups were classified in one way and another, drawing on the newly found concept of "population" that permitted differentiation among peoples. These activities were intimately associated with the rise of the modern state. As part of this transition, the Flemish mathematician Adolphe Quetelet, a key figure in the early history of statistics, put forward the idea of an "ideal type" when investigating human population that was to have a profound influence on the way in which the concept of race became accepted as a biological fact in the latter part of the 19th century.

Interest in "exotic" peoples and attention to physical difference is a very old human preoccupation that has been documented from classical times, and no doubt existed even earlier. Until the 16th century, in those regions that came under the Judeo-Christian sphere of influence, the descent of all people was traced back to Adam and Eve. Although physical differences were recognized, it was nevertheless believed that no fundamental division existed among human beings. A change came about during the early days of global exploration and the founding of colonies, intimately related to the obsessive collection of natural objects that in turn fostered the creation and systematization of typologies, among which was the beginning of comprehensive natural-history taxonomies based on morphology. Identification and depiction of ideal types were central to this process, and items designated as anomalous were set to one side. Such activity is associated with a propensity to make dichotomous distinctions, and difference between designated kinds becomes "the prime negotiated entity in the construction of a classification system."[2] The idea of immutable difference among humans was clearly postulated in the late 17th century by the founder of the Royal Society in England, John Ray, who wrote in 1690 that God had created the "species" and that a "species is never born from the seed of another species."[3]

In the mid–18th century, the best known taxonomist of his day, Carl Linnaeus divided the species *Homo sapiens* into six diurnal varieties: *ferus* (four-footed, mute, hairy); *americanus* (red, choleric, erect); *europaeus* (white, ruddy, muscular); *asiaticus* (yellow, melancholic, inflexible); *afer* (black, phlegmatic, indulgent) and *monstrosus* (further subdivided to include deviant forms from several regions). These diurnal varieties were compared with a single nocturnal one, the troglodytes or cave-dwellers exemplified by *Homo sylvestris* ("man of the woods," or Orang Utan).[4] Well into the 19th century an argument continued as to whether Pygmies, Hottentots, and Orang Utans belonged with the nocturnal or diurnal varieties of humankind, and travelers' tales of the time asserted that the Orang Utan was "equally ardent for women as for its own females."[5]

The French scientist George-Louis Leclerk Buffon is credited with introducing the concept of "race" into the biological literature in 1749,[6] although he argued from the outset that race is an arbitrary classification serving only as a convenient label, and could not designate a definable scientific entity. Buffon and his numerous contemporaries, interested in the taxonomy of humankind, used skin color and the shape of the face and the skull as their key categories of signification; some years later Johann Blumenbach, a German physician, today recognized as the founder of physical anthropology, added hair form to this classificatory system. Prior to the 18th century, it had generally been assumed that when humans migrated out of the Garden of Eden and moved into different environmental niches, a certain amount of "degeneration" from the primordial human form had taken place, accounting for visible physical variation, but this was not inherently valued negatively. However, once the concept of distinct human races was established, the original meaning of degeneration was gradually transformed in a subtle but insidious fashion. Georges Cuvier, for example, a leading scientist of the early 19th century, argued that certain races were "by nature" inevitably degenerate, and could never be stimulated by their physical or social environment to achieve greatness, to become, in essence, whitened, "physically, mentally, or morally."[7] The process of degeneracy was used to assign people to their "correct" place in the new international order, with the result that by the end of the 19th century the urban poor, prostitutes, criminals, and the insane would all be labeled as "degenerate" types; their purported deformed skulls, protruding jaws, and low brain weights marked them as "races apart" from others in whom evolutionary progress was evident.

Louis Agassiz, an enormously influential 19th-century biologist who regarded himself as an intellectual heir to Cuvier, argued vociferously after his arrival in America from Switzerland to take up a position at Harvard University, that God had created blacks and whites as two separate "species."[8] By analogy, similar arguments were made about the intellect and physical bodies of women, who, although of the same race as their menfolk, were nevertheless systematically ranked as lower and inferior to them.[9]

Since the time of its formulation as a biological category, the construct of race has been contested, particularly because it was readily apparent that the so-called races could interbreed successfully, proof that humankind is of one species and therefore biologically alike.[10] However, once Herbert Spencer's theory of social evolution was widely accepted in the second half of the 19th century, the way was opened up for the idea of race to become hardened into an established scientific concept that became increasingly difficult to refute, especially because the slave trade, the arrival of substantial numbers of Europeans in North America, and the subjugation of the indigenous peoples, gave enormous impetus to the study of race and its solidification as a biopolitical category.[11] Ian Hacking reminds us that some of the first European censuses were carried out in the colonies: "Categorization, census, and empire" are an important nexus, he states.[12] In the English-speaking Empire, embroiled in the slavery of Africans, race inevitably became the "natural" category of difference.

Throughout the 20th century several well-known biologists and anthropologists positioned themselves in favor of the fact of race. The geneticist Theodore Dobzhansky stated in the 1960s: "the ideal classification of the races of man is yet to be proposed. The existing ones are tentative ... Yet it does not follow that races are arbitrary and 'mere' inventions of the classifiers; some authors have talked themselves into denying that the human species has any races at all!"[13] The most enduring counter-arguments to this position have been made by Steven J. Gould, Richard Lewontin, and others: "the obvious fact of variability does not require the designation of races" because it is geographic variability, and not race that is self-evident.[14] However, the concept continues to be used, most notably in connection with forensic databases, causing a dilemma for physical anthropologists whose expertise is called on to classify human remains. The majority of physical anthropologists do not accept the existence of human races; nevertheless, forensic anthropologists are able, with considerable accuracy, to evaluate from human skeletal remains whether a deceased individual was of "black," "white," or "native Indian" ancestry. As one anthropologist put it in the early 1990s:

> race identification by forensic anthropologists has little to do with whether or not biological races exist. ... In ascribing a race name to a set of skeletonized remains, the anthropologist is actually translating information about biological traits to a culturally constructed labeling system that was likely to have been applied to a missing person.[15]

This comment highlights the indivisibility of social and biological categories so evident in the history of the concept of race, and that continues to reverberate in human engagements of many kinds wherever they take place.

The material reality – the phenomenon of human difference – cannot be swept to one side simply by asserting a belief that all humans are made equal while racism and discrimination continue to rear their ugly heads at every turn in just about any country one chooses to name. Human interactions are profoundly shaped by our sensitivity to local classifications and social and political uses and abuses of difference marked out very often in terms of skin color. It is customary to subsume such superficial physical difference into recognized social categories of ethnicity, religion, caste, linguistics, race, or some mixture of several of these descriptors. Such biosocial categories are conflated by many with a belief in fundamental biological difference among people; such beliefs existed long before the concept of race began to be made use of in Europe, the Indian caste system being perhaps the most notable example.

Once scientific truth-claims gradually disrupted the authority of pre-Enlightenment thinking, and a belief in the existence of races based on anatomical classification of difference became a dominant ideology among many of the European and North American intelligentsia, often supported by religious commentary, the conflation of social and fundamental biological difference was forcefully reinscribed not simply as the work of God or gods, but as a truth. However, scientific evidence is by definition contestable, and it was possible throughout the 20th century to have public debate and publication of evidence disproving the existence of race, although this by no means resolved the situation. Today the matter is again inflamed by recent findings in population genetics, as current debates about "molecularized race"[16] make abundantly clear. It is in the United States where this contest is most apparent, a country where identity politics has long been characterized as racial.

Molecular Biology and Racial Politics

In the mid-1980s, the United States government began to respond to public pressure to bring about better inclusion of minority and marginalized groups into the purview of health care research. The sociologist Steven Epstein documents comprehensively the various concerns and activities of reformers from many walks of life who participated in bringing pressure on the government, spearheaded initially by people in the women's health movement, but soon also including demands for change in connection with the health of minorities.[17]

A significant outcome of these reform activities was the NIH Revitalization Act of 1993 that included two significant provisions, one being that, as of 1995, women and members of minority groups must be included as subjects in all clinical research funded by the agency. The second provision stated that every NIH-funded clinical trial be "designed and carried out in a manner sufficient to provide for a valid analysis of whether the variables being studied in the trial affect women or members of minority groups, as the case may be, differently from other subjects in the trial."[18] Steven Epstein, in commenting on the changes, notes that this health policy is a product of a "vexed history" of both attending to and ignoring bodily difference, and he highlights how women and minorities are themselves divided as to whether this initiative promotes racism and sexism or, alternatively, is for the general good. Epstein summarizes his own position thus:

> Subpopulation descriptors – "black men," "Asian-American women," and so on – have ... dual character; they pinpoint locations on a reified ... map of social positions and biological properties, but they also designate embodied collective actors engaged in reflexive processes of organizing for political ends, contesting social meanings, and thereby remaking the map.[19]

The demarcation of contestable boundaries for the dual purpose of research and politics, whether by policy-makers, scientists, or activists, lays bare what the majority of researchers in the United States had black-boxed for many years, namely that there may be relevance to such categories in connection with disease incidence. Once findings from molecular genetics began to accumulate, further politicization and disputes about the relationship of biological difference to race were inevitable.

A 2004 special supplement in *Nature Genetics* based on the proceedings of a conference convened at Howard University in Washington made it clear how contentious the question of race has become. Several scientists, including Craig Venter, argued that race is biologically meaningless; however, Francis Collins, former head of the National Human Genome Research Institute, was more circumspect. He noted that ancestral origins may have correlations with "self-identified race" and pointed out that "it is not strictly true that race or ethnicity has no biological connection."[20] Other researchers, however, openly advocated the use of race in making decisions about medical treatment, and in the design of research studies.[21]

The population geneticists Jorde and Wooding remind readers that although humans show little intra-species genetic variation because of our late evolution, as compared with chimpanzees and all other species, even so, each pair of humans differs, on average, by two to three million nucleotide base pairs[22] that constitutes 0.1 percent of the human genome.[23] They add for good measure that numerous studies have shown in a variety of ways that humans first evolved in Africa where genetic diversity accumulated. Later, a small subset of this African population left the continent to found anatomically modern populations that spread around the world – a point that has been popularized by Malcolm Gladwell.[24] These populations show proportionally less genetic variation than do peoples who did not initially migrate out of Africa.[25] Jorde and Wooding reiterate these points to reinforce that there is basic agreement today among the majority of researchers that the human species is of recent, common origin. Acknowledging that population research into molecular genetics embraces a major problem because named populations are superimposed onto raw data, Jorde and Wooding choose instead to focus on findings based on comparison of individuals. This kind of research, of which there is now a great deal, makes clear that individual genotypes tend to cluster according to their ancestral or geographical origins.[26]

Jorde and Wooding argue that it is possible to conclude from this research that Europeans, East Asians, and Africans cluster into distinct populations, encouraging some scientists to argue for the validity of race, but once a large sample of people from the Indian subcontinent are added into the analysis, the picture changes. Considerable overlap then becomes evident between the European and East Asian samples due, no doubt, to the numerous well-documented migrations that took place over the past 10,000 years between Europe and Asia. Most importantly, each individual in any of these four clusters "shares most, but not all, of his or her ancestry with other members of the same cluster."[27] Jorde and Wooding conclude from these findings, as do many other population scientists: "ancestry is a more subtle and complex description of an individual's genetic make-up than is race," and takes into account the continual migrations and "mixing" of human populations throughout history.[28] They argue that the "picture that is beginning to emerge from this and other analyses of human genetic variation is that variation tends to be geographically structured, such that most individuals from the same geographic region will be more similar to one another than to individuals from a distant region."[29] However, most significant, due to continuous migration, this genotypic variation is distributed in a continuous fashion and does not have marked discontinuities.[30] As Barnes and Dupreé have put it, genomes both "individuate" each one of us and, at the same time, "celebrate unity."[31]

Jorde and Wooding are quick to point out that the idea that populations are not "pure" is by no means new, and that Blumenbach, writing in the 1700s, and Charles Darwin, 100 years later, to name just two, argued against "race" as distinctive or constant.[32] They go on to argue strongly that what today is labeled as race in epidemiological and clinical research, cannot be equated with ancestry. They use specific examples to illustrate how, for the majority of common medical conditions and also in connection with the responses of individuals to drugs, the implicated alleles are present across all populations (as is the case for the Alzheimer's illustration in chapter 13), although the alleles are unequally distributed. They elaborate by noting the substantial allelic variation within populations, but emphasize that these variants are nevertheless present across all populations as a result of shared human ancestry. Further, they are careful to note the importance of environmental and other factors, including epigenetic variables, in activating and modifying the function of genes. These authors conclude that further genetic investigation is "likely to render race largely irrelevant in the clinical setting" because testing individual genomes for allelic variation will become feasible, and this will circumvent entirely a need for classification by population.[33] This article makes it abundantly clear that it is the frequency of specific traits, and not dichotomous variables such as the presence or absence of named genes, that is key to the authors' argument. They also reiterate several times throughout their discussion that "populations" are not discrete entities but, rather, are concepts – heuristic devices to enable research.

The Molecularization of Race

Not all genetic researchers take the above approach, and some are actively making use of racial profiling in a search for drugs that they argue have the potential to improve the health of marginalized groups. In observing a laboratory where such research is taking place Fullwiley notes that, because DNA samples are organized and stored for analytical purposes according to the societal descriptors of race (self-defined), a "molecularization of race" is inevitably taking place. Self-defined descriptors of race and ethnicity made use of in laboratories are cementing in place what people in the United States have been obliged to perform for many years when asked to fill out official forms of numerous kinds, including those to do with medical research.[34] Fullwiley notes that the overwhelming similarity among DNA samples could have overridden any interest in breaking down the samples according to race, but this did not happen. An African American scientist suggests that the NIH Revitalization Act, with its emphasis on gender, race, and ethnicity, may well have exacerbated matters, and in the end served to promote racism.[35] A small number of other African American scientists agree with him, but the majority, even though many fully recognize inconsistencies associated with the use of race as a scientific category, nevertheless persist with its use, encouraged to do so because NIH funding sources require that racial distinctions be made. Fullwiley found that the scientists whom she interviewed did not hold a consistent or clear idea of what "race" means to them and her ethnographic inquiry showed clearly that for many, but not all, apparent differences in human biology corresponded to U.S. census categories.[36] Not surprisingly, population geneticists and other scientists working on health-related genomics in other countries do not find such a categorization helpful; on the contrary, many are actively opposed. So too are researchers who argue that it is the effects of living a "racialized" life that primarily account for health disparities, and that a reinscription of race does everyone a disservice.[37]

The anthropologist Michael Montoya probes further into this problem. He writes: "ethnoracial labels do more than identify groups: The labels are used to attribute qualities to groups."[38] He uses the concept of "bioethnic conscription" in his ethnographic research among Mexicans living in Sun County, Texas, on the Mexican–American border, to highlight the way in which, integral to research, the social identities and life conditions of DNA donors are grafted onto explanations about diabetes causality grounded in molecular biology. In other words, Montoya examines how "the complicated social and biological meanings of race and ethnicity simultaneously shape the biomedical production and representation of diabetes knowledge"[39] and in doing so demonstrates how "Mexicana ethnicity" is "naturalized" to account for diabetes etiology. Montoya is adamant that this process is not a simple remaking of the idea of race in the genomic era. He argues that bioethnic conscription takes place in two modes: descriptive and attributive. In descriptive mode ethno/racial classifications are used to pragmatically describe and report about human groups. In attributive mode, ethno/racial labels are used to assign qualities to groups – this second step easily leads, Montoya argues, to racialization. His ethnographic research, involving extensive participation in laboratory activities and interviewing of the involved scientists, enables him to demonstrate that the process of bioethnic conscription happens, in effect, independently of the intentions of human actors. Slippage, much of it inadvertent, frequently takes place between the descriptive and attributive modes of thinking at all stages of knowledge production and dissemination of findings about diabetes causation.

Type 2 diabetes is a major health problem globally and it is estimated that by 2025, 270 million people worldwide will be affected. In 1996 a consortium of diverse researchers was formed because each group of researchers came to the realization that their samples alone were not adequate to carry out the extensive genetic analyses believed necessary to achieve significant results. An "academic, corporate, and state-funded alliance" was formed, composed of molecular, biological, computer and clinical scientists from research sites in Europe, Japan, and the United States. By October 2002 the group had found a polygene candidate for type 2 diabetes, in other words, the interaction of two specific genes appeared significant in diabetes causation, although this does not rule out the possibility of finding that many other genes are also implicated.[40]

Following convention, data sets that are collected and exchanged by the diabetes alliance are organized by two criteria of geography, that is, physical place of origin, and according to named populations. Montoya writes about the extensive discussions that take place among the scientists in connection with the assignment of samples into specific named categories based on these two criteria. For example, when selecting a control group for research in Sun County, debates erupted about the extent of Native American admixture with Puerto Ricans and Mexicans respectively. The debate, and others like it, was settled by referring to the different social histories of Puerto Ricans and Mexicans, on the basis of which it was assumed that less admixture had occurred in Puerto Rico. The scientists willingly acknowledge that the classificatory system they use is imperfect but, nevertheless, it has coherence for them and, above all, facilitates the research they are carrying out in connection with diabetes. They believe that organization of data by populations helps them to achieve the two things most needed for reliable genetic research into complex disease. First, case control comparisons of populations regarded as genetically "homogenous" are needed in order to compare the genomes of individuals affected with the disease in question to those not affected. Second, control is needed for what is known as "population stratification," that is, the different evolutionary histories of groups of people that will have resulted in genetic variation, most of which has no significance for susceptibility to disease, but can create "noise" if not controlled for.

Montoya finds it necessary to deconstruct the dominant ideology in connection with diabetes causation, namely that certain "racial" groups, following United States classification – African Americans, Hispanics/Latinos, American Indians, and Alaskan Natives – are at much greater risk for diabetes than are whites. In reality, the absolute numbers of whites affected is 1.6 times higher than all of these groups combined but, if preference is given to prevalence estimates, as routinely happens, then it can be construed that minority "racial" groups are biologically more vulnerable. Race is therefore reinscribed onto biology in the mundane practices by which scientists, clinicians, and patients alike seek to make sense of illness.

The geneticist James Neel's well known "thrifty gene hypothesis," posited in 1962, has contributed to this bias.[41] Neel postulated that throughout human evolution those people living in difficult environments whose bodies had a so-called "quick insulin trigger" could rapidly convert sugar to fat in times of famine. The assumption is that, today, with an abundance of food and a sedentary lifestyle as the norm, impaired regulation of glucose has become common among these particular peoples. Neel himself emphasized the environmental aspects of his argument and in his later writings emphasized that lifestyle changes were inevitably implicated, and not genes alone. But most researchers have focused on what is assumed to be a proven history of racialized human genetic variation, and the assumptions made and the research methods used by the diabetics research consortium reinforce this approach, although individual researchers are by no means blind to the significance of environmental variables (in this respect their approach is very similar to researchers working on the genetics of Alzheimer's disease).

Montoya concludes: "biogenetic material is so infused with social meaning that those who handle it inevitably reattach (conscript) the sociohistorical context of its production as it travels from the DNA collection site to the laboratory to the journals to clinical practices and back again."[42] But he also richly illustrates the way in which discussion and arguments take place among researchers and with journal editors about when and under what circumstances ethno/racial labels should be disclosed and how, in this particular instance, stereotyping of a vulnerable group of Mexicans living in poverty in the United States should not be further exploited. Their position is in agreement with an editorial published in 2000 in *Nature Genetics*: "epidemiological differences between racially classified groups might indeed be a proxy for discriminatory experiences, diet or other environmental factors,"[43] and hence should be systematically investigated.

Commodifying "Race" and Ancestry

We are living in an era when the 0.1 percent of genomic difference among human kind is being commodified for use in bioscientific research. At the same time this is an era in which public discourse about human rights strives for political action that confirms all people as equal. Commodification of racialized genomes is being carried out primarily for three reasons. The first, discussed all too briefly above, is a search for the contribution of specific segments of DNA to disease incidence, a search in which the majority of involved researchers today are sensitive to a degree about the contribution of history, environment, and social/political factors to disease causation. Genetic determinism is not part of this discourse, and nor is a hard-nosed approach to fundamental difference among human kinds, even though race is usually used as an organizing principle, in the United States, at least.

Second, human genetic variation is actively being made use of by drug companies in efforts to promote "personalized medicine" in which, in theory, the hope is to tailor drugs to individual genotypes. So far, there has been little success with this approach[44] with one notable exception. In a large clinical trial of the drug BiDil, it was not found to prevent heart failure and the FDA refused to license the drug. However, subsequent statistical analyses suggested that in a small group of African Americans, the drug was effective. Although this finding could have been a coincidence, it lead the pharmaceutical firm that sponsored the study to undertake a subsequent trial in African Americans alone. This trial did show that the drug prevented heart failure, allowing the firm to market the drug specifically for this population. The issue of who "counts" as African American, and whether those in the trial were representative of "African Americans" in general, is complicated by the fluid social aspect of this label which the drug company researchers assumed referred to a fixed biological essence. Moreover the trial did not evaluate whether BiDil is better for African Americans relative to whites alone as only the former were included in the study.[45] This was a clever use of a randomized controlled trial to produce evidence to allow the drug to be marketed that nonetheless generated considerable negative publicity as a result of the blatantly self-interested attempt to make use of "statistical mischief"[46] to market BiDil as a "black" drug. This persistent conflation of social categories with supposed dichotomous biological difference suggests that the drug may, in fact, not achieve promised efficacy in the real world where race is a fluid and shifting social and biological category.

The third approach, explicitly encouraged by certain of the scientists who believe that racial difference has scientific value,[47] is the popular activity of searching for one's ancestry by paying for the production of "personalized genetic histories." The anthropologist Stephan Palmié makes it clear how much this activity potentially reignites a belief in fundamental biological difference among humans. His concern is about the "revelations of 'invisible essences' of relatedness and difference" coming about as a result of genomic ancestry making:[48]

> Much like the classical oracular systems on ethnographic record, certain genomically enhanced practices of genealogical identity arbitration in contemporary U.S. society ... perform their cultural work by establishing Wittgensteinian "angles": propositions

around which doubt can turn but that can never be subject to doubt themselves. In the case at hand [African Ancestry projects], such angles pivot on the idea of "racial identity" as an objectively occurring phenomenon whose reality, history and social conventions notwithstanding, ultimately resides in the realm of the biotic.[49]

We do not yet know whether this popular activity of reconstructing genomic pasts, among which African Ancestry projects are a salient example of a more generalized phenomenon visible in many parts of the developed world, will reinforce the naturalization of the idea of race, but clearly this is a possibility. The Nigerian-born geneticist who works in the United States, Charles Rotimi, has expressed great concern about the dubious activity of establishing genetic profiles that supposedly are representative of named African groups, among them Wolof, Zulu, Yoruba, and other tribal entities, whose boundaries have always been extremely fluid. Rotimi cautions that the very real complexities of history are being erased through this spurious genotyping.[50] Palmié is concerned above all that this present round of "racecraft"[51] is precipitating a genealogical amnesia in which "black" people have only "black" ancestors and "white" people only "white" facilitated by the translation of complex histories into supposedly transparent biological "realities" with the assistance of commercial genomic services and certain academic geneticists.[52] Such practices reduce "race – like witchcraft, kinship, class, or, indeed, capital" into a "thing" and not a social relation,[53] with the likely result, as Palmié notes, as does Rotimi, of dehistoricizing race and thus obscuring the very social and political relations that must be kept visible if race and racism are to be diminished. What we are witnessing with the commodification, aestheticization, and dehistoricization of local biologies is exactly what so many social scientists have been concerned about for over half a century – a return to a belief in fundamental difference among human kinds.

Looping Effects

The use of "race" as an epidemiological variable has been criticized explicitly by social scientists for many years as being an inaccurate reflection of biological reality and, further, because the categories are not reliably reproducible.[54] Montoya's findings show clearly that by no means all involved researchers are at ease with the concept. Even though ethnicity and race are mobilized to enable research, in the minds of researchers these categories are not, in their estimation, facts of nature, nor reliably reproducible, and most remain acutely aware of the histories of the social construction of such categories. However, in contrast to the position of most population and molecular geneticists, when it comes to efforts on the part of pharmaceutical companies to create ethno-racially specific drugs, race is deliberately conflated with biology, and biological boundaries of human difference are dichotomized in the interest of making a profit, as the example of BiDil discussed above illustrates.[55]

Ian Hacking argues that "a kind of person" comes into being at the same time as the "kind of being itself" is invented (see chapter 1). He calls this dynamic nominalism: "in some cases ... our classifications and our classes conspire to emerge hand in hand, each egging the other on."[56] On the basis of an examination of the history of several medical conditions, Hacking concludes that people are not simply given disease labels by bureaucrats, medical experts, or other powerful bodies, that they then come to embody. Rather, Hacking insists, labeling and classification – the very act of "making up" people – is more complex than this and actually changes the people who are labeled, so that they become, in effect, moving targets. Hacking calls this the "looping effect." Race is a particularly pernicious example of dynamic nominalism, one with an exceptionally long history. It is a concept that has been remade time and again everywhere that humans have had contact with the "other." Racial labeling of peoples as being of fundamentally different kinds in order to justify exclusion and discrimination is clearly anathema to humanist thinking.

The latest inscription of race grounded in molecular biology raises the fear that it may be possible, this time round, to create an argument that the phenomenon of race is unarguably genetically determined, and thus lend what is apparently scientific support to racist discourse. Virtually all scientists who believe in the value of using racial classifications make great efforts to disassociate themselves from racism, and indeed a good number of population geneticists themselves come from minority groups.[57] The core of the difficulty lies with ascription – with the assignment of value to ethnoracial labeling. This entanglement of phenomena is exceptionally difficult to tear apart as the above discussion makes abundantly clear, and as most people are fully aware from media reporting and, at times, in their own everyday experiences.

Resurgence of the erroneous belief that race has a genetic basis potentially undermines efforts to promote a global recognition of human unity, and also deliberately misinterprets the findings of population and molecular genetics. The result is that efforts to bring about increased understanding of the effects of social inequalities on health outcomes may well be jeopardized if arguments are reduced to those about race and ethnicity. Similarly, the significance of emerging epigenetic findings that show life-long developmental disadvantages as a result of toxic environments and social inequality may be undermined.

Recognition of local biologies as phenomena that are incessantly malleable and unstable, that are produced and transformed over evolutionary and historical time and as a result of human activities for better or worse, works in consort with approaches that foreground social inequality and developmental disadvantages. Such a marriage works most powerfully and successfully to challenge misplaced ideas about fundamental biological difference.

Epilogue

As we finished writing this book, two medical breakthroughs made media headlines. One is about the transplantation of a trachea, the structure of which was created out of the stem cells of the patient herself, thus avoiding the need for immunosuppression. An international consortium of researchers and clinicians were involved in this project, carried out in Spain.[1] The second report was about a remarkable surgical procedure carried out in the Democratic Republic of Congo that involved the successful amputation of an entire arm and shoulder from an adolescent who had been bitten by a hippopotamus. The attending doctor did not have the necessary experience to carry out the surgery and was given instructions by his colleague in London via text messaging on a cell phone.[2] Technological innovations and interventions such as these are remarkable and to be applauded and, of course, so too, for example, are simple effective technologies including vaccination, contraception, and blood pressure medication.

Yet even simple technologies remain out of reach for very many. For instance, while in some of the poorest countries antibiotics and obstetrical services may be available, women continue to die at alarming rates during childbirth. Colleagues working in Mali recently reported to us preliminary results of a study on maternal deaths in this country.[3] Local physicians investigated the cases of 38 women who died of preventable complications of childbirth because of a delay in receiving care. They conducted what are called "social autopsies," which involve reconstructing the events leading up to the deaths, and classified the delays as follows: the first delay comprised the time from the onset of warning signs that labor was going badly (such as fever or excessive pain) to the decision to seek care; the interval between this decision and arrival at the nearest health center was the second delay; and the third delay was between the woman's arrival and the actual performance of the therapeutic intervention, whether this be antibiotics, cesarian section, or assisted delivery. The first delay proved to be the most important factor in the women's deaths, and was attributed to women being ashamed to admit to symptoms and in some cases even refusing to seek care despite the insistence of concerned husbands. Distance and poverty exacerbated the situation by adding to the second delay, and lack of staff and instruments contributed to the third delay. In this story, culture – such as beliefs that difficult labor would result in strong children and that complaining of pain is an admission of weakness – cannot be isolated from economic realities that make health facilities sparse and under-equipped. Meanwhile, the massive roll-out of anti-retroviral drugs, at the time of writing, to over three million people living with HIV in developing countries, registers as a success story in delivering relatively simple, life-saving technologies even to the poorest of the poor. While much is made of the numbers of lives saved through this important effort, men, women, and children continue to die of other common conditions that are easy to prevent and treat. These anecdotes point to the importance of culture as an analytical tool for understanding not only local practices and values that must be acknowledged in addressing health concerns, but the hidden assumptions in global health efforts that value saving some lives above others.

Technologies that are tried and true and those that are high-tech illustrate one of the points we have reiterated throughout – that biomedicine is not (and never was) a monolithic institution largely confined to hospitals and clinics. Increasingly, biomedicine consists of ever-changing assemblages of technologies that include both the apparatus of biomedical research and the dissemination of the resultant knowledge as technological practices organized in a transnational space linked to what many describe as "global capital."[4] We have emphasized that local sites, both in the past and now too, contribute to the global functioning and heterogeneity of these assemblages in the form of provision of research samples, research subjects, and patients; local experiential medical knowledge and practices; local systems of administration and governance often supported regionally and internationally; and by, at times, applying local regimes of value in connection with the uses to which biomedicine is put. The center could not hold without the periphery.

Over the past decade, as biomedical assemblages have become increasingly complex, the respective global consortia conducting research have come to be characterized as "platforms" comprised of specific technologies, institutions, and experts, usually located at many collaborative sites. A major function of these platforms is to produce technologies including diagnostic tools, pharmaceutical products, and so on, that are of direct relevance for use in clinical practice wherever it takes place, an extraordinarily complex process involving practices of standardization and regulation in order to bring about "stabilization" of platforms.[5]

To give just one brief example in closing, that of breast cancer genetics: the first step in attempting to standardize research findings for clinical use today is the production of statistical data based on large population databases and meta-analyses created out of samples collected worldwide. Given that hundreds of mutations have been found for breast cancer, this process involves the continual re-evaluation of epidemiological and molecular data, and of the risk estimates on which collectives of physicians ground their recommendations for clinical decision-making.[6] In countries with the resources, national collectives establish and revise "the conventional arrangements that underlie clinical interventions, such as the risk thresholds above which a particular course of action (search for a family mutation, increased surveillance, mastectomy) is warranted."[7] These collectives also establish criteria to be used when dealing with contradictory evidence. Patients in effect become subjects in what, for the time being at least, is a never-ending experiment during the course of which the criteria of risk for breast cancer are subject to regular readjustments when applied in the clinic. The breast cancer example is by no means unique, and highlights the tensions that are likely to emerge increasingly in clinical care because new genomic technologies are showing what folly it is to act as though biological difference among humans is insignificant when attempting to treat disease. And yet, standardized interventions continue to be systematically deployed on the unexamined assumption that human bodies can readily be standardized about a norm.

There is no doubt that these sophisticated assemblages have the potential to bring about massive changes in global health care, much faster than has been the case to date, but they are unstable, associated with uncertainty, and often subject to fluctuations in the global economy. In the developing world further difficulties arise for three major reasons: first, the shortage of local resources and infrastructure in many countries is worsening due to the global economy; second, embedded assumptions on the part of numerous scientists and clinicians about the universal applicability of biomedical knowledge and technologies persist; and, third, the focus of biomedical research consortia continues to be largely on disease eradication and pharmaceutical research as these are the arenas where profit may accrue. Important though this is, when such an approach is privileged, key facets of health care including preventive medicine and basic primary care are left underfunded and unable to function adequately.

Of course, platforms exist devoted to research on malaria, sleeping sickness, and other "tropical diseases" that kill millions of people and that may well produce valuable findings. However, their effectiveness is likely to be limited because the political, economic, and social conditions contributing to disease prevalence and incidence continue to be largely unattended to, despite incontrovertible and ever-increasing evidence that poverty and worsening lifestyles, driven by exploitative global economic practices, are the greatest contributors to disease. Moreover, with a few notable exceptions, a bottom-up approach to health care, informed by local knowledge, experience, and aspirations is given little support. If people everywhere are to participate in the "age of postgenomics," an era that it appears may well supersede "classical" molecular biology,[8] then close cooperation with individuals and communities directly affected by technological and other forms of interventions is essential. So too is an intimate acquaintance with local histories, politics, local biologies, and other contingencies. Throughout the second half of the 20th century medical anthropologists, certain health care economists, and other researchers involved with health care in developing countries have been arguing in one form or another in opposition to a top-down technological fix, and anthropological research has documented a trail of failed programs that take this approach. These researchers have instead called for bottom-up programs designed to improve public health and health care; however, this call for change, although often noted, has gone largely unheeded to date.[9]

Several chapters in this book have shown how the assumption of the global applicability of biomedical technologies is producing a variety of unanticipated consequences in various locations. The illusion of the universal body, first conceptualized during the colonial enterprise, enables the widespread dissemination of, and longing for, biomedical technologies because such technologies are perceived by large numbers of people today as "neutral" and effective in the alleviation of diseases and unwanted conditions such as infertility or the effects of malnutrition, wherever they are applied. Our arguments have not been set out as a challenge to the efficacy of biomedical technologies per se, but to highlight the ethical and moral dimensions and unexamined values inevitably embedded in their production and application. Access to efficacious medication is clearly on a par with a right to clean water – a fundamental human right that should be supported with no argument. On the other hand, control of populations by governments, resort to assisted reproduction by individuals, with or without government encouragement, and participation in the transfer of human organs, whether carried out legally or otherwise, raise a range of morally debatable situations that can only be fully appreciated in local context. This highlights how biomedical technologies grant individuals unprecedented ability to intervene on their bodies, providing them with powerful tools to transform their lives in ways they were not previously able to accomplish, and sometimes with unexpected or even damaging consequences. These consequences may extend to society at large with long-term repercussions, as in the case of sex selection.

The implementation of highly standardized medical care raises a second set of concerns because the material body is not everywhere the same, and individuals differ in subtle but important ways with respect to disease susceptibility, symptomatology, and response to medications – we have described this variation as local biologies. One unforeseen consequence of the mapping of the human genome was the opening up of a Pandora's box of molecular activity that played havoc with the dogma of genetic determinism and laid bare the extent and significance of biological variation, recognition of which is crucial if medical advances are to be made in a postgenomic era. Human bodies are profoundly and ceaselessly influenced by environmental contexts, historical, social, political, economic, and cultural variables, as illustrative examples throughout the book make abundantly clear. It is undeniable that the changes worked upon the environment by human activity – pesticide use, medication use, toxic waste, unclean water, famine, global warming, and so on, are affecting every kind of living organism, including humans, at a rate greater than ever before. Humans have been described as the "greatest force for evolution"[10] and the biomedical sciences must respond to this situation.

We have argued for recognition of the concept of local biologies to facilitate understanding about how biological difference is implicated in everyday life. Such contingent difference should by no means be construed as essential biological difference among human kinds. The concept of local biologies works in concert with an approach that foregrounds social inequality and developmental disadvantages in disease causation, but it highlights two inter-related matters that are not usually evident in an approach dominated, above all, by a concern about the effects of inequality: first, local knowledge and practices in connection with the body are subject to continual change, increasingly so today, and are not simply the product of unquestioned cultural norms; such knowledge and practice are co-produced and inseparable from history, politics, environments local and global, and medical knowledge of all kinds. Second, local knowledge and practices in connection with health care are informed by subjective and communal assessments of embodiment, discomfort, and disease (in turn produced in part in association with local biologies), and a desire, at a minimum, for the basic necessities relating to life and reproduction.

As a result, our position is that local variables significant for health and illness – social *and* biological – must be taken account of. Moreover, specific measures designed to improve health in local populations should receive serious attention, over the long term, in order that unexpected consequences be identified and addressed. Top-down interventions limited overwhelmingly to technical changes parachuted in – so called "vertical approaches" – should be viewed skeptically, in light of the extensive historical and ethnographic evidence (only a small portion of which has been presented in this book) showing that technologies are very often not effective in the way intended. The potential applicability of research findings of all kinds to local settings should be addressed directly.[11] At the same time, in line with a political economy approach, redistribution of essential public goods including water, clean air, and nutritious food is indispensable if health care infrastructure is to be effective – a situation that at present is bleak in many parts of the world. Given that many people today are reduced to subjecting themselves to clinical trials (the results of which are thus far designed primarily to assist the developed world) in order to gain the basic needs for their very existence and to obtain any form of health care, it is abundantly obvious that the globalized system is failing badly.

Without considerable first-hand experience it is impossible for most people as they go about their daily lives in "advanced" societies to appreciate the extent to which the majority of people in the world live with ceaseless violence, insecurity, political domination, and endless shortages of the amenities for daily life. The daily news clips may well work to dull our sensibilities, and make this untenable situation no longer remarkable. The work of anthropologists to represent and engage effectively with the impact of biomedical technologies at local sites is indispensable in bringing about some change. Throughout this book we have drawn extensively on ethnographic findings. A great deal of this research has focused on how global economic change has uneven impacts among peoples living in diverse societies. We have emphasized heightened internal tensions, including the suffering exacerbated in virtually all sectors of society, accompanying transformations in ideas about personhood, and how desires for individual betterment are acted upon.[12]

Many of the findings we have cited are taken from ethnography writ large in which narratives given by people from all walks of life are interpreted in light of local norms and expectations, past histories of colonization, aspirations for change, defense of "tradition," and so on. However, none of this research adopts the concept of a unified culture as the driving force for social life; instead it highlights differences in responses to introduced technologies and in attitudes of the people who make up the social formations that are being researched. Nor are local informants, whether scientists, medical specialists, patients, or members of the public, understood as providing "truthful" accounts of "reality." Researchers are sensitive to the contribution of relationships of power, dissembling, lies, elaboration, forgetting, and so on, to the narratives that they hear, and some are sensitive as well, to the distortions that they themselves introduce, inadvertently or otherwise, into the retelling of events. Even so, a great deal can be learnt from local accounts; such accounts are not anecdotal, as medical audiences sometimes suggest, but glimpses of great significance into the everyday lives of people that today are subject, as are all our lives, to constant tampering, intrusions, and transformations. People struggle to assemble and reassemble themselves in response to endless assaults of one kind and another; the alternative is to give up and, for many, this means they may, in effect, be obliterated. Of course, we have seen how when some technologies are adopted, local responses are likely to be perceived by outsiders as questionable. Clearly practices of selective abortion based on gender or on genetic testing that suggest that, once born, a child may experience a disease such as breast cancer later in life are troubling. But in such cases attention to local narratives and local circumstances is of particular importance because only then is it possible to understand why people feel pressured or even obliged to act in this way.

However, local accounts are only part of the story we have been telling. The embedded assumptions present in the assemblages of biomedicine, including the distribution with little or no reflection of ever-more technologies worldwide to contain all forms of disease and counter perceived risk, demand attention. Unexamined truth claims of biomedicine are anchored by a moral economy in need of dissection – a task many medical practitioners are themselves engaged in today, one that includes disputes about the status of the unstable knowledge-making associated with techno-medicine. Opposition and obstructions to change will inevitably arise from those whose prime objective in life is to attain ever-greater wealth, but we can no longer forge ahead with business as usual in the global health endeavor.

The time is long overdue for the implementation of a radically new approach, one preceded by public deliberation that transcends disciplinary and factional boundaries, brings unexamined assumptions to light, seeks to drastically reduce inequalities and, at the same time, attends studiously to local voices and local contingencies, biological and social.

Notes

Introduction

1   We use the term biomedicine to refer to what is sometimes called "modern," "Western," or "cosmopolitan" medicine (see Fred L. Dunn, Traditional Asian Medicine and Cosmopolitan Medicine as Adaptive Systems. In Asian Medical Systems, ed. Charles Leslie (Berkeley and Los Angeles: University of California Press, 1976): 133–158). By biomedicine we mean that body of knowledge and associated clinical and experimental practices grounded in the medical sciences that were gradually consolidated in Europe and North America from the 19th century on. Contemporary biomedicine, also referred to as technomedicine at times, is an assemblage of activities at many sites ranging among doctors' offices, clinics, hospitals, laboratories, research consortia, technological units, public health sites, and so on. By biomedical technologies we mean those technologies developed in association with biomedical research and practice.

2   Of course, in practice clinicians know all too well that human bodies are not all the same, but the need to meet the requirements of standardization means that formal recognition of biological diversity is minimized.

3   http://www.who.int/hhr/en

4   Failing the World's Poor. New York Times editorial, September 24, 2008. http://www.nytimes.com/2008/09/24/opinion/24wed2.html

5   Larry Elliott, World Bank Millions Fail to Boost Health of Poor. Guardian Weekly, May 8–14, 2009: 1.

6   Joseph E. Stiglitz, Globalization and Its Discontents (New York: W. W. Norton, 2003): 5.

7   Maude Barlow and Joanne J. Myers, Blue Gold: The Fight to Stop the Corporate Theft of the World's Water (New York: New Press, 2002).

8   Mike Davis, Planet of Slums (New York: Verso, 2006).

9   Lawrence K. Altman, Agent at Border, Aware, Let in Man with TB. New York Times, June 1, 2007. http://www.nytimes.com/2007/06/01/health/01tb.html

10 Robert G. Evans et al., Why Are Some People Healthy and Others Not? The Determinants of Health of Populations (New Brunswick, NJ: Aldine Transaction, 1994).

11 Paul Farmer, Pathologies of Power (Berkeley: University of California Press, 2003); Paul Farmer, Infections and Inequalities (Berkeley: University of California Press, 1998); Paul Farmer et al. eds., Women, Poverty, and AIDS (Monroe, ME: Common Courage Press, 1996); Jody Heyman et al., Healthier Societies: From Analysis to Action (Oxford: Oxford

University Press, 2006); Richard Wilkinson, The Impact of Inequality: How to Make Sick Societies Healthier (New York and London: The New Press, 2005).

12 Don Butler, Antibiotics Don't Kill Viruses. If You Know That, You're in the Minority. The Gazette, Montreal, July 22, 2008: A2.

13 Jerome Groopman, Superbugs: Infections That Are Almost Impossible to Treat. New Yorker, August 11–18, 2008: 46–55.

14 Michael Fischer, Culture and Cultural Analysis as Experimental Systems. Cultural Anthropology 22 (2007): 1–64; Raymond Williams, Keywords: A Vocabulary of Culture and Society (London: Fontana, 1976).

15 Clifford Geertz, Culture Wars. New York Review of Books, November 30, 1995: 4–6 at p. 4.

16 Farmer, Pathologies of Power.

17 Clifford Geertz, After the Fact: Two Decades, Four Countries, One Anthropologist (Cambridge, MA: Harvard University Press, 1995): 43.

18 Marilyn Strathern, The Work of Culture: An Anthropological Perspective. *In* Culture, Kinship and Genes: Towards a Cross-Cultural Genetics, ed. Angus Clarke and Evelyn Parsons (London: Macmillan Press, 1997): 40–53 at p. 42.

19 Roger M. Keesing, Anthropology as Interpretive Quest. Current Anthropology 28 (1987): 161–169.

20 Arjun Appadurai, Disjuncture and Difference in the Global Cultural Economy. Public Culture 2 (1990): 1–24 at p. 5.

21 Appadurai, Disjuncture and Difference: 32.

22 Margaret Lock and Patricia A. Kaufert, Pragmatic Women and Body Politics (Cambridge, New York: Cambridge University Press, 1998); Sjaak Van der Geest and Susan Reynolds Whyte, eds., The Context of Medicines in Developing Countries: Studies in Pharmaceutical Anthropology (Dordrecht: Kluwer, 1989).

23 Duana Fullwiley, Discriminate Biopower and Everyday BioPolitics: Views on Sickle Cell Testing in Dakar. Medical Anthropology 23 (2004): 157–194.

24 Valentine Daniel, Is There a Counterpoint to Culture? Wertheim Lecture, Center for Asian Studies, Amsterdam, 1991.

25 Linda F. Hogle, Recovering the Nation's Body: Cultural Memory, Medicine, and the Politics of Redemption (New Brunswick, NJ: Rutgers University Press, 1999); Margaret Lock, Twice Dead: Organ Transplants and the Reinvention of Death (Berkeley: University of California Press, 2002); Marcia Inhorn, Local Babies, Global Science: Gender, Religion, and *In Vitro* Fertilization in Egypt (New York: Routledge, 2003).

26 Sherry B. Ortner, Introduction. *In* The Fate of "Culture": Geertz and Beyond, ed. Sherry B. Ortner (Berkeley: University of California Press, 1999): 8.

27 Ardys McNaughton Dunn, Cultural Competence and the Primary Care Provider. Journal of Pediatric Health Care 16 (2002): 105; Joseph R. Betancourt, Cultural Competence and Health Care Disparities: Key Perspectives and Trends. Health Affairs 24 (2005): 499.

28 Patricia A. Kaufert, The "Boxification" of Culture: The Role of the Social Scientist. Santé, Culture, Health 7 (1990): 139–145.

29 Arthur Kleinman, Culture and Depression. The New England Journal of Medicine 351 (2004): 951; Alan Nelson, Unequal Treatment: Confronting Racial and Ethnic Disparities in Health Care. Journal of the National Medical Association 94 (2002): 666.

30 Didier Fassin, Culturalism as Ideology. *In* Cultural Perspectives on Reproductive Health, ed. Carla Makhlouf Obermeyer (Oxford: Oxford University Press, 2001): 300–318 at p. 305.

31 Fassin, Culturalism as Ideology.

32 See, for example, Charles Briggs and Clara Mantini-Briggs, Stories in the Time of Cholera: Racial Profiling During a Medical Nightmare (Berkeley: University of California Press,

2003); Farmer, Pathologies of Power; Farmer, Infections and Inequalities; Fassin, Culturalism as Ideology; Wilkinson, The Impact of Inequality.

33 Faye Ginsburg, Aboriginal Media and the Australian Imaginary. Public Culture 5 (1993): 557–578.

34 Fischer, Culture and Cultural Analysis as Experimental Systems: 43.

35 Angela Zito and Tani E. Barlow, eds., Body, Subject and Power in China (Chicago: University of Chicago Press, 1994): 14.

36 George E. Marcus, Ethnography Through Thick and Thin (Princeton: Princeton University Press, 1998).

37 Margaret Lock, Eclipse of the Gene and the Return of Divination. Current Anthropology 46 (2005): S47–S70.

38 Carl Zimmer, Now: The Rest of the Genome. New York Times, November 11, 2008. http://www.nytimes.com/2008/11/11/science/11gene.html

39 Tobias Rees, Plastic Reason: An Anthropological Analysis of the Emergence of Adult Cerebral Plasticity in France. Unpublished PhD dissertation, University of California, Berkeley, 2006.

40 Peter Wright and Andrew Treacher, eds., The Problem of Medical Knowledge: Examining the Social Construction of Medicine. (Edinburgh: University of Edinburgh Press, 1982); Marc Berg and Annemarie Mol, eds., Difference in Medicine: Unraveling Practices, Techniques, and Bodies (Durham, NC: Duke University Press, 1998); Regula Valérie Burri and Joseph Dumit, Biomedicine as Culture: Instrumental Practices, Technoscientific Knowledge and New Modes of Life (New York and London: Routledge, 2007).

41 It has been suggested to us that the dissection of cultural hegemony by anthropologists might be thought of as equivalent to the use of statistics by social epidemiologists to highlight inequities and injustice.

42 This position is different from that inferred by "developmental plasticity" in which lifelong biological changes throughout the lifecycle are at issue. The inseparability of biology (both its material reality and its representation) from culture, language, and social and political variables is key to our approach. Moreover, human agency is recognized as important in contributing to biological change.

1 Biomedical Technologies in Practice

1 See Ludwik Fleck, Genesis and the Development of a Scientific Fact (Chicago: University of Chicago Press, 1979); originally published in German in 1935.

2 Wiebe Bijker et al., The Social Construction of Technological Systems: New Directions in the Sociology and History of Technology (Cambridge, MA: MIT Press, 1989).

3 Michel Foucault, The History of Sexuality, vol. 1 (New York: Pantheon, 1978).

4 Michel Foucault, The History of Sexuality, vol. 2,: The Use of Pleasure (New York: Pantheon, 1986).

5 Ian Hacking, Making up People. In Reconstructing Individualism, ed. Thomas Heller et al. (Stanford: Stanford University Press, 1986): 222–236.

6 Peter Gay, The Enlightenment: An Interpretation (New York: W. W. Norton and Company, 1977); Daniel R. Headrick, The Tools of Empire (Oxford: Oxford University Press, 1981).

7 Cited in George Stocking, Race, Culture, and Evolution (Chicago: Chicago University Press, 1982): 126–127.

8 Edward Tylor, Primitive Culture (New York: J. P. Putnam's Sons, [1871] 1920): 24; see also Alfred Russel Wallace, The Wonderful Century (London: Dodd, Mead, and Company, 1899); Julien Virey, Histoire naturelle du genre humain (Paris: Crochard, 1824).

9   See Charles Taylor, Sources of the Self: The Making of the Modern Identity (Cambridge, MA: Harvard University Press, 1989), especially chapters 22 and 23.

10   Michel Chevalier, L'Europe et la Chine. Revue des Deux Mondes 23 (1840): 209–255.

11   Jenny Uglow, Lunar Men: The Friends Who Made the Future (London: Faber and Faber, 2003).

12   Michael Adas, Machines as the Measure of Man: Science, Technology, and Ideologies of Western Dominance (Ithaca, NY: Cornell University Press, 1989).

13   Isaac Newton, Philosophiae Naturalis Principia Mathematica (London, 1687).

14   Richard S. Westfall, Never at Rest: A Biography of Isaac Newton (Cambridge: Cambridge University Press, 1983), cited in Steven Shapin, The Philosopher and the Chicken: On the Dietetics of Disembodied Knowledge. In Science Incarnate: Historical Embodiments of Natural Knowledge, ed. Christopher Lawrence and Steven Shapin (Chicago: University of Chicago Press, 1998): 41.

15   Vijay Vaitheeswan, Medicine Goes Digital. The Economist, April 16, 2009.

16   Bryan Pfaffenberger, Social Anthropology of Technology. Annual Review of Anthropology 21 (1992): 491–516.

17   Langdon Winner, Autonomous Technology: Technics-out-of-Control as a Theme in Political Thought (Cambridge, MA: MIT Press, 1977).

18   See, for example: Robert L. Heilbroner, Do Machines Make History? Technology and Culture 8 (1967): 335–345.

19   Winner, Autonomous Technology: 16.

20   Pfaffenberger, Social Anthropology of Technology: 495.

21   Lewis Mumford, Technics and Civilization (New York: Harcourt Brace, 1934).

22   See Mario Biagioli, ed., The Science Studies Reader (New York: Routledge, 1999); Sarah Franklin et al., Global Nature, Global Culture (London: Sage, 2000); Donna Haraway, Simians, Cyborgs, and Women: The Reinvention of Nature (New York: Routledge, 1991); Bruno Latour, Aramis, or, the Love of Technology (Cambridge, MA: Harvard University Press, 1996); Bruno Latour, Pandora's Hope: Essays on the Reality of Science Studies (Cambridge, MA: Harvard University Press, 1999); Margaret Lock, Twice Dead: Organ Transplants and the Reinvention of Death (Berkeley: University of California Press, 2002); Hans-Jorg Rheinberger, Beyond Nature and Culture: Modes of Reasoning in the Age of Molecular Biology and Medicine. In Living and Working with the New Biomedical Technologies: Intersections of Inquiry, ed. M. Lock et al. (Cambridge: Cambridge University Press, 2000): 19–30, for example.

23   See, for instance, Uffe Ravnskov, The Cholesterol Myths (Winona Lake, IL: New Trends Publishing, 2002).

24   Lock, Twice Dead; Paul Rabinow, French DNA: Trouble in Purgatory (Chicago: University of Chicago Press, 1999); Marilyn Strathern, Reproducing the Future: Essays on Anthropology, Kinship, and the New Reproductive Technologies (New York: Routledge, 1992).

25   Nikolas Rose, Inventing Our Selves: Psychology, Power and Personhood (Cambridge: Cambridge University Press, 1996): 26.

26   Hannah Landecker, Culturing Life: How Cells Became Technologies (Cambridge, MA: Harvard University Press, 2007): 223.

27   For one of the first arguments of this kind see Marshall Sahlins, Culture and Practical Reason (Chicago: University of Chicago Press, 1976).

28   Strathern, Reproducing the Future, especially pp. 1–7.

29   Foucault, The History of Sexuality, vol. 1: 141.

30   Michel Foucault, Governmentality. Trans. Rosi Braidotti, revised by Colin Gordon, in Graham Burchell et al. (eds.), The Foucault Effect: Studies in Governmentality (Chicago: University of Chicago Press): 87–104.

31 In theory, statistical estimations of risk should be based on population databases, but quite often they are based solely on clinical populations. In practice, this means that extrapolations should not be made from estimates of risk based on clinical populations to the population at large. Very often this is not the case, and knowledge about risk based on estimates calculated from a clinical population become received wisdom about population-wide risk: see, for example, Patricia Kaufert and John Syrotuik, Symptom Reporting at the Menopause. Social Science and Medicine 184 (1981): 173–184.

32 Robert G. Evans et al., Why Are Some People Healthy and Others Not? The Determinants of Health of Populations (New Brunswick, NJ: Aldine Transaction, 1994).

33 Ian Hacking, The Taming of Chance (Cambridge: Cambridge University Press, 1990): 2.

34 Alistair C. Crombie, Philosophical Presuppositions and Shifting Interpretations of Galileo. *In* Theory Change, Ancient Axiomatics and Galileo's Methodology, ed. J. Hintikka et al. (Boston: Reidel, 1981): 271–286.

35 Theodore Porter, Trust in Numbers: The Pursuit of Objectivity in Science and Public Life (Princeton, NJ: Princeton University Press, 1995): 45.

36 Ian Hacking, Making up People. *In* Reconstructing Individualism, ed. Thomas Heller et al. (Stanford: Stanford University Press, 1986): 222–236.

37 Ian Hacking, Making up People. London Review of Books, August 17, 2006: 23–26.

38 Stephen J. Gould, The Median Isn't the Message. Discover, June, 1985: 40–42.

39 Sahra Gibbon, Breast Cancer Genes and the Gendering of Knowledge: Science and Citizenship in the Context of the "New" Genetics (London: Palgrave Macmillan, 2007); Sandra Gifford, The Meaning of Lumps: A Case Study of the Ambiguities of Risk. *In* Anthropology and Epidemiology: Interdisciplinary Approaches to the Study of Health and Disease, ed. Craig R. Janes et al. (Dordrecht: Reidel Publishers, 1986): 213–246; Margaret Lock, Breast Cancer: Reading the Omens. Anthropology Today 14 (1998): 7–16; Deborah Lupton, The Imperative of Health: Public Health and the Regulated Body (London: Sage, 1995).

40 Michel Foucault, Technologies of the Self. *In* Technologies of the Self, ed. Luther Martin et al. (Amherst: University of Massachusetts Press, 1998): 16–49 at p. 18.

41 Veena Das and Deborah Poole, The State and its Margins. *In* Anthropology in the Margins of the State, ed. Veena Das and Deborah Poole (Santa Fe: School of American Research Press, 2004): 3–34 at p. 10.

42 James C. Whorton, Crusaders for Fitness: The History of American Health Reformers (Princeton: Princeton University Press, 1982).

43 Harvey Green, Fit for America: Health Fitness, Sport, and American Society 1830–1940 (New York: Pantheon, 1986).

44 Peter Conrad, Wellness as Virtue: Morality and the Pursuit of Health. Culture, Medicine and Psychiatry 18 (1994): 385.

45 World Health/Diseases of Poverty, http://www.results.org/website/article.asp?id=238.

46 Roy Porter, The Greatest Benefit to Mankind: A Medical History of Humanity (London: HarperCollins, 1998).

47 Georges Canguilhem, Ideology and Rationality in the History of the Life Sciences (Cambridge, MA: MIT Press, 1988); Sarah Franklin, Embodied Progress: A Cultural Account of Assisted Conception (London: Routledge, 1997).

48 Sarah Franklin, Life. *In* The Encyclopedia of Bioethics, ed. W. T. Reich (New York: Simon and Schuster, 1995): 456–462; See also Nikolas Rose, The Politics of Life Itself: Biomedicine, Power, and Subjectivity in the Twenty-First Century (Princeton: Princeton University Press, 2007), especially chapter 2.

49 Rose, The Politics of Life Itself: 44.

50 Erwin Schrödinger, What is Life? (Cambridge: Cambridge University Press, 1944): 22–23.

51 Schrödinger, What is Life?: 22.
52 Evelyn Fox Keller, Reconfiguring Life: Metaphors of Twentieth-Century Biology (New York: Columbia University Press, 1995): xv.
53 Keller, Reconfiguring Life; see also chapter 12 of this book.
54 Donna Haraway, Modest Witness@Second Millennium. FemaleMan Meets OncoMouse: Feminism and Technoscience (New York: Routledge, 1997): 60.
55 Donna Haraway, A Manifesto for Cyborgs: Science, Technology, and Socialist-Feminism in the 1980s. *In* Feminism/Postmodernism, ed. L. J. Nicholson (London: Routledge, 1990): 190–233 at p. 200.
56 Haraway, Modest Witness@Second Millennium: 60.
57 Wade Davis, Passage of Darkness: The Ethnobiology of the Haitian Zombie (Chapel Hill: University of North Carolina Press, 1988).
58 Obviously technologies such as acupuncture and herbal medicines are portable, but their use is therapeutic and they are designed to restore health and revitalize patients, and not to transform them in any fundamental way.
59 Linda F. Hogle, Recovering the Nation's Body: Cultural Memory, Medicine, and the Politics of Redemption (New Brunswick, NJ: Rutgers University Press, 1999): 152.
60 Hogle, Recovering the Nation's Body: 152.
61 Eugene Thacker, The Global Genome: Biotechnology, Politics and Culture (Cambridge, MA: MIT Press, 2005): 28.
62 Informatics is the science of information, the practice of information processing, and the engineering of information systems. Informatics studies the structure, algorithms, behavior, and interactions of natural and artificial systems that store, process, access, and communicate information. With the advent of computers, individuals and organizations increasingly process information digitally and in the worlds of biomedicine and the biotech industry such information is called bioinformatics.
63 Thacker, The Global Genome: 28.
64 Thacker, The Global Genome: 29.

2 The Normal Body

1   Max Weber, From Max Weber: Essays in Sociology. Ed. H. H. Gerth and C. Wright Mills (London: Routledge, [1948 1991): 155.
2   Allan Young, Internalizing and Externalizing Medical Belief Systems: An Ethiopian Example. Social Science and Medicine 10 (1976): 147–156 at p. 148.
3   Stacey Langwick, Devils, Parasites, and Fierce Needles: Healing and the Politics of Translation in Southern Tanzania. Science, Technology, and Human Values 32 (2007): 88–117 at p. 109.
4   Steven Johnson, The Ghost Map: The Story of London's Most Terrifying Epidemic – and how it Changed Science, Cities, and the Modern World (New York: Penguin, 2006).
5   Sandra Hempel, The Medical Detective: John Snow and the Mystery of Cholera (London: Granta Books, 2006): 83.
6   Hempel, The Medical Detective. See especially chapters 13 and 14 for details about the Soho epidemic, Snow's use of disease-mapping, and the Broad Street pump.
7   Johnson, The Ghost Map: 212, see also Hempel, The Medical Detective.
8   Lorraine Daston and Katharine Park, Wonders and the Order of Nature (New York: Zone Books, 1998): 14.
9   Daston and Park, Wonders and the Order of Nature: 14.
10 Lorraine Daston (The Moral Economy of Science. Osiris 10 (1995): 3–26) insists that her use of moral economy is not indebted to E. P. Thompson who first made use of

this concept in Customs in Common (London: The Merlin Press, 1991). Some useful connections can be made between these different applications of the concept, I believe, but space does not permit elaboration (but see Margaret Lock, Le Corps objet: économie morale et techniques d'amélioration. Bulletin d'histoire politique – Corps et Politique, 10 (2002): 33–46).

11 Daston, The Moral Economy of Science.

12 Daston, The Moral Economy of Science: 4.

13 Daston, The Moral Economy of Science: 7.

14 Ian Hacking, Making up People. *In* Reconstructing Individualism: Autonomy, Individuality, and Self in Western Thought, ed. T. C. Heller et al. (Stanford: Stanford University Press, 1986): 222–236; Ian Hacking, World-making by Kind-making: Child Abuse, for Example. *In* How Classification Works: Nelson Goodman among the Social Sciences, ed. Mary Douglas and David Hull (Edinburgh: Edinburgh University Press, 1992): 180–238; Theodore Porter, Trust in Numbers: The Pursuit of Objectivity in Science and Public Life (Princeton: Princeton University Press, 1995).

15 Porter, Trust in Numbers: 3.

16 Porter, Trust in Numbers: 4.

17 Christopher Lawrence and Steven Shapin, eds., Science Incarnate: Historical Embodiments of Natural Knowledge (Chicago: University of Chicago Press, 1998).

18 Lorraine Daston, personal communication with Margaret Lock, May 2008.

19 Lorraine Daston and Peter Galison, Objectivity (New York: Zone Books, 2007): 41.

20 Daston and Galison, Objectivity: 59.

21 Daston and Galison, Objectivity: 382.

22 Daston and Park, Wonders and the Order of Nature.

23 Roy Porter, Medical Science and Human Science in the Enlightenment. *In* Inventing Human Science: Eighteenth Century Domains, ed. Christopher Fox et al. (Berkeley: University of California Press, 1995): 53–87 at p. 56.

24 Porter, Medical Science and Human Science: 58.

25 Cited in Michel Foucault, The Birth of the Clinic: An Archeology of Medical Perception (New York: Vintage Books, 1994): 6.

26 Michel Foucault, The Birth of the Clinic: An Archeology of Medical Perception (New York: Vintage, 1994): 6.

27 Foucault, The Birth of the Clinic.

28 Porter, Medical Science and Human Science: 60.

29 Porter, Medical Science and Human Science: 66.

30 John Passmore, The Perfectibility of Man (London: Gerald Duckworth and Company, 1972).

31 Porter, Medical Science and Human Science: 67.

32 Toby E. Huff, The Rise of Early Modern Science (Cambridge: Cambridge University Press, 2003): 192.

33 Katherine Park, The Life of the Corpse: Division and Dissection in Late Medieval Europe. Journal of the History of Medicine and Allied Sciences 50 (1995): 114; Margaret Lock, Twice Dead: Organ Transplants and the Reinvention of Death (Berkeley: University of California Press, 2002).

34 Shigehisa Kuriyama, The Expressiveness of the Body and the Divergence of Greek and Chinese Medicine (New York: Zone Books, 1999): 8.

35 Kuriyama, The Expressiveness of the Body.

36 Kuriyama, The Expressiveness of the Body: 167.

37 Kuriyama, The Expressiveness of the Body: 272.

38 See also Judith Farquhar, Knowing Practice: The Clinical Encounter in Chinese Medicine (Boulder, CO: Westview Press, 1994).

39 Shigehisa Kuriyama, Between Mind and Eye: Japanese Anatomy in the Eighteenth Century. *In* Paths to Asian Medical Knowledge, ed. Charles Leslie and Allan Young (Berkeley: University of California Press, 1992): 21–43.

40 Matsumoto Ryōzō and Kiyooka Eiichi, The Dawn of Western Science in Japan (Tokyo: Hokuseidô Press, 1969) (the translation cited here has been modified slightly by Shigehisa Kuriyama; see Between Mind and Eye: 21–43).

41 This depiction of reality is described by Daston and Galison in Objectivity as the "truth-to-nature" approach to attaining objectivity.

42 Byron J. Good and Mary-Jo DelVecchio Good, "Learning Medicine": The Construction of Medical Knowledge at Harvard Medical School. *In* Knowledge, Power, and Practice: The Anthropology of Medicine and Everyday Life, ed. Shirley Lindenbaum and Margaret Lock (Berkeley and Los Angeles: University of California Press, 1993): 81–107; Barry Saunders, CT Suite: The Work of Diagnosis in the Age of Noninvasive Cutting (Durham, NC: Duke University Press, 2009).

43 Christopher Lawrence and George Weisz, Greater than the Parts: Holism in Biomedicine, 1920–1950 (Oxford: Oxford University Press, 1998).

44 Saunders, CT Suite.

45 Margaret Lock, Situated Ethics, Culture, and the Brain Death "Problem" in Japan. *In* Bioethics in Social Context, ed. Barry Hoffmaster (Philadelphia: Temple University Press, 2001): 39–68.

46 Lock, Twice Dead.

47 Bruno Latour, We Have Never Been Modern (Cambridge, MA: Harvard University Press, 1993).

48 See Young, Internalizing and Externalizing Medical Belief Systems for a discussion of internalizing and externalizing discourse.

49 This is discussed in chapter 6.

50 Ian Hacking, The Taming of Chance (Cambridge: Cambridge University Press, 1990). See also Georges Canguilhem, The Normal and the Pathological (New York: Zone Books, 1991).

51 Hacking, The Taming of Chance: 164.

52 Canguilhem, The Normal and the Pathological: 228.

53 Foucault, The Birth of the Clinic.

54 Foucault, The Birth of the Clinic: 180.

55 Thomas Schlich, Surgery, Science and Modernity: Operating Rooms and Laboratories as Spaces of Control. History of Science 45 (2007): 237.

56 Stefan Hirschauer, The Manufacture of Bodies in Surgery. Social Studies of Science 21 (1991): 310.

57 Hacking, The Taming of Chance: 160.

58 Hacking, The Taming of Chance: 168.

59 Hacking, The Taming of Chance: 169.

60 Elliot G. Mischler et al., Social Contexts of Health, Illness, and Patient Care (Cambridge: Cambridge University Press, 1981): 4.

61 Fredrick C. Redlich, The Concept of Health in Psychiatry. *In* Explorations in Social Psychiatry, ed. A. H. Leighton et al. (London: Tavistock, 1957): 138–164.

62 Mischler et al., Social Contexts of Health, Illness, and Patient Care: 4.

63 John A. Ryle, The Meaning of Normal. *In* Concepts of Medicine, ed. B. Lush (New York: Pergamon, 1961): 137–149.

64 Charles O. Frake, The Diagnosis of Disease among the Subanum of Mindanao. American Anthropologist 63 (1961): 113–132.

65 American Child Health Association, Physical Defects: The Pathway to Correction (New York: American Child Health Association, 1934): 80–96. This study was cited by Harry

Bakwin as illustrating what he called "The Tonsil–Adenoidectomy Enigma" in the Journal of Pediatrics 52 (1958): 343–344.

66 J. Wennberg and A. Gittelsohn, Variations in Medical Care Among Small Areas. Scientific American 246 (1982): 130; K. McPherson et al., Small-Area Variations in the Use of Common Surgical Procedures: An International Comparison of New England, England, and Norway. New England Journal of Medicine 307 (1982): 1310–1314.

67 A. Macfarlane and M. Mugford, Birth Counts: Statistics of Pregnancy and Childbirth (London: Her Majesty's Stationery Office, 1984).

68 Patricia Leyland Kaufert and John D. O'Neil, Analysis of a Dialogue on Risks in Childbirth: Clinicians, Epidemiologists and Inuit Women. *In* Knowledge, Power, and Practice: The Anthropology of Medicine and Everyday Life, ed. S. Lindenbaum and M. Lock (Berkeley: University of California Press, 1993): 32–54.

69 See C. McClain, Toward a Comparative Framework for the Study of Childbirth: A Review of the Literature. *In* Anthropology of Human Birth, ed. M. A. Kay (Philadelphia: F. A. Davis, 1982): 25–59.

70 Patricia Kaufert, The "Boxification" of Culture. Santé, Culture, Health 7 (1990): 139–148.

71 Carroll Dena and Cecilia Benoit, Aboriginal Midwifery in Canada: Merging Traditional Practices and Modern Science. *In* Reconceiving Midwifery, ed. Ivy Lynn Bourgeault et al. (Montreal: McGill-Queens University Press, 2004): 263–286.

72 The number of births per year in Rankin Inlet has steadily grown since 1993 to between 30 and 40 per year.

73 Alexander Macaulay et al., A Retrospective Audit of the Rankin Inlet Birthing Center, 1993–2004. Unpublished manuscript.

74 Vicki Van Wagner et al., Reclaiming Birth, Health, and Community: Midwifery in the Inuit Villages of Nunavik, Canada. Journal of Midwifery and Women's Health 52 (2007): 384–391.

75 Van Wagner et al., Reclaiming Birth, Health, and Community: 390.

76 See G. C. Bowker and S. L. Star, Sorting Things Out: Classification and Its Consequences (Cambridge, MA: MIT Press, 1999); Hacking, The Taming of Chance.

77 Jocelyn Scott Peccei, A Hypothesis for the Origin and Evolution of Menopause. Maturitas 21 (1995): 83–89; Jocelyn Scott Peccei, A Critique of the Grandmother Hypothesis: Old and New. American Journal of Human Biology 13 (2001): 434–452.

78 Peter McKeown, The Modern Rise of Population (New York: Academic Press, 1976); David Kertzer and Peter Laslett, eds., Aging in the Past: Demography, Society and Old Age (Berkeley: University of California Press, 1995).

79 Margaret Lock, Encounters with Aging: Mythologies of Menopause in Japan and North America (Berkeley: University of California Press, 1993).

80 Helen Jern, Hormone Therapy of the Menopause and Aging (Springfield, IL: Charles C. Thomas, 1973): xiii; A. A. Haspels and P. A. Van Keep, Endocrinology and Management of the Peri-Menopause. *In* Psychosomatics in Peri-Menopause, ed. A. A. Haspels and H. Musaph (Baltimore: University Park Press, 1979): 57–71; Ian Hall Thorneycroft, The Role of Estrogen Replacement Therapy in the Prevention of Osteoporosis. American Journal of Obstetrics and Gynecology 160 (1989): 1306–1310.

81 Patricia Kaufert and Sonja McKinlay, Estrogen-Replacement Therapy: The Production of Medical Knowledge and the Emergence of Policy. *In* Women, Health and Healing: Toward a New Perspective, ed. E. Lewin and V. Oleson (London: Tavistock Publications, 1985).

82 R. B. Greenblatt and A. Z. Teran, Advice to Post-Menopausal Women. *In* The Climacteric and Beyond, ed. L. Zichella et al. (Park Ridge, New Jersey: Parthenon Publishing Group, 1987): 39–53 at p. 39.

83 Institute of Medicine, Committee on Assessing the Need for Clinical Trials of Testosterone Replacement Therapy, Board on Health Science Policies,Testosterone and Aging: Clinical Research Directions, ed. Catharyn T. Liverman and Dan G. Blazer (Washington, D.C.: The National Academies Press, 2004). http://www.nap.edu/openbook.php?isbn=0309090636

84 Ray Moynihan, Drug Company Secretly Briefed Medical Societies on HRT. British Medical Journal 326 (2003): 1161.

85 Moynihan, Drug Company Secretly Briefed Medical Societies: 1161.

86 Tieraona Low Dog, The Role for Botanicals in Menopause. Menopause Management 13 (2004): S51–S53; Alyson L. Huntley and Ernst Edzard, A Systematic Review of Herbal Medicinal Products for the Treatment of Menopausal Symptoms. Menopause 10 (2003): 465–476; Michael J. Murray et al., Soy Protein Isolate with Isoflavones Does Not Prevent Estradidol-Induced Endometrial Hyperplasia in Postmenopausal Women: A Pilot Trial. Menopause 10 (2003): 456–464.

87 Institute of Medicine, Testosterone and Aging.

88 K. Kerlikowske et al., Declines in Invasive Breast Cancer and Use of Postmenopausal Hormone Therapy in a Screening Mammography Population. Journal of the National Cancer Institute 99 (2007): 1335–1339.

89 Merethe Kumle, Declining Breast Cancer Incidence and Decreased HRT Use. The Lancet 372 (2008): 608–610.

90 S. Narod, Ovarian Cancer and HRT in the Million Women Study. The Lancet 369 (2007): 1667–1668.

91 Narod, Ovarian Cancer and HRT.

92 Phillipa Brice, Barcode Babies: Prospects for Genetic Profiling. Biolines, 2004. http://www.cambridgenetwork.co.uk/pooled/profiles/BF_COMP/view.asp?Q=BF_COMP_9786; P. Yoon et al., Public Health Impact of Genetic Tests at the End of the Twentieth Century. Genetics in Medicine 3 (2001): 405–410.

93 Gina Kolata, Studies Show Prostate Test Saves Few Lives. New York Times, March 19, 2009, http://health.nytimes.com/health/; T. A. Stamey et al., Prostate Cancer Screening with the PSA Test. Journal of Urology 172(4) (2004): 1297–1301.

94 Roy Porter, The Greatest Benefit to Mankind: A Medical History of Humanity (London: HarperCollins, 1998); Helaine Selin and Hugh Shapiro, Ed. Medicine Across Cultures: The History and Practice of Medicine in Non-Western Cultures (Dordrecht: Kluwer, 2003); C. R. Ember and M. Ember, eds., Encyclopedia of Medical Anthropology: Health and Illness in the World's Cultures (Dordrecht: Kluwer, 2003).

95 See, for example, the figures for the United States: National Center for Complementary and Alternative Medicine (NCCAM) The Use of Complementary and Alternative Medicine (Washington, D.C.: National Center for Complementary and Alternative Medicine, 2008).

96 Vincanne Adams, Randomized Crime. Social Studies of Science 32 (2002): 659–690; F. Kronenberg and A. Fugh-Berman, Complementary and Alternative Medicine for Menopausal Symptoms: A Review of Randomized, Controlled Trials. Annals of Internal Medicine 137 (2002): 805–813.

97 Regula Valérie Burri and Joseph Dumit, Biomedicine as Culture: Instrumental Practices, Technoscientific Knowledge, and New Modes of Life (New York and London: Routledge, 2007); Margaret Lock and Deborah R. Gordon, eds., Biomedicine Examined (Dordrecht: Kluwer Academic Publishers, 1988); Marc Berg and Annemarie Mol, eds., Difference in Medicine: Unraveling Practices, Techniques, and Bodies (Durham, NC: Duke University Press, 1998); Hannah Landecker, Culturing Life: How Cells Became Technologies (Cambridge, MA: Harvard University Press, 2007); Lynn Payer, Medicine and Culture: Varieties of Treatment in the U.S., England, Germany and France (Austin, TX: Holt, Reinhart, and Winston, 1988).

98 Evelyn Fox Keller, The Century of the Gene (Cambridge, MA: Harvard University Press, 2000).

99 Jean Clottes and David Lewis Williams, The Shamans of Prehistory: Trance and Magic in the Painted Caves (New York: Harry N. Abrams, 1998); J. Lietava, Medicinal Plants in a Middle Paleolithic Grave Shanidar IV?. Journal of Ethnopharmacology 35 (1992): 263–266.

100 Of course the idea of attaining immortality is no doubt as old as humankind, and practices of alchemy were used for this purpose around the world. For excellent coverage on the alchemy of Taoism see Nathan Sivin, Alchemy: Chinese Alchemy. *In* Encyclopedia of Religion, 2nd edn, vol. I (New York: Macmillan Reference, 2005): 237–241.

101 Daston and Galison, Objectivity: 363.

102 Marilyn Strathern, After Nature: English Kinship in the Late Twentieth Century (Cambridge: Cambridge University Press, 1992).

103 Joseph Dumit, Drugs for Life: Growing Health through Facts and Pharmaceuticals (Durham, NC: Duke University Press, forthcoming).

104 Susan R. Whyte et al., Social Lives of Medicines (Cambridge: Cambridge University Press, 2002): 9.

105 Bowker and Star, Sorting Things Out: 13.

106 "QWERTY" refers to the arrangement of the alphabet on the standard American typewriter and computer keyboard. The QWERTY layout was developed to prevent the jamming of typebars (the tiny metal sticks that, once a letter key is pushed, strike the paper in the manual typewriter). It was patented in 1874 and became the standard despite the development of more efficient layouts. It is an oft-cited example of technological "path-dependency" in economic history. See Paul A. David, Understanding the Economics of QWERTY: The Necessity of History. *In* Economic History and the Modern Economist, ed. W. N. Parker (Oxford: Blackwell, 1986): 30–49; Peter Lewin, ed., The Economics of QWERTY: History, Theory, and Policy – Essays by Stan J. Liebowitz and Stephen E. Margolis (New York: New York University Press, 2002).

107 Lewin, The Economics of QWERTY: 14.

3 Anthropologies of Medicine

1 Margaret Lock and Judith Farquhar, eds., Beyond the Body Proper (Durham, NC: Duke University Press, 2007).

2 Bruno Latour, We Have Never Been Modern (Cambridge, MA: Harvard University Press, 1993); Marilyn Strathern, After Nature: English Kinship in the Late Twentieth Century (Cambridge: Cambridge University Press, 1992).

3 Marcel Mauss, The Techniques of the Body. Trans. B. Brewer. Economy and Society 2 (1973): 70–88 (originally published 1935).

4 Robert Hertz, The Pre-Eminence of the Right Hand: A Study in Religious Polarity. *In* Right and Left: Essays on Dual Symbolic Classification, ed. Rodney Needham (Chicago: University of Chicago Press, 1973): 3–21.

5 Lock and Farquhar, Beyond the Body Proper: 22.

6 Lock and Farquhar, Beyond the Body Proper: 22.

7 Russell Keat, The Human Body in Social Theory: Reich, Foucault, and the Repressive Hypothesis. Radical Philosophy 42 (1986): 24.

8 Lock and Farquhar, Beyond the Body Proper: 107.

9 This term comes from Maurice Merleau-Ponty, The Phenomenology of perception (London: Routledge and Kegan Paul, 1962).

10 Judith Farquhar and Margaret Lock, Introduction. *In* Beyond the Body Proper: 2.

11 Terry Eagleton, It Is Not Quite True that I Have a Body and Not Quite True that I Am One Either. London Review of Books May 27 (1993): 7; Rosi Braidotti, Organs Without Bodies. Differences: A Journal of Feminist Cultural Studies (1989): 147–161.

12 Allan Young, The Anthropologies of Illness and Sickness. Annual Review of Anthropology 11 (1982): 257–285; Ronald Frankenberg, Medical Anthropology and Development: A Theoretical Perspective. Social Science and Medicine 14b (1980): 197–207; Peter W. G. Wright and Andrew Treacher, eds., The Problem of Medical Knowledge: Examining the Social Construction of Medicine (Edinburgh: University of Edinburgh Press, 1982).

13 Michel Foucault, The History of Sexuality, vol. 1 (New York: Pantheon Books, 1978); Michel Foucault, Discipline and Punish: The Birth of the Prison (New York: Vintage, 1979).

14 Young, Anthropologies of Illness and Sickness: 257–285 at p. 277.

15 W. H. R. Rivers, Medicine, Magic and Religion (New York: Routledge, 2001).

16 Judith Farquhar, Knowing Practice: The Clinical Encounter in Chinese Medicine (Boulder, CO: Westview Press, 1994); Charles Leslie, The Professionalizing Ideology of Medical Revivalism. In Entrepreneurship and Modernization of Occupational Cultures in South Asia, ed. Milton Singer (Durham, NC: Duke University Press): 16–42; Margaret Lock and Deborah R. Gordon, eds., Biomedicine Examined (Dordrecht: Kluwer Academic Publishers, 1988); Byron J. Good and Mary-Jo DelVecchio Good, "Learning Medicine": The Construction of Medical Knowledge at Harvard Medical School. In Knowledge, Power, and Practice: the Anthropology of Medicine and Everyday Life, ed. S. Lindenbaum and M. Lock (Berkeley: University of California Press, 1993): 141–166; Wright and Treacher, The Problem of Medical Knowledge.

17 E. E. Evans-Pritchard, Witchcraft, Oracles, and Magic among the Azande (Oxford: Clarendon Press, 1937). The seminal contribution of "EP" (as he is affectionately known among anthropologists) to medical anthropology was to show that rationality – the criteria by which we judge the truth and act in consequence – is embedded in social and cultural institutions, and not in some pre-existing structure of the mind. This triggered a vigorous philosophical debate in the 1960s and contributed to an interrogation by sociologists and anthropologists of the cultural and social basis of biomedical rationality in the 1970s.

18 Allan Young, Internalizing and Externalizing Medical Belief Systems: An Ethiopian Example. Social Science and Medicine 10 (1976): 147–156.

19 Melford E. Spiro, Burmese Supernaturalism: A Study in the Explanation and Reduction of Suffering (New York: Prentice-Hall, 1967); Meyer Fortes, Some Reflections on Ancestor Worship in Africa (Oxford: Oxford University Press, 1966); Irving A. Hallowell, The Social Function of Anxiety in Primitive Society. American Sociology Review 6(6) (1941): 869–881; Clyde Kluckhohn, Navaho Witchcraft. Papers of the Peabody Museum of American Archaeology and Ethnology, Harvard University, 22 (1944). Reprinted 1995, Boston: Beacon Press.

20 Gilbert Lewis, Knowledge of Illness in a Sepik Society (Cambridge: Cambridge University Press, 1975).

21 Margaret Lock, East Asian Medicine in Urban Japan: Varieties of Medical Experience (Berkeley: University of California Press, 1980); Farquhar, Knowing Practice; Francis Zimmerman, The Scholar, the Wise Man, and Universals: Three Aspects of Āyurvedic Medicine. In Knowledge and the Scholarly Medical Traditions, ed. Don Bates (Cambridge: Cambridge University Press, 1995): 297–319.

22 Stanley Jeyaraja Tambiah, Magic, Science, Religion, and the Scope of Rationality (Cambridge: Cambridge University Press, 1990).

23 Lock and Farquhar, Beyond the Body Proper.

24 Alan Beals, Strategies of Resort to Curers in South India. *In* Asian Medical Systems: A Comparative Study, ed. Charles Leslie (Berkeley: University of California Press, 1976): 184–200; see p. 184.

25 Charles Leslie, ed., Medical Pluralism in World Perspective. Special Issue on "Medical Pluralism." Social Science and Medicine 14B (4) (1980): 190–196.

26 Beals, Strategies of Resort.

27 Leslie, Medical Pluralism.

28 Margaret Lock, East Asian Medicine in Urban Japan; Vincanne Adams, Modes of Production and Medicine: An Examination of the Theory in Light of Sherpa Medical Traditionalism. Social Science and Medicine 27 (1998): 505–514.

29 Lock, East Asian Medicine in Urban Japan.

30 Paul Brodwin, Medicine and Morality in Haiti: The Contest for Healing Power (Cambridge: Cambridge University Press, 1996).

31 Libbet Crandon-Malamud, From the Fat of Our Souls: Social Change, Political Process, and Medical Pluralism in Bolivia (Berkeley: University of California Press, 1991).

32 Caroline Bledsoe and Monica Goubaud, The Reinterpretation and Distribution of Western Pharmaceuticals: An Example from the Mende of Sierra Leone. *In* The Context of Medicine in Developing Countries: Studies in Pharmaceutical Anthropology, ed. Sjaak Van der Geest and Susan Reynolds Whyte (Dordrecht: Kluwer, 1988): 235–276.

33 Mark Nichter, Idioms of Distress: Alternatives in the Expression of Psychosocial Distress: A Case Study from South India. Culture, Medicine and Psychiatry 5 (1981): 379; see also Byron J. Good, The Heart of What's the Matter: The Semantics of Illness in Iran. Culture, Medicine and Psychiatry 1 (1977): 25; Good and Good, Toward a Meaning Centered Analysis of Popular Illness Categories; Charles Briggs, Theorizing Modernity Conspiratorially: Science, Scale, and the Political Economy of Public Discourse in Explanations of a Cholera Epidemic. American Ethnologist 31 (2004): 164–187; Paul Farmer, AIDS and Accusation: Haiti and the Geography of Blame (Berkeley: University of California Press, 2006).

34 Mark Nichter and Margaret Lock, New Horizons in Medical Anthropology: Essays in Honour of Charles Leslie (London and New York: Routledge, 2002); Laurent Pordié, ed. Tibetan Medicine in the Contemporary World: Global Politics of Medical Knowledge and Practice (London and New York: Routledge, 2008).

35 See, for example, Vincanne Adams and Fei-Fei Li, Integration or Erasure? Modernizing Medicine at Lhasa's Mentsikhang. *In* Tibetan Medicine in the Contemporary World: Global Politics of Medical Knowledge and Practice, ed. Laurent Pordié (London: Routledge, 2008): 105–131.

36 Lock, East Asian Medicine in Urban Japan; Sjaak Van der Geest and Susan Reynolds Whyte, eds., The Context of Medicine in Developing Countries: Studies in Pharmaceutical Anthropology (Dordrecht: Kluwer Academic Publishers, 1988); Stacey Langwick, Devils, Parasites, and Fierce Needles: Healing and the Politics of Translation in Southern Tanzania. Science, Technology, and Human Values 32 (2007) 88–117.

37 Pordié, Tibetan Medicine in the Contemporary World.

38 Lock, East Asian Medicine in Urban Japan); Adams and Li, Integration or Erasure?

39 Vincanne Adams, The Sacred and the Scientific: Ambiguous Practices of Science in Tibetan Medicine. Cultural Anthropology 16 (2002): 542–575.

40 Susan Reynolds Whyte et al., Social Lives of Medicines (Cambridge: Cambridge University Press, 2002).

41 Volker Scheid, Kexue and Guanxixue: Plurality, Tradition and Modernity in Contemporary Chinese Medicine. *In* Plural Medicine, Tradition and Modernity, 1800–2000, ed. W. Ernst (London: Routledge, 2002): 130–152.

42   Steve Ferzacca, Governing Bodies in New Order Indonesia. *In* New Horizons in Medical Anthropology: Essays in Honour of Charles Leslie, ed. M. Nichter and M. Lock (London: Routledge, 2002): 35–57.

43   For other examples see Stacy Leigh Pigg, Too Bold, Too Hot: Crossing "Culture" in AIDS Prevention in Nepal. *In* New Horizons in Medical Anthropology: Essays in Honour of Charles Leslie, ed. M. Nichter and M. Lock (London: Routledge, 2002): 58–80.

44   David Arnold, Colonizing the Body: State Medicine and Epidemic Disease in Nineteenth-Century India (Berkeley: University of California Press, 1993); Charles Leslie, Interpretations of Illness: Syncretism in Modern Āyurveda. *In* Paths to Asian Medical Knowledge: A Comparative Study, ed. C. Leslie and A. Young (Berkeley: University of California Press, 1992):177–208.

45   Cecilia Van Hollen, Nationalism, Transnationalism, and the Politics of Traditional Indian Medicine for HIV/AIDS. *In* Asian Medicine and Globalization, ed. Joseph S. Alter (Philadelphia: University of Pennsylvania Press, 2005): 88–106 at p. 95.

46   Judith Farquhar, Re-Writing Traditional Medicine in Post-Maoist China. *In* Knowledge and the Scholarly Medical Traditions, ed. Don Bates (Cambridge: Cambridge University Press, 1995): 251–276; Volker Scheid, Currents of Tradition in Chinese Medicine 1626–2006 (Seattle: Eastland Press, 2007).

47   Andrew Pickering, The Mangle of Practice: Time, Agency, and Science (Chicago: University of Chicago Press, 1995).

48   Volker Scheid, Chinese Medicine in Contemporary China: Plurality and Synthesis, Science and Cultural Theory (Durham, NC: Duke University Press, 2002).

49   Judith Farquhar, personal communication to Margaret Lock, December 2008.

50   Everett Yuehong Zhang, Switching between Traditional Chinese Medicine and Viagra: Cosmopolitanism and Medical Pluralism Today. Medical Anthropology 26 (2007): 53–96.

51   Langwick, Devils, Parasites, and Fierce Needles: 88–117.

52   World Health Organization, Traditional Medicine (2008). http://www.who.int/ mediacentre/factsheets/fs134/en/

53   Yildiz Aumeeruddy-Thomas and Yeshi C. Lama, Tibetan Medicine and Biodiversity Management in Dolpo, Nepal: Negotiating Local and Global Worldviews, Knowledge and Practices. *In* Tibetan Medicine in the Contemporary World: Global Politics of Medical Knowledge and Practice, ed. Laurent Pordié (London and New York: Routledge, 2008): 160–186.

54   Vincanne Adams, Integrating Abstraction: Modernizing Medicine at Lhasa's Mentsikhang. *In* Soundings in Tibetan Medicine: Anthropological and Historical Perspectives, ed. Mona Schrempf (Leiden: Brill, 2006): 29–44.

55   Vincanne Adams, Randomized Controlled Crime: Postcolonial Sciences in Alternative Medicine Research. Social Studies of Science 32 (2002): 659–690; Adams and Li, Integration or Erasure?; Farquhar, Knowing Practice; Craig Janes, The Transformations of Tibetan Medicine. Medical Anthropology Quarterly 9 (1995): 6–39.

56   Elizabeth Hsu, "The Medicine from China Has Rapid Effects": Chinese Medicine Patients in Tanzania Anthropology and Medicine 9 (2002): 291–313.

57   Langwick, Devils, Parasites, and Fierce Needles: 88; Hsu, "The Medicine from China": 291.

58   Sofia Gruskin, Health and Human Rights: A Reader (New York: Routledge, 1999).

59   Duncan Peterson and Veronica Baruffati, Healers, Deities, Saints and Doctors: Elements for the Analysis of Medical Systems. Social Science and Medicine 29 (1989): 487–496. See also Noel Chrisman and Arthur Kleinman, Popular Health Care, Social Networks, and Cultural Meanings: The Orientation of Medical Anthropology. *In* Handbook of

80 Ann Oakley, Women Confined: Towards a Sociology of Childbirth (Oxford: Martin Robertson 1980); Ann Oakley, The Captured Womb: A History of the Medical Care of Pregnant Women (Oxford: Basil Blackwell, 1984); Shelly Romalis, Childbirth: Alternatives to Medical Control (Austin: University of Texas Press, 1981).

81 Brigitte Jordan, Childbirth in Four Cultures (Montreal: Eden's Press Women's Publications, 1978).

82 Margaret Lock and Patricia A. Kaufert, eds., Pragmatic Women and Body Politics (Cambridge: Cambridge University Press, 1998).

83 Emily Martin, The Woman in the Body: A Cultural Analysis of Reproduction (Boston: Beacon Press. 1987).

84 Peter Conrad, The Medicalization of Society: On the Transformation of Conditions into Treatable Disorders (Baltimore: Johns Hopkins University Press, 2007); Peter Conrad, Up, Down, and Sideways. Social Science and Modern Society 43 (2006): 19–20. See also Kalman Applebaum, Marketing and Commoditization. Social Analysis 44 (2002): 106–128.

85 David Healy, The Creation of Psychopharmacology (Cambridge, MA: Harvard University Press, 2002).

86 Adele E. Clark et al., Technoscience and the New Biomedicalization: Western Roots, Global Rhizomes. Sciences Sociales et Santé 18(2) (2000): 11–42.

87 Sharon Kaufman et al., Revisiting the Biomedicalization of Aging: Clinical Trends and Ethical Challenges. The Gerontologist 44 (2004): 731–738 at p. 731.

88 Susan Sontag, Illness as Metaphor (New York: Farrer, Straus and Giroux, 1978).

89 Arthur Kleinman, Social Origins of Distress and Disease: Depression, Neurasthenia, and Pain in Modern China (New Haven: Yale University Press, 1986); Arthur Kleinman and Byron J. Good, eds., Culture and Depression: Studies in the Anthropology and Cross-Cultural Psychiatry of Affect and Disorder (Berkeley: University of California Press, 1985); Joan Jacobs Brumberg, Fasting Girls: A History of Anorexia Nervosa (Cambridge, MA: Harvard University Press, 1988).

90 Good, The Heart of What's the Matter: 25.

91 Arthur Kleinman, The Illness Narratives: Suffering, Healing and the Human Condition (New York: Basic Books, 1988).

92 Robert J. Barrett, Interpretations of Schizophrenia. Culture, Medicine and Psychiatry 12 (1988): 357–388.

93 Barrett, Interpretations of Schizophrenia: 357; R. J. Barrett, Kurt Schneider in Borneo: Do First Rank Symptoms Apply to the Iban? In Schizophrenia, Culture and Subjectivity: The Edge of Experience, ed. Janice Jenkins and Robert J. Barrett (Cambridge: Cambridge University Press, 2004): 87–109; See also Sue E. Estroff, Identity, Disability, and Schizophrenia: The Problem of Chronicity. In Knowledge, Power and Practice: The Anthropology of Medicine and Everyday Life, ed. S. Lindenbaum and M. Lock (Berkeley: University of California Press, 1993): 247–286.

94 Barrett, Interpretations of Schizophrenia: 357.

95 Kleinman and Good, ed. Culture and Depression.

96 Junko Kitanaka, Society in Distress: The Making of Depression in Contemporary Japan (Princeton: Princeton University Press, forthcoming).

97 Junko Kitanaka, Diagnosing Suicides of Resolve: Psychiatric Practice in Contemporary Japan. Culture Medicine and Psychiatry 32 (2008): 152–176 at p. 171.

98 Kitanaka, Diagnosing Suicides of Resolve:: 172.

99 Lock, East Asian Medicine in Urban Japan.

100 Lawrence Cohen, No Aging in India: Alzheimer's, the Bad Family, and Other Modern Things (Berkeley: University of California Press, 1998): 88.

101 Cohen, No Aging in India: 297–301.

102   See, for example, Mariella Pandolfi, Boundaries Inside the Body: Suffering of the Peasant Women in Southern Italy. Culture Medicine and Psychiatry 2 (1990): 255–273; Margaret Lock, Words of Fear, Words of Power: Nerves and the Awakening of Political Consciousness. Medical Anthropology 11 (1989): 79–90; Margaret Lock, On Being Ethnic: The Politics of Identity Breaking and Making in Canada or, Nevra on Sunday. Culture, Medicine and Psychiatry, 14 (1990): 237–252.

103   Aihwa Ong, The Production of Possession: Spirits and the Multinational Corporation in Malaysia. American Ethnologist 15 (1988): 28–42.

104   Margaret Lock, Flawed Jewels and National Dis/Order: Narratives on Adolescent Dissent in Japan. Journal of Psychohistory 18 (1991): 507–531.

105   Lock, Flawed Jewels.

106   Sachiko Kaneko, Japan's "Socially Withdrawn Youth" and Time Constraints in Japanese Society: Management and Conceptualization of Time in a Support Group for "Hikikomori.". Time and Society 15 (2006): 233–249.

107   Amy Bovery, Japan's Hidden Youth: Mainstreaming the Emotionally Distressed in Japan. Culture Medicine and Psychiatry 32 (2008): 552–576.

108   Arthur Kleinman and Joan Kleinman, How Bodies Remember: Social Memory and Bodily Experience of Criticism, Resistance, and Delegitimation following China's Cultural Revolution. New Literary History 25 (1994): 707–723.

109   Nancy Scheper-Hughes, Death Without Weeping: The Violence of Everyday Life in Brazil (Berkeley: University of California Press, 1992): 187.

110   See also Briggs, Theorizing Modernity Conspiratorially.

111   Claudia Malacrida, Book Review: Ambiguity, Risk and Blame: Critical Responses to Fetal Alcohol Syndrome (FAS). Health 9 (2005): 417–424.

112   R. Bradley and R. Corwyn, Socioeconomic Status and Child Development. Annual Review of Psychology 53 (2002) 169–189.

113   Elizabeth Armstrong, Conceiving Risk, Bearing Responsibility: Fetal Alcohol Syndrome and the Diagnosis of Moral Disorder (Baltimore: Johns Hopkins University Press, 2003).

114   Caroline Tate, The Tip of the Iceberg: The Making of Fetal Alcohol Syndrome in Canada. PhD thesis, Dept. of Anthropology, McGill University, 2003.

115   L. Swartz and A. Levett, Political Repression and Children in South Africa: The Social Construction of Damaging Effects. Social Science and Medicine 28 (1989): 741–750 at p. 747.

116   Swartz and Levett, Political Repression and Children in South Africa: 747, emphasis added.

117   Michael Taussig, Reification and the Consciousness of the Patient. Social Science and Medicine 14B (1980): 3–13.

118   Julio Frenk et al., Elements for a Theory of the Health Transition. Health Transition Review: The Cultural, Social and Behavioural Determinants of Health 1(1) (1991): 21–38.

119   Heinrich Von Staden, The Discovery of the Body: Human Dissection and Its Cultural Contexts in Ancient Greece. Yale Journal of Biology and Medicine 65 (1992): 223–241.

120   Dorothy Porter, Public Health. *In* Companion Encyclopedia of the History of Medicine, vol. 2, ed. W. F. Bynum and R. Porter (London: Routledge, 1993): 1231–1261 at p. 1237.

121   Porter, Public Health: 1237.

122   Crawford, A Cultural Account of "Health".

123   Margaret Lock, Situating Women in the Politics of Health. *In* The Politics of Women's Health: Exploring Agency and Autonomy, ed. Susan Sherwin (Philadelphia: Temple University Press, 1998): 48–63.

124   Robert Crawford, You Are Dangerous to Your Health: The Ideology and Politics of Victim Blaming. International Journal of Health Services 7 (1977): 663–680 at p. 665.
125   John Knowles: comment made at a conference "The Future Direction of Health Care: The Dimensions of Medicine" 1975, cited in Lock, Situating Women in the Politics of Health.
126   Crawford, You Are Dangerous to Your Health.
127   Leon Kass, Regarding the End of Medicine and the Pursuit of Health. Public Interest 40 (1975): 38–39.
128   Anne Somers, Health Care in Transition: Directions for the Future (Chicago: Hospital Research and Educational Trust, 1971): 32.
129   Conrad, Wellness as Virtue.
130   Naomi Adelson, "Being Alive Well": Health and Politics of Cree Wellbeing (Toronto: University of Toronto Press, 2000).

4   Local Biologies and Human Difference

1   Bruno Latour, We Have Never Been Modern (Cambridge, MA: Harvard University Press, 1993): 78.
2   Margaret Lock, Encounters with Aging: Mythologies of Menopause in Japan and North America (Berkeley: University of California Press, 1993).
3   Lock, Encounters with Aging; Margaret Lock, Ideology and Subjectivity: Midlife and Menopause in Japan and North America. In Ethnography and Human Development: Context and Meaning in Social Inquiry, ed. Richard Jessor et al. (Chicago: University of Chicago Press, 1996): 339–369; Margaret Lock, Centering the Household: The Remaking of Female Maturity in Japan. In Re-Imaging Japanese Women, ed. Anne Imamura (Berkeley: University of California Press, 1996): 73–103.
4   See for example, Caroline Bledsoe, Contingent Lives: Fertility, Time, and Aging in West Africa (Chicago: University of Chicago Press, 2002); Melissa Melby et al., Culture and Symptom Reporting at Menopause. Human Reproduction Update 11 (2005): 495–512.
5   Lock, Encounters with Aging: 342.
6   Lock, Encounters with Aging: xxiv–xxxi.
7   Margaret Lock, Contested Meanings of the Menopause. The Lancet 337 (1991): 1270–1291.
8   Melby et al., Culture and Symptom Reporting at Menopause.
9   Steven Epstein, Inclusion: The Politics of Difference in Medical Research (Chicago: University of Chicago Press, 2007).
10   Lock, Encounters with Aging: see chapter 2.
11   Nancy E. Avis and Sonja McKinlay, A Longitudinal Analysis of Women's Attitudes towards the Menopause: Results from the Massachusetts Women's Health Study. Maturitas 13 (1991): 65–79; Patricia Kaufert et al., The Manitoba Project: A Reexamination of the Link Between Menopause and Depression. Maturitas 14 (1992): 143–155; Lock, Encounters with Aging.
12   Lock, Encounters with Aging: see especially chapter 2.
13   Nancy Avis et al., The Evolution of Menopausal Symptoms. Baillières Clinical Endocrinology and Metabolism 7 (1993): 17–32; Lock, Encounters with Aging, for a complete reporting on these findings.
14   Melissa Melby found that some over-reporting of symptoms may have been due to the experience of feeling hot from drinking alcohol and taking Japanese-style hot baths, see Melissa Melby, Vasomotor Symptom Prevalence and Language of Menopause in Japan. Menopause 23(3) (2005): 250–257.

15 Michiko Kasuga et al., Relation between Climacteric Symptoms and Ovarian Hypofunction in Middle-Aged and Elderly Japanese Women Presenting at a Menopausal Clinic. Menopause 11(6) (2004): 631–638.

16 Melissa Melby, Climacteric Symptoms Among Japanese Women and Men: Comparison of 4 Symptom Checklists. Climacteric 9 (2006): 298–304; see also Margaret Lock, Postmodern Bodies, Material Difference, and Subjectivity. *In* Dismantling the East–West Dichotomy: Essays in Honour of Jan van Bremen, ed. J. Hendry and Heung Wah Wong (London: Routledge, 2006): 38–48.

17 Margaret Lock, The Final Disruption? Biopolitics of Post-Reproductive Life. *In* Reproductive Disruptions: Gender, Technology, and Biopolitics in the New Millennium, ed. Marcia Inhorn (New York: Berghahn Books, 2007): 200–224; Melby, Vasomotor Symptom Prevalence.

18 Lock, Encounters with Aging: see chapter 10.

19 Melby, Vasomotor Symptom Prevalence; Melissa K. Melby, Factor Analysis of Climacteric Symptoms in Japan. Maturitas 52 (2005): 205–222.

20 Melby, Vasomotor Symptom Prevalence.

21 E. Gold, Lifestyle and Demographic Factors in Relation to Vasomotor Symptoms: Baseline Results from the Study of Women's Health Across the Nation (SWAN). American Journal of Epidemiology 159(12) (2004): 1189–1199.

22 Melissa Melby et al., Sensitive High-Performance Liquid Chromatographic Method Using Coulometric Electrode Array Detection for Measurement of Phytoestrogens in Dried Blood Spots. Journal of Chromatography 826 (2005): 81–90.

23 Melissa K. Melby, Chilliness: A Vasomotor Symptom in Japan. Menopause 14(4) (2007): 1–8; Melby et al., Culture and Symptom Reporting.

24 Melby, Chilliness.

25 Melissa Melby reports that several women told her that they were prescribed tranquilizers for psychological symptoms. Others told her that they had tried using HRT but did not like the side effects and stopped quite soon after starting. In a postal survey conducted by a Japanese doctor in 2008 only 5% of women surveyed had ever used HRT; personal communication.

26 Margaret Lock and Patricia Kaufert, Menopause, Local Biologies and Cultures of Aging. American Journal of Human Biology, 13 (2001): 494–504; Melby et al., Culture and Symptom Reporting; Jeanne Shea, Cross-Cultural Comparison of Women's Midlife Symptom Reporting: A China Study. Culture Medicine and Psychiatry 30 (2006): 331–362.

27 Jeanne Shea, Women's Midlife Symptom-Reporting in China: A Cross-Cultural Analysis. American Journal of Human Biology 18 (2006): 219–222; Shea, Cross-Cultural Comparison of Women's Midlife Symptom Reporting.

28 Yewoubdar Beyene, Cultural Significance and Physiological Manifestations of Menopause: A Biocultural Analysis. Culture, Medicine, and Psychiatry 10 (1986): 47–71.

29 Carla Makhlouf Obermeyer, Menopause Across Cultures: A Review of the Evidence. Menopause 7 (2000): 184–192.

30 Lynette Leidy Sievert and Erin K. Flanagan, Geographical Distribution of Hot Flash Frequencies: Considering Climatic Differences. American Journal of Physical Anthropology 128 (2005): 437–443.

31 M. J. Boulet et al., Climacteric and Menopause in Seven Southeast Asian Countries. Maturitas 19 (1994): 157–176.

32 E. Gold et al., Factors Associated with Age at Natural Menopause in a Multiethnic Sample of Midlife Women. American Journal of Epidemiology 153(9) (2001): 865–874; S. M. McKinlay et al., The Normal Menopausal Transition. Human Biology 4 (1992): 37–46.

33   Melby et al., Culture and Symptom Reporting; M. Flint et al., eds., Multidisciplinary Perspectives on Menopause (New York: New York Academy of Sciences, 1990); World Health Organization, Research on the Menopause in the 1990s (Geneva: World Health Organization, 1996).

34   Y. Beyene and M. C. Martin, Menopausal Experiences and Bone Density of Mayan Women in Yucatan, Mexico. American Journal of Human Biology 13 (2001): 505–511.

35   M. Martin et al., Menopause Without Symptoms: The Endocrinology of Menopause Among Rural Mayan Indians. American Journal of Obstetrics and Gynecology 168 (1993): 1839–1845.

36   R. R. Freedman, Physiology of Hot Flashes. American Journal of Human Biology 13 (2001): 453–464; F. Kronenberg, Hot Flashes: Epidemiology and Physiology. Annals of the New York Academy of Science 592 (1990): 52–86.

37   Lock, Encounters with Aging.

38   The North American Menopause Society, Estrogen and Progestogen Use in Peri- and Postmenopausal Women: September 2003 Position Statement of the North American Menopause Society. Menopause 10(6) (2003): 497–506; The North American Menopause Society, Treatment of Menopause-Associated Vasomotor Symptoms: Position Statement of the North American Menopause Society. Menopause 11(1) (2004): 11–33; Women's Health Initiative Investigators Writing Group, Risks and Benefits of Estrogen Plus Progestin in Healthy Postmenopausal Women: Principal Results from the Women's Health Initiative Randomized Control Trial. Journal of American Medical Association 288(3) (2002): 321–333.

39   Lock, Encounters with Aging.

40   Atwood Gaines first used the term "local biology" to highlight the cultural construction of biological knowledge, see Atwood D. Gaines, ed. Ethnopsychiatry: The Cultural Construction of Professional and Folk Psychiatries (Albany: State University of New York Press, 1992).

41   William A. Stini, Osteoporosis in Biocultural Perspective. Annual Review of Anthropology, 24 (1995): 397–421.

42   Lock, Encounters with Aging; Byron J. Good, Medicine, Rationality and Experience: An Anthropological Perspective (Cambridge: Cambridge University Press, 1994); Elaine Scarry, The Body in Pain: the Making and Unmaking of the World (Oxford: Oxford University Press, 1985); Byron J. Good and Mary-Jo DelVecchio Good, Clinical Narratives and the Study of Contemporary Doctor–Patient Relationships. In The Handbook of Social Studies in Health and Medicine, ed. Gary L. Albrecht, Ray Fitzpatrick and Susan C. Scrimshaw (London: Sage, 2000): 243–258.

43   Mary-Jo DelVecchio Good et al., Pain as Human Experience: An Anthropological Perspective (Berkeley: University of California Press, 1992); David Kertzer and Jennie Keith, Age and Anthropological Theory (Ithaca: Cornell University Press, 1984).

44   Troy Duster, Buried Alive: The Concept of Race in Science. In Genetic Nature/Culture: Anthropology and Science Beyond the Two-Culture Divide, ed. Alan H. Goodman et al. (Berkeley: University of California Press, 2003): 258–277; Lynn B. Jorde and Stephen P. Wooding, Genetic Variation, Classification and "Race." Nature Genetics 36 (2004): S28–S33.

45   See, for example, Melby, Vasomotor Symptom Prevalence.

46   Richard C. Lewontin, Science and Simplicity. New York Review of Books 50 (2003): 39–42 at p. 39.

47   Lewontin, Science and Simplicity: 39

48   Jonathan Weiner, The Beak of the Finch (New York: Vintage Books, 1994).

49   Alec Wilkinson, Profiles, The Lobsterman. New Yorker, July 31, 2006: 56–65.

50   Karen Barad, Meeting the Universe Half Way: Quantum Physics and the Entanglement of Matter and Meaning (Durham, NC: Duke University Press, 2007): 56.

51   Barad, Meeting the Universe Half Way: 33.

52   Barad, Meeting the Universe Half Way: 33.

53   Barad, Meeting the Universe Half Way: 141.

54   Barad, Meeting the Universe Half Way: 335.

55   Barad, Meeting the Universe Half Way: 140.

56   Barad, Meeting the Universe Half Way: 217.

57   The following discussion draws extensively on an article published by Warwick Anderson, The Possession of *Kuru*: Medical Science and Biocolonial Exchange. Comparative Study of Society and History 42(4) (2000): 713–744 and also on his recent book The Collectors of Lost Souls: Turning *Kuru* Scientists into Whitemen (Baltimore: Johns Hopkins University Press, 2008).

58   Shirley Lindenbaum, *Kuru* Sorcery: Disease and Danger in the New Guinea Highlands (Palo Alto, California: Mayfield, 1978).

59   Anderson, Collectors of Lost Souls: 125.

60   Anderson, The Possession of *Kuru*: 713.

61   Anderson, The Possession of *Kuru*: 723.

62   Anderson, The Possession of *Kuru*: 724.

63   Anderson, The Possession of *Kuru*: 725.

64   Anderson, Collectors of Lost Souls 167.

65   Anderson, Collectors of Lost Souls: 169.

66   Lindenbaum, *Kuru* Sorcery.

67   John D. Matthews et al., *Kuru* and Cannibalism. The Lancet 292(7565) (1968): 449–452 at p. 451.

68   J. Collinge et al., *Kuru* in the twenty-first century – an acquired human prion disease with very long incubation periods. The Lancet 367 (2006): 2068–2074.

69   Collinge et al., *Kuru* in the twenty-first century.

70   J. Rich-Edwards et al., Maternal Experiences of Racism and Violence as Predictors of Preterm Birth: Rationale and Study Design. Paediatric and Perinatal Epidemiology 15 (2001): 124–135 at p. 24.

71   Nancy Krieger, If "Race" Is the Answer, What Is the Question? On "Race," Racism, and Health: A Social Epidemiologist's Perspective. Is Race Real? A web forum organized by the Social Science Research Council, June 7, 2006. http://raceandgenomics.ssrc.org/Krieger/. See p. 3.

72   James W. Collins et al., Very Low Birthweight in African American Infants: The Role of Maternal Exposure to Interpersonal Racial Discrimination. American Journal of Public Health 94 (2004): 2132–2138; James W. Collins et al., Low-Income African-American Mothers' Perception of Exposure to Racial Discrimination and Infant Birth Weight. Epidemiology 11 (2000): 337–339.

73   Krieger, If "Race" Is the Answer: 3

74   Stephen Palumbi, Humans as the World's Greatest Evolutionary Force. Science 293(5536) (2001): 1786–1790.

75   John Ford, The Role of Trypanosomiasis in African Ecology: A Study of the Tsetse Fly Problem (Oxford: Clarendon Press, 1971).

76   R. Reid, Cultural and Medical Perspectives on Geophagia. Medical Anthropology 13 (1992): 337–351; Nina Etkin, The Co-Evolution of People, Plants, and Parasites: Biological and Cultural Adaptations to Malaria. Proceedings of the Nutrition Society 62 (2003): 311–317.

77 This neglect is part of a larger phenomenon, referred to as the "10/90 gap," whereby only 10% of biomedical research money goes into investigating diseases that afflict 90% of the world's population.

78 Naomi E. Aronson, Leishmaniasis in American Soldiers: Parasites from the Front. *In* Emerging Infections 7, ed. W. M. Scheld et al. (Washington, D.C.: ASM Press, 2007): 325–343.

79 Louis-Patrick Haraoui, The Orientalist Sore: Biomedical Discourses, Capital and Urban Warfare in the Colonial Present. MSc thesis, Université de Montreal, 2007.

80 K. N. Harper et al., On the Origin of the Treponematoses: A Phylogenetic Approach. PLoS Neglected Tropical Diseases 2(1) (2008): e148. doi: 10.1371/journal.pntd.0000148

81 C. Briggs and C. Mantini-Briggs, Stories in the Time of Cholera: Racial Profiling During a Medical Nightmare (Berkeley: University of California Press, 2004).

82 Paul Farmer, AIDS and Accusation: Haiti and the Geography of Blame (Berkeley: University of California Press, 2006).

83 Farmer, AIDS and Accusation.

84 Gilles Bibeau and Duncan Pederson, A Return to Scientific Racism: The Case of Sexuality and the AIDS Epidemic in Africa. *In* New Horizons in Medical Anthropology: Essays in Honour of Charles Leslie (London: Routledge, 2002): 141–171.

85 Didier Fassin, Culturalism as Ideology. *In* Cultural Perspectives on Reproductive Health, ed. Carla Makhlouf Obermeyer (Oxford: Oxford University Press, 2001): 300–317.

86 Helen Epstein, The Invisible Cure: Africa, the West and the Fight Against AIDS (New York: Farrar, Straus and Giroux, 2007); Elizabeth Pisani, The Wisdom of Whores: Bureaucrats, Brothels, and the Business of AIDS (New York: W. W. Norton, 2008); James Chin, The AIDS Pandemic: The Collision of Epidemiology with Political Correctness (New York: Radcliffe, 2007).

87 Adam Hochschild, King Leopold's Ghost: A Story of Greed, Terror, and Heroism in Colonial Africa (Boston: Mariner Books, 2006).

88 A. Chitnis et al., Origin of HIV Type 1 in Colonial French Equatorial Africa? AIDS Research and Human Retroviruses 16(1) (2000): 5–8; K. Yusim et al., Using human immunodeficiency virus type 1 sequences to infer historical features of the acquired immune deficiency syndrome epidemic and human immunodeficiency virus evolution. Philosophical Transactions of the Royal Society of London Series B 356(1410) (2001): 855–866.

89 Edward Hooper, The River: A Journey to the Source of HIV and Aids (Harmondsworth: Penguin, 1999).

90 P. Lena and P. Luciw, Polio Vaccine and Retroviruses. Philosophical Transactions of the Royal Society of London Series B 356(1410) (2001): 841–844.

91 Zhiwei Chen et al., Genetic Characterization of New West African Simian Immunodeficiency Virus Sivsm: Geographic Clustering of Household-Derived SIV Strains with Human Immunodeficiency Virus Type 2 Subtypes and Genetically Diverse Viruses from a Single Feral Sooty Mangabey Troop. Journal of Virology 70(6) (1996): 3617–3627.

92 P. A. Marx et al., Serial Human Passage of Simian Immunodeficiency Virus by Unsterile Injections and the Emergence of Epidemic Human Immunodeficiency Virus in Africa. Philosophical Transactions of the Royal Society of London series B 356(1410) (2001): 911–920.

93 M. Lyons, The Colonial Disease (Cambridge: Cambridge University Press, 1992).

94 William Carlsen, Did Modern Medicine Spread an Epidemic? San Francisco Chronicle, January 15, 2001: A11.

95 Christian Apetrei et al., Potential for HIV Transmission Through Unsafe Injections. AIDS 20(7): 1074–1076.

96 Epstein, Inclusion.

5 The Right Population

1 T. R. Malthus, An Essay on the Principle of Population [1798]. Oxford World Classics. 3rd reprint (Oxford: Oxford University Press, 2004): 61.

2 Susan Greenhalgh, Globalization and Population Governance in China. *In* Global Assemblages: Technology, Politics, and Ethics as Anthropological Problems, ed. Aihwa Ong and Steven J. Collier (Oxford: Blackwell Publishing, 2005): 354–372 at p. 357.

3 See, for example, Tola Olu Pearce, Women's Reproductive Practices and Biomedicine: Cultural Conflicts and Transformations in Nigeria. *In* Conceiving the New World Order: The Global Politics of Reproduction, ed. Faye D. Ginsburg and Rayna Rapp (Berkeley: University of California Press, 1995): 195–208.

4 Caroline H. Bledsoe, Contingent Lives: Fertility, Time and Aging in West Africa (Chicago: University of Chicago Press, 2002).

5 Lisa Ann Richey, Women's Reproductive Health and Population Policy: Tanzania. Review of African Political Economy 30 (2003): 273–292.

6 Soheir Morsy, Deadly Reproduction among Egyptian Women: Maternal Mortality and the Medicalization of Population Control. *In* Conceiving the New World Order: The Global Politics of Reproduction, ed. Faye D. Ginsburg and Rayna Rapp (Berkeley: University of California Press, 1995): 162–176.

7 Stacy Leigh Pigg, Too Bold, Too Hot: Crossing "Culture" in AIDS Prevention in Nepal. *In* New Horizons in Medical Anthropology: Essays in Honour of Charles Leslie, ed. Mark Nichter and Margaret Lock (London: Routledge, 2002): 58–80; Steve Ferzacca, Governing Bodies in New Order Indonesia. *In* New Horizons in Medical Anthropology, ed. Mark Nichter and Margaret Lock (London: Routledge, 2002): 35–57.

8 Eric B. Ross, The Malthus Factor: Poverty, Politics and Population in Capitalist Development (London: Zed Books, 1998): 3.

9 Ross, The Malthus Factor: 4.

10 Julian Huxley, Evolutionary Humanism (Melbourne: Australian Institute of International Affairs, 1957).

11 Paul R. Ehrlich, The Population Bomb (New York: Ballantine Books, 1968).

12 Ehrlich, The Population Bomb: 1.

13 *In vitro* techniques are available in which an effort is made to ensure that the conceptus is of one sex rather than another.

14 Gail Kligman, The Politics of Duplicity: Controlling Reproduction in Ceausescu's Romania (Berkeley: University of California Press, 1998).

15 Daniel J. Kevles, Annals of Eugenics: A Secular Faith I. New Yorker, October 8, 1984: 51–115 at p. 85.

16 Kevles, Annals of Eugenics: 85.

17 Kevles, Annals of Eugenics: 92.

18 Charles B. Davenport, Eugenics: The Science of Human Improvement by Better Breeding (New York: Henry Holt, 1910): 12.

19 E. M. East, Hidden Feeblemindedness. Journal of Heredity 8 (1917): 215–217.

20 Daniel Pick, Faces of Degeneration: A European Disorder, c. 1848–1918 (Cambridge University Press, 1993); Nikolas Rose, The Politics of Life Itself: Biomedicine, Power, and Subjectivity in the Twenty-First Century (Princeton: Princeton University Press, 2007).

21 Margaret Sanger, The Pivot of Civilization (Washington, D.C.: Scott-Townsend Publishers, 1922): 98.

22 Sanger, The Pivot of Civilization.

23 S. Otsubo and J. R. Bartholomew, Eugenics in Japan: Some Ironies of Modernity, 1883–1945. Science in Context 11(3–4) (1998): 133–146.

24   Jennifer Robertson, Blood Talks: Eugenic Modernity and the Creation of New Japanese. History and Anthropology 13 (2002): 191–216.

25   Diane B. Paul, The Politics of Heredity: Essays on Eugenics, Biomedicine, and the Nature–Nurture Debate (Albany: State University of New York Press, 1998): 117.

26   Paul, The Politics of Heredity: 128.

27   Harriet Washington, Medical Apartheid: The Dark History of Medical Experimentation on Black Americans from Colonial Times to the Present (New York: Doubleday, 2006): 198.

28   Linda Gordon, The Moral Property of Women: A History of Birth Control Politics in America (Urbana: University of Illinois Press, 2002): 138.

29   Matthew Connelly, Fatal Misconception: The Struggle to Control World Population (Cambridge, MA: Belknap Press of Harvard University Press, 2008).

30   Gordon, The Moral Property of Women: 280.

31   Gordon, The Moral Property of Women: 282.

32   Connelly, Fatal Misconception: 248.

33   Connelly, Fatal Misconception: 247.

34   Helen Epstein, The Strange History of Birth Control. New York Review of Books, August 14, 2008: 57–59 at p. 57; http://www.nybooks.com/contents/20080814. Epstein draws on Simon Szreter, The Idea of Demographic Transition and the Study of Fertility Change: A Critical Intellectual History. *In* Health and Wealth: Studies in History and Policy (Rochester, NY: University of Rochester Press, 2007).

35   Gordon, The Moral Property of Women: 284.

36   Lara Marks, Human Guinea Pigs? The History of the Early Oral Contraceptive Trials. History and Techology 15 (1999): 263–288; see also chapter 7.

37   M. Catherine Maternowska, Reproducing Inequities: Poverty and the Politics of Population in Haiti, Studies in Medical Anthropology (New Brunswick, NJ: Rutgers University Press, 2006): 140.

38   Maternowska, Reproducing Inequities: 111.

39   Susan Greenhalgh, Planned Birth, Unplanned Persons: "Population" in the Making of Chinese Modernity. American Ethnologist 30 (2003): 196–215 at p. 197.

40   Nilanjana Chatterjee, Planning an Indian Modernity: The Gendered Politics of Fertility Control. Signs 26 (2001): 812–845.

41   Chatterjee, Planning an Indian Modernity: 812.

42   Mahmood Mamdani, The Myth of Population Control: Family, Caste, and Class in an Indian Village (New York: Monthly Review Press, 1972).

43   Mamdani, The Myth of Population Control.

44   Chatterjee, Planning an Indian Modernity: 820.

45   Programs designed to improve female literacy were strongly promoted by the World Bank in the 1970s on the assumption that simply providing schooling for illiterate women would reduce fertility rates. These programs have been widely criticized as target driven and decontextualized from the everyday lives of women. It is clear that voluntary reduction of fertility rates is the result of the interaction of a number of variables relating to economic and social security to which female literacy often contributes; see, for example, Caroline Bledsoe et al., eds., Critical Perspectives on Schooling and Fertility in the Developing World (Washington D.C.: National Academies Press, 1992).

46   Emma Tarlo, Body and Space in a Time of Crisis: Sterilization and Resettlement during the Emergency in Delhi. *In* Violence and Subjectivity, ed. A. Kleinman et al. (Berkeley: University of California Press, 2000): 242–270.

47   Tarlo, Body and Space in a Time of Crisis: 248.

48   Tarlo, Body and Space in a Time of Crisis: 249.

49   Veena Das, Critical Events: An Anthropological Perspective on Contemporary India (Delhi, New York: Oxford University Press, 1995).

50 Cecilia Van Hollen, Birth on the Threshold: Childbirth and Modernity in Southern India (Berkeley: University of California Press, 2003).

51 Cecilia Van Hollen, Moving Targets: The Routinization of IUD Insertions in Public Maternity Wards (Berkeley: University of California Press, 2003), see especially chapter 5.

52 http://www.lankalibrary.com/news/reversal.htm

53 http://www.medicalnewstoday.com/articles/21276.php

54 Bledsoe, Contingent Lives.

55 Bledsoe, Contingent Lives.

56 Susan Greenhalgh and Edwin Winckler, Governing China's Population: From Leninist to Neo-Liberal Biopolitics (Stanford, Stanford University Press, 2005): 3.

57 Greenhalgh and Winckler, Governing China's Population: 3.

58 Therese Hesketh et al., The Effect of China's One-Child Family Policy after 25 Years. New England Journal of Medicine 353 (2005): 1171–1176.

59 Susan Greenhalgh, Just One Child: Science and Policy in Deng's China (Berkeley: University of California Press, 2008), see especially chapter 2.

60 Greenhalgh and Winckler, Governing China's Population: 60.

61 Greenhalgh and Winckler, Governing China's Population: 61.

62 Greenhalgh, Just One Child: 5.

63 Greenhalgh, Just One Child: 24.

64 Greenhalgh and Winckler, Governing China's Population: 79.

65 Greenhalgh, Just One Child: 132.

66 Greenhalgh, Just One Child: 143.

67 Greenhalgh, Just One Child: 98.

68 S. Greenhalgh and J. Bongaarts, Fertility Policy in China: Future Options. Science 235 (1987): 1167–1172 at p. 1168.

69 Greenhalgh, Just One Child: 32.

70 Susan Greenhalgh, Managing "the Missing Girls" in Chinese Population Discourse. In Cultural Perspectives on Reproductive Health, ed. Carla Makhlouf Obermeyer (Oxford: Oxford University Press, 2001): 131–152.

71 Hesketh et al., The Effect of China's One-Child Family Policy: 1171–1176.

72 Greenhalgh and Winckler, Governing China's Population: 149.

73 Wei Xing Zhu et al., China's Excess Males, Sex Selective Abortion, and One-Child Policy: Analysis of Data from 2005 National Intercensus Survey. British Medical Journal 338 (2009): 920–936.

74 Wei Xing Zhu et al., China's Excess Males.

75 Greenhalgh and Winckler, Governing China's Population: 247.

76 Greenhalgh and Winckler, Governing China's Population: 251.

77 Greenhalgh and Winckler, Governing China's Population: 272; Junhong Chu, Prenatal Sex Determination and Sex-Selective Abortion in Rural Central China. Population and Development Review 27 (2001): 259–281.

78 Greenhalgh, Managing "the Missing Girls."

79 Andrew Jacobs, Chinese Hunger for Sons Fuels Boys' Abductions. New York Times, April 4, 2009. http://www.nytimes.com/2009/04/05/world/asia/05kidnap.html

80 Ann Anagnost, A Surfeit of Bodies: Population and the Rationality of the State in Post-Mao China. In Conceiving the New World Order: The Global Politics of Reproduction, ed. F. D. Ginsburg and R. Rapp (Berkeley: University of California Press, 1995): 22–41.

81 Jennifer Robertson, Biopower: Blood, Kinship, and Eugenic Marriage. In A Companion to the Anthropology of Japan, ed. Jennifer Robertson (Oxford: Blackwell Publishing, 2005): 329–354.

82 See, for example, Philip Kitcher, The Lives to Come: The Genetic Revolution and Human Possibilities (New York: Simon and Schuster, 1996).

83   Siwan Anderson and Debraj Ray, Missing Women: Age and Disease. Journal of Economic Literature Classification Numbers 11 (in press).

84   Anderson and Ray, Missing Women.

85   Laila Williamson, Infanticide: An Anthropological Analysis. *In* Infanticide and the Value of Life, ed. Marvin Kohl (New York: Prometheus Books, 1978): 61–75.

86   Susan Hanley, Family and Fertility in Four Tokugawa Villages. *In* Family and Population in East Asian History, ed. S. B. Hanley and A. P. Wolf (Stanford: Stanford University Press, 1985): 196–228; William La Fleur, Liquid Life: Abortion and Buddhism in Japan (Princeton: Princeton University Press, 1992).

87   Margaret Lock, Centering the Household: The Remaking of Female Maturity in Japan. *In* Re-Imaging Japanese Women, ed. Anne Imamura (Berkeley: University of California Press, 1996): 73–103.

88   K. Hill and D. M. Upchurch, Gender Differences in Child Health: Evidence from the Demographic and Health Surveys. Population Development Review 21 (1995) 127–151.

89   Elisabeth Croll, Endangered Daughters: Discrimination and Development in Asia (London: Routledge, 2000); Greenhalgh and Winckler, Governing China's Population; Monica Das Gupta et al., State Policies and Women's Agency in China, the Republic of Korea, and India, 1950–2000: Lessons from Contrasting Experiences. *In* Culture and Public Action, ed. V. Rao and M. Walton (Stanford: Stanford University Press, 2004): 234–259; Amartya Sen, More than 100 Million Women are Missing. New York Review of Books 37 (1990): 61–66.

90   Éric Brian and Marie Jaisson, The Descent of Human Sex Ratio at Birth: A Dialogue between Mathematics, Biology and Sociology, Methodos Series, vol. 4 (New York: Springer, 2007): 87–120 at p. 89.

91   Frank van Balen and Marcia C. Inhorn, Son Preference, Sex Selection, and the "New" New Reproductive Technologies. International Journal of Health Services 33 (2003): 235–252.

92   http://www.geneticsandsociety.org/article.php?id=1997; Ted Plafker, Sex Selection in China Sees 117 Boys for Every 100 Girls. British Medical Journal 324 (2002): 1223.

93   Rayna Rapp, Real-Time Fetus: The Role of the Sonogram in the Age of Monitored Reproduction. *In* Cyborgs and Citadels: Anthropological Interventions into Emerging Sciences and Technologies, ed. Gaye Lee Downey and Joseph Dumit (Santa Fe: School of American Research Press, 1997): 31–48.

94   Rapp, Real-Time Fetus: 38.

95   See, for example, Tsipi Ivry, The Ultrasonic Picture Show and the Politics of Threatened Life. Medical Anthropology Quarterly 23 (2009): 189–211.

96   Karen Barad, Meeting the Universe Halfway: Quantum Physics and the Entanglement of Matter and Meaning (Durham, NC: Duke University Press, 2007): 202.

97   Pande Rohini and Anju Malhetra, Son Preference and Daughter Neglect in India. International Center for Research on Women. http://www.icrw.org/docs/2006_son-preference.pdf.

98   Randeep Ramesh, Jailing of Doctor in India Sting Operation Highlights Scandal of Aborted Girl Fetuses. The Guardian, March 30, 2006, 3.

99   Prabhat Jha et al., Low Male-to-Female Sex Ratio of Children Born in India: National Survey of 1.1 Million Households. The Lancet 367(9506) (2006): 211–218.

100 Monica Das Gupta, Selective Discrimination against Female Children in Rural Punjab, India. Population and Development Review, 13 (1987): 77–100; Stephanie Nolen, Land of the Rising Sun. Globe and Mail, September 12, 2009.

101 A. Malpani and A. Malpani, Preimplantation Genetic Diagnosis for Gender Selection for Family Balancing: A View from India. Reproductive BioMedicine Online 4(1) (2001): 7–9. http://humrep.oxfordjournals.org/cgi/content/full/17/1/11

102 Vibhuti Patel, Sex Determination and Sex-Preselection Tests in India: Modern Techniques of Femicide. Bulletin of Concerned Asian Scholars 21(5) (1989): 1153–1156; Jha et al., Low Male-to-Female Sex Ratio; B. D. Miller, The Endangered Sex: Neglect of Female Children in Rural North India (Oxford: Oxford University Press, 1997).

103 Sen, More than 100 Million Women are Missing.

104 Amartya Sen, Missing Women – Revisited: Reduction in Female Mortality Has Been Counterbalanced by Sex Selective Abortions. British Medical Journal 327 (2003): 1297–1298.

105 Preet Rustagi, The Deprived, Discriminated and Damned Girl Child: Story of Declining Child Sex Ratios in India. Women's Health and Urban Life 5 (2006): 16.

106 S. Sudha and S. Irudaya Rajan, Female Demographic Disadvantage in India 1981–1991: Sex Selective Abortions and Female Infanticide. Development and Change 30(3) (1999): 585–618.

107 Rohini and Malhetra, Son Preference and Daughter Neglect.

108 Das Gupta et al., State Policies and Women's Agency in China: 250.

109 Jean Drèze and Amartya Sen, India: Development and Participation (Oxford: Oxford University Press, 2002); see also Satish Balram Agnihotri, Sex Ratio Patterns in the Indian Population: A Fresh Exploration (London: Sage, 2000).

110 Mridula Bandyopadhyay, Missing Girls and Son Preference in Rural India: Looking Beyond Popular Myth. Health Care for Women International 24 (2003): 910–926.

111 Patricia Jeffrey: personal communication with Margaret Lock, September 2008.

112 Sunita Puri, "There Is Such a Thing as Too Many Daughters, But Not Too Many Sons": The Intersection of Medical Technology, Son Preference and Sex Selection Among South Asian Immigrants in the United States (M.Sc. thesis, Department of Anthropology, University of California, 2008).

113 Frank Dikotter, Imperfect Conceptions: Medical Knowledge, Birth Defects, and Eugenics in China (New York: Columbia University Press, 1998).

114 Greenhalgh, Managing "the Missing Girls": 131.

115 Greenhalgh, Managing "the Missing Girls": 139.

116 Greenhalgh, Planned Births, Unplanned Persons.

117 Greenhalgh, Managing "the Missing Girls": 140.

118 Greenhalgh, Managing "the Missing Girls": 143.

119 Greenhalgh, Managing "the Missing Girls": 145.

120 Greenhalgh, Planned Births, Unplanned Persons.

121 Greenhalgh, Planned Births, Unplanned Persons: 207.

122 Greenhalgh, Planned Births, Unplanned Persons: 208.

123 Greenhalgh and Winckler, Governing China's Population: 266.

124 Marcus Gee, The Cruel Irony of China's One-Child Policy. The Globe and Mail, May 8, 2009. http://www.realclearworld.com/2009/05/08/cruel_irony_of_chinas_one-child_policy_100547.html

125 Vanessa Fong, Only Hope: Coming of Age Under China's One-Child Policy (Stanford: Stanford University Press, 2004).

126 Liza Handwerker, The Consequences of Modernity for Childless Women in China: Medicalization and Resistance. In Pragmatic Women and Body Politics, ed. Margaret Lock and Patricia Kaufert (Cambridge: University of Cambridge Press, 1998): 178–205.

127 Chu, Prenatal Sex Determination.

128 Chu, Prenatal Sex Determination: 274.

129 Chu, Prenatal Sex Determination: 269.

130   http://www.chinadaily.com.cn/china/2007-08/content.

131   Jonathan Watts, Villagers Riot Over Family-Planning Law. The Globe and Mail, May 22, 2007, A11.

132   Wei Xing Zhu et al., China's Excess Males.

133   Satish Balram Agnihotri, Sex Ratio Patterns in the Indian Population.

134   Anagnost, A Surfeit of Bodies.

135   Das Gupta et al., State Policies and Women's Agency in China.

136   http://www.nso.go.kr/.

137   Young Rae Oum, Beyond a Strong State and Docile Women: Reproductive Choices, State Policy and Skewed Sex Ratio in South Korea. International Feminist Journal of Politics 5 (2003): 420–446; Homer Williams: personal communication to Margaret Lock, September 2008.

138   Veena Das, Life and Worlds: Violence and the Descent into the Ordinary (Berkeley: University of California Press, 2007): 208.

139   China Daily, China Warned of Risks of Imbalanced Sex Ratio. August 24, 2007.

140   Ketaki Gokhale, Indian Couples Seek Out U.S. Sex Selection Clinics. India West, June 30, 2006, http://news.pacificnews.org/news/view_article.html?article_id=54a58cce91 4f335cb8fb6e722aa1028d.

141   Susannah Baruch et al., Preimplantation Genetic Screening: A Survey of *In Vitro* Fertilization Clinics. Genetics in Medicine 10(9): 685–690; see also D. Almond and L. Edlund, Son-Biased Sex Ratios in the 2000 United States Census. Proceedings of the National Academy of Sciences 105(15) (2008): 5681–5682.

142   http://www.usask.ca/research/files/download.php/National+Post-RogerPierson.pdf

143   Marcia Inhorn, personal communication with Margaret Lock, January 2009.

144   Caroline Bledsoe, personal communication with Margaret Lock, December 2008.

145   Sam Roberts, U.S. Births Hint at Bias for Boys in Some Asians. New York Times, June 15, 2009. http://www.nytimes.com/2009/06/15/nyregion/15babies.html

146   Puri, There Is Such a Thing as Too Many Daughters.

147   Greenhalgh and Winckler, Governing China's Population: 272.

148   Rhoda Ann Kanaaneh, Birthing the Nation: Strategies of Palestinian Women in Israel (Berkeley: University of California Press, 2002): 10.

149   Faye Ginsburg and Rayna Rapp, eds., Conceiving the New World Order: The Global Politics of Reproduction (Berkeley: University of California Press, 1995).

150   Kanaaneh, Birthing the Nation: 22.

151   Kanaaneh, Birthing the Nation: 28. Kanaaneh cites Dov Friedlander and Calvin Goldscheider, The Population of Israel (New York: Columbia University Press, 1979).

152   Kanaaneh, Birthing the Nation: 60. Kanaaneh argues that demographic manipulations happen more on the Jewish than the Palestinian side.

153   Kanaaneh, Birthing the Nation: 76.

154   Kanaaneh, Birthing the Nation: 56.

155   Edward Said, Peace and Its Discontents: Essays on Palestine in the Middle East (New York: Vintage Books, 1995): 18.

156   Kanaaneh, Birthing the Nation: 72.

157   Kanaaneh, Birthing the Nation: 242.

158   Kanaaneh, Birthing the Nation: 166.

159   Kanaaneh, Birthing the Nation: 228.

160   This will be further explored in chapter 10, which will examine how reproductive technologies, be they bio-contraceptives or assisted reproduction, challenge prevailing notions of kinship and relatedness.

6   Colonial Disease and Biological Commensurability

1   Veena Das, Critical Events: An Anthropological Perspective on Contemporary India (Delhi: Oxford University Press).

2   Mark Harrison, Disease and the Modern World: 1500 to the Present Day (Cambridge: Polity Press, 2004): 157.

3   W. F. Bynum, Science and the Practice of Medicine in the Nineteenth Century. (Cambridge, Cambridge University Press, 1994): 146–152.

4   Philip D. Curtin, Disease and Empire: The Health of European Troops in the Conquest of Africa (Cambridge: Cambridge University Press, 1998).

5   David Arnold, Medicine and Colonialism. *In* Companion Encyclopedia of the History of Medicine, ed. W. F. Bynum and Roy Porter (London, New York: Routledge, 1993): 1393–1416.

6   D. Headrick, The Tools of Empire: Technology and European Imperialism in the Nineteenth Century (Oxford: Oxford University Press, 1981): 58–79.

7   W. B. Cohen, Malaria and French Imperialism. Journal of African History 24 (1983): 23–36; Philip D. Curtin, Death by Migration: Europe's Encounter with the Tropical World in the Nineteenth Century (Cambridge: Cambridge University Press, 1989); Mark Harrison, Medicine and the Culture of Command: The Case of Malaria Control in the British Army During the Two World Wars. Medical History 40 (1996): 437–452.

8   Harrison, Medicine and the Culture of Command: 437–452.

9   David Arnold, Colonizing the Body: State Medicine and Epidemic Disease in Nineteenth-Century India (Berkeley: University of California Press, 1993): 28–42.

10   M. Worboys, Tropical Medicine. *In* Companion Encyclopedia to the History of Medicine, vol. I, ed. W. F. Bynum and R. Porter (London: Routledge, 1993): 515.

11   Michael Osborne, Acclimatizing the World: A History of the Paradigmatic Colonial Science. Osiris 15 (2001): 135–151.

12   Caroline Hannaway, Environment and Miasma. *In* Companion Encyclopedia of the History of Medicine, vol. I, ed. W. F. Bynum and R. Porter (London: Routledge, 1993): 304.

13   Ernst Waltraud and Bernard Harris, eds., Race Science and Medicine 1700–1960 (London: Routledge, 1999).

14   Michael Worboys, Tuberculosis and Race in Britain and Its Empire, 1900–50. *In* Race Science and Medicine 1700–1960, ed. Ernst Waltraud and Bernard Harris (London: Routledge, 1999): 144–163 at p. 145.

15   Sheldon Watts, Epidemics and History: Disease, Power and Imperialism (New Haven: Yale University Press, 1997): 121.

16   Douglas Haynes, Framing Tropical Disease in London: Patrick Manson, Filaria perstans, and the Uganda Sleeping Sickness Epidemic, 1891–1902. Social History of Medicine 13 (2000) 467; M. Lyons, The Colonial Disease: A Social History of Sleeping Sickness in Northern Zaire, 1900–1940 (Cambridge: Cambridge University Press, 1992).

17   Haynes, Framing Tropical Disease in London: 472.

18   Anne-Marie Moulin, Tropical without the Tropics: The Turning-Point of Pastorian Medicine in North Africa. *In* Warm Climates and Western Medicine, ed. David Arnold (Amsterdam: Rodopi, 1996): 167.

19   Jean-Pierre Dozon, Une Anthropologie en mouvement: L'Afrique miroir du contemporain (Paris: Quae Éditions, 2008): 123.

20   Jean Pierre Dozon, Quand les Pastoriens traquaient la maladie du sommeil. Sciences Sociales et Santé 3 (1985): 27–56.

21   R. Headrick, Colonialism, Health and Illness in French Equatorial Africa, 1885–1935 (Atlanta: African Studies Association Press, 1994).

22 Myron Echenberg, Plague Ports: The Global Urban Impact of Bubonic Plague,1894–1901 (New York: New York University Press, 2007).

23 Anne-Marie Moulin, The Pasteur Institutes Between the Two World Wars: The Transformation of the International Sanitary Order. *In* International Health Organisations and Movements, 1918–1939, ed. Paul Weindling (Cambridge: Cambridge University Press, 1995): 253.

24 Lyons, The Colonial Disease.

25 Jean Pierre Dozon, D'un tombeau à l'autre. Cahiers d'Études Africaines 31 (1991): 135–157.

26 Quoted in M. Lyons, Sleeping Sickness, Colonial Medicine and Imperialism: Some Connections in the Belgian Congo. *In* Disease, Medicine and Empire, ed. R. Macleod and L. Milton (London: Routledge, 1988): 242–256 at p. 245.

27 Luise White, Tsetse Visions: Narratives of Blood and Bugs in Colonial Northern Rhodesia, 1931–9. Journal of African History 36 (1995): 219–245; Luise White, They Could Make Their Victims Dull: Genders and Genres, Fantasies and Cures in Colonial Southern Uganda. American Historical Review (1995): 1379–1402.

28 Danielle Domergues-Cloarec, Histoire de la santé en Côte-d'Ivoire (Toulouse: Presses Universitaires du Mirail, 1986); Danielle Domergues-Cloarec, Politique coloniale française et réalités coloniale: la santé en Côte d'Ivoire, 1905–1958, 2 vols. (Paris: Académie des science d'Outre-Mer, 1986); Lyons, Sleeping Sickness.

29 David Arnold, ed. Imperial Medicine and Indigenous Societies (Manchester: Manchester University Press, 1988).

30 Ilana Löwy, Virus, moustiques et modernité: La fièvre jaune au Brésil, entre science et politique (Paris: Éditions des Archives Contemporaines, 2001): 87.

31 R. Macleod and M. Lewis, Disease, Medicine and Empire (London: Routledge, 1988).

32 J. Lasker, The Role of Health Services in Colonial Rule: The Case of the Ivory Coast, Culture, Medicine and Psychiatry 1977: 277–297.

33 See Michel Callon, Some Elements of a Sociology of Translation: Domestication of the Scallops and the Fishermen of St Brieuc Bay. *In* Power, Action and Belief: A New Sociology of Knowledge?, ed. J. Law (London: Routledge, 1986): 196–229, at p. 196.

34 Jim Whitman, ed., The Politics of Emerging and Resurgent Infectious Diseases (Basingstoke: Palgrave Macmillan, 2000): 1.

35 P. Basch, Textbook of International Health, 2nd edn. (Oxford: Oxford University Press, 1999).

36 Paul Weindling, International Health Organisations and Movements, 1918–1939 (Cambridge: Cambridge University Press, 1995).

37 David Fidler, SARS: Governance and the Globalization of Disease (London: Palgrave Macmillan, 2004).

38 Paul Farmer, AIDS and Accusation: Haiti and the Geography of Blame (Berkeley: University of California Press, 2006).

39 http://www.who.int/3by5/en/

40 Didier Fassin, When Bodies Remember: Experiences and Politics of AIDS in South Africa (Berkeley: University of California Press, 2007): 54–55.

41 Victor Witter Turner, Forest of Symbols (Ithaca: Cornell University Press, 1967): 93–111.

42 N. R. Hunt, "Le bébé en brousse": European Women, African Birth Spacing and Colonial Intervention in Breast Feeding in the Belgian Congo. International Journal of African Historical Studies 21 (1988): 401–432.

43 Headrick, Colonialism, Health and Illness.

44 Nancy Rose Hunt, A Colonial Lexicon of Birth Ritual, Medicalization, and Mobility in the Congo (Durham, NC: Duke University Press, 1999).

45 Hunt, A Colonial Lexicon: 84.

46 Hunt, A Colonial Lexicon: 248–249.

47 Hunt, A Colonial Lexicon.

48 Babette Müller-Rockstroh, Ultrasound Travels: The Politics of a Medical Technology in Ghana and Tanzania. PhD thesis, Maastricht University, 2007.

49 S. Pedersen, National Bodies, Unspeakable Acts: The Sexual Politics of Colonial Policy-Making. Journal of Modern History 63 (1991): 647–680.

50 Hunt, "Le bébé en brousse"; Carol Summers, Intimate Colonialism: The Imperial Production of Reproduction in Uganda, 1907–1925. Signs 16(4) (1991): 787–807.

51 Janice Boddy, Civilizing Women: British Crusades in Colonial Sudan (Princeton: Princeton University Press, 2007).

52 T. Burke, Lifebuoy Men, Lux Women: Commodification, Consumption, and Cleanliness in Modern Zimbabwe (Durham, NC: Duke University Press, 1996): 44–52.

53 Nancy R. Hunt, Colonial Fairy Tales and the Knife and Fork Doctrine in the Heart of Africa. In African Encounters with Domesticity, ed. Karen Tranberg Hansen (New Brunswick, NJ: Rutgers University Press, 1992): 143–171.

54 Nancy Rose Hunt, Letter-Writing, Nursing Men and Bicycles in the Belgian Congo: Notes Towards the Social Identity of a Colonial Category. In Paths Toward the Past: African Historical Essays in Honor of Jan Vansina, ed. R. W. Harms et al. (Atlanta: African Studies Association Press, 1994): 187–210.

55 Pedersen, National Bodies, Unspeakable Acts.

56 Jean Comaroff, Body of Power, Spirit of Resistance: The Culture and History of a South African People (Chicago: University of Chicago Press, 1985); John Comaroff and Jean Comaroff, Ethnography and the Historical Imagination (Boulder, CO: Westview Press, 1992): 69–94 and 215–264.

57 P. S. Landau, Explaining Surgical Evangelism in Colonial Southern Africa: Teeth, Pain and Faith. Journal of African History 37 (1996): 261–281 at p. 275.

58 Landau, Explaining Surgical Evangelism: 263.

59 Alexander De Waal, Famine Crimes: Politics and the Disaster Relief Industry in Africa (Bloomington: Indiana University Press, 1997).

60 M. Worboys, The Discovery of Colonial Malnutrition Between the Wars. In Imperial Medicine and Indigenous Societies, ed. David Arnold (Manchester: Manchester University Press, 1988): 208–225 at p. 213.

61 Cynthia Brantley, Kikuyu-Maasai Nutrition and Colonial Science: The Orr and Gilks Study in Late 1920s Kenya Revisited. The International Journal of African Historical Studies 30(1) (1997): 49–86.

62 David Arnold, Famine: Social Crisis and Historical Change (Oxford: Blackwell, 1988).

63 K. J. Carpenter, A Short History of Nutritional Science: Part 3 (1912–1944). Journal of Nutrition 133 (2003): 3023–3032.

64 J. Stanton, Listening to the Ga: Cicely Williams' discovery of Kwashiorkor on the Gold Coast. In Women and Modern Medicine, ed. Lawrence Conrad and Anne Hardy (Amsterdam: Rodopi, 2001): 149–171.

65 Stanton, Listening to the Ga: 155.

66 Stanton, Listening to the Ga: 162.

67 Dietrich Bosse et al., Phase I Comparability of Recombinant Human Albumin and Human Serum Albumin. Journal of Clinical Pharmacology 45 (2005): 57–67.

68 Cochrane Injuries Group Albumin Reviewers, Human Albumin Administration in Critically Ill Patients: Systematic Review of Randomised Controlled Trials. British Medical Journal 317 (1998): 235–240.

69 Jing Shao, Fluid Labor and Blood Money: The Economy of HIV/AIDS in Rural Central China. Cultural Anthropology 21 (2006): 535–569 at p. 545.

70   Shao, Fluid Labor and Blood Money: 546.
71   Shao, Fluid Labor and Blood Money: 549.
72   Shao, Fluid Labor and Blood Money.
73   A. Shakir and D. Morley, Measuring Malnutrition. The Lancet 1 (1974): 758–759.
74   Olivier Weber, French Doctors: L'Épopée des hommes et des femmes qui ont inventé la médecine humanitaire (Paris: Robert Laffont, 2000).
75   Peter Redfield, A Less Modest Witness. American Ethnologist, 33 (2006): 3–26.
76   Vinh-Kim Nguyen, Government-by-Exception: Enrolment and Experimentality in Mass HIV Treatment Programmes in Africa. Social Theory and Health 7 (2009): 196–217.
77   While an argument could be made for including obesity and overweight under the rubric of "malnutrition," this term continues to refer to underweight only in biomedical and nutritional literature.
78   Veena Das, personal communication.
79   Michael Pollan, *In* Defense of Food: An Eater's Manifesto (New York: Penguin Press, 2008).
80   J. Sadowsky, Psychiatry and Colonial Ideology in Nigeria. Bulletin of the History of Medicine 71 (1997): 94–111.
81   R. Arnaut, La Folie apprivoisée: L'approche unique du professeur Collomb pour traiter la folie (Paris: De Vecchi, 2006).
82   See Alice Bullard, L'Oedipe africain: A Retrospective. Transcultural Psychiatry 42 (2005): 187.
83   Amy V. Blue and Atwood D. Games, The Ethnopsychiatric Repertoire: A Review and Overview of ethnopsychiatric studies. *In* Ethnopsychiatry: The Cultural Construction of Professional and Folk Psychiatries, ed. Atwood D. Gaines (Binghampton: SUNY Press, 1992): 397–484; Thomas Jovanovski, The Cultural Approach of Ethnopsychiatry: A Review and Critique. New Ideas in Psychology 13 (1995): 281–297; Bullard, L'Oedipe africain.
84   Andrea Tone, The Age of Anxiety: A History of America's Turbulent Affair with Tranquilizers (New York: Beacon Books, 2008). Tone shows how the antidepressant craze of the 1990s was preceded in the 1950s by a craze of anti-anxiety drugs, starting with the drug called Milltown.
85   Andrew Lakoff, Pharmaceutical Reason: Knowledge and Value in Global Psychiatry (Cambridge: Cambridge University Press, 2005).
86   Stefan Ecks, Pharmaceutical Citizenship, Antidepressant Marketing and the Promise of Demarginalization in India. Anthropology and Medicine, 12 (2005): 239–254. See also Junko Kitanaka, Diagnosing Suicides of Resolve: Psychiatric Practice in Contemporary Japan. Culture, Medicine and Psychiatry 32 (2008): 152–176.
87   David Healy, The New Medical Oikumene. *In* Global Pharmaceuticals: Ethics, Markets, Practices, ed. A. Petryna et al. (Durham, NC: Duke University Press, 2006): 61–84.

7   Grounds for Comparison: Biology and Human Experiments

1   W. F. Bynum, Science and the Practice of Medicine in the Nineteenth Century (Cambridge: Cambridge University Press, 1994): 104–106.
2   Bruno Latour, Le Théâtre de la preuve. *In* Pasteur et la révolution pastorienne, ed. Claire Salomon-Bayet (Paris: Payot, 1986): 335–384.
3   Ilana Löwy, The Experimental Body. *In* Companion to Medicine in the Twentieth Century, ed. Roger Cooter and Jonathan Pickstone (London and New York: Routledge, 2000): 435–450 at p. 438.

4   Andrew Cunningham and Perry Williams, eds., The Laboratory Revolution in Medicine (Cambridge: Cambridge University Press, 2002).

5   Bruno Latour, The Pasteurization of France (Cambridge, MA: Harvard University Press, 1988).

6   Bruno Latour, Les Microbes: guerre et paix (Paris: A. M. Métailié, 1984).

7   Jean Pierre Dozon, Quand les Pastoriens traquaient la maladie du sommeil. Sciences Sociales et Santé, 3(3–4) (1985): 27–56.

8   Myron Echenberg, "For Their Own Good": The Pasteur Institute and the Quest for an Anti-Yellow Fever Vaccine in French Colonial Africa. *In* Conquêtes médicales: Histoire de la médecine moderne et des maladies en Afrique, ed. Jean-Paul Bado (Paris: Karthala, 2005): 57–73; G. Lachenal, Franco-African Familiarities: A History of the Pasteur Institute of Cameroon. *In* Hospitals Beyond the West, ed. M. Harrison (New Delhi: Orient Longman, forthcoming); A. M. Moulin, Patriarchal Science: The Network of the Overseas Pasteur Institutes. *In* Science and Empires: Historical Studies About Scientific Development and European Expansion, ed. P. Petitjean et al. (Dordrecht: Kluwer, 1992): 307–322.

9   Paul Weindling, Introduction: Constructing International Health Between the Wars. *In* International Health Organisations and Movements, 1918–1939 (Cambridge: Cambridge University Press, 1995).

10 Latour, Le Théâtre de la preuve: 335–384.

11 Gwendolyn Wright, The Politics of Design in French Colonial Urbanism (Chicago: University of Chicago Press, 1991); Paul Rabinow, French Modern: Norms and Forms of the Social Environment (Cambridge, MA: MIT Press, 1989); John C. Torpey, The Invention of the Passport: Surveillance, Citizenship, and the State (New York: Cambridge University Press, 2000).

12 Warwick Anderson, Colonial Pathologies: American Tropical Medicine, Race, and Hygiene in the Philippines (Durham, NC: Duke University Press, 2006).

13 James Jones, Bad Blood: The Tuskegee Syphilis Experiment (New York: The Free Press, 1981).

14 Löwy, The Experimental Body: 435.

15 Löwy, The Experimental Body: 443.

16 K. Rader, Making Mice: Standardizing Animals for American Biomedical Research 1950–55 (Princeton: Princeton University Press, 2004); Peter Shorett, Of Transgenic Mice and Men. GeneWatch 15 (2002): 3–4; Donna Haraway, Modest_Witness@Second_Millennium: FemaleMan©_Meets_Oncomouse™: Feminism and Technoscience (New York: Routledge, 1997).

17 Robert Proctor, The Nazi War on Cancer (Princeton: Princeton University Press, 2000); Devra Davis, A Secret History of the War on Cancer (New York: Basic Books, 2009).

18 John P. Mackenback, The Mediterranean Diet Story Illustrates the "Why" Questions Are as Important as the "How" Questions in Disease Explanation. Journal of Clinical Epidemiology 60 (2007): 105–109.

19 Harry M. Marks, The Progress of Experiment: Science and Therapeutic Reform in the United States, 1900–1990 (Cambridge: Cambridge University Press, 1997): 45.

20 L. A. Cobb, Evaluation of Internal Mammary Artery Ligation by Double-Blind Technique. New England Journal of Medicine 260 (1959): 1115–1118.

21 Harry Marks, Rigorous Uncertainty: Why R. A. Fisher Is Important. International Journal of Epidemiology 32 (2003): 932–937.

22 Anne Hardy and M. Eileen Magnello, Statistical Methods in Epidemiology: Karl Pearson, Ronald Ross, Major Greenwood and Austin Bradford Hill, 1900–1945. Sozial- und Präventivmedizin/Social and Preventive Medicine 47(2) (2002): 80–89.

23   David Healy, The New Medical Oikumene. *In* Global Pharmaceuticals: Ethics, Markets, Practices, ed. A. Petryna et al. (Durham, NC: Duke University Press, 2006): 61–84; Andrew Lakoff, High Contact: Gifts and Surveillance in Argentina. *In* Global Pharmaceuticals: Ethics, Markets, Practices, ed. A. Petryna et al. (Durham, NC: Duke University Press, 2006): 111–135.

24   Peter Sandner and Karl Ziegelbauer, Product-Related Research: How Research Can Contribute to Successful Lifecycle Management. Drug Discovery Today 13 (2008): 457–463.

25   S. Kaul and G. A. Diamond, Good Enough: A Primer on the Analysis and Interpretation of Noninferiority Trials. Annals of Internal Medicine 145 (2006): 62–69; Anthony N. de Maria, Lies, Damned Lies and Statistics. Journal of the American College of Cardiology 53 (2008): 1430–1431.

26   David Healy, Clinical Trials and Legal Jeopardy. Bulletin of Medical Ethics 153 (1999): 13–18; David Healy, Antidepressant Induced Suicidality. Primary Care Psychiatry 6 (2000): 23–28; David Healy, Let Them Eat Prozac (New York: New York University Press, 2004) (the full relevant correspondence is available on http://www.healyprozac.com); David Healy, Did Regulators Fail Over Selective Serotonin Reuptake Inhibitors? British Medical Journal 333 (2006): 92–95; David Healy, Manufacturing Consensus. Culture, Medicine and Psychiatry 30 (2006): 135–156; Marcia Angell, The Truth About the Drug Companies: How They Deceive Us and What to Do About It (New York: Random House, 2004); Marcia Angell, Drug Companies and Doctors: A Story of Corruption. New York Review of Books 56 (2009): 8–12.

27   Catherine Will, The Alchemy of Clinical Trials. BioSocieties 2 (2007): 85–99 at p. 97.

28   It is not considered ethical to offer more as this would constitute a kind of bribe or coercion, undermining the principle that participants cannot be coerced into human experimentation and must do so of their own free will.

29   A. L. Komaroff, By the Way, Doctor. First It Was Vioxx and Now Avandia. Why Can't Doctors and the Government Screen Out Unsafe Medicines? Harvard Health Letter 32 (2007): 8; J. Avorn, Keeping Science on Top in Drug Evaluation. New England Journal of Medicine 357 (2007): 633–635.

30   In addition to these differences related to culture and environment, there are also, of course, gender differences in connection with the onset, subjective experience, and management of illness, heart disease being one important example.

31   Helen Lambert, Gift Horse or Trojan Horse? Social Science Perspectives on Evidence-Based Health Care. Social Science and Medicine 62 (2006): 2613–2620 at p. 2615.

32   David Armstrong, Professionalism, Indeterminacy and the EBM Project. BioSocieties 2 (2007): 73–84 at p. 75.

33   Gerard Jorland et al. eds., Body Counts: Medical Quantification in Historical and Sociological Perspectives/La Quantification medicale, perspectives historiques et sociologiques (Montreal: McGill-Queens University Press, 2005).

34   Lambert, Gift Horse or Trojan Horse?: 2614.

35   Adriana Petryna, Ethical Variability: Drug Development and the Globalization of Clinical Trials. American Ethnologist 32 (2005): 183–197.

36   A. Petryna et al. eds., Global Pharmaceuticals. Ethics, Markets, Practices (Durham, NC: Duke University Press, 2006): 4.

37   Petryna, Ethical Variability.

38   Adriana Petryna, Globalizing Human Subjects Research. *In* Global Pharmaceuticals: Ethics, Markets, Practices, ed. A. Petryna et al. (Durham, NC: Duke University Press, 2006): 33–60.

39   Adriana Petryna, When Experiments Travel: Clinical Trials and the Global Search for Human Subjects (Princeton: Princeton University Press, 2009).

40   Racing Down the Pyramid: Big Drugmakers' Love Affair with America Is Coming to an End. The Economist, November 15, 2008.

41   This view tends to gloss inequalities in access to biomedical care that of course exist in wealthy nations, most markedly in the U.S. where 30% of the population does not have health insurance.

42   Patrice Trouiller et al., Drug Development for Neglected Diseases: A Deficient Market and a Public Health Policy Failure. The Lancet 359 (2002): 2188–2194.

43   N. King, Security, Disease, Commerce: Ideologies of Postcolonial Global Health. Social Studies of Science 32 (2002): 763–789.

44   See Ilona Kickbusch, New Players for a New Era: Responding to the Global Public Health Challenges. Journal of Public Health Medicine 19 (1997): 171–178, for an early statement to this effect.

45   Susan Okie, Global Health. The Gates–Buffett Effect. New England Journal of Medicine 355 (2006): 1084–1088.

46   See   http://www.guardian.co.uk/business/2009/feb/13/glaxo-smith-kline-cheap-medicine

47   Adriana Petryna, Clinical Trials Offshored: On Private Sector Science and Public Health. BioSocieties 2 (2007): 21–40 at p. 24.

48   Marcia Angell, The Ethics of Clinical Research in the Third World. New England Journal of Medicine 337 (1997): 847–849.

49   Claire L. Wendland, Research, Therapy, and Bioethical Hegemony: The Controversy over Perinatal AZT Trials in Africa. African Studies Review 51(3) (2008): 1–23 at p. 10.

50   A. Phillips, The Life Course of Nevirapine. *In* The Fourth Wave: Gender and HIV in the Twenty First Century, ed. V.-K. Nguyen and J. Klot (New York: Social Science Research Council, in press).

51   This is chronicled in Celia Faber, Out of Control: AIDS and the Corruption of Medical Science. Harper's March, 2006. http://www.harpers.org/archive/2006/03/0080961

52   E. Mills et al., Media Reporting of Tenofovir Trials in Cambodia and Cameroon. BMC International Health and Human Rights 5(6) (2005): doi:10.1186/1472-698X-5-6.

53   Wendland, Research, Therapy, and Bioethical Hegemony: 16.

54   Vincanne Adams, Saving Tibet? An Inquiry into Modernity, Lies, and Beliefs. Medical Anthropology 24 (2005): 71–110.

55   Adams, Saving Tibet?: 76.

56   Adams, Saving Tibet?: 77.

57   Adams, Saving Tibet?: 77.

58   See also Linda Stone and J. Gabriel Campbell, The Use and Misuse of Surveys in International Development: An Experiment from Nepal. Human Organization 43 (1984): 27–37.

59   Adams, Saving Tibet?: 100.

60   J. Fairhead et al., Where Techno-Science Meets Poverty: Medical Research and the Economy of Blood in the Gambia, West Africa. Social Science and Medicine 63 (2006): 1118.

61   Fairhead et al., Where Techno-Science Meets Poverty: 1118.

62   Luise White, Speaking with Vampires. Rumor and History in Colonial Africa (Berkeley: University of California Press, 2000).

63   For instance, Caroline Bledsoe's important study on fertility grew out of a study based at the MRC in the Gambia.

64   J. Fairhead et al., Public Engagement with Science: Local Understandings of a Vaccine Trial in the Gambia. Journal of Biosocial Science 38 (2005): 103–116.

65   Sassy Molyneux and P. Wenzel Geissler, Ethics and the Ethnography of Medical Research in Africa. Social Science and Medicine 67(5) (2008): 685–695 at p. 695.

66   Molyneux and Geissler, Ethics and the Ethnography of Medical Research: 701.
67   Molyneux and Geissler, Ethics and the Ethnography of Medical Research: 702.
68   Personal communication with Vinh-Kim Nguyen.
69   Eric Silla, People Are Not the Same: Leprosy and Identity in Twentieth-Century Mali (London: Heinemann, 1998).
70   V.-K. Nguyen et al., Adherence as Therapeutic Citizenship: Impact of the History of Access to Antiretroviral Drugs on Adherence to Treatment. AIDS 21(5) (2007): S31–S35; F. Dabis et al., 6-Month Efficacy, Tolerance, and Acceptability of a Short Regimen of Oral Zidovudine to Reduce Vertical Transmission of HIV in Breastfed Children in Côte-d'Ivoire and Burkina Faso: A Double-Blind Placebo-Controlled Multicentre Trial. The Lancet 353(6) (1999): 786–793; S. Z. Wiktor et al., Short-Course Oral Zidovudine for Prevention of Mother-to-Child Transmission of HIV-1 in Abidjan, Côte-d'Ivoire: A Randomised Trial. The Lancet 353(6) (1999): 781–785.
71   Nguyen et al. Adherence as Therapeutic Citizenship.
72   Paul Rabinow, Artificiality and Enlightenment: From Sociobiology to Biosociality. *In* Essays on the Anthropology of Reason (New York: Zone Books, 1996): 9–11.
73   Steven Epstein, Inclusion: The Politics of Difference in Medical Research (Chicago: University of Chicago Press, 2007).

8   Who Owns the Body?

1   Karl Marx, Capital, vol. I (New York: International Publishers, 1967): 319.
2   Igor Kopytoff, The Cultural Biography of Things: Commoditization as Process. *In* The Social Life of Things: Commodities in Cultural Perspective, ed. A. Appadurai (Cambridge: Cambridge University Press, 1986): 64–91.
3   Omar el Akkad, Plane Crash Kills Organ Transplant Team. The Globe and Mail, July 12, 2007, A3.
4   Jean Baudrillard, Symbolic Exchange and Death (London: Sage, 1993): 114. In many ways this statement no longer applies to contemporary biomedicine where molecular biology, cell physiology and computerized imaging have all but surpassed gross anatomy.
5   Paul Potter, Herophilus of Chalcedon: An Assessment of his Place in the History of Anatomy. Bulletin of the History of Medicine 50 (1976): 45–60.
6   Katherine Park, The Criminal and the Saintly Body. Renaissance Quarterly 47 (1994): 1–33.
7   Glenn Harcourt, Andreas Vesalius and the Anatomy of Antique Sculpture. Representations 17 (1987): 28–61; Park, The Criminal and the Saintly Body.
8   Ruth Richardson, Death, Dissection, and the Destitute (London: Routledge, 1988); Michael Sappol, The Traffic of Dead Bodies: Anatomy and Embodied Social Identity in Nineteenth-Century America (Princeton: Princeton University Press, 2002).
9   Peter Linebaugh, The Tyburn Riot: Against the Surgeons. *In* Albion's Fatal Tree: Crime and Society in Eighteenth-Century England, ed. P. L. Douglas Hay et al. (London: Allen Lane, 1975): 65–117 at p. 72.
10   Ruth Richardson, Fearful Symmetry: Corpses for Anatomy, Organs for Transplantation. *In* Organ Transplantation: Meanings and Realities, ed. R. C. F. Stuart et al. (Madison: University of Wisconsin Press, 1996): 66–100.
11   Richardson, Fearful Symmetry: 73.
12   Richardson, Death, Dissection, and the Destitute; see especially chapter 3.
13   Giorgio Agamben, *Homo Sacer*: Sovereign Power and Bare Life (Stanford: Stanford University Press, 1988). See pp. 168–171.

14 Hilary Mantel, The Giant, O'Brien (Toronto: Doubleday Canada Limited, 1998).

15 Richardson, Death, Dissection, and the Destitute. See especially chapter 3.

16 Linda Hogle, Transforming "Body Parts" into Therapeutic Tools: A Report from Germany. Medical Anthropology Quarterly 10(4) (1996): 675–682.

17 Marcel Mauss, The Gift (New York: W. W. Norton, 1990 [1950]): 10.

18 Michael Taussig, The Devil and Commodity Fetishism (Chapel Hill: University of North Carolina Press, 1980): 124.

19 David Harvey, Justice, Nature and the Geography of Difference (Oxford: Blackwell, 1996): 232.

20 Michael Taussig, Shamanism, Colonialism, and the Wild Man: A Study in Terror and Healing (Chicago: University of Chicago Press, 1987); see also John and Jean Comaroff, Ethnography and the Historical Imagination (Boulder, CO: Westview Press, 1992).

21 Annette Weiner, Inalienable Possessions: The Paradox of Keeping While Giving (Berkeley: University of California Press, 1992).

22 Patrick J. Geary, Living With the Dead in the Middle Ages (Ithaca: Cornell University Press, 1994); Paul Binski, Medieval Death: Ritual and Representation (Ithaca: Cornell University Press, 1996); Caroline Walker Bynum, Fragmentation and Redemption (New York: Zone Books, 1992); E. E. Evans-Pritchard, Witchcraft, Oracles, and Magic among the Azande (Oxford: Clarendon Press, 1937); Jean Comaroff and John Comaroff, eds., Modernity and its Malcontents: Ritual and Power in Postcolonial Africa (Chicago: University of Chicago Press, 1993); Adam Ashforth, Witchcraft, Violence and Democracy in South Africa (Chicago: University of Chicago Press, 2005).

23 David Hillman and Carla Mazzio, The Body in Parts: Fantasies of Corporeality in Early Modern Europe (New York: Routledge, 1997); Brad Weiss, The Making and Unmaking of the Haya Lived World (Durham, NC: Duke University Press, 1996); James Boyle, Shamans, Softwear, and Spleens: Law and the Construction of Information Society (Cambridge, MA: Harvard University Press, 1996).

24 Margaret Lock, Genetic Diversity and the Politics of Difference. Chicago-Kent Law Review, 75 (1999): 83–111.

25 Lawrence Cohen, Where It Hurts: Indian Material for an Ethics of Organ Transplantation. Daedalus 128(4) (1999): 135–165.

26 Arjun Appadurai, Introduction: Commodities and the Politics of Value. *In* The Social Life of things: Commodities in Cultural Perspective, ed. A. Appadurai (Cambridge: Cambridge University Press, 1986): 3–63.

27 Cohen, Where It Hurts; Nancy Scheper-Hughes, Keeping an Eye on the Global Traffic in Human Organs. The Lancet 361(9369) (2003): 1645–1648.

28 Catherine Waldby and Robert Mitchell, Tissue Economies: Blood, Organs, and Cell Lines in Late Capitalism (Durham, NC: Duke University Press, 2006): 22.

29 New Highly Successful Way of Freezing Human Eggs. Medical News, 2006, http://www.news-medical.net/news/2006/06/19/18516.aspx

30 Appadurai, Introduction: Commodities and the Politics of Value: 17.

31 Kopytoff, The Cultural Biography of Things.

32 Linda Hogle, Standardization across Non-Standard Domains: The Case of Organ Procurement. Science, Technology and Human Values 20 (1995): 482–500.

33 Kopytoff, The Cultural Biography of Things.

34 See Waldby and Mitchell, Tissue Economies, for a discussion about problems associated with resort to arguments for a gift/commodity dichotomy with respect to many kinds of biologicals.

35 Linebaugh, The Tyburn Riots: 65–117.

36 See Joke I. de Witte and Henk ten Have, Ownership of Genetic Material and Information. Social Science and Medicine 45 (1997): 51–60.

37 For details about "presumed consent" see Alberto Abadie and Sebastian Gay, The Impact of Presumed Consent Legislation on Cadaveric Organ Donation: A Cross-Country Study. Journal of Health Economics 25 (2006): 599–620.

38 Janet Radcliffe-Richards, Nepharious Goings on: Kidney Sales and Moral Arguments. Journal of Medical Philosophy 21 (1996): 375–416; Charles A. Erin and John Harris, An Ethical Market in Organs. Journal of Medical Ethics 29 (2003): 137–138.

39 Lesley Sharp, Strange Harvest: Organ Transplants, Denatured Bodies and the Transformed Self (Berkeley: University of California Press, 2006): 11.

40 BCC Research reported that the U.S. market for organ and tissue transplantation generated $18.9 billion in 2007 and that this expected to increase to $20.9 billion in 2008 and $28.2 billion in 2013, for a compound annual growth of 8.3%. BCC Research, Trends in Organ and Tissue Transplantation and Alternative Techniques (Report: HLC012D). Press Release: U.S. Market for Organ and Tissue Transplantation Worth $28.2 Billion in 2013, October 20, 2008: http://www.bccresearch.com/pressroom/press_release.php?rcode=HLC012D

41 Stephen J. Hedges and William Gaines, Donor Bodies Milled into Growing Profits. Chicago Tribune, May 21, 2000. http://chicagotribune.com/news/nationworld/article/0,2669,ART-44908,FF.html

42 Scheper-Hughes, Keeping an Eye on the Global Traffic in Human Organs; Javaad Zargooshi, Iranian Kidney Donors: Motivations and Relations with Recipients. Journal of Urology 165 (2001): 386–393.

43 Renée Fox and Judith P. Swazey, The Courage to Fail: A Social View of Organ Transplants and Dialysis (Chicago: University of Chicago Press, 1978). Other clichéd metaphors have also been put to work, including "sharing of self" and "recycling life." see Donald Joralemon, Organ Wars: The Battle for Body Parts. Medical Anthropology Quarterly 9(3) (1995): 335–356.

44 Richard Titmuss, The Gift Relationship (London: Allen and Unwin, 1971).

45 Mauss, The Gift: 68; Paul Rabinow, French DNA: Trouble in Purgatory (Chicago: University of Chicago Press, 1999): 84.

46 Waldby and Robert Mitchell, Tissue Economies: 4.

47 Waldby and Robert Mitchell, Tissue Economies: 73.

48 Hannah Landecker, Immortality, *in Vitro*: A History of the HeLa Cell Line. In Biotechnology and Culture: Bodies, Anxieties, Ethics, ed. P. E. Brodwin (Indianapolis: Indiana University Press, 2000): 53–74.

49 Waldby and Robert Mitchell, Tissue Economies: 23.

50 Nikolas Rose, The Politics of Life Itself: Biomedicine, Power, and Subjectivity in the Twenty-First Century (Princeton: Princeton University Press, 2007); Sarah Franklin and Margaret Lock, Animation and Cessation: The Remaking of Life and Death. *In* Remaking Life and Death: Towards an Anthropology of the Biosciences, ed. Sarah Franklin and Margaret Lock (Santa Fe: School of American Research Press, 2003): 3–22; Kaushik Sudner Rajan, Biocapital: The Constitution of Postgenomic Life (Durham, NC: Duke University Press, 2006).

51 Charis Thompson, The Biotech Mode of Reproduction. Paper prepared for the School of American Research Advanced Seminar, Animation and Cessation: Anthropological Perspectives on Changing Definitions of Life and Death in the Context of Biomedicine (Santa Fe: New Mexico, 2000). Cited in Franklin and Lock, eds., Remaking Life and Death: 7.

52 Waldby and Robert Mitchell, Tissue Economies; J. L. Burton and M. Wells, The Alder Hey Affair. Archives of Disease in Childhood 86 (2002): 4–7; Boyle, Shamans, Software and Spleens.

53 Alec Russell, Alistair Cooke's Bones Stolen by Transplant Gang. Daily Telegraph, December 23, 2005. http://www.telegraph.co.uk/news/worldnews/northamerica/usa/1506150/Alistair-Cookes-bones-stolen-by-transplant gang

54 Matthew Schmidt and Lisa Jean Moore, Constructing a "Good Catch," Picking a Winner. *In* Cyborg Babies: From Techno-Sex to Techno-Tots, ed. Robbie Davis-Floyd and Joseph Dumit (New York: Routledge, 1998): 21–39.

55 René Almeling, Selling Genes, Selling Gender: Egg Agencies, Sperm Banks, and the Medical Market in Genetic Material. American Sociological Review 72 (2007): 319–340.

56 Sharon Covington and William Gibbons, What is Happening to the Price of Eggs? Obstetrical and Gynecological Survey 62(9) (2007): 589–590.

57 Almeling, Selling Genes, Selling Gender: 320.

58 Almeling, Selling Genes, Selling Gender: 336.

59 Almeling, Selling Genes, Selling Gender: 335.

60 Almeling, Selling Genes, Selling Gender: 338.

61 Schmidt and Moore, Constructing a "Good Catch": 21–39.

62 Schmidt and Moore, Constructing a "Good Catch": 31–32.

63 Schmidt and Moore, Constructing a "Good Catch": 33.

64 Schmidt and Moore, Constructing a "Good Catch": 34.

65 Gisli Pálsson, Biosocial Relations of Production. Comparative Studies in Society and History 51 (2009): 288–313.

66 Leigh Turner, First World Health Care at Third World Prices: Globalization, Bioethics and Medical Tourism. BioSocieties 2 (2007): 303–325 at p. 323.

67 Anne Enright, What's Left of Henrietta Lacks? London Review of Books 22(8) (2000): 8–10.

68 Hannah Landecker, Culturing Life: How Cells Became Technologies (Cambridge, MA: Harvard University Press, 2007): 1.

69 Landecker, Culturing Life: 108.

70 Landecker, Culturing Life: 2.

71 Landecker, Culturing Life: 12.

72 Hannah Landecker, Between Beneficence and Chattel: The Human Biological in Law and Science. Science in Context 12(1) (1999): 203–225 at p. 221.

73 Waldby and Mitchell, Tissue Economies: 88–109.

74 Beth Burrows, Second Thoughts about U.S. Patent #4,438,032. GeneWatch 10 (1996): 4–7.

75 Burrows, Second Thoughts about U.S. Patent #4,438,032: 5.

76 George Annas, Outrageous Fortune: Selling Other People's Cells. Hastings Center Report 20 (1990): 36–39 at p. 36.

77 Carl Feldbaum, Gene Patents Deemed Essential to Next Generation of Cures. GeneWatch 10 (1996): 10. See Jonathan King for a contrary position: Gene Patents Retard the Protection of Human Health. GeneWatch 10 (1996): 10–11.

78 Michael A. Heller and Rebecca S. Eisenberg, Can Patents Deter Innovation? The Anti-commons in Biomedical Research. Science 280(8364) (1998): 698–701.

79 Alberto Cambrosio and Peter Keating, Exquisite Specificity: The Monoclonal Antibody Revolution (New York: Oxford University Press, 1995).

80 Boyle, Shamans, Software and Spleens: ii.

81 Boyle, Shamans, Software and Spleens: iii. See also, Martin Teitel, The Commercialization of Life. GeneWatch 10 (1996): 1–3.

82 Carl Zimmer, Mom and Dad Are Fighting in Your Genes – and in Your Brain. Discover, December 2008, http://www.carlzimmer.com/articles/2008.php

83 Jean Christie, Whose Property, Whose Rights? Cultural Survival Quarterly 20 (1996): 34–36.

84 Yokotam Ibeji and Korowai Gane, The Hagahai Patent Controversy: In Their Own Words. Cultural Survival Quarterly 20 (1996): 33.

85 Christie, Whose Property, Whose Rights?

86 Aroha Te Pareake Mead, Genealogy, Sacredness, and the Commodities Market. Cultural Survival Quarterly 20 (1996): 46.

87 Mead, Genealogy, Sacredness, and the Commodities Market.

88 Paul Ndebele and Rosemary Musesengwa, Will Developing Countries Benefit from Their Participation in Genetics Research? Malawi Medical Journal 20 (2008): 67–69.

89 Harold Cook, Matters of Exchange: Commerce, Medicine and Science in the Dutch Golden Age (New Haven: Yale University Press, 2007).

90 Richard Tutton and Oonagh Corrigan, Genetic Databases: Socio-Ethical Issues in the Collection and Use of DNA (London: Routledge, 2004): 1.

91 Jean E. McEwen, DNA Data Banks. *In* Genetic Secrets: Protecting Privacy and Confidentiality in the Genetic Era, ed. Marc A. Rothstein (New Haven: Yale University Press, 1997): 231–251.

92 Gísli Pálsson, Anthropology and the New Genetics (Cambridge: Cambridge University Press, 2007): 91.

93 Pálsson, Anthropology and the New Genetics, see especially chapter 4.

94 Klaus Hoeyer, Ambiguous Gifts: Public Anxiety, Informed Consent and Biobanks. *In* Genetic Databases: Socio-Ethical Issues in the Collection and Use of DNA, ed. Richard Tutton and Oonagh Corrigan (London: Routledge, 2004): 97–116.

95 Pálsson, Anthropology and the New Genetics: 92.

96 Sarah Franklin, Sheepwatching. Anthropology Today 17(3) (2001): 3–9.

97 Oonagh Corrigan, Informed Consent: The Contradictory Ethical Safeguards in Pharmacogenetics. *In* Genetic Databases: Socio-EthicalIssues in the Collection and Use of DNA, ed. Richard Tutton and Oonagh Corrigan (London: Routledge, 2004): 78–96.

98 Tania Simoncelli and Helen Wallace, Expanding Databases, Declining Liberties. GeneWatch 19(10) (2006): 3–8.

99 Richard Tutton, Person, Property and Gift: Exploring Languages of Tissue Donation. *In* Genetic Databases: Socio-Ethical Issues in the Collection and Use of DNA, ed. Richard Tutton and Oonagh Corrigan (London: Routledge, 2004): 19–38.

100 Tutton, Person, Property and Gift: 24.

101 Tutton, Person, Property and Gift: 27.

102 Tutton, Person, Property and Gift: 32.

103 Rajan, Biocapital.

104 Pálsson, Anthropology and the New Genetics: 55.

105 Rose, From Hype to Mothballs: 185.

106 Pálsson, Anthropology and the New Genetics: 70.

107 Pálsson, Anthropology and the New Genetics: 24.

108 The Book of Icelanders as cited in Pálsson, Anthropology and the New Genetics: 71.

109 Pálsson, Anthropology and the New Genetics: 79.

110 Bob Simpson, Imagined Genetic Communities: Ethnicity and Essentialism in the Twenty-First Century. Anthropology Today 16 (2000): 3–5.

111 Agnar Helgason, The Ancestry and Genetic History of the Icelanders: An Analysis of MTDNA Sequences, Y Chromosome Haplotypes and Genealogy. Doctoral dissertation, Institute of Biological Anthropology, University of Oxford, 2001.

112 Pálsson, Anthropology and the New Genetics: 95.

113 Robin McKie, Icelandic DNA Project Hit by Privacy Storm. The Observer, May 16, 2004.

114 deCODE genetics, SEC Edgar 10-K, 12–31–2006.

115 See http://www.decode.com

116 Firm that Led the Way in DNA Testing Goes Bust. The Independent, November 18, 2009: 18.

117 Gilles Bibeau, Le Quebec transgénique: Science, marché, humanité (Montreal: Boreal, 2004).

118 Bibeau, Le Québec transgénique: 139; translated from the French by V.-K. Nguyen.

119 P³G Observatory, http://www.p3gobservatory.org/

120 Tutton and Corrigan, Genetic Databases; Waldby and Mitchell, Tissue Economies; Shobita Parthasarathy, Architectures of Genetic Medicine. Comparing Genetic Testing for Breast Cancer in the U.S.A. and the U.K.. Social Studies of Science 35(1) (2005): 5–40.

121 Cori Hayden, Taking as Giving: Bioscience, Exchange, and the Politics of Benefit-Sharing. Social Studies of Science 37 (2007): 729–758 at p. 730.

122 Hayden, Taking as Giving: 732

123 Hayden, Taking as Giving: 743.

124 Hayden, Taking as Giving: 747.

125 Margaret Lock, Interrogating the Human Genome Diversity Project. Social Science and Medicine, 39(5) (1994): 603–606; Jenny Reardon, Race to the Finish: Identity and Governance in an Age of Genomics (Princeton, NJ: Princeton University, 2005).

126 Hayden, Taking as Giving: 746.

127 Jon F. Merz et al., Protecting Subjects' Interests in Genetic Research. American Journal of Human Genetics 70 (2002): 965–971 at p. 970.

128 Hayden, Taking as Giving: 753.

129 Eugene Thacker, The Global Genome: Biotechnology, Politics, and Culture (Cambridge, MA: MIT Press, 2005): 300.

9   The Social Life of Organs

1 World Health Organization. WHO Proposes Global agenda on Transplantation. Press release. March 30, 2007. http://www.who.int/mediacentre/news/releases/2007/pr12/en/index.html

2 Lawrence Cohen, Operability, Bioavailability, and Exception. In Global Assemblages: Technology, Politics, and Ethics as Anthropological Problems, ed. Aihwa Ong and Stephen J. Collier (Oxford: Blackwell, 2005): 79–90 at p. 82.

3 Cohen, Operability, Bioavailability and Exception: p. 79.

4 Lawrence Cohen, Where It Hurts: Indian Material for an Ethics of Organ Donation. Daedalus 128(4) (1999): 135–165 at p. 148.

5 Lawrence Cohen, Operability: Surgery at the Margins of the State. In Anthropology in the Margins of the State, ed. Veena Das and Deborah Poole (Santa Fe: School of American Research Press, 2004): 165–190.

6 Lawrence Cohen notes that a well-known transplant surgeon in India informed him that when organ sales were legal he was able to provide follow-up care for donors, something that the surgeon claims he is no longer able to do now that organ sales are illegal; see Cohen, Where It Hurts: 136.

7 Cohen, Where It Hurts: 157.

8 Aslihan Sanal, "Robin Hood" of Techno-Turkey or Organ Trafficking in the State of Ethical Beings. Culture, Medicine, and Psychiatry 28: 281–309.

9 Ahad J. Ghods and Shekourfeh Savaj, Iranian Model of Paid and Regulated Living-Unrelated Kidney Donation. Clinical Journal of the American Society of Nephrology 1(6) (2006): 1136–1145.

10 Ghods and Savaj, Iranian Model of Paid and Regulated Living-Unrelated Kidney Donation.

11 Nancy Scheper-Hughes, Rotten Trade: Millennial Capitalism, Human Values and Global Justice in Organs Trafficking. Journal of Human Rights 2(2) (2003): 197–226.

12 Michael Friedlander, Viewpoint: The Right to Sell or Buy a Kidney: Are We Failing Our Patients? The Lancet 359(9301) (2002): 971–973.

13 Scheper-Hughes, Rotten Trade.

14 Scheper-Hughes, Rotten Trade: 199.

15 Veena Das, The Practice of Organ Transplants: Networks, Documents and Translations. *In* Living and Working with the New Medical Technologies: Intersections of Inquiry, ed. Margaret Lock et al. (Cambridge: Cambridge University Press, 2000): 263–287.

16 Richard Titmuss, The Gift Relationship (London: Allen and Unwin, 1971).

17 Kathleen Erwin, The Circulatory System: Blood Procurement, AIDS, and the Social Body in China. Medical Anthropology Quarterly 20(2) (2006): 139–159.

18 Erwin, The Circulatory System: 148.

19 Burton J. Hendrick, On the Trail of Immortality. McClure's 40 (1913): 304–317.

20 René Kuss cited in Nicholas L. Tilney, Transplant: From Myth to Reality (New Haven: Yale University Press, 2003): 48.

21 Catherine Waldby and Robert Mitchell, Tissue Economies: Blood, Organs, and Cell Lines in Late Capitalism (Durham NC: Duke University Press, 2006): 170.

22 Margaret Lock and Megan Crowley-Matoka, Situating the Practice of Organ Donation in Familial, Cultural, and Political Context. Transplantation Reviews 22(3) (2008): 154–157.

23 Lock and Crowley-Matoka, Situating the Practice of Organ Donation in Familial, Cultural, and Political Context: 155.

24 Sharon R. Kaufman et al., Aged Bodies and Kinship Matters: The Ethical Field of Kidney Transplant. American Ethnologist 33(1) (2006): 81–99.

25 Kaufman et al., Aged Bodies and Kinship Matters: 81.

26 Gabriele Schratzberger and Gert Mayer, Age and Renal Transplantation: An Interim Analysis. Nephrology Dialysis Transplantation 18(3) (2003): 471–476.

27 Kaufman et al., Aged Bodies and Kinship Matters.

28 L. K. Kayler et al., Gender Imbalance and Outcomes in Living Donor Renal Transplantation in the United States. American Journal of Transplantation 3 (2003): 452.

29 Sigmund Freud, Civilization, War, and Death: Selections from Three Works by Sigmund Freud, ed. J. Richman (London: Hogarth Press and the Institute of Psychoanalysis, 1939).

30 Martin Heidegger, Being and Time (New York: Harper and Row, 1962).

31 Ernest Becker, The Denial of Death (New York: Free Press, 1973).

32 Margaret Lock, Twice Dead: Organ Transplants and the Reinvention of Death (Berkeley: University of California Press, 2002).

33 Ad Hoc Committee of the Harvard Medical School to Examine the Definition of Death, A Definition of Irreversible Coma. Journal of the American Medical Association 205(6) (1968): 85–88.

34 Lock, Twice Dead.

35 French doctors were the first to name this new condition as *coma depassé*; the British, under the influence of the eminent neurologist Christopher Pallis, created a concept of brain-stem death, which depends on slightly different criteria than those used to

diagnose whole brain death. Over the years the majority of countries in the "developed" world have recognized either whole brain or brain-stem death legally as the end of life, although adoption of this position involved extensive public debates in some countries including Denmark, Sweden, Germany, and Israel. Japan recognized brain death as death only in 1997 and then under special, limited conditions (Lock, Twice Dead: chapter 4 and especially pp. 124–126).

36 Martin S. Pernick, Back from the Grave: Recurring Controversies over Defining and Diagnosing Death in History. *In* Death: Beyond Whole-Brain Criteria, ed. Richard M. Zaner (Dordrecht: Kluwer Academic Publishers, 1988): 17–74.

37 Jennifer Couzin, Crossing a Frontier: Research on the Dead. Science 299 (2003): 29–30; Rebecca D. Pentz et al., Revisiting Ethical Guidelines for Research with Terminal Wean and Brain-Dead Participants. Hastings Center Report 33 (2003): 22–26; Ronald A. Carson et al., Case Study: Research with Brain Dead Children. Journal of Medical Humanities 3 (1981): 50–53.

38 Lock, Twice Dead; Laura A. Siminoff and Kata Chillag, The Fallacy of "The Gift of Life." Hastings Center Report 29(6) (1999): 34–41.

39 Siminoff and Chillag, The Fallacy of "The Gift of Life."

40 Lock, Twice Dead: 215.

41 Megan Crowley-Matoka and Robert Arnold, The Dead Donor Rule: How Much Does the Public Care ... and How Much Should We Care? Kennedy Institute of Ethics Journal 14 (2004): 319–332; Laura A. Siminoff et al., Death and Organ Procurement: Public Beliefs and Attitudes. Social Science and Medicine 59(11) (2004): 2325–2334.

42 Donald Joralemon, Organ Wars: The Battle for Body Parts. Medical Anthropology Quarterly 9(3) (1995): 335–356.

43 Lock, Twice Dead.

44 Lock, Twice Dead: 145.

45 Leslie A. Sharp, Strange Harvest: Organ Transplants, Denatured Bodies and the Transformed Self (Berkeley: University of California Press, 2006); see especially pp. 74–80.

46 Lock, Twice Dead: 249–255.

47 Lock, Twice Dead: 247.

48 Julius Korein, Terminology, Definitions, and Usage. *In* Brain Death: Interrelated Medical and Social Issue, ed. Julius Korein, Annals of the New York Academy of Sciences 315 (New York: New York Academy of Science, 1978): 9.

49 Ronald Cranford, Even the Dead Are Not Terminally Ill Anymore. Neurology 51(6) (1998): 1530–1531.

50 Margaret Lock, On Making up the Good-as-Dead in a Utilitarian World. *In* Remaking Life and Death: Toward an Anthropology of the Biosciences, ed. Sarah Franklin and Margaret Lock (Santa Fe: School of American Research Press, 2003): 165–192.

51 Caroline Alphonso, Brain-Damaged Man Reawakened. Globe and Mail, August 2, 2007; Keith Andrews, Recovery of Patients after Four Months or More in Persistent Vegetative State. British Medical Journal 306 (1993): 1597–1600.

52 Sharon Kaufman, In the Shadow of Death with Dignity: Medicine and Cultural Quandaries of the Vegetative State. American Anthropologist, 102 (2000): 69.

53 Sharon Kaufman, ... And a Time to Die: How American Hospitals Shape the End of Life (New York: Scribner, 2005): chapter 8.

54 See, for example Richard M. Zaner, ed. Death: Beyond Whole-Brain Criteria (Dordrecht: Kluwer, 1988); Ronald E. Cranford, The Vegetative and Minimally Conscious States: Ethical Implications. Geriatrics, 53(1) (1998): S70–S73.

55 Lock, Twice Dead; Bo Andreassen Rix, Brain Death, Ethics, and Politics in Denmark. *In* The Definition of Death: Contemporary Controversies, ed. S. J. Youngner et al. (Baltimore: Johns Hopkins University Press, 1999): 227–238; Bettina Schöne-Seifert,

Defining Death in Germany: Brain Drain and its Discontents. *In* The Definition of Death: Contemporary Controversies, ed. S. J. Youngner et al. (Baltimore: Johns Hopkins University Press, 1999): 257–271.

56 Lock, Twice Dead; see chapters 5, 6 and 7.

57 The Asahi Shimbun, Diet OKs Revision to Ease Organ Law. July 14, 2009. http://www.asahi.com/english/Herald-asahi/TKY200907140020.html

58 Katō Shinzō, Organ Transplants and Brain-Dead Donors: A Japanese Doctor's Perspective. Mortality 9(1) (2004): 13–26.

59 Susan O. Long, Reflections on Becoming a Cucumber: Images of the Good Death in Japan and the United States. Journal of Japanese Studies 29(1): 33–68.

60 Helen Hardacre, The Response of Buddhism and Shinto to the Issue of Brain Death and Organ Transplants. Cambridge Quarterly of Healthcare Ethics 3 (1994): 585–601.

61 Margaret Lock, Inventing a New Death and Making it Believable. Anthropology and Medicine, 2002(9) (2002): 97–115.

62 Margaret Lock, On Dying Twice: Culture, Technology, and the Determination of Death. *In* Living and Working with the New Medical Technologies: Intersections of Inquiry, ed. Margaret Lock et al. (Cambridge: Cambridge University Press, 2000): 233–262.

63 Lock, Twice Dead: 272–275.

64 Mari Yamaguchi, Japan Lifts Ban on Children Donating Organs. Associated Press, 2009. http://newshopper.sulekha.com/topic/health-fitness.htm/news/japan-to-allow-children-to-receive-organ-donations.htm

65 World Health Organization, WHO Proposes Global Agenda on Transplantation.

66 Yamaguchi, Japan Lifts Ban on Children Donating Organs.

67 Linda Hogle, Recovering the Nation's Body: Cultural Memory, Medicine and the Politics of Redemption (New Brunswick, NJ: Rutgers University Press, 1999): see chapter 3.

68 Hogle, Recovering the Nation's Body: see chapter 2, especially p. 41.

69 Hogle, Recovering the Nation's Body: 192.

70 Leslie Sharp, The Commodification of the Body and Its Parts. Annual Reviews of Anthropology 29 (2000): 287–328.

71 Margaret Lock, Human Body Parts as Therapeutic Tools: Contradictory Discourses and Transformed Subjectivities. Qualitative Health Research 12(10) (2002): 1406–1418.

72 Sharp, Strange Harvest: 83–86.

73 See especially chapter 8 in Lock, Twice Dead.

74 Renée C. Fox and Judith P. Swazey, The Courage to Fail: A Social View of Organ Transplants and Dialysis (Chicago: University of Chicago Press, 1978); Renée C. Fox and Judith P. Swazey, Spare Parts: Organ Replacement in American Society (Oxford: Oxford University Press, 1992); Roberta G. Simmons et al., Gift of Life: The Effect of Organ Transplantation on Individual, Family, and Societal Dynamics (New Brunswick, NJ: Transaction Books, 1987); Lesley A. Sharp, Organ Transplantation as a Transformative Experience: Anthropological Insights into the Restructuring of the Self. Medical Anthropology Quarterly, 9(3) (1995): 357–389.

75 Fox and Swazey, The Courage to Fail: 1168.

76 Margaret Lock, The Alienation of Body Tissue and the Biopolitics of Immortalized Cell Lines. Body and Society 7(2–3) (2001): 63–91.

77 Sharp, Organ Transplantation as a Transformative Experience: 365.

78 Nicholas Thomas, Entangled Objects: Exchange, Material Culture and Colonialism in the Pacific (Cambridge, MA: Harvard University Press, 1991): 27.

79   Sharp, Organ Transplantation as a Transformative Experience.

80   Hogle, Standardization Across Non-Standard Domains: 482–500; Hogle, Recovering the Nation's Body.

81   See also, Megan Crowley-Matoka, Desperately Seeking "Normal": The Promise and Perils of Living with Kidney Transplantation. Social Science and Medicine 61 (2005): 821–831; Lock, Human Body Parts as Therapeutic Tools: 1406–1418.

82   Lock, Twice Dead: 321.

83   Sharp, Organ Transplantation as a Transformative Experience.

84   Lock, Twice Dead: 323.

85   Megan Crowley-Matoka and Margaret Lock, Organ Transplantation in a Globalized World. Mortality 111(2) (2006): 166–181.

86   Lock, Twice Dead: 323.

87   Sharp, Strange Harvest: see introduction and chapter 3.

88   Sharp, Strange Harvest: chapter 3.

89   Crowley-Matoka and Lock, Organ Transplantation in a Globalized World: 172.

90   Megan Crowley-Matoka, Producing Transplanted Bodies: Life, Death and Value in Mexican Organ Transplantation (Durham, NC: Duke University Press, in press).

91   Crowley-Matoka, Producing Transplanted Bodies.

92   Megan Crowley-Matoka, Producing Transplanted Bodies.

93   Crowley-Matoka and Lock, Organ Transplantation in a Globalized World: 176.

94   Crowley-Matoka, Producing Transplanted Bodies.

95   Cited in Crowley-Matoka, Desperately Seeking "Normal": 821–831.

96   Cited in Crowley-Matoka, Desperately Seeking "Normal": 825.

97   See also Farhat Moazam, Bioethics and Organ Transplantation in a Muslim Society: A Study in Culture, Ethnography and Religion (Bloomington: Indiana University Press, 2006).

98   Sherine Hamdy, When the State and Your Kidneys Fail: Political Etiologies in an Egyptian Dialysis Ward. American Ethnologist 35 (2008): 553–569.

99   Hamdy, When the State and Your Kidneys Fail.

100 Hamdy, When the State and Your Kidneys Fail.

101 Rashad S. Barsoum, Overview: End-Stage Renal Disease in the Developing World. Artificial Organs 26(9) (2002): 737–746.

102 Ahmed M. Hassan et al., Study of Ochratoxin A as an Environmental Risk that Causes Renal Injury in Breast-Fed Egyptian Infants. Pediatric Nephrology 21(1) (2005): 102–105; Barsoum, Overview: End-Stage Renal Disease in the Developing World. Artificial Organs 26(9) (2002): 737–746; Jonathan H. Williams et al., Human Aflatoxicosis in Developing Countries: A Review of Toxicology, Exposure, Potential Health Consequences and Interventions. American Journal of Clinical Nutrition 80(5) (2004): 1106–1122.

103 Timothy Mitchell, Rule of Experts: Egypt, Techno-Politics, Modernity (Berkeley: University of California Press, 2002).

104 Hamdy, When the State and Your Kidneys Fail.

105 Hamdy, When the State and Your Kidneys Fail.

106 In Europe presumed consent laws are in place in 14 countries and several of the Swiss cantons. These laws, some modified since their enactment, have strong and weak forms. In the exclusive or "strong" form of the law, if the deceased has not opted out, then organs can be taken without family consent. The "weak" inclusive form involves family consultation. In practice the law is flexible, and it is claimed everywhere that the wishes of the family are not overruled.

107 Crowley-Matoka and Lock, Organ Transplantation in a Globalized World: 177.

108 Crowley-Matoka and Lock, Organ Transplantation in a Globalized World: 179.

10 Kinship, Infertility, and Assisted Reproduction

1 Marcia Inhorn and Frank van Balen, Introduction. *In* Infertility Around the Globe: New Thinking on Childlessness, Gender, and Reproductive Technologies, ed. Marcia Inhorn and Frank Van Balen (Berkeley: University of California Press, 2002): 3–32 at p. 7.

2 Margarete Sandelowski and Sheryl de Lacey, The Uses of a "Disease": Infertility as a Rhetorical Vehicle. *In* Infertility Around the Globe: New Thinking on Childlessness, Gender, and Reproductive Technologies, eds., Marcia Inhorn and Frank van Balen (Berkeley: University of California Press, 2002): 33–51.

3 World Health Organization, Infections, Pregnancies, and Infertility: Perspectives on Prevention. Fertility and Sterility 47 (1987): 964–968.

4 J. A. Collins et al., Treatment-Independent Pregnancy Among Infertile Couples. New England Journal of Medicine 309 (1983): 1201–1206.

5 World Health Organization, Infertility: A Tabulation of Available Data on Prevalence of Primary and Secondary Infertility. Programme on Maternal and Child Health and Family Planning (Geneva: WHO, Division of Family Health, 1991).

6 World Health Organization, Infections, Pregnancies, and Infertility.

7 J. Bongaarts, A Framework for Analyzing the Proximate Determinants of Fertility. Population and Development Review 24 (1978): 15–57.

8 Lori Leonard, Problematizing Fertility: "Scientific" Accounts and Chadian Women's Narratives. *In* Infertility Around the Globe: New Thinking on Childlessness, Gender, and Reproductive Technologies, ed. Marcia Inhorn and Frank van Balen (Berkeley: University of California Press, 2002): 193–214; J. Bongaarts, The Fertility-Inhibiting Effects of the Intermediate Fertility Variables. Studies in Family Planning 13 (1982): 179–198.

9 R. Pressat and C. Wilson, The Dictionary of Demography (New York: Blackwell Science, 1985): 214.

10 Ulla Larsen, Research on Infertility: Which Definition Should We Use? Fertility and Sterility 83 (2005): 846–852.

11 P. A. Marchbanks et al., Research on Infertility: Definition Makes a Difference. American Journal of Epidemiology 130 (1989): 259–267.

12 Nancy Rose Hunt, Colonial Medical Anthropology and the Making of the Central African Infertility Belt. *In* Ordering Africa: Anthropology, European Imperialism and Knowledge, ed. Helen L. Tilley and Robert J. Gordon (Manchester: Manchester University Press, 2007): 252–281.

13 Hunt, Colonial Medical Anthropology: 254.

14 Hunt, Colonial Medical Anthropology: 262.

15 Hunt, Colonial Medical Anthropology: 272.

16 Ulla Larsen, Primary and Secondary Infertility in Sub-Saharan Africa. International Journal of Epidemiology 29 (2000): 285–291. The Demographic and Health Survey (DHS) and the World Fertility Survey (WFS) are standardized surveys of health and fertility based on representative samples of the populations of selected countries.

17 Larsen, Primary and Secondary Infertility in Sub-Saharan Africa: 289.

18 Pamela Feldman-Savelsberg, Is Infertility an Unrecognized Public Health and Population Problem? The View from the Cameroon Grassfields. *In* Infertility Around the Globe: New Thinking on Childlessness, Gender, and Reproductive Technologies, ed. Marcia Inhorn and Frank van Balen (Berkeley, University of California Press, 2002): 215–232.

19 Marcia Inhorn, Global Infertility and the Globalization of New Reproductive Technologies: Illustrations from Egypt. Social Science and Medicine 56 (2003): 1837–1851 at p. 1841.

20 John Caldwell and Pat Caldwell, The Cultural Context of High Fertility in Sub-Saharan Africa. Population and Development Review 13(3) (1987): 409–437.

21 Feldman-Savelsberg, Is Infertility an Unrecognized Public Health and Population Problem?: 219.

22 Feldman-Savelsberg, Is Infertility an Unrecognized Public Health and Population Problem?:229.

23 Feldman-Savelsberg, Is Infertility an Unrecognized Public Health and Population Problem?:229.

24 Karina Kielmann, Barren Ground: Contesting Identities of Infertile Women in Pemba, Tanzania. *In* Pragmatic Women and Body Politics, ed. Margaret Lock and Patricia Kaufert (Cambridge: Cambridge University Press, 1998): 127–163 at p. 128.

25 Kielmann, Barren Ground: 147.

26 Kielmann, Barren Ground: 150.

27 Kielmann, Barren Ground: 153.

28 Kielmann, Barren Ground: 153.

29 Steven Feierman, Explanation and Uncertainty in the Medical World of Ghaambo. Bulletin of the History of Medicine 74 (2000): 317–344. For further accounts of local understanding of infertility as being related to social networks see also Feldman-Savelsberg, Is Infertility an Unrecognized Public Health and Population Problem? and Trudie Gerrits, Infertility and Matrilineality: The Exceptional Case of the Macua of Mozambique. *In* Infertility Around the Globe: New Thinking on Childlessness, Gender, and Reproductive Technologies, ed. Marcia Inhorn and Frank Van Balen (Berkeley: University of California Press, 2002): 233–246.

30 Steven Feierman, (personal communication; see also his Explanation and Uncertainty in the Medical World of Ghaambo.

31 Feierman, Explanation and Uncertainty in the Medical World of Ghaambo: 341.

32 Feierman, Explanation and Uncertainty in the Medical World of Ghaambo: 340.

33 Caroline Bledsoe, Contingent Lives: Fertility, Time, and Aging in West Africa (Chicago: University of Chicago Press, 2002); Caroline Bledsoe, The Politics of Children: Fosterage and the Social Management of Fertility among the Mende of Sierra Leone. *In* Births and Power: Social Change and the Politics of Reproduction, ed. W. P. Handwerker (Boulder, CO: Westview Press, 1990): 81–100; Andrea Cornwall, Looking for a Child: Coping with Infertility in Ado-Odo, South-Western Nigeria. *In* Managing Reproductive Life: Cross-Cultural Themes in Fertility and Sexuality, ed. Soroya Tremayne (New York: Berghahn Books, 2001): 140–156.

34 Lisa Ann Richey, Women's Reproductive Health and Population Policy: Tanzania. Review of African Political Economy 30 (2003): 273–292.

35 Richey, Women's Reproductive Health and Population Policy: 283.

36 Richey, Women's Reproductive Health and Population Policy: 285.

37 Richey, Women's Reproductive Health and Population Policy: 286.

38 H. Standing, Towards Equitable Financing Strategies for Reproductive Health. Institute of Development Studies Working Paper No. 153 (Brighton, U.K.: IDS, 2002).

39 Richey, Women's Reproductive Health and Population Policy: 285.

40 Marilyn Strathern, Reproducing the Future: Anthropology, Kinship and the New Reproductive Technologies (New York: Routledge, 1992): 5.

41 Strathern, Reproducing the Future; Margaret Lock, Flawed Jewels and National Dis/Order: Narratives on Adolescent Dissent in Japan. Festschrift for George DeVos. Journal of Psychohistory 18 (1991): 507–531; Margaret Lock, Encounters with Aging: Mythologies of Menopause in Japan and North America (Berkeley: University of California Press, 1993); Clifford Geertz, The Interpretation of Cultures (New York: Basic Books, 1973).

42 René Almeling, Selling Genes, Selling Gender: Egg Agencies, Sperm Banks, and the Medical Market in Genetic Material. American Sociological Review 72 (2007): 319–340; Matthew Schmidt and Lisa Jean Moore, Constructing a "Good Catch," Picking a Winner: The Development of Technosemen and the Deconstruction of the Monolithic Male. *In* Cyborg Babies:From Techno-Sex to Techno-Tots, ed. R. Davis-Floyd and J. Dumit (New York: Routledge, 1998): 21–39.

43 Strathern, Reproducing the Future: 47.

44 Strathern, Reproducing the Future: 16.

45 Strathern, Reproducing the Future: 17.

46 Strathern, Reproducing the Future: 17.

47 Bledsoe, Contingent Lives; Bledsoe, The Politics of Children: 81–100; Holly Wardlow, Wayward Women: Sexuality and Agency in a New Guinea Society (Berkeley: University of California Press, 2006).

48 Sarah Franklin, Embodied Progress: A Cultural Account of Assisted Conception (London: Routledge, 1997); see also J. Edwards et al., Technologies of Procreation: Kinship in the Age of Assisted Conception (Manchester: Manchester University Press, 1993); Sarah Franklin and Helena Ragone eds., Reproducing Reproduction: Kinship, Power, and Technological Innovation. (Philadelphia: University of Pennsylvania Press, 1998).

49 Franklin, Embodied Progress: 158; See also Charis Cussins, Ontological Choreography: Agency through Objectification in Infertility Clinics. Social Studies of Science 8 (1996): 575–610.

50 Charis Thompson, Making Parents: The Ontological Choreography of Reproductive Technologies (Cambridge, MA: MIT Press, 2005): 115.

51 Thompson, Making Parents: 8.

52 Thompson, Making Parents: 8.

53 Some clinics now specialize in catering to lesbian couples and single mothers, Thompson, Making Parents: 86.

54 Thompson, Making Parents: 86.

55 Thompson, Making Parents: 91.

56 Thompson, Making Parents: 104.

57 Thompson, Making Parents: 141.

58 Thompson, Making Parents: 149.

59 Thompson, Making Parents: 161–163.

60 Thompson, Making Parents: 178.

61 Thompson, Making Parents: 189 and 199.

62 Gay Becker, The Elusive Embryo: How Women and Men Approach New Reproductive Technologies (Berkeley: University of California Press, 2000).

63 Ellen Lewin, Wives, Mothers, and Lesbians: Rethinking Resistance in the U.S. *In* Pragmatic Women and Body Politics, ed. Margaret Lock and Patricia Kaufert (Cambridge: Cambridge University Press, 1998): 164–177.

64 Becker, The Elusive Embryo: 250.

65 Inhorn uses the term IVF, *in vitro* fertilization, to describe the activities in the clinics that she observes. She reserves the term ART (for advanced reproductive technologies) by which she means practices involving surrogacy or sperm donation.

66 Marcia Inhorn, Local Babies, Global Science: Gender, Religion, and *In Vitro* Fertilization in Egypt (London: Routledge, 2003): 1.

67 Faye Ginsburg and Rayna Rapp, Conceiving the New World Order: The Global Politics of Reproduction (Berkeley: University of California Press, 1995): 3.

68 Inhorn, Local Babies: 40.

69 Carol Delaney, The Seed and the Soil: Gender and Cosmology in Turkish Village Society (Berkeley: University of California Press, 1991).

70   Inhorn, Local Babies: chapter 4.

71   Inhorn, Local Babies: 111–121.

72   Inhorn, Local Babies: 152.

73   Inhorn, Local Babies: 163.

74   Inhorn, Local Babies: 238.

75   Inhorn, Local Babies: 256.

76   Inhorn, Local Babies: 192–193.

77   E. D. Yeboah et al., Etiological Factors of Male Infertility in Africa. International Journal of Fertility 37(5) (1992): 300–7.

78   Susan Kahn, Reproducing Jews: A Cultural Account of Assisted Conception in Israel (Durham and London: Duke University Press, 2000): 1.

79   Kahn, Reproducing Jews: 1.

80   Kahn, Reproducing Jews: 71.

81   Kahn, Reproducing Jews: 3.

82   Kahn, Reproducing Jews: 38–39.

83   Kahn, Reproducing Jews: 22.

84   Kahn, Reproducing Jews: 50.

85   Kahn, Reproducing Jews: 89.

86   Kahn, Reproducing Jews: chapter 3.

87   Kahn, Reproducing Jews: 129.

88   Kahn, Reproducing Jews: 131.

89   Kahn, Reproducing Jews: 131.

90   Kahn, Reproducing Jews: 132.

91   Kahn, Reproducing Jews: 138.

92   Kahn, Reproducing Jews: 150.

93   Kahn, Reproducing Jews: 158.

94   Sarah Franklin, Fetal Fascinations: The Construction of Fetal Personhood and the Alton Debate. *In* Off-Centre: Feminism and Cultural Studies, ed. Sarah Franklin et al. (London: Unwin Hyman, 1991): 190–205; Thompson, Making Parents.

95   Margaret Lock, Perfecting Society: Reproductive Technologies, Genetic Testing, and the Planned Family in Japan. *In* Pragmatic Women and Body Politics, ed. Margaret Lock and Patricia Kaufert (Cambridge: Cambridge University Press, 1998): 206–239.

96   Lock, Perfecting Society.

97   Lisa Handwerker, The Politics of Making Modern Babies in China: Reproductive Technologies and the New Genetics. *In* Infertility Around the Globe: New Thinking on Childlessness, Gender and Reproductive Technologies, ed. Marcia Inhorn and Frank van Balen (Berkeley: University of California Press, 2002): 178–205 at p. 182.

98   Handwerker, The Politics of Making Modern Babies in China: 302.

99   Zhang Tingting, China Grapples with Legality of Surrogate Motherhood. June 5, 2006. http://www.china.org.cn/english/2006/Jun/170442.htm

100   Bob Simpson, Localizing a Brave New World: New Reproductive Technologies and the Politics of Fertility in Contemporary Sri Lanka. *In* Reproductive Agency, Medicine and the state: Cultural Transformations in Childbearing, ed. M. Unnithan-Kumar (Oxford and New York: Berghahn Books, 2004): 43–57.

101   Simpson, Localizing a Brave New World: 55.

102   Aditya Bharadwaj, Sacred Conceptions: Clinical Theodicies, Uncertain Science, and Technologies of Procreation in India. Culture, Medicine and Psychiatry 30 (2006): 451–465.

103   Arthur Kleinman, Writing at the Margin: Discourse between Anthropology and Medicine (Berkeley: University of California Press, 1995).

104   Bharadwaj, Sacred Conceptions: 453.

105 Elizabeth Roberts, God's Laboratory: Religious Rationalities and Modernity in Ecuadorian *In Vitro* Fertilization. Culture, Medicine and Psychiatry 30 (2006): 507–536 at p. 529.

106 Rayna Rapp, Preface to a Special Issue, Sacred Conceptions: Religion and the Global Practice of IVF. Culture, Medicine and Psychiatry 30 (2006): 419–421 at p. 421.

11   The Matter of the Self

1   Clifford Geertz, From the Native's Point of View: On the Nature of Anthropological Understanding. *In* P. Rainbow and W. M. Sullivan, Interpretative Social Science (Berkeley: University of California Press, 1979): 225–241 at p. 229.

2   Henri F. Ellenberger, The Pathogenic Secret and Its Therapy. Journal of the History of Behavioral Sciences 2 (January 1966): 29–42.

3   Michel Foucault, The History of Sexuality, vol. 1 (New York: Pantheon, 1978): 26.

4   Foucault, The History of Sexuality, vol. 1: 27 is cited in David Owen, Power, Knowledge and Ethics: Foucault. *In* The Edinburgh Encyclopedia of Continental Philosophy, ed. Simon Glendinning (London: Routledge, 1999): 600.

5   Ian Watt, The Rise of the Novel (Berkeley: University of California Press, 1957).

6   Charles Taylor, Sources of the Self: The Making of the Modern Identity (Cambridge: Harvard University Press, 1992).

7   Henri F. Ellenberger, Discovery of the Unconscious (New York: Basic Books, 1970).

8   Allan Young, The Harmony of Illusions: Inventing Post-Traumatic Stress Disorder (Princeton: Princeton University Press, 1995): 3.

9   Young, The Harmony of Illusions: 4.

10   Ellenberger, The Pathogenic Secret.

11   Young, The Harmony of Illusions.

12   Young, The Harmony of Illusions: 7.

13   R. Rechtman and D. Fassin, L'Empire du traumatisme: enquête sur la condition de victime (Paris: Flammarion, 2006). See also, V. Pupavac, Therapeutic Governance: Psycho-Social Intervention and Trauma Risk Management. Disasters 25(4) (2001): 358–372.

14   Deborah Posel, History as Confession: The Case of the South African Truth and Reconciliation Commission. Public Culture 20(1) (2008): 119–141 at p. 129.

15   Byron J. Good, Medicine, Rationality and Experience: An Anthropological Perspective (Cambridge and New York: Cambridge University Press. 1994): 74.

16   Good, Medicine, Rationality and Experience: 73.

17   S. Hirschauer, The Manufacture of Bodies in Surgery. Social Studies of Science 21 (1991):279–319 at p. 300.

18   Janice Boddy, Remembering Amal: on Birth and the British in Northern Sudan. *In* Beyond the Body Proper: Reading the Anthropology of Material Life, ed. Margaret Lock and Judith Farquhar (Durham, NC: Duke University Press, 2007): 315–329 at p. 317.

19   Claude Lévi-Strauss, Anthropologie structurale (1949; reprint, Paris: Plon, 1974): 205–226.

20   Luc de Heusch, Possession et chamanisme. *In* Pourquoi l'épouser? (Paris, Gallimard, 1971): 226–244.

21   A. Zempléni, L'Enfant Nit Ku Bon. Un tableau psychopathologique traditionnel chez les Wolof et les Lébou du Sénégal. Nouvelle Revue d'Éthnopsychiatrie 4 (1985): 9–41 at p. 10.

22   A. Zempléni, La Dimension thérapeutique du culte des Rab, Ndöp, Tuuru et Samp. Rites de possession chez les Lebou et les Wolof. Psychopathologie Africaine 2(3) (1966): 295–439.

23 A. Zempléni, Des êtres sacrificiels. *In* Sous le masque de l'animal, ed. Michel Cartry (Paris: Presses universitaires de France, 1984):267–317.

24 Zempléni, La Dimension thérapeutique: 422.

25 A. Zempléni, From Symptom to Sacrifice: The Story of Khady Fall. *In* Case Studies in Spirit Possession, ed. V. Crapanzano and V. Garrison (New York: J. Wiley and Sons, 1977): 87–140.

26 WHO, The Ottawa Charter for Health Promotion. (Geneva: WHO, 1986). http://www.who.int/hpr/NPH/docs/ottawa_charter_hp.pdf

27 M. H. Davies, The Origins and Practice of Psychodrama. British Journal of Psychiatry 129 (1976): 201–206.

28 Laura Kim Lee, Changing Selves, Changing Society: Human Relations Experts and the Invention of T Groups, Sensitivity Training and Encounter in the United States, 1938–1980. PhD dissertation, University of California Los Angeles, 2002.

29 Lee, Changing Selves, Changing Society: 100.

30 Walter Truett Anderson, The Upstart Spring: Esalen and the Human Potential Movement: The First Twenty Years (Lincoln, NE: Authors' Guild Backinprint.com, 2004): 82.

31 Anderson, The Upstart Spring: 84.

32 Anderson, The Upstart Spring: 84.

33 J. A. Mills and T. Harrison, John Rickman, Wilfred Ruprecht Bion, and the Origins of the Therapeutic Community. History of Psychology 10(1) (2007): 22–43.

34 João Biehl and Torben Eskerod, Will to Live: AIDS Therapies and the Politics of Survival (Princeton: Princeton University Press, 2007).

35 Carole Cain, Identity Acquisition and Self-Understanding in Alcoholics Anonymous. Ethos 19(2) (1991): 220.

36 See for instance, P. L. F. Heelas and A. J. Lock eds., Indigenous Psychologies: The Anthropology of the Self (London: Academic Press, 1981); Brian Morris, Anthropology of the Self: The Individual in Cultural Perspective (London: Pluto Press, 1995).

37 Veena Das and Ranendra K. Das, Urban Health and Pharmaceutical Consumption in Delhi, India. Journal of Biosocial Science 38 (2005): 69–82.

12 Genes as Embodied Risk

1 Deborah Heath et al., Genetic Citizenship. *In* A Companion to the Anthropology of Politics, ed. David Nugent and Joan Vincent (London: Blackwell, 2004): 152–167; Paul Rabinow, Artificiality and Enlightenment: From Sociobiology to Biosociality. *In* Essays on the Anthropology of Reason (Princeton: Princeton University Press, 1996): 91–111.

2 Paolo Palladino, Between Knowledge and Practice. Social Studies of Science 32 (2002): 137–165.

3 Patricia Jasen, Breast Cancer and the Language of Risk, 1750–1950, Social History of Medicine 15(1) (2002): 17–43.

4 François Ewald, Insurance and Risk. *In* The Foucault Effect: Studies in Governmentality, ed. Graham Burchell et al., (Hemel Hempstead: Harvester Wheatsheaf, 1991): 197–210 at p. 208.

5 Ewald, Insurance and Risk: 208.

6 Mary Douglas, Risk as a Forensic Resource. Daedalus 119 (1990): 1–16.

7 Robert Castel, From Dangerousness to Risk. *In* The Foucault Effect: Studies in Governmentality, ed. Graham Burchell et al. (Chicago: University of Chicago Press, 1991): 289; Michel Foucault, The History of Sexuality, vol. 1 (New York: Pantheon, 1978).

8   Anne M. Kavanagh and Dorothy H. Broom, Embodied Risk: My Body, Myself. Social Science and Medicine 46 (1998): 437–444.

9   Dorothy Nelkin and M. Susan Lindee, The DNA Mystique: The Gene as a Cultural Icon (New York: W. H. Freeman and Company, 1995).

10 Edward J. Yoxen, Constructing Genetic Diseases. *In* The Problem of Medical Knowledge: Examining the Social Construction of Medicine, ed. P. Wright and A. Treacher (Edinburgh: University of Edinburgh, 1982): 144–161.

11 Janet Childerhose, Genetic Discrimination: Biography of an American Problem. PhD dissertation, Dept. of Anthropology, McGill University, Montreal, 2009.

12 Nelkin and Lindee, The DNA Mystique.

13 Ulrich Beck, Risk Society: Towards a New Modernity (London: Sage, 1992).

14 Deborah Lupton, The Imperative of Health: Public Health and the Regulated Body (London: Sage, 1995).

15 David M. Schneider, American Kinship: A Cultural Account (Chicago: Chicago University Press, 1980).

16 Katie Featherstone et al., Risky Relations: Family, Kinship and the New Genetics (Oxford: Berg, 2006): 6.

17 Bruno Latour, The Pasteurization of France (Cambridge, MA: Harvard University Press, 1988): 47.

18 Hans-Jörg Rheinberger, Beyond Nature and Culture: Modes of Reasoning in the Age of Molecular Biology and Medicine. *In* Living and Working with the New Medical Technologies: Intersections of Inquiry, ed. Margaret Lock, Allan Young and Alberto Cambrosio (Cambridge: Cambridge University Press, 2000): 19–30.

19 ETC Group, Extreme Genetic Engineering: An Introduction to Synthetic Biology (2007). http://www.etcgroup.org/en/materials/publications.html?pub_id=602.

20 Rheinberger, Beyond Nature and Culture: 22.

21 Rheinberger, Beyond Nature and Culture: 24.

22 Rheinberger, Beyond Nature and Culture: 25.

23 Rheinberger, Beyond Nature and Culture: 25.

24 Here, Rheinberger makes use of a term coined by Paul Rabinow in Epochs, Presents, Events. *In* Living and Working with the New Medical Technologies, ed. M. Lock, A. Young and A. Cambrosio (Cambridge: Cambridge University Press, 2000): 31–46.

25 Hans-Jörg Rheinberger, Conjunctures, Hybrids, Bifurcations, Experimental Cultures. *In* his Toward a History of Epistemic Things: Synthesizing Proteins in the Test Tube (Stanford: Stanford University Press, 1997): 133–142.

26 Hans-Jörg Rheinberger, What Happened to Molecular Biology? Biosocieties 3 (2008): 303–310.

27 Nukaga Yoshio and Alberto Cambrosio, Medical Pedigrees and the Visual Production of Family Disease in Canadian and Japanese Genetic Counselling Practices. *In* The Sociology of Medical Science and Technology, ed. M. A. Elston (Oxford: Blackwell, 1997): 29–56.

28 Featherstone et al., Risky Relations: 16.

29 Walter Gilbert, A Vision of the Grail. *In* The Code of Codes: Scientific and Social Issues in the Human Genome Project, ed. D. J. Kevles and L. Hood (Cambridge: Harvard University Press, 1992): 83–97 at p. 96.

30 Emphasis added: United States Office of Technology Assessment, Mapping Our Genes, (Washington, D.C.: Government Printing Office, 1988): 86.

31 Daniel Koshland, Sequences and Consequences of the Human Genome. Science 246(4927) (1989): 189.

32 James Watson, Values from a Chicago Upbringing. *In* DNA: The Double Helix, Perspective and Prospective at Forty Years, ed. Donald A. Chambers (New York: New York Academy of Sciences, 1995): 194–197 at p. 197.

33 James Watson, The Road Ahead. *In* Engineering the Human Germline, ed. G. Stock and J. Campbell (Oxford: Oxford University Press, 2000): 73–95 at p. 79.

34 Peter A. Singer and Abdallah S. Daar, Harnessing Genomics and Biotechnology to Improve Global Health Equity. Science 294 (2001): 87–89.

35 Francis Collins, Future Visions: How Will Genetics Change Our Lives? Time Magazine 161(7) (February 17, 2003): 42.

36 Lon Cardon, Translating Complex Disease Genes Into New Medicines. Paper delivered at the Colston Symposium, The New Genomics: Public Health, Social and Clinical Implications, Bristol University, United Kingdom, 2009.

37 Arnold Christianson and Bernadette Modell, Medical Genetics in Developing Countries. Annual Reviews of Genomics and Human Genetics, 5 (2004): 219–265.

38 Performing the polymerase chain reaction (PCR), a technique that is essential to DNA analysis, can be carried out using a simple, portable machine.

39 Christianson and Modell, Medical Genetics in Developing Countries: 258.

40 World Health Organization, Collaboration in Medical Genetics, (Geneva: WHO, 2002).

41 Abby Lippman, Led (Astray) by Genetic Maps: The Cartography of the Human Genome and Human Care. Social Science and Medicine 35 (1992): 1469–1496 at p. 1470.

42 For evidence of this see, for example, Elaine Draper, Risky Business: Genetic Testing and Exclusionary Practices in the Hazardous Workplace (Cambridge: Cambridge University Press, 1991); Troy Duster, Backdoor to Eugenics (New York: Routledge, 1990); Erik Parens and Adrienne Asch, The Disability Rights Critique of Prenatal Genetic Testing: Reflections and Recommendations. Hastings Center Report 229(5) (1999): S1–S22; Diane B. Paul and Hamish G. Spencer, The Hidden Science of Eugenics. Nature 374 (1995): 302–304.

43 A shift towards a molecular approach in biology began in the 1930s; Lily Kay, The Molecular Vision of Life: Caltech, The Rockefeller Foundation, and the Rise of the New Biology (Oxford, Oxford University Press, 1993). This shift was associated with a search for what constitutes "life" and was made possible by the development of several new technologies. For two decades molecular biology focused on protein structure and function. After 1953, when the significance of the discovery of DNA was recognized, emphasis switched dramatically to genes, culminating in the Human Genome Project. In recent years proteomics has again become a major focus in molecular biology and is the sub-discipline that currently holds out the most hope for the development of new, individualized medications and for elucidating the key biological pathways associated with complex disease.

44 Adam Hedgecoe, Schizophrenia and the Narrative of Enlightened Geneticization. Social Studies of Science 31 (2001): 875–911 at p. 877.

45 Pat Spallone, The New Biology of Violence: New Geneticisms For Old? Body and Society 4 (1998): 47–65.

46 Hedgecoe, Schizophrenia and the Narrative of Enlightened Geneticization.

47 Peter McGuffin et al., Toward Behavioral Genomics, Science 291(5507) (2001): 1242–1249.

48 Jon Turney and Jill Turner, Predictive Medicine, Genetics and Schizophrenia. New Genetics and Society 19(1) (2000): 5–22.

49 Nikolas Rose, The Politics of Life Itself: Biomedicine, Power, and Subjectivity in the Twenty-First Century (Princeton: Princeton University Press. 2007): 125.

50 Rose, The Politics of Life Itself: 129; See also, Carlos Novas and Nikolas Rose, Genetic Risk and the Birth of the Somatic Individual. Economy and Society 29(4) (2000): 485–513.

51 John Hodgson, Editorial: Geneticism and Freedom of Choice. Trends in Biotechnology 7(9) (1989): 221.

52   Kimberly A. Quaid and Michael Morris, Reluctance to Undergo Predictive Testing: The Case of Huntington's Disease. American Journal of Medical Genetics 45 (1993): 41–45; Diane Beeson and Teresa Doksum, Family Values and Resistance to Genetic Testing. *In* Bioethics in Social Context, ed. B. Hoffmaster (Philadelphia: Temple University Press, 2001): 153–179; Nancy Wexler, Clairvoyance and Caution: Repercussions from the Human Genome Project. *In* The Code of Codes: Scientific and Social Issues in the Human Genome Project, ed. D. J. Kevles and L. Hood, (Cambridge, MA: Harvard University Press, 1992): 211–243.

53   Shirley A. Hill, Managing Sickle Cell Disease in Low-Income Families (Philadelphia: Temple University Press, 1994); Rayna Rapp, Testing Women, Testing the Fetus: The Social Impact of Amniocentesis, (New York: Routledge, 1999).

54   Kira Apse et al., Perceptions of Genetic Discrimination Among At-Risk Relatives of Colorectal Cancer Patients. Genetics in Medicine 6 (2004): 510–516; Emily A. Peterson et al., Health Insurance and Discrimination Concerns and BRCA1/2 Testing in a Clinic Population. Cancer Epidemiology, Biomarkers and Prevention 11 (2002): 79–87. Both these articles and the PhD thesis of Janet Childerhose (Genetic Discrimination: Biography of an American Problem) suggest that fears about discrimination based on genetic testing may not be fully justified.

55   Rapp, Testing Women, Testing the Fetus.

56   Faye Ginsburg and Rayna Rapp, Conceiving the New World Order: The Global Politics of Reproduction (Berkeley: University of California Press, 1995): 3.

57   Rapp, Testing Women, Testing the Fetus: 250.

58   Rapp, Testing Women, Testing the Fetus: 309.

59   Cited in Rapp, Testing Women, Testing the Fetus: 145.

60   Carole Browner, Can Gender "Equity" in Prenatal Genetic Services Unintentionally Reinforce Male Authority? *In* Reproductive Disruptions: Gender, Technology, and Biopolitics in the New Millennium, ed. Marcia Inhorn (New York: Berghahn Books, 2007): 147–164.

61   Susan Cox and William McKellin, "There's This Thing in Our Family": Predictive Testing and the Construction of Risk for Huntington Disease. *In* Sociological Perspectives on the New Genetics, ed. P. Conrad and J. Gabe (London: Blackwell Publishers, 1999): 121–148 at p. 130.

62   Cox and McKellin, "There's This Thing in Our Family": 140.

63   Cox and McKellin, "There's This Thing in Our Family": 140.

64   Cox and McKellin, "There's This Thing in Our Family": 121–148.

65   Genetic linkage is the phenomenon whereby alleles at loci close together on the same chromosome tend to be inherited together. Until the time that single genes could be mapped, genetic linkage was the method most made use of to ascertain whether or not an individual carried a specific gene or not. This technique had limited use.

66   Elisabeth Almqvist et al., Risk Reversals in Predictive Testing of Huntington Disease, American Journal of Human Genetics 61 (1997): 945–952.

67   Douglas R. Langbehn et al., A New Model for Prediction of the Age of Onset and Penetrance for Huntington's Disease Based on CAG Length. Clinical Genetics, 65(4) (2004): 267–277.

68   Monica Konrad, Narrating the New Predictive Genetic: Ethics, Ethnography and Science (Cambridge: Cambridge University Press, 2005).

69   Konrad, Narrating the New Predictive Genetics: 145. See also, Kaja Finkler, Experiencing the New Genetics: Kinship and Family on the Medical Frontier (Philadelphia: University of Philadelphia Press, 2000); Kaja Finkler, The Kin in the Gene: The Medicalization of Family and Kinship in American Society. Current Anthropology 42 (2001): 235–263.

70 Nina Hallowell, Doing the Right Thing: Genetics Risk and Responsibility. Sociology of Health and Illness 5 (1999): 597–621.

71 Hallowell, Doing the Right Thing: 608.

72 Hallowell, Doing the Right Thing: 609.

73 Mary-Claire King et al., Breast and Ovarian Cancer Risks Due to Inherited Mutations in BRCA1 and BRCA2. Science 302(5645) (2003): 643–646.

74 Sahra Gibbon, Breast Cancer Genes and the Gendering of Knowledge: Science and Citizenship in the Cultural Context of the "New" Genetics (New York: Palgrave Macmillan, 2007).

75 Kaja Finkler et al., The New Genetics and Its Consequences for Family, Kinship, Medicine and Medical Genetics. Social Science and Medicine 57 (2003): 403–412.

76 Ian Hacking, The Looping Effects of Human Kinds. *In* Causal Cognition: a Multi-disciplinary Approach, ed. D. Sperber et al. (Oxford: Oxford Medical Publications, 1995): 351–383.

77 Rayna Rapp et al., Genealogical Disease: Where Hereditary Abnormality, Biomedical Explanation, and Family Responsibility Meet. *In* Relative Matters: New Directions in the Study of Kinship, ed. S. Franklin and S. MacKinnon (Durham, NC: Duke University Press, 2001): 384–412; Rayna Rapp, Cell Life and Death, Child Life and Death: Genomic Horizons, Genetic Diseases, Family Stories. *In* Remaking Life and Death: Toward an Anthropology of the Biosciences, ed. S. Franklin and M. Lock (Santa Fe: School of American Research Press, 2003): 129–164.

78 M. Callon and V. Rabeharisoa, Gino's Lesson on Humanity: Genetics, Mutual Entanglements and the Sociologist's Role. Economy and Society 33 (2004): 1–27; Deborah Heath, Locating Genetic Knowledge: Picturing Marfan Syndrome and Its Travelling Constituencies. Science, Technology, and Human Values 23 (1998): 71–97; Heath et al., Genetic Citizenship: 152–167; Rapp, Cell Life and Death: 129–164; Karen-Sue Taussig et al., Flexible Eugenics: Technologies of the Self in the Age of Genetics. *In* Genetic Nature/Culture: Anthropology and Science beyond the Two-Culture Divide, ed. A. H. Goodman et al. (Berkeley: University of California Press, 2003): 58–76.

79 Taussig et al., Flexible Eugenics: 60.

80 Taussig et al., Flexible Eugenics: 70.

81 Gibbon, Breast Cancer Genes and the Gendering of Knowledge; Palladino, Between Knowledge and Practice; Callon and Rabeharisoa, Gino's Lesson on Humanity; Rapp, Cell Life and Death.

82 Adriana Petryna, When Experiments Travel: Clinical Trials and the Global Search for Human Subjects (Princeton: Princeton University Press, 2009).

83 Rabinow, Artificiality and Enlightenment: 102.

84 Rabinow, Artificiality and Enlightenment.

85 Rabinow, Artificiality and Enlightenment: 102.

86 Rabinow, Artificiality and Enlightenment: 103.

87 Amy Harmon, After DNA Diagnosis: "Hello, Are You Just Like Me?" New York Times, December 28, 2007.

88 Harmon, After DNA Diagnosis.

89 Kelly Raspberry and Debra Skinner, Experiencing the Genetic Body: Parents' Encounters with Pediatric Clinical Genetics. Medical Anthropology 26 (2007): 355–391.

90 Paul Rabinow, Afterword. *In* Biosocialities, Genetics, and the Social Science ed. Sahra Gibbon and Carlos Novas (London: Routledge, 2007): 188–192 at p. 191.

91 Rabinow, Afterword: 191.

92 Sandi Wiggins et al., The Psychological Consequences of Predictive Testing for Huntington's Disease. Obstetrical and Gynecological Survey 48(4): 248.

93   Wiggins et al., Psychological Consequences of Predictive Testing for Huntington's Disease.

94   Carole H. Browner and Mabel H. Preloran Neurogenetic Diagnoses: The Power of Hope and the Limits of Today's Medicine (London: Routledge, forthcoming, 2010).

95   Alice Wexler, Mapping Fate: A Memoir of Family, Risk, and Genetic Research (Berkeley: University of California Press, 1995): 224.

96   Wexler, Mapping Fate: 238.

97   Keith Wailoo and Stephen Gregory Pemberton, The Troubled Dream of Genetic Medicine: Ethnicity and Innovation in Tay-Sachs, Cystic Fibrosis, and Sickle Cell Disease (Baltimore: Johns Hopkins University Press, 2006): 6.

98   Wailoo and Pemberton, The Troubled Dream of Genetic Medicine: 39.

99   An individual who has inherited a matched pair of alleles dominant for a particular gene is said to be homozygous whereas an individual who has inherited a dominant allele from one parent and a recessive allele from the other is described as heterozygous.

100 J. J. Mitchell et al., Twenty-Year Outcome Analysis of Genetic Screening Programs for Tay-Sachs and β-Thalassemia Disease Carriers in High Schools. American Journal of Human Genetics 59 (1996): 793–798.

101 An exception being one program in Cuba for screening sickle cell anemia, see H. Granda et al., Cuban Programme for Prevention of Sickle Cell Disease. The Lancet 337 (1991): 152–153.

102 Barbara Prainsack and Gil Siegal, The Rise of Genetic Couplehood? A Comparative View of Premarital Genetic Testing. BioSocieties 1 (2006): 17–36.

103 J. Ekstein and H. Kazenstein, The Dor Yeshorim story: Community-Based Carrier Screening for Tay-Sachs Disease. Advances in Genetics 44 (2001): 297–310.

104 Wailoo and Pemberton, The Troubled Dream of Genetic Medicine: 39.

105 Madeleine Goodmann and Lenn Goodmann, The Overselling of Genetic Anxiety. Hastings Center Report, October 20–27, 1982: 20.

106 Cited in Gina Kolata, Nightmare or the Dream of a New Era in Genetics? New York Times, December 7, 1993: A1.

107 Lise Stevens, Dr Francis S. Collins, "Genomic Discoveries: Promising and Potentially Dangerous." Neurology Today 2(1) (2002): 14.

108 Stefan Beck and Jörg Niewöhner, Translating Genetic Testing and Screening in Cyprus and Germany: Contingencies, Continuities, Ordering Effects and Bio-Cultural Intimacy. In The Handbook of Genetics and Society: Mapping the New Genomic Era, ed. Paul Atkinson et al. (London: Routledge, 2009): 76–93.

109 Patricia Book, Death at an Early Age: Thalassemia in Cyprus. Medical Anthropology Quarterly: Cross Cultural Studies in Health and Illness 2 (1980): 1–39.

110 Michel Callon, Some Elements of a Sociology of Translation: Domestication of the Scallops and Fishermen of St Brieuc Bay. In Power, Action and Belief: A New Sociology of Knowledge?, ed. J. Law (London: Routledge, 1986): 196–229; Beck and Niewöhner, Translating Genetic Testing and Screening in Cyprus and Germany.

111 Roger Hoedemaekers and Henk ten Have, Geneticization: The Cyprus Paradigm. Journal of Medicine and Philosophy 23 (1998): 274–287.

112 M. Angastiniotis, Cyprus: Thalassaemia Programme. The Lancet 336(8723) (1990): 1119–1120.

113 There is a parallel between these collectivist programs and the recognition of presumed consent in connection with organ donation made use of by certain European nations in which it is assumed that the collectivity, in this case the state, has a right to procure organs for the greater good of society, unless the individual opts out ahead of time (see Margaret Lock, Twice Dead: Organ Transplants and the Reinvention of Death, Berkeley, University of California Press, 2002).

114 Beck and Niewöhner, Translating Genetic Testing and Screening in Cyprus and Germany: 89.

115 Beck and Niewöhner, Translating Genetic Testing and Screening in Cyprus and Germany: 88.

116 Beck and Niewöhner, Translating Genetic Testing and Screening in Cyprus and Germany.

117 Parens and Asch, The Disability Rights Critique of Prenatal Genetic Testing: S1–S22.

118 Karen Kaplan, 25% of Fetuses Found with Disease Aborted. The Gazette, Montreal, September 19, 2007.

119 Wailoo and Pemberton, The Troubled Dream of Genetic Medicine: 48.

120 Wailoo and Pemberton, The Troubled Dream of Genetic Medicine: 48.

121 Frank Livingstone, Malaria and Human Polymorphisms. Annual Review of Genetics 5 (1971): 33–64.

122 Linus Pauling, Reflections on a New Biology: foreword. UCLA Law Review 15 (1968): 269.

123 Duster, Back Door to Eugenics 45.

124 Duster, Back Door to Eugenics: 47.

125 Duster, Back Door to Eugenics: 51.

126 Ginsburg and Rapp, Conceiving the New World Order: 3; See also, Shellee Colen, "Housekeeping" for the Green Card: West Indian Household Workers, the State, and Stratified Reproduction in New York. In At Work in Homes: Household Workers in World Perspective, ed. R. Sanjek and S. Colen (Washington D.C.: American Anthropological Association, 1990): 89–118.

127 Duana Fullwiley, Discriminate Biopower and Everyday Politics: Views on Sickle Cell Testing in Dakar. Medical Anthropology 23 (2004): 157–194.

128 Fullwiley, Discriminate Biopower and Everyday Politics: 161; See also, D. V. Desai and Hiren Dhanani, Sickle Cell Disease: History and Origin. The Internet Journal of Hematology 1, no 2. (2004): http://www.ispub.com/ostia/index, for details about variable symptomatology in sickle cell disease.

129 Fullwiley, Discriminate Biopower and Everyday Politics: 161.

130 Fullwiley, Discriminate Biopower and Everyday Politics: 160.

131 See also Margaret Lock, Perfecting Society: Reproductive Technologies, Genetic Testing, and the Planned Family in Japan. In Pragmatic Women and Body Politics, ed. Margaret Lock and Patricia Kaufert (Cambridge: Cambridge University Press, 1998): 206–239.

132 Mark Henderson, Rooting out the Genes Behind Breast Cancer. The Times, May 9, 2006: http://www.timesonline.co.uk/tol/news/uk/health/article714704.ece

133 Michael R. Debaun et al., Association of In-Vitro Fertilization with Beckwith-Wiedemann Syndrome and Epigenetic Alteration of LIT1 and H19. American Journal of Human Genetics 72 (2003): 156–160; Eamonn R. Maher, Imprinting and assisted reproductive technology. Human Molecular Genetics 14 (2005): R133–R138.

134 Canadian Cancer Society, Canadian Cancer Statistics 2007: Breast Cancer Rate Dropping. http://www.cancer.ca

135 Debora Spar, Reproductive Tourism and the Regulatory Map. New England Journal of Medicine 352(6) (2005): 531–533.

136 See Rapp, Testing Women, Testing the Fetus; Browner, Can Gender "Equity" in Prenatal Genetic Services Unintentionally Reinforce Male Authority?

137 Margaret Lock et al., When it Runs in the Family: Putting Susceptibility Genes into Perspective. Public Understanding of Science 15(3) (2006): 277–300. However, the BRCA genes have greater penetrance than do most susceptibility genes, making increased risk estimates for this condition to date less problematic than those made for other complex diseases.

138 Margaret Lock et al., Susceptibility Genes and the Question of Embodied Identity. Medical Anthropology Quarterly 21(3) (2007): 256–276.

139 Eva Jablonka and Marion J. Lamb, Epigenetic Inheritance and Evolution: The Lamarckian Dimension (Oxford: Oxford University Press, 1995); John Mattick, The Hidden Genetic Program of Complex Organisms. Scientific American 291 (2004): 60–67.

140 Kristin Zeiler, Reproductive Autonomous Choice: A Cherished Illusion? Medicine, Healthcare and Philosophy 7 (2004): 175–183; Sarah Franklin and Celia Roberts, Born and Made: An Ethnography of Preimplantation Genetic Diagnosis (Princeton: Princeton University Press, 2006).

141 Celia Roberts and Sarah Franklin, Experiencing New Forms of Genetic Choice: Findings from an Ethnographic Study of Preimplantation Genetic Diagnosis. Human Fertility 7(4) (2004): 285–293; Franklin and Roberts, Born and Made.

142 Nicholas Wade, The Quest for the $1000 Human Genome. New York Times, July 18, 2006.

143 Arthur Kleinman and Joan Kleinman, The Appeal of Experience: the Dismay of Images: Cultural Appropriations of Suffering in our Times. *In* Social Suffering, ed. Arthur Kleinman et al. (Berkeley: University of California Press, 1997): 1–24 at p. 7.

144 Michael J. Sandel, The Case Against Perfection: Ethics in the Age of Genetic Engineering. (Cambridge, MA: Belknap Press of Harvard University Press, 2007): 86.

145 Sandel, The Case Against Perfection: 87.

146 Leana J. Albertson, ed. Genetic Discrimination (Hauppauge, NY: Nova Science Publishers, 2008).

13   Genomics, Epigenomics, and Uncertain Futures

1 E. E. Evans-Pritchard, Witchcraft, Oracles, and Magic among the Azande (Oxford: Clarendon Press, 1937).

2 Susan Reynolds Whyte, Questioning Misfortune: The Pragmatics of Uncertainty in Eastern Uganda (Cambridge: Cambridge University Press, 1997): 6.

3 Nadia C. Serematakis, The Last Word: Women, Death, and Divination in Inner Mani (Chicago, University of Chicago Press, 1991).

4 The investigation of the roles and functions of single genes is a primary focus of molecular biology. In contrast, genomics is the study of the genomes of cells and of whole organisms. There are several current definitions of the term genome presently in use. The one made use of in this book (following Barry Barnes and John Dupré, Genomes and What to Make of Them (Chicago: University of Chicago Press, 2008): 9) is that a genome can best be understood as a "real" material object constituted out of DNA. Research about single genes does not fall into the field of genomics unless the aim is to elucidate the effect of a specific gene on and its response to the activity of the genome as a whole.

5 Nikolas Rose, The Politics of Life Itself: Biomedicine, Power, and Subjectivity in the Twenty-First Century (Princeton: Princeton University Press, 2007): 19.

6 Edward J. Yoxen, Constructing Genetic Diseases. *In* The Problem of Medical Knowledge: Examining the Social Construction of Medicine, ed. P. Wright and A. Treacher (Edinburgh: University of Edinburgh, 1982): 144–161.

7 Michael Lambek, Knowledge and Practice in Mayotte; Local Discourses of Islam, Sorcery and Spirit Possession (Toronto: University of Toronto Press, 1993); Whyte, Questioning Misfortune; Wikan Unni, Managing Turbulent Hearts: A Balinese Formula for Living (Chicago: University of Chicago Press, 1990).

8 Paul Rabinow and Nikolas Rose, Biopower Today. Biosocieties 1 (2006): 195–218 at p. 211.

9   Barnes and Dupré, Genomes and What to Make of Them: 8.

10 U.K. Biobank – What Is It? http://www.ukbiobank.ac.uk/about/what.php

11 W. Wayt Gibbs, The Unseen Genome: Gems Among the Junk. Scientific American 289(5) (2003): 47–53 at p. 48.

12 RNA is concerned with the inter-relationship between the macro-molecules of DNA (deoxyribonucleic acid) and RNA (ribonucleic acid), and how these molecules synthesize polypeptides, the basic components of all proteins. Only in the past few years has attention turned to the numerous critical activities of RNA that are not directly involved with protein production.

13 Sean R. Eddy, Non-Coding RNA Genes and the Modern RNA World. Nature Reviews/Genetics 2 (2001): 919–929; John S. Mattick, Challenging the Dogma: The Hidden Layer of Non-Protein-Coding RNAs in Complex Organisms. Bioessays 25 (2003): 930–939; John S. Mattick, The Hidden Genetic Program of Complex Organisms. Scientific American 291 (2004): 60–67.

14 Eddy, Non-Coding RNA Genes; Mattick, Challenging the Dogma; Mattick, The Hidden Genetic Program of Complex Organisms.

15 Arturas Petronis, Human Morbid Genetics Revisited: Relevance of Epigenetics. Trends in Genetics 17 (2001): 142–146.

16 The importance of gene regulation was first noted by Jacob and Monod over 40 years ago (1961) but mapping DNA structure was given priority. See François Jacob and Jacques Monod, Genetic Regulatory Mechanisms in the Synthesis of Proteins. Journal of Molecular Biology 3 (1961): 318–356.

17 See Paul Berg, All Our Collective Ingenuity Will Be Needed. Federation of American Societies for Experimental Biology 5(1) (1991): 75–77; and B. D. Davis, The Human Genome and Other Initiatives. Science 4 (1990): 2941–2942 to name just two.

18 S. Pinker, How the Mind Works (New York: W. W. Norton, 1997); D. Buss, Evolutionary Psychology: The New Science of the Mind (Boston: Allyn and Bacon, 2007).

19 Jan Sapp, The Struggle for Authority in the Field of Heredity, 1900–1932: New Perspectives on the Rise of Genetics. Journal of the History of Biology 16(3) (1983): 311–342.

20 Gabriel Gudding, The Phenotype/Genotype Distinction and the Disappearance of the Body. Journal of the History of Ideas 57(3) (1996): 525–545 at p. 526.

21 Cited in Gudding, The Phenotype/Genotype Distinction: 528.

22 Barnes and Dupré, Genomes and What to Make of Them: 8.

23 Lenny Moss, From Representational Preformationism to the Epigenesis of Openness to the World? Reflections on a New Vision of the Organism. *In* From Epigenesis to Epigenetics: The Genome in Context, ed. L. van Speybroeck et al. (New York: New York Academy of Sciences): 219–230.

24 Moss, From Representational Preformationism: 219–220.

25 Moss, From Representational Preformationism: 220.

26 Moss, From Representational Preformationism: 220.

27 Paul E. Griffiths, Developmental Systems Theory. *In* Nature Encyclopedia of Life Sciences (London: Nature Publishing Group, 2001): 4.

28 Moss, From Representational Preformationism: 222.

29 Gertrudis Van de Vijver et al., Epigenetics: A Challenge for Genetics, Evolution, and Development? Annals of New York Academy of Sciences 981 (2002): 1–6.

30 Eva Jablonka and Marion J. Lamb, Epigenetic Inheritance and Evolution: The Lamarckian Dimension, (Oxford: Oxford University Press, 1995): 82.

31 Mia Schmiedeskamp, Preventing Good Brains from Going Bad. Scientific American Special Edition, The Science of Staying Young (2004): 84–91.

32   Barnes and Dupré, Genomes and What to Make of Them: 21.

33   Barnes and Dupré, Genomes and What to Make of Them: 50.

34   Scott F. Gilbert, The Genome in Its Ecological Context: Philosophical Perspectives on Interspecies Epigenesis. Annals of the New York Academy of Sciences 981 (2002): 208–218 at p. 213.

35   Griffiths, Developmental Systems Theory: 4

36   Richard C. Strohman, A New Paradigm for Life: Beyond Genetic Determinism. California Monthly 111 (2001): 4–27 at p. 8.

37   Jablonka and Lamb, Epigenetic Inheritance and Evolution; Margaret Lock, Eclipse of the Gene and the Return of Divination. Current Anthropology 46, S5 (2005): 47–70.

38   F. Champagne and Michael Meaney, Like Mother, Like Daughter: Evidence for Non-Genomic Transmission of Parental Behavior and Stress Responsivity. Progress in Brain Research 133 (2001): 287–302; Petronis, Human Morbid Genetics Revisited: 142–146; Szyf Moshe et al., The Social Environment and the Epigenome. Environmental and Molecular Mutagenesis 49 (2008): 46–60.

39   L. H. Lumey, Decreased Birthweights in Infants After Maternal *in Utero* Exposure to the Dutch Famine of 1944–1945. Paediatric Perinatal Epidemiology 6 (1992): 240–253; J. E. Harding, The Nutritional Basis of the Fetal Origins of Adult Disease. International Journal of Epidemiology 30 (2001): 15–23; Jablonka and Lamb, Epigenetic Inheritance and Evolution; Susan Oyama, Terms in Tension: What Do You Do When All the Good Words Are Taken? in Cycles of Contingency: Developmental Systems and Evolution, ed. Susan Oyama et al. (Cambridge, MA: MIT Press, 2001): 177–193.

40   Strohman, A New Paradigm for Life: 4–27.

41   E. M. Neumann-Held and C. Rehmann-Sutter, Genes in Development: Rereading the Molecular Paradigm (Durham, NC: Duke University Press, 2006): 2.

42   Gudding, The Phenotype/Genotype Distinction.

43   Evelyn Fox Keller, The Century of the Gene (Cambridge, MA: Harvard University Press, 2000).

44   W. Gelbart, Databases in Genomic Research. Science 282 (1998): 660.

45   Keller, The Century of the Gene: 148.

46   Genetic penetrance describes the likelihood that a particular gene will be expressed and result in a disease.

47   P. St George-Hyslop, Molecular Genetics of Alzheimer's Disease. Biological Psychiatry 47 (2000): 183–199.

48   L. Tilley et al., Genetic Risk Factors in Alzheimer's Disease. Journal of Clinical Pathology: Molecular Pathology 51 (1998): 293–304.

49   E. H. Corder et al., Gene Dose of Apolipoprotein E Type 4 Allele and the Risk of Alzheimer's Disease in Late Onset Families. Science 261(5123) (1993): 921–923.

50   Tilley et al., Genetic Risk Factors in Alzheimer's Disease.

51   Dennis J. Selkoe, The Pathophysiology of Alzheimer's Disease. *In* Early Diagnosis of Alzheimer's Disease, ed. L. F. M. Scinto and K. R. Daffner (Totowa, NJ: Humana Press, 2002): 83–104.

52   R. H. Myers et al., Apolipoprotein E ε4 Association with Dementia in a Population-Based Study: The Framingham Study. Neurology 46(3) (1996): 673–7.

53   Deborah Blacker and Rudolph E. Tanzi, Genetic Testing in the Early Diagnosis of Alzheimer's Disease. *In* Early Diagnosis of Alzheimer's Disease, ed. L. F. M. Scinto and K. R. Daffner (Totowa, NJ: Humana Press, 2000): 105–126.

54   J. C. Breitner, The End of Alzheimer's Disease? International Journal of Geriatric Psychiatry 14(7) (1999): 577–586; Peter Whitehouse, The Myth of Alzheimer's Disease:

What You Aren't Being Told About Today's Most Dreaded Diagnosis (New York: St Martin's Press, 2008).

55 David Snowdon, Aging with Grace: What the Nun Study Teaches us About Leading Longer, Healthier, and More Meaningful Lives (New York: Bantam Books, 2001).

56 R. M. Corbo and R. Scacchi, Apolipoprotein E (APOE) Allele Distribution in the World: Is APOEε4 a "Thrifty" Allele? Annals of Human Genetics 63 (1999): 301–310.

57 Lindsay A. Farrer, Familial Risk for Alzheimer's Disease in Ethnic Minorities: Nondiscriminating Genes. Archives of Neurology 57(2) (2000): 28–29; Lindsay A. Farrer et al., Association Between Angiotensin-Converting Enzyme and Alzheimer Disease. Archives of Neurology 57(2) (2000): 210–214.

58 A set of closely linked genetic markers present on one chromosome that tend to be inherited together.

59 Lars Bertram and Rudolph E. Tanzi, Alzheimer's Disease: One Disorder, Too Many Genes? Human Molecular Genetics 13 (2004): R135–R141.

60 Bertram and Tanzi, Alzheimer's Disease: One Disorder, Too Many Genes?: R137.

61 Lars Bertram et al., Systematic Meta-Analyses of Alzheimer Disease Genetic Association Studies: The Alzgene Database. Nature Genetics 39 (2007): 17–23.

62 Mark I. McCarthy et al., Genome-Wide Association Studies for Complex Traits: Consensus, Uncertainty and Challenges. Nature Reviews/Genetics 9 (2008): 356–369.

63 Bruno Latour, We Have Never Been Modern (Cambridge, MA: Harvard University Press, 1993).

64 Paul Rabinow, The Third Culture. History of the Human Sciences 7(2) (1994): 53–64.

65 F. J. Kier and V. Molinari, "Do-It-Yourself" Dementia Testing: Issues Regarding an Alzheimer's Home Screening Test. Gerontologist 43(3) (2003): 295–301.

66 M. R. Farlow et al., Impact of APOE in Mild Cognitive Impairment. Neurology 63 (2004): 1898–1901.

67 Funding for this research was provided by the Social Science and Humanities Research Council of Canada (SSHRC), grant # 205806. The REVEAL project was supported by National Institutes of Health grants HG/AG02213 (The REVEAL Study), AG09029 (The MIRAGE Study), AG13846 (Boston University Alzheimer's Disease Center), and M01 RR00533 (Boston University General Clinical Research Center.

68 Margaret Lock et al., Susceptibility Genes and the Question of Embodied Identity. Medical Anthropology Quarterly 21 (2007): 256–276. Lock was asked to contribute a qualitative component to the REVEAL study and, after much thought, did so having obtained an understanding that the findings might well not support the original objectives of the project. One justification for this research is that testing for susceptibility genes is likely to become increasingly common, especially in the private sector, and therefore knowledge about how people deal with risk information when it is not possible to make predictions with a high degree of confidence is urgently needed. A second justification is that to withhold information about their bodies from people is patronizing. A third justification is that in many families where someone has died of AD some members of the next generation believe that they have a virtually 100% chance of contracting the disease. If individuals can be taught, even if they are homozygous for ApoEε4, their lifetime risk for getting AD is never more than approximately 52% for men and 58% for women, then anxiety levels may well be lowered. The fourth explicit justification for the research is to create a pool of ApoE ε4 individuals whose bloods can be used at any time to enrich clinical trials. The four sites are at Boston University, Case Western University, Cornell University and Howard University. Janalyn Prest and Stephanie Lloyd, formerly affiliated with the Anthropology Department at McGill University, acted as research assistants and conducted and coded the qualitative interviews from Phase I of the REVEAL study.

Heather Lindstrom, in the Anthropology Department at Case Western Reserve also conducted some interviews. Julia Freeman and Gillian Chilibeck, Anthropology Department, McGill University, conducted the interviews at Howard University and transcribed and coded the data.

69 Martin Richards, Lay and Professional Knowledge of Genetics and Inheritance. Public Understanding of Science 5 (1996): 217–230.

70 J. Turney, The Public Understanding of Science – Where Next? European Journal of Genetics in Society 1(2) (1995): 5–22 at p. 12.

71 Lock et al., Susceptibility Genes and the Question of Embodied Identity.

72 Results from the REVEAL quantitative interviews show that 80% of a sub-group of people who tested 3/3 were very positive about the study, and 67% had lower anxiety levels about AD than they did prior to the study: S. LaRusse et al., Genetic Susceptibility Testing Versus Family History-Based Risk Assessment: Impact on Perceived Risk of Alzheimer Disease. Genetic in Medicine 7(1) (2005): 48–53.

73 Arthur Kleinman, The Illness Narratives: Suffering, Healing, and the Human Condition (New York, Basic Books, 1988).

74 A. Kerr et al., The New Human Genetics and Health: Mobilizing Lay Expertise. Public Understanding of Science 7(1) (1998): 41–60.

75 Lock, et al., Susceptibility Genes and the Question of Embodied Identity.

76 Phillipa Brice, Barcode Babies: Prospects for Genetic Profiling. Biolines (2004): http:// www.cambridgenetwork.co.uk/pooled/profiles/BF_COMP/view.asp?Q=BF_COMP_ 9786.

77 P. Yoon et al., Public Health Impact of Genetic Tests at the End of the Twentieth Century. Genetics in Medicine 3 (2001): 405–410.

14   Human Difference Revisited

1 Geoffrey C. Bowker and Susan Leigh Star, Sorting Things Out: Classification and Its Consequences (Cambridge, MA: MIT Press, 1999).

2 Bowker and Star, Sorting Things Out: 231.

3 John Ray, The Wisdom of God Manifested in the Creation (London, 1691).

4 Carl Linnaeus, Systema Naturae (Leiden, 1735).

5 Cited in M. Banton, Racial Consciousness (New York: Longman, 1988): 4.

6 M. F. A. Montagu, The Concept of Race (Toronto: Collier-Macmillan, 1964): 3.

7 Nancy Leys Stepan, Race and Gender: The Role of Analogy in Science. Isis 77 (1986): 261–277.

8 Louis Agassiz, Evolution and Permanence of Type. Atlantic Monthly 33 (1874): 92–101.

9 Stepan, Race and Gender: 263.

10 Montagu, The Concept of Race.

11 L. Bennet, Before the *Mayflower*: A History of the Negro in America 1619–1964, (London: Penguin Books, 1966); R. Cooper and R. David, The Biological Concept of Race and Its Application to Public Health and Epidemiology. Journal of Health Politics, Policy and Law 11(1) (1986): 97–116.

12 Ian Hacking, Why Race Still Matters. Daedalus 134(1) (2005): 102–116 at p. 112.

13 T. Dobzhansky, Mankind Evolving: The Evolution of the Human Species (New Haven: Yale University Press, 1962): 267.

14 S. J. Gould, Ever Since Darwin: Reflections on Natural History (London: Burnett Books, 1973): 232.

15   N. J. Sauer, Forensic Anthropology and the Concept of Race: If Races Don't Exist, Why
     Are Forensic Anthropologists So Good at Identifying Them? Social Science and Medicine
     34 (1992): 109.

16   Duana Fullwiley, The Molecularization of Race: Institutionalizing Human Difference in
     Pharmacogenetics Practice. Science as Culture 16 (2007): 1–30.

17   Steven Epstein, Inclusion: The Politics of Difference in Medical Research (Chicago:
     University of Chicago Press, 2007).

18   National Institutes of Health (NIH) Revitalization Act of 1993. P.L. 103–43, approved
     June 10, 1993. See also Epstein, Inclusion.

19   Steven Epstein, Bodily Difference and Collective Identities: The Politics of Gender and
     Race in Biomedical Research in the United States. Body and Society 10 (2004): 183–203
     at p. 119.

20   Francis S. Collins, What We Do and Don't Know About "Race," "Ethnicity," Genetics
     and Health at the Dawn of the Genome Era, Nature Genetics Supplement 36(11) (2004):
     S13–S15.

21   N. Risch et al., Categorization of Humans in Biomedical Research: Genes, Race and
     Disease. Genome Biology, 3(7) (2002): 1–12; E. G. Burchard et al., The Importance of
     Race and Ethnic Background in Biomedical Research and Clinical Practice. New England
     Journal of Medicine 348(12) (2003): 1170–1175; A. J. Wood, Racial Differences in the
     Response to Drugs – Pointers to Genetic Differences. New England Journal of Medicine
     344(18) (2001): 1393–1396.

22   Nucleotides are the structural units of RNA and DNA.

23   Lynn B. Jorde and Stephen P. Wooding, Genetic Variation, Classification and "Race."
     Nature Genetics 36 (2004): S28–S33.

24   Malcolm Gladwell, The Sports Taboo. New Yorker, May 19, 1997, http://www.
     gladwell.com/1997/1997_05_19_a_sports.htm

25   L. B. Jorde et al., Using Mitochondrial and Nuclear DNA Markers to Reconstruct Human
     Evolution. Bioessays 20(2) (1998): 126–136.

26   M. D. Shriver et al., The Genomic Distribution of Population Substructure in Four
     Populations Using 8,525 Autosomal SNPs. Human Genomics 1(4) (2004): 274–286;
     A. M. Bowcock et al., High Resolution of Human Evolutionary Trees with Polymorphic
     Microsatellites. Nature 368(6470) (1994): 455–457; J. L. Mountain and L. L. Cavalli-
     Sforza, Multilocus Genotypes, a Tree of Individuals, and Human Evolutionary History.
     The American Journal of Human Genetics 61(3) (1997): 705–718; S. A. Tishkoff and
     K. K. Kidd, Implications of Biogeography of Human Populations for "Race" and Medicine.
     Nature Genetics Supplement 36(11) (2004): S21–S27.

27   Jorde and Wooding, Genetic Variation, Classification and "Race": S30.

28   Jorde and Wooding, Genetic Variation, Classification and "Race": S30; M. W. Feldman
     et al., Race: A Genetic Melting-Pot. Nature 424(6947) (2003): 374.

29   Jorde and Wooding, Genetic Variation, Classification and "Race": S30.

30   G. Barbujani et al., An Apportionment of Human DNA Diversity. Proceedings of the
     National Academy of Sciences 94(9) (1997): 4516–4519; L. L. Cavalli-Sforza et al.,
     Demic Expansions and Human Evolution. Science 259(5095) (1993): 639–646.

31   Barry Barnes and John Dupré, Genomes and What to Make of Them (Chicago: University
     Of Chicago Press, 2008): 102.

32   J. F. Blumenbach, On the Natural Varieties of Mankind, trans. and ed. T. Bendyshe
     (1776; reprint, New York: Bergman Publishers, 1969); Charles Darwin, The Descent of
     Man, and Selection in Relation to Sex (London: John Murray, 1871).

33   Jorde and Wooding, Genetic Variation, Classification and "Race": S32.

34   Since 2000 it has been possible in the United States to choose the option "mark one or
     more" when selecting among the possible categories of ethnic/racial affiliation permitted

in the United States, making it possible for individuals who know themselves to be of "mixed race" to give some indication of the situation.

35   Otis W. Brawley, Response to "Inclusion of Women and Minorities in Clinical Trials and the NIH Revitalization Act of 1993 – the Perspective of the NIH Clinical Trialists". Controlled Clinical Trials 16 (1995): 293–295.

36   Fullwiley, The Molecularization of Race: 13–17.

37   L. Braun, Race, Ethnicity, and Health. Perspectives in Biology and Medicine 45(2) (2002): 159–174; R. S. Cooper et al., Race and Genomics. New England Journal of Medicine 348(12) (2003): 1166–1170; M. W. Foster and R. R. Sharp, Race, Ethnicity, and Genomics: Social Classifications as Proxies of Biological Heterogeneity. Genome Research 12(6) (2002): 844–850; S. S. J. Lee et al., The Meanings of Race in the New Genomics: Implications for Health Disparities Research. Yale Journal of Health Policy and Ethics 1 (2001): 33–75; P. Ossorio and T. Duster, Race and Genetics: Controversies in Biomedical, Behavioral, and Forensic Sciences. American Psychologist 60(1) (2005): 115–128 at p. 116.

38   Michael Montoya, Bioethnic Conscription: Genes, Race, and Mexicana/o Ethnicity in Diabetes Research. Cultural Anthropology 22(1) (2007): 94–128 at p. 95.

39   Montoya, Bioethnic Conscription: 94.

40   Montoya, Bioethnic Conscription: 95–96.

41   J. V. Neel, Diabetes Mellitus: A "Thrifty" Genotype Rendered Detrimental by "Progress"? American Journal of Human Genetics 14 (1962): 353–362.

42   Montoya, Bioethnic Conscription: 117; see also Ian Whitmarsh, Hyperdiagnostics: Postcolonial Utopics of Race-Based Biomedicine. Medical Anthropology 28 (2009): 285–315.

43   Montoya, Bioethnic Conscription: 97–98.

44   Adam Hedgecoe, The Politics of Personalised Medicine, Cambridge Studies in Society and the Life Sciences (Cambridge: Cambridge University Press, 2004).

45   Troy Duster, Medicalization of Race. The Lancet 369 (2007): 702–703.

46   Jonathan Kahn, Getting the Numbers Right: Statistical Mischief and Racial Profiling in Heart Failure Research. Perspectives in Biology and Medicine 46 (2003): 473–483.

47   N. E. Risch et al., Categorization of Humans in Biomedical Research: Genes, Race and Disease. Genome Biology 3 (2002); E. G. Buchard, et al., Latino Populations: A Unique Opportunity for the Study of Race, Genetics, and Social Environment in Epidemiological Research. American Journal of Public Health 95 (2003): 2161–2168.

48   Stephan Palmié, Genomics, Divination, "Racecraft." American Ethnology 34(2) (2007): 206.

49   Palmié, Genomics, Divination, "Racecraft": 207.

50   Charles N. Rotimi, Genetic Ancestry Tracing and the African Identity: A Double-Edged Sword? Developing World Bioethics 3 (2003): 151–158.

51   Karen E. Fields, Political Contigencies of Witchcraft in Colonial Central Africa: Culture and the state in Marxist Theory. Canadian Journal of African Studies/Revue Canadienne des Etudes Africaines 16(3) (1985): 567–593.

52   Palmié, Genomics, Divination, "Racecraft": 214.

53   Palmié, Genomics, Divination, "Racecraft": 214.

54   Robert A. Hahn et al., Inconsistencies in Coding of Race and Ethnicity Between Birth and Death in U.S. Infants. A New Look at Infant Mortality, 1983 through 1985. Journal of the American Medical Association 267(2) (1992): 259–263; Nancy Krieger and Mary Bassett, Health of Black Folk: Disease, Class, and Ideology in Science. *In* The Racial Economy of Science: Toward a Democratic Future, ed. Sandra Harding (Indianapolis: Indiana University Press, 1993): 161–169; Tukufu Zuberi, Thicker Than Blood: How Racial Statistics Lie (Minneapolis: University of Minnesota Press, 2001).

55 Jonathon Kahn, How a Drug Becomes "Ethnic": Law, Commerce, and the Production of Racial Categories in Medicine. Yale Journal of Health Policy, Law and Ethics 4 (2004): 1–46.

56 Ian Hacking, Making up People. *In* Reconstructing Individualism: Autonomy, Individuality, and Self in Western Thought, ed. T. C. Heller et al. (Stanford: Stanford University Press, 1986): 222–236; see especially page 228.

57 V. L. Bonham et al., Race and Ethnicity in the Genome Era: The Complexity of the Constructs. American Psychologist 60 (2005): 9–15; Burchard et al., Latino Populations: 2161–2168; Cooper et al., Race and Genomics: 1166–1170; Rick A. Kittles and Kenneth M. Weiss, Race, Ancestry and Genes: Implications for Defining Disease Risk. Annual Review of Genomics and Human Genetics 4(1) (2003): 33–67.

Epilogue

1 Paolo Macchiarini et al., Clinical Transplantation of a Tissue-Engineered Airway. The Lancet 372(9655) (2008): 2023–2030.

2 Daniel Bates, British Surgeon Amputates Teenage Boy's Shoulder in Congo with Instructions Texted from a Friend in London. Daily Mail Online, (December 2, 2008), http://www.dailymail.co.uk/news/worldnews/article-1091315/

3 Pierre Fournier, personal communication.

4 Stephen J. Collier and Aihwa Ong, Global Assemblages, Anthropological Problems. *In* Global Assemblages: Technology, Politics, and Ethics as Anthropological Problems, ed. Aihwa Ong and Stephen J. Collier (Oxford: Blackwell Publishing, 2005): 3–21.

5 Peter Keating and Alberto Cambrosio, Biomedical Platforms: Realigning the Normal and the Abnormal in Twentieth Century Medicine (Cambridge, MA. MIT Press 2003).

6 Pascale Bourret et al., A New Clinical Collective for French Cancer Genetics. Science, Technology and Human Values 31 (2006): 431–464.

7 Alberto Cambrosio et al., Genomic Platforms and Hybrid Formations. *In* The Handbook of Genetics and Society: Mapping the New Genomic Era, ed. Paul Atkinson et al. (London: Routledge, 2009): 502–520.

8 Hans-Jorg Rheinberger, What Happened to Molecular Biology? Biosocieties 3(3) (2008): 303–310.

9 Benjamin Paul ed. Health, Culture and Community: Case Studies of Public Reactions to Health Programs (New York: Russell Sage Foundation 1955); Sandra D. Lane and Robert A. Rubinstein, International Health: Problems and Programs in Anthropological Perspective. *In* Medical Anthropology: Contemporary Theory and Method, ed. Carolyn F. Sargent and Thomas M. Johnson (Westport, CT: Praeger, 1996): 396–424.

10 Stephen Palumbi, Humans as the World's Greatest Evolutionary Force. Science 293(5536) (2001): 1786–1790.

11 See also, Mark Nichter, Global Health: Why Cultural Perceptions, Social Representations, and Biopolitics Matter (Tuscon: University of Arizona Press, 2008).

12 Arthur Kleinman et al., eds., Social Suffering (Berkeley: University of California Press, 1997); Arthur Kleinman and Joan Kleinman, How Bodies Remember: Social Memory and Bodily Experience of Criticism, Resistance, and Delegitimation following China's Cultural Revolution. New Literary History 25 (1994): 707–723; Didier Fassin, When Bodies Remember: Experiences and Politics of AIDS in South Africa (Berkeley: University of California Press, 2007); Veena Das, Critical Events: An Anthropological Perspective on Contemporary India (Delhi: Oxford University Press, 1995).

Bibliography

Abadie, Alberto, and Sebastian Gay
    2006 The Impact of Presumed Consent Legislation on Cadaveric Organ Donation: A Cross-Country Study. Journal of Health Economics 25:599–620.
Adams, Vincanne
    1998 Modes of Production and Medicine: An Examination of the Theory in Light of Sherpa Medical Traditionalism. Social Science and Medicine 27:505–514.
    2002 Randomized Crime. Social Studies of Science 32:659–690.
    2002 The Sacred and the Scientific: Ambiguous Practices of Science in Tibetan Medicine. Cultural Anthropology 16:542–575.
    2005 Saving Tibet? An Inquiry into Modernity, Lies, and Beliefs. Medical Anthropology 24:71–110.
    2006 Integrating Abstraction: Modernizing Medicine at Lhasa's Mentsikhang. In Soundings in Tibetan Medicine: Anthropological and Historical Perspectives. M. Schrempf, ed. Pp. 29–44. Leiden: Brill.
Adams, Vincanne, and Fei-Fei Li
    2008 Integration or Erasure? Modernizing Medicine at Lhasa's Mentsikhang. In Tibetan Medicine in the Contemporary World: Global Politics of Medical Knowledge and Practice. L. Pordié, ed. Pp. 105–131. London: Routledge.
Adas, Michael
    1989 Machines as the Measure of Man: Science, Technology, and Ideologies of Western Dominance. Ithaca: Cornell University Press.
Adelson, Naomi
    2000 "Being Alive Well": Health and Politics of Cree Well-Being. Toronto: University of Toronto Press.
Ad Hoc Committee of the Harvard Medical School to Examine the Definition of Death
    1968 A Definition of Irreversible Coma. Journal of the American Medical Association 205(6):85–88.
Agamben, Giorgio
    1988 Homo Sacer: Sovereign Power and Bare Life. Stanford: Stanford University Press.
Agassiz, Louis
    1874 Evolution and Permanence of Type. Atlantic Monthly 33:92–101.
Agnihotri, Satish Balram
    2000 Sex Ratio Patterns in the Indian Population: A Fresh Exploration. London: Sage.

Akkad, Omar el
    2007 Plane Crash Kills Organ Transplant Team. Globe and Mail. July 12: A3.
Albertson, Leana J., ed.
    2008 Genetic Discrimination. Hauppauge, NY: Nova Science Publishers.
Almeling, René
    2007 Selling Genes, Selling Gender: Egg Agencies, Sperm Banks, and the Medical Market in Genetic Material. American Sociological Review 72:319–340.
Almond, D., and L. Edlund
    2008 Son-Biased Sex Ratios in the 2000 United States Census. Proceedings of the National Academy of Sciences 105(15):5681–5682.
Almqvist, Elisabeth, Shelin Adam, Maurice Bloch, Anne Fuller, Philip Welch, Debbie Eisenberg, et al.
    1997 Risk Reversals in Predictive Testing of Huntington Disease. American Journal of Human Genetics 61:945–952.
Alphonso, Caroline
    2007 Brain-Damaged Man Reawakened. Globe and Mail. August 2.
Altman, Lawrence K.
    2007 Agent at Border, Aware, Let in Man with TB. New York Times, June 1. http://www.nytimes.com/2007/06/01/health/01tb.html
American Child Health Association (ACHA)
    1934 Physical Defects: The Pathway to Correction. New York: American Child Health Association.
Anagnost, Ann
    1995 A Surfeit of Bodies: Population and the Rationality of the State in Post-Mao China. *In* Conceiving the New World Order: The Global Politics of Reproduction. F. D. Ginsburg and R. Rapp, eds. Pp. 22–41. Berkeley: University of California Press.
Anderson, Siwan, and Debraj Ray
    In press. Missing Women: Age and Disease. Journal of Economic Literature Classification Numbers 11.
Anderson, Walter Truett
    2004 The Upstart Spring: Esalen and the Human Potential Movement: The First Twenty Years. Lincoln, NE: Authors Guild Backinprint.com.
Anderson, Warwick
    2000 The Possession of *Kuru*: Medical Science and Biocolonial Exchange. Comparative Studies in Society and History 42(4):713–744.
    2006 Colonial Pathologies: American Tropical Medicine, Race, and Hygiene in the Philippines. Durham, NC: Duke University Press.
    2008 The Collectors of Lost Souls: Turning *Kuru* Scientists into Whitemen. Baltimore: Johns Hopkins University Press.
Andrews, Keith
    1993 Recovery of Patients after Four Months or More in Persistent Vegetative State. British Medical Journal 306:1597–1600.
Angastiniotis, M.
    1990 Cyprus: Thalassaemia Programme. The Lancet 336(8723):1119–1120.
Angell, Marcia
    1997 The Ethics of Clinical Research in the Third World. New England Journal of Medicine 337:847–849.
    2004 The Truth About the Drug Companies: How They Deceive Us and What To Do About It. New York: Random House.
    2009 Drug Companies and Doctors: A Story of Corruption. New York: Review of Books 56:8–12.

Annas, George J.
 1990 Outrageous Fortune: Selling Other People's Cells. Hastings Center Report 20:36–39.
Apetrei, Christian, Joseph Becker, Michael Metzger, Rajeev Gautam, John Engle, Anne Katherine Wales, et al.
 2006 Potential for HIV Transmission Through Unsafe Injections. AIDS 20 (7):1074–1076.
Appadurai, Arjun
 1986 Introduction: Commodities and the Politics of Value. *In* The Social Life of Things: Commodities in Cultural Perspective. A. Appadurai, ed. Pp. 3–63. Cambridge: Cambridge University Press.
 1990 Disjuncture and Difference in the Global Cultural Economy. Public Culture 2:1–24.
Applebaum, Kalman
 2002 Marketing and Commoditization. Social Analysis (44):106–128.
Apse, Kira, Barbara B. Biesecker, Francis M. Giardiello, Barbara P. Fuller, and Barbara A. Bernhardt
 2004 Perceptions of Genetic Discrimination Among At-Risk Relatives of Colorectal Cancer Patients. Genetics in Medicine 6:510–516.
Armstrong, David
 2007 Professionalism, Indeterminacy and the EBM Project. BioSocieties 2:73–84.
Armstrong, Elizabeth M.
 2003 Conceiving Risk, Bearing Responsibility: Fetal Alcohol Syndrome and the Diagnosis of Moral Disorder. Baltimore: Johns Hopkins University Press.
Árnason, Arnar, and Bob Simpson
 2003 Refractions Through Culture: The New Genomics in Iceland. Ethnos 68(4): 533–553.
Arnaut, R.
 2006 La Folie apprivoisée: L'approche unique du professeur Collomb pour traiter la folie. Paris: De Vecchi.
Arnold, David
 1988 Imperial Medicine and Indigenous Societies. Manchester: Manchester University Press.
 1988 Famine: Social Crisis and Historical Change. Oxford: Blackwell.
 1993 Colonizing the Body: State Medicine and Epidemic Disease in Nineteenth-Century India. Berkeley: University of California Press.
 1993 Medicine and Colonialism. *In* Companion Encyclopedia of the History of Medicine. W. F. Bynum and R. Porter, eds. Pp. 1393–1496. London: Routledge.
Aronson, Naomi E.
 2007 Leishmaniasis in American Soldiers: Parasites from the Front. *In* Emerging Infections 7. W. M. Scheld, D. Hooper, and J. Hughes, eds. Pp. 352–343. Washington, D.C.: ASM Press.
Asahi Shimbun, The
 2009 Diet OKs Revision to Ease Organ Law. July 14. http://www.asahi.com/english/Herald-asahi/TKY200907140020.html
Ashforth, Adam
 2005 Witchcraft, Violence and Democracy in South Africa. Chicago: University of Chicago Press.
Aumeeruddy-Thomas, Yildiz, and Yeshi C. Lama
 2008 Tibetan Medicine and Biodiversity Management in Dolpo, Nepal: Negotiating Local and Global Worldviews, Knowledge, and Practices. *In* Tibetan Medicine in the Contemporary World: Global Politics of Medical Knowledge and Practice. L. Pordié, ed. Pp. 160–186. London: Routledge.

Avis, Nancy E., and Sonja McKinlay
    1991 A Longitudinal Analysis of Women's Attitudes towards the Menopause: Results from the Massachusetts Women's Health Study. Maturitas 13:65–79.
Avis, Nancy, Patricia Kaufert, Margaret Lock, Sonja McKinlay, and Kerstin Vass
    1993 The Evolution of Menopausal Symptoms. Baillières Clinical Endocrinology and Metabolism 7:17–32.
Avorn, J.
    2007 Keeping Science on Top in Drug Evaluation. New England Journal of Medicine 35:633–635.
Bakwin, Harry
    1958 The Tonsil–Adenoidectomy Enigma. Journal of Pediatrics 52:343–344.
Bandyopadhyay, Mridula
    2003 Missing Girls and Son Preference in Rural India: Looking Beyond Popular Myth. Health Care for Women International 24:910–926.
Banton, M.
    1988 Racial Consciousness. New York: Longman.
Barad, Karen
    2007 Meeting the Universe Halfway: Quantum Physics and the Entanglement of Matter and Meaning. Durham, NC: Duke University Press.
Barbujani, G., A. Magagni, E. Minch, and L. L. Cavalli-Sforza
    1997 An Apportionment of Human DNA Diversity. Proceedings of the National Academy of Sciences 94(9):4516–4519.
Barlow, Maude, and Joanne J. Myers
    2002 Blue Gold: The Fight to Stop the Corporate Theft of the World's Water. New York: New Press.
Barnes, Barry, and John Dupré
    2008 Genomes and What to Make of Them. Chicago: University of Chicago Press.
Barrett, R. J.
    1988 Interpretations of Schizophrenia. Culture, Medicine and Psychiatry 12:357–388.
    2004 Kurt Schneider in Borneo: Do First Rank Symptoms Apply to the Iban? *In* Schizophrenia, Culture, and Subjectivity: The Edge of Experience. Janice H. Jenkins and Robert J. Barrett eds. Pp. 87–109. Cambridge: Cambridge University Press.
Barsoum, Rashad S.
    2002 Overview: End-Stage Renal Disease in the Developing World. Artificial Organs 26(9):737–746.
Baruch, Susannah, David Kaufman, and Kathy L. Hudson
    2008 Preimplantation Genetic Screening: A Survey of *in Vitro* Fertilization Clinics. Genetics in Medicine 10(9):685–690.
Basch, P.
    1999 Textbook of International Health. 2nd edition. Oxford: Oxford University Press.
Bates, Daniel
    2008 British Surgeon Amputates Teenage Boy's Shoulder in Congo with Instructions Texted from a Friend in London. Daily Mail Online. December 2. http://www.dailymail.co.uk/news/worldnews/article-1091315/
Baudrillard, Jean
    1993 Symbolic Exchange and Death. London: Sage.
BCC Research
    2008 Trends in Organ and Tissue Transplantation and Alternative Techniques (Report: HLC012D). Press Release: U.S. Market for Organ and Tissue Transplantation Worth $28.2 Billion in 2013 (October 20). http://www.bccresearch.com/pressroom/press_release.php?rcode=HLC012D.

Beals, Alan
    1976 Strategies of Resort to Curers in South India. *In* Asian Medical Systems: A Comparative Study. C. Leslie, ed. Pp. 184–200. Berkeley: University of California Press.
Beck, Stefan and Jörg Niewöhner
    2009 Translating Genetic Testing and Screening in Cyprus and Germany: Contingencies, Continuities, Ordering Effects and Bio-Cultural Intimacy. *In* Handbook of Genetics and Society: Mapping the New Genomic Era. P. Atkinson, P. Glasner and M. Lock, eds. Pp. 76–93. London: Routledge.
Beck, Ulrich
    1992 Risk Society: Towards a New Modernity. Trans. Mark Ritter. London: Sage.
Becker, Ernest
    1973 The Denial of Death. New York: Free Press.
Becker, Gay
    2000 The Elusive Embryo: How Women and Men Approach New Reproductive Technologies. Berkeley: University of California Press.
Beeson, Diane, and Teresa Doksum
    2001 Family Values and Resistance to Genetic Testing. *In* Bioethics in Social Context. B. Hoffmaster, ed. Pp. 153–179. Philadelphia: Temple University Press.
Bennet, L.
    1966 Before the *Mayflower*: A History of the Negro in America 1619–1964. London: Penguin Books.
Berg, Marc, and Annemarie Mol, eds.
    1998 Difference in Medicine: Unraveling Practices, Techniques, and Bodies. Durham, NC: Duke University Press.
Berg, Paul
    1991 All Our Collective Ingenuity Will Be Needed. Federation of American Societies for Experimental Biology 5(1):75–77.
Bertram, Lars, and Rudolph E. Tanzi
    2004 Alzheimer's Disease: One Disorder, Too Many Genes? Human Molecular Genetics 13:R135–R141.
Bertram, L., M. B. McQueen, K. Mullin, D. Blacker, and R. E. Tanzi
    2007 Systematic Meta-Analyses of Alzheimer Disease Genetic Association Studies: The AlzGene Database. Nature Genetics 39:17–23.
Betancourt, Joseph R.
    2005 Cultural Competence and Health Care Disparities: Key Perspectives and Trends. Health Affairs 24:499.
Beurton, Peter J., Raphael Falk, and Hans-Jörg Rheinberger
    2000 The Concept of the Gene in Development and Evolution: Historical and Epistemological Perspectives. Cambridge: Cambridge University Press.
Beyene, Yewoubdar
    1986 Cultural Significance and Physiological Manifestations of Menopause: A Biocultural Analysis. Culture, Medicine, and Psychiatry 10:47–71.
Beyene, Y., and M. C. Martin
    2001 Menopausal Experiences and Bone Density of Mayan Women in Yucatan, Mexico. American Journal of Human Biology 13:505–511.
Bharadwaj, Aditya
    2006 Sacred Conceptions: Clinical Theodicies,Uncertain Science, and Technologies of Procreation in India. Culture, Medicine and Psychiatry 30(4):451–465.
Biagioli, Mario, ed.
    1999 The Science Studies Reader. New York: Routledge.

Bibeau, Gilles
    2004 Le Québec transgénique: Science, marché, humanité. Montreal: Boréal Presse.
Bibeau, Gilles, and Duncan Pederson
    2002 A Return to Scientific Racism: The Case of Sexuality and the AIDS Epidemic in
    Africa. London: Routledge.
Biehl, João Guilherme, and Torben Eskerod
    2007 Will to Live: AIDS Therapies and the Politics of Survival. Princeton: Princeton
    University Press.
Bijke, Wiebe, Thomas P. Hughes, and Trevor Pinch
    1989 The Social Construction of Technological Systems: New Directions in the Sociology
    and History of Technology. Cambridge, MA: MIT Press.
Binski, Paul
    1996 Medieval Death: Ritual and Representation. Ithaca: Cornell University Press.
Blacker, Deborah, and Rudolph E. Tanzi
    2000 Genetic Testing in the Early Diagnosis of Alzheimer's Disease. *In* Early Diagnosis
    of Alzheimer's Disease. L. F. M. Scinto and K. R. Daffner, eds. Pp. 105–126. Totowa,
    NJ: Humana Press.
Bledsoe, Caroline
    1990 The Politics of Children: Fosterage and the Social Management of Fertility
    among the Mende of Sierra Leone. *In* Births and Power: Social Change and the
    Politics of Reproduction. W. P. Handwerker, ed. Pp. 81–100. Boulder, CO: Westview
    Press.
    2002 Contingent Lives: Fertility, Time, and Aging in West Africa. Chicago: University
    of Chicago Press.
Bledsoe, Caroline, and Monica Goubaud
    1988 The Reinterpretation and Distribution of Western Pharmaceuticals: An Example
    from the Mende of Sierra Leone. *In* The Context of Medicine in Developing Countries:
    Studies in Pharmaceutical Anthropology. Sjaak Van der Geest and Susan Reynolds Whyte,
    eds. Pp. 253–276. Dordrecht: Kluwer Academic Publishers.
Bledsoe, Caroline, Jennifer A. Johnson-Kuhn, and John G. Haaga, eds.
    1992 Critical Perspectives on Schooling and Fertility in the Developing World. Washington
    D.C.: National Academies Press.
Blue, Amy V., and Atwood D. Gaines
    1992 The Ethnopsychiatric Repertoire: A Review and Overview of Ethnopsychiatric
    Studies. *In* Ethnopsychiatry: The Cultural Construction of Professional and Folk Psy-
    chiatries. A. D. Gaines, ed. Pp. 397–484. Binghampton: State University of New York
    Press.
Blumenbach, J. F.
    1969 [1776] On the Natural Varieties of Mankind. T. Bendyshe trans. and ed. New York:
    Bergman Publishers.
Boddy, Janice
    2007 Civilizing Women: British Crusades in Colonial Sudan. Princeton: Princeton
    University Press.
    2007 Remembering Amal: On Birth and the British in Northern Sudan. *In* Beyond the
    Body Proper: Reading the Anthropology of Material Life. M. Lock and J. Farquhar, eds.
    Pp. 315–329. Durham, NC: Duke University Press.
Bongaarts, J.
    1978 A Framework for Analyzing the Proximate Determinants of Fertility. Population
    and Development Review 24:15–57.
    1982 The Fertility-Inhibiting Effects of the Intermediate Fertility Variables. Studies in
    Family Planning 13:179–198.

Bonham, V. L., E. Warhauer-Baker, and F. S. Collins
2005 Race and Ethnicity in the Genome Era: The Complexity of the Constructs. American Psychologist 60:9–15.

Book, Patricia
1980 Death at an Early Age: Thalassemia in Cyprus. Medical Anthropology Quarterly: Cross Cultural Studies in Health and Illness 2:1–39.

Bosse, Dietrich, Michaela Praus, Peter Kiessling, Lars Nyman, Corina Andresen, Joanne Waters, et al.
2005 Phase I Comparability of Recombinant Human Albumin and Human Serum Albumin. Journal of Clinical Pharmacology 45:57–67.

Boulet, M. J., B. J. Oddens, and P. Lehert
1994 Climacteric and Menopause in Seven South-East Asian Countries. Maturitas 19:157–176.

Bourret, Pascale, Andrei Mogoutov, Claire Julian-Reynier, and Alberto Cambrosio
2006 A New Clinical Collective for French Cancer Genetics. Science, Technology and Human Values 31:431–464.

Bovery, Amy
2008 Japan's Hidden Youth: Mainstreaming the Emotionally Distressed in Japan. Culture Medicine and Psychiatry 32:552–576.

Bowcock, A. M., A. Ruiz-Linares, J. Tomfohrde, E. Minch, J. R. Kidd, and L. L. Cavalli-Sforza
1994 High Resolution of Human Evolutionary Trees with Polymorphic Microsatellites. Nature 368(6470):455–457.

Bowker, G. C., and S. L. Star
1999 Sorting Things Out: Classification and Its Consequences. Cambridge, MA: MIT Press.

Boyle, James
1996 Shamans, Software and Spleens: Law and the Construction of the Information Society. Cambridge, MA: Harvard University Press.

Bradley, R., and R. Corwyn
2002 Socioeconomic Status and Child Development. Annual Review of Psychology 53: 169–189.

Braidotti, Rosi
1989 Organs Without Bodies. Differences: A Journal of Feminist Cultural Studies 1:147–161.

Brantley, Cynthia
1997 Kikuyu-Maasai Nutrition and Colonial Science. The Orr and Gilks Study in Late 1920s Kenya Revisited. International Journal of African Historical Studies 30(1):49–86

Braun, L.
2002 Race, Ethnicity, and Health. Perspectives in Biology and Medicine 45(2):159–174.

Brawley, Otis W.
1995 Response to "Inclusion of Women and Minorities in Clinical Trials and the NIH Revitalization Act of 1993 – the Perspective of the NIH Clinical Trialists." Controlled Clinical Trials 16:293–295.

Breitner, J. C.
1999 The End of Alzheimer's Disease? International Journal of Geriatric Psychiatry 14(7): 577–586.

Brian, Éric, and Marie Jaisson
2007 The Descent of Human Sex Ratio at Birth: A Dialogue between Mathematics, Biology and Sociology. Methodos Series, 4. New York: Springer.

Brice, Phillipa
2004 Barcode Babies: Prospects for Genetic Profiling. Biolines, http://www.cambridgenetwork.co.uk/pooled/profiles/BF_COMP/view.asp?Q=BF_COMP_9786.

Briggs, Charles
2004 Theorizing Modernity Conspiratorially: Science, Scale, and the Political Economy of Public Discourse in Explanations of a Cholera Epidemic. American Ethnologist 31:164–187.
Briggs, Charles L., and Clara Mantini-Briggs
2004 Stories in the Time of Cholera: Racial Profiling During a Medical Nightmare. Berkeley: University of California Press.
Brodwin, Paul
1996 Medicine and Morality in Haiti: The Contest for Healing Power. Cambridge: Cambridge University Press.
Browner, Carole
2007 Can Gender "Equity" in Prenatal Genetic Services Unintentionally Reinforce Male Authority? *In* Reproductive Disruptions: Gender, Technology, and Biopolitics in the New Millennium. M. Inhorn, ed. Pp. 147–164. New York: Berghahn Books.
Browner Carole H. and Mabel H. Preloran
Forthcoming, 2010 Neurogenetic Diagnoses : The Power of Hope and the Limits of Today's Medicine. London: Routledge.
Brumberg, Joan Jacobs
1988 Fasting Girls: A History of Anorexia Nervosa. Cambridge, MA: Harvard University Press.
Bullard, Alice
2005 L'Oedipe africain: A Retrospective. Transcultural Psychiatry 42:187.
Burchard, E. G., E. Ziv, N. Coyle, S. L. Gomez, H. Tang, A. J. Karter, et al.
2003 The Importance of Race and Ethnic Background in Biomedical Research and Clinical Practice. New England Journal of Medicine 348(12):1170–1175.
2003 Latino Populations: A Unique Opportunity for the Study of Race, Genetics, and Social Environment in Epidemiological Research. American Journal of Public Health 95:2161–2168.
Burchell, Graham, Colin Gordon, and Peter Miller
1991 The Foucault Effect: Studies in Governmentality. Chicago: University of Chicago Press.
Burke, T.
1996 Lifebuoy Men, Lux Women: Commodification, Consumption, and Cleanliness in Modern Zimbabwe. Durham, NC: Duke University Press.
Burri, Regula Valérie, and Joseph Dumit
2007 Biomedicine as Culture: Instrumental Practices, Technoscientific Knowledge, and New Modes of Life. New York: Routledge.
Burrows, Beth
1996 Second Thoughts about U.S. Patent #4,438,032. GeneWatch 10:4–7.
Burton, J. L., and M. Wells
2002 The Alder Hey Affair. Archives of Disease in Childhood 86:4–7.
Buss, D.
2007 Evolutionary Psychology: The New Science of the Mind. Boston: Allyn and Bacon.
Butler, Don
2008 Antibiotics Don't Kill Viruses. If You Know That, You're in the Minority; Most Canadians Think They Know the Rules, but Poll Shows Widespread Misinformation. The Gazette, Montreal, July 22.
Bynum, Caroline Walker
1992 Fragmentation and Redemption. New York: Zone Books.
Bynum, W. F.
1994 Science and the Practice of Medicine in the Nineteenth Century. Cambridge: Cambridge University Press.

Cain, Carole
    1991 Identity Acquisition and Self-Understanding in Alcoholics Anonymous. Ethos 19(2):210–253.
Caldwell, John, and Pat Caldwell
    1987 The Cultural Context of High Fertility in Sub-Saharan Africa,. Population and Development Review 13(3):409–437.
Callon, Michel
    1986 Some Elements of a Sociology of Translation: Domestication of the Scallops and the Fishermen of St. Brieuc Bay. *In* Power, Action and Belief: A New Sociology of Knowledge? J. Law, ed. Pp. 196–229. London: Routledge and Kegan Paul.
Callon, M., and V. Rabeharisoa
    2004 Gino's Lesson on Humanity: Genetics, Mutual Entanglements and the Sociologist's Role. Economy and Society 33:1–27.
Cambrosio, Alberto, and Keating, Peter
    1995 Exquisite Specificity: The Monoclonal Antibody Revolution. New York: Oxford University Press.
Cambrosio, Alberto, Peter Keating, and Pascale Bourret
    2009 Genomic Platforms and Hybrid Formations. *In* Handbook of Genetics and Society: Mapping the New Genomic Era. P. Atkinson, P. Glasner, and M. Lock, eds. Pp. 502–520. London: Routledge.
Canadian Cancer Society
    2007 Breast Cancer Rate Dropping. Canadian Cancer Statistics 2007. http://www.cancer.ca/Canada-wide
Canguilhem, Georges
    1988 Ideology and Rationality in the History of the Life Sciences. Cambridge, MA: MIT Press.
    1991 The Normal and the Pathological. New York: Zone Books.
Cardon, Lon
    2009 Translating Complex Disease Genes Into New Medicines. Paper delivered at the Colston Symposium, The New Genomics: Public Health, Social and Clinical Implications. Bristol University, United Kingdom.
Carlsen, William
    2001 Did Modern Medicine Spread an Epidemic? San Francisco Chronicle, January 15: A11.
Carpenter, K. J.
    2003 A Short History of Nutritional Science: Part 3 (1912–1944). Journal of Nutrition 133:3023–3032.
Carson, Ronald A., Jamie L. Frias, and Richard J. Melker
    1981 Case Study: Research with Brain Dead Children. Journal of Medical Humanities 3:50–53.
Castel, Robert
    1991 From Dangerousness to Risk. *In* The Foucault Effect: Studies in Governmentality. G. Burchell, C. Gordon, and P. Miller, eds. Pp. 281–298. Chicago: University of Chicago Press.
Cavalli-Sforza, L. L., P. Menozzi, and A. Piazza
    1993 Demic Expansions and Human Evolution. Science 259(5095):639–646.
Champagne, F., and M. J. Meaney
    2001 Like Mother, Like Daughter: Evidence for Non-Genomic Transmission of Parental Behavior and Stress Responsivity. Progress in Brain Research 133:287–302.
Chatterjee, Nilanjana
    2001 Planning an Indian Modernity: The Gendered Politics of Fertility Control. Signs 26:812–845.

Chen, Zhiwei, Paul Telfer, Agegenehu Gettie, Patricia Reed, Linqi Zhang, David D. Ho et al.
1996 Genetic Characterization of New West African Simian Immunodeficiency Virus Sivsm: Geographic Clustering of Household-Derived SIV Strains with Human Immunodeficiency Virus Type 2 Subtypes and Genetically Diverse Viruses from a Single Feral Sooty Mangabey Troop. Journal of Virology 70(6):3617–3627.

Chevalier, Michel
1840 L'Europe et la Chine. Revue des Deux Mondes 23:209–255.

Childerhose, Janet
2009 Genetic Discrimination: Biography of an American Problem. Ph.D. dissertation, Department of Anthropology, McGill University, Montreal.

Chin, James
2007 The AIDS Pandemic: The Collision of Epidemiology with Political Correctness. New York: Radcliffe.

China Daily
2007 China Warned of Risks of Imbalanced Sex Ratio. August 24.

Chitnis. A., D. Rawls and J. Moore
2000 Origin of HIV Type 1 in Colonial French Equatorial Africa? AIDS Research and Human Retroviruses 16(1):5–8.

Chrisman, Noel, and Arthur Kleinman
1983 Popular Health Care, Social Networks, and Cultural Meanings: The Orientation of Medical Anthropology. *In* Handbook of Health, Health Care, and Health Professions. D. Mechanic, ed. Pp. 569–589. New York: Free Press.

Christianson, Arnold, and Bernadette Modell
2004 Medical Genetics in Developing Countries. Annual Reviews of Genomics and Human Genetics 5:219–265.

Christie, Jean
1996 Whose Property, Whose Rights? Cultural Survival Quarterly 20:34–36.

Chu, Junhong
2001 Prenatal Sex Determination and Sex-Selective Abortion in Rural Central China. Population and Development Review 27:259–281.

Clark, Adele E., Laura Mamo, Janet K. Shim, Jennifer R. Fishman, and Jennifer Ruth Fosket
2000 Technoscience and the New Biomedicalization: Western Roots, Global Rhizomes. Sciences Sociales et Santé 18(2):11–42.

Clottes, Jean, and David Lewis Williams
1998 The Shamans of Prehistory: Trance and Magic in the Painted Caves. New York: Harry N. Abrams.

Cobb, L. A.
1959 Evaluation of Internal Mammary Artery Ligation by Double-Blind Technique. New England Journal of Medicine 260:1115–1118.

Cochrane Injuries Group Albumin Reviewers
1998 Human Albumin Administration in Critically Ill Patients: Systematic Review of Randomised Controlled Trials. British Medical Journal 317:235–240.

Cocks, Michelle, and Anthony Dolk
2000 The Role of "African Chemists" in the Health Care System of the Eastern Cape Province of South Africa. Social Science and Medicine 51:1505–1515.

Cohen, Lawrence
1998 No Aging in India: Alzheimer's, the Bad Family, and Other Modern Things. Berkeley: University of California Press.
1999 Where It Hurts: Indian Material for an Ethics of Organ Transplantation. Daedalus 128(4):135–165.

2004 Operability: Surgery at the Margin of the State. *In* Anthropology in the Margins of the State. V. Das and D. Poole, eds. Pp. 165–190. Santa Fe: School of American Research Press.

2005 Operability, Bioavailability, and Exception. *In* Global Assemblages: Technology, Politics, and Ethics as Anthropological Problems. A. Ong and S. J. Collier, eds. Pp. 79–90. Oxford: Blackwell.

Cohen, W. B.

1983 Malaria and French Imperialism. Journal of African History 24:23–26.

Colen, Shellee

1990 "Housekeeping" for the Green Card: West Indian Household Workers, the State, and Stratified Reproduction in New York. *In* At Work in Homes: Household Workers in World Perspective. American Anthropological Monograph 3. R. Sanjek and S. Colen, eds. Pp. 89–118. Washington D.C.: American Anthropological Association.

Collier, Stephen J., and Aihwa Ong

2005 Global Assemblages, Anthropological Problems. *In* Global Assemblages: Technology, Politics, and Ethics as Anthropological Problems. A. Ong and S. J. Collier, eds. Pp. 3–21. Oxford: Blackwell.

Collinge J., J. Whitfield, E. McKintosh, J. Beck, S. Mead, D. J. Thomas, et al.

2006 *Kuru* in the Twenty-First Century – An Acquired Human Prion Disease with Very Long Incubation Periods. The Lancet 367:2068–2074.

Collins, Francis

2003 Future Visions: How Will Genetics Change Our Lives? Time Magazine 161(7), February 17:42.

2004 What We Do and Don't Know About "Race," "Ethnicity," Genetics, and Health at the Dawn of the Genome Era. Nature Genetics Supplement 36(11):S13–S15.

Collins, J. A., W. Wrixon, L. B. James, and E. H. Wilson 1983 Treatment-Independent Pregnancy Among Infertile Couples. New England Journal of Medicine 309:1201–1206.

Collins, James W., Richard J. David, Arden Handler, Stephen Wall, and Steven Andes

2004 Very Low Birthweight in African American Infants: The Role of Maternal Exposure to Interpersonal Racial Discrimination. American Journal of Public Health 94:2132–2138.

Collins, James W., Richard David, Rebecca Symons, Arden Handler, Stephen Wall, and Lisa Dwyer

2000 Low-Income African-American Mothers' Perception of Exposure to Racial Discrimination and Infant Birth Weight. Epidemiology 11:337–339.

Comaroff, Jean

1985 Body of Power, Spirit of Resistance: The Culture and History of a South African People. Chicago: University of Chicago Press.

1993 The Diseased Heart of Africa. *In* Knowledge, Power, and Practice: the Anthropology of Medicine and Everyday Life. S. Lindenbaum and M. Lock, eds. Pp. 305–329. Berkeley: University of California Press.

Comaroff, Jean and John Comaroff, eds.

1993 Modernity and Its Malcontents: Ritual and Power in Postcolonial Africa. Chicago: University of Chicago Press.

Comaroff, John and Jean Comaroff

1992 Ethnography and the Historical Imagination. Boulder, CO: Westview Press.

Connelly, Matthew

2008 Fatal Misconception: The Struggle to Control World Population. Cambridge, MA: Belknap Press of Harvard University Press.

Conrad, Peter

1992 Medicalization and Social Control. Annual Review of Sociology 18:209–232.

1994 Wellness as Virtue: Morality and the Pursuit of Health. Culture, Medicine, and Psychiatry 18:385–401.

2006 Up, Down and Sideways. Social Science and Modern Society 43:19–20.

2007 The Medicalization of Society: On the Transformation of Conditions into Treatable Disorders. Baltimore: Johns Hopkins University Press.

Conrad, Peter, and Joseph Schneider

1980 Looking at Levels of Medicalization: A Comment on Strong's Critique of the Thesis of Medical Imperialism. Social Science and Medicine 14A:75–79.

Cook, Harold

2007 Matters of Exchange. New Haven: Yale University Press.

Cooper, R. and David, R.

1986 The Biological Concept of Race and Its Application to Public Health and Epidemiology. Journal of Health Politics, Policy and Law 11(1):97–116.

Cooper, R. S., J. S. Kaufman, and R. Ward

2003 Race and Genomics. New England Journal of Medicine 348(12):1166–1170.

Corbo, R. M., and R. Scacchi

1999 Apolipoprotein E (APOE) Allele Distribution in the World: Is APOEε4 a "Thrifty" Allele? Annals of Human Genetics 63:301–310.

Corder, E. H., A. M. Saunders, W. J. Strittmatter, D. E. Schmechel, P. C. Gaskell, G. W. Small, et al.

1993 Gene Dose of Apolipoprotein E Type 4 Allele and the Risk of Alzheimer's Disease in Late Onset Families. Science 261(5123):921–923.

Cornwall, Andrea

2001 Looking for a Child: Coping with Infertility in Ado-Odo, South-Western Nigeria. *In* Managing Reproductive Life: Cross-Cultural Themes in Fertility and Sexuality. S. Tremayne, ed. Pp. 140–156. New York: Berghahn Books.

Corrigan, Oonagh

2004 Informed Consent: The Contradictory Ethical Safeguards in Pharmacogenetics. *In* Genetic Databases: Socio-Ethical Issues in the Collection and Use of DNA. R. Tutton and O. Corrigan, eds. Pp. 78–96. London: Routledge.

Couzin, Jennifer

2003 Crossing a Frontier: Research on the Dead. Science 299:29–30.

Covington, Sharon N., and William E. Gibbons

2007 What Is Happening to the Price of Eggs? Obstetrical and Gynecological Survey 62(9):589–590.

Cox, S, and W. McKellin

1999 "There's This Thing in Our Family": Predictive Testing and the Construction of Risk for Huntington Disease. *In* Sociological Perspectives on the New Genetics. P. Conrad and J. Gabe, eds. Pp. 121–148. London: Blackwell.

Crandon-Malamud, Libbet

1991 From the Fat of Our Souls: Social Change, Political Process, and Medical Pluralism in Bolivia. Berkeley: University of California Press.

Cranford, Ronald

1998 Even the Dead Are Not Terminally Ill Anymore. Neurology 51(6):1530–1531.

1998 The Vegetative and Minimally Conscious States: Ethical Implications. Geriatrics 53(1):S70–S73.

Crawford, Robert

1977 You Are Dangerous to Your Health: The Ideology and Politics of Victim Blaming. International Journal of Health Services 7:633–680.

1985 A Cultural Account of "Health": Control, Release, and the Social Body. *In* Issues in the Political Economy of Health Care. J. B. McKinlay, ed. Pp. 60–106. New York: Tavistock Publications.

Croll, Elisabeth
2000 Endangered Daughters: Discrimination and Development in Asia. London: Routledge.

Crombie, A. C.
1981 Philosophical Presuppositions and the Shifting Interpretations of Galileo. *In* Theory Change, Ancient Axiomatics, and Galileo's Methodology. Volume 1. J. Hintikka, D. Gruender and E. Agazzi eds. Pp. 271–286. Boston: Reidel.

Crosby, Alfred W.
1997 The Measure of Reality: Quantification and Western Society, 1250–1600. Cambridge: Cambridge University Press.

Crowley-Matoka, Megan
2005 Desperately Seeking "Normal": The Promise and Perils of Living with Kidney Transplantation. Social Science and Medicine 61:821–831.
In press. Producing Transplanted Bodies: Life, Death and Value in Mexican Organ Transplantation. Durham, NC: Duke University Press.

Crowley-Matoka, Megan, and Robert M. Arnold
2004 The Dead Donor Rule. How Much Does the Public Care … and How Much Should We Care? Kennedy Institute of Ethics Journal 14:319–332.

Crowley-Matoka, Megan, and Margaret Lock
2006 Organ Transplantation in a Globalised World. Mortality 11(2):166–181.

Cunningham, Andrew, and Perry Williams, eds.
2002 The Laboratory Revolution in Medicine. Cambridge: Cambridge University Press.

Curtin, Philip D.
1989 Death by Migration: Europe's Encounter with the Tropical World in the Nineteenth Century. Cambridge: Cambridge University Press.
1998 Disease and Empire: The Health of European Troops in the Conquest of Africa. Cambridge: Cambridge University Press.

Cussins, Charis
1996 Ontological Choreography: Agency through Objectification in Infertility Clinics. Social Studies of Science 8:575–610.

Dabis, François, Philippe Msellati, Nicolas Meda, Christiane Welffens-Ekra, Bruno You, Olivier Manigart, et al.,
1999 6-Month Efficacy, Tolerance, and Acceptability of a Short Regimen of Oral Zidovudine to Reduce Vertical Transmission of HIV in Breastfed Children in Côte-d'Ivoire and Burkina Faso: A Double-Blind Placebo-Controlled Multicentre Trial. The Lancet 35(6):786–793.

Daniel, Valentine
1991 Is There a Counterpoint to Culture? Wertheim Lecture, Center for Asian Studies, Amsterdam.

Darwin, Charles
1871 The Descent of Man, and Selection in Relation to Sex. London: John Murray.

Das Gupta, Monica
1987 Selective Discrimination against Female Children in Rural Punjab, India. Population and Development Review 13:77–100.

Das Gupta, Monica, Sunhwa Lee, Susan Uberoi, Danning Wang, Lihong Wang, and Xiaodan Zhang
2004 State Policies and Women's Agency in China, the Republic of Korea, and India, 1950–2000: Lessons from Contrasting Experiences. *In* Culture and Public Action. V. Rao and M. Walton, eds. Pp. 234–259. Stanford: Stanford University Press.

Das, Veena
  1995 Critical Events: An Anthropological Perspective on Contemporary India. Delhi: Oxford University Press.
  2000 The Practice of Organ Transplants: Networks, Documents, Translations. *In* Living and Working with the New Medical Technologies: Intersections of Inquiry. M. Lock, A. Young, and A. Cambrosio, eds. Pp. 263–287. Cambridge: Cambridge University Press.
  2007 Life and Worlds: Violence and the Descent into the Ordinary. Berkeley: University of California Press.
Das, Veena, and Ranendra K. Das
  2005 Urban Health and Pharmaceutical Consumption in Delhi, India. Journal of Biosocial Science 36:69–82.
Das, Veena, and Deborah Poole
  2004 The State and its Margins. *In* Anthropology in the Margins of the State. V. Das and D. Poole, eds. Pp. 3–34. Santa Fe: School of American Research Press.
Daston, Lorraine
  1988 Classical Probability in the Enlightenment. Princeton: Princeton University Press.
  1995 The Moral Economy of Science. Osiris 10:3–26.
Daston, Lorraine, and Peter Galison
  2007 Objectivity. New York: Zone Books.
Daston, Lorraine, and Katharine Park
  1998 Wonders and the Order of Nature. New York: Zone Books.
Davenport, Charles B.
  1910 Eugenics: The Science of Human Improvement by Better Breeding. New York: Henry Holt.
David, Paul A.
  1986 Understanding the Economics of QWERTY: The Necessity of History. *In* Economic History and the Modern Economist. W. N. Parker, ed. Pp. 30–49. Oxford: Blackwell.
Davies, M. H.
  1976 The Origins and Practice of Psychodrama. British Journal of Psychiatry 129: 201–206.
Davis, B. D.
  1990 The Human Genome and Other Initiatives. Science 4:2941–2.
Davis, Devra
  2009 A Secret History of the War on Cancer. New York: Basic Books.
Davis, Mike
  2006 Planet of Slums. London: Verso.
Davis, Wade
  1988 Passage of Darkness: The Ethnobiology of the Haitian Zombie. Chapel Hill: University of North Carolina Press.
de Witte, Joke I., and Henk ten Have
  1997 Ownership of Genetic Material and Information. Social Science and Medicine 45:51–60.
Debaun, Michael R., Emily L. Niemitz, and Andrew P. Feinberg
  2003 Association of In-Vitro Fertilization with Beckwith-Wiedemann Syndrome and Epigenetic Alteration of LIT1 and H19. American Journal of Human Genetics 72: 156–160.
Delaney, Carol 1991 The Seed and the Soil: Gender and Cosmology in Turkish Village Society. Berkeley: University of California Press.
Dena, Carroll, and Cecilia Benoit
  2004 Aboriginal Midwifery in Canada: Merging Traditional Practices and Modern Science. *In* Reconceiving Midwifery. I. L. Bourgeault, C. Benoit, and R. Davis-Floyd, eds. Pp. 263–286. Montreal: McGill-Queens University Press.

Desai, D. V., and Hiren Dhanani
  2004 Sickle Cell Disease: History and Origin. The Internet Journal of Hematology 1(2). http://www.ispub.com/ostia/index.php?xmlPrinter=true&xmlFilePath=journals/ijhe/vol1n2/sickle.xml

Dikotter, Frank
  1998 Imperfect Conceptions: Medical Knowledge, Birth Defects, and Eugenics in China. New York: Columbia University Press.

Dobzhansky, T.
  1962 Mankind Evolving: The Evolution of the Human Species. New Haven: Yale University Press.

Domergues-Cloarec, Danielle
  1986 Histoire de la santé en Côte-d'Ivoire. Toulouse: Presses Universitaires du Mirail.
  1986 Politique coloniale française et réalités coloniales: la santé en Côte d'Ivoire, 1905–1958. 2 vols. Paris: Académie des Sciences d'Outre-Mer.

Douglas, Mary
  1990 Risk as a Forensic Resource. Daedalus 119:1–16.

Dozon, Jean Pierre
  1985 Quand les Pastoriens traquaient la maladie du sommeil. Sciences Sociales et Santé 3:27–56.
  1991 D'un tombeau à l'autre. Cahiers d'Études Africaines 31:135–157.
  2008 Une Anthropologie en movement: L'Afrique miroir du contemporain. Paris: Quae Éditions.

Draper, Elaine
  1991 Risky Business: Genetic Testing and Exclusionary Practices in the Hazardous Workplace. Cambridge: Cambridge University Press.

Dreze, Jean, and Amartya Sen
  2002 India: Development and Participation. Oxford: Oxford University Press.

Dumit, Joseph
  Forthcoming Drugs for Life: Growing Health through Facts and Pharmaceuticals. Durham, NC: Duke University Press.

Dunn, Ardys McNaughton
  2002 Cultural Competence and the Primary Care Provider. Journal of Pediatric Health Care 16:105.

Dunn, Fred L.
  1976 Traditional Asian Medicine and Cosmopolitan Medicine as Adaptive Systems. *In* Asian Medical Systems. C. Leslie. ed. Pp. 133–158. Berkeley: University of California Press.

Duster, Troy
  1990 Backdoor to Eugenics. 2nd edition. New York: Routledge.
  2003 Buried Alive: The Concept of Race in Science. *In* Genetic Nature/Culture: Anthropology and Science Beyond the Two-Culture Divide. A. H. Goodman, D. Heath and M. S. Lindee, eds. Pp. 258–277. Berkeley: University of California Press.
  2007 Medicalization of Race. The Lancet 369:702–703.

Eagleton, Terry
  1993 It Is Not Quite True that I Have a Body, and Not Quite True that I Am One Either. London Review of Books. May 27:7.

East, E. M.
  1917 Hidden Feeblemindedness. Journal of Heredity 8:215–217.

Echenberg, Myron
  2005 "For Their Own Good": The Pasteur Institute and the Quest for an Anti-Yellow Fever Vaccine in French Colonial Africa. *In* Conquêtes médicales: Histoire de la médecine moderne et des maladies en Afrique. J.-P. Bado, ed. Pp. 57–73. Paris: Karthala.

2007 Plague Ports: The Global Urban Impact of Bubonic Plague, 1894–1901. New York: New York University Press.

Ecks, Stefan
2005 Pharmaceutical Citizenship, Antidepressant Marketing and the Promise of Demarginalization in India. Anthropology and Medicine 12:239–254.

Economist, The
2008 Racing Down the Pyramid: Big Drugmakers' Love Affair with America Is Coming to an End. November 15.

Eddy, Sean R.
2001 Non-Coding RNA Genes and the Modern RNA World. Nature Reviews/Genetics 2:919–929.

Edwards, J., S. Franklin, E. Hirsch, F. Price, and M. Strathern
1993 Technologies of Procreation: Kinship in the Age of Assisted Conception. Manchester: Manchester University Press.

Russell, Alec
2005 Alistair Cooke's Bones Stolen by Transplant Gang. Daily Telegraph, December 23. http://www.telegraph.co.uk/news/worldnews/northamerica/usa/1506150/Alistair-Cookes-bones-stolen-by-transplant-gang.html

Ehrlich, Paul R.
1968 The Population Bomb. New York: Ballantine Books.

Ekstein, J., and H. Katzenstein
2001 The Dor-Yeshorim Story: Community-Based Carrier Screening for Tay-Sachs Disease. Advances in Genetics 44:297–310.

Ellenberger, Henri F.
1970 Discovery of the Unconscious. New York: Basic Books.
1966 The Pathogenic Secret and Its Therapy. Journal of the History of Behavioral Sciences 2:29–42.

Elliott, Larry
2009 World Bank Millions Fail to Boost Health of Poor. Guardian Weekly, May 8–14:1.

Ember, C. R., and M. Ember, eds.
2003 Encyclopedia of Medical Anthropology: Health and Illness in the World's Cultures. Dordrecht: Kluwer Academic Plenum Publishers.

Enright, Anne
2000 What's Left of Henrietta Lacks? London Review of Books 22(8):8–10. http://www.lrb.co.uk/v22/n08/enri01_.html

Epstein, Helen
2007 The Invisible Cure: Africa, the West and the Fight Against AIDS. New York: Farrar, Straus and Giroux.
2008 The Strange History of Birth Control. New York Review of Books. August 14:57–59. http://www.nybooks.com/contents/20080814

Epstein, Steven
2004 Bodily Difference and Collective Identities: The Politics of Gender and Race in Biomedical Research in the United States. Body and Society 10:183–203.
2007 Inclusion: The Politics of Difference in Medical Research. Chicago: University of Chicago Press.

Erin, Charles A., and John Harris
2003 An Ethical Market in Human Organs. Journal of Medical Ethics 29:137–138.

Erwin, Kathleen
2006 The Circulatory System: Blood Procurement, AIDS, and the Social Body in China. Medical Anthropology Quarterly 20(2):139–159.

Estroff, Sue E.

1993 Identity, Disability and Schizophrenia: The Problem of Chronicity. *In* Knowledge, Power, and Practice: The Anthropology of Medicine and Everyday Life. S. Lindenbaum and M. Lock, eds. Pp. 247–286. Berkeley: University of California Press.

ETC Group

2007 Extreme Genetic Engineering: An Introduction to Synthetic Biology. http://www. etcgroup.org/en/materials/publications.html?pub_id=602

Etkin, Nina

2003 The Co-Evolution of People, Plants, and Parasites: Biological and Cultural Adaptations to Malaria. Proceedings of the Nutrition Society 62:311–317.

Evans, Robert G., Morris L. Barer, and Theodore R. Marmor, eds.

1994 Why Are Some People Healthy and Others Not? The Determinants of Health of Populations. New Brunswick, NJ: Aldine Transaction.

Evans-Pritchard, E. E.

1937 Witchcraft, Oracles, and Magic among the Azande. Oxford: Clarendon Press.

Ewald, François

1991 Insurance and Risk. *In* The Foucault Effect: Studies in Governmentality. G. Burchell, C. Gordon, and P. Miller, eds. Pp. 197–210. Hemel Hempstead: Harvester Wheatsheaf.

Faber, Celia

2006 Out of Control. AIDS and the Corruption of Medical Science. Harper's, March. http://www.harpers.org/archive/2006/03/0080961

Fairhead, J., M. Leach, and M. Small

2005 Public Engagement with Science: Local Understandings of a Vaccine Trial in the Gambia. Journal of Biosocial Science 38:103–116.

2006 Where Techno-Science Meets Poverty: Medical Research and the Economy of Blood in the Gambia, West Africa. Social Science and Medicine 63:1118.

Farlow, M. R., Y. He, S. Tekin, J. Xu, R. Lane, and H. C. Charles

2004 Impact of APOE in Mild Cognitive Impairment. Neurology 63:1898–1901.

Farmer, Paul

1998 Infections and Inequalities. Berkeley: University of California Press.

2003 Pathologies of Power: Health, Human Rights, and the New War on the Poor. California Series in Public Anthropology 4. Berkeley: University of California Press.

2006 AIDS and Accusation: Haiti and the Geography of Blame. Updated edition with a new preface. Comparative Studies of Health Systems and Medical Care. Berkeley: University of California Press.

Farmer, Paul, Margaret Connors, and Janie Simmons, eds.

1996 Women, Poverty, and AIDS. Monroe, ME: Common Courage Press.

Farquhar, Judith

1994 Knowing Practice: The Clinical Encounter in Chinese Medicine. Boulder, CO: Westview Press.

1995 Re-Writing Traditional Medicine in Post-Maoist China. *In* Knowledge and the Scholarly Medical Tradition. D. Bates, ed. Pp. 251–276. Cambridge: Cambridge University Press.

Farrer, Lindsay A.

2000 Familial Risk for Alzheimer's Disease in Ethnic Minorities: Nondiscriminating Genes. Archives of Neurology 57:28–29.

Farrer, Lindsay A., Tatyana Sherbatich, Sergey A. Keryanov, Galina I. Korovaitseva, Ekaterina A. Rogaeva, Svetlana Petruk, et al.

2000 Association Between Angiotensin-Converting Enzyme and Alzheimer Disease. Archives of Neurology 57(2):210–214.

Fassin, Didier
2001 Culturalism as Ideology. *In* Cultural Perspectives on Reproductive Health. C. M. Obermeyer, ed. Pp. 300–318. Oxford: Oxford University Press.
2007 When Bodies Remember: Experiences and Politics of AIDS in South Africa. Berkeley: University of California Press.

Featherstone, Katie, Paul Atkinson, Aditya Bharadwaj, and Angus Clarke
2006 Risky Relations: Family, Kinship and the New Genetics. Oxford: Berg.

Feierman, Steven
2000 Explanation and Uncertainty in the Medical World of Ghaambo. Bulletin of the History of Medicine 74:317–344.

Feldbaum, Carl
1996 Gene Patents Deemed Essential to Next Generation of Cures. GeneWatch 10:10.

Feldman, M. W., R. C. Lewontin, and M. C. King
2003 Race: A Genetic Melting-Pot. Nature 424(6947):374.

Feldman-Savelsberg, Pamela
2002 Is Infertility an Unrecognized Public Health and Population Problem? The View from the Cameroon Grasslands. *In* Infertility Around the Globe: New Thinking on Childlessness, Gender, and Reproductive Technologies. M. Inhorn and F. van Balen, eds. Pp. 215–232. Berkeley: University of California Press.

Fernandez-Llimos, F., L. Tuneu, M. I. Baena, A. Garcia-Delgado, M. J. Faus
2004 Morbidity and Mortality Associated with Pharmacotherapy: Evolution and Current Concepts of Drug-Related Problems. Current Pharmaceutical Design 10(31):3947–3967.

Ferzacca, Steve
2002 Governing Bodies in New Order Indonesia. *In* New Horizons in Medical Anthropology: Essays in Honour of Charles Leslie. M. Nichter and M. Lock, eds. Pp. 35–57. London: Routledge.

Fidler, David
2004 SARS: Governance and the Globalization of Disease. London: Palgrave Macmillan.

Fields, Karen E.
1985 Political Contigencies of Witchcraft in Colonial Central Africa: Culture and the State in Marxist Theory. Canadian Journal of African Studies/Revue Canadienne des Etudes Africaines 16(3):567–593.

Finkler, Kaja
2000 Experiencing the New Genetics: Kinship and Family on the Medical Frontier. Philadelphia: University of Pennsylvania Press.
2001 The Kin in the Gene: The Medicalization of Family and Kinship in American Society. Current Anthropology 42:235–263.

Finkler, Kaja, Cécile Skrzynia, and James P. Evans
2003 The New Genetics and Its Consequences for Family, Kinship, Medicine, and Medical Genetics. Social Science and Medicine 57:403–412.

Fischer, Michael
2007 Culture and Cultural Analysis as Experimental Systems. Cultural Anthropology 22:1–64.

Fleck, Ludwik
1979 (1935). Genesis and the Development of a Scientific Fact. Chicago: University of Chicago Press.

Flint, M., F. Kronenberg, and W. Utian, eds. 1990 Multidisciplinary Perspectives on Menopause. New York: New York Academy of Sciences.

Fong, Vanessa 2004 Only Hope: Coming of Age Under China's One-Child Policy. Stanford: Stanford University Press.

Ford, John
1971 The Role of Trypanosomiasis in African Ecology: A Study of the Tsetse Fly Problem. Oxford: Clarendon Press.

Fortes, Meyer
1966 Some Reflections on Ancestor Worship in Africa. Oxford: Oxford University Press.

Foster, M. W., and R. R. Sharp
2002 Race, Ethnicity, and Genomics: Social Classifications as Proxies of Biological Heterogeneity. Genome Research 12(6):844–850.

Foucault, Michel
1978 The History of Sexuality, vol. 1: The Will to Knowledge. Trans. Robert Hurley. New York: Pantheon.
1979 Discipline and Punish: The Birth of the Prison. New York: Vintage.
1986 The History of Sexuality, vol. 2: The Use of Pleasure. Trans. Robert Hurley. New York: Pantheon Books.
1991 Governmentality. Trans. Rosi Braidotti and revised by Colin Gordon. *In* The Foucault Effect: Studies in Governmentality. Graham Burchell, Colin Gordon, and Peter Miller, eds. Pp. 87–104. Chicago: University of Chicago Press.
1994 The Birth of the Clinic: An Archeology of Medical Perception. New York: Vintage Books.
1998 Technologies of the Self. *In* Technologies of the Self. Luther Martin, H. Gutman, and P. H. Hutton, eds. Pp. 16–49. Boston: University of Massachusetts Press.

Fox, Renée, and Judith P. Swazey
1978 The Courage to Fail: A Social View of Organ Transplants and Dialysis. Chicago: University of Chicago Press.
1992 Spare Parts: Organ Replacement in American Society. Oxford: Oxford University Press.

Frake, Charles O.
1961 The Diagnosis of Disease among the Subanum of Mindanao. American Anthropologist 63:113–132.

Frankenberg, Ronald
1980 Medical Anthropology and Development: A Theoretical Perspective. Social Science and Medicine 14b:197–207.

Franklin, Sarah
1991 Fetal Fascinations: The Construction of Fetal Personhood and the Alton Debate. *In* Off-Centre: Feminism and Cultural Studies. S. Franklin, C. Lury, and J. Stacey, eds. Pp. 190–205. London: Unwin Hyman.
1995 Life. *In* The Encyclopedia of Bioethics. W. T. Reich, ed. Pp. 456–462. New York: Simon and Schuster.
1997 Embodied Progress: A Cultural Account of Assisted Conception. London: Routledge.
2001 Sheepwatching. Anthropology Today 17(3):3–9.

Franklin, Sarah, and Margaret Lock
2003 Animation and Cessation: The Remaking of Life and Death. *In* Remaking Life and Death: Toward an Anthropology of the Biosciences. S. Franklin and M. Lock, eds. Pp. 3–22. Santa Fe: School of American Research Press.

Franklin, Sarah, and Helena Ragone, eds.
1998 Reproducing Reproduction: Kinship, Power, and Technological Innovation. Philadelphia: University of Pennsylvania Press.

Franklin, Sarah, and Celia Roberts
2006 Born and Made: An Ethnography of Preimplantation Genetic Diagnosis. Princeton: Princeton University Press.

Franklin, Sarah, Jackie Stacey, and Celia Lury
    2000 Global Nature, Global Culture London: Sage.
Freedman, R. R.
    2001 Physiology of Hot Flashes. American Journal of Human Biology 13:453–464.
Frenk, Julio, José Luis Bobadilla, Claudio Stern, Tomas Frejka, and Rafael Lozano
    1991 Elements for a Theory of the Health Transition. Health Transition Review: The
    Cultural, Social and Behavioural Determinants of Health 1(1):21–38.
Freud, Sigmund
    1939 Civilization, War, and Death: Selections from Three Works by Sigmund Freud.
    J. Richman, ed. London: Hogarth Press and the Institute of Psychoanalysis.
Friedlander, Dov, and Calvin Goldscheider
    1979 The Population of Israel. New York: Columbia University Press.
Friedlander, M. M.
    2002 Viewpoint: The Right to Sell or Buy a Kidney: Are We Failing Our Patients? The
    Lancet 359(9310):971–973.
Fukuyama, Francis
    2002 Our Posthuman Future: Consequences of the Biotechnology Revolution. New
    York: Farrar, Straus, and Giroux.
Fullwiley, Duana
    2004 Discriminate Biopower and Everyday Politics: Views on Sickle Cell Testing in Dakar.
    Medical Anthropology 23:157–194.
    2007 The Molecularization of Race: Institutionalizing Human Difference in Pharma-
    cogenetics Practice. Science as Culture 16(1):1–30.
Gaines, Atwood D., ed.
    1992 Ethnopsychiatry: The Cultural Construction of Professional and Folk Psychiatries.
    Albany: State University of New York Press.
Gajdusek, Carlton D., ed.
    1963 *Kuru* Epidemiological Patrols from the New Guinea Highlands to Papua 1957.
    Bethesda, MD: National Institutes of Health.
Gay, Peter
    1977 The Enlightenment: An Interpretation. New York: W. W. Norton and
    Company.
Geary, Patrick J.
    1994 Living With the Dead in the Middle Ages. Ithaca: Cornell University Press.
Gee, Marcus
    2009 The Cruel Irony of China's One-Child Policy. The Globe and Mail. May 8. http://
    www.realclearworld.com/2009/05/08/cruel_irony_of_chinas_one-child_policy_
    100547.html
Geertz, Clifford
    1973 The Interpretation of Cultures. New York: Basic Books.
    1995 After the Fact: Two Decades, Four Countries, One Anthropologist. Cambridge
    MA: Harvard University Press.
    1995 Culture War. New York Review of Books. November 30:4–6.
Gelbart, W.
    1998 Data Bases in Genomic Research. Science 282:660.
Gerrits, Trudie
    2002 Infertility and Matrilineality: The Exceptional Case of the Macua of Mozambique.
    In Infertility Around the Globe: New Thinking on Childlessness, Gender, and Reproduc-
    tive Technologies. M. Inhorn and F. van Balen, eds. Pp. 233–246. Berkeley: University
    of California Press.

Ghods, A. J., and S. Savaj
    2006 Iranian Model of Paid and Regulated Living-Unrelated Kidney Donation. Clinical Journal of the American Society of Nephrology 1(6):1136–1145.
Gibbon, Sahra
    2007 Breast Cancer Genes and the Gendering of Knowledge: Science and Citizenship in the Context of the "New" Genetics. London: Palgrave Macmillan.
Gibbon, Sahra, and Carlos Novas, eds.
    2007 Biosocialities, Genetics, and the Social Sciences. London: Routledge.
Gibbs, W. Wayt
    2003 The Unseen Genome: Gems Among the Junk. Scientific American 289(5):47–53.
Gifford, Sandra
    1986 The Meaning of Lumps: A Case Study of the Ambiguities of Risk. *In* Anthropology and Epidemiology: Interdisciplinary Approaches to the Study of Health and Disease. C. R. Janes, R. Stall, and S. M. Gifford, eds. Pp. 213–246. Dordrecht: Reidel.
Gilbert, Scott F.
    2002 The Genome in Its Ecological Context: Philosophical Perspectives on Interspecies Epigenesis. Annals of the New York Academy of Sciences 981:202–218.
Gilbert, Walter
    1992 A Vision of the Grail. *In* The Code of Codes: Scientific and Social Issues in the Human Genome Project. D. J. Kevles and L. Hood, eds. Pp. 83–97. Cambridge, MA: Harvard University Press.
Ginsburg, Faye
    1993 Aboriginal Media and the Australian Imaginary. Public Culture 5:557–578.
Ginsburg, F, and Rayna Rapp
    1995 Conceiving the New World Order: The Global Politics of Reproduction. Berkeley: University of California Press.
Gladwell, Malcolm
    1997 The Sports Taboo. New Yorker, May 19. http://www.gladwell.com/1997/1997_05_19_a_sports.htm
Gokhale, Ketaki
    2006 Indian Couples Seek Out U.S. Sex Selection Clinics. India West, June 30. http://news.pacificnews.org/news/view_article.html?article_id=54a58cce914f335cb8fb6e722aa1028d
Gold, E, G. Block, S. Crawford, L. Lachance, G. Fitzgerald, H. Miracle, and S. Sherman
    2004 Lifestyle and Demographic Factors in Relation to Vasomotor Symptoms: Baseline Results from the Study of Women's Health Across the Nation (SWAN). American Journal of Epidemiology 159(12):1189–1199.
Gold, E., J. Bromberger, S. Crawford, S. Samuels, G. Greendale, S. Harlow, and J. Skurnick
    2001 Factors Associated with Age at Natural Menopause in a Multiethnic Sample of Midlife Women. American Journal of Epidemiology 153(9):865–874.
Good, Byron J.
    1977 The Heart of What's the Matter: The Semantics of Illness in Iran. Culture, Medicine and Psychiatry 1:25–58.
    1994 Medicine, Rationality, and Experience: An Anthropological Perspective. Cambridge: Cambridge University Press.
Good, Byron J., and Mary-Jo DelVecchio Good
    1982 Toward a Meaning Centered Analysis of Popular Illness Categories: "Fright Illness" and "Heart Distress" in Iran. *In* Cultural Conceptions of Mental Health and Therapy. A. Marsella and G. White, eds. Pp. 141–166. Dordrecht: D. Reidel.

1993 "Learning Medicine": The Construction of Medical Knowledge at Harvard Medical School. *In* Knowledge, Power, and Practice: the Anthropology of Medicine and Everyday Life. S. Lindenbaum and M. Lock, eds. Pp. 81–107. Berkeley: University of California Press.

2000 Clinical Narratives and the Study of Contemporary Doctor–Patient Relationships. *In* The Handbook of Social Studies in Health and Medicine. G. L. Albrecht, R. Fitzpatrick, and S. C. Scrimshaw, eds. Pp. 243–258. London: Sage.

Good, Mary-Jo DelVecchio, Byron J. Good, Paul E. Brodwin, and Arthur Kleinman
1992 Pain as Human Experience: An Anthropological Perspective. Berkeley: University of California Press.

Goodmann, Madeleine, and Lenn Goodmann
1982 The Overselling of Genetic Anxiety. Hastings Center Report, October 20–27: 20.

Gordon, Linda
2002 The Moral Property of Women: A History of Birth Control Politics in America. Urbana: University of Illinois Press.

Gould, S. J.
1973 Ever Since Darwin: Reflections on Natural History. London: Burnett Books.
1985 The Median Isn't the Message. Discover. June:40–42.

Granda, H., S. Gispert, A. Dorticos, M. Martin, Y. Cuadras, and M. Calvo
1991 Cuban Programme for Prevention of Sickle Cell Disease. The Lancet 337:152–153.

Green, Harvey
1986 Fit for America: Health Fitness, Sport, and American Society 1830–1940. New York: Pantheon.

Greenblatt, R. B., and A. Z. Teran
1987 Advice to Post-Menopausal Women. *In* The Climacteric and Beyond. L. Zichella, M. Whitehead, and P. A. V. Keep, eds. Pp. 39–53. Park Ridge, NJ: Parthenon Publishing Group.

Greenhalgh, Susan
2001 Managing "the Missing Girls" in Chinese Population Discourse. *In* Cultural Perspectives on Reproductive Health. C. M. Obermeyer, ed. Pp. 131–152. Oxford: Oxford University Press.
2003 Planned Birth, Unplanned Persons: "Population" in the Making of Chinese Modernity. American Ethnologist 30(2):196–215.
2005 Globalization and Population Governance in China. *In* Global Assemblages: Technology, Politics, and Ethics as Anthropological Problems. A. Ong and S. J. Collier, eds. Pp. 354–372. Oxford: Blackwell.
2008 Just One Child: Science and Policy in Deng's China. Berkeley: University of California Press.

Greenhalgh, S. and J. Bongaarts
1987 Fertility Policy in China: Future Options. Science 235:1167–1172.

Greenhalgh, Susan, and Edwin A. Winckler
2005 Governing China's Population: From Leninist to Neoliberal Biopolitics. Stanford: Stanford University Press.

Griffiths, Paul E.
2001 Developmental Systems Theory. *In* Nature Encyclopedia of the Life Sciences. London: Nature Publishing Group.

Groopman, Jerome
2008 Superbugs: Infections That Are Almost Impossible to Treat. New Yorker, August 11–18:46–55.

Gruskin, Sofia
    1999 Health and Human Rights: A Reader. New York: Routledge.
Gudding, Gabriel
    1996 The Phenotype/Genotype Distinction and the Disappearance of the Body. Journal of the History of Ideas 57(3):525–545.
Habermas, Jürgen
    2003 The Future of Human Nature. Cambridge: Polity Press.
Hacking, Ian
    1975 The Emergence of Probability. Cambridge: Cambridge University Press.
    1986 Making up People. *In* Reconstructing Individualism: Autonomy, Individuality, and Self in Western Thought. T. C. Heller, M. Sosna and D. E. Wellbery, eds. Pp. 222–236. Stanford: Stanford University Press.
    1990 The Taming of Chance. Cambridge: Cambridge University Press.
    1992 World-Making by Kind-Making: Child Abuse For Example. *In* How Classification Works: Nelson Goodman among the Social Sciences. M. Douglas and D. Hull, eds. Pp. 180–238. Edinburgh: Edinburgh University Press.
    1995 The Looping Effects of Human Kinds. *In* Causal Cognition: A Multidisciplinary Approach. D. Sperber, D. Premack, and A. J. Premack, eds. Pp. 351–383. Oxford: Oxford Medical Publications.
    1996 The Disunities of Science. *In* The Disunity of Science: Boundaries, Contexts and Power. P. Galison and D. Stump, eds. Pp. 37–74. Stanford: Stanford University Press.
    2005 Why Race Still Matters. Daedalus 134(1):102–116.
    2006 Making up People. London Review of Books, August 17:23–26. http://www.lrb.co.uk/contributors/hack01
Hahn, Robert A., Joseph Mulinare, and Steven M. Teutsch
    1992 Inconsistencies in Coding of Race and Ethnicity Between Birth and Death in U.S. Infants. A New Look at Infant Mortality, 1983 through 1985. Journal of the American Medical Association 267(2):259–263.
Hallowell, Irving A.
    1941 The Social Function of Anxiety in Primitive Society. American Sociology Review 6(6):869–81.
Hallowell, Nina
    1999 Doing the Right Thing: Genetic Risk and Responsibility. Sociology of Health and Illness 5:597–621.
Hamdy, Sherine
    2008 When the State and Your Kidneys Fail: Political Etiologies in an Egyptian Dialysis Ward. American Ethnologist 35:553–569.
Handwerker, L.
    1998 The Consequences of Modernity for Childless Women in China: Medicalization and Resistance. *In* Pragmatic Women and Body Politics. M. Lock and P. A. Kaufert, eds. Pp. 178–205. Cambridge: Cambridge University Press.
    2002 The Politics of Making Modern Babies in China: Reproductive Technologies and the New Genetics. *In* Infertility Around the Globe: New Thinking on Childlessness, Gender, and Reproductive Technologies. M. Inhorn and F. van Balen, eds. Pp. 298–314. Berkeley: University of California Press.
Hanley, Susan
    1985 Family and Fertility in Four Tokugawa Villages. *In* Family and Population in East Asian History. S. B. Hanley and A. P. Wolf, eds. Pp. 196–228. Stanford: Stanford University Press.
Hannaway, Caroline
    1993 Environment and Miasma. *In* Companion Encyclopedia of the History of Medicine, vol. I. W. F. Bynum and R. Porter, eds. P. 304. London: Routledge.

Haraoui, Louis-Patrick
2007 The Orientalist Sore: Biomedical Discourses, Capital and Urban Warfare in the Colonial Present. MSc thesis, Université de Montreal.

Haraway, Donna
1990 A Manifesto for Cyborgs: Science, Technology, and Socialist-Feminism in the 1980s. *In* Feminism/Postmodernism. L. J. Nicholson, ed. Pp. 190–233. London: Routledge.
1991 A Cyborg Manifesto: Science, Technology, and Socialist-Feminism in the Late Twentieth Century. *In* Simians, Cyborgs, and Women: The Reinvention of Nature. Pp. 149–181. New York: Routledge.
1991 Simians, Cyborgs, and Women: The Reinvention of Nature. New York: Routledge.
1997 Modest_Witness@Second_Millennium: FemaleMan©_Meets_Oncomouse™: Feminism and Technoscience. New York: Routledge.

Harcourt, Glenn
1987 Andreas Vesalius and the Anatomy of Antique Sculpture. Representations 17: 28–61.

Hardacre, Helen
1994 The Response of Buddhism and Shinto to the Issue of Brain Death and Organ Transplants. Cambridge Quarterly of Healthcare Ethics 3:585–601.

Harding, J. E.
2001 The Nutritional Basis of the Fetal Origins of Adult Disease. International Journal of Epidemiology 30:15–23.

Hardy, Anne, and M. Eileen Magnello
2002 Statistical Methods in Epidemiology: Karl Pearson, Ronald Ross, Major Greenwoood and Austin Bradford Hill, 1900–1945. *Sozial- und Präventivmedizin/Social and Preventive Medicine* 47(2):80–89.

Harmon, Amy
2007 After DNA Diagnosis: "Hello, Are You Just Like Me?" New York Times, December 28.

Harper, K. N., Paolo S. Ocampo, Bret M. Steiner, Robert W. George, Michael S. Silverman, Shelly Bolotin, et al.
2008 On the Origin of the Treponematoses: A Phylogenetic Approach. PLoS Neglected Tropical Diseases 2(1):e148. doi:10.1371/journal.pntd.0000148

Harrison, Mark
1996 Medicine and the Culture of Command: The Case of Malaria Control in the British Army during the Two World Wars. Medical History 40:437–452.
2004 Disease and the Modern World: 1500 to the Present Day. Cambridge: Polity Press.

Harvey, David
1996 Justice, Nature and the Geography of Difference. Oxford: Blackwell.

Haspels, A. A., and P. A. Van Keep
1979 Endocrinology and Management of the Peri-Menopause. *In* Psychosomatics in Peri-Menopause. A. A. Haspels and H. Musaph, eds. Pp. 57–71. Baltimore: University Park Press.

Hassan, Ahmed M., Hussein A. Sheashaa, Mohamed F. Abdel Fattah, Alla Z. Ibrahim, Osama A. Gaber, and Mohamed A. Sobh
2006 Study of Ochratoxin A as an Environmental Risk that Causes Renal Injury in Breast-Fed Egyptian Infants. Pediatric Nephrology 21(1):102–105.

Hayden, Cori
2007 Taking as Giving: Bioscience, Exchange, and the Politics of Benefit-Sharing. Social Studies of Science 37(5):729–758.

Haynes, Douglas
2000 Framing Tropical Disease in London: Patrick Manson, *Filaria Perstans*, and the Uganda Sleeping Sickness Epidemic, 1891–1902. Social History of Medicine 13:467–493.

Headrick, Daniel R.
1981 The Tools of Empire: Technology and European Imperialism in the Nineteenth Century. Oxford: Oxford University Press.
Headrick, R.
1994 Colonialism, Health and Illness in French Equatorial Africa, 1885–1935. Atlanta: African Studies Association Press.
Healy, David
1999 Clinical Trials and Legal Jeopardy. Bulletin of Medical Ethics 153:12–18.
2000 Antidepressant Induced Suicidality. Primary Care Psychiatry 6:23–28.
2000 Good Science or Good Business? Hastings Center Report 30:19–23.
2002 The Creation of Psychopharmacology. Cambridge, MA: Harvard University Press.
2004 Let Them Eat Prozac. New York: New York University Press.
2006 Did Regulators Fail Over Selective Serotonin Reuptake Inhibitors? British Medical Journal 333:92–95.
2006 Manufacturing Consensus. Culture, Medicine, and Psychiatry 30:135–156.
2006 The New Medical Oikumene. *In* Global Pharmaceuticals: Ethics, Markets, Practices. A. Petryna, A. Lakoff, and A. Kleinman, eds. Pp. 61–84. Durham, NC: Duke University Press.
Heath, Deborah
1998 Locating Genetic Knowledge: Picturing Marfan Syndrome and Its Traveling Constituencies. Science, Technology, and Human Values 23(1):71–97.
Heath, Deborah, Rayna Rapp, and Karen-Sue Taussig
2004 Genetic Citizenship. *In* A Companion to the Anthropology of Politics. D. Nugent and J. Vincent, eds. Pp. 152–167. London: Blackwell.
Hedgecoe, Adam
2001 Schizophrenia and the Narrative of Enlightened Geneticization. Social Studies of Science 31:875–911.
2004 The Politics of Personalised Medicine, Cambridge Studies in Society and the Life Sciences. Cambridge: Cambridge University Press.
Hedges, Stephen J., and William Gaines
2000 Donor Bodies Milled Into Growing Profits, Chicago Tribune, May 21. http://chicagotribune.com/news/nationworld/article/0,2669,ART-44908,FF.html
Heelas, P. L. F., and A. J. Lock, eds.
1981 Indigenous Psychologies: The Anthropology of the Self. London: Academic Press.
Heidegger, Martin
1962 Being and Time. New York: Harper and Row.
Heilbroner, Robert L.
1967 Do Machines Make History? Technology and Culture 8:335–345.
Helgason, Agnar
2001 The Ancestry and Genetic History of the Icelanders: An Analysis of MTDNA Sequences, Y Chromosome Haplotypes and Genealogy, Doctoral dissertation. Institute of Biological Anthropology, University of Oxford.
Heller, Michael A., and Rebecca S. Eisenberg
1998 Can Patents Deter Innovation? The Anticommons in Biomedical Research. Science 280(5364):698–701.
Hempel, Sandra
2006 The Medical Detective: John Snow and the Mystery of Cholera. London: Granta Books.
Henderson, Mark
2006 Rooting out the Genes Behind Breast Cancer. The Times, May 9. http://www.timesonline.co.uk/tol/news/uk/health/article714704.ece

Hendrick, Burton J.
1913 On the Trail of Immortality. McClure's 40:304–317.

Hertz, Robert
1973 The Pre-eminence of the Right Hand: a Study in Religious Polarity. *In* Right and Left: Essays on Dual Symbolic Classification. R. Needham, ed. Pp. 3–21. Chicago: University of Chicago Press.

Hesketh, Therese, Li Lu, and Zhu Wei Xing
2005 The Effect of China's One-Child Family Policy after 25 Years. New England Journal of Medicine 353:1171–1176.

Heusch, Luc de
1971 Possession et chamanisme. *In* Pourquoi l'épouser? Pp. 226–244. Paris: Gallimard.

Heyman, Jody, Clyde Hertzman, Morris L. Barer, and Robert G. Evans, eds.
2006 Healthier Societies: From Analysis to Action. Oxford: Oxford University Press.

Hill, K., and D. M. Upchurch
1995 Gender Differences in Child Health: Evidence from the Demographic and Health Surveys. Population Development Review 21:127–151.

Hill, Shirley A.
1994 Managing Sickle Cell Disease in Low-Income Families. Philadelphia: Temple University Press.

Hillman, David, and Carla Mazzio
1997 The Body in Parts: Fantasies of Corporeality in Early Modern Europe. New York: Routledge.

Hirschauer, Stefan
1991 The Manufacture of Bodies in Surgery. Social Studies of Science 21:279–319.

Hochschild, Adam
2006 King Leopold's Ghost: A Story of Greed, Terror, and Heroism in Colonial Africa. Boston: Mariner Books.

Hodgson, John
1989 *Editorial*: Geneticism and Freedom of Choice. Trends in Biotechnology 7(9): 221–226.

Hoedemaekers, Roger, and Henk ten Have
1998 Geneticization: The Cyprus Paradigm. Journal of Medicine and Philosophy 23: 274–287.

Hoeyer, Klaus
2004 Ambiguous Gifts: Public Anxiety, Informed Consent and Commercial Genetic Biobank Research. *In* Genetic Databases: Socio-Ethical Issues in the Collection and Use of DNA. R. Tutton and O. Corrigan, eds. Pp. 97–116. London: Routledge.

Hogle, Linda F.
1995 Standardization Across Non-Standard Domains: The Case of Organ Procurement. Science, Technology and Human Values 20:482–500.
1996 Transforming "Body Parts" into Therapeutic Tools: A Report from Germany. Medical Anthropology Quarterly 10(4):675–682.
1999 Recovering the Nation's Body: Cultural Memory, Medicine and the Politics of Redemption. New Brunswick, NJ: Rutgers University Press.

Hooper, Edward
1999 The River: A Journey to the Source of HIV and Aids. Harmondsworth: Penguin.

Hsu, Elizabeth
2002 "The Medicine from China Has Rapid Effects": Chinese Medicine Patients in Tanzania. Anthropology and Medicine 9:291–313.

Huff, Toby E.
2003 The Rise of Early Modern Science. Cambridge: Cambridge University Press.

Hunt, Nancy R.
1988 "Le bébé en brousse": European Women, African Birth Spacing and Colonial Intervention in Breast Feeding in the Belgian Congo. International Journal of African Historical Studies 21:401–432.
1992 Colonial Fairy Tales and the Knife and Fork Doctrine in the Heart of Africa. *In* African Encounters with Domesticity. K. T. Hansen, ed. Pp. 143–171. New Brunswick, NJ: Rutgers University Press.
1994 Letter-Writing, Nursing Men and Bicycles in the Belgian Congo: Notes Towards the Social Identity of a Colonial Category. *In* Paths Toward the Past: African Historical Essays in Honor of Jan Vansina. R. W. Harms, Joseph C. Miller and David S. Newbury, eds. Pp. 187–210. Atlanta: African Studies Association Press.
1999 A Colonial Lexicon of Birth Ritual, Medicalization, and Mobility in the Congo. Durham, NC: Duke University Press.
2007 Colonial Medical Anthropology and the Making of the Central African Infertility Belt. *In* Ordering Africa: Anthropology, European Imperialism, and Knowledge. H. L. Tilley and R. J. Gordon, eds. Pp. 252–281. Manchester: Manchester University Press.
Huntley, Alyson L., and Ernst Edzard
2003 A Systematic Review of Herbal Medicinal Products for the Treatment of Menopausal Symptoms. Menopause 10(5):465–476.
Huxley, Julian
1957 Evolutionary Humanism. Melbourne: Australian Institute of International Affairs.
Ibeji, Yokotam, and Korowai Gane
1996 The Hagahai Patent Controversy: In Their Own Words. Cultural Survival Quarterly 20 (Summer):33.
Illich, Ivan D.
1976 Medical Nemesis. New York: Pantheon
Independent, The
2009 Firm that Led the Way in DNA Testing Goes Bust. November 18:18.
Inhorn, Marcia
1996 Infertility and Patriarchy: The Cultural Politics of Gender and Family Life in Egypt. Philadelphia: University of Pennsylvania Press.
2003 Global Infertility and the Globalization of New Reproductive Technologies: Illustrations from Egypt. Social Science and Medicine 56:1837–1851.
2003 Local Babies, Global Science: Gender, Religion and *In Vitro* Fertilization in Egypt. New York: Routledge.
Inhorn, Marcia, and Frank van Balen
2002 Introduction. *In* Infertility Around the Globe: New Thinking on Childlessness, Gender, and Reproductive Technologies. M. Inhorn and F. van Balen, eds. Pp. 3–32. Berkeley: University of California Press.
Institute of Medicine Committee on Assessing the Need for Clinical Trials of Testosterone Replacement Therapy, Board on Health Science Policies
2004 Testosterone and Aging: Clinical Research Directions. Catharyn T. Liverman and Dan G. Blazer, eds. Washington, D.C.: The National Academies Press. http://www.nap.edu/openbook.php?isbn=0309090636
Ivry, Tsipi
2009 The Ultrasonic Picture Show and the Politics of Threatened Life. Medical Anthropology Quarterly 23:189–211.
Jablonka, Eva, and Marion J. Lamb
1995 Epigenetic Inheritance and Evolution: The Lamarckian Dimension. Oxford: Oxford University Press.
2005 Evolution in Four Dimensions: Genetic, Epigenetic, Behavioral, and Symbolic Variation in the History of Life, Life and Mind. Cambridge, MA: MIT Press.

Jacob, François, and Jacques Monod
1961 Genetic Regulatory Mechanisms in the Synthesis of Proteins. Journal of Molecular Biology 3:318–356.

Jacobs, Andrew
2009 Chinese Hunger for Sons Fuels Boys' Abductions. New York Times. April 4. http://www.nytimes.com/2009/04/05/world/asia/05kidnap.html

Janes, Craig
1995 The Transformations of Tibetan Medicine. Medical Anthropology Quarterly 9:6–39.

Jasanoff, Sheila, ed.
2004 States of Knowledge: The Co-Production of Science and Social Order: London: Routledge.

Jasen, Patricia
2002 Breast Cancer and the Language of Risk, 1750–1950. Social History of Medicine 15(1):17–43.

Jern, Helen
1973 Hormone Therapy of the Menopause and Aging. Springfield, IL: Charles C. Thomas.

Jha, Prabhat, Rajesh Kumar, Priya Vasa, Neeraj Dhingra, Deva Thiruchelvam, and Rahim Moineddin
2006 Low Male-to-Female Sex Ratio of Children Born in India: National Survey of 1.1 Million Households. The Lancet 367(9506):211–218.

Johnson, Steven
2006 The Ghost Map: The Story of London's Most Terrifying Epidemic – and How It Changed Science, Cities, and the Modern World. New York: Penguin.

Jones, James
1981 Bad Blood: The Tuskegee Syphilis Experiment. New York: The Free Press.

Joralemon, Donald
1995 Organ Wars: The Battle for Body Parts. Medical Anthropology Quarterly 9(3): 335–356.

Jordan, Brigitte
1978 Childbirth in Four Cultures. Montreal: Eden's Press Women's Publications.

Jorde, Lynne B., and Stephen P. Wooding
2004 Genetic Variation, Classification, and "Race". Nature/Genetics 36:S28–S33.

Jorde, L. B., M. Bamshad, and A. R. Rogers
1998 Using Mitochondrial and Nuclear DNA Markers to Reconstruct Human Evolution. BioEssays 20(2):126–136.

Jorland, Gerard, Annick Opinel, and George Weisz, eds.
2005 Body Counts: Medical Quantification in Historical and Sociological Perspectives// La Quantification medicale, perspectives historiques et sociologiques. Montreal: McGill-Queens University Press.

Jovanovski, Thomas
1995 The Cultural Approach of Ethnopsychiatry: A Review and Critique. New Ideas in Psychology 13:281–297.

Kahn, Jonathan
2003 Getting the Numbers Right: Statistical Mischief and Racial Profiling in Heart Failure Research. Perspectives in Biology and Medicine 46:473–483.
2004 How a Drug Becomes "Ethnic": Law, Commerce, and the Production of Racial Categories in Medicine. Yale Journal of Health Policy, Law, and Ethics 4:1–46.

Kahn, Susan
2000 Reproducing Jews: A Cultural Account of Assisted Conception in Israel. Durham, NC: Duke University Press.

Kanaaneh, Rhoda Ann
2002 Birthing the Nation: Strategies of Palestinian Women in Israel. Berkeley: University of California Press.

Kaneko, Sachiko
2006 Japan's "Socially Withdrawn Youth" and Time Constraints in Japanese Society: Management and Conceptualization of Time in a Support Group for "Hikikomori". Time and Society 15:233–249.

Kaplan, Karen
2007 25% of Fetuses Found with Disease Aborted. The Gazette, Montreal, September 19.

Kass, Leon
1975 Regarding the End of Medicine and the Pursuit of Health. Public Interest 40(summer):38–39.

Kasuga, Michigo, Kazuya Makita, Ken Ishitani, Kiyoshi Takamatsu, Kenji Watanabe, Gregory A. Plotnikoff, et al.
2004 Relation between Climacteric Symptoms and Ovarian Hypofunction in Middle-Aged and Elderly Japanese Women Presenting at a Menopausal Clinic. Menopause 11(6): 631–638.

Katō, Shinzō
2004 Organ Transplants and Brain-Dead Donors: A Japanese Doctor's Perspective. Mortality 9(1):13–26.

Kaufert, Patricia
1990 The "Boxification" of Culture: The Role of the Social Scientist. Santé, Culture, Health 7:139–148.

Kaufert, Patricia, and Sonja McKinlay
1985 Estrogen-Replacement Therapy: The Production of Medical Knowledge and the Emergence of Policy. *In* Women, Health and Healing: Toward a New Perspective. E. Lewin and V. Oleson, eds. Pp. 113–138. London: Tavistock Publications.

Kaufert, Patricia Leyland, and John D. O'Neil
1993 Analysis of a Dialogue on Risks in Childbirth: Clinicians, Epidemiologists and Inuit Women. *In* Knowledge, Power, and Practice: The Anthropology of Medicine and Everyday Life. S. Lindenbaum and M. Lock, eds. Pp. 32–54. Berkeley: University of California Press.

Kaufert, Patricia, and John Syrotuik
1981 Symptom Reporting at the Menopause. Social Science and Medicine 184:173–184.

Kaufert, Patricia, Penny Gilbert, and Robert Tate
1992 The Manitoba Project: a Reexamination of the Link Between Menopause and Depression. Maturitas 14:143–155.

Kaufman, Sharon
2000 In the Shadow of Death with Dignity: Medicine and Cultural Quandaries of the Vegetative State. American Anthropologist 102:69–83.
2005 … And a Time to Die: How American Hospitals Shape the End of Life. New York: Scribner.

Kaufman, Sharon R., Ann J. Russ, and Janet K. Shim
2006 Aged Bodies and Kinship Matters: The Ethical Field of Kidney Transplant. American Ethnologist 33(1):81–99.

Kaufman, Sharon, Janet K. Shim, and Ann J. Russ
2004 Revisiting the Biomedicalization of Aging: Clinical Trends and Ethical Challenges. The Gerontologist 44:731–738.

Kaul, S., and G. A. Diamond
2006 Good Enough: A Primer on the Analysis and Interpretation of Noninferiority Trials. Annals of Internal Medicine 145:62–69.

Kavanagh, Anne M., and Dorothy H. Broom
1998 Embodied Risk: My Body, Myself. Social Science and Medicine 46:437–444.

Kay, Lily 1993 The Molecular Vision of Life: Caltech, The Rockefeller Foundation, and the Rise of the New Biology. Oxford: Oxford University Press.

Kayler, L. K., C. S. Rasmussen, and D. M. Dykstra
2003 Gender Imbalance and Outcomes in Living Donor Renal Transplantation in the United States. American Journal of Transplantation 3:452.

Keat, Russell
1986 The Human Body in Social Theory: Reich, Foucault, and the Repressive Hypothesis. Radical Philosophy 42:24.

Keating, Peter, and Alberto Cambrosio
2003 Biomedical Platforms: Realigning the Normal and the Abnormal in the Twentieth Century. Cambridge, MA: MIT Press.

Keesing, Roger M.
1987 Anthropology as Interpretive Quest. Current Anthropology 28:161–169.

Keller, Evelyn Fox
1995 Reconfiguring Life: Metaphors of Twentieth-Century Biology. New York: Columbia University Press.
2000 Is there an Organism in this Text? In Controlling Our Destinies: Historical, Philosophical, Ethical, and Theological Perspectives on HGP. P. Sloan, ed. Pp. 273–290. South Bend, IN: Notre Dame University Press.
2000 The Century of the Gene. Cambridge, MA: Harvard University Press.

Kerlikowske, K., D. F. Miglioretti, and D. S. Buist
2007 Declines in Invasive Breast Cancer and Use of Postmenopausal Hormone Therapy in a Screening Mammography Population. Journal of the National Cancer Institute 99:1335–1339.

Kerr, A., S. Cunningham-Burley, and A. Amos
1998 The New Human Genetics and Health: Mobilizing Lay Expertise. Public Understanding of Science 7(1):41–60.

Kertzer, David, and Jennie Keith
1984 Age and Anthropological Theory. Ithaca: Cornell University Press.

Kertzer, David, and Peter Laslett, eds.
1995 Aging in the Past: Demography, Society and Old Age. Berkeley: University of California Press.

Kevles, Daniel J.
1984 Annals of Eugenics: A Secular Faith I. New Yorker, October 8:51–115.

Kickbusch, Ilona
1997 New Players for a New Era: Responding to the Global Public Health Challenges. Journal of Public Health Medicine 19:171–178.

Kielmann, Karina
1998 Barren Ground: Contesting Identities of Infertile Women in Pemba, Tanzania. In Pragmatic Women and Body Politics. M. Lock and P. Kaufert, eds. Pp. 127–163. Cambridge: Cambridge University Press.

Kier, F. J., and V. Molinari
2003 "Do-It-Yourself" Dementia Testing: Issues Regarding an Alzheimer's Home Screening Test. Gerontologist 43(3):295–301.

King, Jonathan
1996 Gene Patents Retard the Protection of Human Health. GeneWatch 10: 10–11.

King, Mary-Claire, Joan H. Marks, Jessica B. Mandell, and the New York Breast Cancer Study Group

2003 Breast and Ovarian Cancer Risks Due to Inherited Mutations in BRCA1 and BRCA2. Science 302(5645):643–646.

King, N.
2002 Security, Disease, Commerce: Ideologies of Postcolonial Global Health. Social Studies of Science 32:763–789.

Kitanaka, Junko
2008 Diagnosing Suicides of Resolve: Psychiatric Practice in Contemporary Japan. Culture, Medicine and Psychiatry 32:152–176.
2009 Japanese Psychiatry and the Discovery of Depression. Princeton: Princeton University Press.
Forthcoming Society in Distress: The Making of Depression in Contemporary Japan. Princeton: Princeton University Press.

Kitcher, Philip
1996 The Lives to Come: The Genetic Revolution and Human Possibilities. New York: Simon and Schuster.

Kittles, Rick A., and Kenneth M. Weiss
2003 Race, Ancestry and Genes: Implications for Defining Disease Risk. Annual Review of Genomics and Human Genetics 4(1):33–67.

Kleinman, Arthur
1986 Social Origins of Distress and Disease: Depression, Neurasthenia, and Pain in Modern China. New Haven: Yale University Press.
1988 The Illness Narratives: Suffering, Healing, and the Human Condition. New York: Basic Books.
1995 Writing at the Margin: Discourse Between Anthropology and Medicine. Berkeley: University of California Press.
2004 Culture and Depression. New England Journal of Medicine 351:951.

Kleinman, Arthur, and Byron Good, eds.
1985 Culture and Depression: Studies in the Anthropology and Cross-Cultural Psychiatry of Affect and Disorder. Berkeley: University of California Press.

Kleinman, Arthur, and Joan Kleinman
1994 How Bodies Remember: Social Memory and Bodily Experience of Criticism, Resistance, and Delegitimation following China's Cultural Revolution. New Literary History 25:707–723.
1997 The Appeal of Experience: The Dismay of Images: Cultural Appropriations of Suffering in Our Times. *In* Social Suffering. A. Kleinman, V. Das, and M. Lock, eds. Pp. 1–24. Berkeley: University of California Press.

Kleinman, Arthur, Veena Das, and Margaret Lock, eds.
1997 Social Suffering. Berkeley: University of California Press.

Kligman, Gail
1998 The Politics of Duplicity: Controlling Reproduction in Ceausescu's Romania. Berkeley: University of California Press.

Kluckhohn, Clyde
1995[1944] Navaho Witchcraft. Papers of the Peabody Museum of American Archaeology and Ethnology, Harvard University 22. Boston: Beacon Press.

Kolata, Gina
1993 Nightmare or the Dream of a New Era in Genetics? New York Times, December 7:A1.
2009 Studies Show Prostate Test Saves Few Lives. New York Times, March 19. http://health.nytimes.com/health/

Komaroff, A. L.
2007 By the Way, Doctor. First It Was Vioxx and Now Avandia. Why Can't Doctors and the Government Screen Out Unsafe Medicines? Harvard Health Letter 32:8.

Konrad, Monica
2005 Narrating the New Predictive Genetics: Ethics, Ethnography, and Science, Cambridge Studies in Society and the Life Sciences. Cambridge: Cambridge University Press.

Kopytoff, Igor
1986 The Cultural Biography of Things: Commoditization as Process. *In* The Social Life of Things: Commodities in Cultural Perspective. A. Appadurai, ed. Pp. 64–91. Cambridge: Cambridge University Press.

Korein, Julius
1978 The Problem of Brain Death: Development and History. Annals of the New York Academy of Sciences 315:19–38.
1978 Terminology, Definitions, and Usage. *In* Brain Death: Interrelated Medical and Social Issues. J. Korein, ed. Annals of the New York Academy of Science 315:9.

Koshland, Daniel
1989 Sequences and Consequences of the Human Genome. Science 246(4927):189.

Kramer, Peter D.
1997 Listening to Prozac. New York: Penguin Books.

Krieger, Nancy
2006 If "Race" Is the Answer, What Is the Question? On "Race," Racism, and Health: A Social Epidemiologist's Perspective. Is Race Real? A web forum organized by the Social Science Research Council. June 7. http://raceandgenomics.ssrc.org/Krieger/

Krieger, Nancy, and Mary Bassett
1993 Health of Black Folk: Disease, Class, and Ideology in Science. *In* The Racial Economy of Science: Toward a Democratic Future. S. Harding, ed. Pp. 161–169. Indianapolis: Indiana University Press.

Kronenberg, F.
1990 Hot Flashes: Epidemiology and Physiology. Annals of the New York Academy of Science 592:52–86.

Kronenberg, F., and A. Fugh-Berman
2002 Complementary and Alternative Medicine for Menopausal Symptoms: A Review of Randomized, Controlled Trials. Annals of Internal Medicine 137:805–813.

Kumle, Merethe
2008 Declining Breast Cancer Incidence and Decreased HRT use. The Lancet 372: 608–610.

Kuriyama, Shigehisa
1992 Between Mind and Eye: Japanese Anatomy in the Eighteenth Century. *In* Paths to Asian Medical Knowledge. C. Leslie and A. Young, eds. Pp. 21–43. Berkeley: University of California Press.
1999 The Expressiveness of the Body and the Divergence of Greek and Chinese Medicine. New York Zone Books.

Lachenal, G.
Forthcoming Franco-African Familiarities: A History of the Pasteur Institute of Cameroon. *In* Hospitals Beyond the West. M. Harrison ed. New Delhi: Orient Longman.

La Fleur, William
1992 Liquid Life: Abortion and Buddhism in Japan. Princeton: Princeton University Press.

Laing, R. D.
1960 The Divided Self. London: Tavistock Publications.

Lakoff, Andrew
2005 Pharmaceutical Reason: Knowledge and Value in Global Psychiatry. Cambridge: Cambridge University Press.
2006 High Contact: Gifts and Surveillance in Argentina. *In* Global Pharmaceuticals: Ethics, Markets, Practices. A. Petryna, A. Lakoff, and A. Kleinman, eds. Pp. 111–135. Durham, NC: Duke University Press.

Lam, C. L., M. G. Catarivas, C. Munro, and I. J. Lauder
1994 Self-Medication among Hong Kong Chinese. Social Science and Medicine 39(12): 1641–1647.

Lambek, Michael
1993 Knowledge and Practice in Mayotte: Local Discourses of Islam, Sorcery, and Spirit Possession. Toronto: University of Toronto Press.

Lambert, Helen
2006 Gift Horse or Trojan Horse? Social Science Perspectives on Evidence-Based Health Care. Social Science and Medicine 62:2613–2620.

Landau, P. S.
1996 Explaining Surgical Evangelism in Colonial Southern Africa: Teeth, Pain and Faith. Journal of African History 37:261–281.

Landecker, Hannah
1999 Between Beneficence and Chattel: The Human Biological in Law and Science. Science in Context 12(1):203–225
2000 Immortality, *in Vitro*: A History of the HeLa Cell Line. *In* Biotechnology and Culture: Bodies, Anxieties, Ethics. P. E. Brodwin, ed. Pp. 53–74. Indianapolis: Indiana University Press.
2007 Culturing Life: How Cells Became Technologies. Cambridge, MA: Harvard University Press.

Lane, Sandra D., and Robert A. Rubinstein
1996 International Health: Problems and Programs in Anthropological Perspective. *In* Medical Anthropology: Contemporary Theory and Method. C. F. Sargent, and T. M. Johnson, eds. Pp. 396–424. Westport, CT: Praeger.

Langbehn, Douglas R., Ryan R. Brinkman, Daniel Falush, Jane S. Paulsen, and Michael R. Hayden
2004 A New Model for Prediction of the Age of Onset and Penetrance for Huntington's Disease Based on CAG Length. Clinical Genetics 65(4):267–277.

Langwick, Stacey
2007 Devils, Parasites, and Fierce Needles: Healing and the Politics of Translation in Southern Tanzania. Science, Technology and Human Values 32:88–117.

Larsen, Ulla
2000 Primary and Secondary Infertility in Sub-Saharan Africa. International Journal of Epidemiology 29:285–291.
2005 Research on Infertility: Which Definition Should We Use? Fertility and Sterility 83:846–852.

LaRusse, S., J. S. Roberts, T. M. Marteau, H. Katzen, E. L. Linnenbringer, M. Barber, et al.
2005 Genetic Susceptibility Testing Versus Family History-Based Risk Assessment: Impact on Perceived Risk of Alzheimer Disease. Genetics in Medicine 7(1):48–53.

Lasker, J.
1977 The Role of Health Services in Colonial Rule: The Case of the Ivory Coast. Culture, Medicine and Psychiatry 1:277–297.

Latour, Bruno
1984 Les microbes: guerre et paix. Paris: A. M. Métailié.
1986 Le Théâtre de la preuve. *In* Pasteur et la révolution pastorienne. C. Salomon-Bayet, ed. Pp. 335–384. Paris: Payot.
1987 Science in Action: How to Follow Scientists and Engineers Through Society. Milton Keynes: Open University Press.
1988 The Pasteurization of France. Cambridge, MA: Harvard University Press.
1993 We Have Never Been Modern. Cambridge, MA: Harvard University Press.
1996 Aramis, or, The Love of Technology. Cambridge, MA: Harvard University Press.

1999 Pandora's Hope: Essays on the Reality of Science Studies. Cambridge, MA: Harvard University Press.

Lawrence, Christopher, and Steven Shapin, eds.
1998 Science Incarnate: Historical Embodiments of Natural Knowledge. Chicago: University of Chicago Press.

Lawrence, Christopher, and George Weisz
1998 Greater than the Parts: Holism in Biomedicine, 1920–1950. Oxford: Oxford University Press.

Lee, Laura Kim
2002 Changing Selves, Changing Society: Human Relations Experts and the Invention of T Groups, Sensitivity Training and Encounter in the United States, 1938–1980. PhD dissertation, University of California Los Angeles.

Lee, S. S. J., J. Mountain, and B. A. Koenig
2001 The Meanings of Race in the New Genomics: Implications for Health Disparities Research. Yale Journal of Health Policy and Ethics 1:33–75.

Leidy-Sievert, Lynette, and Erin K. Flanagan
2005 Geographical Distribution of Hot Flash Frequencies: Considering Climatic Differences. American Journal of Physical Anthropology 128:437–443.

Lena, P. and P. Luciw,
2001 Polio Vaccine and Retroviruses. Philosophical Transactions of the Royal Society of London Series B 356(1410):841–844.

Leonard, Lori
2002 Problematizing Fertility: "Scientific" Accounts and Chadian Women's Narratives. *In* Infertility Around the Globe: New Thinking on Childlessness, Gender, and Reproductive Technologies. M. Inhorn and F. van Balen, eds. Pp. 193–214. Berkeley: University of California Press.

Leslie, Charles
1973 The Professionalizing Ideology of Medical Revivalism. *In* Entrepreneurship and Modernization of Occupational Cultures in South Asia. M. Singer, ed. Pp. 16–42. Durham NC: Duke University Press.
1980 Medical Pluralism in World Perspective. Special Issue "Medical Pluralism," Social Science and Medicine 14B(4):190–196.
1992 Interpretations of Illness: Syncretism in Modern Āyurveda. *In* Paths to Asian Medical Knowledge: A Comparative Study. C. Leslie and A. Young, eds. Pp. 177–208. Berkeley: University of California Press.

Lévi-Strauss, Claude
1974 [1949] Anthropologie structurale. Paris Plon.

Levy, S., G. Sutton, P. C. Ng, L. Feuk, A. L. Halpern, B. P. Walenz, et al.
2007 The Diploid Genome Sequence of an Individual Human. PLoS Biology 5(10):e254. http://www.ncbi.nlm.nih.gov/pubmed/17803354

Lewin, Ellen
1998 Wives, Mothers, and Lesbians: Rethinking Resistance in the U.S. *In* Pragmatic Women and Body Politics. M. Lock and P. Kaufert, eds. Pp. 164–177. Cambridge: Cambridge University Press.

Lewin, Peter, ed.
2002 The Economics of QWERTY: History, Theory, and Policy – Essays by Stan J. Liebowitz and Stephen E. Margolis. New York: New York University Press.

Lewis, Gilbert
1975 Knowledge of Illness in a Sepik Society. Cambridge: Cambridge University Press.

Lewontin, Richard C.
2003 Science and Simplicity. New York Review of Books 50:39–42.

Lietava, J.
  1992 Medicinal Plants in a Middle Paleolithic Grave Shandihar IV? Journal of Ethnopharmacology 35:263–266.
Lindenbaum, Shirley
  1978 *Kuru* Sorcery: Disease and Danger in the New Guinea Highlands. Palo Alto, CA: Mayfield.
Linebaugh, Peter
  1975 The Tyburn Riot: Against the Surgeons. *In* Albion's Fatal Tree: Crime and Society in Eighteenth-Century England. D. Hay, P. Linebaugh, J. Rule, E. T. P. Thompson, and C. Winslow, eds. Pp. 65–117. London: Allen Lane.
Linnaeus, Carl
  1735 Systema Natura. Leiden.
Lippman, Abby
  1992 Led (Astray) by Genetic Maps: The Cartography of the Human Genome and Human Care. Social Science and Medicine 35:1469–1496.
Livingstone, Frank
  1971 Malaria and Human Polymorphisms. Annual Review of Genetics 5:33–64.
Lock, Margaret
  1980 East Asian Medicine in Urban Japan: Varieties of Medical Experience. Berkeley: University of California Press.
  1989 Words of Fear, Words of Power: Nerves and the Awakening of Political Consciousness. Medical Anthropology 11:79–90.
  1990 On Being Ethnic: The Politics of Identity Breaking and Making in Canada or, Nevra on Sunday. Culture, Medicine and Psychiatry 14:237–252.
  1991 Contested Meanings of the Menopause. The Lancet 337:1270–1291.
  1991 Flawed Jewels and National Dis/Order: Narratives on Adolescent Dissent in Japan. Festschrift for George DeVos. Journal of Psychohistory 18:507–531.
  1993 Encounters with Aging: Mythologies of Menopause in Japan and North America. Berkeley: University of California Press.
  1994 Interrogating the Human Diversity Genome Project. Social Science and Medicine 39(5):603–606.
  1996 Centering the Household: the Remaking of Female Maturity in Japan. *In* Re-Imagining Japanese Women. A. Imamura, ed. Pp. 73–103. Berkeley: University of California Press.
  1996 Ideology and Subjectivity: Midlife and Menopause in Japan and North America. *In* Ethnography and Human Development: Context and Meaning in Social Inquiry. R. Jessor, A. Colby and R. Schweder, eds. Pp. 339–369. Chicago: University of Chicago Press.
  1998 Breast Cancer: Reading the Omens. Anthropology Today 14:7–16.
  1998 Perfecting Society: Reproductive Technologies, Genetic Testing, and the Planned Family in Japan. *In* Pragmatic Women and Body Politics. M. Lock and P. A. Kaufert, eds. Pp. 206–239. Cambridge: Cambridge University Press.
  1998 Situating Women in the Politics of Health. *In* The Politics of Women's Health: Exploring Agency and Autonomy. S. Sherwin, ed. Pp. 48–63. Philadelphia: Temple University Press.
  1999 Genetic Diversity and the Politics of Difference. Chicago-Kent Law Review 75: 83–111.
  2000 On Dying Twice: Culture, Technology, and the Determination of Death. *In* Living and Working with the New Medical Technologies: Intersections of Inquiry. M. Lock, A. Young, and A. Cambrosio, eds. Pp. 233–262. Cambridge: Cambridge University Press.
  2001 The Alienation of Body Tissue and the Biopolitics of Immortalized Cell Lines. Body and Society 7(2–3):63–91.

2001 Situated Ethics, Culture, and the Brain Death "Problem" in Japan. *In* Bioethics in Social Context. B. Hoffmaster, ed. Pp. 39–68. Philadelphia: Temple University Press.

2002 Le Corps objet: économie morale et techniques d'amélioration. Bulletin d'histoire politique – Corps et Politique 10:33–46.

2002 Human Body Parts as Therapeutic Tools: Contradictory Discourses and Transformed Subjectivities. Qualitative Health Research 12(10):1406–1418.

2002 Inventing a New Death and Making it Believable. Anthropology and Medicine 2002(9):97–115.

2002 Twice Dead: Organ Transplants and the Reinvention of Death. Berkeley: University of California Press.

2003 On Making up the Good-as-Dead in a Utilitarian World. *In* Remaking Life and Death: Toward an Anthropology of the Biosciences. S. Franklin and M. Lock, eds. Pp. 165–192. Santa Fe: School of American Research Press.

2005 Eclipse of the Gene and the Return of Divination. Current Anthropology 46(S5): 47–70.

2006 Postmodern Bodies, Material Difference, and Subjectivity. *In* Dismantling the East–West Dichotomy: Essays in Honour of Jan van Bremen. J. Hendry and H. W. Wong, eds. Pp. 38–48. London: Routledge.

2007 The Final Disruption? Biopolitics of Post-Reproductive Life. *In* Reproductive Disruptions: Gender, Technology, and Biopolitics in the New Millennium. M. Inhorn, ed. Pp. 200–224. New York: Berghahn Books.

Lock, Margaret, and Megan Crowley-Matoka
2008 Situating the Practice of Organ Donation in Familial, Cultural, and Political Context. Transplantation Reviews 22(3):154–157.

Lock, Margaret, and Judith Farquhar, eds.
2007 Beyond the Body Proper. Durham, NC: Duke University Press.

Lock, Margaret, and Deborah R. Gordon, eds.
1988 Biomedicine Examined. Dordrecht: Kluwer Academic Publishers.

Lock, Margaret, and Patricia Kaufert, eds.
1998 Pragmatic Women and Body Politics. Cambridge: Cambridge University Press.
2001 Menopause, Local Biologies, and Cultures of Aging. American Journal of Human Biology 13:494–504.

Lock, Margaret, Julia Freeman, Gillian Chilibeck, Briony Beveridge, and Miriam Padolsky
2007 Susceptibility Genes and the Question of Embodied Identity. Medical Anthropology Quarterly 21(3):256–276.

Lock, Margaret, Julia Freeman, Rosemary Sharples, and Stephanie Lloyd
2006 When It Runs in the Family: Putting Susceptibility Genes in Perspective. Public Understanding of Science 15(3):277–300.

Loewe, Michael
1981 China. *In* Oracles and Divination. M. Loewe, C. Blacker, and L. C. Radha, eds. Pp. 38–62. Boulder, CO: Shambhala Publications.

Long, Susan O.
2003 Becoming a Cucumber: Culture, Nature, and the Good Death in Japan and the United States. Journal of Japanese Studies 29(1):33–68.

Low Dog, Tieraona
2004 The Rule for Botanicals in Menopause. Menopause Management 13:S51–S53.

Löwy, Ilana
2000 The Experimental Body. *In* Companion to Medicine in the Twentieth Century. R. Cooter and J. Pickstone, eds. Pp. 435–450. London: Routledge.
2001 Virus, moustiques et modernité: La fièvre jaune au Brésil, entre science et politique. Paris: Éditions des archives contemporaines.

Lumey, L. H.
    1992 Decreased Birthweights in Infants after Maternal *in Utero* Exposure to the Dutch Famine of 1944–194. Paediatric Perinatal Epidemiology 6:240–253.
Lupton, Deborah
    1995 The Imperative of Health: Public Health and the Regulated Body. London: Sage.
Lyons, M.
    1988 Sleeping Sickness, Colonial Medicine and Imperialism: Some Connections in the Belgian Congo. *In* Disease, Medicine and Empire. R. Macleod and L. Milton, eds. Pp. 242–256. London: Routledge.
    1992 The Colonial Disease: A Social History of Sleeping Sickness in Northern Zaire, 1900–1940. Cambridge: Cambridge University Press.
Macaulay, Alexander, Anne Durcan, Johanna Geraci, Norman Hartlevik, and Nowyah Williams.
    n.d. A Retrospective Audit of the Rankin Inlet Birthing Center, 1993–2004. Unpublished manuscript available from the first author.
McCarthy, Mark I., Goncalo R. Abscasis, Lon R. Cardon, David B. Goldstein, Julian Little, John P. A. Ionnidid, et al.
    2008 Genome-Wide Association Studies for Complex Traits: Consensus and Challenges. Nature Reviews/Genetics 9:356–369.
Macchiarini, Paolo, Philipp Jungebluth, Tetsuhiko Go, M. Adelaide Asnaghi, Louisa E. Rees, Tristan A. Cogan, et al.
    2008 Clinical Transplantation of a Tissue-Engineered Airway. The Lancet 372(9655): 2023–2030.
McClain, C.
    1982 Toward a Comparative Framework for the Study of Childbirth: A Review of the Literature. *In* Anthropology of Human Birth. M. A. Kay, ed. Pp. 25–59. Philadelphia: F. A. Davis.
McClintock, Barbara
    1967 Regulation of Pattern of Gene Expression by Controlling Elements in Maize. Carnegie Institute of Washington 65:563–578.
McEwen, Jean E.
    1997 DNA Data Banks. *In* Genetic Secrets: Protecting Privacy and Confidentiality in the Genetic Era. M. A. Rothstein, ed. Pp. 231–251. New Haven: Yale University Press.
Macfarlane, A., and M. Mugford
    1984 Birth Counts: Statistics of Pregnancy and Childbirth. London: Her Majesty's Stationery Office.
McGuffin, Peter, Brien Riley, and Robert Plomin
    2001 Toward Behavioral Genomics. Science 291(5507):1242–1249.
Mackenback, John P.
    2007 The Mediterranean Diet Story Illustrates the "Why" Questions Are as Important as the "How" Questions in Disease Explanation. Journal of Clinical Epidemiology 60:105–109.
McKeown, Peter
    1976 The Modern Rise of Population New York: Academic Press.
McKie, Robin
    2004 Icelandic DNA Project Hit by Privacy Storm. The Observer, May 16.
McKinlay, S. M., D. Brambilla, and J. Posner
    1992 The Normal Menopausal Transition. Human Biology 4:37–46.
Macleod, R., and M. Lewis
    1988 Disease, Medicine, and Empire. London: Routledge.

Mcpherson, K., J. E. Wennberg, O. B. Hovind, and P. Clifford
1982 Small-Area Variations in the Use of Common Surgical Procedures: An International Comparison of New England, England, and Norway. New England Journal of Medicine 307:1310–1314.

Maher, Eamonn R.
2005 Imprinting and Assisted Reproductive Technology. Human Molecular Genetics 14:R133–R138.

Malacrida, Claudia
2005 *Book review*: Ambiguity, Risk and Blame: Critical Responses to Fetal Alcohol Syndrome (FAS). Health 9:417–424.

Malpani, A., and A. Malpani
2001 Preimplantation Genetic Diagnosis for Gender Selection for Family Balancing: A View from India. Reproductive BioMedicine Online 4(1):7–9. http://humrep. oxfordjournals.org/cgi/content/full/17/1/11

Malthus, T. R.
2004[1798] An Essay on the Principle of Population [1698]. Oxford World Classics. 3rd reprint. Oxford: Oxford University Press.

Mamdani, Mahmood
1972 The Myth of Population Control: Family, Caste and Class in an Indian Village. New York: Monthly Review Press.

Mantel, Hilary
1998 The Giant, O'Brien. Toronto: Doubleday.

Marchbanks, P. A., H. B. Peterson, G. L. Rubin, and P. A. Wingo
1989 Research on Infertility: Definition Makes a Difference. American Journal of Epidemiology 130:259–267.

Marcus, George E.
1998 Ethnography through Thick and Thin. Princeton: Princeton University Press.

Maria, Anthony N. de
2008 Lies, Damned Lies and Statistics. Journal of the American College of Cardiology 53:1430–1431.

Marks, Harry
1997 The Progress of Experiment: Science and Therapeutic Reform in the United States, 1900–1990. Cambridge: Cambridge University Press.
2003 Rigorous Uncertainty: Why R. A. Fisher Is Important. International Journal of Epidemiology 32:932–937.

Marks, Lara
1999 Human Guinea Pigs? The History of the Early Oral Contraceptive Trials. History and Technology 15:263–288.

Martin, Emily
1987 The Woman in the Body: A Cultural Analysis of Reproduction. Boston: Beacon Press.

Martin, M., J. Block, S. Sanchez, C. Arnaud, and Y. Beyene
1993 Menopause Without Symptoms: The Endocrinology of Menopause Among Rural Mayan Indians. American Journal of Obstetrics and Gynecology 168:1839–1845.

Marx, Karl
1967 Capital: A Critique of Political Economy. Vol. 1. New York: International Publishers.

Marx, P. A., P. G. Alcabes, and E. Drucker,
2001 Serial Human Passage of Simian Immunodeficiency Virus by Unsterile Injections and the Emergence of Epidemic Human Immunodeficiency Virus in Africa. Philosophical Transactions of the Royal Society of London Series B 356(1410):911–920.

Maternowska, M. Catherine
    2006 Reproducing Inequities: Poverty and the Politics of Population in Haiti, Studies in Medical Anthropology. New Brunswick, NJ: Rutgers University Press.
Matthews, John D., Robert Glasse, and Shirley Lindenbaum
    1968 *Kuru* and Cannibalism. The Lancet 292(7565):449–452.
Mattick, John
    2003 Challenging the Dogma: The Hidden Layer of Non-Protein-Coding RNAs in Complex Organisms. Bioessays 25:930–939.
    2004 The Hidden Genetic Program of Complex Organisms. Scientific American 291: 60–67.
Mauss, Marcel
    1973[1935] The Techniques of the Body. Trans. B. Brewer. Economy and Society 2:70–88.
    1990[1950] The Gift. New York: W. W. Norton.
Mayeux, R., R. Ottman, G. Maestre, C. Ngai, M. X. Tang, H. Ginsberg, M. Chun, B. Tycko, and M. Shelanski
    1995 Synergistic Effects of Traumatic Head Injury and Apolipoprotein-ε4 in Patients with Alzheimer's Disease. Neurology 45:555–557.
Mead, Aroha Te Pareake
    1996 Genealogy, Sacredness, and the Commodities Market. Cultural Survival Quarterly 20:46.
Medical News
    2006 New Highly Successful Way of Freezing Human Eggs. http://www.news-medical.net/news/2006/06/19/18516.aspx
Melby, Melissa
    2005 Vasomotor Symptom Prevalence and Language of Menopause in Japan. Menopause 23(3):250–257.
    2005 Factor Analysis of Climacteric Symptoms in Japan. Maturitas 52:205–222.
    2006 Climacteric Symptoms Among Japanese Women and Men: Comparison of 4 Symptom Checklists. Climacteric 9:298–304.
    2007 Chilliness: A Vasomotor Symptom in Japan. Menopause 13(4):1–8.
Melby, Melissa, Margaret Lock, and Patricia Kaufert
    2005 Culture and Symptom Reporting at Menopause. Human Reproduction Update 11:495–512.
Melby, Melissa, S. Watanabe, P. L. Whitten, and C. M. Worthman
    2005 Sensitive High-Performance Liquid Chromatographic Method Using Coulometric Electrode Array Detection for Measurement of Phytoestrogens in Dried Blood Spots. Journal of Chromatography 826:81–90.
Merleau-Ponty, Maurice
    1962 The Phenomenology of Perception. London: Routledge and Kegan Paul.
Merz, Jon, David Magnus, Mildred K. Cho, and Arthur Caplan
    2002 Protecting Subjects' Interests in Genetic Research. American Journal of Human Genetics 70:965–971.
Miller, B. D.
    1997 The Endangered Sex: Neglect of Female Children in Rural North India. Oxford: Oxford University Press.
Mills, Edward, Beth Rachlis, Ping Wu, Elaing Wong, Kumanan Wilson, and Sonal Singh
    2005 Media Reporting of Tenofovir Trials in Cambodia and Cameroon. BMC International Health and Human Rights 5(6): doi:10.1186/1472–698X-5-6
Mills, J. A. and T. Harrison
    2007 John Rickman, Wilfred Ruprecht Bion, and the Origins of the Therapeutic Community. History of Pyschology 10(1):22–43.

Mischler, Elliot G., Lorna Amarasingham Rhodes, Stuart T. Hauser, Samuel D. Osherson, Nancy E. Waxler, and Ramsay Liem
1981 Social Contexts of Health, Illness, and Patient Care. Cambridge: Cambridge University Press.

Mitchell, J. J., A. Capua, C. Clow, and C. R. Scriver
1996 Twenty-Year Outcome Analysis of Genetic Screening Programs for Tay-Sachs and β-Thalassemia Disease Carriers in High Schools. American Journal of Human Genetics 59:793–798.

Mitchell, Timothy
2002 Rule of Experts: Egypt, Techno-Politics, Modernity. Berkeley: University of California Press.

Moazam, Farhat
2006 Bioethics and Organ Transplantation in a Muslim Society: A Study in Culture, Ethnography, and Religion. Bloomington: Indiana University Press.

Molyneux, Sassy and P. Wenzel Geissler
2008 Ethics and the Ethnography of Medical Research in Africa. Social Science and Medicine 67(5):696–707.

Montagu, M. F. A.
1964 The Concept of Race. Toronto: Collier-Macmillan.

Montoya, Michael J.
2007 Bioethnic Conscription: Genes, Race, and Mexicana/o Ethnicity in Diabetes Research. Cultural Anthropology 22(1):94–128.

Morris, Brian
1995 Anthropology of the Self: The Individual in Cultural Perspective. London: Pluto Press.

Morsy, Soheir
1995 Deadly Reproduction among Egyptian Women: Maternal Mortality and the Medicalization of Population Control. *In* Conceiving the New World Order: The Global Politics of Reproduction. F. D. Ginsburg and R. Rapp, eds. Pp. 162–176. Berkeley: University of California Press.

Moshe, Szyf, Patrick McGowan, and Michael J. Meaney
2008 The Social Environment and the Epigenome. Environmental and Molecular Mutagenesis 49:46–60.

Moss, Lenny
2001 Deconstructing the Gene and Reconstructing Molecular Developmental Systems. *In* Cycles of Contingency: Developmental Systems and Evolution edited by S. Oyama, P. E. Griffiths and R. D. Gray, eds. Pp. 85–98. Cambridge, MA: MIT Press.
2002 From Representational Preformationism to the Epigenesis of Openness to the World? Reflections on a New Vision of the Organism. *In* From Epigenesis to Epigenetics: The Genome in Context. Annals of the New York Academy of Sciences. L. Van Speybroeck, G. Van de Vijver, and D. De Waele, eds. Pp. 219–230. New York: New York Academy of Sciences.

Moulin, A. M.
1992 Patriarchal Science: The Network of the Overseas Pasteur Institutes. *In* Science and Empires: Historical Studies About Scientific Development and European Expansion. P. Petitjean, C. Jami, and A. M. Moulin, eds. Pp. 307–322. Dordrecht: Kluwer.
1995 The Pasteur Institutes between the Two World Wars: The Transformation of the International Sanitary Order. *In* International Health Organisations and Movements, 1918–1939. Paul Weindling, ed. Pp. 244–265. Cambridge: Cambridge University Press.
1996 Tropical without the Tropics: The Turning-Point of Pastorian Medicine in North Africa. *In* Warm Climates and Western Medicine. David Arnold, ed. Pp. 160–180. Amsterdam: Rodopi.

Mountain, J. L., and L. L. Cavalli-Sforza
    1997 Multilocus Genotypes, a Tree of Individuals, and Human Evolutionary History. American Journal of Human Genetics 61(3):705–718.
Moynihan, Ray
    2003 Drug Company Secretly Briefed Medical Societies on HRT. British Medical Journal 326:1161.
Müller-Rockstroh, Babette
    2007 Ultrasound Travels: The Politics of a Medical Technology in Ghana and Tanzania. PhD thesis, Maastricht University.
Mumford, Lewis
    1934 Technics and Civilization. New York: Harcourt Brace.
Murray, Michael J., William R. Meyer, Bruce A. Lessey, Richard H. Oi, Rebecca E. DeWire, and Marc A. Fritz
    2003 Soy Protein Isolate with Isoflavones Does Not Prevent Estradidol-Induced Endometrial Hyperplasia in Postmenopausal Woman: A Pilot Trial. Menopause 10(5): 456–464.
Myers, R. H., E. J. Schaefer, P. W. Wilson, R. D'Agostino, J. M. Ordovas, A. Espino, et al.
    1996 Apolipoprotein E ε4 Association with Dementia in a Population-Based Study: The Framingham Study. Neurology 46(3):673–677.
Narod, S.
    2007 Ovarian Cancer and HRT in the Million Women Study. The Lancet 369(9574): 1667–1668.
National Center for Complementary and Alternative Medicine (NCCAM)
    2008 The Use of Complementary and Alternative Medicine. Washington: National Center for Complementary and Alternative Medicine.
Nature Genetics
    2000 *Editorial*: Census, Race and Science. Nature Genetics 24:97–98.
Ndebele, Paul and Rosemary Musesengwa
    2008 Will Developing Countries Benefit from Their Participation in Genetics Research? Malawi Medical Journal 20:67–69.
Neel, J. V.
    1962 Diabetes Mellitus: A "Thrifty" Genotype Rendered Detrimental by "Progress"? American Journal of Human Genetics 14:353–362.
Nelkin, Dorothy, and M. Susan Lindee
    1995 The DNA Mystique: The Gene as a Cultural Icon. New York: W. H. Freeman and Company.
Nelson, Alan
    2002 Unequal Treatment: Confronting Racial and Ethnic Disparities in Health Care. Journal of the National Medical Association 94:666.
Neumann-Held, E. M., and C. Rehmann-Sutter
    2006 Genes in Development: Rereading the Molecular Paradigm. Durham, NC: Duke University Press.
Newton, Isaac
    1687 Philosophiae Naturalis Principia Mathematica. London.
New York Times
    2008 *Editorial*: Failing the World's Poor. September 24: A26.
Nguyen, Vinh-Kim
    2009 Government-by-Exception: Enrolment and Experimentality in Mass HIV Treatment Programmes in Africa. Social Theory and Health 7:196–217.
Nguyen, Vinh-Kim, C. Y. Ako, P. Niamba, A. Sylla, and I. Tiendrebeogo
    2007 Adherence as Therapeutic Citizenship: Impact of the History of Access to Antiretroviral Drugs on Adherence to Treatment. AIDS 21(5):S31–S35.

Nichter, Mark
   1981 Idioms of Distress: Alternatives in the Expression of Psychosocial Distress: A Case Study from South India. Culture, Medicine and Psychiatry 5:379.
   2008 Global Health: Why Cultural Perceptions, Social Representations, and Biopolitics Matter. Tucson: University of Arizona Press.
Nichter, Mark, and Margaret Lock
   2002 New Horizons in Medical Anthropology: Essays in Honour of Charles Leslie. London: Routledge.
Nolen, Stephanie
   2009 Land of the Rising Sun. Globe and Mail, September 12.
North American Menopause Society
   2003 Estrogen and Progestogen Use in Peri- and Postmenopausal Women: September 2003 Position Statement. Menopause 10(6):497–506.
   2004 Treatment of Menopause-Associated Vasomotor Symptoms: Position Statement of the North American Menopause Society. Menopause 11(1):11–33.
Novas, Carlos, and Nikolas Rose
   2000 Genetic Risk and the Birth of the Somatic Individual. Economy and Society 29(4):485–513.
Oakley, Ann
   1980 Women Confined: Towards a Sociology of Childbirth. Oxford: Martin Robertson.
   1984 The Captured Womb: A History of the Medical Care of Pregnant Women. Oxford: Basil Blackwell.
Obermeyer, Carla Makhlouf
   2000 Menopause Across Cultures: A Review of the Evidence. Menopause 7:184–192.
Okie, Susan
   2006 Global Health. The Gates–Buffett Effect. New England Journal of Medicine 355:1084–1088.
Ong, Aihwa
   1988 The Production of Possession: Spirits and the Multinational Corporation in Malaysia. American Ethnologist 15:28–42.
Ortner, Sherry B.
   1999 Introduction. *In* The Fate of "Culture": Geertz and Beyond. S. B. Ortner, ed. Pp. 1–13. Berkeley: University of California Press.
Osborne, Michael
   2001 Acclimatizing the World: A History of the Paradigmatic Colonial Science. Osiris 15:135–151.
Ossorio, P., and T. Duster
   2005 Race and Genetics: Controversies in Biomedical, Behavioral, and Forensic Sciences. American Psychologist 60(1):115–128.
Otsubo, S., and J. R. Bartholomew
   1998 Eugenics in Japan: Some Ironies of Modernity, 1883–1945. Science in Context 11(3–4):133–146.
Oum, Young Rae
   2003 Beyond a Strong State and Docile Women: Reproductive Choices, State Policy and Skewed Sex Ratio in South Korea. International Feminist Journal of Politics 5:420–446.
Owen, David
   1999 Power, Knowledge and Ethics: Foucault. *In* The Edinburgh Encyclopedia of Continental Philosophy. Simon Glendinning ed. P. 600. London: Routledge.
Oyama, Susan
   2001 Terms in Tension: What Do You Do When All the Good Words Are Taken? *In* Cycles of Contingency: Developmental Systems and Evolution. S. Oyama, P. E. Griffiths, and R. D. Gray, eds. Pp. 177–194. Cambridge, MA: MIT Press.

Oyama, Susan, Paul E. Griffiths, and Russell D. Gray
2001 Cycles of Contingency: Developmental Systems and Evolution, Life and Mind. Cambridge, MA: MIT Press.

Palladino, Paolo
2002 Between Knowledge and Practice. Social Studies of Science 32:137–165.

Palmié, Stephan
2007 Genomics, Divination, "Racecraft." American Ethnology 34(2):205–222.

Pálsson, Gisli
2007 Anthropology and the New Genetics. Cambridge: Cambridge University Press.
2009 Biosocial Relations of Production. Comparative Studies in Society and History 51:288–313.

Palumbi, Stephen
2001 Humans as the World's Greatest Evolutionary Force. Science 293(5536):1786–1790.

Pandolfi, Mariella
1990 Boundaries Inside the Body: Suffering of the Peasant Women in Southern Italy. Culture, Medicine and Psychiatry 2:255–273.

Parens, Erik, and Adrienne Asch
1999 The Disability Rights Critique of Prenatal Genetic Testing: Reflections and Recommendations. Hastings Center Report 229(5):S1–S22.

Park, Katherine
1994 The Criminal and the Saintly Body. Renaissance Quarterly 47:1–33.
1995 The Life of the Corpse: Division and Dissection in Late Medieval Europe. Journal of the History of Medicine and Allied Sciences 50:114.

Parthasarathy, Shobita
2005 Architectures of Genetic Medicine: Comparing Genetic Testing for Breast Cancer in the U.S.A. and the U.K. Social Studies of Science 35(1):5–40.

Passmore, John
1972 The Perfectibility of Man. London: Gerald Duckworth and Company.

Patel, Vibhuti
1989 Sex Determination and Sex-Preselection Tests in India: Modern Techniques of Femicide. Bulletin of Concerned Asian Scholars 21(5):1153–1156.

Paul, Benjamin, ed.
1955 Health, Culture and Community: Case Studies of Public Reactions to Health Programs. New York: Russell Sage Foundation.

Paul, Diane B.
1998 The Politics of Heredity: Essays on Eugenics, Biomedicine, and the Nature–Nurture Debate. Albany: State University of New York Press.

Paul, Diane B., and Hamish G. Spencer
1995 The Hidden Science of Eugenics. Nature 374:302–304.

Pauling, Linus
1968 Foreword: Reflections on a New Biology. UCLA Law Review 15:269.

Payer, Lynn
1988 Medicine and Culture: Varieties of Treatment in the U.S., England, Germany and France. Austin, TX: Holt, Reinhart, and Winston.

Pearce, Tola Olu
1995 Women's Reproductive Practices and Biomedicine: Cultural Conflicts and Transformations in Nigeria. *In* Conceiving the New World Order: The Global Politics of Reproduction. F. D. Ginsburg and R. Rapp, eds. Pp. 195–208. Berkeley: University of California Press.

Peccei, Jocelyn Scott 1995 A Hypothesis for the Origin and Evolution of Menopause. Maturitas 21:83–89.

2001 A Critique of the Grandmother Hypothesis: Old and New. American Journal of Human Biology 13:434–452.

Pedersen, S.
1991 National Bodies, Unspeakable Acts: The Sexual Politics of Colonial Policy-Making. Journal of Modern History 63:647–680.

Pentz, Rebecca D., Anne L. Flamm, Renata Pasqualini, Christopher J. Logothetis, and Wadih Arap
2003 Revisiting Ethical Guidelines for Research with Terminal Wean and Brain-Dead Participants. Hastings Center Report 33:20–26.

Pernick, Martin S.
1988 Back from the Grave: Recurring Controversies over Defining and Diagnosing Death in History. *In* Death: Beyond Whole-Brain Criteria. R. M. Zaner, ed. Pp. 17–74. Dordrecht: Kluwer Academic Publishers.

Peterson, Duncan, and Veronica Baruffati
1989 Healers, Deities, Saints and Doctors: Elements for the Analysis of Medical Systems. Social Science and Medicine 29:487–496.

Peterson, Emily A., Kara J. Milliron, Karen E. Lewis, Susan D. Goold, and Sofia D. Merajver
2002 Health Insurance and Discrimination Concerns and BRCA1/2 Testing in a Clinic Population. Cancer Epidemiology, Biomarkers, and Prevention 11:79–87.

Petronis, Arturas
2001 Human Morbid Genetics Revisited: Relevance of Epigenetics. Trends in Genetics 17:142–146.

Petryna, Adriana
2005 Ethical Variability: Drug Development and the Globalization of Clinical Trials. American Ethnologist 32:183–197.
2006 Globalizing Human Subjects Research. *In* Global Pharmaceuticals: Ethics, Markets, Practices. A. Petryna, A. Lakoff, and A. Kleinman, eds. Pp. 33–60. Durham, NC: Duke University Press.
2007 Clinical Trials Offshored: On Private Sector Science and Public Health. BioSocieties 2:21–40.
2009 When Experiments Travel: Clinical Trials and the Global Search for Human Subjects. Princeton: Princeton University Press.

Petryna, A, A. Lakoff, and A. Kleinman, eds.
2006 Global Pharmaceuticals. Ethics, Markets, Practices. Durham, NC: Duke University Press.

Pfaffenberger, Bryan
1992 Social Anthropology of Technology. Annual Review of Anthropology 21:491–516.

Phillips, A.
In press The Life Course of Nevirapine. *In* The Fourth Wave: Gender and HIV in the Twenty First Century. Vinh-Kim Nguyen and Jennifer Klot, eds. New York: Social Science Research Council. http://blogs.ssrc.org/fourthwave/2008/11/29/phillips/

Pick, Daniel
1993 Faces of Degeneration: A European Disorder, c. 1848–1918. Cambridge: Cambridge University Press.

Pickering, Andrew
1995 The Mangle of Practice: Time, Agency, and Science. Chicago: University of Chicago Press.

Pigg, Stacy Leigh
2002 Too Bold, Too Hot: Crossing "Culture" in AIDS Prevention in Nepal. *In* New Horizons in Medical Anthropology: Essays in Honour of Charles Leslie. M. Nichter and M. Lock, eds. Pp. 58–80. London: Routledge.

Pinker, S.

1997 How the Mind Works. New York: W. W. Norton.

Pisani, Elizabeth

2008 The Wisdom of Whores: Bureaucrats, Brothels, and the Business of AIDS. New York: W. W. Norton.

Plafker, Ted.

2002 Sex Selection in China Sees 117 Boys for Every 100 Girls. British Medical Journal 324:1223.

Pollan, Michael

2008 In Defense of Food: An Eater's Manifesto. New York: Penguin Press.

Pordié, Laurent, ed.

2008 Tibetan Medicine in the Contemporary World: Global Politics of Medical Knowledge Practice. London: Routledge.

Porter, Dorothy

1993 Public Health. *In* Companion Encyclopedia of the History of Medicine, vol. 2. W. F. Bynum and R. Porter, eds. Pp. 1231–1261. London: Routledge.

1999 Health, Civilization and the State: A History of Public Health from Ancient to Modern Times. London: Routledge.

Porter, Roy

1995 Medical Science and Human Science in the Enlightenment. *In* Inventing Human Science: Eighteenth Century Domains. C. Fox, R. Porter, and R. Wokler, eds. Pp. 53–87. Berkeley: University of California Press.

1995 Medicine in the Enlightenment, Wellcome Institute Series in the History of Medicine. Amsterdam: Rodopi.

1998 The Greatest Benefit to Mankind: A Medical History of Humanity. London: HarperCollins.

Porter, Theodore

1995 Trust in Numbers: The Pursuit of Objectivity in Science and Public Life. Princeton: Princeton University Press.

Posel, D.

2005 Sex, Death and the Fate of the Nation: Reflections on the Politicization of Sexuality in Post-Apartheid South Africa. Africa 75(2):125–153.

2008 History as Confession: The Case of the South African Truth and Reconciliation Commission. Public Culture 20(1):119–141.

Potter, Paul

1976 Herophilus of Chalcedon: An Assessment of His Place in the History of Anatomy. Bulletin of the History of Medicine 50:45–60.

Prainsack, Barbara, and Gil Siegal

2006 The Rise of Genetic Couplehood? A Comparative View of Premarital Genetic Testing. BioSocieties 1:17–36.

Pressat, R., and C. Wilson

1985 The Dictionary of Demography. New York: Blackwell Science.

Proctor, Robert

2000 The Nazi War on Cancer. Princeton: Princeton University Press.

Pupavac, V.

2001 Therapeutic Governance: Psycho-Social Intervention and Trauma Risk Management. Disasters 25(4):358–372.

Puri, Sunita

2008 "There Is Such a Thing as Too Many Daughters, But Not Too Many Sons": The Intersection of Medical Technology, Son Preference and Sex Selection among South Asian Immigrants in the United States. MSc dissertation, Department of Anthropology, University of California, Berkeley.

Quaid, Kimberly A., and Michael Morris
1993 Reluctance to Undergo Predictive Testing: The Case of Huntington's Disease. American Journal of Medical Genetics 45:41–45.

Rabinow, Paul
1989 French Modern: Norms and Forms of the Social Environment. Cambridge, MA: MIT Press.
1994 The Third Culture. History of the Human Sciences 7(2):53–64.
1996 Artificiality and Enlightenment: From Sociobiology to Biosociality. *In* Essays on the Anthropology of Reason. Pp. 91–111. Princeton: Princeton University Press.
1999 Epochs, Presents, Events. *In* Living and Working with the New Medical Technologies: Intersections of Inquiry. M. Lock, A. Young, and A. Cambrosio, eds. Pp. 31–48. Cambridge: Cambridge University Press.
1999 French DNA: Trouble in Purgatory. Chicago: University of Chicago Press.
2007 Afterword. *In* Biosocialities, Genetics, and the Social Sciences. S. Gibbon and C. Novas, eds. Pp. 188–192. London: Routledge.

Rabinow, Paul, and Nikolas Rose
2006 Biopower Today. BioSocieties 1:195–218.

Rabinow, Paul, and W. M. Sullivan
1979 Interpretative Social Science. Berkeley: University of California Press.

Radcliffe-Richards, Janet
1996 Nepharious Goings on: Kidney Sales and Moral Arguments. Journal of Medical Philosophy (21):375–416.

Rader, K.
2004 Making Mice: Standardizing Animals for American Biomedical Research 1950–55. Princeton: Princeton University Press.

Rajan, Kaushik Sudner
2006 Biocapital: The Constitution of Postgenomic Life. Durham, NC: Duke University Press.

Ramesh, Randeep
2006 Jailing of Doctor in India Sting Operation Highlights Scandal of Aborted Girl Fetuses. The Guardian, March 30.

Rapp, Rayna
1997 Real-Time Fetus: The Role of the Sonogram in the Age of Monitored Reproduction. *In* Cyborgs and Citadels: Anthropological Interventions into Emerging Sciences and Technologies. G. L. Downey and J. Dumit, eds. Pp. 31–48. Santa Fe: School of American Research Press.
1999 Testing Women, Testing the Fetus: The Social Impact of Amniocentesis. New York: Routledge.
2003 Cell Life and Death, Child Life and Death: Genomic Horizons, Genetic Diseases, Family Stories. *In* Remaking Life and Death: Toward an Anthropology of the Biosciences. S. Franklin and M. Lock, eds. Pp. 23–60. Santa Fe: School of American Research Press.
2006 Preface to a Special Issue. Sacred Conceptions: Religion and the Global Practice of IVF. Culture, Medicine, and Psychiatry 30:419–421.

Rapp, Rayna, Deborah Heath, and Karen-Sue Taussig
2001 Genealogical Disease: Where Hereditary Abnormality, Biomedical Explanation, and Family Responsibility Meet. *In* Relative Matters: New Directions in the Study of Kinship. S. Franklin and S. MacKinnon, eds. Pp. 384–412. Durham, NC: Duke University Press.

Raspberry, Kelly, and Debra Skinner
2007 Experiencing the Genetic Body: Parents' Encounters with Pediatric Clinical Genetics. Medical Anthropology 26:355–391.

Ravnskov, Uffe
2002 The Cholesterol Myths. Winona Lake, IL: New Trends Publishing.

Ray, John
    1691 The Wisdom of God Manifested in the Creation. London.
Reardon, Jenny
    2005 Race to the Finish: Identity and Governance in an Age of Genomics. Princeton: Princeton University Press.
Recthman, R., and D. Fassin
    2006 L'Empire du traumatisme: enquête sur la condition de victime. Paris: Flammarion.
Redfield, Peter
    2006 A Less Modest Witness. American Ethnologist 33:3–26.
Redlich, F. C.
    1957 The Concept of Health in Psychiatry. *In* Explorations in Social Psychiatry. A. H. Leighton, J. N. Clausen, and R. N. Wilson, eds. Pp. 138–164. London: Tavistock.
Rees, Tobias
    2006 Plastic Reason: An Anthropological Analysis of the Emergence of Adult Cerebral Plasticity in France. Unpublished PhD thesis, University of California, Berkeley.
Reid, R.
    1992 Cultural and Medical Perspectives on Geophagia. Medical Anthropology 13: 337–351.
Rheinberger, Hans-Jörg
    1997 Toward a History of Epistemic Things: Synthesizing Proteins in the Test Tube. Stanford: Stanford University Press.
    2000 Beyond Nature and Culture: Modes of Reasoning in the Age of Molecular Biology and Medicine. *In* Living and Working with the New Medical Technologies: Intersections of Inquiry. M. Lock, A. Young, and A. Cambrosio, eds. Pp. 19–30. Cambridge: Cambridge University Press.
    2008 What Happened to Molecular Biology? BioSocieties 3(3):303–310.
Richards, Martin
    1996 Lay and Professional Knowledge of Genetics and Inheritance. Public Understanding of Science 5:217–230.
Richardson, Ruth
    1988 Death, Dissection, and the Destitute. London: Routledge.
    1996 Fearful Symmetry: Corpses for Anatomy, Organs for Transplantation. *In* Organ Transplantation: Meaning and Realities edited by R. C. Fox, L. J. O'Connell, and S. J. Youngner, eds. Pp. 66–100. Madison: University of Wisconsin Press.
Rich-Edwards, J., Nancy Krieger, Joseph Majzoub, Sally Zierler, Ellice Lieberman, and Matthew Gillman
    2001 Maternal Experiences of Racism and Violence as Predictors of Preterm Birth: Rationale and Study Design. Paediatric and Perinatal Epidemiology 15:124–135.
Richey, Lisa Ann
    2003 Women's Reproductive Health and Population Policy: Tanzania. Review of American Political Economy 30:273–292.
Risch, N., E. Burchard, E. Ziv, and H. Tang
    2002 Categorization of Humans in Biomedical Research: Genes, Race and Disease Genome Biology 3(7):1–12.
Rivers, W. H. R.
    2001 Medicine, Magic and Religion. New York: Routledge.
Rix, Bo Andreassen
    1999 Brain Death, Ethics, and Politics in Denmark. *In* The Definition of Death: Contemporary Controversies. S. J. Youngner, R. M. Arnold, and R. Shapiro, eds. Pp. 227–238. Baltimore: Johns Hopkins University Press.

Roberts, Celia, and Sarah Franklin
2004 Experiencing New Forms of Genetic Choice: Findings from an Ethnographic Study of Preimplantation Genetic Diagnosis. Human Fertility 7(4):285–293.

Roberts, Elizabeth
2006 God's Laboratory: Religious Rationalities and Modernity in Ecuadorian *In Vitro* Fertilization. Culture, Medicine, and Psychiatry 30:507–536.

Roberts, Sam
2009 U.S. Births Hint at Bias for Boys in Some Asians. New York Times, June 15. http://www.nytimes.com/2009/06/15/nyregion/15babies.html

Robertson, Jennifer
2002 Blood Talks: Eugenic Modernity and the Creation of New Japanese. History and Anthropology 13:191–216.
2005 Biopower: Blood, Kinship, and Eugenic Marriage. *In* A Companion to the Anthropology of Japan. J. Robertson, ed. Pp. 329–354. Oxford: Blackwell.

Rohini, Pande, and Anju Malhetra
2006 Son Preference and Daughter Neglect in India: International Center for Research on Women. http://www.icrw.org/docs/2006_son-preference.pdf

Romalis, Shelly
1981 Childbirth: Alternatives to Medical Control. Austin: University of Texas Press.

Rose, Hilary
2006 From Hype to Mothballs in Four Years: Troubles in the Development of Large-Scale DNA Biobanks in Europe. Community Genetics 9(3):184–189.

Rose, Nikolas
1994 Medicine, History, and the Present. *In* Reassessing Foucault: Power, Medicine and the Body. C. Jones and R. Porter, eds. Pp. 48–72. London: Routledge.
1996 Inventing Our Selves: Psychology, Power, and Personhood Cambridge: Cambridge University Press.
2007 Beyond Medicalization. The Lancet 369:700–702.
2007 The Politics of Life Itself: Biomedicine, Power, and Subjectivity in the Twenty-First Century. Princeton: Princeton University Press.

Rose, Steven
1997 Lifelines: Life Beyond the Gene. Oxford: Oxford University Press.

Ross, Eric B.
1998 The Malthus Factor: Poverty, Politics and Population in Capitalist Development. London: Zed Books.

Rothman, Barbara Katz
1998 Genetic Maps and Human Imaginations: The Limits of Science in Understanding Who We Are. New York: W. W. Norton and Company.

Rotimi, Charles N.
2003 Genetic Ancestry Tracing and the African Identity: A Double-Edged Sword? Developing World Bioethics 3:151–158.

Rustagi, Preet
2006 The Deprived, Discriminated and Damned Girl Child: Story of Declining Child Sex Ratios in India. Women's Health and Urban Life 5:6–26.

Ryle, J.
1961 The Meaning of Normal. *In* Concepts of Medicine. B. Lush, ed. Pp. 137–149. New York: Pergamon.

Ryōzō, Matsumoto, and Kiyooka Eiichi
1969 The Dawn of Western Science in Japan. Tokyo: Hokuseidō Press.

Sadowsky, J.
1997 Psychiatry and Colonial Ideology in Nigeria. Bulletin of the History of Medicine 71:94–111.

Sahlins, Marshall
1976 Culture and Practical Reason. Chicago: University of Chicago Press.

Said, Edward
1995 Peace and Its Discontents: Essays on Palestine in the Middle East. New York: Vintage Books.

St George-Hyslop, P.
2000 Molecular Genetics of Alzheimer's Disease. Biological Psychiatry 47:183–199.

Sanal, Aslihan.
2004 "Robin Hood" of Techno-Turkey or Organ Trafficking in the State of Ethical Beings. *Culture, Medicine, and Psychiatry* 28:281–309.

Sandel, Michael J.
2007 The Case Against Perfection: Ethics in the Age of Genetic Engineering. Cambridge, MA: Belknap Press of Harvard University Press.

Sandelowski, Margarete, and Sheryl de Lacey
2002 The Uses of a "Disease": Infertility as a Rhetorical Vehicle. *In* Infertility Around the Globe: New Thinking on Childlessness, Gender, and Reproductive Technologies. M. Inhorn and F. van Balen, eds. Pp. 33–51. Berkeley: University of California Press.

Sandner, Peter, and Karl Ziegelbauer
2008 Product-Related Research: How Research Can Contribute to Successful Life-Cycle Management. Drug Discovery Today 13:457–463.

Sanger, Margaret
1922 The Pivot of Civilization. Washington, D.C.: Scott-Townsend Publishers.

Sapp, Jan
1983 The Struggle for Authority in the Field of Heredity, 1900–1932: New Perspectives on the Rise of Genetics. Journal of the History of Biology 16(3):311–342.

Sappol, Michael
2002 The Traffic of Dead Bodies: Anatomy and Embodied Social Identity in Nineteenth-Century America. Princeton: Princeton University Press.

Sauer, N. J.
1992 Forensic Anthropology and the Concept of Race: If Races Don't Exist, Why Are Forensic Anthropologists So Good at Identifying Them? Social Science and Medicine 34:107–111.

Saunders, B.
2009 CT Suite: The Work of Diagnosis in the Age of Noninvasive Cutting. Durham, NC: Duke University Press.

Scarry, Elaine
1985 The Body in Pain: The Making and Unmaking of the World. Oxford: Oxford University Press.

Scheid, Volker
2002 *Kexue* and *Guanxixue*: Plurality, Tradition and Modernity in Contemporary Chinese Medicine. *In* Plural Medicine, Tradition and Modernity, 1800–2000. W. Ernst, ed. Pp. 130–152. London: Routledge.
2002 Chinese Medicine in Contemporary China: Plurality and Synthesis, Science and Cultural Theory. Durham, NC: Duke University Press.
2007 Currents of Tradition in Chinese Medicine 1626–2006. Seattle: Eastland Press.

Scheper-Hughes, Nancy
1992 Death Without Weeping: The Violence of Everyday Life in Brazil. Berkeley: University of California Press.

2003 Keeping an Eye on the Global Traffic in Human Organs. The Lancet 361(9369): 1645–1648.

2003 Rotten Trade: Millennial Capitalism, Human Values and Global Justice in Organs Trafficking. Journal of Human Rights 2(2):197–226.

Schlich, Thomas

2007 Surgery, Science, and Modernity: Operating Rooms and Laboratories as Spaces of Control. History of Science 45(3):231–256.

2007 The Art and Science of Surgery: Innovation and Concepts of Medical Practice in Operative Fracture Care, 1960s–1970s. Science, Technology and Human Values 32: 65–88.

Schmidt, Matthew, and Lisa Jean Moore

1998 Constructing a "Good Catch," Picking a Winner: The Development of Technosemen and the Deconstruction of the Monolithic Male. *In* Cyborg Babies: From Techno-Sex to Techno-Tots. R. Davis-Floyd and J. Dumit, eds. Pp. 21–39. New York: Routledge.

Schmiedeskamp, Mia

2004 Preventing Good Brains from Going Bad. Scientific American Special Edition, The Science of Staying Young:84–91.

Schneider, David M.

1980 American Kinship: A Cultural Account. Chicago: Chicago University Press.

Schöne-Seifert, Bettina

1999 Defining Death in Germany: Brain Drain and its Discontents. *In* The Definition of Death: Contemporary Controversies. R. M. Arnold, R. Shapiro, and S. J. Youngner, eds. Pp. 257–272. Baltimore: Johns Hopkins University Press.

Schratzberger, Gabriele, and Gert Mayer

2003 Age and Renal Transplantation: An Interim Analysis. Nephrology Dialysis Transplantation 18(3):471–476.

Schrödinger, Erwin

1944 What is Life? Cambridge: Cambridge University Press.

Selin, Helaine, and Hugh Shapiro, eds.

2003 Medicine Across Cultures: The History and Practice of Medicine in Non-Western Cultures. Dordrecht: Kluwer.

Selkoe, Dennis J.

2002 The Pathophysiology of Alzheimer's Disease. *In* Early Diagnosis of Alzheimer's Disease. L. F. M. Scinto and K. R. Daffner, eds. Pp. 83–104. Totowa, NJ: Humana Press.

Sen, Amartya

1990 More than 100 Million Women are Missing. New York Review of Books 37:61–66.

2003 Missing Women – Revisited: Reduction in Female Mortality Has Been Counterbalanced by Sex Selective Abortions. British Medical Journal 327:1297–1298.

Serematakis, Nadia C.

1991 The Last Word: Women, Death, and Divination in Inner Mani. Chicago: University of Chicago Press.

Shakir, A., and D. Morley

1974 Measuring Malnutrition. The Lancet 1:758–759.

Shao, Jing

2006 Fluid Labor and Blood Money: The Economy of HIV/AIDS in Rural Central China. Cultural Anthropology 21:535–569.

Shapin, Steven

1998 The Philosopher and the Chicken: On the Dietetics of Disembodied Knowledge. *In* Science Incarnate: Historical Embodiments of Natural Knowledge. C. Lawrence and S. Shapin, eds. Pp. 21–50. Chicago: University of Chicago Press.

Sharp, Lesley

1995 Organ Transplantation as a Transformative Experience: Anthropological Insights into the Restructuring of the Self. Medical Anthropology Quarterly 9(3):357–389.

2000 The Commodification of the Body and Its Parts. Annual Review of Anthropology 29:287–328.

2006 Strange Harvest: Organ Transplants, Denatured Bodies and the Transformed Self. Berkeley: University of California Press.

Shea, Jeanne

2006 Cross-Cultural Comparison of Women's Midlife Symptom Reporting: A China Study. Culture, Medicine and Psychiatry 30:331–362.

2006 Women's Midlife Symptom-Reporting in China: A Cross-Cultural Analysis. American Journal of Human Biology 18:219–222.

Shorett, Peter

2002 Of Transgenic Mice and Men. GeneWatch 15:3–4.

Shriver, M. D., G. C. Kennedy, E. J. Parra, H. A. Lawson, V. Sonpar, J. Huang, et al. 2004 The Genomic Distribution of Population Substructure in Four Populations Using 8,525 Autosomal SNPs. Human Genomics 1(4):274–286.

Silla, Eric

1998 People Are Not the Same: Leprosy and Identity in Twentieth-Century Mali. London: Heinemann.

Siminoff, Laura A., and Kata Chillag

1999 The Fallacy of "The Gift of Life." Hastings Center Report 29(6):34–41.

Siminoff, Laura A., Christopher Burant, and Stuart J. Youngner

2004 Death and Organ Procurement: Public Beliefs and Attitudes. Social Science and Medicine 59(11):2325–2334.

Simmons, Roberta G., Susan K. Marine, and Robert L. Simmons

1987 Gift of Life: The Effect of Organ Transplantation on Individual, Family, and Societal Dynamics. New Brunswick, NJ: Transaction Books.

Simoncelli, Tania, and Helen Wallace

2006 Expanding Databases, Declining Liberties. GeneWatch 19(1):3–8.

Simpson, Bob

2000 Imagined Genetic Communities: Ethnicity and Essentialism in the Twenty-First Century. Anthropology Today 16(3):3–6.

2004 Localizing a Brave New World: New Reproductive Technologies and the Politics of Fertility in Contemporary Sri-Lanka. *In* Reproductive Agency, Medicine, and the State: Cultural Transformations in Childbearing. M. Unnithan-Kumar, ed. Pp. 43–58. New York, Oxford: Berghahn Books.

Singer, Peter A., and Abdallah S. Daar

2001 Harnessing Genomics and Biotechnology to Improve Global Health Equity. Science 294:87–89.

Sivin, Nathan

2005 Alchemy: Chinese Alchemy. *In* Encyclopedia of Religion and Nature. 2nd edition. Bron R. Taylor and Jeffrey Kaplan eds. Vol. 1. Pp. 237–241. New York: Macmillan Reference.

Snowdon, David

2001 Aging with Grace: What the Nun Study Teaches Us about Leading Longer, Healthier, and More Meaningful Lives. New York: Bantam Books.

Somers, Anne

1971 Health Care in Transition: Directions for the Future. Chicago: Hospital Research and Educational Trust.

Sontag, Susan
1978 Illness as Metaphor. New York: Farrar, Straus and Giroux.

Spallone, Pat
1998 The New Biology of Violence: New Geneticisms for Old? Body and Society 4:47–65.

Spar, Debora
2005 Reproductive Tourism and the Regulatory Map. New England Journal of Medicine 352(6):531–533.

Spiro, Melford E.
1967 Burmese Supernaturalism: A Study in the Explanation and Reduction of Suffering. New York: Prentice-Hall.

Stamey, T. A., M. Caldwell, J. E. McNeal, R. Nolley, M. Hemenez, and J. Downs
2004 Prostate Cancer Screening with the PSA Test. Journal of Urology 172(4):1297–1301.

Standing, H.
2002 Towards Equitable Financing Strategies for Reproductive Health. Institute of Development Studies Working Paper No. 153. Brighton, U.K: IDS.

Stanton, J.
2001 Listening to the Ga: Cicely Williams' Discovery of Kwashiorkor on the Gold Coast. *In* Women and Modern Medicine. L. Conrad and A. Hardy, eds. Pp. 149–171. Amsterdam: Rodopi.

Stepan, Nancy Leys
1986 Race and Gender: The Role of Analogy in Science. Isis 77:261–277.

Stevens, Lise
2002 Dr Francis S. Collins: "Genomic Discoveries: Promising and Potentially Dangerous." Neurology Today 2(1):14.

Stiglitz, Joseph E.
2003 Globalization and Its Discontents. New York: W. W. Norton.

Stini, William A.
1995 Osteoporosis in Biocultural Perspective. Annual Review of Anthropology 24:397–421.

Stocking, George
1982 Race, Culture, and Evolution Chicago: Chicago University Press.

Stolberg, Sheryl Gay
2002 Trials are Halted on a Gene Therapy. New York Times, October 4.

Stone, Linda, and J. Gabriel Campbell
1984 The Use and Misuse of Surveys in International Development: An Experiment from Nepal. Human Organization 43:27–37.

Strathern, Marilyn
1992 After Nature: English Kinship in the Late Twentieth Century. Cambridge: Cambridge University Press.
1992 Reproducing the Future: Essays on Anthropology, Kinship, and the New Reproductive Technologies. New York: Routledge.
1997 The Work of Culture: An Anthropological Perspective. *In* Culture, Kinship, and Genes: Towards a Cross-Cultural Genetics. A. Clarke and E. Parsons, eds. Pp. 40–53. London: Macmillan Press.

Strittmatter, W. J., A. M. Saunders, D. Schmechel, M. Pericak-Vance, J. Enghild, G. S. Salvesen, et al.
1993 Apolipoprotein E: High-Avidity Binding to Beta-Amyloid and Increased Frequency of Type 4 Allele in Late-Onset Familial Alzheimer's Disease. Proceedings of the National Academy of Sciences 90(5):1977–1981.

Strohman, Richard C.
1993 Ancient Genomes, Wise Bodies, Unhealthy People: Limits of a Genetic Paradigm in Biology and Medicine. Perspectives in Biology and Medicine 37(1):112–145.
2001 A New Paradigm for Life: Beyond Genetic Determinism. California Monthly 111:4–27

Strong, P. M.
1979 Sociological Imperialism and the Profession of Medicine: A Critical Examination of the Thesis of Medical Imperialism. Social Science and Medicine 13A:199–215.

Sudha, S., and S. Irudaya Rajan
1999 Female Demographic Disadvantage in India 1981–1991: Sex Selective Abortions and Female Infanticide. Development and Change 30(3):585–618.

Summers, Carol
1991 Intimate Colonialism: The Imperial Production of Reproduction in Uganda, 1907–1925. Signs 16(4):787–807.

Swartz, L., and A. Levett
1989 Political Repression and Children in South Africa: The Social Construction of Damaging Effects. Social Science and Medicine 28:741–50.

Szasz, Thomas
1961 The Myth of Mental Illness. New York: Harper and Row.

Szreter, Simon
2007 Health and Wealth: Studies in History and Policy. Rochester, NY: University of Rochester Press.

Tambiah, Stanley Jeyaraja
1990 Magic, Science, Religion, and the Scope of Rationality. Cambridge: Cambridge University Press.

Tarlo, Emma
2000 Body and Space in a Time of Crisis: Sterilization and Resettlement during the Emergency in Delhi. *In* Violence and Subjectivity. A. Kleinman, V. Das, M. Ramphaele, and P. Reynolds, eds. Pp. 242–270. Berkeley: University of California Press.

Tate, Caroline
2003 The Tip of the Iceberg: The Making of Fetal Alcohol Syndrome in Canada, PhD thesis, Department of Anthropology, McGill University.

Taussig, Karen-Sue, Rayna Rapp, and Deborah Heath
2003 Flexible Eugenics: Technologies of the Self in the Age of Genetics. *In* Genetic Nature/Culture: Anthropology and Science beyond the Two Culture Divide. A. H. Goodman, D. Heath, and M. S. Lindee, eds. Pp. 58–76. Berkeley: University of California Press.

Taussig, Michael
1980 The Devil and Commodity Fetishism. Chapel Hill: University of North Carolina Press.
1980 Reification and the Consciousness of the Patient. Social Science and Medicine 14B:3–13.
1987 Shamanism, Colonialism, and the Wild Man: A Study in Terror and Healing Chicago: University of Chicago Press.

Taylor, Charles
1989 Sources of the Self: The Making of the Modern Identity. Cambridge, MA: Harvard University Press.

Teitel, Martin
1996 The Commercialization of Life. GeneWatch 10:1–3.

Templeton, A. R.
   1998 The Complexity of the Genotype–Phenotype Relationship and the Limitations of Using Genetic "Markers" at the Individual Level. Science in Context 11(3–4):373–389.

Thacker, Eugene
   2005 The Global Genome: Biotechnology, Politics, and Culture. Cambridge, MA: MIT Press.

Thomas, Lewis
   1983 The Youngest Science: Notes of a Medicine-Watcher. New York: Viking Press.
   2005 Making Parents: the Ontological Choreography of Reproductive Technologies. Cambridge, MA: MIT Press.

Thomas, Nicholas
   1991 Entangled Objects: Exchange, Material Culture and Colonialism in the Pacific. Cambridge, MA: Harvard University Press.

Thompson, Charis
   2005 The Ontological Choreography of Reproductive Technologies. Cambridge, MA: MIT Press.

Thompson, E. P.
   1991 Customs in Common. London: Merlin Press.

Thorneycroft, Ian Hall
   1989 The Role of Estrogen Replacement Therapy in the Prevention of Osteoporosis. American Journal of Obstetrics and Gynecology 160:1306–1310.

Tilley, L., K. Morgan, and N. Kalsheker
   1998 Genetic Risk Factors in Alzheimer's Disease. Journal of Clinical Pathology: Molecular Pathology 51:293–304.

Tilney, Nicholas L.
   2003 Transplant: From Myth to Reality. New Haven: Yale University Press.

Tingting, Zhang.
   2006 China Grapples with Legality of Surrogate Motherhood. June 5. http://www.china.org.cn/english/2006/Jun/170442.htm

Tishkoff, S. A., and K. K. Kidd
   2004 Implications of Biogeography of Human Populations for "Race" and Medicine. Nature Genetics Supplement 36(11):S21–S27.

Titmuss, Richard
   1971 The Gift Relationship. London: Allen and Unwin.

Tone, Andrea
   2008 The Age of Anxiety: A History of America's Turbulent Affair with Tranquilizers. New York: Beacon Books.

Torpey, John C.
   2000 The Invention of the Passport: Surveillance, Citizenship, and the State. New York: Cambridge University Press.

Trouiller, Patrice
   2002 Drug Development for Neglected Diseases: A Deficient Market and a Public Health Policy Failure. The Lancet 359:2188–2194.

Turner, Leigh
   2007 First World Health Care at Third World Prices: Globalization, Bioethics and Medical Tourism. BioSocieties 2(03):303–325.

Turner, Victor Witter
   1967 Forest of Symbols: Ithaca: Cornell University Press.

Turney, J.
   1995 The Public Understanding of Science – Where Next? European Journal of Genetics in Society 1(2):5–22.

Turney, Jon, and Jill Turner
    2000 Predictive Medicine, Genetics and Schizophrenia. New Genetics and Society 19(1):5–22.
Tutton, Richard
    2004 Person, Property and Gift: Exploring Languages of Tissue Donation. *In* Genetic Data Bases: Socio-ethical Issues in the Collection and Use of DNA. R. Tutton and O. Corrigan, eds. Pp. 19–38. London: Routledge.
Tutton, Richard, and Oonagh Corrigan
    2004 Genetic Databases: Socio-Ethical Issues in the Collection and Use of DNA. London: Routledge.
Tylor, Edward
    1920[1871] Primitive Culture. New York: J. P. Putnam's Sons.
Uglow, Jenny
    2003 Lunar Men: The Friends Who Made the Future. London: Faber & Faber.
United States Office of Technology Assessment
    1988 Mapping Our Genes. Washington, D.C.: Government Printing Office.
Unni, Wikan
    1990 Managing Turbulent Hearts: A Balinese Formula for Living. Chicago: University of Chicago Press.
Vaitheeswan, Vijay
    2009 Medicine Goes Digital. The Economist. April 16.
van Balen, Frank, and Marcia C. Inhorn
    2003 Son Preference, Sex Selection, and the "New" New Reproductive Technologies. International Journal of Health Services 33(2):235–252.
Van de Vijver, Gertrudis, Linda Van Speybroeck, and Dani De Waele
    2002 Epigenetics: A Challenge for Genetics, Evolution, and Development? Annals of New York Academy of Sciences 981:1–6.
Van der Geest, Sjaak
    1987 Self-Care and the Informal Sale of Drugs in South Cameroon. Social Science and Medicine 25:293–305.
Van der Geest, Sjaak, and Susan Reynolds Whyte, eds.
    1989 The Context of Medicines in Developing Countries: Studies in Pharmaceutical Anthropology. Dordrecht: Kluwer.
Van Hollen, Cecilia
    2003 Birth on the Threshold: Childbirth and Modernity in Southern India (Berkeley: University of California Press, 2003).
    2003 Moving Targets: The Routinization of IUD Insertions in Public Maternity Wards. Berkeley: University of California Press.
    2005 Nationalism, Transnationalism, and the Politics of Traditional Indian Medicine for HIV/AIDs. *In* Asian Medicine and Globalization. J. S. Alter, ed. Pp. 88–106. Philadelphia: University of Pennsylvania Press.
Virey, Julien
    1824 Histoire naturelle du genre humain. Paris: Crochard.
Von Staden, Heinrich
    1992 The Discovery of the Body: Human Dissection and Its Cultural Contexts in Ancient Greece. Yale Journal of Biology and Medicine 65:223–241.
Waal, Alexander De
    1997 Famine Crimes: Politics and the Disaster Relief Industry in Africa Bloomington: Indiana University Press.
Wade, Nicholas
    2006 The Quest for the $1000 Human Genome. New York Times, July 18.

Wagner, Vicki Van, Brenda Epoo, Julie Nastapoka, and Evelyn Harney
    2007 Reclaiming Birth, Health, and Community: Midwifery in the Inuit Villages of Nunavik, Canada. Journal of Midwifery and Women's Health 52:384–391.
Wailoo, Keith, and Stephen Gregory Pemberton
    2006 The Troubled Dream of Genetic Medicine: Ethnicity and Innovation in Tay-Sachs, Cystic Fibrosis, and Sickle Cell Disease. Baltimore: Johns Hopkins University Press.
Waldby, Catherine, and Robert Mitchell
    2006 Tissue Economies: Blood, Organs and Cell Lines in Late Capitalism. Durham, NC: Duke University Press.
Wallace, Alfred Russel
    1899 The Wonderful Century. London: Dodd, Mead, and Company.
Waltraud, Ernst, and Bernard Harris, eds.
    1999 Race, Science and Medicine 1700–1960. London: Routledge.
Wardlow, Holly
    2006 Wayward Women: Sexuality and Agency in a New Guinea Society. Berkeley: University of California Press.
Washington, Harriet A.
    2006 Medical Apartheid: The Dark History of Medical Experimentation on Black Americans from Colonial Times to the Present. New York: Doubleday.
Watson, James
    1995 Values from a Chicago Upbringing. *In* DNA: The Double Helix, Perspective and Prospective at Forty Years. D. A. Chambers, ed. Pp. 194–197. New York: New York Academy of Sciences.
    2000 The Road Ahead. *In* Engineering the Human Germline. G. Stock and J. Campbell, eds. Pp. 73–95. Oxford: Oxford University Press.
Watt, Ian
    1957 The Rise of the Novel. Berkeley: University of California Press.
Watts, Jonathan
    2007 Villagers Riot over Family-Planning Law. Globe and Mail, May 22:A11.
Watts, Sheldon
    1997 Epidemics and History: Disease, Power and Imperialism. New Haven: Yale University Press.
Weber, Max
    1991[1948] From Max Weber: Essays in Sociology. Ed. H. H. Gerth and C. Wright Mills. London: Routledge.
Weber, Olivier
    2000 French Doctors: L'Épopée des hommes et des femmes qui ont inventé la médecine humanitaire. Paris: Robert Laffont.
Weindling, Paul, ed.
    1995 International Health Organisations and Movements, 1918–1939. Cambridge: Cambridge University Press.
Weiner, Annette
    1992 Inalienable Possessions: The Paradox of Keeping While Giving. Berkeley: University of California Press.
Weiner, Jonathan
    1994 The Beak of the Finch. New York: Vintage Books.
Weiss, Brad
    1996 The Making and Unmaking of the Haya Lived World. Durham, NC: Duke University Press.
Wendland, Claire L.
    2008 Research, Therapy, and Bioethical Hegemony: The Controversy over Perinatal AZT Trials in Africa. African Studies Review 51(3):1–23

Wennberg, J., and A. Gittelsohn
    1982 Variations in Medical Care Among Small Areas. Scientific American 246:120–133.
Westfall, Richard S.
    1983 Never at Rest: A Biography of Isaac Newton. Cambridge: Cambridge University Press.
Wexler, Alice
    1995 Mapping Fate: A Memoir of Family, Risk, and Genetic Research. Berkeley: University of California Press.
Wexler, Nancy
    1992 Clairvoyance and Caution: Repercussions from the Human Genome Project. *In* The Code of Codes: Scientific and Social Issues in the Human Genome Project. D. J. Kevles and L. Hood, eds. Pp. 211–243. Cambridge, MA: Harvard University Press.
White, Luise
    1995 They Could Make Their Victims Dull: Genders and Genres, Fantasies and Cures in Colonial Southern Uganda. American Historical Review 100:1379–1402.
    1995 Tsetse Visions: Narratives of Blood and Bugs in Colonial Northern Rhodesia, 1931–9. Journal of African History 36:219–245.
    2000 Speaking with Vampires. Rumor and History in Colonial Africa. Berkeley: University of California Press.
Whitehouse, Peter
    2008 The Myth of Alzheimer's Disease: What You Aren't Being Told About Today's Most Dreaded Diagnosis. New York: St Martin's Press.
Whitman, Jim, ed.
    2000 The Politics of Emerging and Resurgent Infectious Diseases. Basingstoke: Palgrave Macmillan.
Whitmarsh, Ian
    2009 Hyperdiagnostics: Postcolonial Utopics of Race-Based Biomedicine. Medical Anthropology 28:285–315.
Whorton, James C.
    1982 Crusaders for Fitness: The History of American Health Reformers. Princeton: Princeton University Press.
Whyte, Susan Reynolds
    1997 Questioning Misfortune: The Pragmatics of Uncertainty in Eastern Uganda. Cambridge: Cambridge University Press.
Whyte, Susan R., Sjaak Van der Geest, and Anita Hardon
    2002 Social Lives of Medicines. Cambridge: Cambridge University Press.
Wiggins, S., P. Whyte, M. Huggins, S. Adam, J. Theilmann, M. Bloch, et al.
    1993 The Psychological Consequences of Predictive Testing for Huntington's Disease. Obstetrical and Gynecological Survey 48(4):248.
Wiktor, Stefan Z., Ehounou Ekpini, John M. Karon, John Nkengasong, Chantal Maurice, Sibailly T. Severin, et al.
    1999 Short-Course Oral Zidovudine for Prevention of Mother-to-Child Transmission of HIV-1 in Abidjan, Côte-d'Ivoire: A Randomised Trial. The Lancet 353(6):781–785
Wilkinson, Alec
    2006 Profiles, "The Lobsterman." New Yorker, July 31:56–65.
Wilkinson, Richard G.
    2005 The Impact of Inequality: How to Make Sick Societies Healthier. New York: New Press.
Will, Catherine
    2007 The Alchemy of Clinical Trials. BioSocieties 2:85–99.
Williams, Jonathan H., Timothy D. Phillips, Pauline E. Jolly, Jonathan K. Stiles, Curtis M. Jolly, and Deepak Aggarwal

2004 Human Aflatoxicosis in Developing Countries: A Review of Toxicology, Exposure, Potential Health Consequences, and Interventions. American Journal of Clinical Nutrition 80(5):1106–1122.

Williams, Raymond
1976 Keywords: A Vocabulary of Culture and Society. London: Fontana.

Williamson, Laila
1978 Infanticide: An Anthropological Analysis. *In* Infanticide and the Value of Life. M. Kohl, ed. Pp. 61–75. New York: Prometheus Books.

Winner, Langdon
1977 Autonomous Technology: Technics-out-of-Control as a Theme in Political Thought. Cambridge, MA: MIT Press.

Women's Health Initiative Investigators Writing Group
2002 Risks and Benefits of Estrogen Plus Progestin in Healthy Postmenopausal Women: Principal Results from the Women's Health Initiative Randomized Control Trial. Journal of American Medical Association 288(3):321–333.

Wood, A. J.
2001 Racial Differences in the Response to Drugs – Pointers to Genetic Differences. New England Journal of Medicine 344(18):1393–1396.

Worboys, M.
1988 The Discovery of Colonial Malnutrition Between the Wars. *In* Imperial Medicine and Indigenous Societies. D. Arnold, ed. Pp. 208–225. Manchester: Manchester University Press.
1993 Tropical Medicine. *In* Companion Encyclopedia to the History of Medicine, vol I. W. F. Bynum and R. Porter, eds. Pp. 512–536. London: Routledge.
1999 Tuberculosis and Race in Britain and Its Empire, 1900–50. *In* Race, Science and Medicine, 1700–1960. Ernst Waltraud and Bernard Harris, eds. Pp. 144–163. London: Routledge.

World Health Organization (WHO)
1986 The Ottawa Charter for Health Promotion. Geneva: WHO. http://www.who.int/hpr/NPH/docs/ottawa_charter_hp.pdf
1987 Infections, Pregnancies, and Infertility: Perspectives on Prevention. Fertility and Sterility 47:964–968.
1991 Infertility: A Tabulation of Available Data on Prevalence of Primary and Secondary Fertility. Programme on Maternal and Child Health and Family Planning. Geneva: WHO Division of Family Health.
1996 Research on the Menopause in the 1990s. Geneva: WHO.
2002 Collaboration in Medical Genetics. Geneva: WHO.
2007 WHO Proposes Global Agenda on Transplantation. Press release, March 30. http://www.who.int/mediacentre/news/releases/2007/pr12/en/index.html
2008 Traditional Medicine. Available from http://www.who.int/mediacentre/factsheets/fs134/en/.
2008 WHO Health and Human Rights. Available from http://www.who.int/hhr/en/.

Wright, Gwendolyn
1991 The Politics of Design in French Colonial Urbanism. Chicago: University of Chicago Press.

Wright, Peter
1988 Babyhood: The Social Construction of Infant Care as a Medical Problem in England in the Years Around 1900. *In* Biomedicine Examined. M. Lock and D. Gordon, eds. Pp. 299–330. Dordrecht: Kluwer Academic Publishers.

Wright, Peter W. G., and Andrew Treacher, eds.
1982 The Problem of Medical Knowledge: Examining the Social Construction of Medicine. Edinburgh: University of Edinburgh Press.

Yamaguchi, Mari
    2009 Japan Lifts Ban on Children Donating Organs. Associated Press. http://
    newshopper.sulekha.com/topic/health-fitness.htm/news/japan-to-allow-children-to-
    receive-organ-donations.htm
Yeboah, E. D., J. M. Wadhwani, and J. B. Wilson
    1992 Etiological Factors of Male Infertility in Africa. International Journal of Fertility
    37(5):300–307.
Yoon, P., W. Bin Chen, A. Faucett, M. Clyne, M. Gwinn, I. Lubin, et al.
    2001 Public Health Impact of Genetic Tests at the End of the Twentieth Century.
    Genetics in Medicine 3:405–410.
Yoshio, Nukaga, and Alberto Cambrosio
    1997 Medical Pedigrees and the Visual Production of Family Disease in Canadian and
    Japanese Genetic Counselling Practices. In The Sociology of Medical Science and
    Technology. M. A. Elston, ed. Pp. 29–56. Oxford: Blackwell.
Young, Allan
    1976 Internalizing and Externalizing Medical Belief Systems: An Ethiopian Example.
    Social Science and Medicine (10):147–156.
    1982 The Anthropologies of Illness and Sickness. Annual Review of Anthropology
    11:257–285.
    1995 The Harmony of Illusions: Inventing Post-Traumatic Stress Disorder. Princeton:
    Princeton University Press.
Yoxen, Edward J.
    1982 Constructing Genetic Diseases. In The Problem of Medical Knowledge: Examining
    the Social Construction of Medicine. P. Wright and A. Treacher, eds. Pp. 144–161.
    Edinburgh: University of Edinburgh.
Yusim, K., M. Peeters, O. G. Pybus, T. Battacharya, T. Delaporte, and C. Mulanga
    2001 Using Human Immunodeficiency Virus Type 1 Sequences to Infer Historical
    Features of the Acquired Immune Deficiency Syndrome Epidemic and Human Immuno-
    deficiency Virus Evolution. Philosophical Transactions of the Royal Society of London
    Series B 356(1410):855–866.
Zaner, Richard M.
    1988 Death: Beyond Whole-Brain Criteria. Dordrecht: Kluwer.
Zargooshi, Javaad
    2001 Iranian Kidney Donors: Motivations and Relations with Recipients. Journal of
    Urology 165:386–393.
Zeiler, Kristin
    2004 Reproductive Autonomous Choice: A Cherished Illusion? Medicine, Healthcare and
    Philosophy 7:175–183.
Zempléni, A.
    1966 La Dimension thérapeutique du culte des Rab, Ndöp, Tuuru et Samp. Rites de
    possession chez les Lebou et les Wolof. Psychopathologie Africaine 2(3):295–439.
    1977 From Symptom to Sacrifice: The Story of Khady Fall,. In Case Studies in Spirit
    Possession. V. Crapanzano and V. Garrison, eds. Pp. 87–140. New York: J. Wiley and
    Sons.
    1984 Des êtres sacrificiels. In Sous le masque de l'animal. M. Cartry, ed. Pp. 267–317.
    Paris: Presses Universitaires de France.
    1985 L'Enfant Nit Ku Bon. Un tableau psychopathologique traditionnel chez les Wolof
    et les Lébou du Sénégal. Nouvelle Revue d'Éthnopsychiatrie 4:9–41.
Zhang, Everett Yuehong
    2007 Switching between Traditional Chinese Medicine and Viagra: Cosmopolitanism and
    Medical Pluralism Today. Medical Anthropology 26:53–96.

Zhu, Wei Xing, Li Lu, and Therese Hesketh
    2009 China's Excess Males, Sex Selective Abortion, and One Child Policy: Analysis of Data from 2005 National Intercensus Survey. British Medical Journal 338:920–936.
Zimmer, Carl
    2008 Mom and Dad Are Fighting in Your Genes – and in Your Brain. Discover, December. http://www.carlzimmer.com/articles/2008.php
    2008 Now: The Rest of the Genome. New York Times, November 11. http://www.nytimes.com/2008/11/11/science/11gene.html
Zimmerman, Francis
    1995 The Scholar, the Wise Man, and Universals: Three Aspects of Ayurvedic Medicine. *In* Knowledge and the Scholarly Medical Traditions. D. Bates, ed. Pp. 297–319. Cambridge: Cambridge University Press.
Zita, Jacquelyn N.
    1998 Body Talk: Philosophical Reflections on Sex and Gender. New York: Columbia University Press.
Zito, Angela, and Tani E. Barlow, eds.
    1994 Body, Subject, and Power in China. Chicago: University of Chicago Press.
Zola, Irving
    1972 Medicine as an Institution of Social Control. Sociological Review 20:487–504.
Zuberi, Tukufu
    2001 Thicker Than Blood: How Racial Statistics Lie. Minneapolis: University of Minnesota Press.

Index

An Anthropology of Biomedicine

Margaret Lock and Vinh-Kim Nguyen

WILEY-BLACKWELL

A John Wiley & Sons, Ltd., Publication

This edition first published 2010
© 2010 Margaret Lock and Vinh-Kim Nguyen

Blackwell Publishing was acquired by John Wiley & Sons in February 2007. Blackwell's publishing program has been merged with Wiley's global Scientific, Technical, and Medical business to form Wiley-Blackwell.

Registered Office
John Wiley & Sons Ltd, The Atrium, Southern Gate, Chichester, West Sussex, PO19 8SQ, United Kingdom

Editorial Offices
350 Main Street, Malden, MA 02148–5020, USA
9600 Garsington Road, Oxford, OX4 2DQ, UK
The Atrium, Southern Gate, Chichester, West Sussex, PO19 8SQ, UK

For details of our global editorial offices, for customer services, and for information about how to apply for permission to reuse the copyright material in this book please see our website at www.wiley.com/wiley-blackwell.

The right of Margaret Lock and Vinh-Kim Nguyen to be identified as the authors of this work has been asserted in accordance with the UK Copyright, Designs and Patents Act 1988.

Library of Congress Cataloging-in-Publication Data

Lock, Margaret.
    An anthropology of biomedicine / by Margaret Lock and Vinh-Kim Nguyen.
      p.   cm.
    Includes bibliographical references and index.
    ISBN 978-1-4051-1072-3 (hardcover : alk. paper) – ISBN 978-1-4051-1071-6 (pbk. : alk. paper)
  1. Medical anthropology.   2. Public health–Anthropological aspects.   3. Human body–Social aspects.
  I. Nguyen, Vinh-Kim.   II. Title.
      GN296.L63 2010
      306.4′61–dc22

                                        2009040192

A catalogue record for this book is available from the British Library.

Set in 10/12.5 pt Galliard by Toppan Best-set Premedia Limited
Printed in Singapore by Ho Printing Singapore Pte Ltd

05   2013